D1716567

Welcome to PEARSON mystratlab™

Your Strategic Management course is personalized by you, it is NOT the same as the course taught down the hall. So, shouldn't your online resources be personalized as well? MyStratLab is an easy to use on-line tool that personalizes course content and provides robust assessment and reporting to measure student and class performance.

What Is MyStratLab?

Your course can include textbook assignments, case analysis, simulations, readings, and financial analysis. Now, all the resources both professors and students need for course success are in one place — easily organized and adapted for your course. *MyStratLab* is the ONLY **Strategic Management** tool which includes: Readiness Quizzes, Cases, Case Teaching Notes, Video Cases, Case Analysis Tools, Financial Templates, Team Evaluation Tools, **InterActive** How Would You Do Thats.

Features for Instructors

- *MyStratLab* matches the organization of this textbook. Preloaded content for every chapter of this book allows instructors to use *MyStratLab* as is or to customize *MyStratLab* with their own materials
- **Strategic Management Cases**-Almost every case from the book is available online in MyStratLab
- **Case Teaching Notes** which each include: Case at a Glance, Case Learning Objectives, Case Synopsis, Case Questions and Discussion, What if Discussions
- **Financial Analysis Tools**-Generic financial statement templates and pre-loaded financials from selected cases
- **Test Item File** and TestGen Test Generating Software
- **PowerPoint™** slides: 2 Sets—Both chapter specific and case specific
- **Team** evaluation tools
- **Built-in Electronic Gradebook** to track students' progress on the assessments and remediation activities
- **Interactive How Would You Do Thats**-Using Excel, students have the chance to experience the impact of management decisions and the interdepence of formulation and implementation

Features for Students

- **Chapter Readiness Quizzes**—Give students the opportunity to make sure they understand key chapter concepts and to prepare for Case Analysis. Readiness Quizzes test students on chapter learning outcomes and create a personalized study plan based on their results. Students can track their own progress through the course and use the personalized study plan activities to help them achieve success in the classroom and in their professional lives

- **Customized Study Plan**—Based upon the results of the Readiness Quizzes, students receive a plan to help them remediate important concepts and applications where they need improvement. Study Plans correlate to the Learning Objectives from the textbook and analysis tools to help students understand and apply the concepts. Some of the tools include: **Ebook pages, Powerpoint presentations, Strategic Management videos**

- **Financial Statement Templates**-Generic Financial Statement Templates and pre-loaded financials from selected cases

- **Interactive How Would You Do Thats**-Using Excel, students have the chance to experience the impact of management decisions and the interdepence of formulation and implementation

- **Chapter Resources**—Students have access to standard reference resources throughout *MyStratLab* to use as needed including: cases from the book, case writing guidelines, team guidelines

Your Strategy. Your Course.

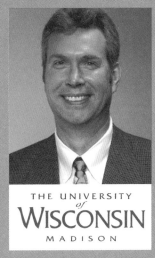

THE UNIVERSITY
of
WISCONSIN
MADISON

BYU
BRIGHAM YOUNG
UNIVERSITY

We're often asked....

WHAT IS A DYNAMIC PERSPECTIVE ON STRATEGY AND WHY IS IT IMPORTANT?

Dynamic perspective on strategy gives students a means of connecting the dots between internal resources and capabilities, ever- and increasingly rapid-changing external conditions, and firm and industry survival and profitability. Taking a dynamic perspective on strategy allows students to see that change is inevitable in strategy and can occur rapidly or slowly.

WHAT IS STRATEGIC LEADERSHIP AND WHY IS IT IMPORTANT?

Strategic Leadership is the role that top and middle-managers play in strategy and formulation and implementation. Strategic Leadership is important in regards to dynamic strategy because managers are often the key sources of dynamic capabilities that allow firms to complete in rapidly changing competitive environments. Students can see how the strategic tone is set at the top but that successful implementation is dependent on individuals.Instructors have an opportunity to talk about the personalities of executives in cases they use and how these personalities play out in formulation and implementation.

WHAT IS THE INTERDEPENDENCE
OF FORMULATION AND IMPLEMENTATION AND WHY IS IT IMPORTANT?

Executives often say "I would rather have a mediocore strategy with great implementation than a great strategy with mediocore implementation." Students will have a clear understanding that formulation and implementation are interdependent and that effective formulation take implementation details into account early in the strategy process.

To sum it up....

Our treatment of the process of strategic management—managing the firm's strategy formulation and implementation over time—**allows us to bring management back into strategy**. By returning strategic leadership into the teaching strategy, we believe students at all levels can more readily see themselves as instrumental in the strategic management process.

Mason Carpenter

Wm. Gerard Sanders

Be Dynamic. Be Strategic.

The Fundamentals of Economic Logic

Ratios	How Calculated	Relevance of Concept
Profitability Indicators		
EBIT (Earnings before interest and taxes)	Net sales – operating expenses (also called operating profit)	Represents the amount of cash that such a company will be able to use to pay off creditors.
EBITDA (Earnings before interest, taxes, depreciation, and amortization)	EBIT + depreciation expenses + amortization expenses	A good way of comparing companies within and across industries. EBITDA is essentially the income that a company has free for interest payments.
Net Profit Margin	$\dfrac{\text{Profits after taxes}}{\text{Sales}}$	This number is an indication of how effective a company is at cost control. The higher the net profit margin is, the more effective the company is at converting revenue into actual profit.
Gross Profit Margin	$\dfrac{\text{Sales} - \text{Cost of goods sold}}{\text{Sales}}$	A good indication of what the company has left over to cover administrative costs after it has cover the cost of the goods sold
Return on assets	$\dfrac{\text{Return after taxes}}{\text{Total assets}}$ or $\dfrac{\text{Profits after taxes} + \text{interest}}{\text{Total Assets}}$	A measure of how effectively a firm uses its total assets.
Return on capital employed (ROCE)	$\dfrac{\text{EBIT}}{\text{Total assets} - \text{current liabilities}}$	A measure of the returns that a company is realizing from its capital employed. The ratio can also be seen as representing the efficiency with which capital is being utilized to generate revenue. It is commonly used as a measure for comparing the performance between businesses and for assessing whether a business generates enough returns to pay for its cost of capital.
Return on Equity (ROE)	$\dfrac{\text{Profits after taxes}}{\text{Total stockholders' equity}}$	A measure of how well a company has used reinvested earnings to generate additional earnings.
Return on Investment (ROI)	$\dfrac{\text{Operating income}}{\text{Total assets}}$	How effectively the firm uses its capital to generate profit; the higher the ROI, the better.
Return on Invested Capital (ROIC)	$\dfrac{\text{Profits after taxes} - \text{Preferred stock dividends}}{\text{Total stockholders' equity} + \text{total debt} - \text{par value of preferred stock}}$	How effectively a company uses the money (borrowed or owned) invested in its operations.
EBITDA margin	$\dfrac{\text{EBITDA}}{\text{Total revenue}}$	Measures the extent to which cash operating expenses use up revenue.
Operating Profit Margin	$\dfrac{\text{EBIT}}{\text{Total revenue}}$	A measure of a company's earnings power from ongoing operations. Operating profit margin indicates how effective a company is at controlling the costs and expenses associated with their normal business operations.

Ratios (continued)	How Calculated	Relevance of Concept
Activity Indicators		
Asset turnover	$$\frac{\text{Sales}}{\text{Total Assets}}$$	How efficiently sales are using the firm's asset base.
Inventory turnover	$$\frac{\text{Sales}}{\text{Inventory of finished goods}}$$	How efficiently a firm is able to convert inventory into sales.
Working Capital Turnover	$$\frac{\text{Sales}}{\text{Working capital}}$$	How efficiently a firm is able to convert working capital into sales.
Accounts receivable turnover	$$\frac{\text{Annual credit sales}}{\text{Accounts receivable}}$$	How quickly a firm is collecting on the monies owed it.
Accounts payable turnover	$$\frac{\text{Cost of goods sold}}{\text{Accounts payable}}$$	How quickly a firm is pay creditors.
Leverage Indicators		
Debt to equity ratio	$$\frac{\text{Total debt}}{\text{Total stockholders' equity}}$$	One measure of financial leverage. A higher debt/equity ratio may be riskier, especially in times of rising interest rates, due to the additional interest that has to be paid out for the debt.
Debt to assets	$$\frac{\text{Total debt}}{\text{Total assets}}$$	Another measure of leverage. If the ratio is greater than one, most of the company's assets are financed through debt. Companies with high debt/asset ratios are said to be "highly leveraged."
Interest coverage ratio	$$\frac{\text{Profits before interest and taxes}}{\text{Total interest charges}}$$	A calculation of a company's ability to meet its interest payments on outstanding debt. The lower the interest coverage, the larger the debt burden is on the company.
Liquidity Indicators		
Quick ratio (Acid Test Ratio)	$$\frac{\text{Current assets – Inventory}}{\text{Current liabilities}}$$	Using the firm's most liquid assets (typically cash + AR), is an "acid test" of a firm's ability to meet current financial obligations.
Current ratio	$$\frac{\text{Current assets}}{\text{Current liabilities}}$$	Using all the firm's current assets, is an indication of a firm's ability to meet current financial obligations.
Other Key Indicators		
Sustainable growth rate	ROE * (1– dividend-payout ratio)	Evaluates a firm's financial health by determining the rate of growth the company can sustain with its current capital structure.
Operating leverage	$$\frac{\text{Gross margin (or gross profit)}}{\text{Net profit margin}}$$	Indicates how sensitive a firm's profits are to small increases or decreases in revenue.
Weighted average cost of capital (WACC)	$$\frac{\text{Debt}}{\text{Cost of debt}} + \frac{\text{Equity}}{\text{Cost of equity}}$$	Represents the overall required return on the firm as a whole and is often used internally by company directors to determine the economic feasibility of expansionary opportunities and mergers.

Concepts

Strategic Management

A Dynamic Perspective

SECOND EDITION

Mason A. Carpenter
University of Wisconsin–Madison

Wm. Gerard Sanders
Brigham Young University

PEARSON
Prentice
Hall

Upper Saddle River, New Jersey 07458

Library of Congress Cataloging-in-Publication Data
Carpenter, Mason Andrew
    Strategic management : a dynamic perspective concepts / Mason A. Carpenter, Wm. Gerard Sanders. — 2nd ed.
    p. cm.
    Includes bibliographical references and index.
    ISBN 978-0-13-234140-0
1. Strategic planning. I. Sanders, William Gerard II. Title.
  HD30.28.C377 2007b
  658.4'012—dc22

                              2007040203

Editor-in-Chief: David Parker
Executive Editor: Wendy Craven
Development Editor: Claire Hunter
Manager, Product Development: Ashley Santora
Project Manager, Editorial: Christina Volpe
Assistant Editor, Media: Valerie Patruno
Director of Marketing Manager: Patrice Jones
Senior Managing Editor: Judy Leale
Project Manager, Production: Kevin H. Holm
Permissions Project Manager: Charles Morris
Senior Operations Supervisor: Arnold Vila
Operations Specialist: Arnold Vila
Creative Director: John Christiana
Interior and Cover Design: John Christiana
Cover Illustration/Photo: ©Adam Peiperl
Director, Image Resource Center: Melinda Patelli
Manager, Rights and Permissions: Zina Arabia
Manager: Visual Research: Beth Brenzel
Manager, Cover Visual Research & Permissions: Karen Sanatar
Image Permission Coordinator: Nancy Seise
Photo Researcher: Diane Austin
Composition: S4Carlisle Publishing Services
Full-Service Project Management: S4Carlisle Publishing Services
Printer/Binder: Courier/Kendallville; Coral Graphics
Typeface: Minion 10/12

Credits and acknowledgments borrowed from other sources and reproduced, with permission, in this textbook appear on appropriate page within text (or on page 480).

Pearson Education LTD.
Pearson Education Singapore, Pte. Ltd
Pearson Education Canada, Ltd
Pearson Education—Japan

Pearson Education Australia PTY, Limited
Pearson Education North Asia Ltd
Pearson Educación de Mexico, S.A. de C.V.
Pearson Education Malaysia, Pte. Ltd.

10 9 8 7 6 5 4 3 2 1
ISBN-13: 978-0-13-234140-0
ISBN-10: 0-13-234140-9

Dedication

My work on this book is dedicated to my wife Lisa , and to our boys Wesley and Zachary.

—MAC

This book is dedicated to my family—my wife Kathy, and our children Ashley, Adam, and Noelle—for providing the patience and support necessary to complete this project.

—WGS

Brief Contents

v

Contents

4 Exploring the External Environment: Macro and Industry Dynamics 102

PART THREE BUSINESS, CORPORATE, AND GLOBAL STRATEGIES

5 Creating Business Strategies 144

6 Crafting Business Strategy for Dynamic Contexts 180

7 Developing Corporate Strategy 214

8 Looking at International Strategies 252

Preface

Intended Audience

This book is designed for undergraduate and MBA students and is most often used in strategic management or business policy courses. This book is available in two versions:

Strategic Management 2e Concepts and Cases, **ISBN: 0-13-234138-7**

Strategic Management 2e Concepts, **ISBN: 0-13-234140-9**

New and Enhanced in This Edition

With strategic management evolving so rapidly, textbooks and learning packages must evolve just as quickly. Here are highlights of the revisions in this edition:

- **New and Substantially Revised Chapter Opening Vignettes:** All chapter openers highlight dynamic companies and their leaders who make the strategic decisions. For example, Chapter 1 highlights UnderArmour and the decisions its founder Kevin Plank needed to make; and Chapter 2 highlights Anne Mulcahy, the first female CEO in Xerox history.

- **Interactive How Would You Do That (HWDYT) features:** We've pushed the envelope and in every chapter, students have a chance to place themselves in the role of a strategic decision maker at a well-known (and interesting) company. Using Excel, HWYDTs clearly show students the interdependence of formulation and implementation and lets them practice their decision-making skills. For example, see Mapping Your Social Network in Chapter 2 and Creating a Value Curve in Chapters 4 and 6.

- **NEW Ethical Questions in Every Chapter:** These questions require students to think about the ethical implications of strategic decision making.

- **NEW Emphasis on Financial Implications and Decision Making:** Key Economic Indicator ratios included at the front of the book AND Excel-based financial templates and selected case financials can be found at www.mystratlab.com.

Resources For Instructors

INSTRUCTOR'S RESOURCE CENTER: REGISTER. REDEEM. LOGIN.

At www.prenhall.com/irc, instructors can access a variety of print, digital, and presentation resources available with this text in downloadable format. Registration is simple and gives you immediate access to new titles and new editions. As a registered faculty member, you can download resource files and receive immediate access and instructions for installing course management content on your campus server.

The following supplements are available to adopting instructors at www.prenhall. com/irc

- www.mystratlab.com

- Instructor's Manual

- Test Item File

- TestGen Test Generating Software.

- PowerPoint Slides

- Author Podcasts

Need Help? Our dedicated Technical Support team is ready to help with the media supplements that accompany this text. Visit www.247.prenhall.com for answers to frequently asked questions and toll-free user support phone numbers.

PEARSON
mystratlab

Welcome to MyStratLab

www.mystratlab.com

Your Strategic Management course is personalized by you and is NOT the same as the course taught down the hall. So, shouldn't your online resources be personalized as well? MyStratLab is an easy to use online tool that personalizes course content and provides robust assessment and reporting to measure student and class performance.

Your course can include textbook assignments, case analysis, simulations, readings, and financial analysis. Now, all the resources both professors and students need for course success are in one place — easily organized and adapted to your course. MyStratLab is the ONLY Strategic Management tool that includes: Readiness Quizzes, Cases, Case Teaching Notes, Case Analysis Tools, Financial Templates, Team Evaluation Tools, and InterActive How Would You Do That features.

FEATURES FOR INSTRUCTORS

- *MyStratLab* matches the organization of this textbook. Preloaded content for each chapter of this book allows instructors to use MyStratLab as-is or to customize MyStratLab with their own materials.

- Strategic Management Cases: Almost every case from the book is available online in MyStratLab.

- Case Teaching Notes that each include: Case at a Glance, Case Learning Objectives, Case Synopsis, Case Questions and Discussion, and What If Discussions

- Financial Analysis Tools: Generic financial statement templates and preloaded financials from selected cases

- Test Item File and TestGen Test Generating Software

- PowerPoint™ Slides: Two sets—both chapter and case specific

- Team Evaluation Tools

- Built-in Electronic Gradebook: Track student progress on the assessments and remediation activities.

- **Interactive How Would You Do That Features:** Using Excel, students have the chance to experience the impact of management decisions and the interdependence of formulation and implementation.

FEATURES FOR STUDENTS

- **Chapter Readiness Quizzes:** Give students the opportunity to make sure they understand key chapter concepts and prepare for Case Analysis. Readiness Quizzes test students on chapter learning outcomes and create a personalized study plan based on results. Students can track their own progress through the course and use the personalized study plan activities to help them to achieve success in the classroom and in their professional lives.

- **Customized Study Plan:** Based upon the results of the Readiness Quizzes, students receive a plan to help them remediate important concepts and applications where they need improvement. Study Plans correlate to the Learning Objectives from the textbook and analysis tools to help students understand and apply the concepts. Some of the tools include: **Ebook pages, Powerpoint presentations, Strategic Management videos**

- **Financial Statement Templates:** Generic Financial Statement Templates and preloaded financials from selected cases

- **Interactive How Would You Do That features:** Using Excel, students have the chance to experience the impact of management decisions and the interdependence of formulation and implementation

- **Chapter Resources:** Students have access to standard reference resources throughout *MyStratLab* to use as needed, including: almost all cases from the book, Case Writing Guidelines, and Team Guidelines.

CourseSmart Textbooks Online

CourseSmart Textbooks Online is an exciting new *choice* for students looking to save money. As an alternative to purchasing the print textbook, students can *subscribe* to the same content online and save up to 50% off the suggested list price of the print text. With a CourseSmart etextbook, students can search the text, make notes online, print out reading assignments that incorporate lecture notes and bookmark important passages for later review. For more information, or to subscribe to the CourseSmart eTextbook, visit www.coursesmart.com.

Acknowledgments

Many people were involved in reviewing the First Edition of the book and the Second Edition manuscript. Others were instrumental in developing MyStratLab and all of the teaching and learning material. All deserve to be recognized.

Chapter Reviewers

Robert DeFillippi *Suffolk University*

Scott Droege *Western Kentucky University*

Varghese George *University of Massachusetts Boston*

Manuela Hoehn-Weiss *University of Washington*

Necmi Karagozoglu *Sacramento State University*

Ismatilla Mardanov *Southeast Missouri State University*

Jeffrey Nystrom *University of Colorado at Denver and Health Sciences Center*

Timothy Palmer *Western Michigan University*

Abe Qastin *Lakeland College*

Steven Samaras *Longwood University*

Paul Thurston *Siena College*

Kenneth Wendeln *Indiana University*

Virtual Focus Group Attendees

Peter Antoniou *California State University*

LaKami Baker *Mississippi State University*

Greg Berezewski *Robert Morris College*

Steven Boivie *University of Arizona*

Aruna Chandra *Indiana State University*

Scott Elston *Iowa State University*

Robert DeFillippi *Suffolk University*

Betty Deiner *Barry University*

Scott Gallagher *James Madison University*

Debbie Gillard *Metropolitan State College, Denver*

Alan Miller *University of Nevada, Las Vegas*

Roman Nowacki *Northern Illinois University*

??? Phelan *University of Nevada, Las Vegas*

Douglas Polley *St. Cloud State University*

Katsu Shimizu *University of Texas, San Antonio*

John Upson *Florida State University*

Edward Ward *St. Cloud State University*

Marta White *Georgia State University*

Case Survey Respondents

Garry Adams *Auburn University*

Todd Alessandri *Syracuse University*

Errol Alexander *Menlo College*

A. Alkhafaji

Brent Allred *The College of William and Mary*

A Amason *The University of Georgia*

Clarence Anderson *Walla Walla College*

Rex Anderson *Gardner Webb University*

Steve Andersen *Black Hills State University*

Anthony Avallone *Saint Peter's College*

Warren Baker *Roanoke College*

Paul Bell *Southwest Wisconsin Technical College*

Richard Birkenbeuel *University of Dubuque*

Sylvia Black *North Carolina A & T State University*

William Boulton *Auburn University*

Thomas Box *Pittsburg State University*

Robert Brown *Idaho State University*

Scott Bryant *Montana State University*

Patricia Buhler *Goldey-Beacom College*

Thomas Butte *Humboldt State University*

Anthony Cantarella *Murray State University*

Samuel Cappel *Southeastern Louisiana University*

Steven Carr *Texas A & M University*

Tim Carroll *Georgia Tech University*

Ronald Clement *Pittsburg State University*

Robert Cline *Binghamton University*

Bob Comerford *University of Rhode Island*

Robert Corsini *Bryant University*

Peter Crowell *Fordham University*

Refik Culpan *Pennsylvania State University at Harrisburg*

Don Daake *Olivet Nazarene University*

William Davig *Eastern Kentucky University*

Peter Davis *The University of Memphis*

Rolf Dixon *Weber State University*

Bambi Douma *University of Montana*

Scott Droege *Western Kentucky University*

Robert Edelson *Wilmington College*

Cathy Enz *Hotel School*

Rangamohan Eunni *Youngstown State University*

Ronald Ferner *Philadelphia Biblical University*

Robert Ferrari *Marymount College*

Phyllis Flott *Tennessee State University*

Richard Gendreau *Bemidji State University*

Armand Gilinsky *Sonoma State University*

Bill Godair *College of Saint Joseph*

Anita Gorham *Central Michigan University*

Peter Goulet *University of Northern Iowa*

Shane Greenstein *Kellogg School of Management*

Bill Gregory *Northwestern Oklahoma State University*

Allen Harmon *University of Minnesota Duluth*

Tom Holubik *Texas Tech University*

Andrew Hoh *Creighton University*

Peter Hom *Arizona State University*

Stephen Horner *Arkansas State University*

Peter Hughes *University of New Hampshire*

Alan Jackson *College of Saint Mary*

Stuart Johnston *Texas Christian University*

Susan Anne Kadlec *Dillard University*

Rick Koza *Chadron State College*

Scott Latham *University of Massachusetts, Lowell*

Ted Legatski *Texas Christian University*

Art Lekacos *State University of New York, Stony Brook*

Annette Lohman *California State University Long Beach*

Patricia Luoma *Quinnipiac University*

Sean Lux *Florida State University*

Barbara MacLeod *Ohio Wesleyan University*

Paul Mallette *Colorado State University*

Alfred Marcus *University of Minnesota*

Theresa Marron-Grodsky *University of Maryland University College*

Richard McCabe *Graziadio School of Business and Management*

Paul McCullough *Aquinas College Primetime*

Sal Monaco *Graduate School of Management and Technology*

Ann Mooney *Wesley J. Howe School*

Rebecca Morris *University of Nebraska at Omaha*

Alisa Mosley *Jackson State University*

Robert Moussetis *North Central College*

Art Padilla *North Carolina State University*

C. Patrick Palmer *Siena Heights University*

Ralph Parrish *University of Central Oklahoma*

Sharon Peck *Capital University*

Christine Pence *California State University*

Phillip Phan *Rensselaer Polytechnic Institute*

A Pillutla *St. Ambrose University*

Carol Pope *Alverno College*

Burt Reynolds *Southern New Jersey University*

Barbara Ribbens *Western Illinois University*

Nancy Robinson *East Tennessee State University*

Charles Roe *Arkansas State University*

Marty Rogoff *Philadelphia University*

Robert Roller *LeTourneau University*

Robert Rottman *Kentucky State University*

L. Alan Schafler *Florida Atlantic University*

Randolph Schewering *Rockhurst University*

Frank Schultz *Michigan State University*

Mark Seabright *Western Oregon University*

Bob Seigel *Buena Vista University*

Matthew Semadeni *Moore School of Business/University of South Carolina*

Jeffrey Sherlock *Tri-State University*

Chris Shook *Auburn University*

Nicolaj Siggelkow *Wharton School*

Patty Silfies *Western Kentucky University*

Quentin Skrabec *University of Findlay*

Jeff Slattery *Northeastern State University*

Anne Smith *University of Tennessee*

Howard Smith *University of New Mexico*

Marion Smith *Texas Southern University*

Stephen Standifird *University of San Diego*

Paul Stepanovich *Southern Connecticut State University*

Bill Stevens *School of Business Administration*

Roy Suddaby *University of Iowa*

Mohammad Syed *Miles College*

Michael Sykuta *University of Missouri*

Qingjiu Tao *Lehigh University*

Doug Thomas *University of New Mexico*

Paul Tiffany *University of California*

Bert Turner *Arkansas State University*

Steve Varga-Sinka *Saint Leo University, Atlanta Center*

Robert Von der Ohe *Rockford College*

Alan Wallace *Mesa State College*

Peter Wallace *Stonehill College*

Rod Walter *Western Illinois University*

Al Warner *Penn State*

Morrison Webb *Manhattanville College*

Paula Weber *St. Cloud State University*

William Worthington *Texas A & M University*

Russell Wright *University of Utah*

Ray Zammuto *University of Colorado, Denver*

"Live" Focus Group Attendees

Adam Fremeth *University of Minnesota*
Cynthia Lengick-Hall *University of Texas, San Antonio*
Santo Marabella *Moravian College*
Michele Masterfano *Drexel University*
Jacquelyn Palmer *Wright State University*

Sandu Petru *Elizabethtown College*
Peter Stanwick *Auburn University*
Paul Thurston *Siena College*
Margaret White *Oklahoma State*
Douglas Ross *Towson University*

Teaching Package and MyStratLab

Cara Cantarella *Pace University*
Robert Panco *Pace University*
Noushi Rahman *Pace University*

Paul Thurston *Siena College*
Diana Wong *Eastern Michigan University*

Personal Acknowledgments from the Authors

We wrote this Second Edition to build on the success of our First Edition and further improve the student and faculty experience with learning and teaching about strategic management. We take the perspective of practicing managers, and want to acknowledge the students, faculty, and managers who were directly and indirectly engaged in developing this new edition of *Strategic Management: A Dynamic Perspective.* This includes our own students and colleagues at the University of Wisconsin–Madison and Brigham Young University, the many executives and managers we have consulted with and brought into our classes, and those we worked with in our travels as we developed this new edition.

Although we had a specific vision for the book, we cannot take full credit for all the content that supports that vision. In particular, we want to acknowledge the contributions of the many researchers whose work helps managers understand and cope with the challenges of crafting and implementing revolutionary strategies in changing times. You will see their work cited throughout the text, and we encourage you to read the original studies (including our own) upon which the content of this book is based. We also want to acknowledge the many managers whose views and daily challenges helped us develop a theoretically rigorous, yet practically relevant and readable approach to strategic management. At many points along the way these colleagues challenged us with observations like, "That's nice, but how would you do that?" and forced us to continually refine our writing to connect the dots—from concept to action—so to speak.

Out of this group, one team of researchers continues to deserve particular note: Don Hambrick at Penn State University and Jim Fredrickson at the University of Texas at Austin. These talented and prolific researchers and award-winning teachers have been leading the bandwagon to put managers back into strategy, and have been exceptional mentors to both of us. You can see their imprint in our early research, in the managerial orientation of our textbook, and in the strategy diamond that ties all the chapters together. This strategy diamond will endure long after they are done writing; it will create a rich and relevant learning environment for students of strategy, and it will provide managers a tool for thinking through and answering in the affirmative, "Yes, I really have a strategy!"

We thank our team at Pearson Prentice Hall for making the book a reality. We wanted a publishing partner that shared and supported our vision and high aspirations for the next generation of undergraduate and MBA strategy textbooks, and with Pearson Prentice Hall we got one.

Feedback   The authors and the product team would appreciate hearing from you! Let us know what you think about this textbook by writing to college_marketing@prenhall.com. Please include "Feedback about Carpenter/Sanders 2e" in the subject line.

About the Authors

Mason A. Carpenter

Professor Carpenter is the M. Keith Weikel Professor of Leadership at the Wisconsin School of Business. He has a B.S. in Business Administration from California State University (Humboldt) and University of Copenhagen, Denmark, and an M.B.A. from California State University (Bakersfield). He also completed graduate studies in enology at the University of Bordeaux, France. Before obtaining his Ph.D. in strategy at the University of Texas, Austin, he worked in banking, management consulting, and software development. His research concerns corporate governance, top management teams, and the strategic management of global firms, and is published in Strategic Management Journal, Academy of Management Journal, Academy of Management Review, Academy of Management Executive, Journal of Management, and Human Resource Management. He serves on the editorial boards of the Academy of Management Journal, Academy of Management Review, Journal of Management Studies, and the Strategic Management Journal, was voted Professor of the Year by M.B.A. students, and identified as one of the most popular professors in the BusinessWeek M.B.A. poll. He recently received the Larson Excellence in Teaching award from the School of Business, and the University of Wisconsin's Emil H. Steiger Distinguished Teaching Award.

Wm. Gerard Sanders

Professor Sanders is an associate professor and the Department Chair in Organization Leadership and Strategy at the Marriott School of Management at Brigham Young University. He earned a Ph.D. in strategic management from the University of Texas at Austin. In 1996, Professor Sanders joined the faculty at BYU, where he teaches strategic management. He has also been a visiting professor at Penn State University. His research is in the area of corporate governance and its affects on firm strategy and performance. He has published extensively in the Academy of Management Journal, Strategic Management Journal, Journal of Management, Human Resource Management, among other outlets. His work on the effects of stock option pay has been featured in such outlets as the New York Times, the Economist, BusinessWeek, CFO, and on National Public Radio's Marketplace. Professor Sanders is an Associate Editor of the Academy of Management Journal. In 2001 he received the Marriott School's J. Earl Garrett Fellowship and in 2003 he was designated a University Young Scholar. Prior to entering graduate school, Dr. Sanders spent twelve years in industry managing the acquisitions and financing of large portfolios of commercial real estate.

Concepts

Strategic Management
A Dynamic Perspective

1 Introducing Strategic Management

In This Chapter We Challenge You To >>>

1. Understand what a *strategy* is and identify the difference between business-level and corporate-level strategy.

2. Understand why we study *strategic management*.

3. Understand the relationship between *strategy formulation* and *implementation*.

4. Describe the determinants of *competitive advantage*.

5. Recognize the difference between the *fundamental* and *dynamic* views of *competitive advantage*.

Click Clack—
David Challenging Goliath

*T*welve years ago, Kevin Plank was a walk-on football player for the University of Maryland Terrapins. He hated how his cotton T-shirts became soaking wet with sweat during every practice. The wet T-shirts would cause chaffing, gain several pounds in weight, and generally just feel very uncomfortable. He wondered why, in an era of microfiber fabric with moisture-wicking properties, he and other football players had to put up with uncomfortable cotton T-shirts under their shoulder pads. Runners, bicyclists, and others were already benefiting from clothing made of advanced materials to make their workouts more comfortable. Plank, who grew up always looking for a way to make money, went to a fabric store and bought a bolt of moisture-wicking fabric and paid a tailor to make several prototype shirts. Plank's teammates envied his new shirts, so he set out to make more samples. He officially launched his company out of his grandmother's basement and called his product Under Armour®. As you can see from the snapshot in Exhibit 1.1, sales in 2006 were $430 million, and the company's equity was valued at over $1.8 billion.[1] With such dominant incumbents as Nike and adidas, how did Plank successfully enter and grow his company into one of the best performing companies on Wall Street? Apparently, at least early on, its competitors did not heed Under Armour's savvy and mega-successful advertising campaign titled "Click-Clack: I think you hear us coming!" Although Under Armour has been successful to date, surely Nike and others did not stand idly by while watching its customers migrate to the new upstart. What can Under Armour do to maintain and grow its position in the industry? Let's first look at the industry, then we'll review Under Armour's strategy for entering and competing in this dynamic industry.

Exhibit 1.1   Under Armour at a Glance

	1996	2006
Revenues	$17,000	$430,000,000
Net Income	0	57,300,000
Equity Value	0	1,800,000,000

Revenue Distribution

Apparel

men's 59.4%
women's 19.9%
youth 7.4%

footwear 6.2%
accessories 3.5%
licensing revenues 3.6%

Brands and Trademarks		Under Armour®, HeatGear®, ColdGear®, AllSeasonGear®, LooseGear®, Under Armour design mark, Protect This House™, Duplicity™, I Think You Hear Us Coming™ and Click Clack™
NYSE Ticker (Went public in August 2005)		UA
Kevin Plank's Vision		To become the #1 performance athletic brand in the world

The Performance Apparel Industry Under Armour participates in the sports apparel market, which NPD Group, a leading provider of consumer and retail market research information, estimated was a $45 billion market in 2006. Approximately 30 percent of the market is synthetic product and purchased for use in active sport or exercise. While one might assume that Nike dominates the market, in fact the active sports apparel market is fragmented—10 brands combine to comprise the top 30 percent of the market.

Historically, exercise clothing consisted of products made with relatively unsophisticated design and generic fabrics. The most common shirt used in exercise was a standard cotton T-shirt, often decorated with logos and company or team names. In segments like running and basketball, there were specialized jerseys made of synthetic fibers and tank top designs that improved performance. Lycra® revolutionized sportswear in the late twentieth century, and the microfibers revolutionized the market later. Fabrics like fleece and Sympatex® were specifically developed for fluctuations in weather conditions. It is unlikely that street fashion would have adopted them so readily if there had not been the status association of sporting prowess. When this was combined with effective functional utility, a fabric fashion was born that encompassed all ages from young skateboarders to mature golfers. Moisture-management fibers were developed to accommodate the desire for more comfortable sportswear. According to Dupont, who invented Coolmax® and Tactel®, function is paramount. These fibers are used commonly today not only in sports apparel, but in other products ranging from socks to lingerie.

The performance apparel segment of the sports apparel market is growing more rapidly than other segments. This growth is fueled by demographic trends and increased consumer awareness and participation in active lifestyles. During the past two decades, consumers have continued to spend heavily in the areas of weight loss and dieting, fitness center memberships, and sports and athletic equipment. And sports enthusiasts tend to spend more for their equipment than casual users, which translates to the possibility for higher price points and greater margins.

As upstarts like Under Armour in sports apparel and Sketchers in specialized footwear have gained strong footholds in emerging segments, industry giants like Nike and adidas have taken notice and responded in kind with their own specialized products. However, while the market is large and growing rapidly, incumbents in traditional segments of the industry have not grown as rapidly.

Under Armour's Entry The original Under Armour shirt that Kevin Plank designed was made as a form-fitting compression using microfiber that would wick perspiration away from the body and dry quickly. The shirts he shared with teammates were a big hit and this led him to believe there was a market for these "performance shirts." He guessed there would be a big market for his shirts among professional and amateur athletes who, like himself, were irritated by working out in cotton shirts but continued to do so simply because there were few alternatives. Kevin Plank figured he had a winning product that was quite different from current products. His product has three distinct features. First, the fabric wicks moisture and dries quickly (a sweat-soaked cotton T-shirt can weigh two to three pounds). Second, Plank used a compression design—tight, form-fitting cuts that reduced the amount of fabric and improved comfort when worn under a uniform (and equipment like shoulder pads). Third, Under Armour shirts were made with a tagless design; conventional tags on the collar often irritate the neck of athletes. Plank designed a way to heat-seal the tag information directly to the fabric rather than needing to sew on a separate tag.

With a superior product designed for a specific market, Plank still faced the issue of how to get his product to market. Like many entrepreneurs, he started with who he knew—former teammates from college and prep school who were now playing in the NFL. He figured that if he could get some professional athletes to use the product, teammates would hound them for their own shirts, much like his college teammates did at Maryland. While working on getting athletes to demand his product, Plank also went about securing wholesale and retail accounts. Early NFL players who started wearing Under Armour shirts included quarterbacks Jeff George and Frank Wycheck (a former Maryland teammate) and all pro and hall of fame receiver Jerry Rice. In baseball, Roger Clemens got Under Armour rolling by being an early adopter of the new shirts. Today, Under Armour is available via the Internet, catalogs, and 12,000 sporting goods stores worldwide.

With the early success of the basic product, Under Armour set out to find natural product extensions. The first product growth came in expanding from the basic shirt, known as AllSeason Gear®, to HeatGear® and ColdGear®, products designed to be worn in hot climates or cold temperatures while still providing the basic performance technology of the original product. Later, Under Armour looked for additional growth from new geographic areas. The major targets for international expansion today are Europe and Asia. More recently, Under Armour has expanded into new product and sports segments. In 2006, Under Armour launched what has proved to be a highly successful line of footwear. The specific target area? Football and baseball cleats. Why did Under Armour pick this particular segment? Plank says that the Under Armour strategy is not to be a niche player in football (or baseball) cleats. Rather, this segment is designed to be the platform from which to launch into a broader athletic footwear position at a later time. Because so many football and baseball players were already using Under Armour performance shirts, Under Armour felt that they would be a very receptive audience for footwear. The highly successful "Click-Clack" advertising campaign propelled Under Armour to a fabulous first year in footwear; in its first year of marketing cleats, Under Armour captured 20 percent market share overall, and an amazing 40 percent of the market for cleats priced over $70! In 2007, Under Armour launched lines of performance sunglasses and sports watches, both targeted at the premium price segments.

Under Armour's targets for growth in the near future focus on three main areas. First, Plank plans to continue to reinvigorate the core products, which are men's and women's apparel. And, Under Armour is just beginning to grow in the women's market. Within the basic product segment, Under Armour sees room to expand into other sports. For instance, within the last year, Under Armour started to notice that their shirts were showing up on golf courses. Golfers who used the products in other activities saw the benefits of the product while spending hours on the golf course. That led Under Armour to start marketing a specific polo-style shirt line through golf stores and later to start a full line of golf apparel. Similarly, Under Armour now targets outdoor adventure seekers (climbers, hikers, skiers), largely because they noticed the product being used in those venues. In addition, Under Armour sees lots of growth opportunity in footwear. Football and baseball cleats are seen as a mechanism to get Under Armour into this vast and potentially lucrative market. Analysts are anxious to know when Under Armour will move into other sports shoes (e.g., running, basketball). Plank simply responds: "When the time is right." Finally, Under Armour has just begun to get serious about international expansion. Under Armour recently opened a European office to lead negotiations with local athletes and distributors.

In a recent conference call with financial analysts covering Under Armour's stock, Kevin Plank was asked how Nike and adidas could have been taken by surprise by Under Armour's entry into the performance apparel segment. Indeed, Under Armour is now credited with creating the sports performance segment because former products are seen

Exhibit 1.2   Under Armour's Cumulative Total Stock Market

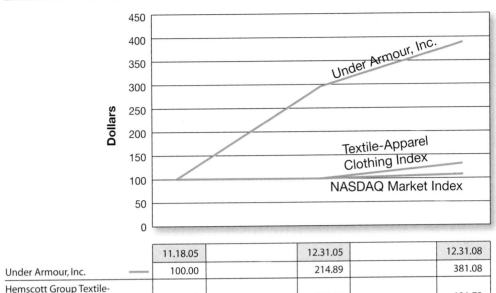

		11.18.05		12.31.05		12.31.08
Under Armour, Inc.	———	100.00		214.89		381.08
Hemscott Group Textile-Apparel Clothing Index	-------	100.00		113.00		131.72
NASDAQ Market Index	—— —	100.00		98.78		101.82

as so technologically backwards. Analysts posed the question: "How was the door left so wide open (for your entry)?" Plank's response was telling: "I don't know, but our job is to close that door." He went on to comment that nobody thought consumers would spend $25 to $35 for a T-shirt. He concluded by noting that when you give the consumer some tangible benefit, you're able to reinvent entire product categories. Evidently, as summarized in Exhibit 1.2, in its first year of trading as a public company, Wall Street appeared to like Plank's plays as much as consumers did.[2]

Why are some firms incredibly successful while others are not? And why is it that once they're successful, so few can sustain a high level of success? We are sure that you are familiar with many once successful firms, that today no longer enjoy such success. In this text, we'll introduce you to the concepts that you'll need to answer questions about gaining and sustaining success in the world of business competition. <<<

Three Overarching Themes

As you've probably gathered from the topic of this book—*strategic management*—a firm's performance is directly related to the quality of its strategy and its competency in implementing it. You also need to understand that concerns about strategy, sometimes referred to as *business policy*, preoccupy the minds of many top executives. Their responsibility is to see that the firm's whole is ultimately greater than the sum of its parts—whether these parts are distinct business units, such as Under Armour's men's apparel and footwear, or simply the functional areas that contribute to the performance of one particular business, such as Under Armour's distribution through national sporting goods chains. Good strategies are affected by, and affect all of, the functional areas of the firm, including marketing, finance, accounting, and operations. Thus, we'll also introduce you to the concepts and tools that you'll need to analyze the conditions of a firm and its industry, to formulate appropriate strategies, and to determine how to implement a chosen strategy.

Three themes that run throughout this book are critical to developing competency in the field of strategic management:

1. **Firms and industries are *dynamic* in nature.** In recent years, theories and research have emerged on issues regarding dynamic markets and the importance of developing dynamic capabilities to create value. Our first theme, then, is the dynamic nature of both firms and their competitive environments. It's easy, for instance, to look at a financial snapshot of Under Armour and understand the competitive position that it commands in its industry. But we need to see Under Armour not as a snapshot at one particular moment in time but as an ongoing movie. Under Armour's current position isn't the result of a single strategic decision but rather the product of many decisions made over time. Under Armour's current stock of resources and capabilities weren't always available to the firm; they had to be developed dynamically. For instance, entering segments dominated by companies such as Nike and adidas required it to develop exceptional capabilities in design and marketing. And as tempting as it is to use hindsight to see some of Under Armour's competitors as inept, they didn't sit idly by while Under Armour ascended, created new market segments, and stole market share in existing segments. Indeed, Nike now has its own line of compression performance sports apparel. For pedagogical simplicity, we first introduce some fundamental concepts in strategic management and then move on to discuss the concepts and tools that managers use to think of strategy in dynamic terms.

2. **To succeed, the *formulation* of a good strategy and its *implementation* should be inextricably connected.** Unfortunately, many managers tend to focus on formulating a plan of attack and give too little thought to implementing it until it's too late. Likewise, they may similarly give short shrift to the importance of strategic leadership in effectively bridging strategy formulation and implementation. In fact, research suggests that, on average, managers are better at formulating strategies than they are at implementing them. This problem has been described as a "knowing–doing gap."[3] Effective managers realize that successfully implementing a good idea is at least as important as generating one. To implement strategies, the organization's leaders have numerous levers at their disposal. Levers such as organization structure, systems and processes, and people and rewards are tools that help strategists achieve alignment—that is, the need for all of the firm's activities to complement each other and support the strategy.

3. **Strategic leadership is essential if a firm is to both formulate and implement strategies that create value.** Strategic leaders are those responsible for formulating firms' strategies, such as Kevin Plank at Under Armour. They have this responsibility as a consequence of their hierarchical status in management. In addition, strategic leadership plays two critical roles in successful strategy implementation, and it's important to highlight them here so that you can incorporate them into your own assessment of a strategy's feasibility as well as ensure that you include these roles in your implementation plans. Specifically, strategic leadership is responsible for (1) making substantive implementation-lever and resource-allocation decisions and (2) developing support for the strategy from key stakeholders.

What Is Strategic Management?

strategic management
Process by which a firm manages the formulation and implementation of a strategy.

Strategic management is the process by which a firm manages the formulation and implementation of its strategy. But we still need to ask ourselves: What is the *goal* of strategic management? What does "having a *strategy*" mean? Even if we're pretty sure that we have a strategy and a goal for it, how do we know whether we have a good strategy or a bad one?

THE STRATEGIC LEADER'S PERSPECTIVE

The word *strategy* is derived from the Greek *strategos*. Roughly translated, it means "the general's view," and thinking about military ranks and responsibilities is one way to focus on the difference between the general's view (and the CEO's view) and that of some lower-level officer (like line or middle managers). The primary responsibility of a lower-level officer might be supply logistics, infantry, or heavy armored vehicles. Thus, lower-level officers may not be too concerned with the overall plan because of their attention to detail in specific areas of responsibility. The general, however, must not only understand how *all* of the constituent parts interrelate, but must use that understanding to draw up a plan that will lead to victory—a strategy. In the business context, the idea of strategy, therefore, suggests a big-picture perspective on the firm and its context. We call this holistic view of the organization the *strategic leader's perspective.*

The success of a military strategy depends not only on the quality of the general's planning and the vision behind it, but also on the execution of the strategy by the forces under the general's command. In business settings, likewise, a strategy is of little use if it is not well-executed by line managers. In addition, the quality of a strategy is often dependent on the leader's soliciting and utilizing the advice of other senior and midlevel leaders. In other words, a good leader can't afford to devise a strategy in isolation from the lower-level leaders who are responsible for executing it.

The ideas of strategy need not focus exclusively on military analogies just because the root of the word is from this context. You can see ideas analogous to the difference between the general's view and the lower-level officer's view in sports, education, personal life, and business. The important thing about the Greek derivation of the word *strategy* is that the big-picture perspective is fundamentally different from the detail of operational tactics.

In business, strategy requires a big-picture perspective. Up to this point, most of your business courses have probably focused on important but limited aspects of business. Indeed, most business-education classes are devoted to specialized areas of study on specific functional areas, such as finance or marketing. In strategic management, however, we're concerned with an overall, holistic view of the firm and its environment and the ways in which such a view determines the competitive decisions that businesspeople have to make. For this reason, when studying strategic management we generally take the perspective of the strategic leader. Recognize, however, that strategies often emerge from bottom-up processes and from fortuitous circumstances that the leader could not have anticipated. The strategic leader's perspective does not mean to suggest that plans are formulated in some linear fashion by a single leader. Rather, the strategic leader's perspective is the holistic consideration of the business and its environment rather than the myopic focus on a single functional area.

WHY STUDY STRATEGY?

You may wonder why it is important to study strategy when your career is unlikely to begin at the level of strategic leadership. From a practical standpoint, employers expect you to be functionally fluent in accounting, marketing, or some other specialization. They also expect that you will understand the "big picture"—strategic management gives you the tools to understand and describe the big picture. If strategy is the means by which an organization goes about pursuing its overarching objectives, then studying and gaining an understanding of the principles, theories, and tools of strategic management will be an important aid for you even early in your career. This course will help you in several areas critical to your career: you will be in a better position to understand your firm's objectives (or what they should be), you will be equipped to analyze and understand how competition will interfere with attaining your objectives and what can be done to minimize these threats, you will comprehend how effective strategy formulation and implementation requires complementary organizational resources and capabilities, and you will be able to identify which of these key factors may be missing in your organization. In addition, while the ultimate responsibility for strategy lies with senior management, the process of strategic management is one that requires the coordinated cooperation of employees at all levels of the organization. Top executives are not lone wolves when it comes to devising and implementing strategy. They rely on lower-level managers to collect and analyze data regarding competition and commercial opportunities. Consequently, the better employees understand the firm's strategy, the better they'll be able to make choices that are consistent with it. It's critical, therefore, that managers at every level understand the firm's strategy and work toward implementing its strategic initiatives.

WHAT IS STRATEGY?

strategy The coordinated means by which an organization pursues its goals and objectives.

The idea of "strategy" means different things to different people (and a lot of these ideas aren't particularly accurate).[4] In fact, experts in the field have formulated various definitions of *strategy*. We've adopted the simple and direct definition; **strategy** is the coordinated means by which an organization pursues its goals and objectives.[5] A strategy thus encompasses the pattern of actions that have been taken and those that are planned to be taken by an organization in pursuing its objectives.[6]

Because firms are attempting to sell products or services to potential customers, an implication of strategy in this context is that the firm is attempting to gain an advantage over other potential providers of those products and services. Virtually all firms face some level of competition. A strategy helps a firm accomplish its objectives in the face of competition. Strategy is not, however, necessarily a zero-sum game in which one firm wins and one loses. In many instances, firms cooperate in some aspects of business and compete in others.

Exhibit 1.3 outlines the strategic management process that you will be exploring and applying throughout this textbook.[7] From the exhibit, you can see how vision, goals and objectives, internal and external analysis, and implementation levers can be used to help formulate and implement strategy. Strategy outlines the means by which a firm intends to create unique value for customers and other important stakeholders.[8] This definition of strategy is important because, as you will see later, it forces managers to think holistically and dynamically about what the firm does and why those activities consistently lead customers to prefer the firm's products and services over those of its competitors.

BUSINESS STRATEGY VERSUS CORPORATE STRATEGY

In studying strategy, you'll find it useful to distinguish between strategic issues at the *business level* and those at the *corporate level*. Some firms are focused sharply on their *business* strategy: They compete in only one or very few industries. Other firms compete in many industries. The opening vignette on Under Armour paints a picture of a firm that has a very specific core business (athletic apparel). Some firms, such as General Electric (GE) or United Technologies, are called *conglomerates* because they're so diversified that it's difficult to pigeonhole them into any specific industry.

Consider the two largest competitors in the aircraft-engine industry. The largest is General Electric (GE), with $11 billion in aircraft-engine sales; the second largest is Rolls-Royce PLC, with approximately $8.4 billion in total sales. Rolls-Royce gets most of its revenue—approximately 74 percent—from this industry. (The firm no longer makes luxury cars; the operation was parceled off to BMW and Volkswagen in 1998.) In contrast, GE is involved in hundreds of businesses, including such diverse enterprises as manufacturing light bulbs, medical devices, and commercial jet engines; providing home mortgages; broadcasting (it

Exhibit 1.3 The Strategic Management Process

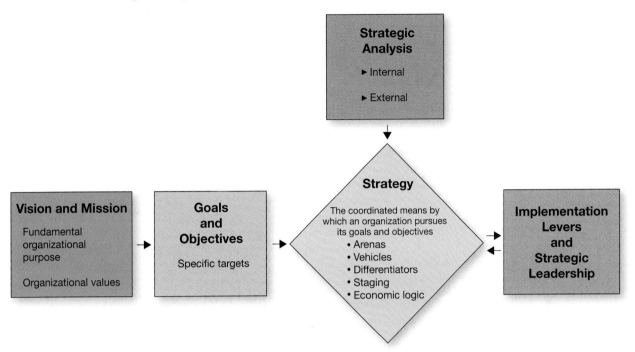

owns NBC); and operating self-storage facilities. It derives less than 10 percent of its revenue from aircraft engines. Within this industry, of course, both GE and Rolls-Royce face the same competitive pressures, such as determining how to compete against each other and such rivals as Pratt & Whitney (the third-largest firm in the industry). In managing its portfolio of businesses, GE faces strategic issues that are less relevant to Rolls-Royce.

Business Strategy What sort of issues are these? **Business strategy** refers to the ways a firm goes about achieving its objectives within *a particular industry* or *industry segment.* In other words, one of GE's business strategies would be how it pursues its objectives within the jet engine business. This strategy may encompass such things as how it competes against Rolls-Royce for contracts from Boeing and Airbus, how it cooperates with other suppliers of technology it uses in designing its engines, and the decision to ramp up scale in an effort to reduce its costs. When Under Armour managers decide how to compete with Nike for consumer dollars, they, too, are engaged in business strategy. Business strategy, therefore, focuses on *achieving a firm's objectives within a particular business line.*

Increasingly, business strategy also takes into account the changing competitive landscape in which a firm is located. Two critical questions that business strategy must address are (1) how the firm will achieve its objectives *today,* when other companies may be competing to satisfy the same customers' needs, and (2) how the firm plans to compete *in the future.* In later chapters, we'll focus specifically on issues related to business strategy.

Corporate Strategy Many firms are involved in more than one line of business. Large corporations like 3M and GE can be involved in dozens or hundreds of separate business activities. Under Armour started with a focus on men's performance apparel, but has expanded into other apparel like footwear. **Corporate strategy** addresses issues related to

business strategy Strategy for competing against rivals within a particular industry or industry segment.

corporate strategy Strategy for guiding a firm's entry and exit from different businesses, for determining how a parent company adds value to and manages its portfolio of businesses, and for creating value through diversification.

three fundamental questions associated with managing a company that operates in more than one business:

1. **In what businesses will we compete?** In the 1970s and 1980s, for instance, Sears chose to branch out of retailing into credit cards, stock brokerage, and real estate. Later, it decided that many of these moves were ill-advised and it divested most of these new businesses. GE managers address corporate-strategy questions when deciding whether the firm should enter a new business. All of the decisions about what businesses to compete in (including decisions to exit businesses) are issues of corporate strategy.

2. **How can we, as a corporate parent, add value to our various lines of business?** At GE, for instance, senior management might be able to orchestrate synergies and learning across its commercial- and consumer-finance groups, which are two separate business units. Under Armour sees an opportunity to create synergies by operating in the related businesses of performance apparel and athletic footwear. These synergies, if they are to materialize, will require the corporate office to help the business units to work in a cooperative manner. Sears once thought that it could provide one-stop shopping at retail outlets for everything from tools to life insurance. Thus, corporate strategy also deals with *finding ways to create value by having two or more owned businesses cooperate and share resources.*

3. **How will diversification or our entry into a new industry help us to compete in our other industries?** Under Armour thinks that by entering athletic footwear they may be better positioned to sell more performance apparel. In addition, because Nike operates in both markets, it puts them in a better competitive position in both industries relative to this large incumbent. Wal-Mart has found that diversification into the grocery business segment of retailing has increased retail foot traffic and boosted sales of nongrocery retail products.

Strategy Formulation and Implementation

strategy formulation Process of developing a strategy.

strategy implementation Process of executing a strategy.

Earlier we defined *strategy* as the means by which an organization pursues its goals and objectives. **Strategy formulation** is the process of *deciding what to do;* **strategy implementation** is the process of performing all the activities necessary *to do what has been planned.*[9] Because neither can succeed without the other, the two processes are iterative and interdependent from the standpoint that implementation should provide information that is used to periodically modify business and corporate strategy. Our opening vignette focused mostly on Under Armour's strategy. However, as the company has grown, it found that in order to implement this strategy, it had to invest heavily in organizational structure, systems, and processes.

The Under Armour example also shows how good strategies represent solutions to complex problems. They help to solve problems *external* to the firm by enabling the production of goods or services that both beat the competition and have a ready market. They solve problems *internal* to the firm by providing all employees, including top executives, with clear guidelines as to what the firm should and should not be doing.

STRATEGY FORMULATION

So now we know that strategy formulation means deciding what to do. Some strategies result from rational and methodical planning processes based on analyses of both internal resources and capabilities and the external environment. Others emerge over time and are adopted only after an unplanned pattern of decisions or actions suggests that an unfolding idea may unexpectedly lead to an effective strategy. Sometimes the recognition of a strategically good idea is accidental or "lucky," but corporate innovation and renewal are increasingly the products of controlled experiments and the opportunistic exploitation of surprise.[10] As you can see in Exhibit 1.4, these different aspects of strategy are referred to as intended, deliberate, realized, emergent, and unrealized.[11] You can think of intended strategy as the initial plan, whereas the realized strategy is what actually is put in place and succeeds. Thus, parts of the realized strategy can be credited to deliberate choices and actions (i.e., intended strategies that are realized), and parts are due to unplanned ones (i.e., realized strategies that were not deliberate but nevertheless emerged). Finally, some aspect of the initial strategic plan is not realized at all, and drops by the wayside.

You can see these various aspects of intended and realized strategy through the experience of Intel. During its early years, for instance, the chipmaker Intel was consciously focused on the design and manufacture of dynamic, random-access memory chips (DRAMs), and through the 1970s and early 1980s virtually all of the firm's revenue came from DRAMs. Intel's participation in the DRAM market was intentional and planned virtually from the moment of its founding. By 1984, however, 95 percent of the company's revenue came from the microprocessor segment of the industry. Ironically, Intel's participation in this segment of the industry was not planned by senior management. Rather, it evolved from an experimental venture to make processors for Busicom, a Japanese maker of calculators.[12] Unbeknownst and unforeseen by top management was the fact that market demand was shifting dramatically from DRAMs to microprocessors. Only through the Busicom experiment—and Intel's willingness to follow the signals this experiment sent them in terms of market-demand shifts—was the firm able to dramatically change its business strategy. To this day, Intel officials give credit for the firm's dominance in the microprocessor market to a strategy that emerged originally from a lower-level management initiative—one that, at the time, wasn't greeted with unanimous enthusiasm by senior management.[13]

Exhibit 1.4   Intended and Realized Strategies

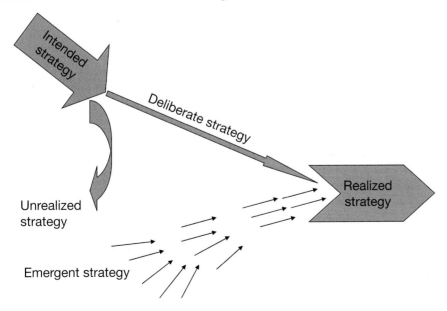

You might be more familiar with Rolls-Royce's automobiles than its jet engines. The fact is, however, that Rolls-Royce PLC no longer even makes luxury automobiles. The company's core business is now jet engines. Jet engines generate 72 percent of its revenues.

Since their lucky foray into the microprocessor market, Intel managers have obviously focused on effective strategies for maintaining the firm's advantages in the segment while at the same time promoting experiments and exploiting surprises like Busicom to keep abreast of significant underlying market-demand shifts.

The Strategy Diamond and the Five Elements of Strategy

Good strategy formulation means refining the elements of the strategy.[14] Remember, first of all, not to confuse *part* of a strategy—for example, being a low-cost provider or first mover in an industry—for strategy itself. Being a low-cost provider or first mover may be part of a strategy, but it's not a complete strategy.

As we noted earlier, a strategy is the means by which a firm will achieve its goals and objectives. This is, of course, the *intended strategy* (referring back to Exhibit 1.4), although through this process managers have a good chance of shaping the *realized strategy* as well. In a for-profit firm, a business strategy will generally address how it will compete against its rivals and make a profit. For instance, if a firm has an objective to be one of the top two firms in a particular industry, this is a complex objective. As result, a strategy designed to pursue this objective will consist of an *integrated set of choices*. These choices can be categorized as five related elements of strategy based on decisions that managers make regarding *arenas, vehicles, differentiators, staging,* and *economic logic*. We refer to this constellation of elements, which are central to the strategic management process outlined in Exhibit 1.3, as the *strategy diamond*. Unfortunately, many naïve managers only focus on one or two such elements, often leaving large gaps in the overall strategy. Or, they may have all five pieces, but not understand how they need to fit together. Only when you have answers to your questions about *each of these five elements* can you determine whether your strategy is an integrated whole; you'll also have a better idea of the areas in which your strategy needs to be revised or overhauled. As Exhibit 1.5 shows, a good strategy diamond provides answers to all five questions:[15]

1. **Arenas.** Where will we be active?

2. **Vehicles.** How will we get there?

3. **Differentiators.** How will we win in the marketplace?

4. **Staging and pacing.** What will be our speed and sequence of moves?

5. **Economic logic.** How will we obtain our returns?

Let's take a closer look at each of these elements.

Arenas By **arenas**, we mean areas in which a firm will be active. Decisions about a firm's arenas may encompass its products, services, distribution channels, market segments, geographic areas, technologies, and even stages of the value-creation process. Unlike vision statements, which tend to be fairly general, the identification of arenas must be very specific: It will clearly tell managers what the firm should and should not do. In addition, because firms can contract with outside parties for everything from employees to manufacturing services, the choice of arenas can be fairly narrowly defined for some firms.

For example, Under Armour made the choice to compete in performance apparel for men, women, and children. Historically, their target market has been in the U.S., but they recently expanded into Europe. More recently, they also targeted users in new market segments and moved into athletic footwear. They sell their products primarily through sporting goods stores. In addition to these arena choices, Under Armour has entirely outsourced the production of its products to outside textile firms, mostly in Asia.

Vehicles Vehicles are the means for participating in targeted arenas. For instance, a firm that wants to go international can achieve that objective in different ways. Under Armour sent their own personnel to Europe to open those operations. Wal-Mart, in recent moves to

arena Area (product, service, distribution channels, geographic markets, technology, etc.) in which a firm participates.

Exhibit 1.5 The Business Strategy Diamond

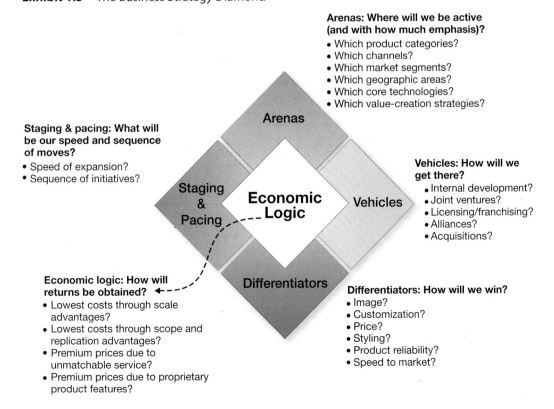

enter certain international markets (such as Argentina and China), has both acquired local retail chains and opened new stores on its own in order to gain more immediate presence. Likewise, a firm that requires a new technology could develop it through investments in R&D. Or, it could opt to form an alliance with a competitor or supplier who already possesses the technology, thereby accelerating the integration of the missing piece into its set of resources and capabilities. Finally, it could simply buy another firm that owns the technology. In this case, then, the possible vehicles for entering a new arena include acquisitions, alliances, and organic investment and growth.

Differentiators A firm that understands why its customers regularly choose its products or services over those of competitors has identified its **differentiators**. The output of differentiators can be seen in the features and attributes of a company's products or services that help it win sales. Firms can be successful in the marketplace along a number of common dimensions, including *image, customization, technical superiority, price,* and *quality and reliability.* Under Armour gains sales in the marketplace through both image and technical superiority. Toyota and Honda have done very well by providing effective combinations of differentiators. They sell both inexpensive cars and cars with high-end, high-quality features, and many consumers find the value that they provide hard to match. As you will learn later in this course, while effective strategies often combine differentiators, it is important to make very specific choices about what your product or service is and what it is not. It is impossible to be all things to all consumers. It's difficult to imagine, for instance, a single product that boasts both state-of-the-art technology and the lowest price on the market. Part of the problem is perceptual—consumers often associate low quality with low price. Part of it is practical—leading-edge technologies cost money to develop and command higher prices because of their uniqueness or quality.

There are two critical factors in selecting differentiators:

■ **These decisions must be made early.** Key differentiators rarely materialize without significant up-front decisions, and without valuable differentiators, firms tend to lose marketplace battles.

■ **Identifying and executing successful differentiators means making tough choices—tradeoffs.** Managers who can't make tough decisions about tradeoffs often end up trying to satisfy too broad a spectrum of customer needs; as a result, they make too many strategic compromises and execute poorly on most dimensions.

Audi provides an example of a company that has aligned these two factors successfully. In the early 1990s, Audi management realized that its cars were perceived as low-quality, high-priced German automobiles—obviously a poor position from which to compete. The firm decided that it had to move one way or another—up market or down market. It had to do one of two things: (1) lower its costs so that its pricing was consistent with customers' perceptions of product quality or (2) improve quality sufficiently to justify premium pricing. Given limited resources, the firm could not go in both directions—that is, produce cars in both the low-price and high-quality strata. Audi made a decision to invest heavily in quality and image; it invested significantly in quality programs and in refining its marketing efforts. Ten years later, the quality of Audi cars has increased significantly, and customer perception has moved them much closer to the level of BMW and Mercedes. Audi has reaped the benefits of premium pricing and improved profitability, but the decisions behind the strategic up-market move entailed significant tradeoffs.[16]

Differentiators are what drive potential customers to choose one firm's offerings over those of competitors. The earlier and more consistent the firm is at defining and driving these differentiators, the greater the likelihood that customers will recognize them.

differentiator Feature or attribute of a company's product or service (e.g., image, customization, technical superiority, price, quality, and reliability) that helps it beat its competitors in the marketplace.

Staging **Staging** refers to the timing and pace of strategic moves. Staging choices typically reflect available resources, including cash, human capital, and knowledge. At what point, for example, should Under Armour enter specific international markets? Perhaps if the company pursues global opportunities too early, it may redirect resources that are needed to exploit its existing opportunities in the U.S. And, when it is time to expand internationally, it is critical to decide which countries they will enter first and which will come later. Furthermore, as product lines are expanded, it is critical to decide which products make the most sense to enter next, and which should be saved for a later time. For instance, there are many possible expansion moves for Under Armour in sporting goods. They have sacrificed some of these possible opportunities for the time being (e.g., running shoes) in order to focus on other activities first (e.g., football cleats). Wal-Mart explicitly decided to delay its international moves so that it could focus first on dominating the U.S. market, which is, after all, the largest retail market in the world. Despite mixed results overseas, Wal-Mart is the undisputed leader in global retailing and has recently increased its emphasis on international markets as the basis for future growth.[17]

Staging decisions should be driven by several factors: resources, urgency, credibility, and the need for early wins. Because few firms have the resources to do everything they'd like to do immediately, they usually have to match opportunities with available resources. In addition, not all opportunities to enter new arenas are permanent; some have only brief windows. In such cases, early wins and the credibility of certain key stakeholders may be necessary to implement a strategy.

Economic Logic Most of the firms you will study in this course are likely to be for-profit firms. As such, a key objective of these firms is to earn an economic profit. The previous four elements of strategy just reviewed (arenas, vehicles, differentiators, and staging) will only make sense for a for-profit firm to the extent that they combine to earn a profit. **Economic logic** is the fifth element of strategy and it refers to *how* the firm will earn a profit—that is, how the firm will generate positive returns over and above its cost of capital. Economic logic is the "fulcrum" for profit creation. Earning normal profits, of course, requires a firm to meet all of its fixed, variable, and financing costs, and achieving desired returns over the firm's cost of capital is a tall order for any organization. In analyzing a firm's economic logic, think of both costs and revenues. Sometimes economic logic resides primarily on the *cost* side of the equation. Southwest Airlines, for example, can fly passengers for significantly lower costs per passenger mile than any major competitor. At other times, economic logic may rest on the firm's ability to increase the customer's willingness to pay premium prices for products (in other words, prices that significantly exceed the costs of providing enhanced products).

When the five elements of strategy are aligned and mutually reinforcing, the firm is generally in a position to perform well. The discussion in the box entitled "How Would *You* Do That? 1.1" demonstrates how you would apply the strategy diamond to JetBlue airlines. High performance levels, however, ultimately mean that a strategy is also being executed well, and we now turn to strategy implementation. It is important to note that you can apply the strategy diamond at multiple levels—at a product level (product strategy), business level (business strategy), corporate level (corporate strategy), and global level (international strategy). The strategy diamond will become a powerful and flexible tool in your strategic management and business policy toolkit.

STRATEGY IMPLEMENTATION LEVERS

Whatever the origin of a strategic idea, whether it was carefully planned from the outset or evolved over time by means of luck or experimentation, successful strategies are dependent on effective implementation. As discussed earlier in the chapter, *strategy implementation* is the process of executing the strategy—of taking the actions that put the strategy into effect and ensure that organizational decisions are consistent with it.[18] The

staging Timing and pace of strategic moves.

economic logic Means by which a firm will earn a profit by implementing a strategy.

The Five Elements of Strategy at JetBlue

To experience how you might apply the strategy diamond, let's consider a recent entrepreneurial success story. The major U.S. airlines lost over $7 billion between 1998 and 2002. David Neeleman, however, confounded the experts when he decided that despite the industry's horrendous performance, the time was right to step down from his executive position at Southwest Airlines to launch a new airline. JetBlue took off on February 11, 2000, with an inaugural flight between New York City's John F. Kennedy International Airport and Fort Lauderdale, Florida. Today, the airline serves more than 50 cities around the country and in the Caribbean and intends to expand further. If you follow the financial fortunes of commercial airlines you will know that JetBlue has obviously done something right. As shown in Exhibit 1.6, even after suffering some recent setbacks that have severely affected profitability, it is second only to Southwest Airlines in profitability over the past three years.[19] To begin applying the strategy diamond to JetBlue, let's quickly review JetBlue's vision, which is to "bring humanity back to air travel" through product innovation and excellent service. It intends to be a low-fare, low-cost passenger airline that provides high-quality customer service. Using the strategy diamond, and public documents posted at www.jetblue.com, we can determine what strategy JetBlue has pursued in order to meet its stated objective.

Exhibit 1.6 Performance of JetBlue

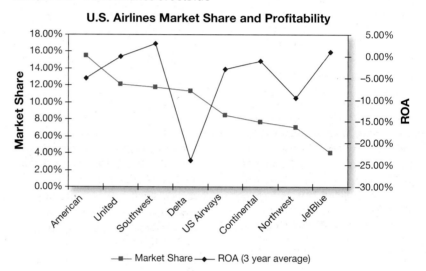

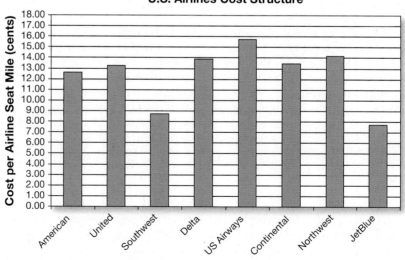

- **In what arenas does JetBlue compete?** Management states that the company competes as a low-fare commercial air carrier, and caters to underserved but overpriced U.S. cities. Its main base of operations is John F. Kennedy airport in New York City, which serves the largest travel market in the country.

- **What vehicles does JetBlue use to enter the arenas in which it competes?** JetBlue started from scratch and has achieved all of its growth in flights per day through internal growth. The firm could have grown by purchasing regional airlines, but chose not to.

- **What are its differentiators?** Price is a big part of JetBlue's strategy for winning new customers, but it also wants to develop the image that it is a low-fare airline with high-quality service. Although it offers only one class of service, the level of service is rather high for a low-fare airline. For instance, it offers leather seating and individual in-seat live satellite TV. Thus, JetBlue states that it aims to create a new segment in airline travel based on value, service, and style.

- **How does JetBlue's staging—the speed of its expansion and the sequence of its growth initiatives—reflect its timetable for achieving its objectives?** JetBlue has grown from 1 route between 2 cities to routes that serve more than 50 cities in just 7 years. At first, it limited itself to the East Coast (between its JFK home base and destinations in Florida and upstate New York), but it soon proceeded westward, establishing locations in the west. Expansion in the east has filled in many more cities, and destinations

When former Southwest Airlines employee and JetBlue founder David Neeleman (shown vacuuming a plane) announced that he was launching a new airline company, people were aghast. Although the airline industry as a whole is losing money, JetBlue has found a way to prosper by effectively aligning the five elements of its strategy that is both internally consistent and externally generates great market demand. The strategy includes low-fare but upscale service, complete with leather seats and satellite TV.

in the Caribbean were also added. JetBlue has targeted more cities for future expansion.

- **What's the economic logic of JetBlue's strategy?** JetBlue's income statements show that its costs are significantly lower than industry averages. Indeed, in 2006 JetBlue had the lowest costs per airline seat mile of any major airline (with Southwest a close second). These cost advantages appear to come from an *ability to perform key tasks in ways that are fundamentally less expensive* than those of competitors. By flying only one make of aircraft that is relatively fuel efficient, JetBlue also keeps maintenance and training costs down. By securing a home base at JFK at a time when the New York Port Authority was anxious to attract more air traffic, JetBlue secured lower

airport fees. Locating in secondary locations (Long Beach instead of Los Angeles International Airport, Fort Lauderdale instead of Miami) also means lower-than-average airport fees. On the revenue side, although JetBlue offers very low fares, it wins customers from competitors and uses its low-cost incentive as a means to convert non-fliers to JetBlue customers. It has also attracted customers by concentrating on underserved, high-priced routes. As a result, it now boasts the highest load factor of any major airline.

As you can see, walking through JetBlue's strategy diamond helps illustrate its strategy. The plan looks sound, but what is required to implement such a plan? The next sections of this chapter provide an overview of this critical issue.

process of implementation also encompasses the refinement, or change, of a strategy as more information is made available through early implementation efforts. The goal of implementation is twofold:

- To make sure that strategy formulation is comprehensive and well informed
- To translate good ideas into actions that can be executed (and sometimes to use execution to generate or identify good ideas)

In sports, a coach's play-calling is only as good as the excellence with which the players execute it. Likewise in business: The value of a firm's strategy is determined by its ability to carry it out. "Any strategy," says Michael Porter, one of the preeminent writers on the subject, ". . . is only as good as its execution."[20] Adds Peter Drucker, one of our most prolific writers on management: "The important decisions, the decisions that really matter, are strategic. . . . [But] more important and more difficult is to make effective the course of action decided upon."[21]

Strategy implementation is usually studied in business school graduate courses, and it's the subject of hundreds of books in business school libraries. We don't intend to supplant the results of all of this study, but we do want you to focus on the implications of a very basic fact: *The processes of strategy formulation and strategy implementation are inextricably linked.* The five elements of strategy, for instance, are related to both formulation and implementation. Good implementation means that an organization coordinates resources and capabilities and uses structure, systems, processes, and strategic leadership to translate a deliberate strategy into a realized strategy and to positive bottom-line results. Throughout the text we help you to see the relationship between formulation and implementation. Chapter 2 introduces you to the role of strategic leadership, and Chapter 11 drills down much deeper into our implementation framework. At this point, and in order to help you consider the complexity of implementing a strategy, we introduce you to just the basic ideas of strategic leadership and implementation.

To implement strategies, organization leaders have numerous levers at their disposal. The framework summarizing these levers is shown in Exhibit 1.7.[22] We categorize these levers into three broad categories: (1) *organization structure,* (2) *systems and processes,* and (3) *people and rewards.* The strategist uses these tools to test for alignment, which is the need for all of the firm's activities to complement each other and support the strategy.

Exhibit 1.7
Implementation Framework

Implementation Levers
- Organizational structure
- Systems and processes
- People and rewards

Intended Strategy

Realized Strategy

Strategic Leadership
- Lever- and resource-allocation decisions
- Develop support among stakeholders

In addition, strategic leadership engages in a few activities related to implementing the strategy that are unique to their positional authority. As the exhibit suggests, implementation includes the activities carried out by the organization that are aimed at executing a particular strategy. Often, the strategy that is realized through these implementation efforts are somewhat different from the original plan. Ideally, these deviations from the original plan are a result of explicit alterations of the strategy that result from feedback during early implementation efforts as well as from the exploitation of serendipitous opportunities that were not anticipated when the strategy was formulated.

Organization Structure   Structure is the manner in which responsibilities, tasks, and people are organized. It includes the organization's authority, hierarchy, units, divisions, and coordinating mechanisms. At this point, we just need to remind ourselves of a few key questions that managers must consider when implementing a strategy:

- Is the current structure appropriate for the intended strategy?

- Are reporting relationships and the delegation of authority set up to execute the strategic plan?

- Is the organization too centralized (or decentralized) for the strategy?

Systems and Processes   Systems are all the organizational processes and procedures used in daily operations. Obviously, these include control and incentive systems, resource-allocation procedures, information systems, budgeting, distribution, and so forth.

People and Rewards   The *people and rewards* lever of the model underscores the importance of using all of the organization's members to implement a strategy. Regardless of your strategy, at the end of the day, it's your people who will have implemented it. Competitive advantage is generally tied to your human resources.[23] Successful implementation depends on having the right people and then developing and training them in ways that support the firm's strategy. In addition, rewards—how you pay your people—can accelerate the implementation of your strategy or undermine it. We have all seen instances in which unintended consequences happen because a manager rewards "A" while hoping for "B."[24]

STRATEGIC LEADERSHIP

Strategic leadership plays two critical roles in successful strategy implementation, and it is important to highlight them here so that you can incorporate them into your own assessment of a strategy's feasibility as well as ensure that you include these roles in your implementation plans. Specifically, as will be discussed in greater detail in Chapter 11, strategic leadership is responsible for (1) making substantive implementation lever and resource-allocation decisions and (2) developing support for the strategy from key stakeholders. Kevin Plank at Under Armour obviously spends a lot of time deciding what needs to be done, such as which new products to launch next, which markets to enter, and which suppliers and distributors to use. However, he also spends a significant amount of time talking to analysts at large U.S. brokerage firms, mutual funds, and pension funds. Why? Because he must keep these key financial stakeholders and shareholders abreast of what Under Armour is doing so that they retain confidence in the firm.

A successful strategy is not generally formulated just by a single person or a small group of leaders. Strategic leadership requires involving the right people in critical decisions because key information may be widely dispersed within the firm. In addition, successful strategy implementation requires active leadership to ensure that what emerges and what is realized are desirable and that needed changes of course are detected before it is too late.

What Is Competitive Advantage?

Earlier we defined *strategy* as the means by which a firm will achieve its objectives. We noted that within a firm's business operations, its objectives will generally encompass some notion of being successful at selling products or services to customers. Because virtually all firms face competition when trying to serve these customers, to achieve its objectives, a firm will have to be perceived by at least some customers as superior to its competition. Thus, the concept of strategy suggests a relationship between strategy on the one hand and performance and competitive advantage on the other. Specifically, we explained that a strategy encompasses the pattern of actions taken by a firm to achieve its objectives. These premises lead us to a logical conclusion: The activities of strategic management are based on the assumption that *firms attempt to achieve a position of competitive advantage over their rivals when serving target customers.*[25] Or, to put it another way: Firms prefer to be winners in their respective industries rather than subpar or even average performers. This leads us to define **competitive advantage** as a firm's ability to create *value* in a way that its rivals cannot.

> **competitive advantage** A firm's ability to create value in a way that its rivals cannot.

Performance itself, however, is not competitive advantage; it's merely a result of it. A firm may achieve relatively high short-term performance levels without gaining any substantial advantage over its rivals. Maybe the company just had an unusually good year or took drastic measures to cut costs (perhaps to unsustainably low levels). By the same token, a firm may enjoy significant competitive advantage in some lines of business but still perform more poorly than its competitors because of other underperforming business units or because it chooses to keep prices lower than its competitive position would otherwise allow. For instance, a firm with a competitive advantage may desire to gain additional market share. Alternatively, it may keep prices lower than its competitive position would otherwise allow to avoid regulators' or competitors' attention.

The question that we now want to answer is: *Why are some firms able to achieve greater advantages over rivals than other firms?* All firms are not alike. For many years, Dell, for example, seemed to have some capabilities that other computer manufacturers, such as Hewlett-Packard and IBM, were unable to duplicate. Thus, for many years Dell sustained a competitive advantage which only recently may have been neutralized by Hewlett-Packard and IBM. Toyota enjoys a similar advantage in the automotive industry. In some industries, we see new entrants quickly outmaneuver incumbents. For instance, why has Under Armour been able to enter an industry with some very formidable incumbents and still be able to earn very good profits? Most industries are *not* accurately characterized by the theoretical condition of perfect competition that you likely learned about in micro econonics (i.e., in perfect competition firms can only earn "normal" profits because super normal profits will attract new entrants and this additional competition will drive profits down). In reality, many industries have one or more companies that earn more than "normal" profits for many years. In addition, some firms appear to outperform competitors consistently, which is likely an indication that they have some form of competitive advantage over their rivals. As we will see, however, it's become increasingly difficult for any one firm to sustain a competitive advantage over a long period of time.[26]

DETERMINANTS OF COMPETITIVE ADVANTAGE

The field of strategic management focuses on explanations for competitive advantage—on the reasons why companies experience above- and below-normal rates of returns. In other words, strategic management offers theories and models that help us understand why some firms perform better than others, and more to the point, offers managers tools to help their firm obtain a competitive advantage and perform better than the competition. Generally speaking, as summarized in Exhibit 1.8, there are three primary perspectives on this issue (perspectives that, as we shall see, reflect contrasting but complementary points of view):

- The *internal perspective* focuses on resources and capabilities as internal sources of uniqueness that allow firms to beat the competition.

- The *external perspective* focuses on the structure of industries and the ways in which firms can position themselves within them for competitive advantage.

- The *dynamic perspective,* which bridges the internal and external perspectives, is a third view of competitive advantage. This view helps explain why competitive advantages do not typically last over long periods of time.

Let's examine each of these perspectives, or theories, more closely.

The Internal Perspective   The first of the two fundamental perspectives on competitive advantage is an internal one. It is often called the *resource-based view of the firm.* This perspective suggests that no two firms are identical because they possess resources and capabilities of different qualities. The advantage goes to the firms with superior resources and capabilities. Proponents of this theory argue that a firm gains an advantage by obtaining valuable and rare resources and developing the capability to utilize these resources to drive customers toward their products and services at the expense of competitors. As a result, firms with superior resources and capabilities enjoy competitive advantage over other firms.[27] This advantage makes it relatively easier for these firms to achieve consistently higher levels of performance than competitors. Competitive advantage, therefore, arises when a company's resources allow its products, services, or businesses to compete

Exhibit 1.8   Three Perspectives on Competitive Advantage

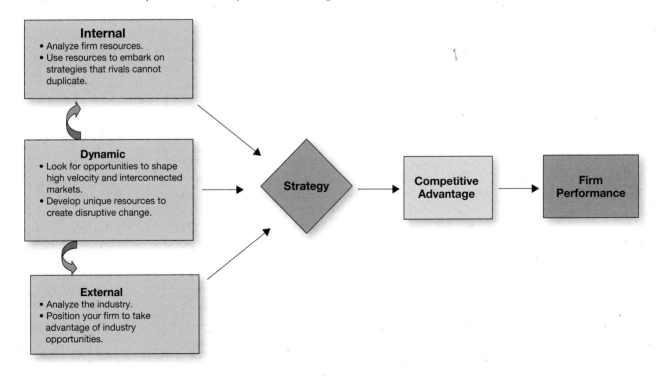

successfully against rival firms in the same industries. According to this perspective, the objective for managers is to determine what resources and capabilities offer the most potential value, to acquire them if they are lacking, and then to leverage those specific resources in executing the firm's strategy. The resource-based view also holds that a firm's bundle of resources may either hinder or help its entry into new businesses—an idea that we'll explore further in later chapters.[28]

The External Perspective

The second fundamental perspective on competitive advantage contends that variations in firms' competitive advantage and performance are primarily a function of industry attractiveness and the *position* of firms within the industry relative to competitors. Thus, this external perspective suggests that competitive advantage comes from a firm's positioning within the competitive business environment.

The seminal work supporting this approach is Michael Porter's work on competitive strategy.[29] Porter's theory—sometimes called *industrial organization economics* (I/O economics)—suggests that firms should do one of two things: (1) position themselves to compete in attractive industries or (2) adopt strategies that will make their current industries more attractive. In some countries, for instance, carmakers lobby for import tariffs in order to make their domestic markets more attractive. When the strategy works, the access of foreign manufacturers to the market is limited, and the cost of participating in it is higher. (In later chapters, we'll explore in more detail the theoretical models and tools that help managers analyze, understand, and shape a firm's competitive environments.)

The Dynamic Perspective

In addition, the two fundamental perspectives that focus on internal and external determinants of competitive advantage, some industries or market segments are less stable than others. Not surprisingly, competitive advantage is more likely to endure in stable markets than in unstable ones. Conversely, the competitive advantage held by one firm over another tends to change very slowly in stable markets but more quickly in unstable ones. As a result of current or possible future changes in the competitive environment, strategies need to be dynamic in nature. The greater the degree of change in the environment, the greater will need be the dynamism of the strategy.

The global chocolate industry, for example, is a relatively stable environment because a few firms—notably, M&M/Mars, Nestlé, and Hershey— dominate it in terms of both size and brands. In addition, demand for chocolate is relatively stable, growing with population growth. To stimulate growth, large companies try to formulate new candy bars. However, this type of growth is rather incremental and predictable. Smaller companies carve out niches in which to offer differentiated products, but this generally does not result in any significant upheaval of market position. In such stable contexts, fundamental theories of competitive advantage usually explain most economic facts. The external (or positional) view of strategy tends to dominate questions of strategy formulation and implementation. Why? Because a firm's current market position, as gauged by market share or some other criterion, may be a good indicator of competitive advantage and provides a relatively accurate predictor of future performance. This view also tends to assume that industries are clearly defined, that competition is predictable, and that the future doesn't hold many surprises.

But what about dynamic industries—such as computer chips or laser printers or medical products—in which it seems that competitive advantage can shift in a matter of months or even days simply because of a new product release or some other technological breakthrough?[30] A so-called *dynamic perspective* on competitive advantage has become increasingly important in explaining the economic facts in such industries in which markets converge, technologies rapidly change competitive conditions, capital markets become increasingly impatient, firms compete in multiple markets and multiple industries against common rivals, and the costs of establishing a competitive position soar (and so increase dramatically the cost of failure). The dynamic perspective suggests that a firm's current market position or competitive advantage is *not* an accurate predictor of future performance or sustainable competitive advantage. Why not? Because current market position itself is not a competitive advantage, but rather an outcome of past competitive activities. Consequently, as the competitive environment changes, new leaders may be past leaders, new entrants, or prior incumbents who are better positioned for the future state of the industry. From the dynamic perspective, we look to the past for clues about how the firm arrived at its current position and to the future in an effort to predict the look of the new competitive landscape.

The External Dimension of the Dynamic Perspective Of course, the dynamic strategy perspective has both external and internal dimensions as well. On the external side, it's useful in analyzing "high-velocity" markets—markets that are changing rapidly and unpredictably.[31] Often, such changes result from technology. For instance, the personal music player market has seen tremendous upheaval in the status quo as digital formats replaced analog devices. However, as we noted earlier, there are usually several contributing factors. The dynamic perspective is also a good tool for examining industries characterized by *multimarket competition*—those in which firms tend to encounter the same rivals in multiple markets.[32] Goodyear, Michelin, and Bridgestone, for instance, compete head-to-head in tire markets around the world. Another form of multimarket competition is illustrated by Nestlé and Mars; these companies battle it out in global industries ranging from pet foods to snack foods and will often use resources from one industry to bolster competitive position in another—say, by offering retailer discounts on pet food in exchange for shelf space for snack foods. For instance, Proctor & Gamble's entry into Vietnam appears to be less driven by the profit motive (P&G tends to lose money on Vietnamese soap sales) than by a determination to keep rival Unilever in check. If P&G had not entered the Vietnamese market, Unilever could have reaped monopoly-like profits and proceeded to use the windfall to pay for competitive efforts against P&G in other markets. By competing with Unilever in a market in which it has no competitive advantage (and may not even seek one), P&G's strategy reduces Unilever's ability to wage war on other fronts.

The Internal Dimension of the Dynamic Perspective The dynamic perspective can also help us to focus on a firm's resources and capabilities, particularly those that lead to a *continuous flow* of advantages in resources or market position and those that strengthen the firm's ability to embrace (and even foster) continuous and sometimes disruptive *change*. Risk taking, experimentation, improvisation, and continuous learning are—at least from the dynamic perspective—key features of successful firms. Later in the text, we will explore several relevant analytical tools for shaping strategy formulation. You'll also learn how to combine your analysis of an industry's cumulative technological development with your assessment of whether a firm can exploit an innovative product or disruptive technology through its entire life cycle or whether it must instead leap from product to product at strategically defined crossover points.

As suggested by our opening vignette on Under Armour, note that the dynamic perspective also provides valuable insight into the formulation and implementation of strategies at firms competing in ostensibly stable markets and industries. Few observers classified the men's athletic apparel market as a dynamic industry. While there were many competitors in various segments, Nike was viewed as the Goliath of the industry that led much of the innovation of new products. Under Armour entered the industry with an innovative product targeted at an underserved market. Under Armour's compression performance wear products were able to generate significant price premiums over incumbents' products (remember, $25 to $35 for a T-shirt). Yet, while the creation and design of the concept was proprietary to Under Armour, they used off-the-shelf technology from third-party suppliers. Consequently, in order to successfully enter and capitalize on his idea, Kevin Plank needed to be able to marshal organizational resources to implement his plan and gain market share before he awoke the giant incumbents. By the time Under Armour appeared on Nike's and adidas' radar, it had already created and was in position to defend a rather dominant position in the performance apparel segment. You will find the same theme in stories about Amazon.com versus Barnes & Noble and U.S. mini-mills versus major steel producers.[33]

Summary of Challenges

1. *Understand what* **strategy** *is and identify the difference between business-level and corporate-level strategy.* Strategic management is the process by which a firm manages the formulation and implementation of its strategy. A *strategy* is the central, integrated, externally oriented concept of how a firm will achieve its objectives. Strategies typically take one of two forms: business strategy or corporate strategy. The objective of a business strategy is to spell out how the firm plans to compete. This plan integrates choices regarding arenas (where the firm will be active), vehicles (how it will get there), differentiators (how it will win), staging (the speed and sequence of its moves), and economic logic (how it obtains its returns). The objective of corporate strategy is to spell out which businesses a firm will compete in, how ownership by the corporate parent adds value to the business, and how this particular diversification approach helps each business compete in its respective markets.

2. *Understand why we study* **strategic management.** It should be clear to you by now that strategic management is concerned with firm performance. Strategic management holds clues as to why firms survive when performance suffers. Strategy helps you to understand which activities are important and why and how a plan, absent good execution, is perhaps only as valuable as the paper it's printed on.

3. *Understand the relationship between* **strategy formulation** *and* **implementation.** *Strategy formulation* is the determination of what the firm is going to do; *strategy implementation* is how the firm goes about doing it. These two facets of strategy are linked and interdependent. This interdependence is made strikingly clear by the strategic management process (Exhibit 1.3) you are introduced to in this chapter, examples throughout the text, and the specific treatment of implementation levers in Chapter 11.

4. *Describe the determinants of competitive* **advantage.** Competitive advantage is realized when one firm creates value in ways that its competitors cannot, such that the firm clearly performs better than its competitors. Advantage is not simply higher relative performance; rather, superior performance signals the ability of a firm to do things in ways its direct competitors cannot. The two primary views of competitive advantage—internal and external—are complementary and together are used to help formulate effective strategies. The internal view portrays competitive advantage to be a function of unique, firm-specific resources and capabilities. The external view holds that a firm's performance is largely a function of its position in a particular industry or industry segment given the overall structure of the industry. Profitable industries are considered attractive, and therefore, high firm performance is attributed to a firm's position in the industry relative to the characteristics of the industry or industry segment.

5. *Recognize the difference between the* **fundamental** *and* **dynamic views of competitive advantage.** The two fundamental views of competitive advantage are characterized by a largely internal or external orientation toward competitive advantage, research shows that few firms persist in their dominance over competitors over prolonged periods of time. For most firms, therefore, competitive advantage is considered to be temporary. The dynamic perspective assumes that a firm's current market position is not an accurate predictor of future performance because position itself is not a competitive advantage. Instead, the dynamic perspective looks at the past for clues about how the firm arrived at its present position and to the future to divine what the new competitive landscape might look like. It also holds that it's possible for the firm to influence the future state of the competitive landscape.

Review Questions

1. What is strategic management?

2. What are the key components of the strategic management process?

3. How does business strategy differ from corporate strategy?

4. What is the relationship between strategy formulation and strategy implementation?

5. What five elements comprise the strategy formulation diamond?

6. What are the internal and external perspectives of competitive advantage?

7. What are the fundamental and dynamic perspectives of competitive advantage?

8. Why should you study strategic management?

Experiential Activities

Group Exercises

1. Identify the characteristics of a firm that the members of your group would like to work for and try to identify an example of this type of firm. What's the difference between business and corporate strategy at this firm? How might that affect your experiences and opportunities in that organization? Use your knowledge of the firm's strategy to construct a high-impact job application cover letter to apply for a job with this firm.

2. How is international expansion related to business and corporate strategy? Identify a firm that may be thinking of expanding into new international markets. Apply the staging element of the strategy diamond to the firm's international expansion opportunities or plans. Which markets should it target first and why?

Ethical Debates

1. Should ethics be a formal and explicit part of strategy formulation and implementation? What would you do to achieve this type of objective?

2. For many of the firms you will study in this class, competitive advantage is measured by some form of financial profitability. How should you evaluate ethical choices in terms of accounting costs and benefits?

How Would
YOU DO THAT?

1. Go to Warren Buffet's *Letter to Shareholder's* page at www.berkshirehathaway.com/letters/letters.html and read the most recent letter. How many of the strategy topics covered in this chapter are referenced in the letter? Pick one of the businesses owned by Berkshire Hathaway and draft a strategy formulation diamond similar to the one outlined in the JetBlue example in the box entitled "How Would *You* Do That? 1.1."

2. Go back to the discussion of JetBlue in the box entitled "How Would *You* Do That? 1.1." Use the strategy implementation model in Exhibit 1.7 to identify what would be necessary to successfully implement JetBlue's strategy. How would the implementation levers be different for JetBlue than for some of the major airlines?

Go on to see How Would You Do That at www.prenhall.com/carpenter&sanders

Endnotes

1. Under Armour, Inc., *2006 Annual Report.*

2. Under Armour, Inc., *2006 Annual Report.*

3. J. Pfeffer and R. I. Sutton, *The Knowing-Doing Gap: How Smart Companies Turn Knowledge into Action* (Boston: Harvard Business School Press, 2000).

4. M. Porter, "What Is Strategy?" *Harvard Business Review* 74:6 (1996), 61–78.

5. D. C. Hambrick and J. W. Fredrickson, "Are You Sure You Have a Strategy?" *Academy of Management Executive* 15:4 (2001), 48–59.

6. K. R. Andrews, *The Concept of Corporate Strategy* 3rd ed. (Homewood, IL: Irwin, 1987).

7. Adapted from D. C. Hambrick and J. W. Fredrickson, "Are You Sure You Have a Strategy?" *Academy of Management Executive* 15:4 (2001), 48–59.

8. R. H. Waterman, T. J. Peters, and J. R. Phillips, "Structure Is Not Organization," *Business Horizons* 23:3 (1980), 14–26.

9. Andrews, *The Concept of Corporate Strategy* 3rd ed. (Homewood, IL: Irwin, 1987).

10. S. Brown and K. Eisenhardt, *Competing on the Edge* (Boston: Harvard Business School Press, 1998); R. A. Burgelman and L. Sayles, *Inside Corporate Innovation* (New York: Free Press, 1986).

11. Adapted from H. Mintzberg, "The Strategy Concept I: Five Ps for Strategy" *California Management Review* 30:1 (1987): 11–24.

12. R. A. Burgelman, "Fading Memories: A Process Theory of Strategic Business Exit in Dynamic Environments," *Administrative Science Quarterly* 39 (1993): 24–56.

13. Burgelman, "Fading Memories"; Grove, *Only the Paranoid Survive.*

14. This section draws extensively from Hambrick and Fredrickson, "Are You Sure You Have a Strategy?"

15. Adapted from D. C. Hambrick and J. W. Fredrickson, "Are You Sure You Have a Strategy?" *Academy of Management Executive* 15:4 (2001), 48–59.

16. Personal interviews with company executives.

17. T. Carl, "After Growing on Small Towns, Wal-Mart Looks to World for More Expansion," Associated Press Newswires, March 26, 2003.

18. *The Strategy Execution Imperative: Leading Practices for Implementing Strategic Initiative* (Washington, D.C.: Corporate Executive Board, 2001); Christensen, "Making Strategy."

19. Data obtained from *JetBlue 2006 Annual Report*, Transportation Workers Union, TWU Airline Industry Review, at www.twuatd.org; Bureau of Transportation, *TransStats Reports*, at www.transtats.bts.gov.

20. M. F. Porter, "Know Your Place: How to Assess the Attractiveness of Your Industry and Your Company's Position in It," *Inc.*, September 1991, 90.

21. P. F. Drucker, *The Practice of Management* (New York: HarperCollins, 1954), 352–353.

22. Adapted from D. Hambrick and A. Cannella, "Strategy Implementation as Substance and Selling," *Academy of Management Executive* 3:4 (1989), 278–285.

23. See J. B. Barney and P. M. Wright, "On Becoming a Strategic Partner: The Role of Human Resources in Gaining Competitive Advantage," *Human Resource Management* 37:1 (1998), 31–46; J. Pfeffer, *Competitive Advantage Through People* (Boston: HBS Press, 1994).

24. S. Kerr, "On the Folly of Rewarding A, While Hoping for B," *Academy of Management Journal* 18:4 (1975), 769–783.

25. J. B. Barney, "Firm Resources and Sustained Competitive Advantage," *Journal of Management* 17:1 (1991), 99–121; M. A. Peteraf, "The Cornerstones of Competitive Advantage: A Resource-Based View," *Strategic Management Journal* 14:3 (1993), 179–191.

26. R. R. Wiggins and T. W. Ruefli, "Sustained Competitive Advantage: Temporal Dynamics and the Incidence and Persistence of Superior Economic Performance," *Organization Science* 13:1 (2002), 82–105.

27. Barney, "Firm Resources and Sustained Competitive Advantage"; Peteraf, "The Cornerstones of Competitive Advantage"; B. Wernerfelt, "A Resource Based View of the Firm," *Strategic Management Journal* 5:2 (1984), 171–180.

28. Peteraf, "The Cornerstones of Competitive Advantage"; C. A. Montgomery and S. Hariharan, "Diversified Expansion by Large Established Firms," *Journal of Economic Behavior* 15:1 (1991), 71–99.

29. M. Porter, *Competitive Strategy* (New York: Free Press, 1980).

30. C. M. Christensen, *The Innovator's Dilemma: When New Technologies Cause Great Firms to Fail* (Boston: Harvard Business School Press, 1997).

31. Brown and Eisenhardt, *Competing on the Edge.*

32. J. Gimeno and C. Woo, "Multimarket Contact, Economies of Scope, and Firm Performance," *Academy of Management Journal* 42:3 (1999), 239–259.

33. Christensen, *The Innovator's Dilemma.*

2

Leading Strategically Through Effective
Vision and Mission

In This Chapter We Challenge You To >>>

1. Explain how strategic leadership is essential to strategy formulation and implementation.

2. Understand the relationships among vision, mission, values, and strategy.

3. Understand the roles of vision and mission in determining strategic purpose and strategic coherence.

4. Identify a firm's stakeholders and explain why such identification is critical to effective strategy formulation and implementation.

5. Explain how ethics and biases may affect strategic decision making.

The Xerox Vision

*O*ur strategic intent is to help people find better ways to do great work—by constantly leading in document technologies, products and services that improve our customers' work processes and business results.

How to Pull a $15-Billion Cow Out of a Ditch[1] From an outsider's perspective, there was very little in Anne Mulcahy's background at Xerox to suggest that she'd be prepared for the kind of crisis management that awaited her. Most recently, she'd been vice president for human resources and chief staff officer to former chief executive officer (CEO) Paul A. Allaire. The Xerox board promoted Mulcahy to president in May 2000, ousting G. Richard Thoman after a mere 13 months and reinstalling Chairman Allaire as CEO.

When Allaire stepped down on August 1, 2001, Mulcahy became the first female CEO in Xerox history. When Mulcahy's promotion to CEO was announced, Xerox stock took a 15% nosedive. "Not a big confidence boost," Mulcahy said. She also knew that even some of her fellow senior managers did not have confidence in her leadership. So she quickly called a meeting of all senior Xerox leaders and told them point blank that if any of them wanted to leave she would help. Mulcahy did this because she needed the entire team to buy into her plan. "To my surprise, four people asked to leave from the leadership team. But those who stayed became very active. They were stretched, but I did not want armchair quarterbacks criticizing my every move. We needed to work quickly," she said.

The Fall from the Nifty 50 The Xerox story is pretty well known. Introduced in 1959, the Xerox 914 copier transformed office work and installed Xerox as a charter member of the so-called "Nifty 50"—the 50 stocks most favored by institutional investors. Since the 1970s, however, Xerox had been crippled by competition (mostly Japanese), repeated failures to capitalize on innovations coming out of its own Palo Alto Research Center (PARC), and tardiness in embracing digital imaging. After years of weak sales, the company was foundering, and employees were as disgruntled as customers. Then things went from bad to worse. In October 2001, Xerox reported its first quarterly loss in 16 years, and as debt piled up, the Securities and Exchange Commission began investigating the company's accounting practices.

Although the move from senior executive to CEO was a huge jump, Mulcahy was given the chance because she'd instilled confidence in the board. "She has the strategic mind and toughness to serve as CEO," said board member (and Johnson & Johnson CEO) Ralph Larsen.

Mulcahy was a popular manager with years of experience in dealing with customers. Granted, she'd never been involved in product development and didn't boast Allaire's financial expertise, but she'd demonstrated smart decision-making skills as head of the company's $6-billion division for small-office equipment. She'd also put together one of its biggest acquisitions—the $925-million purchase from Tektronix Inc. of a color-printing division that's now a source of fast-growing revenues (in large part because Mulcahy had preserved the division's autonomy and many of its business practices).

Running the Gamut from Enthusiasm to Pragmatism If there was ever any uncertainty about her qualifications as a CEO, they were soon dispelled. Mulcahy refined the Xerox vision and went out of her way to remind Xerox employees that the core values embedded in the company's mission statement had always been part of the firm's deep culture. More important, she moved decisively to align the firm's operations with its refined statement of mission and values.

On the less philosophical side, she sold Xerox's China and Hong Kong operations, and in March 2001 she raised $1.3 billion by selling half of its stake in a joint venture with Fuji. Mulcahy also proved willing to make other tough decisions. In June 2001, she closed down the unit that made desktop inkjet printers in Rochester, New York—a business that she'd once supported. Soon after taking the reins, she eliminated the company's stock dividend and announced that PARC would be spun off as a separate company.

Internally, she spread her message with a regular memo called "Turnaround Talk," which alternates between enthusiasm ("Together We Can Do It!") and pragmatism ("When we shut off the bottled water, it's not because we want to be mean-spirited. It's because all these little expenses can spell the difference between losing money and turning a profit"). By 2002, stressing fidelity to the Xerox mission and long-term vision, she'd cut annual expenses by $1.7 billion, sold $2.3 billion worth of noncore assets, and reduced long-term debt to $9.2 billion, down from a high of $15.6 billion in 2000. Xerox returned to full-year profitability in 2002, generating $1.9 billion in operating-cash flow and $91 million in net income on $15.8 billion in sales.

The Next Chapter In July 2003, with Xerox gaining market share in important segments with new-product introductions, Mulcahy announced that the current chapter in the Xerox "turnaround story" had been closed. Her new challenge would be reigniting growth. Even during weak sales years, she'd invested $1 billion annually in research and development. Her investment in R&D paid off. By 2006, two-thirds of Xerox revenues came from new products that had been introduced just two years prior. "I would say the most important way we foster innovation is our funding of research, which so many companies have walked away from," Mulcahy said. In 2006, the company introduced 49 new products. In the first four months of 2007, Xerox introduced 19 more new products. Mulcahy also bet big on growth through such service businesses as document-management flow and computer networking and achieved a win there as well. In the first quarter of 2007, 70 percent of revenue came from supplies and services.

The task of turning Xerox around has taken its toll on Mulcahy's personal life. Friends say that she laughs when asked about hobbies and executive-suite privileges like golf. Nowadays, reports *Business Week,* Mulcahy "only has time for work and her family, including her two teenage sons." But that, concludes the article, is "the kind of effort it takes to pull a $15-billion cow out of a ditch—and then try to make it run." <<<

Strategic Leadership

Imagine starting a new job and then finding out that your job description includes the following items:

- You'll be personally responsible for the entire company's performance—success, or failure.

- You'll be relatively powerless to control most of what goes on in the organization.

- You'll have more authority than any other employee, but in using that authority, you'll make some people so unhappy that they'll harbor personal grudges against you.[2]

Congratulations: You're a CEO.

The basic responsibility of a CEO—*strategic leadership*—is so important that you'll find chapters on it in every management and organizational behavior book you pick up. Stories about leaders and leadership regularly command the covers and fill the pages of major business publications around the world. Some business leaders become celebrities.

What do these leaders do when they're on the job? *Leadership* is the task of exerting influence on other people's pursuit of goals in an organizational context. **Strategic leadership** is the task of managing an overall enterprise and influencing key organizational outcomes, such as company-wide performance, competitive superiority, innovation, strategic change, and survival. As the process of communicating the vision and mission that top executives espouse and model through their own actions, strategic leadership also sets the stage for strategy creation and implementation. Strategic leadership is often associated with individuals like Anne Mulcahy, but increasingly it's being exercised by teams of top executives. Given the complexity and speed of competitive change and uncertainty facing most firms today, this shift shouldn't be surprising.

strategic leadership Task of managing an overall enterprise and influencing key organizational outcomes.

WHAT THIS CHAPTER IS ABOUT

Most of this section explains why top executives, through their decisions and behavior, have both a symbolic and a substantive impact on the outcomes that concern a firm's key stakeholders. What we can tell you at this point, however, is that executives tend to be reactive and defensive in their decisions when their firms don't have clear strategies, and that is generally not a desirable situation for a manager. Thus we start by introducing the roles filled by top individual managers and management teams as they exercise strategic leadership. We'll discuss the functions of individuals and executive teams, as well as the conditions under which strategic-leadership efforts may flourish or founder. We will then discuss the ways in which vision, mission, values, and strategy relate to one another, and we'll show how vision and mission are reflected in the properties of strategy that we call *purpose* and *coherence*. Next, we'll introduce the principles of stakeholder analysis and explain why the best strategic leaders consider stakeholder interests when developing organizational vision and mission and strategies for realizing them. We conclude by showing how unethical and biased judgments can undermine even the best-laid strategic-leadership plans.

THE ROLES LEADERS FILL

What do senior managers do? What occupies their days and nights and fills up their personal digital assistants (PDAs)? As our opening vignette suggests, their jobs are complex and multifaceted, and we can understand the CEO's job only by analyzing it in some detail.[3] Let's start by dividing executive activities into the three basic roles illustrated in Exhibit 2.1: *interpersonal, informational,* and *decisional.*[4]

Exhibit 2.1   The Roles That Leaders Play

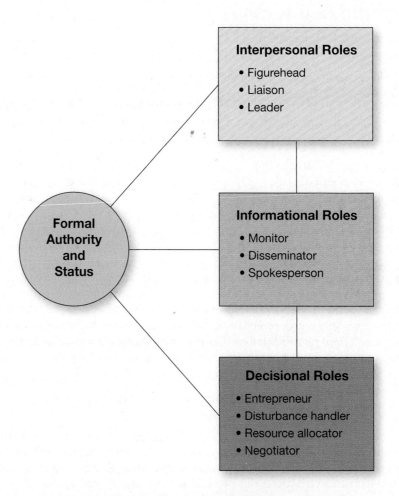

Interpersonal Roles   Some executive tasks derive from the status and formal authority that come with the job. They're often interpersonal in nature and have a degree of symbolic value. Many of these roles may seem to have little to do with the practical exigencies of running a company, but they frequently occupy a great of deal of a CEO's time in all firms, from the smallest to the very largest.

Figurehead and Liaison   As *figureheads,* top executives perform various ceremonial tasks, such as breaking ground at new facilities, hosting retirement dinners, and even fielding calls from irate stakeholders. As *liaisons,* they maintain relationships with external stakeholders, thus strengthening the company's links with its external environment. In this role, they serve on the boards of other companies, meet with suppliers and customers, and participate in charities and civic organizations.

Leader   Whereas the role of liaison is horizontal in nature, leadership is a vertical relationship: Top executives are *leaders* because employees and other stakeholders who don't possess their authority look to them for motivation and direction. In this chapter, we'll focus on senior-leadership responsibilities, such as providing vision, purpose, and direction.

Informational Roles   Informational roles include those of monitor, disseminator, and spokesperson. As *monitor,* the executive taps into a larger network of contacts, colleagues, and employees to collect and collate the information needed to understand the organization and its environment. An effective monitor, says strategic-leadership expert Henry Mintzberg, "seeks information in order to detect changes, to identify problems and opportunities, to build up knowledge about his milieu, to be informed when information must be disseminated and decisions made."[5]

Sharing Information: Disseminator and Spokesperson   Not surprisingly, information is never in short supply; in fact, information overload is a common condition of executive life. Top managers are bombarded with reports, analyses, and projections and information about both internal operations and external events. Obviously, the good monitor must know what to do with all of this information. Much of it, of course, is passed on to people both inside and outside the firm who can put it to use. In passing information to internal stakeholders, executives are *disseminators;* in passing it to external stakeholders, they're *spokespersons.*

As disseminators, CEOs communicate not only factual information, such as data received from bankers and consultants, but also what's often called *value-based information.* In leading Xerox through a period of change, for example, Anne Mulcahy spent much of her time communicating value statements to both internal and external stakeholders.

As spokespersons, CEOs perform such communications tasks as lobbying, public relations, and formal reporting. CEOs communicate with both boards of directors, to whom they report, and the general public. Needless to say, being an effective spokesperson means focusing on the most current, accurate, and relevant information.

Decisional Roles   Perhaps the most obvious—some will say the most important—role of top managers is making key decisions about the company's strategy and future. In developing and implementing strategy, top executives may play any or all of four decisional roles: *entrepreneur, disturbance handler, resource allocator,* and *negotiator.*

The Entrepreneur   As entrepreneur, the CEO designs the firm's strategy. Clearly, many people are involved in the process, but the CEO must ultimately authorize major strategic initiatives and supervise their implementation.

The Disturbance Handler   Whereas the entrepreneurial role focuses on voluntary and proactive initiatives, disturbance handling deals with unforeseen situations or those in which the firm is involved involuntarily. Any number of "disturbances" can threaten the successful implementation of a strategy, including both internal and external conflicts. Internal conflicts, such as infighting by divisions or managers over responsibilities and authority, often require the CEO's arbitration. Likewise, the CEO will probably have to take action to smooth out conflicts in the distribution channel (a key supplier's announcement, for example, that it will no longer deal with the company on an exclusive basis).

The Resource Allocator The role of resource allocator is crucial both to the task of formulating strategy and to the task of executing it successfully. If resources aren't effectively allocated, even a well-formulated strategy has little chance of success. With authority over the organization's financial, material, and human resources, the CEO is the only person who can manage the tradeoffs among competing strategic projects.

The Negotiator As a negotiator, the CEO is usually concerned with nonroutine transactions involving other organizations. Such decisions as whether to acquire or merge with another firm, to sell a major division, or to renegotiate a labor contract require significant participation from the CEO.

The Surprised CEO Obviously, then, being a CEO isn't easy.[6] What's astonishing, however, is the result of recent research showing that many new CEOs are quite surprised by many aspects of their jobs. Some report, for instance, that they're surprised at having to work with limited information and insufficient time to accomplish what they're expected to do. Others are surprised that being a CEO means that they can no longer run day-to-day operations the way they once did. As heads of divisions or small companies, managers are much more deeply involved in nuts-and-bolts operations, but when they move into the executive suite of a large organization, they no longer have the time for hands-on management.

Yet other new CEOs learn the hard way that being the most powerful person in the organization doesn't mean that that you can use power as liberally as you please; power is a privilege best indulged in moderation. Conversely, many CEOs reach the top rung on the organizational ladder only to be reminded—sometimes rudely—that they still have to answer to a board of directors. Finally, new CEOs are often surprised at how hard they have to work to make their brilliant strategies understood and get them accepted by a broad range of stakeholders.

In addition, as demonstrated by Anne Mulcahy's situation, many who rise to senior leadership positions in large organizations often pay a price—sacrificing their personal and family lives in order to meet their managerial responsibilities. Roger Deromedi, the recently appointed CEO of Kraft Foods, notes that "I travel about 40 percent of the time, so life is a balancing act. People often don't make time with their spouse that's separate from time with their kids. I prioritize my wife and family, which means I don't have as much time for outside interests."[7]

THE SKILL SET OF THE EFFECTIVE STRATEGIC LEADER: THE LEVEL 5 HIERARCHY

What does it take to be an effective organizational leader? Obviously, neither all leaders nor leadership challenges are created equal. A diverse set of skills, therefore, can come in handy. In this section, we'll discuss the development of leadership skill sets in terms of a model called the **Level 5 Hierarchy**, which was popularized by management researcher Jim Collins in the book *From Good to Great*.[8] The key to this framework is the idea that leadership requires a wide range of abilities, some of which are hierarchical in nature—in other words, that before mastering certain higher-level abilities, one must first master certain lower-level skills.[9] Collins proposes the five levels of leadership skills summarized in Exhibit 2.2.[10]

Level 5 Hierarchy Model of leadership skills calling for a wide range of abilities, some of which are hierarchical in nature.

- **Level 1.** Before becoming an effective leader, you must prove highly competent in your work. On the first level of leadership, therefore, productive contributions of your talent, knowledge, hard work, and skills must be made.

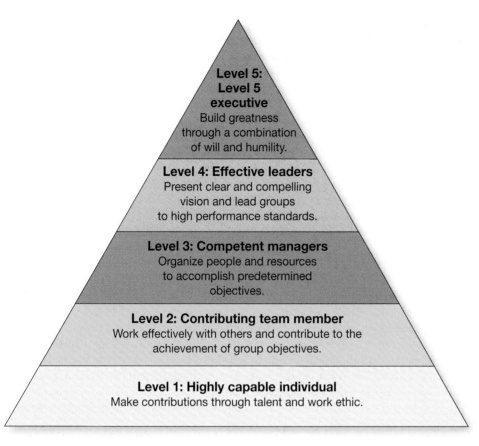

Exhibit 2.2 Level 5 Leaders: A Hierarchy of Capabilities

- **Level 2.** Senior management is often a team endeavor, and CEOs must be able to delegate major responsibilities to teams of senior executives. At level 2, therefore, you must also show the ability to work effectively as a member of a team.

- **Level 3.** After teamwork abilities have been demonstrated, you need to show the ability to manage other people—the ability to organize people and marshal resources to achieve specific objectives.

- **Level 4.** Next, you must prove capable of leading a larger organization by generating broad commitment to a clear vision of the organization's future. At level 4, you need to show the ability to lead a group to superior levels of performance. Anne Mulcahy, for example, didn't reverse Xerox's fortunes by herself. She assembled a team with diverse backgrounds and capabilities and drew upon their collective abilities.

- **Level 5.** Level 5 leadership tends to feature an unusual, even paradoxical, combination of skills. Level 5 executives not only express an unwavering resolve, or *professional will*, to achieve higher goals but demonstrate a surprising degree of *professional modesty*. Let's take a closer look at these two managerial attributes.

Professional Will   Carrying out bold strategy moves requires commitment across the entire organization. A level 5 leader can translate strategic intent into the resolve needed to pursue a strategy—and usually to make hard choices—over a period of time.

Here's a good illustration. Walgreen Company was founded in 1901 by Chicago pharmacist Charles Walgreen. Eight years later, Walgreen began serving lunch at a new soda fountain, where, by the 1920s, he was doing his part to popularize the milk shake. Although food services remained a key part of Walgreen's business, the company realized during the 1960s that its classic soda-fountain operations were draining profits from the modern self-service retail operations that generated far greater sales per square foot. Now, to many people, soda fountains were a Walgreen hallmark, and because its history of food service was part of the firm's identity, there was considerable internal resistance to the idea of closing down the soda-fountain operations. In fact, CEO Charles Walgreen III found that phasing out food-service operations was more easily said than done; simply announcing his plan by no means ensured organization-wide cooperation. Ultimately, Walgreen set a deadline of five years, admonishing senior executives that "the clock is ticking." When reminded six months later that management had only five years to get out of the restaurant business, Walgreen reasserted his resolve to stick to the schedule: "Four and a half years," he replied.[11] In the final analysis, it was largely Walgreen's resolve that transformed the old model of the drugstore chain into a new (and more profitable) retail model.

Professional Modesty

Oddly, level 5 executives also tend to be modest people—a fairly rare trait among people with upward career trajectories. Most research suggests that hubris is much more common than humility in the upper echelons of Corporate America, and given the drive that's needed to found or lead a successful firm, that fact shouldn't be surprising. And although examples abound of successful leaders who would not be described as modest, Collins' research suggests that companies that improve from average profitability and then beat the market over the long haul tend to be led by people who prefer to share credit rather than hog it. They tend to shun public attention, act with calm determination, and exercise their ambitions on the company's behalf rather than their own. They're also concerned about the future welfare of the company as well as its performance record during their own tenures.

WHAT DOES IT TAKE TO BE A CEO?

Having established the fact that senior executives influence the formation and implementation of strategy through both judgment and behavior, we know that it's worthwhile to understand what makes them think and act the way they do. We'll start by focusing on the characteristics of individual executives and the roles that they play in shaping strategic-leadership abilities.

Are you CEO material? Just what does it take? Charisma? Integrity? An Ivy League MBA? International management experience? Not surprisingly, there's no single answer to these seemingly simple questions. Although some answers involve such personality differences as charisma and emotional intelligence, others point to such demographic characteristics as gender, race, education, or work experience. There's little consensus on the issue of whether personality or background counts more, but understanding their actions is important if you want to understand successful leaders. With this fact in mind, let's take a closer look at all three perspectives on leadership characteristics: *personality differences, background and demographic differences,* and *differences in competence and actions.*

Personality Differences

Largely because psychological traits can be measured through surveys and other quantitative approaches, a large amount of research has been done on the personality or psychological determinants of strategic leadership. Many of these studies focus on four personality characteristics: *locus of control, need for achievement, tolerance for risk or ambiguity,* and *charisma and emotional intelligence.*[12]

What's Your Tolerance for Ambiguity? Analyzing all of these characteristics goes beyond the purpose of this chapter, but you may find it instructive to investigate how you measure up on one key personality attribute—tolerance for ambiguity—compared to typical executives. *Tolerance for ambiguity* means that one tends to perceive situations as promising rather than threatening. If you are intolerant of ambiguity, then uncertainty or a lack of information, for example, would make you uncomfortable. Ambiguity arises from three main sources: novelty, complexity, and insolubility. You can use the ambiguity scale in Exhibit 2.3 to see how you measure up in terms of tolerance for ambiguity.[13]

Personality Traits Versus Leadership Abilities   If there is indeed a correspondence between certain personality characteristics and leadership abilities, then (at least in theory) boards of directors could sift through applicant pools and choose CEOs on psychological grounds. Unfortunately, the jury is still out on the question of whether "natural" leaders can be classified according to personality differences or identified through psychological test instruments. In fact, some researchers warn against placing undue importance on trendy personality screens. In short, personality characteristics may be important in some respects, but defining and isolating effective leadership abilities is a complex task.

Background and Demographic Differences   *Background* differences typically refer to such factors as work experience and education, whereas *demographics* refers to such factors as gender, nationality, race, religion, network ties, and so forth.[14] Obviously, many factors of both kinds will figure prominently on your résumé.

Historically, the profile of the typical *Fortune*-500 top executive was a white male between the ages of 45 and 60 with a law, finance, or accounting degree from an Ivy League school.[15] Sociologists explain this pattern by pointing out that, for a long time, a large portion of the educated population—and thus of the managerial talent pool—consisted of white males. Moreover, white males were favored by certain structural features of the executive-employment market, including the usual prejudice of people to show favoritism toward people who are like them (in this case, white males).

Changes in demographics of business school students, as well as legal and social influence from lawsuits and legislation, have helped to diversify management ranks. Although there are significantly more female and minority managers at the start of the twenty-first century than there were just 20 years ago, few women and minorities have ascended to the level of CEO at the largest American companies. For instance, as of 2007 there were only twelve female CEOs among the 500 largest U.S. companies (2.4 percent), up from nine in 2005 and more than double the number a decade ago. In addition, 16 percent of the corporate officers of these same companies are female, suggesting that change is happening, even if only gradually. It is interesting to note that the diversity of CEOs among privately owned smaller companies is much more reflective of the U.S. population. Although the diversity of large public companies has been slow to change, the diversity of leadership in smaller companies is much greater and growing.

Although there are still a lot of white males in the upper echelons of American business, most of today's CEOs don't have an Ivy League pedigree, and we're now finding much greater diversity on other dimensions among top-management teams.[16] Again, however, we need to remember that boards don't rely on any single criterion when choosing a CEO. In fact, our opening vignette features a CEO who came up not by following the usual accounting or finance track but rather through strategic human resource management.

Beside the fact that it's unethical (and, in many countries, illegal) to discriminate in hiring and promotion, a number of practical explanations account for the increasing diversity in the ranks of top managers, both in the U.S. and elsewhere:

- Although an advanced degree remains a typical prerequisite for promotion, college education is now available to more people than ever before. All around the world, schools compete for the best and brightest regardless of race, gender, or religion, and employers reap the benefits of more diverse talent pools.

Exhibit 2.3 Can You Tolerate Ambiguity?

You may have taken this survey earlier in the semester in preparation for this course. By definition, ambiguity characterizes strategic management and the study of strategy through cases. Your response to the case method itself is a function of your own attitude toward ambiguity. Take the following survey and tabulate your score to find out your tolerance for ambiguous situations.

Please respond to the following statements by indicating the extent to which you agree or disagree with them. Fill in the blanks with the number from the rating scale that best represents your evaluation of the item. There's a scoring key at the end of the survey.

1	Strongly disagree	5	Slightly agree
2	Moderately disagree	6	Moderately agree
3	Slightly disagree	7	Strongly agree
4	Neither agree nor disagree		

_____ 1. An expert who doesn't come up with a definite answer probably doesn't know too much.

_____ 2. I would like to live in a foreign country for a while.

_____ 3. There is really no such thing as a problem that can't be solved.

_____ 4. People who fit their lives to a schedule probably miss most of the joy of living.

_____ 5. A good job is one where what is to be done and how it is to be done are always clear.

_____ 6. It is more fun to tackle a complicated problem than to solve a simple one.

_____ 7. In the long run it is possible to get more done by tackling small, simple problems rather than large and complicated ones.

_____ 8. Often the most interesting and stimulating people are those who don't mind being different and original.

_____ 9. What we are used to is always preferable to what is unfamiliar.

_____ 10. People who insist upon a yes or no answer just don't know how complicated things really are.

_____ 11. A person who leads an even, regular life in which few surprises or unexpected happenings arise really has a lot to be grateful for.

_____ 12. Many of our most important decisions are based upon insufficient information.

_____ 13. I like parties where I know most of the people more than ones where all or most people are complete strangers.

_____ 14. Teachers or supervisors who hand out vague assignments give one a chance to show initiative and originality.

_____ 15. The sooner we all acquire similar values and ideals, the better.

_____ 16. A good teacher is one who makes you wonder about your way of looking at things.

To score the instrument, **the even-numbered items must be reverse scored.** That is, the 7s become 1s, 6s become 2s, 5s become 3s, and 4s remain the same. After reversing the even-numbered items, sum the scores for all 16 items to get your total score. High scores indicate a greater intolerance for ambiguity. Use the comparison scores provided below to benchmark your own score, and read the following paragraphs to interpret such results.

Total Score

Subscores (follow same even/odd reverse scoring)

(N) Novelty score (sum 2, 9, 11, 13)   _____

(C) Complexity score (sum 4, 5, 6, 7, 8, 10, 14, 15, 16)   _____

(I) Insolubility score (sum 1, 3, 12)   _____

Being intolerant of ambiguity (relatively high score) means that an individual tends to perceive situations as threatening rather than promising. Lack of information or uncertainty, for example, would make such a person uncomfortable. Ambiguity arises from three main sources: *novelty, complexity, and insolubility.* These three subscales exist within the instrument you just completed.
Comparison total scores: Senior executives 44–48, MBAs 55–60.

▪ Groups tend to make better decisions when they can draw on heterogeneous perspectives, especially when facing turbulent or uncertain environments. When uncertainty makes it difficult to predict the future, top-management teams make better strategic decisions when they get input from diverse sources.[17]

▪ Companies today need top managers with strong international skills gained through work experience abroad. Because these skills are still fairly rare, even among college graduates, firms must look harder and farther to find them.[18]

▪ Firms increasingly seek competitive advantage through the quality of their human capital—the people who work for them. Because human capabilities are color, gender, and ethnicity blind, people with greater background and demographic diversity are rising to the ranks of upper management. Indeed, any form of bias that prevents talented employees from being promoted will put a firm at a distinct competitive disadvantage, particularly in terms of its ability to attract and retain talented people.

Competence and Actions   Do actions speak louder than words (or perhaps even louder than personality, background, or demographic differences)? Among the main reasons that Anne Mulcahy rose to the top at Xerox was her experience as vice president and staff officer for customer operations in South and Central America, Europe, Asia, Africa, and China. Increasingly, the consensus on what it takes to make it to the top-executive ranks goes beyond skin color, gender, and even line items on a résumé. More companies are placing value on substantive work experience—looking as much for the knowledge gleaned from mistakes as for the successes accumulated along the way.

Mulcahy had already demonstrated courage and toughness when it came to making and sticking to decisions, and although such toughness may be a product of experience, many experts argue that superior executives are distinguished by a talent for strategic thinking. Mulcahy was promoted because of her proven strength as a business strategist as well as her decision-making toughness. What, exactly, does a "talent for strategic thinking" add to "toughness"? By *toughness,* we mean a willingness and ability to change an organization's strategic course even when that change represents a significant departure from its traditional way of doing business. Whereas the average manager emphasizes the efficient execution of a given plan, the strategic leader works not only to develop the plan in the first place, but to empower the organization to realize the vision behind it.

Strategists and nonstrategists differ in how they think about problems. Like personality differences, these differences are too broad to review in detail in this chapter. However, a few of these dimensions of strategic thinking are reviewed in the "Are You a Strategist?" exercise in Exhibit 2.4. Test yourself on a few dimensions of strategic leadership by taking the survey.[19] As you can see, strategists are characterized by having a spirit of entrepreneurship and an eye to the future.

WHAT MAKES AN EFFECTIVE EXECUTIVE TEAM?

In reality, of course, organizations need good managers as well as great leaders, just as armies need hard-working soldiers and inspirational generals. Ironically, one hallmark of great leadership is knowing when and how to follow the lead of others. In this section, we'll discuss the ways in which the interaction of members of a top-management team can influence—for better or for worse—the contributions of a strategic leader. (We'll also discuss the importance of top-management teams and teamwork in strategic leadership in later chapters as well.) At the very least, the team has the advantage of a division of labor, and in any case, no single person, regardless of talent and ability, can single-handedly attend to all the details encountered at the top of today's complex organizations.

Exhibit 2.4 Are You a Strategist?

Answer each question with "Yes," "Mostly Yes," "Mostly No," or "No." Tally up the percentage of answers in each category.	Yes	Mostly Yes	Mostly No	No
1. Do you like to be entrepreneurial and come up with new ideas or plans but are also comfortable having others execute them? _____	☐	☐	☐	☐
2. Do you have clear guiding values for your actions (i.e., strategic intent and coherence)? _____	☐	☐	☐	☐
3. Do you think about your strengths and weaknesses before making major life choices? _____	☐	☐	☐	☐
4. Do you engage in activities that are in concert with your vision of the future and personal guiding values? _____	☐	☐	☐	☐
5. When you work with others, do you try to foster a climate where your colleagues can act freely in the interests of the objective you are seeking to achieve? _____	☐	☐	☐	☐
6. When you are working with others to achieve a certain objective, do you actively and regularly involve them in formulating the strategy to achieve that objective? _____	☐	☐	☐	☐
7. When working with others to achieve an objective do you seek harmony in matching your group's culture with your strategy? _____	☐	☐	☐	☐
8. Do you point out new directions and take novel approaches? _____	☐	☐	☐	☐
9. Have you been lucky so far (strategic leadership includes the ability to place oneself in positions that favor being lucky)? _____	☐	☐	☐	☐
10. Do you make a contribution to society and yourself (strategic leaders leave a legacy)? _____	☐	☐	☐	☐

If you answered "Yes" or "Mostly Yes" to these questions, congratulations—you have the makings of a strategic leader!

Teamwork and Diversity   What does effective teamwork mean if the team consists of top-management personnel? Basically, effective teamwork requires four criteria:

1. The team responds to a complex and changing environment.

2. The team can manage the needs of interdependent but often diverse units, arenas, or functional areas.

3. The team has a valuable and effective **social network**.

4. The team is able to develop a coherent plan for executive succession.

There's a common key to satisfying the first two criteria: A team can accommodate diverse input while acting as an integrated unit. In other words, the team is composed of people who have diverse backgrounds in terms of demographics and experience but who can nevertheless work well together as a network and take advantage of the resources and knowledge they have access to by virtue of each team member's personal and professional networks. Large firms typically can afford, and often have, larger top-management teams than do smaller firms, which also means that executives in larger firms have access to broader personal and professional networks.

Social Networks The third area, which we will call the team's social network, reflects the personal or professional set of relationships between individuals that extend beyond the management team. Social networks represent both a collection of ties between people and the strength of those ties. A related concept is **social capital**. Social capital is a core concept in business, economics, organizational behavior, political science, and sociology, defined as the advantage created by a person's location in a structure of relationships. So, when you say that a manager or management team has valuable social capital, you are actually talking about the value created by their social network. Often used as a measure of social "connectedness", recognizing the size and other characteristics of social networks assists in determining how information moves throughout groups, and how trust can be established and fostered. Just as a team can often accomplish more than a given individual, so too can network differences allow one management team to be more effective than another, by virtue of the information or other resources the network allows them to access. For instance, a firm that plans to use acquisitions as a growth vehicle is well-served when members of the management team have established good relationships with bankers and the managers of possible acquisition targets. It is possible for you to map out other important characteristics of social networks, as shown in the box entitled "How Would *You* Do That? 2.1," which is another reason that you should add social network analysis to your strategy toolkit.

Succession Planning The fourth area, succession planning, has received increased attention in recent years as turnover among upper-echelon executives has increased. This is the case even among small firms, although the process is often made more complex by the fact that potential successors may include family members, in addition to current executives and outsiders hired from other companies. As a practical matter, succession planning has become more important because the rate of CEO dismissals by relatively large public firms has increased by 170 percent from 1995 to 2004 (from 30 out of 2,500 to 75). Globally, CEO job security is declining, with average tenure decreasing by 23 percent between 1995 and 2004, to a low of 7.6 years. Twenty-eight percent of the 238 CEOs who departed in 2004 were outsiders—the highest proportion in any year since 1995.[20]

Experts agree that a well-planned and executed succession process is essential for a successful transition. **Succession planning** is typically overseen by the board, often with an outside consulting firm, and usually involves the current CEO. In most cases, succession is typically considered final only when the new CEO is in place and the old one has departed. Why? Given the power that sitting CEOs may command, it's often better that a long-term CEO leave the company entirely. Boards, says Jeffrey Sonnenfeld, an expert on CEO succession, "should recognize that creators have a strong tendency to act like monarchs or generals, and both kinds have trouble giving things up."[21]

Even with CEO succession planning becoming more established and accepted in corporations around the world, its practice is a science tempered by a strong dose of art. The science part involves the development of a methodical approach to identifying desirable CEO characteristics and then drawing out a short-list of candidates from a broad field of wanna-be

social network The collection of ties between people and the strength of those ties.

social capital The advantage created through the characteristics of a person's network.

succession planning Process of managing a well-planned and well-executed transition from one CEO to the next with positive outcomes for all key stakeholders.

Mapping Your Social Network

Social networks exist to accomplish specific tasks, manage careers, or in relation to hobbies or leisure. Obviously, social networks are not just for the workplace. For instance, you are probably familiar with popular social networking websites such as Friendster.com, MySpace.com, or Classmates.com, or perhaps you already manage a professional network through LinkedIn.com, or another business-related networking site. While you probably know that social networks are important, particularly for managers, what network characteristics should you pay attention to? Here is a step-by-step process to help you answer that question.

First, imagine a particular objective, be it getting a job or being effective in your current job. Next, make a list of the people you communicate with on a regular basis, who are also relevant to the objective you identified. These are your network ties—that is, the people who tie you into the social network. Remember, this list is based only on who you interact with, and not whether you work with them, go to school with them, and so on. If they are relevant to the objective, they should be on your list. To give you an idea of how many names you might have, a 35-year-old manager would list 10 to 20 contacts. Now that you have your list, the third step in this mapping process is to categorize your relationships. While you can use any criteria that you want, we will use "closeness" here. Very close relationships are those characterized by

high degrees of liking, trust, and mutual commitment. Distant relationships are those characterized by not knowing the person very well, or by having very little liking, trust, and mutual commitment. A problematic relationship is still a network relationship if it is related to your

objective. The fourth and final step is to calculate the density of your social network. To do this, you create a simple grid where you indicate who knows who in your network. Tally up the number of unique pairs then calculate your network density as follows:

---

a) Total number of people in your network

Pat's N = 10

N = _____

b) Maximum Density (i.e., if everyone in your network knew each other). *Pat's maximum density is (10*9) ÷ 2 = 45.*

$[N * (N - 1)] \div 2 = M$

M = _____

c) Total number of checkmarks on your network grid (i.e., the number of relationships among people in your network).

Pat's C = 19.

C = _____

d) Density of Your Network. *Pat's D = 19 ÷ 45 = .42* (will be between 0.00 and 1.00)

$C \div M = D$

D = _____

Now we are ready to talk about your social network. The number of people on your list is obviously the size of your social network. In the example shown here in Exhibit 2.5, the network is comprised of 10 people, plus you. More people means more information, and possibly access to greater resources. But notice that not all of the ties in the example are equally close. You can compare absolute numbers here, or boil these down into percentages—for instance, 20 percent of these ties are very close, and 10 percent are distant. For most people, it would be hard to

manage a huge network where all the ties are very close, just by virtue of the amount of time and energy it takes to satisfy the conditions for closeness. Moreover, there is a natural tradeoff between closeness and number of ties, or network size. Though this also means that some people in your network may be less useful than others, in terms of the resources and information they would readily and voluntarily provide you. You can use other characteristics to categorize these ties as well, such as demographics or hierarchy. For instance, what

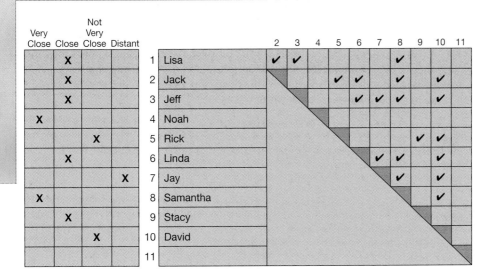

Exhibit 2.5 Sample of Pat's Social Network Grid

Very Close	Close	Not Very Close	Distant	#	Name	2	3	4	5	6	7	8	9	10	11
	X			1	Lisa	✔	✔					✔			
	X			2	Jack				✔	✔		✔		✔	
	X			3	Jeff				✔	✔	✔			✔	
X				4	Noah										
		X		5	Rick								✔	✔	
	X			6	Linda						✔	✔		✔	
			X	7	Jay							✔		✔	
X				8	Samantha									✔	
	X			9	Stacy										
		X		10	David										
				11											

percentage of your network ties are the same age, gender, or nationality as you? What percentage come from the same organization, or are lower or higher than you on the organization chart?

This brings us back to the density of your network. At this point you are probably getting some idea about the nature of your social network, and how and why information and resources may flow through it. Density is important because, if it is close to 1.00, then everyone in your network knows everyone else. This is great if everyone in your network has their own network density close to 0.00, because you are very central in the network, have access to diverse information and resources, and provide a common link to the others in the network. If you were to map out the connections between network members you could clearly see examples of individuals who are more or less central in this particular network. Unfortunately though, if your network density is high, then so is theirs, and you all have access to the same information. Why is this bad? Well, if you are a team of music industry executives, and only have experience with that industry, then you might not be aware of opportunities or threats emerging in, say, a little place called the Internet! More generally, the more dense the network, the less that new information will come into it, and that is probably not a good thing in a changing world. We also know that, on average, your social network is likely to change in structure over time as a function of things like your tenure in one industry. For instance, the longer you have been in one industry, the more likely it is that you will see your network size begin to shrink and that its density increases.

Now that you understand how social networks operate and can map them, you can also begin to evaluate and manage them. With this map, identify the people on whom you are dependent. Focus your energies on cultivating relationships with those dependencies, or network ties that bypass or co-opt them. Develop strategies for networking with difficult targets—individuals who would make your network more useful. Two broad organizing principles will assure that you have a useful network—similarity and exchange. The similarity principal suggests that relationships develop spontaneously between people with common backgrounds, values, and interests; the exchange principal suggests that "difference" is what makes ties useful, in that it increases the likelihood that each party has a complementary resource. Through this exercise you should have also learned something else—your attitude toward networks and perhaps some intuition about your networking style. That knowledge alone provides you a good start.

CEOs. As you can see, the art part comes into play when making the difficult judgments about who should make the short list and then ranking those candidates realistically in terms of their ability to meet the firm's strategic needs.

When the succession process flounders, it can destroy the CEO's legacy—not to mention the company's health—by undermining investor confidence, depressing the stock price, creating dissension on the board, disrupting the continuity of ongoing initiatives, and even crippling the organization for years. Conversely, when the process goes well, a smooth transition fosters positive outcomes for the company and its stakeholders. General Electric, for example, conducted a meticulous search over several years before appointing Jeffrey Immelt, who ran the company's medical-systems division, to succeed CEO Jack Welch. By the time a final decision was made, according to insiders, Immelt had in effect been running the company for most of a year—planning acquisitions, attending employee reviews, and overseeing management team meetings. Similarly, when the founder and CEO of Boston auto-wash chain ScrubaDub sought to turn the leadership of the business over to his two sons, he did so only after they had thoroughly hashed out their respective roles and titles, the company's vision and mission, and their respective compensation and stock ownership packages. One brother now serves as CEO, responsible for R&D and operations, and the other serves as president, responsible for training, sales, and marketing.[22]

Sometimes, of course, the timing of a transition can't be predicted. In such cases, an even higher premium is placed on good managerial bench strength and prior planning. At McDonald's, for example, the promotion of Charlie Bell only hours after the sudden death of CEO Jim Cantalupo reassured employees and investors that the firm was under competent leadership. The smooth transition was possible only because the plan for Bell's succession was already in place, and a year later, when Bell himself resigned because of illness, the board already had Jim Skinner waiting in the wings. "The worst-case scenario planning of most companies," points out Jeffrey Sonnenfeld, "is only a Band-Aid transitional solution, not a strategic solution. McDonald's directors, by immediately naming a battle-tested insider, showed the wisdom of having a succession plan in place."[23]

The Imprint of Strategic Leadership: Vision and Mission

Top executives provide the context for strategy formulation and implementation through the vision and mission that they espouse and model with their own actions. Sometimes, they're the originators of the vision and mission; at other times, they're caretakers or stewards who work to sharpen employees' shared understanding of the vision and mission. In any case, the vision and mission remain central, and that's why the overarching model of strategic management that we introduced in Chapter 1 starts with vision and mission.

DEFINING *VISION* AND *MISSION*

vision Simple statement or understanding of what the firm will be in the future.

Vision is a simple statement of where a firm is going, and what the firm's leaders want it to be in the future. A statement of vision is forward-looking and identifies the firm's desired long-term status. Think of the vision statement like a car's headlights, perhaps its high beams, and the illuminating or guiding role they might play for a driver who is negotiating a curvy road on a dark, stormy night. Vision statements can be very brief, even just a couple of words or sentences. They describe what the firm wants to look like many years from now, or how the organization aims to fulfill customers' future needs and expectations. In contrast, a **mission** is a declaration of what a firm stands for in relation to key organizational stakeholders like employees, customers, investors, government, and the environment—the

mission Declaration of what a firm is and what it stands for—its fundamental values and purpose.

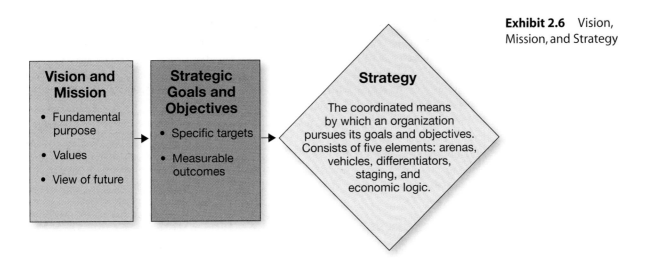

Exhibit 2.6 Vision, Mission, and Strategy

fundamental values and purpose that its leaders believe are shared and prized among those stakeholders. Because it's difficult to execute a strategy if it can't be described or understood, firms with clearly and widely understood visions and missions find it easier to make strategic decisions entailing difficult tradeoffs.

Thus, as you can see in Exhibit 2.6, vision and mission influence strategy formulation and implementation.[24] Sometimes this influence is exercised when leaders focus explicitly on defining or refining a firm's vision, as was the case with Mulcahy at Xerox. More often, however, an organization's vision and mission are well established and functional. In these cases, leaders work to formulate the firm's strategy in a manner that's consistent with the fundamental values and purpose expressed in its statements of core beliefs. Discussion of the vision and mission provides shared understanding of the firm's direction and values, and thus helps guide both executives and employees in their daily decisions and actions. Similarly, when external stakeholders like investors or customers understand the vision and mission, they may have a better understanding of why a particular strategy is pursued. Vision and mission, therefore, reinforce and support strategy; conversely, strategy provides a coherent plan for realizing vision and mission.

Once you've finished this and the next section, you should be able to identify a firm's vision and mission and understand their roles in more complex organizational activities. You'll understand how vision and mission are translated into strategic action, and you'll be able to make recommendations for improving organizational performance or competitive position. You'll see how vision and mission contribute to the organizational functions that we call *strategic purpose* and *strategic coherence*. Because strategy can be successful only to the extent that key stakeholders (customers, suppliers, government, and employees) facilitate its implementation, you'll also learn how to use the tool that we call *stakeholder analysis*.

WHAT SHOULD VISION AND MISSION STATEMENTS ENCOMPASS?

A study by the consulting firm Bain and Company reports that 90 percent of 500 firms surveyed issue some form of vision and mission statements.[25] Toward what end? Together, vision and mission statements not only express a firm's identity and describe its work but inform both managers and employees of the firm's direction. They're not strategies in and of themselves, but they convey organizational identity and purpose to critical stakeholders both inside and outside the firm.

Vision: The Uses of Ambition and Ambiguity   In the early 1950s, Sony stated its vision of "becoming the company that most changes the worldwide image of Japanese products as being of poor quality." Back in 1915, CitiBank (now CitiGroup aka Citi) announced its grandiose vision of becoming "the most powerful, the most serviceable, the most far-reaching world financial institution the world has ever seen."[26] As these two examples suggest, vision statements generally express long-term action horizons, and they're ambitious by design, because ambition forces the firm to stretch both by challenging external competitors and by questioning the internal status quo. Because they're often ambiguous, they don't inhibit the firm from reaching for the stars (or at least aspiring to reach for the stars). Ambiguity also enables flexibility for changing strategy or implementation tactics when it looks as if business as usual isn't going to realize the expressed vision.

Mission: The Uses of Core Values   A firm will use its mission statement to identify certain core concepts, such as its purpose, or *raison d'être;* values and beliefs; standards of behavior; or corporate-level aims.[27] All employees are supposed to internalize core ideals and call upon them to guide their decisions and actions. At 3M, for example, a core value is the innovative solution of problems. Merck wants employees to preserve and improve human life, and Wal-Mart wants them to devote themselves to selling ordinary folks the same things that affluent people buy.[28]

WHY VISION AND MISSION STATEMENTS ARE NOT SUBSTITUTES FOR STRATEGY

Research suggests that the best-performing firms boast clear visions and missions.[29] However, it should be obvious by now that clearly articulated, coherent, and widely understood vision and mission statements are not substitutes for strategy. Nevertheless, we need to spend a little time on this point.

In 1993, when outsider Lou Gerstner was hired as CEO and charged with the daunting task of saving IBM from potential ruin, he announced that "the last thing IBM needs (right now) is a vision." The statement was widely circulated (although press reports usually edited out the words "right now"),[30] as was Gerstner's charge that IBM's vision was nothing but a litany of platitudes, like those of firms who declare commitment to "total quality" or "customer service." Having discovered that some divisions at IBM were busier squabbling over the distribution of revenue than responding to customer needs, Gerstner was more interested in consistent and tangible managerial action.

Likewise, vision statements don't help much if managers view them as cure-alls for organization ailments or if they paint pictures of a future that's clearly unattainable. Sometimes, a vision is so irrelevant to organizational reality that employees and customers simply reject it. Small firms, in particular, need a clear vision and mission to provide them with focus, but they also need a concrete strategy to translate concepts and resource constraints into profitable action. In the case of IBM, an enormous firm, Gerstner wanted to send a strong message to all employees that serious changes were needed if the company was to survive—changes that would extend far beyond any revamped statement of vision.

Vision and mission can be powerful tools, but because they're general and ambiguous by design, they must be realized through carefully crafted and executed strategy. Firms undergoing strategic change are especially susceptible to serious discrepancies between a new vision statement that's crafted on high and the organizational processes designed to realize it on the factory floor. As you can see from Exhibit 2.7, Gerstner did in fact have a clear vision for IBM (namely, to get it back to the top spot in its industry), but he first set out to anchor this vision in specific goals and objectives derived from a focused and clearly articulated strategy.[31] IBM's prospects were gloomy back in 1993, but thanks to Gerstner's clear-headed understanding of the relationship between strategy and vision (and his talent for leadership), IBM is once again one of America's most admired companies.

GOALS AND OBJECTIVES

If talk of visions and missions conjures up images of crystal balls and astrology, don't be too surprised. Some executives treat vision and mission statements as symbolic pronouncements, and in many organizations they exist on a different plane than actual strategy and strategic actions. Such discrepancies are symptomatic of various conditions. Perhaps the firm is floundering from a lack of clear or unique strategic direction; perhaps its strategy is too complex; maybe management has lost sight of the competitive realities facing the company.

What is one of the key determinants of whether a vision and mission are judged to be effective? The answer appears to be found when leaders have spelled out a set of clear and specific quantitative or qualitative **goals and objectives** that provide a bridge between the vision and the strategy. Progress toward a certain goal or achievement of an objective serve as indicators of how well the strategy is delivering on the aspirations laid out in the vision and mission. Employee pay can also be tied to such progress. Firms can choose from a myriad number of goals and objectives, and a subset of these are shown in Exhibit 2.7. A goal can be as simple as a single performance figure, like sales growth or **return on invested capital (ROIC)**. Single goals like this are also called **superordinate goals**, because they serve as an overarching reference point for other goals and objectives. Wal-Mart's annual report, for example, states that the company will grow sales and profits by 20 percent per year; Ryanair says that it will be Europe's largest airline in seven years; Matsushita intends to become a "Super Manufacturing Company." Ultimately, the strength with which a firm's vision and mission are anchored in relevant goals and objectives will determine which ones walk the talk and which ones just . . . talk.

Increasingly, managers track their strategic progress against goals and objectives with a tool called a **balanced scorecard**, which is a system for bridging vision and strategy. The general idea here is that shareholder value (and value created for other stakeholders) is a function of firm productivity and growth. However, because financial measures of productivity

goals and objectives Combination of a broad indication of organizational intentions (*goals*) and specific, measurable steps (*objectives*) for reaching them.

return on invested capital (ROIC) How effectively a company uses the money (borrowed or owned) invested in its operations.

superordinate goal Overarching reference point for a host of hierarchical subgoals.

balanced scorecard Strategic management support system for measuring vision and strategy against business- and operating-unit-level performance.

Exhibit 2.7 Key Elements of Gerstner's 1993 Vision for IBM

- IBM will not be split up and its many parts will be even more closely coordinated.

- IBM will reassert its identity as customers' primary computing resource.

- The company will be the dominant supplier of technology in the industry.

- PowerPC, a new microprocessor design, will be IBM's centerpiece. Built into many future computers, it will run a wide range of standard industry software. And it will steeply cut manufacturing costs.

- Mainframes are no longer central to the strategy, but IBM will still make them, now with microprocessors.

- IBM is its own worst enemy. Employees must waste fewer opportunities, minimize bureaucracy, and put the good of the company before their division's.

and growth are typically retrospective (for instance, ROIC or month-to-month sales increases, respectively), they don't readily provide managers with the information to monitor or influence their underlying determinants. If managers can map out the financial, customer, and organizational factors that feed productivity, growth, or both, then they can better measure and set goals for these finer-grained indicators of eventual performance. Typically, the best scorecards let managers know how the strategy is going before they see the financial numbers, or even provide a glimpse into the future. For example, one of GE's goals is to have better relationships with customers such that they refer more business to GE, and GE is investing in marketing and innovation skills to support that objective. GE actually measures progress on this objective by asking customers "Would GE be the first company you would refer a colleague to?" And because GE has found that this measure is an accurate predictor of business growth, it can tie it to managerial pay as well.

Strategic Purpose and Strategic Coherence

An overview of the examples presented in this chapter should tell you that it's relatively easy to compose a snappy vision statement. You should also have gathered by now that having vision and mission statements doesn't guarantee higher levels of performance. For one thing, some statements are more effective than others. How so? Research suggests the importance of the process used to develop and articulate statements. Performance, for example, is positively correlated with the integration of internal stakeholders—in other words, manager and employee satisfaction with the statement-development process.[32] This is yet one more reason why we'll focus on the stakeholder-analysis tool in the next section and why we stress the importance of considering stakeholders in the practice of strategic leadership. First, however, let's focus on the two most critical aspects of effective vision and mission statements: *strategic purpose* and *strategic coherence.*

STRATEGIC PURPOSE

strategic purpose Simplified, widely shared mental model of the organization and its future, including anticipated changes in its environment.

Vision and mission statements are actually statements of organizational identity and purpose that can guide executives in making corporate decisions. After all, one individual—even a group of individuals—can cope with only so much complexity in a problem. Vision and mission statements provide all employees with **strategic purpose**: a simplified, widely shared model of the organization and its future, including anticipated changes in its environment.

Tradeoffs, Options, and Other Decisions Most major strategic decisions require tradeoffs—deciding on one course of action may necessarily eliminate other options. In addition, although some courses of action may satisfy the needs of some stakeholders, they may adversely affect others.

The consumer-products companies Mars Inc. and SC Johnson, for example, remain private corporations. When you visit either firm's Web site, you'll see that independence is a core value for both. Moreover, private ownership means greater flexibility in strategic choices: Because neither firm must cater to the stock market as a stakeholder, each can choose to make costly investments in the kinds of socially responsible programs that often draw fire from the shareholders of public companies. And the tradeoffs? The growth potential of each firm is limited, and it's more difficult to arrange for employee ownership, whether through direct share ownership or stock options.

Newman's Own, founded by actor Paul Newman and a partner in 1982, makes and sells salad dressing, lemonade, popcorn, salsa, steak sauce, and other food items through major grocery chains in the U.S. and abroad. In 2003, McDonald's announced that it would use Newman's Own dressings exclusively in its new Premium Salad line. Newman expects this alliance to increase profits by 25 percent. The firm's success derives from two policies anchored in its vision: (1) It insists on top-quality products with no artificial ingredients or preservatives and (2) It donates all after-tax profits to educational and charitable organizations, including UNICEF, Habitat for Humanity, and the Hole in the Wall Gang Camp for seriously ill children. The determination to combine commerce with philanthropy underlies a fairly unique vision, but it's guided the company's strategy for more than two decades. The tradeoff? Although adhering to a strongly held corporate philosophy helps managers choose certain courses of action over others, the decision to use more expensive natural ingredients means sacrificing higher short-term profitability.

Even a company with a more traditional profit orientation can be guided by a fairly simple vision. Michael Dell founded Dell Computers in 1984 on an investment of $1,000. His vision was to sell computer systems directly to customers. The company now has more than 78,000 employees and boasted revenues in excess of $57 billion in 2006.[33] Such rapid growth, however, means that the great majority of Dell employees are relative newcomers to the corporate family, which puts pressure on the company to preserve the values that guided it in its early years. Dell training, therefore, strives to imbue all employees with the "Soul of Dell"—the set of values that guides all of the firm's business practices.

As you can see in Exhibit 2.8, Matsushita Electric, the Japanese parent company of Panasonic, is preparing to stretch by comparing what the company does today with what it will have to do to become a "Super Manufacturing Company" in the future.[34] Such a company, explains Matsushita CEO Kunio Nakamura, "must in essence be 'light and speedy.' Now when the nature of business is changing, emphasis will be placed on the maintenance, broadening and strengthening of IT, on R&D and marketing. Moreover, Matsushita at present is like a heavy lead ball loaded with assets. In the future we need to cast off superfluous assets and become a company that can move lightly like a soccer ball."[35]

The Challenge of Closing the Gap The challenge posed by a strategic purpose is to close the gap between the firm's aspirations and its current capabilities and market positions. All strategies, for example, address the tradeoff between efficiency and effectiveness, and a firm can easily fall into the trap of adhering to its current strategy (say, becoming more efficient) even though customers no longer value its products (in other words, becoming less effective). Like long-term personal goals, the forward-looking aspect of strategic purpose means more than merely setting long-term goals that require stretch. Rather, an effective strategic purpose must be tied to a coherent set of activities, near-term goals, and objectives anchored in *measurable strategic outcomes*—that is, *strategic coherence*.

Matsushita's Goal: To Become a 21st-Century "Super Manufacturing Company"		
	Today: A Conventional Manufacturing Company	**Tomorrow: A 21st-Century Super Manufacturing Company**
Role	Providing goods	Providing solutions
Investment	Principally capital investment	Expansion of R&D, marketing, and IT investment
Information	From the company	Interactive/direct contact with customers
Organization	Pyramid	Flat and web

Exhibit 2.8 Creating Strategic Purpose at Matsushita

STRATEGIC COHERENCE

strategic coherence
Symmetric coalignment of the five
elements of the firm's strategy, the
congruence of functional-area
policies with these elements, and the
overarching fit of various businesses
under the corporate umbrella.

An effective strategy is coherent. As we saw in Chapter 1, a firm's strategy entails an integrated set of choices regarding the five elements of the *strategy diamond*. **Strategic coherence** (versus *incoherence*) is the symmetrical coalignment of the five elements of the firm's strategy, the congruence of policies in such functional areas as finance, production, and marketing with these elements, and the overarching fit of various businesses under the corporate umbrella. Successful firms depend on dozens of critical elements operating in concert and in balance. These elements are integrated so that everyone from design to manufacturing to marketing to accounting understands them in the same way.

In practice, some firms suffer from incoherent and fragmented strategies. For instance, a firm's decision to grow rapidly through acquisitions may be out of sync with its attempts to differentiate its products on the basis of strong brand equity. Some firms lack coherence because functional areas are treated like independent domains, as if they were silos of business activity that don't need orchestrated cooperation. Finally, some firms lack a coherent strategy because they move in and out of new businesses, as AT&T has done over the past two decades.

Applying the Strategy Diamond   How can firms achieve strategic coherence? The answer seems to be serious commitment to, and widespread communication of, well-understood and shared organizational vision and values. The strategy diamond framework is useful in testing the coherence of the elements of a strategy. Specifically, do the five diamond facets—arenas, differentiators, vehicles, staging, and economic logic—all add up to an internally consistent, externally-relevant set of choices that allow the firm to realize its vision and mission? From an internal perspective, a coherent strategy aligns all of the strategy's strategic, tactical, and design elements. From an external perspective, coherence is an alignment of the strategy with the industry environment and the vision of where and how the firm will be positioned in that environment in the future. Incoherence tends to plague firms that allocate resources primarily in response to competitors' strategies. That is, instead of working on an internally-consistent strategy, the firm is trying to keep up with diverse competitors by mimicking their strategies and tactics. As a result, it will appear as if their actions and functions are about average for the industry. In reality, of course, there's nothing distinctive about such a firm because it has in effect allowed its competitors to determine its strategy.

The Clear and Compelling Vision Statement   In many ways, strong vision statements function as guidelines for clear and compelling strategies that distinguish a firm from its competitors. What do we mean by "compelling"? Namely, that the underlying strategy is not only coherent but is accepted as truthful and useful by employees, customers, and other key stakeholders.[36] A clear vision of what the organization wants to achieve, coupled with an unambiguous understanding of its mission, helps managers make coherent strategic decisions.

Stakeholders, Stakeholder Analysis, and Stakeholder Planning

stakeholder   Individual or group
with an interest in an organization's
ability to deliver intended results and
maintain the viability of its products
and services.

Stakeholders are individuals or groups who have an interest in an organization's ability to deliver intended results and maintain the viability of its products and services. We've already stressed the importance of stakeholders to a firm's vision and mission. We've also explained that firms are usually accountable to a broad range of stakeholders, including shareholders, who can make it either more difficult or easier to execute a strategy. This is the main reason why strategy formulators must consider stakeholders' interests, needs, and preferences. Considering these factors in the development of a firm's vision and mission is a good place to start, but first, of course, you must identify critical stakeholders, get a handle on their short- and long-term interests, calculate their potential influence on your strategy, and take into consideration how the firm's strategy might impact stakeholders (beneficially or adversely).

As we've already seen, for instance, one key stakeholder group is composed of the CEO and the members of the top-management team. This group is important for at least three reasons:

1. Its influence as either originator or steward of the organization's vision and mission

2. Its responsibility for formulating a strategy that realizes the vision and mission

3. Its ultimate role in strategy implementation (a role that we'll discuss in more detail in Chapter 11)

Typically, stakeholder evaluation of both quantitative and qualitative performance outcomes will determine whether or not strategic leadership is effective. We summarized some relevant performance outcomes in Exhibit 2.9. Different stakeholders may place more emphasis on some outcomes than other stakeholders who have other priorities.

STAKEHOLDERS AND STRATEGY

Stakeholder analysis is the technique used to identify the key people who have to be won over. You then use stakeholder planning to build the support that helps you succeed.

The benefits of using a stakeholder-based approach are that:

■ You can use the opinions of the most powerful stakeholders to shape your strategy and tactics at an early stage. Not only does this make it more likely that they will support you, their input can also improve the quality of your strategy

■ Gaining support from powerful stakeholders can help you to win more resources—this makes it more likely that your projects will be successful

■ By communicating with stakeholders early and frequently, you can ensure that they fully understand what you are doing and understand the benefits of your project—this means they can support you actively when necessary

■ You can anticipate what people's reaction to your project may be, and build into your plan the actions that will win people's support.

Financial Performance Metrics	Nonfinancial Performance Metrics
▶ Return on sales	▶ Customer retention
▶ Return on assets	▶ Customer satisfaction
▶ Return on equity	▶ Customer complaints
▶ Return on invested capital	▶ Employee turnover
▶ Sales per employee	▶ Product returns
▶ Sales growth	▶ Product quality
▶ Inventory turn	▶ Patents
▶ Accounts receivable turn	▶ New products released
▶ Debt ratio	▶ Product development speed
▶ Current ratio	▶ Reputation
▶ Cost reduction	▶ Web traffic

Exhibit 2.9 Some Financial and Nonfinancial Performance Metrics

STAKEHOLDER ANALYSIS

The first step in stakeholder analysis is identifying major stakeholder groups. As you can imagine, the groups of stakeholders who will be affected either directly or indirectly by or have an effect on a firm's strategy and its execution can run the gamut from employees to customers to competitors to governments.

Let's pause for a moment to consider the important constituencies charted on our stakeholder map. Before we start, however, we need to remind ourselves that stakeholders can be individuals or groups—communities, social or political organizations, and so forth. In addition, we can break groups down demographically, geographically, by level and branch of government, or according to other relevant criteria. In so doing, we're more likely to identify important groups that we might otherwise overlook.

With these facts in mind, you can see that, externally, a map of stakeholders will include such diverse groups as governmental bodies, community-based organizations, social and political action groups, trade unions and guilds, and even journalists. National and regional governments and international regulatory bodies will probably be key stakeholders for global firms or those whose strategy calls for greater international presence. Internally, key stakeholders include shareholders, business units, employees, and managers.

Steps in Identifying Stakeholders

Identifying all of a firm's stakeholders can be a daunting task. In fact, as we will note again shortly, a list of stakeholders that is too long actually may reduce the effectiveness of this important tool by overwhelming decision makers with too much information. Again, the goal of stakeholder analysis is to identify the key players, not every single possible player (otherwise your list of stakeholders will begin to look like a telephone book!). To simplify the process, we suggest that you start by identifying groups that fall into one of four categories: *organizational, capital market, product market,* and *social*. Let's take a closer look at this step.

Step 1: Determining Influences on Strategy Formulation One way to analyze the importance and roles of the individuals who comprise a stakeholder group is to identify the people and teams who should be consulted as strategy is developed or who will play some part in its eventual implementation. These are *organizational stakeholders,* and they include both high-level managers and frontline workers. *Capital-market stakeholders* are groups that affect the availability or cost of capital—shareholders, venture capitalists, banks, and other financial intermediaries. *Product-market stakeholders* include parties with whom the firm shares its industry, including suppliers and customers. *Social stakeholders* consist broadly of external groups and organizations that may be affected by or exercise influence over firm strategy and performance, such as unions, governments, and activists groups.

Step 2: Determining the Effects of Strategic Decisions on the Stakeholder Step 2 in stakeholder analysis is to determine the nature of the effect of the firm's strategic decisions on the list of relevant stakeholders. Not all stakeholders are impacted equally by strategic decisions. Some effects may be rather mild, and any positive or negative effects may be secondary and of minimal impact. At the other end of the spectrum, some stakeholders bear the brunt of firm decisions, good or bad.

At this stage, it's critical to determine the stakeholders who are most important based on how the firm's strategy impacts the stakeholders. You must determine which of the groups still on your list have direct or indirect material claims on firm performance or which are potentially adversely impacted. For instance, it is easy to see how shareholders are affected by firm strategies—their wealth either increases or decreases in correspondence with firm actions. Other parties have economic interests in the firm as well, such as parties the firm interacts with in the marketplace, such as suppliers and customers. The effects on other parties may be much more indirect. For instance, governments have an economic interest in firms doing well—they collect tax revenue from them. However, in cities that are well diversified with many employers, a single firm has minimal economic impact on what the government collects. Alternatively, in other areas individual firms represent a significant contribution to local employment and tax revenue. In those situations, the impact of firm actions on the government would be much greater.

Step 3: Determining Stakeholders' Power and Influence over Decisions The third step of stakeholder analysis is to determine the degree to which a stakeholder group can exercise power and influence over the decisions the firm makes. Does the group have direct control over what is decided, veto power over decisions, nuisance influence, or no influence? Recognize that although the degree to which stakeholders are affected by firm decisions (i.e., step 2) is sometimes highly correlated with their power and influence over the decision, this is often not the case. For instance, in some companies, frontline employees may be directly affected by firm decisions but have no say in those decisions. Power can take the form of formal voting power (boards of directors and owners), economic power (suppliers, financial institutions, and unions), or political power (dissident stockholders, political action groups, and governmental bodies). Sometimes the parties that exercise significant power over firm decisions don't register as having a significant stake in the firm (step 2). In recent years, for example, Wal-Mart has encountered significant resistance in some communities by well-organized groups who oppose the entry of the megaretailer. Wal-Mart executives now have to anticipate whether a vocal and politically powerful community group will oppose its new stores or aim to reduce their size, which decreases Wal-Mart's per-store profitability. Indeed, in many markets, such groups have been effective at blocking new stores, reducing their size, or changing building specifications.

Once you've determined who has a stake in the outcomes of the firm's decisions as well as who has power over these decisions, you'll have a basis on which to allocate prominence in the strategy-formulation and strategy-implementation processes. The framework in Exhibit 2.10 will also help you categorize stakeholders according to their influence in determining strategy versus their importance to strategy execution.[37] For one thing, this distinction may help you identify major omissions in strategy formulation and implementation.

		Power of the Stakeholder over Strategic Decisions			
		Unknown	Little/no power	Moderate degree of power	Significant power
Effect of Strategy on the Stakeholder	Unknown				
	Little/no effect				
	Moderate effect				
	Significant effect				

Exhibit 2.10 Mapping Stakeholder Influence and Importance

Having identified stakeholder groups and differentiated them by how they are affected by firm decisions and the power they have to influence decisions, you'll want to ask yourself some additional questions:

- Have I identified any vulnerable points in either the strategy or its potential implementation?

- Which groups are mobilized and active in promoting their interests?

- Have I identified supporters and opponents of the strategy?

- Which groups will benefit from successful execution of the strategy and which may be adversely affected?

- Where are various groups located? Who belongs to them? Who represents them?

Although the stakeholder-analysis framework summarized in Exhibit 2.10 is a good starting point, you'll find that many of the strategic-analysis tools that we introduce in later chapters will also help you determine which stakeholders may be most critical to the success of your chosen strategy (and why). Ultimately, because vision and mission are necessarily long-term in orientation, identifying important stakeholder groups will help you to understand which constituencies stand to gain or lose the most if they're realized.

STAKEHOLDER PLANNING

Now that you have identified and analyzed your key stakeholders, you can develop your plan for managing them. Stakeholder planning involves mapping out your communications and actions so that you can win stakeholder support for your strategy. Stakeholder planning is the means by which to orchestrate this sometimes highly political process.

Steps in Stakeholder Planning
Planning builds on the analysis you have completed so far. It takes the stakeholders you have identified and asks that you develop a communication and action plan for dealing with them to gain or retain their support for your strategy. Exhibit 2.11 provides you with an excellent starting point for organizing this process.

Step 1. Fill in Names of Key Stakeholders Based on the stakeholder map you created in your stakeholder analysis, enter the stakeholders' names, their influence and interest in your strategy, and your current assessment of where they stand with respect to it.

Step 2. Plan Your Approach to Stakeholder Management The amount of time you should allocate to stakeholder management depends on the size and difficulty of the projects and goals related to your strategy, the time you have available for communication, and the amount of help you need to achieve the results you want. Consider the amount of time that will be taken to manage this and the time you will need for communication.

Step 3. Evaluate What You Want from Each Stakeholder Next, work through your list of stakeholders and consider the levels of support you want from them and the roles you would like them to play (if any). Consider the actions you would like them to perform. Write this information down in the 'Desired Support', 'Desired Strategy Role', and 'Actions Desired' columns.

Step 4. Identify the Messages You Need to Convey Next, identify the messages that you need to convey to your stakeholders to persuade them to support you and engage in your strategy or goals. Typical messages will show the benefits of your strategy or goals to the person or organization, and will focus on key performance drivers like increasing profitability or delivering real improvements relevant to that stakeholder.

Step 5. Identify Actions and Communications Finally, work out what you need to do to win and manage the support of these stakeholders. With the time and resources you have

Exhibit 2.11   Your Stakeholder Management Plan

Stakeholder Name	Communication Approach	Key Interests and Issues	Current Status	Desired Support	Desired Role in Strategy	Actions Desired	Messages/ Actions Needed	Action and Communication

available, identify how you will manage the communication to and the input from your stakeholders. Focusing on the high-power/high-effect stakeholders first and the low-effect/low-power stakeholders last, devise a practical plan that communicates with people as effectively as possible and that communicates the right amount of information in a way that neither under- nor over-communicates. Consider what you need to do to keep your best supporters engaged and on-board. Plan how to win over or neutralize the opposition of skeptics. Where you need the active support of people who are not currently interested in what you are doing, consider how you can engage them and raise their level of interest.

The effective application of stakeholder analysis and planning for a newly appointed manager is described in the box entitled "How Would *You* Do That? 2.2." From this example, you can see why stakeholder management should be an important input into both strategy formulation and implementation and how the roles of certain stakeholders create important interdependencies between formulation and implementation.

Ethics, Biases, and Strategic Decision Making

Because the stakes are so high when executives make strategic decisions, they must do everything they can to make sure that those decisions are sound. You should thus weigh two additional factors before committing yourself to a major strategic endeavor: (1) whether the decision is ethical and (2) whether any potential biases have clouded your strategic decision-making process.

It should be obvious by now that our conception of strategy is that it is a means to accomplish organizational goals. The fact that we see numerous examples in the media of corporate scandals suggests the unfortunate observation that some people justify any means to accomplish a desired goal. Although it would be unfair to suggest that most corporations engage in

Driving Stakeholder Analysis at Tritec Motors

The first challenge in managing stakeholders is stakeholder analysis—determining how stakeholders are affected by a firm's decisions and how much influence they have over the implementation of the decisions that are made. Not all stakeholders are affected in the same way, and not all stakeholders have the same level of influence in determining what a firm does. When stakeholder analysis is executed well, as you will see from the following example of the Tritec joint venture in Curitiba, Brazil, stakeholder planning will give the resulting strategy a better chance of succeeding, because the entities you might rely on in the implementation phase also helped to formulate the strategy.

THE STALLED MOTOR MAKER

Formed in 2001, the Tritec joint venture between Daimler-Chrysler and BMW represented a $400-million state-of-the-art engine manufacturing facility in Curitiba, Brazil. From the start, however, production problems with the new motors were wreaking havoc with BMW's newly minted line of wildly successful Mini Coopers. On the Chrysler side, Daimler's acquisition of the U.S. firm resulted in the triage of the main line of vehicles that would receive engines from the Curitiba plant. In sum, the Curitiba plant was producing poor-quality engines for BMW, and Daimler was paying for half

of a factory that it was barely even using.

In stepped Bob Harbin, a 25-year employee of Chrysler. Bob was given 90 days to come up with a plan to fix Tritec's problems. This was a make-or-break assignment for Harbin. Fortunately, Harbin knew how to apply stakeholder analysis and stakeholder planning, and he knew that the key players he involved in designing the turnaround strategy would likely be instrumental in executing it as well. In some cases, even if they did not have a role in implementation, certain stakeholders, such as the Brazilian government, could actually hurt Tritec's turnaround chances.

THE DISCOVERY PROCESS

Harbin spent the first five days of his assignment meeting with top executives at Daimler and BMW, both to gain an understanding of their needs and expectations and to determine how much discretion they would afford him if drastic changes were needed. After all, the corporate partners were essentially Tritec's financial backers and its only customers. Next, he spent two weeks in Curitiba meeting with everyone from the shop-floor employees to his future management team. He also spent time with key local parts suppliers as well as members of the newly installed Brazilian government. The government was particularly important because of the

tax incentives and export credits that it had put into place to entice Tritec to Brazil; however, the change in government meant that those credits were in danger of being annulled. Throughout this discovery process, Harbin reiterated a common vision: "If we can't produce quality engines and get them to BMW on time, then the plant will likely be closed. No jobs, no tax revenues, no engines. Period." Not only did this quickly gain each stakeholder's attention, it also fostered cooperation and a sense of urgency among all the key players.

SENDING MESSAGES AND IMPLEMENTING A PLAN

After the first 30 days, Harbin assembled his leadership team based on impressions gained during his early interviews. Most of his team were Brazilians, which sent a strong message of confidence to the Brazilian workforce as well as to the Brazilian government. Together, Harbin and his team put together a rescue plan for the engine-manufacturing process; he then took this plan back to Germany for endorsement by both BMW and Daimler. With the key pieces of the plan in place and the most important stakeholders squarely behind the plan—the alliance partners, the Brazilian government, Tritec's employees, and the new Tritec management team—Harbin began the steady process of turning around Tritec.

Although there were some minor setbacks along the way, within one year the factory was a world benchmark plant in many areas for both Daimler and BMW. By 2005, Tritec's production quality and efficiency were so high that even Toyota executives considered it one of the world's best-run auto-engine plants.

PLOTTING ROLES

Although every firm has multiple stakeholders, in this particular case the major stakeholders can be identified as BMW, Daimler-Chrysler, local employees, suppliers, the Brazilian and Curitiba governments, the Tritec leadership team (including Harbin), and competitors. What roles did these stakeholders play in the tough decisions faced by Harbin? Let's take each stakeholder individually and plot them on the stakeholder-analysis grid (see Exhibit 2.12). In some cases you may find you fill in every cell, but since the goal is to narrow the set of stakeholders down to those that are key, most of the time several of the cells will be left empty. Though empty cells are also an opportunity to ask yourself whether you have identified all the relevant players.

What role does BMW play in this situation? BMW is an owner/investor in the Tritec joint venture; thus on the power dimension BMW would be plotted in the far-right column, because it has voting and veto rights over all major decisions. However, BMW plays another role as well; it is the customer buying most of the engines made in this factory. Thus, BMW simultaneously has an economic interest apart from its ownership stake. Daimler-Chrysler's position is similar; it is an equity investor in the plant—thus it has an equity interest—and it has voting rights over all major decisions. Daimler is also a customer, but buys a fraction of the production used by BMW.

What position do the suppliers have? In terms of interests, they have a nonownership economic interest in the health of the plant. If the plant were to close, they would lose a major buyer. What influence/power do they have over decisions? They do not have major decisional power.

What about employees? Employees do not directly influence factory

decisions, but they do have an economic, nonequity stake in the factory. Individually, though, they are relatively powerless. What about the Brazilian or Curitiba government? The government clearly has a stake in ensuring that local businesses are prosperous. However, that stake is not as direct or significant as an equity stake or employees' or suppliers' economic interest. The national and local government can, however, dictate key issues like domestic content requirements, transfer pricing, or union and labor policies that affect the viability of Tritec's strategy. Competitors have no real power over this strategy, and at this point it is unclear of the impact of the strategy on them.

What does this analysis suggest? It suggests that if BMW does not get on board, all bets are off. Moreover, the government is a critical stakeholder; at this stage of the game Tritec should actively manage its relationship with the Brazilian government and make sure suppliers, employees, and management implement a plan that keeps BMW and Daimler-Chrysler satisfied.

Exhibit 2.12 Stakeholder-Analysis Grid for Tritec

	Power of the Stakeholder over Strategic Decisions			
	Unknown	Little/no power	Moderate degree of power	Significant power
Effect of Strategy on the Stakeholder — Unknown				
Little/no effect			Brazilian Government	
Moderate effect				Tritec Leadership Team
Significant effect		Tritec Suppliers Employees		BMW Daimler-Chrysler

deliberate acts of malfeasance to accomplish their goals, and that all executives are crooks, it would likewise be unwise to ignore such potential problems and the safeguards that can help firms avoid unethical behavior. Although there's no reason why a sound strategy has to have any hint of unethical motives or tactics, managers must take precautions to ensure that their firms don't figure in the next headline trumpeting the ethical bankruptcy of Corporate America.

In addition to ethical lapses, strategic decision making can be subject to a number of common decision-making biases. When executives fail to recognize and account for them, they may unwittingly pursue a course of action that they'd otherwise avoid. In this section, we'll review some of the ethics- and bias-related issues that may arise in the course of strategic decision making.

ETHICS AND STRATEGY

A quick survey of business history and recent business news will give you a good idea of the disastrous effects that questionable strategies can have on shareholders, clients, and even decision makers themselves. Enron is the most notorious recent example, but it's certainly not the only—nor even the most egregious—case. In early 2004, for example, Royal Dutch/Shell Group announced that executives had knowingly overstated oil and gas reserves by 4.5 million barrels, or 23 percent. In October of that year, Shell announced that it would have to "restate" its reserves by another million barrels. Investors were naturally unhappy at being misled about the firm's key assets, and its management ranks soon underwent a major shakeup.[38] Executives at other companies—notably Adelphia, a telecommunications provider, and Tyco, a diversified manufacturer and services provider—have been indicted (and some convicted) for diverting firm resources to private use. In other instances, misbehavior has taken the form of fraud; at the hospital chain HealthSouth, for example, no fewer than five onetime CFOs have been convicted in a $2.5-billion case of accounting fraud.[39]

Why Organizations Are Vulnerable to Ethics Violations In some of these cases, a few key executives were responsible for the violations of legal and ethical standards. In others, the misdeeds required a larger cast of characters. So why shouldn't organizations

In February 2004, former Enron CEO Jeffrey Skilling (handcuffed) appeared in federal court in Houston, Texas, where he was charged with 35 counts of conspiracy, securities fraud, wire fraud, and insider trading. According to the government, Skilling presided over accounting schemes to inflate the energy-trading company's earnings, leading to its collapse (and the loss of thousands of jobs) in 2001. Some say Enron's flawed incentive system was to blame. Employees were lavishly rewarded for making the company look good, whether their actions were legal or not. He was convicted in 2006 of multiple felony charges and was sentenced to a 24-year term in a Federal Correctional Facility in Waseca, Minnesota.

just be careful to hire principled people? For one thing, companies are often vulnerable because of organization-level conditions. In this section, we'll review two of these conditions—*authority structures* and *incentive systems*—and show how avoiding certain pitfalls can reduce a firm's risk.

Authority Structures Whereas some organizational characteristics foster potential opportunities for exploiting the system, others discourage potential whistle-blowers from alerting the proper authorities.[40] For example, because responsibility is distributed throughout an organization and tasks are specialized, there's a tendency for people to assume that someone else will blow the whistle on suspicious activity. The phenomenon, of course, can also be observed in society at large, as in cases in which bystanders will ignore an accident or criminal activity on the assumption that someone else will intervene.

The authority structure of modern organizations also inhibits lower-level employees from disclosing questionable practices. People who are relatively obedient tend to follow the directions of legitimate authorities even when they know that what they're doing is dubious.[41] And, of course, whistle-blowing is not an attractive option when those who are engaged in the questionable behavior occupy positions of authority.

Incentive Systems The larger the potential reward, the more some people are willing to compromise their standards. Research shows, for instance, that business-unit managers are more likely to defer income to subsequent accounting periods when earnings targets in their bonus plans won't be met or when they've already reached maximum payouts.[42]

More recently, some analysts have questioned whether stock-option pay induces executives to make decisions designed to improve near-term stock prices rather than to enhance the firm's long-term competitive position. Because of the potential effect that financial incentives can have on managerial behavior, firms must take stronger measures to ensure that they're not "rewarding A, while hoping for B."[43]

The Role of Corporate Governance

We'll discuss *corporate governance*—the roles of owners, directors, and managers in making corporate decisions—in more detail in Chapter 13. Here, we'll mention only that good corporate governance can reduce the risk of unethical and illegal activities. Because many unethical deeds are the work of individuals acting alone, quality governance can't guarantee ethical behavior. However, *poor* corporate governance provides a breeding ground for *un*ethical behavior. More and more firms are thus using governance mechanisms to discourage undesirable activities.

The Role of Decision Making Lapses

When managers aren't fully aware of the biases influencing their judgment and strategic decision making, lapses in the quality of strategic decision making may lead to ethical lapses. In this section, we'll sort potential biases into three sets of theories that we may hold about the conditions under which we make decisions: *theories about ourselves, theories about other people,* and *theories about the world.*[44]

Theories About Ourselves It shouldn't come as any surprise to hear that your self-perceptions influence your judgment and decisions. For instance, because strategic decision making is characterized by uncertainty and ambiguity, you'd expect that most senior executives are confident in their ability to make judgments under such conditions. When self-confidence, however, borders on the belief in one's own superiority, rational decision making may be impaired. Confidence, for example, can lead people to give themselves more credit for their successes and take less responsibility for their failures. It can also lead people to underestimate the prospect of negative future events while overestimating the prospect of positive outcomes. And when managers are confident they are more likely to believe that they are in greater control of a situation than rational analysis would support. Research, for example, shows that when people are allowed to touch a playing card before it's been reshuffled into the deck, they're more likely to believe that they can find it again on a random draw than if they hadn't touched it. In reality, of course, their odds are the same under both circumstances.

Importantly, this set of theories about ourselves also contribute to a decision-making bias called **escalation of commitment**—the willingness to commit additional resources to a failing course of action. Obviously, this particular bias might well influence an executive's decision to change a strategy, to pursue an acquisition even though the bidding has reached astronomical levels, or to continue or discontinue a particular project related to current strategy.

Similarly, research shows that a manager who initiates a project is less likely to perceive that it's failing, more likely to remain committed to it, and more likely to continue funding it than the manager who comes on board after the project is underway. People also tend toward increased commitment to innovative products than to less innovative products. Such findings suggest that simply giving managers better information won't necessarily lead to better decisions. They also indicate that escalation of commitment is a more serious problem during new-product development than after a product has been rolled out.[45] In short, escalation of commitment seems to be a particularly dangerous decision-making bias, especially when we consider the ambiguity and uncertainty inherently involved in most strategic decisions.

So, what are the potential ethical consequences of these theories about ourselves? The worst-case upshot of confidence-related biases is that some executives believe that they aren't subject to the same rules as everyone else. Top managers may delude themselves that they can get away with unethical or even felonious behavior because they believe either that they won't be caught or that, if they are, their status will protect them from the consequences. According to some researchers, executives believe that they are fair people and want to act in ways that are perceived as fair and just. Like most people, however, they usually do a better job of tracking their own contributions to a project and thus tend to take more credit for good outcomes than they give. As a result of this tendency, executives may rationalize lavish pay and perks on the grounds that they earned them because they contributed more than others.

Theories About Other People In many ways, our theories about other people reflect our theories about ourselves:

- We give ourselves more credit than we deserve and others less.

- We expect more credit and reward and expect others to accept less.

- We view positive future outcomes as more likely than negative outcomes but believe that the outcomes achieved by others are more likely to fail.

- We think that we're better than others at judging uncertain futures and so give more credence to our plans than to those of others.

- We believe that although we're acting on the best knowledge of present and future conditions, others are acting on imperfect knowledge.

In addition to these obvious biases, our theories about other people also encompass both *ethnocentrism* and *stereotyping*. **Ethnocentrism** is a belief in the superiority of one's own ethnic group, but it can be interpreted more broadly as the conviction that one's own national, group, or cultural characteristics are "normal" and ordinary. That belief, of course, renders everyone else foreign, strange, and perhaps dangerous.

In fact, we're all ethnocentric to some degree. Your ethnocentrism accounts for your opinion of foreigners' speech patterns and favored cuisines. Being ethnocentric, then, doesn't necessarily mean that you're hostile toward other groups, but it does mean that you probably regard your group as superior. Ethnocentrism is dangerous because it's automatic and often subtle: we tend to believe that our own group has multiple dimensions, whereas other groups can be characterized according to one relatively homogeneous characteristic—say, nationality, gender, or ethnicity. When you've reached this stage, you're engaged in

escalation of commitment Decision-making bias under which people are willing to commit additional resources to a failing course of action.

ethnocentrism Belief in the superiority of one's own ethnic group or, more broadly, the conviction that one's own national, group, or cultural characteristics are "normal."

stereotyping—relying on a conventional or formulaic conception of another group based on some common characteristic. The fallacy of ethnocentrism, then, is the belief in your own group's superiority; the fallacy of stereotyping lies in ascribing limiting characteristics to an entire set of people.

stereotyping Relying on a conventional or formulaic conception of another group based on some common characteristic.

Stereotyping puts executives at risk of making unethical, unfair, and sometimes illegal decisions because it limits their evaluations of other people to group affiliation while ignoring individual qualities. Ethnocentrism exposes businesspeople to rationally and ethically unsound decisions because it exaggerates the differences between us and them.

In terms of strategic decision making, ethnocentrism and stereotyping can have disastrous results. U.S. automakers, for example, ignored the Japanese competitive threat for decades because of a twofold mistaken belief: (1) that American car manufacturers were the best in the world and (2) that Japanese automakers could never produce high-quality vehicles. Thus ethnocentrism and stereotypes combined to blind U.S. (and European) carmakers to the emergence of extremely formidable rivals.

Theories About the World Today's top executives must be able to understand global events—or at least know where to get the information they need. Otherwise, it's too easy to misjudge the risks and consequences of an action with international ramifications. The trick, of course, is knowing what you don't know. Granted, it's often impossible to foresee all the possible consequences of a strategic choice, but a good starting point is the premise that "you can never do just one thing."[46] All actions, in other words, have multiple consequences, some intended, some unintended.

For example, the management of Levi Straus & Co. (LS&CO.) has a firm commitment to its corporate values. LS&CO. quickly stepped in to enforce a policy of not using contractors who employ child labor. Upon finding that a subcontractor in Bangladesh was employing children younger than 14, LS&CO. made the factory rectify the situation. Levi's decision to demonstrate its commitment to ethical practices and global social responsibility by discouraging child labor had an unintended consequence: Because factory jobs were no longer available, poor families that depended on their daughters' incomes resorted to pushing them into prostitution. Where did Levi Straus go wrong? Arguably, a few fallacious theories about the world resulted in a faulty perception of certain stakeholders: LS&CO. looked initially only at the situation of the girls and inadvertently ignored the needs of their families. Once discovering the complication, LS&CO. decided to pay for the underage children to go to school and guarantee jobs in the factory once they were of age.

Similarly, imperfect theories about the world may lead executives to discount low-probability events or to underestimate the probability of certain activities becoming public. The effects of such poor judgment can snowball into strategic and ethical blunders. In the early 1970s, for example, internal safety tests on the Ford Pinto revealed that under rare rear-impact conditions the gas tank could explode. The defect could be remedied with a $10 part, but Ford opted for a less costly response and, what's worse, covered up its own test results when the fatal rear-end crash turned out to be more common and more deadly than the company had figured.[47] The more recent example of how Ford proactively responded to tire problems from its chief supplier Bridgestone/Firestone, which caused some SUVs to roll when experiencing a flat, suggests that Ford may have learned its lesson.

Related to these imperfections in strategic decision making is the fact that we tend to discount the future and to place lower values on collective outcomes. In other words, we often focus on today's problems because we believe them to be more important than those that may be encountered down the road. Similarly, because we're prone to underestimate the consequences of our actions on large groups, we tend to ignore collective outcomes. Ford's behavior in the Pinto case, for example, contributed to public perception that the auto industry couldn't, or wouldn't, police itself on the issue of safety—a reaction that, in turn, led to an unprecedented raft of auto-safety regulations.

Summary of Challenges

1. *Explain how strategic leadership is essential to strategy formulation and implementation.* **Strategic leadership** is concerned with the management of an overall enterprise and the ways in which top executives influence key organizational outcomes, such as performance, competitive superiority, innovation, strategic change, and survival. Leaders typically play three critical roles—interpersonal, informational, and decisional—all of which support the firm's vision and mission and the implementation of its strategy. The **Level 5 Hierarchy** is a model of leadership skills that calls for a wide range of abilities, some of which are hierarchical in nature. Leaders can be distinguished by personality and demographic differences, and strategic leadership can be exercised either by individuals or groups.

2. *Understand the relationships among vision, mission, values, and strategy.* An organizational **vision** is a simple forward-looking statement or understanding of what the firm will be in the future. A **mission** is a declaration of what a firm is and what it stands for—its fundamental values and purpose. Together, mission and vision statements express the identity and describe the work of a firm. They also state the firm's direction. Vision and mission statements support strategy, which provides a coherent plan for realizing the firm's vision and mission.

3. *Understand the roles of vision and mission in determining strategic purpose and strategic coherence.* Guidance in making decisions is important because there's only so much complexity in a given problem with which any individual or group can reasonably cope. Vision and mission statements are thus useful because they inform all employees of the firm's **strategic purpose**—a simplified, widely shared model of the organization and its future, including anticipated changes in its environment. The challenge posed by a defined strategic purpose is closing the gap between aspirations on the one hand and current capabilities and market positions on the other. **Strategic coherence** refers to the symmetrical coalignment of the five elements of the firm's strategy, the congruence of functional-area policies with these elements, and the overarching fit of various businesses under the corporate umbrella.

4. *Identify a firm's stakeholders and explain why such identification is critical to effective strategy formulation and implementation.* Stakeholder analysis improves the understanding of the range and variety of parties who have a vested interest in the formulation and implementation of a firm's strategy or some influence on firm performance. The first step in stakeholder analysis is identifying stakeholder groups that are affected by or that may affect the firm's strategy. The second step calls for identifying those stakeholders who are important for strategy formulation and implementation, those for whom the strategy will be important, and those who are influential in determining the strategy. The third step involves categorizing stakeholders according to their influence in determining strategy versus their importance in its execution. Stakeholder analysis also helps expose any major omissions in strategy formulation and implementation.

5. *Explain how ethics and biases may affect strategic decision making.* Strategic leadership and strategic decision making have much in common. Indeed, strategic leadership can be characterized by strategic decision making and the actions in which it results. The effectiveness of strategic decision making is threatened when managers act unethically or without being fully aware of the biases influencing their judgment. Ethical lapses may reflect an individual shortcoming, but they can often be traced to a lack of clear organizational mechanisms for making individuals accountable for their actions. Decision-making biases, or threats to rational decision making in general, result from theories about oneself, theories about other people, and theories about one's world. They may impair both rational and ethical decision making and even an organization's ability to realize its vision and mission.

Review Questions

1. Why is strategic leadership important for effective strategy formulation and implementation?

2. How do the characteristics of strategic leadership differ between individuals and teams?

3. What is a vision? A mission?

4. How are vision and mission related to strategy? What roles does strategic leadership play in realizing vision and mission?

5. How does strategy differ from vision and mission?

6. What is strategic purpose?

7. What is strategic coherence?

8. Who are a firm's stakeholders? Why are they important?

9. What tools can you use to identify the impact of various stakeholders on the firm and the impact of the firm on various stakeholders?

10. Why are ethics and biases relevant to strategic decision making and strategic leadership?

Experiential Activities

Group Exercises

1. (a) Craft a vision and mission statement for your business school and then for your college or university as a whole. How are these statements related? How are they similar? How do they differ? How are they similar or different from those that you might craft for a for-profit organization? (b) Using the vision and mission you crafted, develop a list of key stakeholders for your school and their relative power and stake in the school. Which of these stakeholder groups is accounted for in your vision and mission statement, and which ones are left out? Did you identify any stakeholder groups that could negatively affect your realization of this vision and mission?

2. What roles should strategic leadership play in the realization of the vision and mission statements that you articulated in the previous question? Whom have you identified as strategic leaders?

Ethical Debates

1. A slogan on an ethics poster for Boeing states: "Between right and wrong is a troublesome gray area." What aspects of this statement do you agree or disagree with? As a future business leader, what should you be doing to manage the "gray area"?

2. When reading the business press, it seems that leaders are regularly challenged by ethical dilemmas. Is this a function of the individual leader or the situation, or both?

How Would YOU DO THAT?

1. Building on the CEO-successor selection process described in the box entitled "How Would *You* Do That? 2.1," devise a succession plan for the dean of your business school. Be sure to include the following in your succession-planning process: (a) Translate your school's strategy into actual operating needs and key activities; (b) identify the skills needed for these operating needs and activities; (c) outline an internal and external candidate search process; and (d) develop a list of goals and milestones and a compensation structure that ties actions to the strategic drivers of success at your school.

2. Based on the framework applied to Tritec Motors in the box entitled "How Would *You* Do That? 2.2," use the opening vignette on Anne Mulcahy at Xerox to map out the key stakeholders in her turnaround effort. Which stakeholders would you expect to be most resistant? Most supportive? Create a 90-day action plan for Mulcahy, following the example laid out by Bob Harbin in "How Would *You* Do That? 2.2."

Go on to see How Would You Do That at www.prenhall.com/ carpenter&sanders

Endnotes

1. W. M. Bulkeley and J. S. Lublin, "Xerox Appoints Insider Mulcahy to Execute Turnaround as CEO," *Wall Street Journal* (Eastern edition), July 27, 2001, A3; P. Moore, "Anne Mulcahy: She's Here to Fix Xerox," *Business Week,* August 6, 2001, 47; A. Klein, "Xerox to Expand Color-Printing Business," *Wall Street Journal* (Eastern edition), September 23, 1999, B12; J. Bandler, "Xerox Profit Falls, but CEO Sees a 'Breakthrough,'" *Wall Street Journal* (Eastern edition), July 29, 2003, A3; J. Bandler, "Xerox Corp.: CEO Sees Improving Finances, Broadening Product Offering," *Wall Street Journal* (Eastern edition), May 16, 2003, B6; O. Kharif, "Anne Mulcahy Has Xerox by the Horns," *Business Week Online,* May 29, 2003 (accessed June 21, 2005), at www.businessweek.com/technology/content/may2003/`tc20030529_1642_tc111.htm; Marc Ferranti, "Mulcahy: Innovation, Services Key to Xerox Future," *InfoWorld,* October 2, 2006, p3; Paolo Del Nibletto, "The Saviour," *Computer Dealer News,* September 8, 2006, p30; Claudi H. Deutsch, "Prices Are Lower, but Profit Is Up at Xerox," *New York Times,* April 21, 2007.

2. M. Porter, J. Lorsch, and N. Nohria, "Seven Surprises for New CEOs," *Harvard Business Review* 82:10 (2004), 62–72.

3. This discussion of the nature of CEO job responsibilities draws heavily from the seminal work of H. Mintzberg, *The Nature of Managerial Work* (New York: Harper and Row, 1973).

4. Exhibit is adapted from H. Mintzberg, *The Nature of Managerial Work* (New York: Harper and Row, 1973).

5. Mintzberg, *The Nature of Managerial Work,* 67.

6. Information in this paragraph is based on Porter, Lorsch, and Nohria, "Seven Surprises for New CEOs," 62–72.

7. Stanford Graduate School of Business Alumni Profiles (accessed July 12, 2005), at www.gsb.stanford.edu/news/profiles/deromedi.shtml.

8. J. Collins, *Good to Great: Why Some Companies Make the Leap . . . and Others Don't* (New York: HarperBusiness, 2001).

9. Collins, "Level 5 Leadership: The Triumph of Humility and Fierce Resolve," *Harvard Business Review* 79:1 (2001), 67–76.

10. Exhibit is adapted from Collins, "Level 5 Leadership: The Triumph of Humility and Fierce Resolve," *Harvard Business Review* 79:1 (2001), 67–76.

11. Collins, "Level 5 Leadership," 73.

12. For a review of this material, see D. Whetten and K. Cameron, *Developing Management Skills,* 5th ed. (Upper Saddle River, NJ: Prentice Hall, 2002).

13. Source: S. Budner, "Intolerance of Ambiguity as a Personality Variable," *Journal of Personality* 30 (1982), 29–50.

14. For a comprehensive review of this literature, see M. A. Carpenter, W. G. Sanders, and M. A. Geletkanycz, "The Upper Echelons Revisited: The Antecedents, Elements, and Consequences of TMT Composition," *Journal of Management* 30 (2004), 749–778.

15. M. Useem and J. Karabel, "Pathways to Corporate Management," *American Sociological Review* 51 (1986), 184–200.

16. 'Any College Will Do' Nation's Top Chief Executives Find Path to the Corner Office Usually Starts at State University, *Wall Street Journal* (2006), B1.

17. S. L. Keck, "Top Management Team Structure: Differential Effects by Environmental Context," *Organization Science* 8 (1997), 143–156.

18. M. A. Carpenter, W. G. Sanders, and H. B. Gregersen, "International Experience at the Top Makes a Bottom-Line Difference," *Human Resource Management* 39:2/3 (2000), 277–285; Carpenter, Sanders, and Gregersen, "Bundling Human Capital with Organizational Context: The Impact of International Experience on Multinational Firm Performance and CEO Pay," *Academy of Management Journal* 44 (2001), 493–512.

19. Adapted from H. Hinterhuber and W. Popp, "Are You a Strategist or Just a Manager?" *Harvard Business Review* 70:1 (January–February 1992), 105–113.

20. C. Lucier, R. Schuyt, and J. Handa, "CEO Succession 2003: The Perils of 'Good' Governance" (accessed June 21, 2005), at www.boozallen hamilton.com.

21. S. Hamm, "Former CEOs Should Just Fade Away," *Business Week,* April 12, 2004 (Online Extra) (accessed July 12, 2005), at www.businessweek. com/magazine/content/04_15/b3878092_mz063.htm; J. Sonnenfeld, *The Hero's Farewell: What Happens when CEOs Retire* (New York: Oxford University Press, 1991).

22. P. Estess, "Twos Company," entrepreneur.com, May 1997 (accessed June 22, 2005), at www.entrepreneur.com/article/0,4621,227207,00.html.

23. C. Hymowitz and J. S. Lublin, "McDonald's CEO Tragedy Holds Lessons," *Wall Street Journal,* April 20, 2004, B1.

24. Adapted from D.C. Hambrick and J.W. Fredrickson, "Are You Sure You Have a Strategy?" *Academy of Management Executive* 15:4 (2001), 48–59.

25. C. K. Bart and M. C. Baetz, "The Relationship Between Mission Statements and Firm Performance: An Exploratory Study," *Journal of Management Studies* 35 (1998), 823–853.

26. J. C. Collins and J. I. Porras, *Build to Last* (New York: Harper Business, 1997).

27. Bart and Baetz, "The Relationship Between Mission Statements and Firm Performance"; A. Campbell and S. Yeung, "Creating a Sense of Mission," *Long Range Planning* 24:4 (1991), 10–20; P. Drucker, *Management: Tasks, Responsibilities, and Practices* (New York: Harper and Row, 1974); R. D. Ireland and M. A. Hitt, "Mission Statements: Importance, Challenge and Recommendations for Development," *Business Horizons* 35:3 (1992), 34–42.

28. Collins and Porras, *Build to Last.*

29. J. Collins and J. Porras, "Building a Visionary Company," *California Management Review* 37 (1995), 80–100; W. Kim and R. Mauborgne, "Charting Your Company's Future," *Harvard Business Review* 80:6 (2002), 5–11.

30. D. Kirkpatrick, "Gerstner's New Vision for IBM," *Fortune,* November 15, 1993, 119–124.

31. D. Kirkpatrick, "Gerstner's New Vision for IBM," *Fortune,* November 15, 1993, 119–124.

32. Bart and Baetz, "The Relationship Between Mission Statements and Firm Performance."

33. "Company Background: The History and Overview of Dell" (accessed July 12, 2005), at www1.us.dell.com/content/topics/global.aspx/corp/background/en/index?c=us&l=en&s=corp.

34. Panasonic, "In the Pursuit of a Super Manufacturing Company" (accessed July 18, 2005), at matsushita.co.jp/corp/vision/president/interview2/en/index.html.

35. Panasonic, "About Panasonic: Vision" (accessed January 11, 2005) at panasonic.co.jp/global/about/vision/index.html.

36. Kim and Mauborgne, "Charting Your Company's Future."

37. Adapted from R.E. Freeman, *Strategic Management: A Stakeholder Approach* (Boston, MA: Pitman, 1984).

38. M. Curtin, "THE SKEPTIC: Thorough Shell Revamp, But Where's the Oil?" *Dow Jones International News*, October 28, 2004.

39. B. Berkrot, "First HealthSouth Sentencing Set for Wednesday," Reuters, November 11, 2003.

40. This discussion draws heavily on R. Gandossy and J. Sonnenfeld, "I See Nothing, I Hear Nothing: Culture, Corruption, and Apathy," in Gandossy and Sonnenfeld (eds.), *Leadership and Governance from the Inside Out* (Hoboken, NJ: Wiley, 2004), 3–26.

41. S. Milgram, *Obedience to Authority* (New York: Harper, 1974).

42. P. M. Healy and J. M. Wahlen, "A Review of the Earnings Management Literature and Its Implications for Standard Setting," *Accounting Horizons* 13 (1999), 365–383.

43. S. Kerr, "On the Folly of Rewarding A, While Hoping for B," *Academy of Management Journal* 18 (1975), 769–783.

44. This material draws from behavioral decision theory. Excellent references are D. Kahneman, P. Slovic, and A. Tversky, *Judgment Under Uncertainty* (Cambridge: Cambridge University Press, 1982); M. Bazerman, *Judgment in Managerial Decision Making* (New York: John Wiley, 1994); J. Janis, *Groupthink* (Boston: Houghton-Mifflin, 1982).

45. J. Schmidt and R. Calantone, "Escalation of Commitment During New Product Development," *Journal of the Academy of Marketing Science* 30:2 (2002), 103–118.

46. G. Hardin, *Filters Against Folly* (New York: Penguin Books, 1985).

47. R. Nader, *Unsafe at Any Speed* (New York: Grossman, 1965).

Examining the Internal Environment

3

Resources, Capabilities, and Activities

In This Chapter We Challenge You To >>>

1. Explain the *internal context of strategy*.

2. Identify a firm's resources and capabilities and explain their role in firm performance.

3. Define *dynamic capabilities* and explain their role in both strategic change and firm performance.

4. Explain how value-chain activities are related to firm performance and competitive advantage.

5. Explain the role of managers with respect to resources, capabilities, and value-chain activities.

Strategy
Inside Intel

*P*aul Otellini, the current CEO of Intel, joined the company right after getting his MBA in 1974. "I consider myself a product guy," Otellini said in an interview. "I've had my fingerprints on products for 20 years. I ran the microprocessor division for a decade, during the 486 [and] Pentium days. I get into products. I like them, I use them."

Intel is, at its core, an engineering company. Intel was founded in 1968 by three engineers—Robert Noyce, Gordon Moore, and Andy Grove—who left secure jobs at Fairchild Semiconductor to create a new company that would develop technology for silicon-based semiconductor chips. From that small start, Intel has gone on to become the world's largest computer chip maker. The $35 billion company's strengths lie in technology innovations and manufacturing capability. When Otellini took over as CEO, he reiterated Intel's key strengths in R&D, manufacturing and technology: "You're going to see Intel combine its R&D innovation, manufacturing and technology leadership with energy-efficient micro-architectures and powerful multicore processors to deliver unique platforms best tailored to individual needs." Otellini is only Intel's fifth CEO, and he sees a continuity of strategy across the CEOs. Intel's current chairman, Craig Barrett, summarized the strategy and each CEO's contribution: "Robert Noyce and Gordon Moore were the two founders of the company, and they founded the company on the very simple premise of doing something with integrated-circuit technology and commercializing integrated circuits. I look at their era as heavily focused on advancing technology," Barrett said. Andy Grove, CEO from 1987–1997, "took over when the PC started to build, and that's when he had the most influence on the company; he drove us hard in that direction, and we achieved a more reasonable market signature, market penetration, with the microprocessor," Barrett said. Reflecting on his own tenure as CEO from 1998–2005, Barrett said, "What did we do in the seven years I was CEO that will reap Intel benefits seven years hence? We clearly invested in basic R&D and process technology, extreme-UV lithography and all sorts of good stuff that I think will allow us to continue to be at the front of the parade in Moore's Law and driving transistors. I think we made the investments in manufacturing, and we'll continue to reap those benefits to the next decade."

A key facet of Intel's strategy is its choice to build its differentiators based on massive investments in R&D. "You have two choices with R&D, lead or be led," Barrett said. "R&D drives the next level of innovation. You can have the best business model in the world, but if it's creating last year's technology, it will not be successful." Intel starts with an innovation, gets a toehold in the new field, and then methodically exploits its financial and technical resources to gain an advantage. In server chips, for instance, Intel had a negligible market share in 1995 when the Pentium Pro, the company's first chip specifically designed for servers, debuted. Now, more than 80 percent of servers coming out of factories run on Intel chips.

Intel invests in innovation through thick and thin. Barrett often quoted Gordon Moore's adage that a chip company can't save its way out of a recession. "You invest your way out of a recession," Barrett said. Intel uses recessions and downturns to continually develop new products and better position itself for the next expansion. The 2001 recession was no exception. Barrett and Grove explained the strategy in the company's 2001 Annual Report: "[W]e know that a downturn is no time to shy away from strategic spending. Consequently, during this downturn, we did what may seem counterintuitive: We accelerated our capital investments, spending $7.3 billion in 2001, compared with approximately $10 billion in capital spending over the previous two years combined. We also invested $3.8 billion in research and development in 2001." The payoff for Intel was handsome. When the 2002–3 recovery came, Intel was able to quickly launch new products such as its Centrino mobile processor technology. Consequently, Intel had a banner year in 2003, with revenues increasing 13 percent and net income rising 81 percent over the previous year. By 2006, however, the company was again facing challenges, especially from rival chipmaker AMD. Otellini responded to the challenge in characteristic Intel fashion: "We accelerated the introduction of new products, leading the industry into an era of energy-efficient, multi-core computing and ending the year with one of the strongest product lineups in our history." The year ended on a strong note and Intel reported its 20th consecutive year of profitability.

Processing Competitive Threats Initially, Intel (the name is a contraction of "*int*egrated *el*ectronics") made read-only memory chips for computers and experienced early success in the industry. Before long, however, Asian competitors stepped up their competitive practices, using low-cost capital financing, large advantages in economies of scale, and aggressive pricing to dominate global market share. In addition, technological improvements in new generations of memory chips continued at lightning speed. These forces converged to create an extremely volatile market. As a result, Intel and other U.S. memory-chip companies suffered financially.

Fortunately for Intel, just when competition was intensifying in the memory-chip business, a new microprocessor technology that Intel had developed earlier was paying off and picking up some of the slack. In 1971, Intel introduced the world's first commercial microprocessor, the 4004. When a subsequent generation of the chip (the 8088) was chosen for the IBM PC in 1981, Intel secured its place as the standard setter in the microprocessor business.

A Few Knowledgeable Workers Go a Long Way Intel's transition from a memory-chip company to the leading manufacturer of microprocessors was not planned. In fact, the official corporate strategy was to compete primarily in the memory-chip market, not the microprocessor market, based on Intel's senior executives' views that the firm's historic success in memory chips could be carried into the future. Rather, the company's production managers started shifting manufacturing capacity from memory chips to microprocessors because the yields per wafer square inch were higher. They followed a rather simple managerial rule—allocate production capacity based on a "margin-per-wafer-start." Margins on memory wafers were declining and margins for microprocessor wafers were increasing. In light of this change, Intel production managers shifted production capacity toward microprocessors, and they did so rapidly, because Intel's incentive and accountability systems rewarded plant managers based on wafer yields. Moreover, the chairman and CEO of Intel, Andy Grove, had successfully nurtured a strong internal culture that encouraged open debate about strategic initiatives and discouraged the use of hierarchy or position over the power of knowledge to make key decisions. The confluence of these factors—Intel's experiment with microprocessors, IBM's selection of the Intel chip, the excessive price competition in the memory market, and Intel's organizational processes that enabled plant managers to make these changes without explicit approval from senior management— enabled Intel to change rapidly from a memory-chip company to a microprocessor company.

Taking Strategic License An important benefit of the change to microprocessors was the evolution of Intel's capabilities beyond narrow technical design to the implementation of complex design architectures in logic products, which gave Intel a much larger market domain. As the standard setter and chief supplier for the world's largest PC maker, Intel became a formidable player in the microprocessor industry. IBM, however, was reluctant to allow a small company to be the sole supplier of such a key technology. Consequently, Intel chose to license the technology to other companies to satisfy IBM's concern. It licensed its next chip design, the 286, to other semiconductor firms, such as Advanced Micro Devices (AMD). Licensing reinforced Intel's status as an industry technology architecture leader, and it also enabled the company to supplement profits from its own sales with the healthy fees paid by licensees.

With a patent on the microprocessor design that had become the industry standard, Intel controlled a valuable intellectual property. The licensing fees paid by other firms were substantial; nevertheless, Intel moved to ease its dependence on outside manufacturers by adopting a three-pronged approach to improving its competitive position:

■ The company used revenues from licensing agreements and profits from chip sales to fund the expansion of its manufacturing capacity and manufacturing-processing capabilities. Intel realized that if it could improve the manufacturing process, it would not only control the technology that semiconductor firms used to make processors, but it might also be able to generate cost savings. With a superior manufacturing process in hand, Intel then increased manufacturing capacity by building larger fabrication plants (called "fabs"), which also resulted in superior economies of scale.

■ At the same time that Intel was building both innovation and manufacturing capability for microprocessors, the PC industry was expanding and credible threats to IBM were emerging. Compaq decided to adopt the 486 chip design after IBM decided to delay adoption of the chip, and other small PC companies soon followed Compaq's lead. The new chip proved to be a success with consumers. Because Intel had been investing in additional capacity in its fabs, it was able to exploit these new dynamics in the PC industry. Intel started revoking licensing agreements from other semiconductor companies for future generations of the Intel microprocessor. This move allowed Intel to capture a larger market share and boosted profits because canceling licenses eliminated competitors and the number of PC makers was increasing dramatically.

■ Intel set out to brand its product in order to make it the microprocessor of choice among end users, even if similar products entered the market. PC manufacturers, of course, preferred to source their technology from multiple suppliers. Thus, Intel still faced the threat that AMD or some other upstart would begin to compete aggressively and weaken its market share. Intel responded by advertising its product to end users—the individual consumers who purchase PCs from computer makers. The campaign was so successful that consumers turned out to be willing to pay higher prices for PCs with "Intel Inside." **<<<**

Internal Drivers of Strategy and Competitive Advantage

In this chapter, we'll introduce theories and models that explain why some firms outperform their rivals and others lag behind. You have probably been introduced to a very simple tool in other classes (such as marketing) called *SWOT analysis*. Recall that SWOT is an acronym for *s*trengths, *w*eaknesses, *o*pportunities, and *t*hreats. This chapter deals primarily with firms' strengths and weaknesses, or the resource-based inputs into the strategy process. These are internal characteristics of firms. Firms within an industry generally have different strengths and weaknesses, and those differences often have a strong bearing on which firms win competitive interactions. We will introduce you to more rigorous models that help managers diagnose their strengths and weaknesses and prescribe future actions to exploit their strengths or remedy their weaknesses. Of course, a complete understanding of a firm's strengths and weaknesses requires an understanding of competitors. Chapter 4 will introduce the basic tools for analyzing competitors, thereby enabling you to evaluate firms relative to their competitors.

 This chapter focuses on firms' resources and capabilities, the choices managers make when configuring the activities they chose to perform internally (versus outsourcing), and the role of managers in allocating, reconfiguring, and exploiting firm resources and capabilities. All firms, of course, must consider the external context when formulating and implementing strategy, but focusing on the internal perspective reminds us that firms differ in terms of resources and capabilities. Indeed, the internal perspective should help you describe and understand the *differentiators* facet of the strategy diamond for a given firm. ◆ If you can identify the key resources and capabilities that allow it to differentiate its products or services in its targeted arenas, you are well on your way to understanding its strategy and strategic opportunities. To this end, we'll examine several models and analytical tools that will help you analyze and formulate competitive strategies.

◆ **Differentiators**

Our opening vignette has already given us some insight into the internal sources of competitive advantage. Although the microprocessor industry is extremely competitive, Intel has been able to maintain its competitive advantage over most of its rivals for an extended period of time. This fact suggests that Intel has access to internal resources and capabilities that other firms do not. Many firms in the industry, for example, are capable of making innovations in chip design. Intel, however, has always been able to get new products to market faster than its competitors and get them there in the volume necessary to achieve significant cost advantages. Speed to market is thus an Intel differentiator. It is a differentiator because Intel is relatively unique in this area, and because speed to market is highly valued by its customers. This advantage in speed to market results, in part, from Intel's ability to convince computer makers to use its products and from its ability to move new products into production in a timely manner.

However, as we also noted in the opening vignette, at one point Intel was forced to license its technology to other manufacturers because its chief customer demanded multiple sourcing options. Being forced to license the technology to other firms meant that Intel didn't have the immediate in-house capacity to manufacture chips fast enough and in large enough quantities to satisfy market demand. The firm addressed this problem by investing heavily to improve its manufacturing processes. The related judgment and willingness of management to undertake such a risk—new semiconductor plants cost over $1 billion to build and take several years to complete—may be considered another of Intel's internal strengths. This combination of speed to market and manufacturing-process capability means that Intel can charge significant price premiums during the first months following a new-product release. Competitors who get to market later must settle for lower profits because prices have fallen.

As our description of Intel's history, strategy, and performance suggests, the firm's advantage is due, in part, to its use of engineering expertise to create valuable technologies, operational efficiencies to make its new products proprietary standards in the industry, and marketing skills to exploit its ability to speed products to market. Not surprisingly, its competitive advantage translates into higher levels of performance.

Firms in many other industries have also managed to do what Intel has done—namely, to outperform major competitors for extended periods of time. As you can see in Exhibit 3.1, such firms can be found in industries ranging from semiconductors to retail grocers. Notice that the average profitability (return on sales and return on assets) for firms within these very different industries varies significantly across firms over long periods of time. Intel's average return on assets (ROA) and return on sales (ROS), which are measures of financial performance that gauge profits as a percentage of total sales and total assets, respectively, dwarf those of its nearest competitor, Texas Instruments. In the exhibit, note that the only competitors who approach Intel's average returns are much smaller companies focused on specialized niches. In the grocery industry, Publix, Whole Foods, and Weis appear to perform much better on average than other grocery chains even though they are much smaller than the largest firms in the industry. The exhibit only illustrates two industries, but these are representative of what you would generally find in most industries. Whether we look at high-tech industries, such as semiconductors or a retail business, such as grocery stores, within industries some firms perform much better than others over time.

Exhibit 3.1   Comparative Performance in Selected Industries

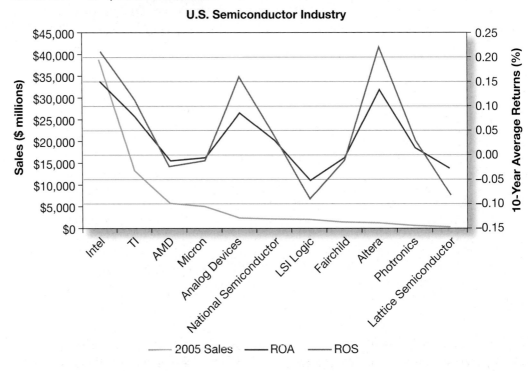

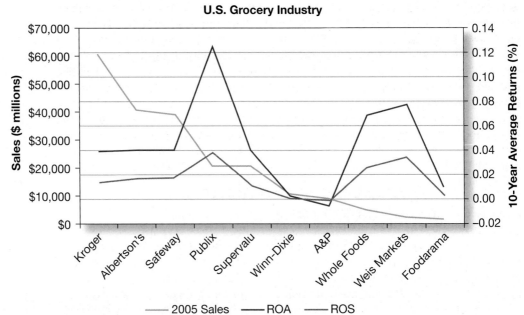

One of the primary purposes of this chapter is to help you understand how such differences in profitability materialize as a result of firms being able to use their resources and capabilities to create differentiators, and perhaps other unique choices related to facets of the strategy diamond, and what firms can do to improve their performance relative to firms in their industry.

INTERNAL MODELS OF COMPETITIVE ADVANTAGE

This chapter presents the two dominant models regarding internal sources of competitive advantage; they help to explain how and why some firms perform better than others. Recall in Chapter 1 we told you that there are three perspectives of competitive advantage: internal, external, and dynamic. The two models presented in this chapter are distinct but complementary theories that both suggest that differences in long-term-performance outcomes across firms within the same industry are derived largely from different levels of internal sources of competitive advantage. However, the source of competitive advantage differs between these theories. The first explanation as to why some firms perform better than others attributes this success to fundamental differences in the resources firms control as well as their capabilities to perform certain aspects of value creation activities. The dynamic perspective introduced in Chapter 1 is necessary to understand how these differences in resources and capabilities evolve over time. The second theory for why firms differ within industries focuses not on resources, but on *the specific value chain activities firms choose to engage in.* This activity perspective, treated toward the end of this chapter, relies heavily on the value chain and the advantages firms might gain by configuring value-chain activities in ways to add more value to their products or services than competitors. We'll explain how these two theories help to determine which firms are able to develop a competitive advantage and potentially perform above industry averages and which ones suffer from liabilities and struggle to keep up.

STRATEGIC LEADERSHIP

Finally, whether we trace a firm's competitive advantage to its resources and capabilities or to the organization of its value-chain activities, we must always consider the role played by its managers. Senior and mid-level managers make key decisions about how to acquire, allocate, and discard resources, and they're also in charge of organizing a firm's value-chain activities. This is why we include managers' strategic leadership as a potentially valuable internal input into strategy. Exhibit 3.2 provides an overview of how resources, capabilities, and managerial decision making are interdependent; all are necessary to understand how and why firms perform differently within similar industry environments. As we'll explain in more detail later, notice how the role of management is both to use the resources and capabilities to devise strategies and to make decisions about reconfiguring resources and

Exhibit 3.2   Resources, Capabilities, and Managerial Decisions

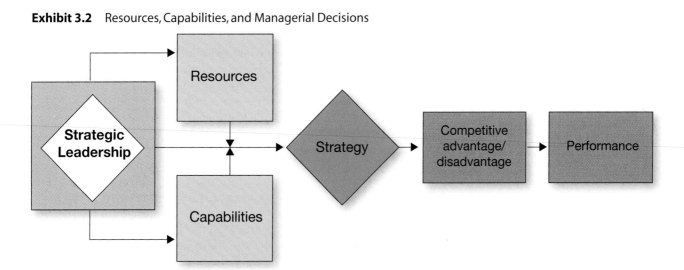

capabilities. Indeed, managers play the unique role of being a resource for the firm, having capabilities which they use to manage the firm, and making choices about the stewardship and deployment of other resources and capabilities (our opening vignette on Intel is an example here).

Resources and Capabilities

Resources and capabilities are the fundamental building blocks of a firm's strategy. The choices made by firms' managers relative to the five elements of a strategy, as organized by the strategy diamond, require resources and capabilities. For instance, if a firm wants to enter new arenas, it will need appropriate resources and capabilities in order to compete there. In addition, no matter how a firm plans to differentiate its products—whether on quality, image, or price—it needs the right resources and capabilities to make the differentiation real. Likewise, when a firm is deciding on the best way to enter a new market—whether by means of acquisition, alliance, or internal development—it has to consider its available resources and capabilities. Sometimes a firm uses a vehicle such as an acquisition or an alliance specifically for the purpose of acquiring resources or capabilities that it does not currently own.[1] Not surprisingly, successful strategies exploit the resources and capabilities that a firm enjoys and put the firm on a path to acquire missing resources and capabilities and upgrade existing ones; whereas unsuccessful strategies often reflect the fact that critical resources and capabilities are lacking.

RESOURCES

resources   Inputs used by firms to create products and services.

What, exactly, do we mean by *resources?* **Resources** are the inputs that firms use to create goods or services. Some resources are rather undifferentiated inputs that any firm can acquire. For instance, land, unskilled labor, debt financing, and commodity-like inventory are inputs that are generally available to most firms. Other resources are more firm-specific in nature.[2] They are difficult to purchase through normal supply chain channels. For instance, managerial judgment, intellectual property, trade secrets, and brand equity are resources that are not easily purchased or transferred. From this description, it is clear that some resources have physical attributes; these are referred to as *tangible* resources. Other resources, such as knowledge, organizational culture, location, patents, trademarks, and reputation are *intangible* in nature. Some resources have both tangible and intangible characteristics. Land, for instance, has physical properties and satisfies certain functional needs. At the same time, some properties may have value as a resource by virtue of their location, which is an intangible benefit arising from unique proximity to customers or suppliers due to preferences or relative location.

Because tangible resources are easier to identify and value, they may be less likely to be a source of competitive advantage than intangible resources. This is because their tangible nature gives competitors a head start on imitation or substitution. But some tangible resources are quite instrumental in helping firms achieve favorable competitive positions, partly because of their intangible benefits. Wal-Mart, for example, enjoys near-monopoly status in many rural locations. As the first large retailer in a rural market, Wal-Mart has locked out potential competitors who won't build facilities in locations that can't support two stores. Thus, one reason for Wal-Mart's formidable competitive position in rural markets is its tangible real estate. Similarly, Union Pacific Railroad's control of key rail property gives it a competitive advantage in the transportation of certain materials, such as hazardous chemicals.

Likewise, McDonald's controls much more than a valuable brand name (an intangible resource that does in fact convey a significant advantage). Like Wal-Mart, it also controls a great deal of valuable real estate by virtue of its location near high-traffic centers. Indeed, without its prime real-estate locations, McDonald's would have a less valuable brand name. Obviously, the pace at which McDonald's grew required a certain capability in finding the needed real estate.

CAPABILITIES

Capabilities refer to a firm's skill in using its resources (both tangible and intangible) to create goods and services. A synonym that is often used to describe the same concept is *competences*. For simplicity, we use the term *capabilities*. Capabilities may be possessed by individuals or embedded in company-wide rules and routines.[3] In essence, they are the combination of procedures and expertise that the firm relies on to engage in distinct activities in the process of producing goods and services. Several examples of companies and their capabilities are listed in Exhibit 3.3.[4] For instance, Wal-Mart is widely regarded as having excellent capabilities related to the management of logistics, which it uses to exploit resources such as large stores, store locations, its trucking fleet, and massive distribution centers.

Capabilities span from the rather simple tasks that firms must perform to accomplish their daily business, such as taking and fulfilling orders, to more complex tasks, such as designing sophisticated systems, creative marketing, and manufacturing processes. Collectively, these capabilities are the activities that constitute a firm's **value chain**. Not all capabilities are of equal value to the firm—a fact that has, in turn, given rise to the rapid growth of **outsourcing**. Outsourcing is contracting with external suppliers to perform certain parts of a company's normal value chain of activities. Later in the chapter, you will be introduced to a special class of capabilities known as *dynamic capabilities*.

Two other special classes of capabilities with which you should be familiar, if for no other reason than that they are part of the generally used business vocabulary, are *distinctive competences* and *core competences*. **Distinctive competences** (or *distinctive capabilities*) are the capabilities that set a firm apart from other firms. They are the capabilities that are unique to the firm within its competitive landscape. **Core competences** (or *core capabilities*) are those capabilities that are central to the main business operations of the firm; they are the capabilities that are common to the principal businesses of the firm and that enable the firm to generate new products and services in these businesses. Thus, a core competence at GE, which operates in many unrelated businesses, is

capabilities A firm's skill at using its resources to create goods and services; combination of procedures and expertise on which a firm relies to produce goods and services.

value chain Total of primary and support value-adding activities by which a firm produces, distributes, and markets a product.

outsourcing Activity performed for a company by people other than its full-time employees.

distinctive competence Capability that sets a firm apart from other firms; something that a firm can do which competitors cannot.

core competence Capability which is central to a firm's main business operations and which allow it to generate new products and services.

Company	Capability	Result
Wal-Mart	Logistics—distributing vast amounts of goods quickly and efficiently to remote locations.	200,000 percent return to shareholders during first 30 years since IPO.
The Vanguard Group	Extraordinarily frugal system using both technological leadership and economies of scale for delivering the lowest cost structure in the mutual-fund industry.	25,000 percent return to shareholders during the 30+ year tenure of CEO John Connelly. Shareholders in Vanguard equity funds pay, on average, $30 per $10,000 versus a $159 industry average. With bond funds, the bite is just $17 per $10,000.
3M	Generating new ideas and turning them into innovative and profitable products.	30 percent of revenue from products introduced within the past four years.

Exhibit 3.3 A Few Extraordinary Capabilities

its general management capability; GE is able to manage a portfolio of businesses based on sound business principles when most firms cannot manage such unrelated business simultaneously.

The relationship between resources and capabilities can be further illustrated by a few more examples. Intel's manufacturing capacity (i.e., its plants, equipment, and production engineers), its patented microprocessor designs, and its well-established brand name are among its key resources. Like its capabilities in speed-to-market, these other internal factors contribute to its strategic differentiators, in terms of the strategy diamond. Intel has also demonstrated the organizational capability to design new generations of leading-edge microprocessors and to do so rapidly. In addition, Intel has demonstrated marketing adroitness by creating the "Intel Inside" campaign, which stimulated greater demand and higher switching costs among end users—the customers of Intel's customers. This clearly suggests a marketing capability. The combination of Intel's resources and capabilities collectively comprise its differentiators, and enable its managers to execute a value-creating strategy and achieve a formidable competitive advantage in the microprocessor industry.

In the oil industry, too, we can see that resources and capabilities aren't uniformly developed by all competitors. Some firms, for example, are highly integrated. These integrated firms are involved in every stage of the value chain, including risky and time-consuming oil exploration and extraction activities. BP, ChevronTexaco, ExxonMobil, and Royal Dutch/Shell all possess significant capabilities in exploration and extraction, refining, distribution, and marketing. As a result, they also own rights to significant petroleum deposits around the world, and these reserves are potentially valuable tangible resources. In contrast, other oil companies are involved primarily in "downstream activities." These companies gear their capabilities to refining, distribution, and marketing. Valero Energy and Sunoco, for instance, are the largest independent U.S. oil refiners and distributors. Neither, however, is active in exploration. Their resources include refineries, pipelines, distribution networks, and equipment, but both buy crude oil from other companies.

The important complementary relationship between one of McDonald's tangible resources (real estate) and one of its capabilities (its site-location skills) are highlighted in the following example. Few people go out for the sole purpose of buying a hamburger or a taco. Most fast-food purchases are impulse buys, and this fact points to just one reason why site location is so important in the fast-food industry. Like magazines and candies strategically placed at supermarket checkout counters, fast-food outlets are situated by design. At one time, McDonald's used helicopters to assess the growth of residential areas: Basically, planners looked for cheap land alongside thoroughfares that would one day run through well-populated suburbs.

Today, the site-location process is even more high-tech. In the 1980s, McDonald's turned to satellite photography to predict urban sprawl. The company has developed a software package called *Quintillion,* which integrates information from satellite images, detailed maps, demographic information, CAD drawings, and sales data from existing stores. With all of this information at its disposal, McDonald's has taken the strategy of site location to new heights. Prime locations, of course, command prime dollars: The difference between the cost of a prime location and a mediocre site could be three times the price per square foot.[5]

THE VRINE MODEL

In a given industry, then, all competitors do not have access to the same resources and capabilities—a fact that should have significant implications for the strategies that they develop. In addition, one firm's resources or capabilities aren't necessarily as effective as an-

Exhibit 3.4   Applying the VRINE Model

	The Test	The Competitive Implication	The Performance Implication
Is it valuable?	Does the resource or capability allow the firm to meet a market demand or protect the firm from market uncertainties?	If so, the company is able to compete in an industry, but value by itself does not convey an advantage.	Valuable resources and capabilities have the *potential* to contribute to *normal profits* (profits that cover the cost of all inputs, including capital).
Is it rare?	Assuming that the resource or capability is valuable, is it scarce relative to demand or is it widely possessed by competitors?	Valuable resources that are also rare contribute to a *competitive advantage*, but that advantage may be only temporary.	A *temporary competitive advantage* can contribute to *above-normal profits*, at least until the advantage is nullified by other firms.
Is it inimitable and/or nonsubstitutable?	Assuming that the resource is both valuable and rare, how difficult is it for competitors either to imitate it or substitute other resources and capabilities that yield similar benefits?	Valuable and rare resources and capabilities that are also difficult to imitate or substitute can contribute to *sustained competitive advantage*.	A sustained competitive advantage can contribute to *above-normal profits for extended periods of time* (until competitors find ways to imitate or substitute or environmental changes nullify the advantage).
Is it exploitable?	If the resource or capability satisfied any or all of the preceding VRINE criteria, can the firm actually exploit it?	Resources and capabilities that satisfy the first four VRINE criteria but that cannot be exploited do not convey competitive advantage. In fact, they may increase opportunity costs.	Firms that control but don't exploit their VRINE resources and capabilities (even after they satisfy the V, R, I, and N criteria) generally suffer from lower levels of financial performance and depressed market valuations *relative to what they would enjoy if they could in fact exploit them* (although they won't be in as bad a shape as competitors who don't control any VRINE-certified resources and capabilities).

other's in helping it develop or sustain a competitive advantage. Why do some resources and capabilities enable some firms to develop a competitive advantage? Exhibit 3.4 summarizes five basic characteristics that determine whether a resource or capability can help a firm compete and, indeed, achieve superior performance: (1) value, (2) rarity, (3) inimitability, (4) nonsubstitutability, and (5) exploitability.[6]

According to the **VRINE model** (for *v*alue, *r*arity, *i*nimitability, *n*onsubstitutability, and *e*xploitability), resources and capabilities contribute to competitive advantage to the extent that they satisfy the five components of the model. VRINE analysis helps managers systematically test the importance of particular resources and capabilities and the desirability of acquiring new resources and capabilities. VRINE analysis also suggest to you how a firm might use its resources and capabilities to differentiate its products or services in valuable ways that competitors cannot imitate; that is, it suggests what the firm might do in terms of the differentiator facet of the strategy diamond. In the following sections, we'll explain and provide examples of each VRINE characteristic.

VRINE model   Analytical framework suggesting that a firm with resources and capabilities which are valuable, rare, inimitable, nonsubstitutable, and exploitable will gain a competitive advantage.

Value   A resource or capability is *valuable* if it enables a firm to take advantage of opportunities or to fend off threats in its environment.[7] Union Pacific (UP) Railroad, for example, maintains an extensive network of rail-line property and equipment on the U.S. Gulf Coast. It operates in the western two-thirds of the United States, serving 23 states, linking every major West Coast and Gulf Coast port and reaching east through major gateways in Chicago, St. Louis, Memphis, and New Orleans. UP also operates in key north-south corridors (see Exhibit 3.5).[8] It's the only U.S. railroad to serve all six gateways to Mexico, and it interchanges traffic with Canadian rail systems.

Its rail system is a tangible resource that enables UP to compete with other carriers in the long-haul transportation of a variety of goods. UP is, for example, the nation's largest hauler of chemicals, and much of that traffic originates along the Gulf Coast near Houston, Texas. The company enjoys this advantage because it owns the physical resources necessary to compete in this market—the railway rights of way through strategic areas—and because it has the specialized capability to transport chemicals safely and cost effectively. Government studies indicate that railroads are very efficient compared to alternative forms of transportation (such as truck and air) for the transportation of chemicals. Thus, railroad assets are valuable because they enable the company to provide a cost-effective means of transporting chemicals. In addition, because the Gulf Coast is the source for most chemical production in the United States, this network permits UP to take advantage of a market opportunity.

Alternatively, UP owns many rights of way that are no longer active. These resources would appear to convey no value to UP unless it can find a new use for these properties although UP's ownership of them is a deterrent to new railroad industry entrants. Consequently, UP frequently sells these abandoned railway rights of way to communities for such things as bike trails, and not to competing railroad operators.

Finally, it is worthwhile to remember that some resources that can be sources of value can also be abused and consequently become sources of corporate overhead. For instance,

Exhibit 3.5   The Union Pacific Right-of-Way System

Source: Union Pacific, "System Map" (accessed August 4, 2005), at www.uprr.com/aboutup/maps/sysmap/index.shtml.

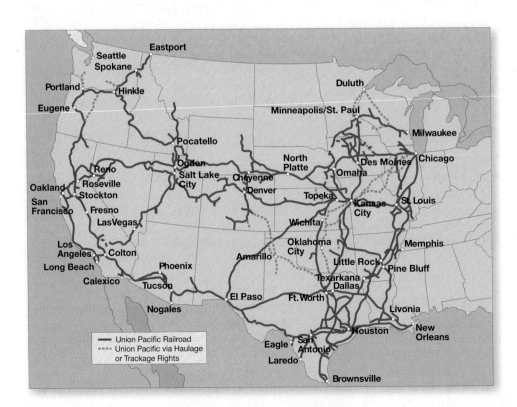

consider a small fleet of business jets owned by a company. Occasionally, the company may need to be able to get top executives in and out of remote or congested locations quickly, which would make the jets a valuable resource. However, in other situations, the jets may be a costly convenience and an example of corporate excess that provide no real economic value.

If a firm cannot use a resource to minimize threats or take advantage of opportunities, then it probably doesn't enhance its competitive position. In fact, some experts suggest that owning resources that *don't* meet the VRINE criteria for value actually puts a firm at a competitive *disadvantage*. Why? Because the capital tied up in the resource could be put to better use,[9] the capital could be reinvested in other resources that do satisfy the value requirement of VRINE, or the capital could be redistributed to shareholders.

Rarity   *Rarity* is defined as scarcity relative to demand. An otherwise valuable resource that isn't rare won't necessarily contribute to competitive advantage: Valuable resources that are available to most competitors simply enable a firm to achieve parity with everyone else. Sometimes such resources may be called *table stakes,* as in poker, because they are required to compete in the first place. But when a firm controls a valuable resource that's also rare in its industry, it's in a position to gain a competitive advantage. Such resources, for example, may enable a company to exploit opportunities or fend off threats in ways that competitors cannot. When McDonald's signs an agreement to build a restaurant inside a Wal-Mart store, it has an intangible location advantage over Burger King and Wendy's that is not only valuable but also rare because it has an exclusive right to that geographic space.

How rare does a resource have to be in order to offer potential competitive advantage? It's a difficult question to answer with any certainty. At the two extremes, of course, *only one* firm has the resource or *every* firm has it, and the answer is fairly obvious. If only one firm possesses a given resource, it has a significant advantage. Monsanto, for instance, enjoyed an advantage for many years because it owned the patent to aspartame, the chemical compound in NutraSweet. As the only legal seller of aspartame, Monsanto dominated the artificial-sweetener market. Such is typically the case in the pharmaceutical industry for those who are first or second to patent and market a therapy for a particular disease.

Satisfying the rarity condition, however, doesn't necessarily require *exclusive* ownership. When a resource is controlled by a handful of firms, those firms will have an advantage over the rest of the field. Pfizer was first to the market for a drug to treat erectile dysfunction with its Viagra product, but it was later joined by two other products offered by competitors (Levitra and Cialis). Pfizer no longer has a monopoly in the market to treat this condition, but the three firms collectively control resources that are scarce relative to demand. Thus, Pfizer's resource, the patent for Viagra, would still seem to satisfy both the value and the rarity requirements of VRINE. Consider an example from another context. Both Toyota and Honda, for example, can build high-quality cars at relatively low cost, and the products of both firms regularly beat those of rivals in both short-term and long-term quality ratings. The criterion of rarity requires only that a resource be scarce *relative to demand.* It also follows, of course, that the more exclusive the access to a valuable resource, the greater the benefit of having it.

A firm that controls a valuable and scarce resource or capability may create a competitive advantage, but there is no assurance that the advantage will persist. We now turn to the two criteria that must be satisfied if the advantage is to be sustained.

Inimitability and Nonsubstitutability   A valuable and rare resource or capability will grant an advantage only so long as competitors don't gain possession of it or find a close substitute. We review these two criteria jointly because they work in similar fashions. The criterion of *inimitability* is satisfied if competitors cannot acquire the valuable and rare resource quickly or if they face a cost disadvantage in doing so. The *nonsubstitutability* criterion is satisfied if a competitor cannot achieve the same benefit using

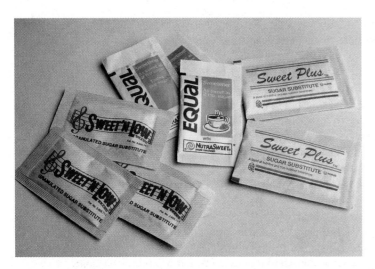

Monsanto enjoyed a competitive advantage for many years because it owned the patent to aspartame, the chemical compound in NutraSweet. The patent on aspartame ran out in 1992, and in 2000 Monsanto sold NutraSweet to private investors. NutraSweet now faces fierce competition from other aspartame-containing products, and newer and more popular nonaspartame-based sweeteners.

different combinations of resources and capabilities. When a resource or capability is valuable and rare and contributes to a firm's advantage, one can assume that competitors will do all they can to get it. Of course, firms can acquire needed resources or capabilities in a number of different ways, including internal investment, acquisitions, and alliances. They can, for instance, form alliances in order to learn from and internalize a partner's capabilities.[10]

Some firms find alternative resources or capabilities that "mimic" the benefits of the original. For several years, for example, Barnes & Noble and Borders enjoyed formidable advantages in the retail-book industry. Their sheer size gave them an immense advantage over smaller players: Because they had access to more customers, they were able to take advantage of greater buying power. Eventually, however, Amazon.com's ability to substitute online for conventional retail marketing provided a feasible substitute for geographic accessibility to consumers. Generally speaking, then, valuable and rare resources can provide competitive advantage only as long as they're difficult to imitate or substitute.

The High Cost of Imitation and Substitution Several factors can make some resources and capabilities difficult to duplicate or substitute. A rival might, for instance, try to acquire a competitor or supplier that possesses the resource it needs.[11] But acquisitions of this kind often entail large premiums that result in a buyer paying more for a resource than it cost competitors to develop the original.[12] In 1999, for example, when Cisco purchased Cerent in order to acquire fiber-optic data-transfer capabilities, it ended up paying $6.9 billion for a startup company with just $10 million in sales.[13] Cisco desperately wanted the capabilities of Cerent, but managers felt it would take too long to develop those capabilities internally. Absent Cisco's excellent capabilities in merger integration and new product distribution, therefore, the firm would be at a cost disadvantage relative to any competitor who could develop the same collective capabilities for less money.

Inimitability, Nonsubstitution, and Property Rights Perhaps the most straightforward cause of resources and capabilities being difficult to imitate or substitute is property rights. Competitors can be prevented from copying resources if they are protected by ownership rights. For instance, patented items or processes cannot be directly copied during the term of the patent without the imitator being subject to severe legal repercussions. Media companies own copyrights on titles in their libraries. Because of this, it is very difficult for competitors to substitute for Mickey Mouse. However, property rights alone do not protect all resources and capabilities from imitation or substitution.

Inimitability, Nonsubstitution, and Time Another factor that can make resources and capabilities difficult to imitate or substitute is the unique historical conditions surrounding their development or the fact that their acquisition requires the passage of time.[14] Sometimes a firm's resources and capabilities are the result of unique historical events that converged to its benefit. For instance, in order to build troop morale during World War II, General Dwight D. Eisenhower requested that Coca-Cola be available to all American servicemen and servicewomen. To ensure that GIs could buy Coke for five cents a bottle, the government and Coca-Cola cooperated to build 64 bottling plants around the world. In the long term, Coke gained the competitive advantage of instant global presence, both in bottling capacity and brand recognition.[15] At war's end, Coke ramped up its overseas production and marketing and succeeded in penetrating new markets. In effect, Coke's market entry had been subsidized by the government, and rival Pepsi faced considerable cost disadvantages in competing with Coke's international presence. Coke's global advantage over Pepsi remains even today. Of Coke's $24.1 billion sales in 2006, fully 71 percent were from outside North America; whereas just 57 percent of PepsiCo's $22.5 billion in beverage sales were from outside North America.[16]

The simple passage of time creates inimitability and nonsubstitutability as well, typically because the original owner may have built up the value of the resource or capability through a process of gradual learning and improvement that can't be matched through catch-up programs. For instance, firms that invest a given rate of R&D spending over an extended time period appear to produce larger gains in knowledge and intellectual property than firms that invest at twice the same level over half the time.[17] Thus, we can say that a resource is difficult to imitate if shorter development time results in inferior imitations.

Causal Ambiguity   Another factor that makes imitation difficult is **causal ambiguity**. For a number of reasons, it may be difficult to *identify* or *understand* the causal factors of a resource or capability—the complex combination of factors that make it valuable.[18] For instance, what makes Apple, Google, 3-M, and Toyota so much more innovative than their direct competitors? There is clearly something special about these firms but you would be hard-pressed to create a carbon copy from scratch, even if you had the money to do so. Firms may enjoy resources that have resulted from a complex convergence of activities that the company itself doesn't fully understand.[19] For example, 3M enjoys an enviable capacity for innovation that, at least in part, is a function of company culture. A competitor may copy certain 3M policies—say, allowing employees to spend 10 percent of their time experimenting on potential new products—but it will be more difficult to imitate the complex culture of cooperation and rewards that facilitates innovation at 3M. The causal process, in other words, would be difficult to identify because it's *socially complex*. Products that are technologically complex are relatively easier to duplicate (say, by adopting such processes as reverse engineering) than are socially complex organizational phenomena.[20] Firms with socially complex resources and capabilities like this must strive to appreciate what contributes to them—even if they can't be fully understood or quantified—so that strategic choices continue to protect and nourish such unique underlying sources of competitive advantage.

causal ambiguity   Condition whereby the difficulty of identifying or understanding a resource or capability makes it valuable, rare, and inimitable.

Exploitability   The fifth and final VRINE criterion reminds us that mere possession of or control over a resource or capability is necessary but not sufficient to gain a competitive advantage: A firm must be able to *exploit* it; that is, the firm must be able to nurture and take advantage of the resources and capabilities that it possesses.

The question of exploitability is, of course, quite broad, but in this case, we're focusing on *a company's ability to get the value out of any resource or capability that it may generate.* Thus, the issue of an organization's exploitative capability incorporates all of the dimensions of a firm's value-adding processes. Although we may not deal directly with organizational processes until the final criterion in the VRINE model, bear in mind that, without this skill, a firm won't get much benefit from having met any of the first four VRINE criteria. A valuable resource or capability that is also possessed by many other competitors has the potential to give the firm competitive parity, but only if the firm also has the exploitative capabilities to implement a strategy that utilizes the resource or capability. Likewise, a firm that possesses a valuable and rare resource will not gain a competitive advantage unless it can actually put that resource to effective use.

In fact, many firms do have valuable and rare resources that they fail to exploit (in which case, by the way, their competitors aren't under much pressure to imitate them). For many years, for instance, Novell's core NetWare product gave it a significant advantage in the computer networking market. In high-tech industries, however, staying on top requires continuous innovation, and according to many observers, Novell's decline in the 1990s reflected an inability to innovate in order to meet the demands of changing markets and technology. But shortly after he was hired from Sun Microsystems to turn Novell around, new CEO Eric Schmidt (now CEO of Google) arrived at a different conclusion: "I walk down Novell hallways," he reported, "and marvel at the incredible potential for innovation here. But Novell has had a difficult time in the past turning innovation into products in the marketplace."[21] The company, Schmidt confided to a few key executives, was suffering from "organizational constipation."[22] According to its new CEO, Novell had the resources and capabilities needed to innovate, but it lacked the exploitative capability (especially in its product-development and marketing processes) to get innovative products to market in a timely manner.

Xerox, too, went through a period when it was unable to exploit its resources to innovate products. At a dedicated facility in Palo Alto, California, Xerox established a successful research team known as Xerox PARC. Scientists in this group invented an impressive list of innovative products, including laser printers, Ethernet, graphical-interface software, computers, and the computer mouse. All of these products were commercially successful, but, unfortunately for Xerox shareholders, they were commercial successes for other firms. Xerox couldn't get information about them to the right people in a timely fashion. Why? Largely because the company's bureaucracy tended to suffocate ideas before they had a chance to flow through the organization. Compensation policies ignored managers who fostered innovations and rewarded immediate profits over long-term success.[23]

The VRINE model can be used to assess any resource or capability in order to determine if it is a source or potential source of competitive advantage and, if so, whether that advantage is likely to be temporary or sustained. To illustrate how this is done, we use the VRINE model in Exhibit 3.6 to analyze Pfizer's ownership of the patents for Zoloft as a possible source of competitive advantage.[24]

Where Do Resources Come From?   Our earlier definitions of *resources* and *capabilities* describe them as something the firm may own or possess. However, we have also suggested that many resources and capabilities cannot be easily purchased. Brand equity, for example, can't be readily purchased unless a company purchases an existing brand from another company. Otherwise, a brand will need to be developed, and that takes time. The brand equity of Coke, for example, has been developed through decades of marketing efforts with investments in the hundreds of millions per year. Toyota's reputation for quality automobiles has been developed through stringent quality-control methods; Intel's R&D capability is the result of years of investment. In other words, intangible resources such as brand equity, reputation, and innovative capability result from policies and strategies that have been implemented over extended periods of time; they can't be acquired through one-time purchases.

Dynamic Capabilities

Thus far, our discussion of resources and capabilities has portrayed a rather static view. However, the process of developing, accumulating, and losing resources and capabilities is inherently dynamic. We now introduce two concepts to demonstrate the dynamic aspects of resources and capabilities. The first deals with *stocks versus flows;* the second deals with a special class of capability referred to as a *dynamic capability*.

RESOURCES AS STOCKS AND FLOWS

Resources can be thought of as both stocks and flows. A firm's stock of resources and capabilities is what it possesses at any given point in time. However, that stock of resources and

Exhibit 3.6 Putting Pfizer's Drug Patents up to the VRINE Test

	Putting Pfizer's Drug Patents up to the VRINE test	Answers
	Let's walk through the VRINE model as applied to Pfizer's patents for Zoloft (sertraline HCl), an antidepressant known as a selective serotonin reuptake inhibitor (SSRI). If you were studying Pfizer and the pharmaceutical industry using the VRINE model, you would probably identify a number of resources and capabilities that may be the source of competitive advantage. You would probably identify patents, R&D capabilities, and marketing as key resources and capabilities that drive the differentiator facet of its strategy.	
Value: Do Pfizer's two patents on Zoloft provide value?	In any given year, about 7 percent of the U.S. population (approximately 20 million people) will experience a depressive disorder. Approximately 16 percent of adults will experience depression at some point in their lives. Women are twice as likely as men to experience depression. Thus, it appears that having a patent for a treatment for depression would enable a pharmaceutical company to take advantage of a large market opportunity.	Yes
Rarity: Are they rare?	Pfizer's patents on Zoloft give it the exclusive right to use the chemical compound sertraline HCl to treat depression (the patents expired in June, 2006). When the patents expire, generic drug makers will be able to sell copied versions of the drug. The patents for Zoloft are definitely rare during the term of the patents, but will not be after they expire (assuming that several generic companies make the drug, its scarcity relative to demand will decline).	Yes, but not after they expire.
Inimitability?	Pfizer is certainly not the only large pharmaceutical company that desires to profit from therapies for depression. However, a patent makes direct imitation illegal until the patent expires.	
Nonsubstitutability: Is there protection against ready substitutes?	Competitors can and do attempt to find substitute compounds that have similar effects. Indeed, Zoloft itself was a Pfizer innovation in the face of Eli Lilly's patent for Prozac. Zoloft is not the only treatment for depression; other SSRIs include Prozac, Paxil, and others. The patents for Zoloft may convey temporary advantage, but Pfizer's value from them will probably erode over time as others invent substitute compounds and as the patents expire, resulting in direct imitation.	Not completely.
Exploitability: Is there evidence these are exploitable?	To satisfy this VRINE criterion, Pfizer needs to be able to move drugs from successful clinical trial to market distribution. Fortunately for Pfizer, marketing and distribution are two of its core competences. Indeed, Pfizer has more drug representatives than any other pharmaceutical company. Pfizer also has large cash reserves that can be used to bring sufficient quantities of the product quickly to market prior to the lapsing of the patents.	Yes
The verdict?	As you may have guessed by now, Pfizer's patents on Zoloft largely stand up to the VRINE framework, suggesting that patents are a resource that can generate competitive advantage. The expiration of those patents could largely diminish the VRINE advantages they provided. Note, however, that Zoloft is such a resource not just because of patents. Pfizer also possesses the complementary VRINE resources and capabilities underlying its exploitability.	Yes

capabilities was created over time through a combination of initial endowment and accumulated investment. Consider the resource stock represented by a patent. To a large degree, the value of the patent depends on the level of innovation its original discovery represented, and that discovery was probably the result of years of investment and a process of trial and error. However, continual resource inflows may augment the value of the patent. For instance, additional R&D investments may lead to further discoveries that can be bundled with the original patent. Alternatively, investments in marketing efforts can spur demand, which leads to increased value. However, value also dissipates over time, as in the gradual expiration of the patent. The key point is that the value of resources and capabilities is a function of both the level (or stock) of resources and capabilities and the net effect of additional investment and depreciation.

This stock can be increased through development activities and sustained investment. It can be reduced through the divestiture of business units, loss of key personnel, and shifts in the competitive environment that alter the value of given resources. Remember, too, that strategic resources and capabilities are accumulated *over time*. Thus, the *process* of resource accumulation through dynamic capabilities is fundamentally different from the static possession of stocks of resources and capabilities.

REBUNDLING RESOURCES AND CAPABILITIES

Beyond making investments to augment the accumulation of resources and capabilities, firms can make decisions about how resources and capabilities are utilized and configured, and thereby change their fundamental value. And although a firm can't easily change its stock of resources and capabilities, it can reconfigure or integrate them in new ways. **Dynamic capabilities** are processes by which a firm integrates, reconfigures, acquires, or divests resources in order to achieve new configurations of resources and capabilities.[25] In fact, the term *dynamic* is added to the description of these special kinds of capabilities because it refers to a firm's ability to modify and revise its resources and capabilities to match a shifting environment. The ability to reconfigure firm resources and capabilities is especially critical in markets that move quickly, and it is typically seen in complex areas of the firm, such as its culture, knowledge base, and ability to learn.

Dynamic capabilities are manifest in several ways. The ability to integrate different resources and capabilities to create new revenue-producing products and services is a dynamic capability.[26] Disney, for instance, recently launched its "Princess Line," which brings together merchandise based on famous female Disney characters. The effort required that Disney integrate development and marketing campaigns geared toward groups of characters that had before been developed and marketed separately.[27] Reconfiguring or transferring resources and capabilities from one division to another is another form of a dynamic capability. Mail Boxes Etc. (MBE), the postal center that was recently purchased by UPS, illustrates this fact. By encoding its knowledge of how to start up a master-area franchise, MBE created "templates" for future franchisees. New master-area franchisees are required to duplicate the template exactly prior to making any adjustments to meet local market needs. This is because their internal research shows that master-area franchisees who duplicate the template significantly outperform those who first customize the model.[28] The opening vignette about Intel also illustrates how resource-allocation rules can result in a dynamic capability to reallocate resources to new uses.

The rebundling of resources and capabilities is also accomplished through alliances and acquisitions. Resources and capabilities can both be acquired and lost through these vehicles. Cisco has been able to launch many new products by strategically acquiring bits and pieces of network architecture through acquisitions.[29]

The dynamic view of resources and capabilities differs somewhat from the traditional view. It emphasizes the need to renew resources and capabilities, either in order to keep pace with a

dynamic capabilities A firm's ability to modify, reconfigure, and upgrade resources and capabilities in order to strategically respond to or generate environmental changes.

changing environment or to reconfigure the organization proactively (i.e., to change the environment). One or both of these capabilities—the ability to adapt to change or to initiate it—is particularly important in industries in which time to market is critical, technological change is rapid, and future competition is difficult to forecast.[30] When incumbent firms, even strong companies, don't have such capabilities, they're likely to be outmaneuvered by new competitors who are ready to introduce new industry standards.[31] Consequently, the value of a firm's portfolio of resources and capabilities is directly affected by its dynamic capability to reconfigure resources and capabilities to the evolving requirements of the competitive environment.

More complex forms of dynamic capabilities are typically associated with dynamic or turbulent environments. As we saw in our opening vignette, for example, Intel's internal organizational processes and organizational culture enabled it to make a dramatic change from one technological platform to another.[32] Specifically, the firm was able to shift scarce manufacturing resources from the memory-chip business to the emerging microprocessor business in a very brief period of time.

The Value Chain

Earlier in the chapter, we demonstrated that firms in the same industry differ in their resources, capabilities, and dynamic capabilities and that these differences account for much of the variance in firm performance that we see within industries. This is because such differences allow firms to create products and services with hard to imitate *differentiators* in their strategy diamond.

Firms in the same industry may also differ in the scope and type of their value-chain activities. As we saw in our discussion of the *strategy diamond* model in Chapters 1 and 2, firms can also make unique decisions about the value-chain *arenas* in which they'll participate within a given industry. ◆ So, just as firms might be making choices about what industry arenas they should compete in, so too can they make choices about what internal functions to emphasize, de-emphasize, or outsource entirely. It is the differentiators, in conjunction with the choices about value chain arenas, that further solidifies internal sources of competitive advantage. Returning to the oil industry, which we discussed earlier, Valero and Sunoco make very different choices about which value-chain activities to engage in (e.g., refining and distribution but not exploration) relative to the major integrated oil companies. Even if two firms possess similar resources and capabilities, it is still possible for one firm to gain the upper hand and achieve a competitive advantage. One way this can be done is by having a different configuration of value-adding activities.[33]

 Arenas

Firms make products or provide services by engaging in many different activities. The basic structure of these activities is embodied in the firm's value chain. Value-chain activities are of two types: primary activities and support activities. *Primary activities* include inbound logistics, operations, outbound logistics, marketing and sales, and service. *Support activities* include human resources, accounting and finance operations, technology, and procurement. The term *support activities* may seem to minimize the importance of these operations, but bear in mind that all activities—primary and support—are potential sources of competitive advantage (or disadvantage).

Exhibit 3.7 depicts the value chain for Under Armour, the performance apparel company introduced in Chapter 1.[34] Notice that the primary activities are located along the horizontal axis and represent the value-added activities that are necessary to produce and sell a product. For instance, Under Armour needs to purchase raw materials to have its apparel products manufactured. Notice, however, that a critical step in the value chain is outsourced—Under Armour outsources virtually all of its manufacturing to third party firms. To fulfill orders, the outbound logistics steps of the value chain would include matching the merchandise with the order and organizing the shipping to the customer. This is

Exhibit 3.7 The Value Chain for Under Armour

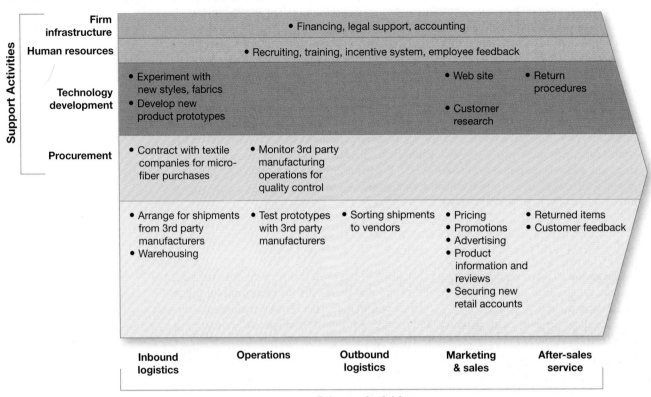

handled from one central warehouse in Maryland. Marketing and service functions are directed both at Under Armour's wholesale clients, like national sporting goods retailers, and directly at consumers through television and print advertising.

Support activities are represented on the top half of the vertical axis. Again, although these activities are generally portrayed as not being a part of the primary logistics involved in securing inputs, adding value, and fulfilling orders, when you see the types of activities performed by support functions, you begin to realize that any company would be hard-pressed to fulfill orders without these functions being performed. For instance, much of the value of Under Armour's products is a function of the advanced technological design of their performance apparel. They were the first to design tight-fitting compression athletic apparel made with moisture-wicking properties. Likewise, Under Armour's innovation of shirts with different properties for use in hot, cold, or moderate weather was a first—prior to that, athletes simply bundled on more, or removed, layers according to the temperature. So, technological design and other support activities can be sources of competitive advantage if they allow the firm to deliver products or services with unique differentiators.

Firms can use value-chain activities to create value by either finding *better* ways to perform the same activities or by finding *different* ways to perform them. However, any advantage obtained by doing the same activities but better than competitors may be short-lived. The VRINE framework that you studied earlier in this chapter should tell you that. Best practices in activities are often rapidly diffused throughout industries. Eventually, rivals improve performance in activities that they once performed less efficiently than industry leaders. For instance, a beverage distributor located in Kern County, Central California, sends its trucks to Los Angeles to pick up its products, and makes the 120-mile return trip to sell them in Bakersfield and other cities in Kern County. Obviously, transportation can be a huge cost for distributors and sending a fleet of empty trucks to Los Angeles represented a significant opportunity cost. Fortunately, this enterprising distributor found a Bakersfield manufacturing company that needed its products trucked to Los Angeles, and now the beverage company makes money as a shipper (transporting goods from Bakersfield to Los Angeles) and in its core business as a distributor in Kern County. Thus, even though shipping is not part of the beverage company's strategy, this value-chain choice directly, and positively, affects the firm's profitability and economic logic. However, logistical tactics that prove efficient at one firm often show up at rival firms through consultants or as a result of outsourcing. Thus, performing the same activities better than rivals usually results in a temporary advantage. Alternatively, configuring value-chain activities in different ways than competitors makes it harder for rivals to imitate those activities. This is due to what is known as *tradeoff protection.*

TRADEOFF PROTECTION

By organizing their value-chain activities in unique and specific ways, firms may be able to make imitation quite difficult. Gaining advantage through value-chain configuration usually involves a rather complex system of activities. When a firm reconfigures the value chain, it exercises some tradeoffs. By adding or dropping certain activities, it may necessitate the elimination or addition of other activities. Rivals find it very difficult and costly to imitate a system of interdependent activities because they have made some investments in their system of activities that may be irreversible. For example, in early competitive battles between global tractor makers Caterpillar and newcomer Komatsu, Komatsu invested in the development of tractors that required little service and easy maintenance. In contrast, industry incumbent Caterpillar made big profits in parts and service for its tractors, so was very hesitant to invest in making more reliable tractors (hence less need for parts and repairs). Generally, as shown with Caterpillar and Komatsu, companies won't imitate activities if doing so would mean abandoning one or more activities that are essential to their own strategies.[35] In other words, they'll balk at the tradeoff.

To further illustrate this point, let's consider some differences between the value-chain activities of Southwest Airlines and those of most other major U.S. airlines, which are summarized in Exhibits 3.8 and 3.9.[36] Despite the fact that other low-cost carriers have emerged,

	Southwest	Major Airlines
Technology and design	• Single aircraft	• Multiple types of aircraft
Operations	• Short-segment flights • No meals • No seat assignments • Single class of service • No baggage transfers to other airlines • Smaller markets and secondary airports in major markets	• Hub-and-spoke system • Meals • Seat assignments • Multiple classes of service • Baggage transfers to other airlines
Marketing	• Limited use of travel agents • Word of mouth	• Extensive use of travel agents

Exhibit 3.8 Key Value-Chain Activities in the U.S. Airline Industry

Exhibit 3.9   Comparative Revenues and Costs for U.S. Airlines

	2006 Revenue ($ millions)	2006 Cost of Available Seat Miles	2006 Revenue per Available Seat Miles	Difference
Low-Cost Carriers				
AirTran	1,893.40	9.80	12.9	3.10
ATA	1,160.00	9.36	13.1	3.74
Frontier	994.30	10.78	11.7	0.92
JetBlue	2,363.00	7.54	9.7	2.16
Southwest	9,086.00	8.50	12.4	3.90
Sector Average		9.40	11.8	
Major Carriers				
Alaska	3,334.40	11.70	13.9	2.20
American	22,563.00	12.50	12.8	0.30
Continental	13,128.00	13.30	12.2	−1.10
Delta	17,171.00	13.62	11.8	−1.82
Northwest	12,286.00	14.28	13.1	−1.18
United	19,340.00	13.06	12.2	−0.86
US Airways	7,117.00	15.36	13.2	−2.16
Sector Average		13.32	12.5	

Transportation Workers Union, TWU Airline Industry Review, *at www.twuatd.org; Bureau of Transportation,* TransStats Reports, *at www.transtats.bts.gov.*

Southwest has achieved unrivaled cost advantages among large airlines by radically pruning the number of activities that it performs and by undertaking others in nontraditional ways. Consequently, the configuration of its value chain is fundamentally different from those of most other airlines. Southwest, for example, uses only one type of aircraft—a strategy that reduces maintenance and training costs. In addition, the chosen aircraft is efficient for the kind of shorter flights that comprise most of Southwest's schedule. Southwest has also cut many of the services normally provided by major carriers (such as baggage transfers, meals, and assigned seats).

As a result of its unique configuration of activities, Southwest operates at a significantly lower cost than its competitors. We can confirm this conclusion by taking a look at a factor known as *CASM* (cost of available seat miles), which is a common measure of costs in the airline industry. As you can see in Exhibit 3.9, Southwest's CASM is significantly lower than that of every major competitor. Moreover, Southwest is generating greater revenue per seat mile, suggesting that many of the major airlines are trying to compete with it by lowering their prices. Why don't other major airlines imitate Southwest's value chain? Primarily because doing so would mean ceasing certain activities that are fundamental to their operations. Although many airlines have stopped serving meals to save costs, they can't stop transferring luggage, abandon the hub-and-spoke system, or convert exclusively to Boeing 737s. So many tradeoffs would mean changing their business model completely. Thus, Southwest has protected its advantage by configuring its value-chain activities in such a way that imitating them is not attractive to competitors.

Further analysis of Exhibit 3.9 reveals another important insight. The airline with the lowest CASM is actually JetBlue. This recent startup has been able to imitate much of Southwest's value chain and then make a few modifications that have further lowered costs (e.g., newer, more fuel-efficient planes, low-cost labor). This illustrates that although it may be very difficult for an established competitor to imitate the successful value-chain configuration of a leading company, a new entrant has much more flexibility to do so. A new firm that hasn't already made irreversible commitments to another value-chain configuration may be in a better position to imitate a successful value-chain configuration and even make improvements upon that model.

Innovation and Integration in the Value Chain IKEA, a Swedish furniture company, has built a hugely successful business by almost completely reconfiguring the value-chain activities of the furniture industry by transferring delivery and assembly to the customer. IKEA's stores double as warehouses. The furniture is shipped in flat-packed boxes. Customers shop among display models, but then take the unassembled furniture off the shelves and assemble it at home. This significantly lowers the costs of production and distribution.

Similarly, Dell's success is based on an innovative reconfiguration of sales, distribution, and customer-service activities in the personal-computer industry that exploits the growing base of knowledgeable PC consumers around the world. Dell PCs use components manufactured entirely by suppliers. In addition, its distribution and marketing operations rest on a direct-sales model that avoids retailers. This combination of strategies—outsourcing component manufacturing and distributing finished products directly—was a radical departure from the business models that prevailed in the industry.

Many competitors have tried to imitate this model, but at Dell the model supports—and is integrally linked to—a *chain* of value-adding activities. Large, established PC firms have never been able to duplicate Dell's cost structure because they haven't been willing or able to make all of the tradeoffs that would be necessary to imitate its value-chain activities.

The message in each of these examples is pretty much the same: The key to the value-chain approach to competitive advantage is not only developing value-chain activities that differ from those of rivals but also configuring them so that they're integrally related and can't be imitated without significant tradeoffs. *Value-chain fit* is important, Michael Porter reminds us, because it locks out imitators by "creating a chain of activities that is as strong as its strongest link."[37] By this we mean that strong links have positive spillover effects into the costs and benefits of other activities. For instance, Southwest's use of one type of jet, gives it greater flexibility with pilots, more reliable maintenance by ground crews, and faster turnarounds (and thus happier customers) at airport gates.

SEEKING CLUES TO VALUE CHAIN ADVANTAGES THROUGH FINANCIAL ANALYSIS

How might you intuit, at least in a rough way, if a firm is exploiting value chain advantage or particular resources or capabilities to create competitive advantage? Remembering that firms compete based on lower costs, an ability to gain higher prices for comparable products, or a combination of both, one tool you can use is the basic DUPONT financial analysis. You may have encountered this analytical tool in an accounting or finance course, and it is a very useful strategic analysis tool as well. The DuPont formula helps you break down determinants of a firm's profitability based on the equation where ROA = Net Profit Margin × Asset Turnover. A more detailed version of the basic formula is presented in Exhibit 3.10, and applied in "How Would *You* Do That? 3.1".

Beyond the math part, what does the formula tell you? The DuPont formula integrates the income statement and balance sheet to show how a firm's return on assets can be disaggregated into two components—asset turnover and profit margins. Asset turnover measures the firm's efficiency at generating revenues from its assets, while profit margin measures the firm's ability to garner higher prices to generate the revenues.

Exhibit 3.10   DuPont Analysis Formula

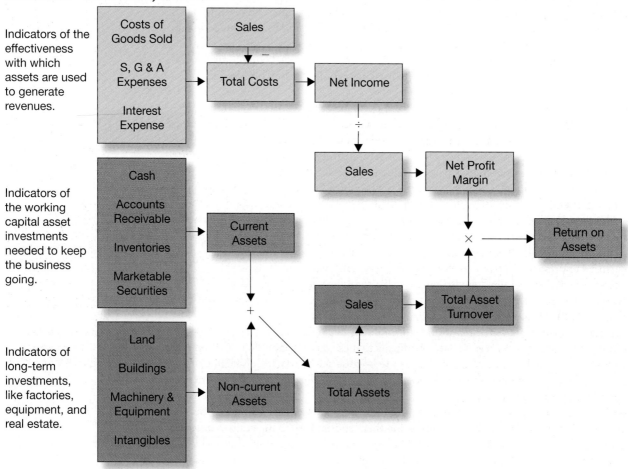

OUTSOURCING, OFFSHORING, AND THE VALUE CHAIN

Given that strategy is about making tradeoffs, one of the most fundamental tradeoffs managers make today is whether to outsource a historically integral value-chain activity. **Outsourcing** is simply sourcing the function, product, or service of a value chain activity from another company. **Offshoring** is taking that activity from a high-cost country to a low-cost country. We often commingle the two concepts of outsourcing and offshoring but a firm can do the former, the latter, or both. Indeed, value chain analysis gives you an opportunity to identify activities and capabilities the firm must possess itself, and those that can be performed outside of the firm. Referring back to IKEA, one of IKEA's innovations was to outsource furniture assembly to the end consumer, and 70% of the inputs into Boeing's new Dreamliner are outsourced to its commercial airframe partners.

Outsourcing and offshoring are not new; it is just that they have become so prevalent, and sometimes contentious, especially when it involves the loss of domestic jobs, that they may seem relatively new. Part of this prevalence is due to the broad number of choices managers have in terms of outsourcing and offshoring; they are able to outsource or offshore nearly any activity that they please. Although outsourcing or offshoring a value-chain activity may be feasible and lower a firm's direct costs and overhead, based on what you have learned about the resource and capability perspective, you should know that caution must be exercised. For instance, if a firm outsources its marketing or distribution function, it may lose access to the knowledge of customer preferences that inspired its early product breakthroughs in the first place. This perhaps explains why brand leaders such as Nike and Pacific Cycle (Schwinn brand) have outsourced functions such as manufacturing to low-cost countries (hence, offshoring that activity) and have instead focused their efforts on activities surrounding product development, logistics, brand management, and customer retention and expansion.

While outsourcing and offshoring remain as much an art as it is a science, they are an integral part of your strategy toolkit. What functions do you outsource? Offshore? Again, there is no perfect recipe but your strategy, and the VRINE-based value chain analysis should be a good starting point in answering that question. A firm may be better served by improving technologies or shaking up existing operations, instead of outsourcing the broken parts to lower-cost overseas locales. If you give the green light to outsourcing certain activities, then you will need to decide if you run it yourself in a cheaper offshore location (offshoring) or contract for the service from an outside provider. Again, outsourcing does not always mean the latter. For instance, Boeing Co. opened its own center in Moscow, where it employs 1,100 skilled but relatively low-cost aerospace engineers on a range of projects, including the design of titanium parts for the new 787 Dreamliner jet. Likewise, Chicago-based law firm Baker & McKenzie has its own English-speaking team in Manila that drafts documents and does market research.

Southwest Airlines founder and former CEO Herb Kelleher created a value chain for his company unlike that of any of his competitors. Using a low-fare, no-frills, no-reserved seating approach, Southwest has managed to earn a profit for 30 years straight—an astonishing feat in the airlines industry.

Whether value chain activities are outsourced or kept internally but sent offshore, three criteria appear to be common among successful outsourcing and offshoring arrangements:

Commit Time and Effort   Firms typically choose outsourcing and/or offshoring to lower their costs. However, such cost reductions are typically a one-time event. Beyond the first year, the firm must be committed to invest in quality control and training to keep the outsourced or offshored activity competitive and efficient.

Treat Outsourcing Partners as Partners   Many outsourced operations, in particular, are run by a third party. So, whereas the function was historically internally managed, the firm now contracts for that function with an external supplier. There is a temptation to treat such suppliers as order-takers, instead of taking advantage of the relationship to learn new things about product and process innovations.

Involve Middle Management   As you will learn from the following section, middle managers are the life-blood of strategy execution. Outsourcing and offshoring are undertaken to improve competitiveness in a function or set of functions, and not because the function is unimportant. For example, aerospace engineering is very important to Boeing and any other airplane manufacturer. However, the offshoring arrangement in Moscow gives Boeing access to a greater quantity of engineering expertise and at a lower cost than it could manage domestically. Middle managers play the role of bridging the offshored activities with the internal ones, and putting additional outsourcing arrangements into place as opportunities arise.

Applying DuPont Analysis to Understand Competitive Advantage in Retailing

Let's see if we can apply the DuPont tool to some "big box" retailers—Wal-Mart, Sears, and Kohl's—to better understand where they might be gaining their competitive advantage. We start by going to their company websites, or sites like Yahoo finance or Hoover's that provide balance sheet and income statement information on public firms.

In Exhibit 3.11, notice how straightforward the information-gathering is. We simply put together a small grid, and transferred a few pieces of financial information for each company. Since we were already gathering data, we decided to look at each firm's total equity as well—and we will show you how this small piece of information can add further depth to your DuPont toolkit. Also, we picked a single recent year for the data, but you

could take an average of several years, if you like. The important thing is that you have chosen a time period where you think that the differences across firms are fairly reflective of what they might be doing in the future.

When we look at the information in Exhibit 3.11, we can see that Wal-Mart is the largest firm of the three, in terms of assets and sales. They also have the greatest amount of profits. The problem, though, is that this information does not tell us much about how efficiently or effectively each firm is managing its sales or assets. For example, Wal-Mart has sales that are 23 times greater than those of Kohl's, but only 12 times greater profit. And even though Wal-Mart is so much bigger than Kohl's, it looks like Kohl's is much more profitable in terms of the returns it generates for a given asset

base. The DuPont analysis will help us understand the source of these differences.

With the data you have compiled in Exhibit 3.11, you can calculate the pieces of the DuPont formula. For instance, net profit margin is simply net profits divided by total sales, and so on. With this analysis in hand, we are now able to better understand the underlying determinants of these firms' performance. That is, you can explain why Kohl's has a higher return on assets than does Wal-Mart, despite the obvious size differences. This information, in turn, should provide you with clues as to the resources, capabilities, and value chain choices that might be part and parcel to each firm's strategy.

For instance, DuPont analysis shows that Kohl's has a very high net

Exhibit 3.11
Comparative Financial Information

Company	Total Assets ($ millions)	Total Sales ($ millions)	Net Profit ($ millions)	Total Equity ($ millions)
Wal-Mart	94,685	244,524	8,039	39,337
Sears	50,409	41,366	1,584	6,753
Kohl's	6,315	9,120	643	3,511

profit margin—7.1%, or $7.10 for every $100 of sales—relative to the others. This means that it is able to sell products for higher prices than competitors, or manage a higher priced mix of products. This suggests that one of Kohls' differentiators, in terms of the strategy diamond, might be the ability to merchandise higher-margin products. In contrast, you probably know that Wal-Mart competes with its low prices, so that it is willing to make a tradeoff between greater sales and lower relative margins. Thus, even though Kohl's and Wal-Mart are both "discount" retailers, each is using a somewhat different set of differentiators to arrive at net profits. You can further see this with asset turns, where Wal-Mart has nearly twice the asset turns as Kohl's. This difference means that Wal-Mart is very efficient with its assets, and for every $1 in assets it is generating $2.60 in sales. Indeed, Wal-Mart has made a set of very unique choices in terms of how it manages its value chain, and through DuPont analysis we can see where it is clearly the low cost leader. And what about Sears? Well, it looks like Sears is stuck in the middle—net profit margins are ok, but asset turns

are horrible.[38] The combination leaves Sears with the lowest relative ROA of the three.

Finally, recall that we jotted down total equity since we were collecting financial data on our sample of discount retailers. If you divide total assets by total equity, you arrive at an equity multiplier—in other words, for every $1 of equity, this is the dollar amount of assets it supports. You will be interested to know that you can multiply ROA by this number to arrive at a firm's return on equity, or ROE. This is called the Extended DuPont Analysis (Exhibit 3.12). Higher equity multipliers mean that a firm is using a greater amount of debt to finance its productive assets.

This can tell you that the firm's management has a greater appetite for debt, and risk, and is perhaps good at managing this type of risk. Conversely, you know that debt requires fixed payments of principle and interest. If these payments are not made, the firm can be forced into bankruptcy. Therefore, extremely high levels of debt (and a correspondingly high equity multiplier) represent poor capital structure management. Only by comparing one firm's multiplier against

others in its industry, as well as its own cash flow, can you judge whether such debt is excessive.

As with all financial analysis, you should remember that the DuPont formula only provides a snapshot of what a firm is doing. Ratios can vary from year to year as well as by industry, so it is important to calculate them across several years for each firm and compare them to other firms in the industry or industry averages to get a sense of their consistency and trends. Also, if you have applied the VRINE tool and concluded that a firm has resources and capabilities that are valuable, rare, and difficult to imitate, but the firm still is performing worse than its competitors, then you may conclude that the *exploitability* dimension is the problem. Again, the DuPont framework is a useful starting point in determining the degree to which the firm has advantages based on identifiable resources and capabilities. It also provides some indication of where the firm's resources and capabilities might be found, and can therefore help you to evaluate differentiators and their alignment with internal and external arenas.

Exhibit 3.12 Extended DuPont Analysis

Company	Net Profit Margin	×	Total Asset Turn	=	ROA	×	Equity Multiplier	=	ROE
Wal-Mart	3.3%		2.6		8.5%		241.1%		20.4%
Sears	3.8%		0.8		3.1%		175.4%		23.5%
Kohl's	7.1%		1.4		10.2%		179.4%		18.3%

Strategic Leadership: Linking Resources and Capabilities to Strategy

The opening vignette in this chapter notes the central role of leaders in managing a firm's resources and capabilities. It is important to not lose sight of the fact that it is a firm's managers who scan its external and internal environments and consequently decide how to use resources and capabilities and how to configure value-chain activities based on their assessment of those sometimes rapidly changing environments. Indeed, the role of managers is so critical that some experts include managerial human capital among a firm's resources; others include management among a company's dynamic capabilities.[39] A recent McKinsey consulting report concluded that "companies that overlook the role of leadership in the early phases of strategic planning often find themselves scrambling when it's time to execute. No matter how thorough the plan, without the right leaders it is unlikely to succeed."[40] To incorporate these views, we regard managers as *decision agents*—the people who put into motion the processes that use the firm's resources and capabilities.

SENIOR MANAGERS

In addition to deciding how to use resources and capabilities and configuring a firm's value-chain activities, senior managers also set the context that determines how frontline and middle managers can add value. Recall from the opening vignette that senior managers did not change Intel's strategy from memory chips to microprocessors—at least not until frontline managers made that change a *fait accompli*.

Strategy research has shown that senior managers in the most effective firms around the globe view their organizations as portfolios of processes—specifically, entrepreneurial, capability-building, and renewal processes—and key people, such as those who comprise the firm's middle and frontline managerial ranks.[41] Collectively, these processes may be seen as part of a firm's culture.

The *entrepreneurial process* encourages middle managers to be externally oriented—to seek out opportunities and run their part of the business as if they owned it. Senior managers who foster this process are stepping back from the notion that they are the sole visionaries and saviors of the company and instead seek to share this responsibility with the managers on the front lines. The *capability-building process* also looks to middle managers to identify, grow, and protect new ways to create value for the organization and its key stakeholders. In many ways, this process is the internal side of the externally oriented entrepreneurial process. Finally, the *renewal process* is senior managers' way of shaking up the firm and challenging its historic ways of operating; however, this process is based on information learned through current business activities performed elsewhere in the firm.

We can see all three of these processes taking place in the opening vignette about Intel. Senior management implemented processes and a culture that encouraged entrepreneurial activities. Similarly, middle management helped the firm to develop new capabilities to capitalize on the microprocessor opportunity. Finally, senior management stepped in to validate this major change in strategy, based on upgraded organizational resources and capabilities related to logic-device architecture. The only piece missing from the opening case is the role played by senior management in the selection, retention, and promotion of middle and frontline managers.

Of course, not all senior managers are equipped equally to act effectively. Obviously, basic managerial talent isn't bestowed equally on all managers, even if they have risen to the highest levels in the organization. Moreover, specific experiences and backgrounds will make some managers better qualified to work with a specific bundle of resources. Researchers have discovered, for instance, that multinational firms (those with operations in several countries) achieve higher levels of performance when their CEOs have had some experience in foreign operations.[42] In addition, entrepreneurial operations must often rely on few or no valuable or rare resources. Managers of these enterprises generally start with ideas and goals and not much more. In such situations, the positive influence of managers is even more important.[43] Likewise, in firms facing financial or competitive turmoil, the galvanizing and enabling effects of superior senior management are also more pronounced.

MIDDLE MANAGERS

From the discussion on senior managers, you should be able to see that middle managers play a key role in what the firm is doing and what it may be adept at doing in the future. The entrepreneurial, capability-building, and renewal processes all require the involvement, choices, and actions of middle and frontline managers. Executives must consider their leadership pool as they shape strategy and align their leadership-development programs with long-term aspirations. Particularly in large firms, the effect of senior executives on firm performance is a function of the choices they have made about the context in which frontline managers work and the appointment of particular managers themselves.

Strategic leadership researcher Quy Nguyen Huy has identified four areas where middle managers are better positioned to contribute to competitive advantage and corporate success than are senior executives:[44]

- **Entrepreneur.** Middle managers are close enough to the front lines to spot fires, yet far enough away to understand the bigger picture. Because middle management ranks are typically more diverse in terms of ethnicity, gender, experience, and geography, this group has the potential to contribute richer ideas than the senior management team.

- **Communicator.** Middle managers are typically long tenured and have very broad social networks. This gives them great credibility with employees, and they are therefore better able to move change initiatives in nonthreatening ways. Their tenure also gives them deep knowledge about how to get things done in the organization.

- **Psychoanalyst.** Internal credibility also enables middle managers to be more effective in quelling alienation and chaos, as seen by high productivity among anxious employees during times of great change. Because they know their troops, frontline managers also know when and how to provide one-on-one support and problem solving.

- **Tightrope walker.** Particularly in the case of dynamic capabilities and dynamic environments, firms are faced with the need to balance continuity and radical change. Middle managers are well poised to accomplish this balancing act. With the right process in place courtesy of senior executives, middle managers can help the firm avoid inertia and too little change or slow change and also avoid the paralyzing chaos accompanying too much change too quickly.

In many ways, it's the central role of upper and middle management that distinguishes the internal perspective on strategy from the external perspective that we'll discuss in Chapter 4. After all, if competitive advantage results from the different characteristics of firms, then the key task in the role of management is to identify resources and capabilities, specify the resources that will create competitive advantage, locate an attractive industry in which to deploy them, and then select the strategy to get the most out of them. Finally, it's the job of managers to choose *when* to change a firm's mix of resources, capabilities, and targeted markets. As you learned in Chapter 2, the managements of smaller firms typically differ from those of larger firms in terms of their overall number, not the roles that they play. This means that in smaller firms, senior leaders—often the owners or company founders—may wear many, if not all, of the middle and frontline manager hats described.

Summary of Challenges

1. Explain the internal context of strategy. Firms facing similar industry conditions achieve different levels of competitive advantage and performance based on their internal characteristics and managerial choices. Although firms must always take the external context into account when formulating and implementing strategy, the internal perspectives stress the differences among firms in terms of the unique resources and capabilities that they own or control. These perspectives offer important models and analytical tools that will help you to analyze and formulate competitive strategies.

2. Identify a firm's resources and capabilities and explain their role in its performance. Resources are either tangible or intangible. Resources and capabilities that help firms establish a competitive advantage and secure higher levels of performance are those that are valuable, rare, and costly to imitate. The VRINE model helps you analyze resources and capabilities. A resource or capability is said to be valuable if it enables the firm to exploit opportunities or negate threats in the environment. In addition, the firm must have complementary organizational capabilities to exploit resources and capabilities that meet these three conditions. Rare resources enable firms to exploit opportunities or negate threats in ways that those lacking the resource cannot. Competitors will try to find ways to imitate valuable and rare resources; a firm can generate an enduring competitive advantage if competitors face a *cost disadvantage* in acquiring or substituting the resource that is lacking. Unique historical conditions that have led to resource or capability development, time-compression diseconomies, and causal ambiguity all make imitation more difficult. Firms often use alliances, acquisitions, and substitution with less costly resources as mechanisms to gain access to difficult-to-imitate resources.

3. Define dynamic capabilities and explain their role in both strategic change and a firm's performance. The process of development, accumulation, and possible loss of resources and capabilities is inherently dynamic. The resource-accumulation process and dynamic capabilities are fundamentally different from the static pos-

session of a stock of resources and capabilities. Dynamic capabilities are processes that integrate, reconfigure, acquire, or divest resources in order to use the firms' stocks of resources and capabilities in new ways. The ability to adapt to changing conditions or to proactively initiate a change in the competitive environment is particularly important in industries in which time-to-market is critical, technological change is rapid, and future competition is difficult to forecast.

4. Explain how value-chain activities are related to firm performance and competitive advantage. Firms produce products or offer services by engaging in many activities. The basic structure of firm activities is illustrated by the firm's value chain. The value chain is divided into primary and support activities. One way a company can outperform rivals is to find ways to perform some value-chain activities better than its rivals or to find different ways to perform the activities altogether. Selective outsourcing of some value-chain activities is one way to perform activities differently. Competitive advantage through strategic configuration of value-chain activities only comes about if the firm can either deliver greater value than rivals or deliver comparable value at lower cost. The essence of the activity-based value-chain perspective of competitive advantage is to choose value-chain activities that are different from those of rivals and to configure these activities in a way that are internally consistent and that requires significant tradeoffs should a competitor want to imitate them.

5. Explain the role of managers with respect to resources, capabilities, and value-chain activities. Managers make decisions about how to employ resources in the formulation and implementation of strategy. Managers are the decision agents who put into motion the use of all other firm resources and capabilities; they are key to the success of a firm's strategy. Managers with specific experiences and backgrounds may be more qualified to work with a specific bundle of resources owned by a firm. The influence of managers is more pronounced in contexts such as entrepreneurial phases, turnarounds, and competitive turmoil.

Review Questions

1. What are resources? How do different types of resources differ?

2. What is a capability?

3. What are the five components of the VRINE model?

4. How do time and causal ambiguity relate to the value, rarity, and inimitability of a resource or capability?

5. What is the difference between a stock of resources and capabilities and a flow of resources and capabilities?

6. What are dynamic capabilities? How do they differ from general capabilities?

7. What is a firm's value chain? How does it figure into a firm's competitive advantage?

8. What is your role as a manager in linking resources and capabilities to strategy and competitive advantage?

Experiential Activities

Group Exercises

1. What is the role of luck in gaining possession of a particular resource or capability? Can a firm manage luck? Give an example of a resource or capability that a firm garnered through luck and determine whether it was subsequently well-managed.

2. Some firms' products are so well known that the entire category of products offered in the industry (including rivals' products) is often referred to by the leading firm's brand name (which is called an *eponym*). Identify one such product and discuss whether its brand recognition gives the leading firm a competitive advantage. Why or why not?

Ethical Debates

1. Companies are increasingly looking to India for outsourced IT and knowledge work. To attract and accommodate an even greater influx of foreign firms, the government has given a contract to Reliance, a local company, to turn a vast area of farmland near Mumbai into a new high-tech city. And, in the process, the government has given Reliant essentially the powers of eminent domain and the power to evict farmers whose families have worked the land for generations. Does this pose a problem for foreign firms looking to India for outsourcing opportunities?

2. What are some of the ethical issues that seem to accompany discussions of outsourcing or offshoring? What tradeoffs might a management team be weighing with a particular outsourcing or offshoring option?

How Would YOU DO THAT?

1. In the box entitled "How Would *You* Do That? 3.1," we walked through how to apply the DuPont analysis to better understand the value chain choices, and possibly resources and capabilities, that support a firm's strategy. Pick two competing firms, and develop a DuPont analysis on both of them. What conclusions do you draw from this analysis and comparison?

2. Based on your analysis, are there activities that this organization performs differently than its rival? Start by looking at the firm's products, services, or target markets. Do any of the rival firm's value-chain activities give them a competitive advantage? If so, why don't others imitate these activities? What resources and capabilities does your focal organization possess? What are the resources and capabilities possessed by the rival? How do your focal organization's resources and capabilities fare relative to those of the rivals' when you apply the VRINE model to them?

Go on to see How Would You Do That at www.prenhall.com/carpenter&sanders

Endnotes

1. J. Haleblian and S. Finkelstein, "The Influence of Organizational Acquisition Experience on Acquisition Performance: A Behavioral Learning Perspective," *Administrative Science Quarterly* 44:1 (1999), 29–56; F. Vermeulen and H. Barkema, "Learning Through Acquisitions," *Academy of Management Journal* 44:3 (2001), 457–476.

2. D. J. Teece, G. Pisano, and A. Shuen, "Dynamic Capabilities and Strategic Management," *Strategic Management Journal* 18 (1997), 509–529.

3. R. R. Nelson and S. G. Winter, *An Evolutionary Theory of Economic Change* (Cambridge, MA: Belknap Press of Harvard University Press, 1982).

4. G. Stalk, P. Evans, and L. E. Shulman, "Competing on Capabilities: The New Rules of Corporate Strategy," *Harvard Business Review* 70:2 (1992), 54–65; R. Makadok, "Doing the Right Thing and Knowing the Right Thing to Do: Why the Whole Is Greater Than the Sum of the Parts," *Strategic Management Journal* 24:10 (2003), 1043–1054.

5. english.pravda.ru/usa/2001/11/03/20045.html and www.restaurantreport.com/qa/location.html (accessed June 28, 2005).

6. This framework is consistent with the larger literature on the resource-based view of the firm. For another helpful discussion, see J. B. Barney, "Looking Inside for Competitive Advantage," *Academy of Management Executive* 9:4 (1995), 49–61.

7. J. B. Barney, "Firm Resources and Sustained Competitive Advantage," *Journal of Management* 17:1 (1991), 99–120.

8. Union Pacific, "System Map" (accessed August 4, 2005), at www.uprr.com/aboutup/maps/sysmap/index.shtml.

9. Barney, "Firm Resources and Sustained Competitive Advantage."

10. C. K. Prahalad and G. Hamel, "The Core Competence of the Corporation," *Harvard Business Review* 68:3 (1990), 79–92.

11. L. Capron and W. Mitchell, "The Role of Acquisitions in Reshaping Business Capabilities in the International Telecommunications Industry," *Industrial and Corporate Change* 7:4 (1998), 715–730.

12. P. R. Haunschild, "How Much Is That Company Worth? Interorganizational Relationships, Uncertainty, and Acquisition Premiums," *Administrative Science Quarterly* 39:3 (1994), 391–414.

13. B. Labaris, "Has Your Vendor Gone Buyout Crazy?" *Computerworld* 33:36 (1999), 34–35.

14. J. B. Barney, "Looking Inside for Competitive Advantage," Academy of Management Executive 9:4 (1995), 49–61; I. Dierickx and K. Cool, "Asset Stock Accumulation and Sustainability of Competitive Advantage," *Management Science* 35:12 (1989), 1504–1511.

15. M. Pendergrast, *For God, Country and Coca-Cola* (New York: Basic Books, 1993).

16. Coca-Cola, *2006 Annual Report*; PepsiCo, *2006 Annual Report*.

17. Dierickx and Cool, "Asset Stock Accumulation and Sustainability of Competitive Advantage."

18. Dierickx and Cool, "Asset Stock Accumulation and Sustainability of Competitive Advantage."

19. Nelson and Winter, *An Evolutionary Theory of Economic Change*.

20. Barney, "Looking Inside for Competitive Advantage"; Dierickx and Cool, "Asset Stock Accumulation and Sustainability of Competitive Advantage."

21. Author's personal communication with Margaret Haddox, Novell Corporate Librarian, October 2003.

22. Author's personal communication with former Novell executives, September 2003.

23. D. T. Kearns and D. A. Nadler, *Prophets in the Dark* (New York: Harper-Collins, 1992); Barney, "Looking Inside for Competitive Advantage."

24. "Could Cymbalta Bring Cheer for Lilly?" *IMS Health.com*, August 23, 2004 (accessed August 4, 2005), at open.imshealth.com; C. Baysden, "Report: Blockbuster Drug Marketing Costs Average $239M," *Triangle Business Journal*, February 24, 2005 (accessed August 4, 2005), at triangle.bizjournals.com; "Medication for Depression: Antidepressant Medications," *Psychology Information Online* (accessed August 4, 2005), at www.psychologyinfo.com.

25. Eisenhardt and Martin, "Dynamic Capabilities."

26. Eisenhardt and Martin, "Dynamic Capabilities."

27. B. Orwall, "In Disney Row, an Aging Heir Who's Won Boardroom Bouts," *Wall Street Journal*, December 5, 2003, A1.

28. G. Szulanski and R. J. Jensen, "Overcoming Stickiness: An Empirical Investigation of the Role of the Template," *Managerial Decision Economics*, 25: 6–7 (2004:) 347–363.

29. Eisenhardt and Martin, "Dynamic Capabilities."

30. Teece, Pisano, and Shuen, "Dynamic Capabilities and Strategic Management."

31. C. Christensen, *The Innovator's Dilemma* (New York: Harper Business Press, 1997).

32. R. Burgelman, "Fading Memories: A Process Theory of Strategic Business Exit in Dynamic Environments," *Administrative Science Quarterly* 39:1 (1994), 24–56.

33. M. E. Porter, "What Is Strategy?" *Harvard Business Review* 74:6 (1996), 61–78.

34. The generic value chain model was developed by M. E. Porter, *Competitive Advantage: Creating and Sustaining Superior Performance* (New York: The Free Press, 1985), p. 47.

35. Porter, "What Is Strategy?"

36. Transportation Workers Union, TWU Airline Industry Review, at www.twuatd.org; Bureau of Transportation, *TransStats Reports*, at www.transtats.bts.gov.

37. Porter, "What Is Strategy?"

38. Sears' and Kohls' asset turns and return on assets are much more similar when you capitalize Kohls' leases as part of its asset figure, though Kohl's still outperforms Sears after this adjustment.

39. Barney, "Firm Resources and Sustained Competitive Advantage."

40. T. Hseih and S. Yik, "Leadership as the Starting Point of Strategy," *McKinsey Quarterly* 1 (2005), 11–26.

41. S. Ghoshal and C. A. Bartlett, "Changing the Role of Top Management: Beyond Structure to Processes," *Harvard Business Review* 73:3 (1995), 86–96; C. A. Bartlett and S. Ghoshal, "Changing the Role of Top Management: Beyond Systems to People," *Harvard Business Review* 73:3 (1995), 132–134.

42. M. A. Carpenter, W. Sanders, and H. Garegersen, "Bundling Human Capital with Organizational Context: The Impact of International Assignment Experience on Multinational Firm Performance and CEO Pay," *Academy of Management Journal* 44:3 (2001), 493–512.

43. M. A. Carpenter, T. G. Pollock, and M. M. Leary, "Testing a Model of Reasoned Risk-Taking: Governance, the Experience of Principals and Agents, and Global Strategy in High-Technology IPO Firms," *Strategic Management Journal* 24:9 (2003), 803–820.

44. Q. Huy, "In Praise of Middle Managers," *Harvard Business Review* 79:8 (2001), 72–79.

Exploring the External Environment

Macro and Industry Dynamics

In This Chapter We Challenge You To >>>

1. Explain the importance of the external context for strategy and firm performance.

2. Use PESTEL to identify the macro characteristics of the external context.

3. Identify the major features of an industry and the forces that affect industry profitability.

4. Understand the dynamic characteristics of the external context.

5. Show how industry dynamics may redefine industries.

A Chronicle
of the Cola War

Coca Cola sells a billion servings—in cans, bottles, and glasses—every day. You can grab a Coke in almost 200 countries. Its archrival, Pepsi, isn't too far behind. Like Ford versus Chevy, theirs is a battle not just for customer dollars, but for their hearts and minds as well.

—The History Channel, "Empires of Industry: Cola Wars"

As the environment changes, companies are forced to change as well. Often, the change is challenging. PepsiCo, for example, saw its sales drop from $31 billion in 1999 to $25 billion in 2002. Pepsi's leaders needed to transform the company to meet the new industry realities. As Indra Nooyi, Pepsi's President and CEO said, "In a perfect world, I'd be able to tell you we executed this restructuring flawlessly. Naturally, that's not the case. The process was neither smooth nor seamless. Many times it felt like baptism by fire."

For generations, the soft drink industry has been one of the most profitable industries. Experts estimate that gross margins in soft drink concentrate are approximately 83 percent and net margins about 35 percent. Coke had long been the dominant player while Pepsi fought hard to win market share. The "Cola Wars" between the two giants defined the industry, as we'll see in more detail below. But as the two companies battled intently with each other, the battleground around them was changing.

"Some dark clouds moved in," Nooyi recalls. "After years of investing aggressively, too aggressively in retrospect, our international beverage businesses suffered dramatic losses." During the battle, Pepsi had also entered the restaurant business—buying Taco Bell, Pizza Hut, and KFC—to block Coke from further gains in the fountain market. Coke dominated the fountain market with a strategic partnership with McDonalds, which accounted for 75–100 million gallons of Coke sold each year in the U.S. alone. Pepsi bought the three chains to ensure that those restaurants sold only Pepsi products.

Although buying the restaurants seemed a good strategic move, it brought Pepsi into an unfamiliar industry, and the venture started sapping Pepsi's profits. Nooyi and her colleagues realized that the restaurant business had to go. As Nooyi's then-boss Roger Enrico explained, "The central part of her proposition was that we weren't retailers ourselves, and we didn't have the expertise to run them the way they could and should be run." Nooyi therefore created a new company, Yum Brands, that consisted of the three restaurant chains, and sold it off. "You have to think of a business like any investment. You have to know when to get in, but more important, when to get out. Getting out can be a lot tougher, especially if you develop an emotional tie to the business. But the world changes, and so should the models we apply to our businesses."

The core carbonated soft drinks business started changing, too. Both Coke and Pepsi face challenges as consumers become more health conscious and start to substitute juice and water for soda. In order to appeal to investors and stay relevant, Coca-Cola's Chairman-CEO Neville Isdell switched from using the word "carbonated" to using the term "sparkling," and using the word "still" in place of "noncarbonated." "Sparkling beverages," he said, "are what we simply define as nonalcoholic, ready-to-drink consumer beverages with carbonation." Coke's press releases have been changed so say that Coke "markets four of the world's top five nonalcoholic sparkling brands." Industry expert Gary Hemphill, managing director of the Beverage Marketing Group, sees the change in nomenclature as a shift: "It signals a changing marketplace," he said. "'Sparkling' spans multiple categories like carbonated soft drinks, energy drinks, sparkling water, and sparkling juice; whereas the term 'carbonated' is mostly associated solely with carbonated soft drinks." In fact, Pepsi recently acquired Izze Beverage, known for its all-natural, sparkling fruit juices, and both Coke and Pepsi have begun marketing some sodas as sparkling, including Coke's Fresca and Enviga and Pepsi's Tava.

In another move to stay relevant, Pepsi's Nooyi is shifting Pepsi's strategy to address health issues. Born in India, Nooyi understands the concerns over nutrition, and she has promised that at least half of all new Pepsi products will now be comprised of "essentially healthy" ingredients or offer "improved health benefits". Under her new strategy, Pepsi's North American drinks business is now led by noncarbonated, "healthier" options: waters, "enhanced" waters, and teas and energy drinks, which all show double-digit growth. PepsiCo's Aquafina brand is the number-one bottled water in the U.S. and has so-called functional variants that include B-Power, Calcium+, Daily C, and Multi-V in 20-ounce bottles.

Despite the new strategy, Nooyi is aware that strategic wins are a moving target. "The minute you've developed a new business model, it's extinct, because somebody is going to copy it," she said.

And indeed, in classic cola-war fashion, Coke vowed to invest an additional $400 million annually in 2005 on innovation and is trademarking a fortified fruit drink and energy-enhanced diet drink.

Let's take a look at the history of cola wars. Its roots can be traced back to 1886, when a pharmacist in Atlanta, Georgia, concocted a headache tonic that he sold for five cents a glass. His bookkeeper named the remedy "Coca-Cola" and committed its secret formula to writing. About a decade later, and just a few hundred miles away in New Bern, North Carolina, another pharmacist created Pepsi Cola.

Over a century later, the stakes in the soft-drink industry are enormous. The average American consumes 53 gallons of carbonated beverages per year—about 29 percent of the total consumption of all liquids! Given gross margins on soft drink concentrate that can be as high as 83 percent, enormous profit is potentially at stake. It's no wonder that Coke and Pepsi go to great lengths to defend their turf.

Trading Punches Although Coke has long been dominant, Pepsi has worked hard to weaken its enemy's position. In 1950, for example, Pepsi recruited a former Coke marketing manager and proclaimed the battle cry "Beat Coke." In the 1960s, Pepsi launched its "Pepsi Generation" campaign to target younger buyers. In the mid-1970s, spurred by the success of blind taste tests in Texas, Pepsi launched a nationwide offensive called the "Pepsi Challenge." Coke, however, refused to retreat, countering with such tactics as retail price cuts and aggressive advertising.

Coke's tactics intensified after Roberto Goizueta became CEO in 1981. Once in command, Goizueta more than doubled advertising, switched to lower-priced sweeteners, sold off noncarbonated beverage businesses, and introduced new flavors and diet versions of existing brands. Coke's victories included Diet Coke, the most successful new product introduction of the 1980s. Then, however, Coke made a serious tactical error: It tried to reformulate the 100-year-old recipe for Coke. When consumers rebelled, Coke was forced to retreat to the original formula. Pepsi proclaimed the effort to reformulate Coke as an admission that Pepsi had a superior taste.

The value-chain activities that bring carbonated beverages to market are centered on four functions: production (producing concentrate), marketing (managing a portfolio of brands), packaging (bottling finished products), and distribution (distributing products for resale). Concentrate is the syrup that provides the distinctive flavor to soft drinks. Historically, the major beverage companies focused on the production of concentrate and marketing, and independent regional bottlers were tasked with packaging and distribution. Bottlers mixed the soft drink concentrate with sweetener and carbonated water and then packaged and distributed the finished product in cans, bottles, or bulk (for restaurant and other on-premises sales). In the early years, both Coke and Pepsi expanded rapidly by granting franchises to independent bottlers around the country. This strategy avoided huge investments in capital-intensive bottling operations.

Bottling Operations However, as the industry matured, the economics of bottling operations changed. Two trends resulted in a change in the bottling industry. First, a few bottling companies saw an opportunity to buy up local franchises in contiguous markets and restructure local operations by building large plants with greater economies of scale designed to serve multiple markets. As these bottling operations began to grow in size, they also grew in power relative to Coke and Pepsi, which posed a legitimate threat to Coke and Pepsi. This threat led to the second trend in the bottling industry. Even though bottling operations generated much less than half the operating margins of concentrate production, both Coke and Pepsi entered the bottling industry. They began buying up independent bottling operations, consolidating territories, and building newer, more efficient facilities.

Although entering the bottling industry could have diluted Coke's and Pepsi's earnings, they actually were able to use this move to improve their overall performance. They did this in two ways. First, by purchasing the bottling operations based on existing profitability, they were able to buy these strategic operations cheaply relative to their value once they restructured operations and made them more efficient. Second, both Coke and Pepsi later divested part of their holdings by spinning off bottling subsidiaries (based on higher profitability) but retaining significant holdings in these now partially owned subsidiaries. These ownership positions enabled them to counteract any power that these operations may have had in negotiations were they to be completely independently owned and operated.

A New Age An outside observer might think that such a fierce battle for market share would gradually erode the combatants' profitability. Since the mid-1960s, however, both Coke and Pepsi have increased market share by about 11 percent, and both enjoy healthy profits. Entry barriers created by large market shares, tremendous brand equity, and ownership or control of regional bottlers explain much of this profitability. Of course, that increased market share had to be captured from weaker rivals, although competitors like Cadbury Schweppes and private label suppliers are making up ground as well. Perhaps the only thing that is certain at this point is that the global hostilities between the two cola superpowers are far from over. **<<<**

The External Context of Strategy

To formulate an effective strategy—one that has a good chance of helping you achieve your objectives—it is crucial that you understand the external environment. In the broadest sense, the external environment consists of a wide array of economic and sociopolitical factors. In the narrowest sense, the external environment is the specific market arenas that the firm has chosen in its strategy. It is the external environment that provides the business opportunities—ultimately in the form of its chosen arenas—to the firm. ◆ However, the external environment is also a source of threats—forces that may impede the successful implementation of a strategy. The external environment in which firms compete exerts a strong influence on firms' profitability.

 Arenas

As we noted at the start of Chapter 3, where we discussed some tools for identifying the internal determinants of a firm's strengths and weaknesses, you should think of the chapters on the internal and external contexts of strategy as related sections of a single unit. Individually, each discussion provides you with only half of the information you need to analyze a firm's strategy.

In this chapter, you'll learn how to identify the external opportunities and threats that affect every firm's strategy. Taken together, these two chapters provide the tools that will enable you to perform a rigorous analysis of the firm's competitive environment and its capabilities to implement a strategy. In previous coursework, you probably approached these issues with a *SWOT analysis*, which is a relatively simple tool. The tools provided in Chapters 3 and 4 will help you systematically analyze what you could only do intuitively with the SWOT tool.

The long-term profitability of both Coke and Pepsi has probably been influenced by the structure of the soft drink industry. Many enterprising entrepreneurs have seen this long-term propensity to make lots of money in the soft drink industry and have desired to share in that wealth. Many small, profitable companies have emerged; yet, none has succeeded in becoming a major player alongside Coke and Pepsi. In this chapter, you will begin to understand why some industries are more profitable than others, why some industries are easier to enter than others, and what firms can do to influence these environmental factors in their favor.

Exhibit 4.1   Comparative Industrywide Levels of Profitability, 1996–2006

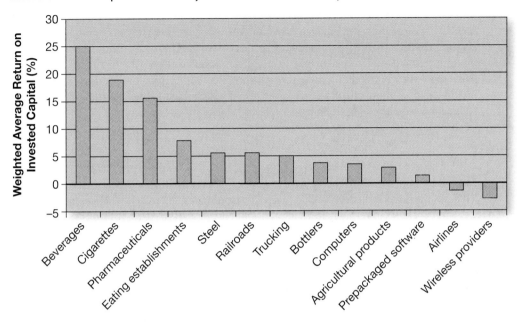

INDUSTRY- AND FIRM-SPECIFIC FACTORS

Knowing what industry- and firm-specific factors affect a firm is critical to understanding its competitive position and determining what strategies are viable. We can examine the complementary roles of industry- and firm-specific factors on firm performance in many different industries. For instance, consider the venerable position of Coca-Cola in the soft drink industry. Clearly, Coca-Cola has some firm-level advantages over its competitors. However, what happened when Coca-Cola entered the wine industry? The entry of Coca-Cola into the wine industry won't change at least two fundamental facts; namely, there is relatively little brand loyalty in wine, and the sale and distribution of the product is heavily regulated in most parts of the world. In 1977, Coke swallowed up industry giants Taylor Wine and Sterling Vineyard. As a beverage, wine is not entirely unrelated to Coke's core products, but unfortunately, Coke never mastered the complexities of a production and distribution process that's often as much an art as a science. After ringing up huge losses for a few years, Coke sold off its wine businesses—for much less than it initially paid for them. Evidently, some things don't go better with Coke.

As shown in Exhibit 4.1, profitability varies widely from industry to industry.[1] Even without the analytical tools to which you'll be introduced in this chapter, you can see that there must be some things about the airline industry relative to the pharmaceutical industry that result in such drastic differences in profitability. Likewise, there are probably factors about the soft drink industry that have helped Coke and Pepsi maintain such high profits over such an extended period of time. Why *are* some industries more profitable than others? For instance, why is the beverage concentrate industry (e.g., Coke, Pepsi, and their competitors) so much more profitable than the bottling industry?

What is needed to answer these questions are tools that allow you to systematically analyze a firm's external context. In the following sections you will be introduced to these tools. The proper use of these tools will help identify some of the major reasons industries differ so much in their long-term profitability.

We'll start this chapter by introducing methods for analyzing the macro environment and firms' industries. We then draw attention to the dynamic facets of the external environment.

FUNDAMENTAL CHARACTERISTICS OF THE EXTERNAL CONTEXT

Identifying the industry in which a firm competes is a logical starting point for analyzing its external context. By the fundamental characteristics of an industry, we mean those factors that are relevant to firm performance at a given point in time—the distinct features that you'd see if you could take an industry snapshot. Remember, too, that industry analysis will include many, but not all, of a firm's key external stakeholders. Thus, in order to avoid blind spots in an industry analysis, managers should always integrate their analysis of a firm's industry with a broader stakeholder analysis like that discussed in Chapter 2.

KEY QUESTIONS

Managers should ask the following questions when analyzing the firm's external context: "What is the firm's industry?" "What macro environmental conditions will have a material effect on our ability to implement our strategy successfully?" "What appear to be unstoppable trends?" "What are the characteristics of the industry?" and "How stable are these characteristics?" By addressing such questions, managers can gain a better sense of a firm's strategic options and challenges. Managers must remain focused on the industry, not on a particular firm operating within it. Focusing on Coca-Cola alone will not provide much information on the general characteristics of the soft drink industry, especially given the fact that Coke is far from average in terms of resources and capabilities. In addition, an industry analysis examines much more than simply the competitors in the industry. Our goal throughout this chapter is to present a deeper understanding of the external context in which *all* firms in an industry operate.

The external environment has two major components: the macro environment and the industry environment. The industry environment is composed of strategic groups—groupings of firms that seem to be more similar in certain ways than other members of the larger industry. The various levels of analysis necessary to examine a firm's external context are summarized in Exhibit 4.2. We will start with the macro environment most removed from the firm and work our way toward more micro analysis.

Exhibit 4.2 The External Environment of the Organization

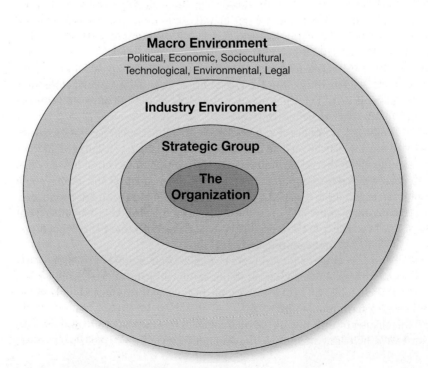

Macro Environment
Political, Economic, Sociocultural, Technological, Environmental, Legal

Industry Environment

Strategic Group

The Organization

Macro Environment

The macro environment refers to the larger political, economic, social, technical, environmental, and legal issues that confront the firm. To analyze the macro environment, we introduce the PESTEL model and present the determinants and consequences of globalization.

PESTEL ANALYSIS

A simple but important and widely used tool that can be used to develop an understanding of the big picture of a firm's external environment is **PESTEL analysis**. PESTEL is an acronym for the *p*olitical, *e*conomic, *s*ociocultural, *t*echnological, *e*nvironmental, and *l*egal context(s) in which a firm operates. It provides a nonexhaustive list of potential influences of the environment on the organization. It helps managers gain a better understanding of the opportunities and threats they face and consequently aids them in building a better vision of the future business landscape and how the firm might compete profitably. The PESTEL analysis is a useful tool for understanding market growth or decline. Its primary focus is on the future impact of macro environmental factors.

Firms need to understand the macro environment to ensure that their strategy is aligned with the powerful forces of change that are affecting their business landscape. When firms exploit changes in the environment, they are more likely to be successful than when they simply try to survive or oppose change. A good understanding of PESTEL also helps managers avoid strategies that may be doomed to failure for reasons beyond their control. Finally, understanding PESTEL is a good starting point for entering into a new country or region.

The fact that a strategy is congruent with PESTEL in the home environment gives no assurance that it will be so aligned in new geographic arenas. For example, when the online clothier Lands' End sought to expand its operations from the United States to Germany in 1996 it ran into local laws prohibiting Lands' End from offering unconditional guarantees on its products. In the United States, Lands' End had built its reputation for quality on its no-questions-asked money-back guarantee. However, this practice was considered illegal under Germany's regulations governing incentive offers and price discounts. The political skirmish between Lands' End and the German government finally came to an end in 2001, when the regulations were abolished. Although the regulations did not put Lands' End out of business in Germany, they did slow its growth there until the laws against advertising unconditional guarantees were abolished.

A PESTEL analysis involves three steps. First, you should consider the relevance of each of the PESTEL factors to your particular context. Second, you identify and categorize the information that applies to these factors. Third, you analyze the data and draw conclusions. A mistake too many students make is to stop after the second step. A second common mistake is to assume that your initial analysis and conclusions are correct without testing your assumptions and investigating alternative scenarios.

The PESTEL analysis framework is detailed in Exhibit 4.3. It has six sections, one for each of the PESTEL headings. The table includes sample questions or prompts, the answers to which will help you determine the nature of opportunities and threats in the macro environment. The questions are not meant to be exhaustive; rather, they are merely examples of the types of issues that you should be concerned about in the macro environment.

Political Factors   The political environment can have a significant influence on businesses as well as affect consumer confidence and consumer and business spending. Managers need to consider numerous types of political factors. For instance, the stability of the political environment is particularly important for companies entering new markets. In addition, government policies with respect to regulation and taxation vary from state to state and across national boundaries. Political considerations also encompass trade treaties, such

Exhibit 4.3 The Dimensions of PESTEL Analysis

Political
- How stable is the political environment?
- What are local taxation policies and how do these affect your business?
- Is the government involved in trading agreements such as EU, NAFTA, ASEAN, or others?
- What are the foreign-trade regulations?
- What are the social-welfare policies?

Economic
- What are current and projected interest rates?
- What is the level of inflation, what is it projected to be, and how does this projection reflect the growth of your market?
- What are local employment levels per capita and how are they changing?
- What are the long-term prospects for gross domestic product (GDP) per capita and so on?
- What are exchange rates between critical markets and how will they affect production and distribution of your goods?

Sociocultural
- What are local lifestyle trends?
- What are the current demographics and how are they changing?
- What is the level and distribution of education and income?
- What are the dominant local religions and what influence do they have on consumer attitudes and opinions?
- What is the level of consumerism and what are popular attitudes toward it?
- What pending legislation affects corporate social policies (e.g., domestic-partner benefits or maternity/paternity leave)?
- What are the attitudes toward work and leisure?

Technological
- What is the level of research funding in government and industry and are those levels changing?
- What is the government and industry's level of interest and focus on technology?
- How mature is the technology?
- What is the status of intellectual-property issues in the local environment?
- Are potentially disruptive technologies in adjacent industries creeping in at the edges of the focal industry?

Environmental
- What are local environmental issues?
- Are there any pending ecological or environmental issues relevant to your industry?
- How do the activities of international pressure groups (e.g., Greenpeace, Earth First, PETA) affect your business?
- Are there environmental-protection laws?
- What are the regulations regarding waste disposal and energy consumption?

Legal
- What are the regulations regarding monopolies and private property?
- Does intellectual property have legal protections?
- Are there relevant consumer laws?
- What is the status of employment, health-and-safety, and product-safety laws?

as NAFTA, and regional trading blocks, such as ASEAN and the European Union (EU). Such treaties and trading blocks tend to favor trade among the member countries and to impose penalties or less favorable trade terms on nonmembers.

Economic Factors   Managers also need to consider the macroeconomic factors that will have near- and long-term effects on the success of their strategies. Factors such as inflation rates, interest rates, tariffs, the growth of the local and foreign national economies, and exchange rates are critical. Unemployment rates, the availability of critical labor, and the local labor costs also have a strong bearing on strategy, particularly as it relates to where to locate disparate business functions and facilities.

Sociocultural Factors   The social and cultural influences on business vary from country to country. Depending on the type of business the firm operates, factors such as the local languages, the dominant religions, leisure time, and age and lifespan demographics may be critical. Local sociocultural characteristics also vary on such things as attitudes toward consumerism, environmentalism, and the roles of men and women in local society. Making assumptions about local sociocultural norms derived from your experience in your home market is a common cause of early failure when entering new markets. However, even home-market norms can change over time, often caused by shifting demographics due to immigration or aging populations. For example, Coca-Cola and Pepsi have grown in international markets due to increasing levels of consumerism outside of the United States.

Technological Factors   The critical role of technology will be discussed in more detail later in the chapter. For now, suffice it to say that technological factors have a major bearing on the threats and opportunities firms encounter. Does technology enable products and services to be made more cheaply and to a better standard of quality? Do technologies provide the opportunity for more innovative products and services, such as online stock trading, reduction in communications costs, and increased remote working? How might distribution of products or services be affected by new technologies? All of these factors have the potential to change the face of the business landscape.

Environmental Factors   The environment has long been a factor in firm strategy, primarily from the standpoint of access to raw materials. Increasingly, however, this factor is best viewed as a direct- and indirect-operating cost for the firm, as well as from the lens of the footprint left by a firm on its respective environments in terms of waste, pollution, and so on. For consumer products companies such as Pepsi, for example, this can mean waste management and organic farming practices in the countries from which raw materials are obtained. Similarly, in consumer markets it may refer to the degree to which packaging is biodegradable or recyclable.

Legal Factors   Finally, legal factors reflect the laws and regulations relevant to the region and the organization. Legal factors may include whether the rule of law is well established and how easily or quickly laws and regulations may change. It may also include the costs of regulatory compliance. For instance, Coca-Cola's market share in Europe is greater than 50 percent, and as a result, regulators have asked that Coke give up shelf space to competitors' products in order to provide greater consumer choice.

As you can see, many of the PESTEL factors are interrelated. For instance, the legal environment is often related to the political environment in that laws and regulations will change only when politicians decide that such changes are needed.

GLOBALIZATION

Over the past decade, as new markets have been opened to foreign competitors, whole industries have been deregulated and state-run enterprises have been privatized; globalization has become a fact of life in almost every industry.[2] Because of this, the topic of globalization spans both the subjects of PESTEL analysis and industry analysis in both relatively stable and dynamic contexts. We define **globalization** as the evolution of distinct geographic product markets into a state of globally interdependent product markets.

globalization Evolution of distinct geographic product markets into a state of globally interdependent product markets.

Exhibit 4.4 Factors in Globalization

Pressures Favoring Industry Globalization			
Markets	**Costs**	**Governments**	**Competition**
• Homogeneous customer needs • Global customer needs • Global channels • Transferable marketing approaches	• Large scale and scope economies • Learning and experience • Sourcing efficiencies • Favorable logistics • Arbitrage opportunities • High R&D costs	• Favorable trade policies • Common technological standards • Common manufacturing and marketing regulations	• Interdependent countries • Global competitors

Globalization entails much more than a company simply exporting products to another country. Some industries that aren't normally considered global do in fact have strictly domestic players, but they're often competing alongside firms with operations in many countries, and in many cases, both sets of firms are doing equally well. In contrast, in a truly global industry, the core product is standardized, the marketing approach is relatively uniform, and competitive strategies are integrated in different international markets.[3] In these industries, competitive advantage clearly belongs to the firms that can compete globally.

A number of factors reveal whether an industry has globalized or is in the process of globalizing. In Exhibit 4.4, we've grouped them into four categories: *market, cost, government,* and *competition*.[4]

Markets The more similar markets in different regions become, the greater the pressure for an industry to globalize. Coke and Pepsi, for example, are fairly uniform around the world because the demand for soft drinks is largely the same in every country. The airframe-manufacturing industry, dominated by Boeing and Airbus, also has a highly uniform market for its products because airlines all over the world have the same needs when it comes to large commercial jets. When the distribution channels used to take products to market have already globalized, an incumbent that globalizes early will gain an advantage over other competitors. Thus, if distribution channels are global in nature, waiting to become a global player will put a firm at a disadvantage that may never be overcome. Finally, when similar marketing approaches are widely transferable across geographic markets, there will be pressure to globalize in order to reap the benefits of economies in scale in advertising (i.e., spreading the fixed-cost component of the advertising campaign across more customers).

Costs Anytime fixed costs are extremely high, there will be pressure to globalize in order to spread fixed costs across more customers. In both the automobile and airframe-manufacturing industries, costs also favor globalization. For instance, Boeing and Airbus can invest millions in new-product R&D only because the global market for their products is so large. Coke and Pepsi make huge investments in marketing and promotion, and because they're promoting coherent images and brands, they can leverage their marketing dollars around the world. Pharmaceuticals spend billions of dollars researching and developing new therapies and applications. Consequently, again, there is tremendous pressure to sell products in any economy that might have demand for the drug to help recoup this investment.

Governments can have a huge impact on trade by setting industry-wide standards and regulations. In some parts of Western Europe, for example, people and freight can't travel easily from country to country without switching railroads. Because each country's rail standards and technology are different from its neighbors', rail lines are in some cases incompatible with one another.

Beyond leveraging fixed costs, there are several other cost pressures to globalize. For instance, in many industries the only way to have competitive manufacturing costs is to move these operations to locations outside the home country and into one of the emerging economies that offers significantly lower wages. Finally, the improvement in logistics and transportation capabilities within companies and in the logistics service industry generally make it very easy to enter new markets. Thus, the cost to globalize has been reduced significantly over the past several decades. This means that competitors seeking growth will globalize; failing to do so in your own company could negatively affect your competitive position.

Governments and Competition   Obviously, favorable trade policies encourage the globalization of markets and industries. Governments, however, can also play a critical role in globalization by determining and regulating technological standards. Railroad gauge—the distance between the two steel tracks—would seem to favor a simple technological standard. In Spain, however, the gauge is wider than in France. Why? Because back in the 1850s, when Spain and neighboring France were hostile to one another, the Spanish government decided that making Spanish railways incompatible with French railways would hinder a French invasion.

The cell-phone industry offers a more recent example. The EU has mobilized around one GSM standard, whereas most of the North American market adheres to another GSM standard or the CDMA standard that originally dominated most of the U.S. market. Although recent breakthroughs have made multistandard phones possible, these differences still create fragmented markets for cell-phone manufacturers, such as Motorola and Nokia. Moreover, the interdependence of the European and North American markets means that manufacturers must maintain a strong regional presence. Finally, recent entrants into the industry, including Samsung and NEC, already engage in other global operations. Thus, the problem of multiple standards and the entry of large global competitors both spur globalization in the industry.

Several of the examples reviewed above in the other categories (e.g., markets and costs) suggested that competition was a strong factor affecting globalization. With the exception of niche players, an incumbent may need to globalize simply because competitors are doing so. This will be the case when competitors' globalization gives them any form of advantage that is applicable across their markets.

Now that you understand how PESTEL analysis and an assessment of globalization can help you characterize the general conditions of the macro environment, you are prepared to delve deeply into industry analysis. The next section reviews critical information that will help you analyze the structure of an industry and better understand your competitors.

Industry Analysis

Neoclassical microeconomics has long held the position that in market economies where competition is encouraged and monopolies are not allowed, firms should be able to earn only "normal" profits—that is, enough return to cover the cost of production and the cost of capital. Why? Because of competition. When there is perfect competition, there are numerous sellers and buyers (no monopolies), perfect information, relatively homogenous products offered by different firms, and no barriers to entry or exit. What happens if firms earn greater-than-normal profits (as most managers and shareholders are trying hard to accomplish)? Competition will increase, usually through the entry of new firms into the industry, and profits will be driven back to normal levels. Conversely, if profits fall *below* normal levels, some firms will exit, easing competition and allowing profits to increase to normal levels. However, even a casual reexamination would suggest that most industries must not be held to the laws of perfect competition because we see industries with long-run average profits far exceeding normal levels and others with profits way below such levels.

In this book, however, we have asserted more than once that the strategist's goal is to develop a *competitive advantage* over rivals. When one firm enjoys an inherent advantage over other firms in its industry, above-normal returns are possible (at least for the firm with the advantage) because competition under these conditions is not perfect. In contrast to the conditions of perfect competition, imperfect competition is characterized by relatively few competitors, numerous suppliers and buyers, asymmetric information, heterogeneous products, and barriers that make entry into an industry difficult. Industry analysis helps managers determine the nature of the competition, the possible sources of imperfect competition in the industry, and the possibility of the firm earning above-normal returns.

I/O ECONOMICS AND KEY SUCCESS FACTORS

The insights that help managers analyze an industry originate in a discipline called *industrial organization (I/O) economics*. Fortunately, one does not need to be an economist to understand the basic tools of industry analysis. These tools enable managers to understand the business landscape in which the firm operates. These tools and the insights derived from their use should be used iteratively with the tools of internal analysis. However, for simplicity's sake we will hold constant the internal condition of the firm and focus on external conditions in this chapter.

One implication of industry analysis is that firms perform best when they select a strategy that fits the industry environment. Researchers often argue that the goal of managers should be to acquire the necessary skills and resources, often called the **key success factors** (**KSFs**), to compete in their industry environment.[5] For example, KSFs in the soft drink industry might include (1) the ability to meet competitive pricing; (2) extensive distribution capabilities, including ownership of vending machines and cold-storage cases; (3) marketing skills to raise consumer brand awareness in a highly crowded marketplace; (4) a broad mix of products, including diet and noncaffeinated beverages; (5) global presence; and (6) well-positioned bottlers and bottling capacity.

key success factor (KSF)
Key asset or requisite skill that all firms in an industry must possess in order to be a viable competitor.

On the surface, this strategy-development process is similar to the process of strategy formulation and implementation that we discussed in Chapter 3, with one critical difference: According to the I/O approach, the appropriate strategy, key assets, and requisite skills are dictated by *industry* characteristics. Why do I/O researchers regard KSFs as a function of the industry? Simply because all firms in an industry must possess them in order to be viable. Thus, KSFs fit the definition of valuable resources as defined in Chapter 3 because they are like table stakes in a poker game: You need the stakes just to get a seat at the poker table. The soft drink example shows that these stakes actually create barriers to entry because they are complex and costly to put in place. While KSFs are resources and skills that would satisfy the *value* criteria from the VRINE model introduced in Chapter 3, by definition they will not satisfy the *rareness* criterion. Thus, possessing KSFs will not grant a firm a competitive advantage over other key players in the industry, but it will permit it to compete against such firms.

I/O researchers also argue that the analyst should focus primarily on the industry as a whole, and not on a particular firm, because KSFs are easily transferred from one firm to another. Thanks to relatively efficient markets, firms can readily buy the KSFs they need. In summary, the I/O approach suggests that managers should study an industry in order to understand which strategies are rewarded most profitably and to acquire the industry-relevant KSFs required to implement them.

WHAT IS AN INDUSTRY?

Economists define an *industry* as a firm or group of firms that produce or sell the same or similar products to the same market. Is there such a thing as a one-firm industry? If a firm holds a *monopoly*—if it's the only seller in the market—then it's the only firm in the industry. Many utilities operate as monopolies within specific geographic areas (and are typically regulated or owned outright by government bodies). Most industries have several or many competitors. But even some industries that have many competitors are dominated by a few powerful firms.

Fragmentation and Concentration   In a *duopoly* or *oligopoly,* the market is dominated by only two or a few large firms, and the industry is characterized as concentrated. In our opening vignette on the Cola War, it is clear that the soft drink industry is very concentrated. At the other end of the spectrum, industries in which there's no clear leader are characterized as fragmented.

How can we determine the extent to which an industry is concentrated or fragmented? One useful tool is the *concentration ratio,* which represents the combined revenues of the largest industry participants as a ratio of total industry sales. For manufacturing industries, the U.S. Department of Commerce calculates these ratios at different levels, according to the number of firms treated as the industry's largest—4, 8, 20, or 50. Thus, we refer to these ratios as C4, C8, C20, and C50, respectively. Industry concentration is one of several important factors in industry analysis, because concentration affects the intensity of competition in an industry. For instance, fragmented markets are believed to be more competitive than concentrated markets, whereas concentrated markets are more difficult to enter.

To determine what constitutes an industry, it is necessary to identify clear classifications of products or markets. In the case of Coke and Pepsi, for instance, the industry could be defined as the *beverage industry.* This industry would include every firm that manufactures beverages—Lipton (tea), Starbucks (coffee), Seagram's (liquor), Heineken (beer), Mondavi (wine), Ocean Spray (juice), Coke and Pepsi (soft drinks), and so on. However, such a broad definition makes analysis very difficult and probably obscures important micro-level structural features. Coke and Pepsi's industry could alternatively be defined as the *carbonated soft-drink* industry. There is no definitive rule as to where to draw the boundaries when analyzing an industry. The key is to not be so inclusive that important factors that differ across heterogeneous markets cannot be detected (e.g., Are there key differences between alcoholic beverage markets and soft drink markets?) nor so exclusive that important threats are missed (e.g., Does excluding bottled water from the carbonated soft-drink industry miss the main growth segments?).

Defining Industry Boundaries Indeed, the answer to the question "What industry am I in?" is not as simple as it might seem, even if you're only thinking about something to drink. You'll probably be surprised by the implications of different answers that can be given to this deceptively simple question. This is because industries are typically composed of many segments with different structural characteristics. In the midst of the Cola War, both antagonists were looking for ways to grow. Hard-nosed head-to-head competition was one option, but a simpler strategy involved merely redefining what industry each company was in—say, *beverages* in general or, more particularly, *soft-drink beverages*. Toward this end, Coke bought Minute Maid in 1960, and since then Coke and Pepsi seem to have agreed that they're in the *nonalcoholic beverage* industry, which includes not only soda but also juices and teas. Pepsi purchased Tropicana (juices) in 1999 and South Beach Beverage in 2000. Coke bought Odwalla (juices) in 2001.

Today, the hottest new-product area in the nonalcoholic beverage business is water—bottled water, to be exact. Bottled water is a multibillion-dollar growth industry, and it's well on its way to becoming the most consumed beverage in America (except for soft drinks). With an active market consisting of nearly half of all Americans, bottled water is on track to surpass beer, milk, and coffee to become the second-best-selling beverage in the United States.

Although Coke is big in soda, it comes in a distant third in the global bottled water business.[6] With 70 brands in 160 countries, Nestlé, a Swiss company, controls nearly a third of the market, and its share is growing. In North America alone, Nestlé sells nine domestic brands, including Arrowhead, Poland Spring, and Deer Park; and five imported brands, including San Pellegrino and Perrier. Pepsi, with a nearly 10 percent share, comes in second with Aquafina, the top-selling single-serve bottled water in the United States. Coca-Cola is third (though not last) with Dasani, which has 8 percent of the market. Recently, however, Coke entered into a partnership with France's Groupe Danone that may vault it into second place once it begins producing, marketing, and distributing Danone's niche brands, which include Evian.

At least one thing should be clear by now: Before getting into an industry, the firm's managers must know the type of product and the geographic market that they're considering. Exhibit 4.5 underscores the importance of drawing industry boundaries in a way that enables managers to understand the dynamics of competition.[7] As shown in Exhibit 4.5, concentration ratios vary dramatically among segments within the same broad industry group. In comparison to other industries, for example, the food industry is relatively fragmented: The four largest manufacturers account for only 14 percent of sales. Within this broad grouping, however, some areas are highly concentrated; the four largest competitors, for instance, account for a full 83 percent of breakfast cereal sales. The apparel industry also consists of numerous segments. Concentration ratios in the men's and boys' segment are quite different from those in the women's and girls' segment: Sales are much more concentrated in the former. The differences in concentration ratios remind us that industry dynamics vary dramatically across various sectors of the same industry. As demonstrated by such differences in concentration ratios, the definition of an industry is critical to gaining an understanding of the competitive dynamics facing firms that operate in it and, ultimately, to the formulation of a strategy for competing in it.

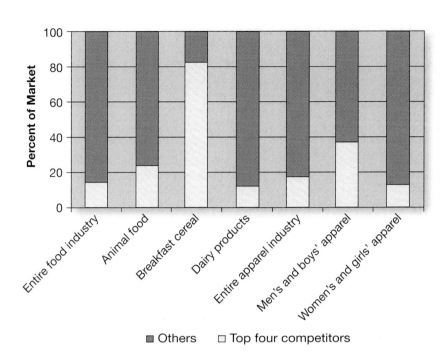

Exhibit 4.5 Concentrati on in Selected U.S. Industries

■ Others   □ Top four competitors

A MODEL OF INDUSTRY STRUCTURE

Once the boundaries of the industry to be analyzed have been identified, the next step is to examine the industry's fundamental characteristics and structure. The model shown in Exhibit 4.6 identifies five forces that determine the basic structure of an industry.[8] We've added a sixth force, complementors, to the model because it's an increasingly critical industry force, and therefore an input into your strategic analysis (you will learn more on complementors below).

These five forces were identified by Michael Porter as the industry **five-forces model**.[9] The horizontal axis is a stylized version of the industry value chain. An industry purchases inputs, or supplies, from other industries. Likewise, an industry sells its products or services to customers, which are often other businesses but may be retail consumers as well. In negotiations with suppliers and buyers, transactions are not always between parties of equal negotiating strength. The five-forces model draws attention to factors that systematically alter the negotiating strength in favor of suppliers, industry members, or buyers. Likewise, the model draws attention to threats posed by the possibility of new entrants (and conversely, the difficulty of exit) and possible substitute products from other industries or industry segments, either of which can pose threats to industry participants.

It's sometimes useful to think of these forces as countervailing sources of power all vying for a larger piece of the industry's total profits. Recall that when an industry is characterized by perfect competition, rivals in an industry will achieve normal levels of profitability—enough to pay for all factors of input, including the cost of capital. However, industries actually vary considerably in their average level of returns. A key reason for this variance in industry profitability is differences in the power of these five forces across different industries.

Rivalry Firms can compete in an industry in many ways. The intensity of competition is known as **rivalry**. The key questions to ask when analyzing the degree of rivalry in an industry include: Who are the competitors? How do rival firms compete? Which firms will be identified as competitors? Because an understanding of the nature of rivalry is so important, we include a separate section on competitor analysis that details ways in which the future actions of competitors can be more accurately predicted.

five-forces model Framework for evaluating industry structure according to the effects of rivalry, threat of entry, supplier power, buyer power, and the threat of substitutes.

rivalry Intensity of competition within an industry.

Exhibit 4.6 The Five Forces of Industry Structure

Source: Adapted from M. E. Porter, Competitive Strategy: Techniques for Analyzing Industries and Competitors (New York: Free Press, 1980)

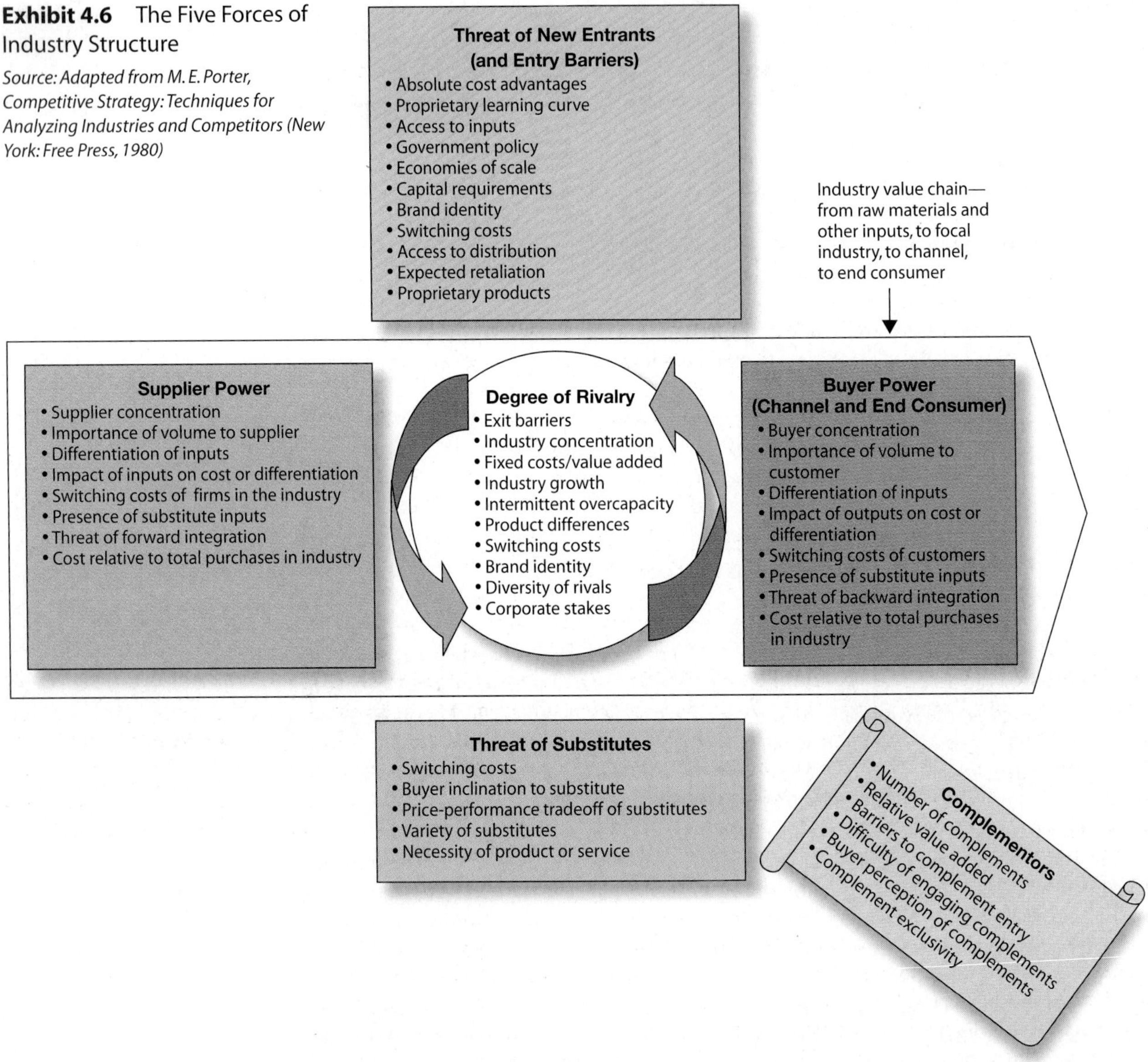

Threat of New Entrants (and Entry Barriers)
• Absolute cost advantages
• Proprietary learning curve
• Access to inputs
• Government policy
• Economies of scale
• Capital requirements
• Brand identity
• Switching costs
• Access to distribution
• Expected retaliation
• Proprietary products

Industry value chain— from raw materials and other inputs, to focal industry, to channel, to end consumer

Supplier Power
• Supplier concentration
• Importance of volume to supplier
• Differentiation of inputs
• Impact of inputs on cost or differentiation
• Switching costs of firms in the industry
• Presence of substitute inputs
• Threat of forward integration
• Cost relative to total purchases in industry

Degree of Rivalry
• Exit barriers
• Industry concentration
• Fixed costs/value added
• Industry growth
• Intermittent overcapacity
• Product differences
• Switching costs
• Brand identity
• Diversity of rivals
• Corporate stakes

Buyer Power (Channel and End Consumer)
• Buyer concentration
• Importance of volume to customer
• Differentiation of inputs
• Impact of outputs on cost or differentiation
• Switching costs of customers
• Presence of substitute inputs
• Threat of backward integration
• Cost relative to total purchases in industry

Threat of Substitutes
• Switching costs
• Buyer inclination to substitute
• Price-performance tradeoff of substitutes
• Variety of substitutes
• Necessity of product or service

Complementors
• Number of complements
• Relative value added
• Barriers to complement entry
• Difficulty of engaging complements
• Buyer perception of complements
• Complement exclusivity

At this stage of the analysis, it is important simply to come to a better sense of the overall nature of rivalry within an industry. The outcome associated with high degrees of rivalry is generally defined in terms of price competition. The most aggressive forms of competition include price wars. When firms are willing to sacrifice their margins through significantly lower prices, it can be assumed that the nature of the rivalry is very intense. This is not to say that competition isn't serious in industries in which price wars are not common. Rather, in those industries firms have found nonprice-based forms of competition. From this definition of rivalry, it is easy to see that higher degrees of rivalry result in lower levels of average industry profitability: As price competition increases, average prices decline, resulting in lower levels of profitability.

What factors tend to increase rivalry? These factors can be categorized into attributes about firms within the industry and attributes about the products or markets themselves. First we will review the attributes of firms that make them likely to compete on prices. When there are numerous competitors, price competition is typically more intense than when there are only a few competitors. Consider the Cola War reviewed in the opening vignette. As intense as that rivalry has been, competition in most periods has focused on nonprice factors. Although advertising to build brand loyalty has been very expensive for Coke and Pepsi, it has been less harmful to profits than intense price wars. More generally, recall that the definition of perfect competition assumes that there are numerous buyers and sellers. In addition, price competition increases when competitors are of relatively equal size and power. Thus, rivalry is affected not only by the number of firms competing but also by how similar those firms are. For instance, the software industry includes many competitors, but Microsoft's size relative to most firms has the effect of marginalizing the threat of price competition.

Another factor that increases the threat of price competition is the degree to which the industry is strategically important to competitors. Recall that many firms are diversified and compete in multiple industries. Price competition tends to be fiercer when the industry is a key business for the major players in that industry.

Characteristics about the products and markets within an industry can also have a strong influence on the degree of price competition. Price competition tends to be fiercer in industries that are growing slowly. When a company's products are difficult to differentiate from those of competitors, they are forced to compete on price. Price competition is reduced when firms are able to create the impression that their products are different from those of competitors. Coke and Pepsi, for example, have spent billions of dollars to build brand equity and loyalty. Likewise, when there are very low costs for buyers to switch from one firm's offerings to another's, then competitors feel compelled to motivate buyer loyalty with aggressive pricing. Conversely, when customers face high switching costs, there is less pressure to keep prices low because a firm's buyers are somewhat locked in. Industries characterized by high fixed costs, such as the airline industry, are also more prone to price wars.

Finally, recall that the concept of perfect competition suggested that if profits dropped too low, some competitors would choose to exit the industry, resulting in profits rising back to normal levels. However, in some industries firms may face high **exit barriers** when it is very costly to leave an industry or market, particularly given the opportunity set possessed by any given incumbent. Firms with high exit barriers are typically forced to compete aggressively. So, exit barriers tend to increase rivalry and price competition. For instance, the exit barriers in the airline industry are very high because air carriers have few opportunities outside of air travel, and those firms that exit the industry are likely to do so only by selling off their business or otherwise dissolving the firm.

Indeed, a firm may remain in an industry due to high exit barriers even when the business is not profitable. As an example, Litton Industries was very successful in building ships for the U.S. Navy in the 1960s. However, when the Vietnam war ended and defense spending plummeted, Litton was so heavily invested in shipbuilding that it could not feasibly exit the industry, particularly given the high specialized investment in now-unattractive shipbuilding facilities. As a result, Litton was forced to stay in the shipbuilding market even though it was unattractive and in decline.

Threat of Entry   Not surprisingly, industries that boast relatively high average profitability attract the attention of firms operating elsewhere that are looking for promising new arenas in which to compete. Paradoxically, industries with consistently high average profitability also tend to be those that are the most difficult to enter. The degree to which new competitors may enter an industry and make rivalry more intense is known as the **threat of new entry**. Conditions that make it difficult to enter an industry are known as **barriers to entry**. Note that perfect competition is characterized by the absence of barriers to entry. Several industry characteristics contribute to such barriers, including strong brands, proprietary technologies, and other bases for product differentiation. Certain technologies, for instance, give their owners cost advantages that new entrants can't readily match or compensate for. In some industries, restricted access to investment capital or distribution channels constitutes barriers. Other industries, such as computer-chip manufacturing, require large incremental

exit barriers Barriers that impose a high cost on the abandonment of a market or product.

threat of new entry Degree to which new competitors can enter an industry and intensify rivalry.

barrier to entry Condition under which it is more difficult to join or compete in an industry.

capital investments in specialized manufacturing facilities. In others, the need for location-based or preferential access to distribution networks can hinder or block entry by new players.

The concept of barriers to entry and their effect on industry structure is illustrated in Exhibit 4.7. Competitors A, B, and C are incumbents in this industry. If D were to enter, the competition in the industry would increase (each incumbent would now have three competitors instead of two). A variety of factors and associated illustrative examples are detailed in the exhibit. Some industries possess more than one of these barriers. But, the more of these barriers that exist, the harder it will be for D to enter.

Let's consider the soft drink industry from our chapter-opening vignette as an illustration. The soft drink industry is shown as an example of access to distribution as a barrier to entry in Exhibit 4.7. But this industry actually has several barriers making it difficult for new entrants to compete nationally with Coke and Pepsi. With such perennially high levels of profit experienced by Coke and Pepsi, one would expect the industry to attract envious firms and entrepreneurs. And to be certain, there have been many new entrants at the margins and in newer segments not yet dominated by Coke and Pepsi. However, there has yet to be a successful entrant to the cola segment that has been able to capture a significant share of the market. A number of brave companies have tried. For instance, Sir Richard Bransen's Virgin Group has tried twice to enter the soft drink market. In 1998, the British billionaire rode into New York's Times Square atop a tank, promising a battle with Coke and Pepsi. Virgin tried extensive hard-edge advertising to gain market awareness. However, it found it nearly impossible to secure premium shelf space in traditional retail outlets. Thus, difficulty gaining access to distribution is a major stumbling block for companies wanting to enter the industry. Branson also faced considerable brand awareness problems; he discovered that the cost and time required to create brand awareness posed another monumental problem. Indeed, the difficulty gaining shelf space and lack of brand awareness were mutually reinforcing weaknesses. Retailers didn't want to allocate much shelf space to a new brand, and Virgin couldn't succeed in making the brand more well-known without shelf space. After pulling out of the U.S. for a period, Virgin is giving it another try in America. The strategy this time is to be a niche player, having secured a deal for distribution through 7-Eleven stores.[10] Thus, entry barriers in the soft drink industry include both extreme levels of brand loyalty and virtual control of prime distribution channels. The only competitive space available for new entrants in the near term appears to be on the periphery of the market. Thus, new entry is most often seen with local brands, private label offerings, and specialty drinks.

Exhibit 4.7 Barriers to Entry

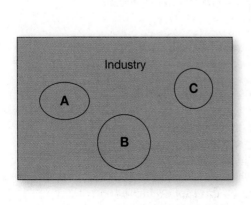

- Scale economics
  —Aerospace
- Scope economies
  —Retailing
- Capital requirements
  —Automobiles
- Switching costs
  —Computer operating systems
- Access to distribution
  —Soft drinks
- Regulation
  —Pharmaceuticals

The greater the degree of difficulty that potential entrants face in accumulating the resources necessary to compete in an industry, the higher the barriers to entry; and high barriers to entry have the effect of reducing potential competition by limiting supply and reducing rivalry. This results in higher prices and higher levels of average profitability than in industries in which there are fewer barriers to entry.

Supplier Power   In transactions between industry participants and firms in supply industries, the relative power of each party affects both the pricing of transactions and the profitability of each industry. The degree to which firms in the supply industry are able to dictate favorable contract terms and thereby extract some of the profit that would otherwise be available to competitors in the focal industry is referred to as **supplier power**. When focal-industry participants have negotiating strength, suppliers have limited bargaining power, and the focal industry acts to reduce supplier industry performance rather than the other way around. Suppliers are powerful when they control such factors as prices, delivery lead times, minimum orders, postpurchase service, and payment terms.

Supplier power arises when the suppliers are relatively concentrated, control a scarce input, or are simply bigger than their customers. In some cases, firms in a focal industry need a unique product or service and have only a few alternative suppliers to which to turn. In these instances, of course, suppliers can demand higher prices.

For instance, from the opening vignette it is easy to see that the soft drink industry is very consolidated and the two major players are very large. They purchase most of their inputs in commodity markets (e.g., sweeteners, food coloring). As a result, suppliers have no leverage over soft drink manufacturers. In contrast, consider the situation from the point of view of the bottlers, who buy soft drink concentrate from manufacturers like Coke and Pepsi and cans and bottles from canning companies. The bottling industry faces significant supplier-power problems because their concentrate suppliers are heavily consolidated. When a firm has a franchise to bottle Coke (or Pepsi), the contract is exclusive, meaning that it has agreed to let Coke or Pepsi be its supplier in perpetuity. By contract, the bottler cannot buy cola products from any other concentrate maker. Thus, soft drink bottlers face a condition of considerable supplier power.

Likewise, the jewelry business requires access to diamonds. Because South Africa's DeBeers controls over 50 percent of the world's diamond supply, it is in the position to force jewelry makers to pay high prices for its diamonds.

Even when an industry is sourcing products that may be considered commodities, such as textiles or wood, suppliers can impose payment terms that implicitly raise the cost of the resource for the focal industry. Such is the case when the supplier industry is more consolidated than the focal industry. Because the furniture industry, for example, is highly fragmented, no single manufacturer has much power when bargaining with the larger wood and fabric suppliers who provide the industry's primary raw materials. Suppliers of wood have many possible firms to which to sell.

Supplier power is also high when firms in the supply industry present a threat of forward integration—that is, if it's possible for them to manufacture finished products rather than just sell components to manufacturers. Coke and Pepsi, for example, could easily integrate forward into bottling instead of just supplying bottlers with concentrate. They have demonstrated this by purchasing bottlers in the past. This potential gives them significant power in negotiating prices with their bottling networks.

Finally, suppliers are powerful when firms in the focal industry face significant switching costs when changing suppliers. For instance, companies purchasing enterprise resource planning (ERP) software have several supplier choices, including SAP, Oracle, and PeopleSoft. However, once a firm purchases from one supplier and incurs the significant implementation costs associated with ERP, it will be very reluctant to switch to another supplier because the costs of doing so are significant. Because of the high costs involved in switching ERP systems, firms switch suppliers less frequently than one would expect in a market with many sellers.

supplier power   Degree to which firms in the supply industry are able to dictate terms to contracts and thereby extract some of the profit that would otherwise be available to competitors in the focal industry.

South Africa's DeBeers controls half of the world's diamonds. As such, it wields a great deal of buyer and supplier power and controls the prices that it both pays and charges for diamonds.

In summary, in transactions between industry participants and firms in supply industries, the relative power of each party affects both the pricing and profitability of each industry. When focal-industry participants have negotiating strength, suppliers have limited bargaining power, and the focal industry acts to reduce the supplier-industry performance rather than the other way around.

Buyer Power

buyer power Degree to which firms in the buying industry are able to dictate terms on purchase agreements that extract some of the profit that would otherwise go to competitors in the focal industry.

The mirror image of supplier power, **buyer power** is the degree to which firms in the buyers' industry are able to dictate favorable terms on purchase agreements that extract some of the profit that would otherwise be available to competitors in the focal industry. When firms in the focal industry sell to their customers (i.e., buyers), those transactions are subject to the same bargaining forces just reviewed for supplier power. Buyers, for example, whether in a business-to-business or business-to-consumer relationship, compete with sellers by trying to force prices down.

Several factors lead to buyers having high degrees of relative power over their suppliers. A buyer group has greater power in the exchange relationship with its suppliers when the buyers are prestigious and when their purchases represent a significant portion of the sellers' sales. By the same token, if a product has little value for the buyer group, buyers are more powerful negotiating with firms in the industry. A buyer group is also powerful when it has numerous choices, such as when the products and prices of multiple competitors are easy to compare. Tire makers, for instance, have little power over carmakers because their product is standardized and there are many competitors in the industry. If a tire maker tried to raise prices, large automobile manufacturers would turn to one of several other firms that could fill their needs. Conversely, when buyers have few alternatives, their power is minimal, and industry prices increase, resulting in higher-than-average industry profitability.

Consider the extreme case of the Green Bay Packers of the National Football League. The Packers have maintained a waiting list for season tickets for the past 45 years; the average wait is 30 years. Because there are few other entertainment alternatives in Green Bay, Wisconsin, there is essentially one seller and many buyers for the opportunity for professional sports entertainment. The team is certainly under no pressure to discount prices.[11]

Information also provides buyers with power, particularly when they have choices, when the products are relatively inexpensive, or when products are not heavily regulated. New-car buyers, for example, are relatively powerful not only because there are numerous makes and models in every category, but because they can now use the Internet to compare products and prices online. In contrast, dealers don't have a corresponding advantage when negotiating with carmakers because operating agreements require them to sell certain manufacturers' products.

Finally, buyers are powerful to the extent that they pose a threat of backward integration. Large brewers, for instance, could conceivably make their own beer cans (in fact, some do). The implicit threat that these buyers of aluminum cans could move backward into a supplier's industry naturally diminishes the supplier's price-setting power.

What About Retail Consumers? Let's make a final—and critical—point about the role of buyer power in any definition of an industry. Note that the industry is the unit that we're analyzing: The focal point of our assessment of rivalry in an industry is the industry segment that we've chosen to analyze. Consequently, when we talk about buyers, we don't mean end retail consumers (unless, of course, we're analyzing a retail-market segment—grocery stores, new-car dealers, department stores, etc.). Japan's Matsushita Electric Industrial, for example, markets many well-known electronics brands, including Panasonic, Quasar, and JVC. When Matsushita markets Panasonic TVs, its targeted customers are not household consumers but, rather, large retail chains and electronics wholesalers. Certainly, retail consumers are important, but they don't negotiate directly with manufacturers, and they don't wield any direct power in nonretail segments. Consumers affect industry profits indirectly when they exercise power as the last link in an industry value chain. An analysis of Panasonic's industry segment would examine the relative power of Matsushita and its rivals in negotiating with retailers, such as Best Buy and Circuit City, who carry their products.

Threat of Substitutes Sometimes products in other industries can satisfy the same demand as the products of the focal industry (see Exhibit 4.8). The degree to which this is the case is known as the **threat of substitutes**. Recall, for example, our earlier discussion of bottled water and soft drinks. These two different types of products may be substituted for one another in satisfying the demand of some customers. If we defined Coke and Pepsi's industry as soft drinks, then bottled water would be a substitute to which we'd have to pay attention. Consider the case of the movie rental business. Blockbuster faces direct competition from Hollywood Video, Movie Gallery, Netflix, and other regional and local chains. What are substitutes for DVD and video rental services? Customers' options seem to be increasing. Cable and satellite TV would seem to be a separate industry from movie rentals. However, movie channels available through these outlets are clear substitutes for movie rentals. And, more recently, the availability of on-demand movie streaming through cable and satellite providers seems to provide an even closer substitute product. Thus, the prices that Blockbuster and other movie rental businesses can charge is held in check to some extent by the availability of these viable substitutes.

Even when market segments aren't as closely related as cable and satellite TV are to the movie rental industry, products may still be potential substitutes. In the broadest sense, a *substitute* is any product that satisfies a common need or desire. The desire for leisure, for instance, can be satisfied with both books and travel. Narrowing the classification scheme, consider substitute products between segments in the travel industry. At Southwest Airlines, for example, the primary competition for many shorter flights comes not from other airlines but, rather, from competitors in the automobile- and bus-transportation segments. Thus, within certain geographic limitations, automobiles and bus service are substitutes for airline travel.

It should be clear by now that the prevalence of viable substitute products from other industries places pressures on the prices that can be charged in the focal industry. When there are no viable substitutes, there is less pressure on price. Consequently, average industry profits tend to be lower when clear substitutes are available.

The Impact of Complementors As we noted at the beginning of this discussion, the five forces that we've just described comprise a model of industry structure proposed by

> **threat of substitutes** Degree to which products of one industry can satisfy the same demand as those of another.

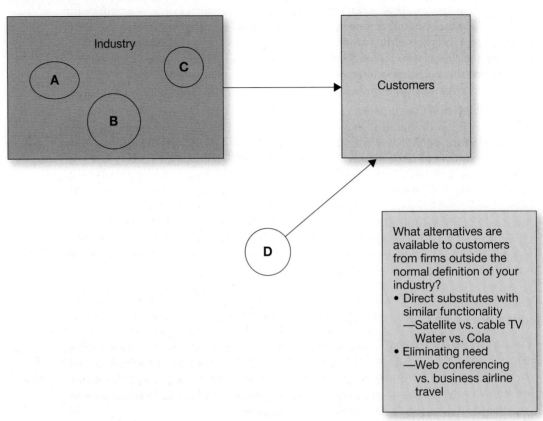

Exhibit 4.8 Threat of Substitutes

Michael Porter. When these forces are strong, industry profitability tends to be reduced. More recently, some researchers have argued that the players outlined in the five-forces model do not always compete exclusively in zero-sum games. Sometimes these players work together to create value jointly rather than competing to divide the market. **Complementors** are players who provide complementary rather than competing products and services.[12]

Factors affecting the importance of complementors in a given industry are shown in Exhibit 4.6. Firms in the music and electronics industries, for example, sell products that must be used together—such as Ipods, headphones, and music. Each benefits from the other's presence. Likewise, when people buy hot dogs, an increase in sales of buns, condiments, and beverages is likely. These three products are marketed by complementary industry segments (which is why grocers can sell buns below cost to stimulate sales of higher-margin hot dogs). Sometimes firms in the same industry or suppliers and buyers simultaneously play the role of complementors. For instance, United and Delta compete fiercely in trying to attract customers to fill their seats. However, when upgrading their fleets to a newer plane, both airlines are probably better off when they jointly order a new model from Boeing or Airbus. Because both are in the market for new planes at the same time, aircraft manufacturers are able to achieve greater economies of scale with larger orders, thereby lowering the cost of new planes.

This example helps introduce a more formal definition of *complementor:* A complementor is any factor that makes it more attractive for suppliers to supply an industry on favorable terms or that makes it more attractive for buyers to purchase products or services from an industry at prices higher than it would pay absent the complementor. However, even though a firm or industry segment fulfills a complementor role, it may still compete with firms in the focal industry. A firm or industry segment may simultaneously play the roles of complementor and competitor (as in the Delta/United example). In addition, a complementor that results in increased focal-industry sales will not necessarily share equally in the increased bounty. These relationships still have elements of bargaining power akin to supplier and buyer relationships; one party to a complementor relationship may receive more of the benefit than the other even though both are better off.

Customers, then, are likely to put a higher value on the products of one industry segment when they already have or have access to complementary products from another segment.[13] The value of computer peripherals obviously increases as the number of personal computers increases. Likewise, the value of a commercial real estate development is enhanced if there are neighboring amenities valued by business tenants, such as restaurants, entertainment venues, and transportation facilities. More new cars are sold when affordable financing is easier to get or dealers offer extended service warranties. Thus, financing and warranty arrangements can be regarded as complementors to the retail new-car market.

Finally, note one important difference between complementors and the other five forces in this model of industry analysis: Whereas the five forces typically work to *decrease* industry profitability, the presence of strong complementors may *increase* profits by increasing demand for an industry's products.

Using the Industry-Structure Model An understanding of the five industry forces and complementors can help managers evaluate the general attractiveness of an industry as well as the specific opportunities and threats facing firms in their focal segment. An industry is most attractive—that is, has the highest profit potential—when attractive complementors create positive externalities and when the effects of the other five forces are minimal. The pressure on operating margins will be significantly lower than in industries in which suppliers or buyers exercise high levels of power, in which entry barriers are low, and in which abundant substitute products are available.

How does industry analysis affect strategy formulation? First, a good industry analysis will enable an executive to answer a few basic questions with much greater certainty than could be done before the analysis. Some of these questions include the following: Does the firm's current strategy fit with current industry conditions—specifically, the industry conditions relevant to the firm's chosen industry arenas? What changes in the industry may result in misalignment? Which elements of the firm's strategy will need to be altered to exploit future industry conditions? Second, a high quality strategy will be one that helps the firm adapt to the five forces so that they are more in the favor of the firm. Specifically, a successful strategy will help minimize buyer power, offset supplier power, avoid excessive rivalry, raise the barriers to entry, and reduce the threat of substitution. A firm might minimize buyer power by attempting to build customer loyalty through specific differentiators. Supplier power can be offset by assuring that there are multiple sources of key inputs. Excessive rivalry can be avoided by attempting to grow in emerging segments rather than attacking competitors in mature markets. Barriers to entry might be built by making preemptive investments that reduce the incentives for new entrants. Finally, the threat of substitutes can be reduced by understanding the benefits that substitutes offer and then incorporating those in your own products or services.

When using the five-forces model to formulate strategy, remember that these forces are not static. The actions of various industry players keep industry conditions in an almost constant state of flux. Consequently, unattractive industry structure isn't necessarily an omen that profitability is destined to be marginal. Wise strategists use information gleaned from the study of industry structure to formulate strategies for dealing with threats highlighted by industry analysis.

Remember, too, that this type of analysis views industry forces from an overall industry perspective and not from that of any particular firm. The industry-wide effect of these forces will determine whether an industry is attractive or not. We walk through the use of Porter's five-forces analysis in the box entitled "How Would *You* Do That? 4.1."

How Would
YOU DO THAT? 4.1

A Five-Forces—Plus Complementors—Analysis of the U.S. Airline Industry[14]

Let's apply the five-forces model to the U.S. airline industry to illustrate how it is used in practice. Examination of data maintained by the U.S. Department of Transportation reveals that the Department categorizes the airline industry into four groups: international, national, regional, and cargo. Let's focus on national airlines (with sales of at least $1 billion). This will include all U.S. international airlines because they are also large, national airlines.

To perform an industry analysis using the Porter model, it is often useful to translate the concepts into quantitative data. One way to do this is to assign points to each sub-factor of the 5 forces. For illustrative purposes, we will use a scale of 1–5. If the particular force is strong, meaning the threat to firms in the industry is very high on account of that particular sub-factor, we will assign it 5 points. If the particular sub-factor poses no threat to firms in the industry, we will set it equal to 0. Points in between can be used for various gradations.) After identifying each relevant sub-factor for a particular force, you will then take the *average* score for sub-factors associated with that force. So, for illustrative purposes, let's assume we're analyzing the threat of substitutes for an industry. Refer to Exhibit 4.6 and rate this industry on the five sub-factors identified on the exhibit.

A word of caution: The validity of your analysis is only as good as (1) your identification of sub-factors associated with each particular force and (2) your subjective evaluation of each sub-factor. Exhibit 4.6 is intended to be a guide for determining these sub-factors, but is not necessarily an exhaustive list (threats could be industry-specific in many cases).

RIVALRY

The first step is to identify the key players in the national passenger-airline market. Who are the rivals? You could turn to numerous available data sources to identify the key players. Using hoovers.com, we identify the top three competitors as United, American, and Delta; other competitors include AirTran, Alaska Air, America West, Continental Airlines, Hawaiian Air, JetBlue, Northwest Airlines, Southwest Airlines, and US Airways. How competitive is this industry? Is competition based on price or nonprice competition? It would not take a lot of research to discover that this is a highly competitive industry. Most airlines make extremely low returns; indeed, many are currently losing money. Let's assume that, after studying the industry data, you evaluate the sub-factors as outlined below. A score of 3.6 leads you to determine that this industry has an above average level

of rivalry, which will hurt margins for most players.

Exit barriers:	4
Industry concentration:	3
Fixed costs:	5
Industry growth:	4
Overcapacity:	4
Product differences:	3
Switching costs:	3
Brand identity:	2
Diversity of rivals:	4
Corporate stakes:	3
Average:	3.6

POWER OF SUPPLIERS

Who are the suppliers to national airlines? Most, such as caterers, airports, airplane manufacturers, and security firms, are oligopolies, meaning that the airlines are in a less advantageous position. Key suppliers include makers of aircraft; two companies, Boeing and Airbus, dominate that market and are able to garner significant profits at the airlines' expense by virtue of their specialized positions and government subsidies. The other key supply for airlines is fuel. Due to oil shortages, the price of fuel is currently proving a very problematic issue for airlines. However, this is not a function of supplier power but, rather, conditions in the oil market.

After studying the industry data, you evaluate the sub-factors as outlined below. A score of 2.4 indicates that this force is relatively neutral. Airlines and their suppliers have points of bargaining power that about cancels out the other.

Supplier concentration:	5
Importance of volume:	1
Input differentiation:	3
Input effect on company differentiation:	1
Switching costs of firms in industry:	2
Presence of substitute inputs:	5
Threat of forward integration:	1
Cost relative to total purchases in supplier industry:	1
Average:	2.4

POWER OF BUYERS

To whom do national airlines sell their services? Buyers can be categorized into three primary groups: business travelers, leisure travelers, and buyers of large blocks of seats known as consolidators, who buy excess seat inventory at large discounts. What bargaining power do these customers have? Switching costs are very low, though airlines have increased them somewhat through frequent flier programs. Buyers are price sensitive, but they have very little individual buyer power.

Again, you study the industry data and you evaluate the sub-factors as outlined below. A score of 2.5 indicates that this force is neutral. Each party (firms in your industry and customers) has points of bargaining power that about cancels out the other.

Buyer concentration:	1
Importance of volume:	1
Differentiation in airline industry:	3
Switching costs of customers:	4
Presence of substitute inputs:	1
Threat of backward integration:	1
Price sensitivity:	4
Buyer information:	4
Average:	2.5

THREAT OF SUBSTITUTES

What is the likelihood that airline customers will use alternative means of transportation? When it comes to business travelers, this would seem minimal. However, communication technology has proven to be a viable substitute for some forms of business travel. For leisure travelers, the threat of substitutes is mainly for shorter flights. Thus, alternatives such as auto and bus transportation are more viable substitutes for regional airlines and national airlines that specialize in shorter flights (e.g., Southwest).

After studying the industry data and evaluating the sub-factors, you determine the ratings outlined below. A score of 1.8 indicates that this force is relatively in the industry's favor—substitutes exist, but they don't seem to be a major threat.

Switching costs:	4
Buyer inclination to substitute:	1
Price-performance tradeoff of substitute:	2
Variety of substitutes:	1
Necessity of product or service:	2
Average:	1.8

THREAT OF NEW ENTRANTS

The capital intensity of the airline industry appears to pose an entry barrier. However, JetBlue, AirTran, and other entrants have proven that financing is available when there is a convincing business plan and when economic conditions are conducive to the business model proposed. Brand name and frequent flier plans also seem to be deterrents to entry. However, JetBlue's success demonstrates that customers are willing to switch airlines if the price is right.

On balance, in this analysis you rate the threat of new entry as only moderate. The structural factors make it unlikely the industry will attract many profitable new entrants.

Average profitability of incumbents:	1
Incumbents have a cost advantage:	5
Learning curve advantage for incumbents:	3
Access to inputs:	5
Government policy (regulation):	2
Economies of scale:	3
Capital requirements:	2
Brand identity:	2
Switching costs:	3
Access to distribution (gates):	2
Expected retaliation:	1
Proprietary products:	5
Average:	2.8

THE ROLE OF COMPLEMENTORS

Your analysis of complementors suggests that there are complementors such as credit cards and rental cars, that they are unlikely to become direct competitors, but that it is hard to tie up these complementors in exclusive relationships that competitors can't duplicate with the same or comparable complementor.

Number of complementors:	2
Relative value added:	3
Barriers to complement entry:	2
Difficulty of engaging complements:	1
Buyer perception of complements:	2
Complement exclusivity:	5
Average:	2.5

In summary, it appears that supplier power, buyer power, and substitutes do not pose ominous threats to the airline industry. Complementors, while present, do not make the industry overly attractive. The only two forces that seem to account for the poor performance of the industry are moderately low entry barriers and intense competitive rivalry.

COMPETITOR ANALYSIS

The industry analysis that we've discussed so far has focused on the broad industry definition. Another purpose of an industry analysis is to develop a clear understanding of who the firm's competitors are and what their behaviors are likely to be in the future in its chosen industry arena or arenas. Consequently, after completing a five-forces analysis, it is critical to investigate the strategies and behaviors of the firm's competitors. That is, after understanding the five forces, we want to dive deeply into the study of the firm's rivals. There are many ways you might study a firm's rivals. We present a model that can be used to map out who the competitors are and the strategies they're pursuing. This type of competitor analysis will then be used when turning to the formulation of your firm's strategy, which will be discussed in detail in Chapters 5 and 6. This tool, explored in "How Would *You* Do That? 4.2," is known as the *value curve* and it offers an intuitive way to map competitors' strategies using the industry KSFs discussed earlier in the chapter.

Mapping Competitors

Mapping competitors within an industry starts by identifying who the competitors are. This is usually the easiest step. Firms generally know who they compete against for sales. It is perhaps more problematic when the firm only currently competes in a niche market and doesn't encounter all the competitors with regularity. Nevertheless, there are numerous data sources that will list the companies in specific industries. Once identifying the primary competitors, the next step is to document how these firms go about competing within the industry. What you will generally find is that specific types of competitors emerge—groups of competitors will follow similar strategies along the KSFs, and the various groups will be distinct in how they go about doing this.

The fact that we can segment market competitors into their central locations in the business landscape doesn't mean, of course, that firms with similar strategies only compete amongst themselves. However, firms with relatively similar strategies are more likely to be mutual threats than are groups with significantly different characteristics. For instance, Trek, which manufactures high-quality performance bicycles that are sold through independent dealers, faces more competition from Specialized than it does from Huffy, which makes mass market bikes with lower-end components that are sold through mass merchandisers like Wal-Mart and Target. However, for its lower-end models, Trek does experience some competition with Schwinn, who sells its bikes both in mass merchants and independent bicycle dealers. Similarly, luxury hotel chains face a greater threat from high-quality business hotels than from the economy hotel market.

We analyze competitors' strategies to get a more detailed look at the competitive environment in which firms operate. Through such an analysis as the value curve, we can more readily identify a firm's closest competitors (something that most decision makers can usually do intuitively). More importantly, however, we can also better identify any probable *future competition* that we might otherwise ignore or underestimate. Likewise, analyzing competitors like this also helps us identify growth opportunities because it makes us focus on potential competitive positions that are compatible with a firm's unique set of resources and capabilities.

THE VALUE CURVE

value curve A graphical depiction of how a firm and major groups of its competitors are competing across its industry's factors of completion.

Now that we have described why firms need to have a deep understanding of their competitors, we'll describe the **value curve**, a convenient tool to help managers visualize their competitive landscape. An intuitive way to do this is to use the key success factors discussed earlier in this chapter and use a rating system to compare the various competitors on how they score on these dimensions. In "How Would *You* Do That? 4.2," we walk you through this exercise using the U.S. wine industry. The tool's purpose is to visually plot how major groups of firms compete. This tends to reveal the underlying assumptions firms make about the market and customers. The first step is to determine the existing key success factors as perceived by incumbents. List these factors along the horizontal axis. The vertical axis is used to rate the level of delivery of the major groups of firms. For instance, if room comfort were one of the key success factors that you identified when evaluating the hotel industry, then you would rate establishments like Hyatt and Marriott much higher than hotels like Motel 6 and Best Western. The scale you use is not as important as your judgment in segregating different levels of products and services along the key success factors. For illustrative purposes, we use a scale of 1–5. Generally, you can plot firms by the central tendency of clusters of firms following similar strategies. We call these clusters **strategic groups.**

After ranking the firms or groups on each dimension, connect the points for each firm or group. Connecting the points, which is drawing the value curve for that respective company or group, reveals a visual representation of the various ways rivals compete in the industry. For instance, if you were mapping the airline industry, even without plotting them you would assume that most of the major airlines would have very similar value curves and, therefore, constitute one strategic group. Plotting Southwest Airlines, as well as Southwest's imitators, such as JetBlue or Air Tran (or Ryanair in Europe), would probably reveal a strikingly different value curve. It is often convenient to consolidate similar competitors into a single value curve. The value curves in the industry visually represent the underlying logic incumbents use in positioning their products. Being able to visualize how competitors perform along these differentiators helps reveal industry assumptions. Understanding how competitors compete and surmising their assumptions are essential steps in predicting their future behaviors.

Predicting Competitors' Behaviors After identifying the firm's closest rivals, it is important to gain a better understanding of their likely future behaviors. The specific rivals that are most pertinent to the analysis are those in the firm's same strategic group, those likely to move into the group, and those operating in groups that the firm may enter in the future. In the opening vignette on the Cola War, it is clear that Coke and Pepsi care deeply about what the other is doing. Neither wants to be caught off guard by a move the other may make in the future. Likewise, as new strategic groups have emerged in the beverage industry, such as in the flavored ice teas or premium sodas, they have had to pay more attention to these upstarts.

Several goals can be achieved by closely analyzing the firm's closest competitors. For instance, you may gain a better understanding of the competitors' future strategies. Similarly, you may gain a better appreciation for how competitors will respond to your strategic initiatives. Finally, you may also conclude that your firm's actions may influence competitors' behaviors, and some of these reactions may be to your benefit (or detriment). Although the firm's strategy should not be *determined* by competitors' behaviors, it should be *influenced* by what you think your competitors' behaviors are likely to be.

Porter suggests a four-step approach for making predictions about competitors. The first step in predicting the behaviors of competitors is to understand their objectives. These objectives are often surprisingly easy to determine if the companies are publicly-held firms, because their objectives are usually communicated regularly to shareholders through disclosure documents. The second step is to determine the competitors' current strategies. If you have already completed a strategic-group map, you probably have a good idea of those strategies. Further insight can be gained by using the strategy diamond and using public documents to see what competitors are doing in terms of arenas, vehicles, differentiators, staging, and economic logic. The third step is a bit more difficult, but it is critical to understanding the competitors' future behaviors: What assumptions does each competitor hold about the industry and about itself? People's behaviors are strongly influenced by the assumptions they make about themselves and the world. Again, communications between top executives and shareholders often hold insights into what these assumptions may be. Finally, the competitors' future behaviors will likely be related to the resources and capabilities they possess. What are the competitors' key strengths and weaknesses?

strategic group Subset of firms which, because of similar strategies, resources, and capabilities, compete against each other more intensely than with other firms in an industry.

Evaluating the Value Curve in the Wine Industry[15]

et's uncork an example of the value curve in action. With over $20 billion in annual revenues, the U.S. market is the largest contiguous wine market in the world. However, the market is intensely competitive, and California wines command two-thirds of all U.S. wine sales. This intense competition is further fueled by the fact that wines are produced and imported from almost every continent on the planet, and new entrants increasingly sell their wines at very low prices.

The threat of new entrants to the wine industry is very high; suppliers (wine-grape growers) are powerful; wineries are concentrated (C8 is 75 percent); sales channels are powerful because of consolidation; consumers are powerful because of the breadth of choices; and substitutes (any beverage) are many. Moreover, complements, such as the *Wine Spectator* and wine experts such as Robert Parker, are also powerful, because they rank wines based on taste and price, potentially swaying

Exhibit 4.9 A Value Curve for the U.S. Wine Industry

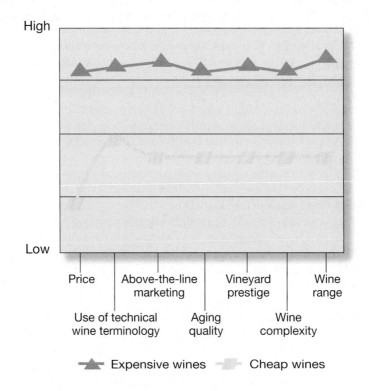

channel and consumer purchases. These factors suggest that the industry is not very attractive to new entrants. In fact, an old saying in the wine industry is that if you want to make $5 million, you need to start with $40 million!

So what does this mean with regard to the value curve and dynamic strategy? If we map the wine industry based on the characteristics of the dominant players and those factors considered essential to success, we would produce a map similar to the one in Exhibit 4.9. Notice that Exhibit 4.9 captures the dominant strategic groups—wineries competing in the budget or high-price segments. A new entrant could fight it out in the already hypercompetitive and overcapacity high-price or budget wine segments, or it could try to have a presence in both segments and use the resulting scale to its advantage.

You can use the value curve to see how incumbents are competing, map the strategic groups in an industry, and suggest how a new entrant might reconfigure the way it defines being a winery. In Chapter 6 you will learn how to use the value curve tool to craft a truly revolutionary strategy, and see such application in action by a wine company known as [yellow tail]®.

After addressing these four primary questions, you are in a position to make reasonable predictions about what your competitors are likely to do in the future. For instance, are they about to change their strategy? You may also gain insights into their likely reaction to any initiatives you are pondering.

Dynamic Characteristics of the External Context

The various models and analytical tools that we've discussed so far can provide an excellent snapshot of a firm's external context. In some industries, such a snapshot view gives a fairly accurate portrayal of the business landscape in the foreseeable future. In other cases, however, a snapshot captures little more than a first impression: The essential features of many industries are often undergoing gradual or rapid change. What's worse, snapshot views may give an overblown picture of a firm's competitive advantage: All we see may be a firm that's staked out a nice position in an attractive market, reaps enormous profits, and regularly makes large deposits in the bank. But if you reflect on the opening story of Coke and Pepsi, you know that competitors do not typically stand still and that overconfidence in the strength of one's competitive position is often a prelude to organizational decline.

Research increasingly shows that the durability of competitive advantages varies by industry or market.[16] For instance, the structural characteristics of some industries, such as utilities, will shift very little in the absence of significant regulatory changes. Other industries or markets may be undergoing gradual changes that may evolve into the kind of dramatic changes that we described in our story about Sears and Wal-Mart, where the change in market structure was dramatic but evolved over a long period of time. This is typically the case in the consumer products industry. As a rule, the relatively static analysis afforded by the five-forces model, plus the complementors dimension, applies best to industries such as these.

Industries in a third category, however, may be undergoing substantial change, whether because of the scale and scope of environmental changes, the rapid pace of such changes, or a combination of both. Dramatic change, for instance, can result from deregulation, which may bring about significant changes in key success factors and completely redesign the competitive playing field. Deregulation in the airline industry gave rise to discount carriers such as Southwest Airlines and JetBlue. Once a segment of niche players, the discount segment now poses a serious threat to the traditional hub-and-spoke segment dominated by American and United Airlines.

Changes in technology can dramatically change the business landscape and alter the nature of competitive advantage within an industry. In such cases, a relatively stable industry can be thrown into disarray until a new equilibrium is reached. Up until the mid-1980s, for example, the pineapple industry was relatively sleepy and fragmented. Then, Fresh Del Monte (a Cayman Island company separate from the U.S. Del Monte) introduced a new variety developed by scientists at the Pineapple Research Institute. This "Extra Sweet Gold" pineapple has a bright gold color, rather than the pale yellow of the traditional pineapple; it is sweeter, less acidic, and highly resistant to parasites and rotting. Early introductions into the U.S. market were limited to a few cities on the East Coast. The pineapple was so well received that Fresh Del Monte quickly raised prices and exported the pineapple to all major U.S. markets. Despite higher prices, the Extra Sweet Gold captured 70 percent of the market.

What propelled Fresh Del Monte to the top of the market and allowed it to maintain the lion's share of what one would normally consider to be a commodity market? Fresh Del Monte successfully exploited a technological development that other firms ignored. Once it proved successful, Fresh Del Monte claimed proprietary rights to this particular strain of pineapple and was able to forestall other producers from planting the same variety. Eventually, the courts ruled that Fresh Del Monte did not have exclusive legal rights to this strain of pineapple, and companies such as Chiquita and Dole are now converting much of their production to this particular strain. Once again, dominance in the pineapple industry is up for grabs.

In this part of the chapter, we'll describe some tools for analyzing industries and formulating strategy in a dynamic context. We start by reviewing the most fundamental reason why some industries are more dynamic than others—the fact that the five forces or essential complementors are changing, not static. We then discuss two macro-level drivers of industry change: the *industry life cycle* and *discontinuities*. Although globalization itself is a profoundly important driver of change, as you read earlier in the chapter, it often goes hand-in-hand with the changes that accompany industry evolution and technological discontinuities.

DRIVERS OF CHANGE: MAKING THE FIVE-FORCES MODEL DYNAMIC

While learning to apply the various facets of industry analysis, you probably observed that some of your conclusions about industry structure would have to be modified if a given factor, such as the competitive behavior of one or more firms, altered any one of the five forces. One way to focus on the dynamic nature of the external context is to stop thinking of your analysis in terms of an industry snapshot and start thinking of it in terms of a "storybook" that shows how an industry structure is changing or may change. Any of the five forces that we have described so far can change significantly, and when that happens, the industry's structure and balance of power will probably be upset. Again, remember that some industries are dynamic simply because of the *rapid pace* of change. Think about the almost daily releases of new products in such markets as cell phone handsets, laser printers, and digital cameras.

Exhibit 4.10 lists a few potential sources of change and their effects on industry structure and profitability. Entry barriers, for instance, may be weakened, perhaps because of changes in technology.[17] The industry may be in its early stages, with many firms jockeying for position, many of whom will probably go out of business or be acquired as the industry matures. As the industry becomes more dynamic, such factors as substitutes and complementors may become more important. Finally, as an industry matures, buyers become more knowledgeable about product features and costs. We'll start our discussion of industry-change drivers by examining how industries often evolve over time.

Industry Life Cycle   Where do new industries come from? A new industry emerges when entirely new products are developed that satisfy customer demands in ways that existing products and technologies could not. The automobile industry emerged after Karl Benz developed an automobile powered by an Otto gasoline engine in 1885 and granted a patent in the following year.[18] Prior to that time, personal transportation was largely accomplished by means of horse and carriage, or trains for longer trips. Much like living organisms, industries evolve over time. The **industry life cycle** is a model that describes this evolution from inception through to its current state and possible future states. You have probably learned of a similar concept in your studies of marketing relating to the product life cycle. It so happens that competitive dynamics often follow a similar evolution at the industry level—from the point at which an industry emerges to the point at which it matures or perhaps even stagnates. The industry life cycle is a powerful driver of industry dynamics because it's a phenomenon characterized by change. Exhibit 4.11 illustrates the basic trajectory of the industry life cycle as well as numerous examples of industries at different stages of evolution.[19]

industry life cycle   Pattern of evolution followed by an industry inception to current and future states.

Evolution and Commoditization   One common result of this evolution is that an industry tends to become characterized by price competition, partly because many or most of its incumbents acquire similar resources and capabilities and so offer fairly similar products.

Exhibit 4.10 Dynamics of Industry Structure

Industry Rivalry
- *Increase in industry growth* ➔ Reduced rivalry and less pressure on prices
- *Globalization of industry* ➔ Increased rivalry as new foreign players enter the market, pressure for scale economies leading to consolidation, and market domination by fewer but larger competitors
- *Change in mix between fixed and variable costs* ➔ Shift to greater fixed costs creating more pressure to maintain sales levels and leading to greater propensity to compete on price

Threat of New Entrants
- *Decline in scale necessary to compete effectively* ➔ Increased rivalry because it's easier for start-ups to enter and effectively compete
- *Increases in customer heterogeneity* ➔ Easier entry because some customer segments are likely to be underserved plus increased ability to protect those segments that the firm serves well
- *Increased customer concentration* ➔ Reduces threat of new entry, leading to less pressure to compete on price

Bargaining Power of Suppliers
- *Increasing concentration of firms in supply industries* ➔ Greater supplier power and likelihood of reduced profitability in focal industry
- *Forward-integration by some key suppliers* ➔ Loss of power in focal industry because of reduction in number of viable suppliers
- *Emergence of substitute inputs that are good enough to satisfy basic needs* ➔ Reduction of supplier power and increased profits for focal industry

Bargaining Power of Buyers
- *Increased fragmentation of buyers' industry* ➔ Reduction in buyer power as the number of potential buyers increases and size of buyer industry declines relative to size of focal industry
- *Improvement in buyer information* ➔ Increased buyer power because of ability to compare
- *Emergence of new distribution channels* ➔ Reduction in buyer power because focal industry has more options

Threat of Substitutes
- *Emergence of a new substitute* ➔ Reduced ability to maintain high prices due to more buyer alternatives
- *Decline in the relative price performance of a substitute* ➔ Reduction in the threat of substitutes and pressure to maintain lower prices

Role of Complementors
- *Emergence of new complementors* ➔ Increased demand and less pressure on prices in focal industry
- *Higher barriers to entry in complementor industry* ➔ Greater complementor leverage and ability to profit from complementary relationship
- *Lower barriers to entry in complementor industry* ➔ Reduction in leverage of individual complementors leading to net increase of possible firms who can serve as complementors and increased demand

---

Source: Adapted from M. E. Porter, Competitive Strategy: Techniques for Analyzing Industries and Competitors (New York: Free Press, 1980)

commoditization Process during industry evolution by which sales eventually come to depend less on unique product features and more on price.

This trend is called **commoditization**—the process by which sales eventually come to depend less on unique product features and more on price.[20] Commoditization even affects technologically sophisticated products. Take the cell phone industry for example. Although handset sales are booming thanks to the addition of cameras, music players, and fancy software, cell phone voice services are fast becoming a basic commodity distinguished primarily by price. It is a pattern that other industries, from airlines to personal computers, have followed in recent decades as onetime technological breakthroughs became widely available.

Some cell phone service providers are introducing new services, such as picture messaging and video downloads, but the revenue they generate is minuscule alongside the

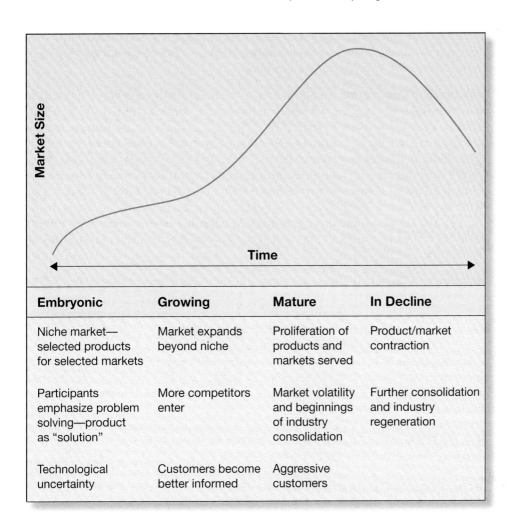

Exhibit 4.11 Industry Life Cycle Curve

Embryonic	Growing	Mature	In Decline
Niche market—selected products for selected markets	Market expands beyond niche	Proliferation of products and markets served	Product/market contraction
Participants emphasize problem solving—product as "solution"	More competitors enter	Market volatility and beginnings of industry consolidation	Further consolidation and industry regeneration
Technological uncertainty	Customers become better informed	Aggressive customers	

vast sums spent on voice calls, and their growth is expected to be slow. In Europe, there has been an influx of so-called no-frills service providers that basically use a model similar to that of low cost airlines. Even the U.S. market, although still growing, has already become more commoditized, with prices plunging and companies locked in fierce competition for new customers. A marked slowdown in revenue growth could exacerbate the long-running price war in the U.S., where competition has pushed the average per-minute cost of a call down more than 65 percent in the past four years, according to Yankee Group, a consulting firm.[21] One effect of the slowdown is increasing globalization and consolidation in the cell phone industry, as some of Europe's big service providers look for revenue growth by expanding outside their home markets. Demand for cell phone services is growing much faster than analysts had expected in Southeast Asia, Africa, Latin America, and other emerging markets, which tend to be dominated by a couple of local players.

Evolution and Reinvigoration As some industries mature, however, certain segments may emerge to reinvigorate them, sometimes even restoring their status as growth industries (as a matter of fact, it's hard to imagine any industry that doesn't have at least one growth segment). The bicycle industry, for example, has existed for more than 200 years, and during that time, technological advances have periodically increased the product's popularity and given rise to growth segments in an otherwise stagnant industry. In the 1960s, for instance, the emergence of children's bike designs and the 10-speed accelerated sales. More recently, the mountain bike has not only spurred sales growth but has spawned many new specialized bike manufacturing companies.

Evolution and Information Although most of the factors involved in the evolution of an industry are fairly obvious, the role of information and customer learning has only recently begun to attract the attention of researchers.[22] We're beginning to see, for example, that the effects of learning, information, and competition can conspire to enable newer entrants to replace industry leaders, especially in the later stages of industry-wide change. The emergence of computer retailer Dell is an excellent example. Originally, because Dell targeted sophisticated buyers—buyers who were technologically savvy and who needed little education on the uses of a personal computer—it was able to invest less money in pre- and postsales activities. Dell could sell leading-edge PCs at a relatively low price and still make a profit, and as the market matured and price competition became more intense, Dell was able to leapfrog IBM and other larger companies.

Evolution and Tactics The effect of customer learning and information often isn't apparent until later in the life cycle. In the early stages, because there's usually a lack of knowledge and information about new products, customers tend to look to industry incumbents not only as a source of education but as a form of insurance in the way of more extensive product support. During the transition from introduction to growth, as once-new products establish themselves and become accepted, incumbents often add extra services, such as shipping, training, or extended warrantees at little or no cost in order to retain sales momentum through the growth phase. Taken together, these factors usually mean higher *average* margins in the early stages of growth because high and increasing operating costs are usually offset by relatively high prices. Again, such was the case in the early years of the PC market, when it was dominated by such players as IBM and Compaq. Discounters like Dell were considered fringe players back when they occupied a small, specialized market niche.

Technological Discontinuities
The link between technological discontinuities and industry change should be readily apparent from our discussion of industry evolution as a driver of change.[23] Moreover, technology is one of the key factors in the PESTEL framework you learned about earlier in the chapter: Discontinuities are a special, intensive case of technological change in action. Get in the habit of thinking broadly about the nature of the changes that create technological discontinuities. Technological discontinuities are much more extreme than mere incremental technological change.

To examine these extreme forms of change, it is important to understand first that technological discontinuities include both changes in science-based technologies (such as innovations) and business-process technologies (such as new business models). The two major forms of technology are *process technology* and *product technology*. Process technology refers to the devices, tools, and knowledge used to transform inputs into outputs. Product technology creates new products.[24] Needless to say, technological changes can have traumatic effects on industries and firms.[25] Indeed, major technological changes often alter firm environments and industry structures significantly. Of course, not all technological changes affect competitors and industries equally. Some, for example, work to the advantage of incumbents, others to that of new entrants.

Disruptive Product-Related Change Patterns of technological change often reflect gradual *incremental* evolutionary change. However, other forms of episodic change are also prone to punctuate industry evolution; we characterize these forms of change as *discontinuous* change.[26] Discontinuous technological change occurs when breakthrough technologies appear, sometimes sustaining the competencies of incumbent firms and sometimes destroying them. Competency-sustaining technologies are typically introduced by incumbents.

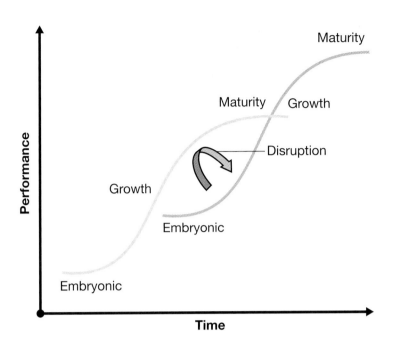

Exhibit 4.12 Discontinuity in the Industry Life Cycle

Those that destroy incumbents' competencies are called **disruptive technologies.** In many instances, these disruptions have been introduced by new firms.[27] A disruptive change introduced by a new technology also has the effect of altering the industry life cycle. The industry is reinvigorated and rather than proceeding into decline accelerates into new phases of growth, as illustrated by Exhibit 4.12.

As an illustration of this process, consider the minicomputer industry. Out of 116 major innovations introduced in the minicomputer industry (the precursor to the personal computer), 111 were incremental sustaining technological improvements and only 5 were disruptive. All 111 sustaining technologies were introduced by incumbents, whereas all 5 disruptive technologies were introduced by outsiders—firms specializing in new personal computers. In the disk drive industry, virtually every new generation of technology has led to the demise of the market leader. The arrival of the personal computer, for example, heralded the downfall of every major competitor in the minicomputer industry. [28] This process, known as the **innovator's dilemma**, unfolds in established industries when incumbents continue to develop competency-enhancing innovations, while new entrants develop disruptive innovations.[29] Specifically, the *dilemma* for incumbents is that their economic incentives are to continue developing evolutionary improvements in their existing technology and to avoid sponsoring disruptive innovations, even when the disruptive technology may eventually supplant the existing technology.

What are these incentives that usually persuade incumbents to maintain a course of incremental, sustaining innovations rather than adopting the disruptive innovation? Sustaining innovations are introduced to satisfy the needs of firms' best customers; those who demand the most from their products and who pay the highest margins to receive such service. In the case of minicomputers, firms like DEC were satisfying their largest business customers by continually improving the speed and power of their top-of-the-line minicomputers. These units would sell for tens of thousands of dollars and have margins of 25 percent or more. The new personal computers that new entrants were producing would sell for only a few thousand dollars, and the margins may have been ten percentage points or more less. Thus, you could say that DEC was being entirely rational to avoid this market. However, that calculus ignores the new business landscape that disruptive innovations will create in the not-too-distant future. ◆

disruptive technology
Breakthrough product- or process-related technology that destroys the competencies of incumbent firms in an industry.

innovator's dilemma
When incumbents avoid investing in innovative and disruptive technologies because those innovations do not satisfy the needs of their mainstream and most profitable clients.

Economic Logic

Exhibit 4.13 The Innovator's Dilemma

Adapted from C. M. Christensen, The Innovator's Dilemma (Cambridge, MA: Harvard Business Press, 1997).

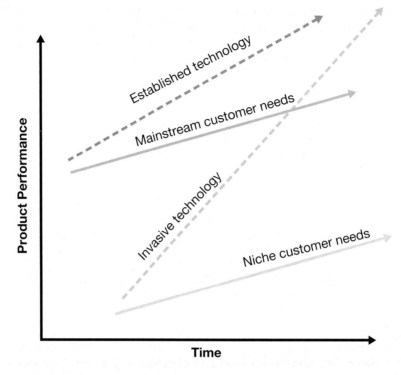

The process of disruptive change is illustrated in Exhibit 4.13. Incumbents tend to serve the needs of their best customers. Ironically, they are executing and improving upon the *economic logic* of their existing strategy, even though the other facets—*differentiators* and *arenas*—of the strategy will be made dramatically obsolete by the innovator's products or services. Consequently, over time, their products tend to migrate away from the center of the market; they out-innovate the needs of most customers. Disruptive technological innovations are often initially aimed at a small segment of the market, perhaps the lower end—those customers for whom incumbents' innovations are really more than they need. The margins for these innovations are often much lower than the margins on new, competency-enhancing innovations. It isn't until the disruptive innovation goes through several phases of refinement and improvement that it eventually migrates up the industry product hierarchy that it eventually steals more valued customers from incumbents. By this time the new entrants have improved their products sufficiently that they satisfy most of the needs of the larger market, and they do so for a fraction of the cost of incumbents.

Exhibit 4.13 demonstrates the interplay between incumbents' innovation and new entrants' innovation. Notice how established companies sometimes follow an innovation trajectory that leads them to overshoot the majority of their mainstream customers' needs. The invasive technology, however, which may be initially targeted at lower-end customers eventually migrates upstream to be good enough for the basic needs of many mainstream customers. This process, while not universally true in all industries, has been documented as the source of dynamic change in many industries. A few examples are notebook computers and handheld digital appliances, full-service stock brokerage and on-line stock brokerage, printed greeting cards and free on-line greeting cards, classroom- and campus-based higher education and distance education, offset printing and digital printing, and cardiac surgery and angioplasty, just to name a few.[30]

Disruptive Process-Related Change It's important to remember that disruptive technologies can be process-related as well as product-related. The development of manufacturing (TQM) methods, for instance, eventually elevated the Japanese auto industry to world-class status. TQM programs such as *six sigma* and *lean* are process innovations. No automaker in the world can now ignore the competitive threat posed by such firms as Toyota and Honda, and, in fact, many who once did are now struggling to emulate the TQM methods pioneered by these one-time fringe players.

Southwest Airlines radically changed the business model that had long dominated the industry, but established full-service airlines originally took little notice. Why? Because Southwest's new process couldn't help them meet the needs of their most profitable customers. In time, however, the number and length of Southwest's flights reached the point at which the services provided by its model could satisfy the demands of customers who normally used larger airlines.

Likewise, Wal-Mart's business model was originally of little threat to Sears because it focused on rural areas that Sears was happy to ignore. Eventually, Wal-Mart's model was transferable to larger markets, but it was too late for Sears to respond. A similar pattern unfolded in the U.S. steel industry. At first, large firms such as U.S. Steel ignored the emergence of so-called "mini-mills" because their unsophisticated technology was efficient only in turning out the least profitable products. But as the capabilities of mini-mill technology improved, so did the ability of the new firms to enter more profitable segments of the industry.

WHEN INDUSTRIES DIVIDE

The industry life cycle model is too simplistic to describe the evolution of many industries. In some cases, one industry becomes two or more distinct but related industries. One cause of such a split is the decision by a firm to divest a once-core business that has been separated from the firm's original core because of industry changes. As a rule, the divestiture is prompted by the emergence of a new market.

Such was the case with 3Com Corporation and its Palm division. 3Com originally specialized in modems, which have both hardware and software components. In developing this interface, 3Com innovated a new product that linked the two components. It was called the PalmPilot, and it soon defined the new personal data assistant (PDA) industry. Once convinced that the PDA industry was distinct from its core business in the modem industry, 3Com sold off its Palm division in a public stock offering. New entrants into the PDA industry began to specialize in either the software or hardware side of the business, with Sony, Compaq, and Dell making hardware and Palm and Microsoft selling software. Now Palm is weighing the idea of breaking up into two smaller firms—one that specializes in software and one that develops hardware. Remember: Before 3Com's original innovation, there was no such thing as a PDA industry—let alone any subindustries.

Finally, industries may divide when the market for a particular product becomes large enough that firms can economically justify dedicating a distribution channel to it. This type of division typically results in new industry *segments* or *subindustries* rather than in new industries. A good example is the emergence of so-called *category killers* in various retail industries—industry segments composed of large, highly specialized retail chains, such as PetSmart or Home Depot and Lowe's. They're called "category killers" because they aim to dominate whatever category they participate in by offering the broadest possible assortment of goods at the lowest possible prices. The Internet has spawned a number of such segments and some well-known firms, including Amazon.com and BarnesandNoble.com in books and Travelocity.com and Expedia.com in travel.

WHEN INDUSTRIES COLLIDE

Although some changes lead to industry division, others result in new industry definitions that consolidate two or more separate industries into one. As you read this section of the chapter, note the distinction between industry *consolidation* and industry *concentration*. Whereas *concentration* results in an industry with fewer players, *consolidation* results in fewer industries. Ironically, changes in concentration can lead to either consolidation or division.[31]

Today, for example, both the global media and entertainment industries seem to be agglomerations of many once-distinct industries. The definition of the media industry now includes firms with a significant presence in both program distribution (they own or control television networks) and program content (they own or develop new shows). The largest incumbents are often called media and entertainment *conglomerates* (which suggests organizations composed of unrelated divisions), but in reality the dominant players, including Fox, Disney, Viacom, and VivendiUniversal, have consolidated a broad range of functions that were once performed by suppliers, substitutes, complementors, or even customers.

Industry division and convergence happens over time. Opportunities to create significant value tend to be greatest for firms that lead the charge in convergence and division of industries. However, when firms define their industries very broadly, performing external analysis becomes much more complicated. For instance, framing a printing company like FedEx/Kinko's as a simple printer versus a marketing-communications firm connotes a broadly different set of industry conditions.

Now that you're familiar with a few key drivers of industry change, it is important that you understand the particular implications of technological and business-model breakthroughs for both the pace and extent of industry change. The *rate* of change may vary significantly from one industry to the next. The rate of change in the computing industry, for example, has been much faster than in the steel industry. Nevertheless, changes in both industries has prompted complete reconfigurations of industry structure and the competitive positions of various players. The idea that all industries change over time and that business environments are in a constant state of flux is relatively intuitive. As a strategic decision maker, therefore, the question you need to keep asking yourself is, how accurately does current structure (which is relatively easy to identify) predict future industry conditions?

Summary of Challenges

1. *Explain the importance of the external context for strategy and firm performance.* In order to understand the threats and opportunities facing an organization, you need a thorough understanding of its external context, including not only its industry, but the larger environment in which it operates. The proper analysis of the external context, together with the firm-level analysis you learned in Chapter 3 (e.g., VRINE, value-chain), allow you to complete a rigorous analysis of a firm and its options. You could say that with these tools you can now perform a thorough and systematic (rather than intuitive) *SWOT analysis;* that is, an assessment of a firm's *s*trengths, *w*eaknesses, *o*pportunities, and *t*hreats.

2. *Use PESTEL to identify the macro characteristics of the external context.* PESTEL analysis and an understanding of the drivers of globalization can be used to characterize the macro characteristics of the firm's external environment. PESTEL is an acronym for the *p*olitical, *e*conomic, *s*ociocultural, *t*echnological, *e*nvironmental, and *l*egal contexts in which a firm operates. Managers can use the PESTEL analysis to gain a better understanding of the opportunities and threats faced by the firm. By knowing the firm's opportunities and threats, managers can build a better vision of the future business landscape and identify how the firm may compete profitably. By examining the drivers of globalization, managers can identify how market, cost, governments, and competition work to favor the globalization of an industry.

3. *Identify the major features of an industry and the forces that affect industry profitability.* The major factors to be analyzed when examining an industry are rivalry, the power of suppliers, the power of buyers, the threat of substitutes, and the threat of new entrants. When suppliers and buyers have significant power, they tend to be able to negotiate away some of the profit that would otherwise be available to industry rivals. Thus, profits tend to be lower than average in industries that face high levels of supplier and buyer power. Likewise, as the threat of new entrants and the availability of substitutes increases, the ability of rivals in the industry to keep prices high is reduced. Rivalry within an industry decreases profitability. High levels of rivalry result in heavy emphasis on price-based competition. Rivalry is reduced when products are differentiated. Strategic-group analysis is used to gain a better understanding of the nature of rivalry. Whereas industry profits tend to be reduced when any of the five forces are strong, the presence of complementors results in the opposite; they increase the ability of firms to generate profits. Finally, an analysis of competitors' objectives, current strategies, assumptions, and resources and capabilities can help managers predict the future behaviors of their competitors.

4. *Understand the dynamic characteristics of the external context.* The various models and analytical tools presented can provide an excellent snapshot of a firm's external context. In some industries, such a snapshot view gives an accurate portrayal of the look of the business landscape for the foreseeable future. The five forces of industry structure change, and very rapidly in some industries; other drivers of change to which managers must be attuned include the stage and pace of transition in the industry life cycle and technological discontinuities.

5. *Show how industry dynamics may redefine industries.* In some cases, one industry becomes two or more distinct, but often related, industries. Industries may also divide when the market for a particular product becomes large enough that firms can economically justify dedicating a distribution channel to it. Whereas some changes lead to industry division, others result in new industry definitions that consolidate two or more separate industries into one. Industry convergence and division happen over time, and firms that identify such changes and initiate early changes have a better opportunity to create value.

Review Questions

1. What constitutes the external context of strategy?

2. What are the five forces affecting industry structure?

3. What are complementors?

4. What is a key success factor (KSF)?

5. What are strategic groups?

6. What factors increase industry dynamics?

7. What is the industry life cycle?

8. What is a technological discontinuity?

9. What is the innovator's dilemma?

10. How does globalization affect the external context of strategy?

11. What is industry redefinition?

Experiential Activities

Group Exercises

1. Pick two of the industries listed in Exhibit 4.1, one on the high end of profitability and one on the low end. What are the boundaries of these industries? What are their market and geographic segments? Who are the key players? Draw up a five-forces model of each industry and compare and contrast their industry structure. Now shift your analysis to the dynamic five-forces model. What dimensions of the five-forces model are most likely to change in the near future? Which are most likely to stay relatively stable? Answer these questions for both 5- and 10-year windows.

Ethical Debates

1. Genetically modified organisms (GMOs) include food products in which genetics have been used to extend product shelf life, deter pests, and other product innovations. Much of the food consumed in the U.S. is genetically modified, while many other developing countries prohibit them for ethical and other reasons. Ethical objections to GMO foods typically center on the possibility of harm to persons or other living things. What do you believe explains this striking difference in ethical views about GMO food between the U.S. and other global markets?

2. Despite the pharmaceutical industry's notable contributions to human progress, including the development of miracle drugs for treating cancer, AIDS, and heart disease, there is a growing ethical tension between the industry and the public. What are some of the key ethical questions, and how does that affect your analysis of the pharmaceutical industry?

How Would
YOU DO THAT?

1. The box entitled "How Would *You* Do That? 4.1" illustrates the five-forces model for the airline industry. Use the analysis there as an example and perform a five-forces analysis for one of the following industries: soft drinks, cable television, or cell phone service providers. What are the one or two most important issues from your analysis that managers in that industry must take into account when they revisit their strategies?

2. Using the value curve model illustrated in "How Would *You* Do That? 4.2," map the strategic groups in the soft drink industry. What groups are there other than the two dominant companies? How do they compete relative to Coke and Pepsi?

Go on to see How Would You Do That at www.prenhall.com/ carpenter&sanders

Endnotes

1. Data from Standard & Poor's Compustat.

2. G. Yip, "Global Strategy in a World of Nations," *Sloan Management Review* 31:1 (1989), 29–40.

3. M. Porter, *Competition in Global Industries* (Boston: Harvard Business School Press, 1986); Yip, "Global Strategy in a World of Nations."

4. Adapted from M. E. Porter, *Competition in Global Industries* (Boston: Harvard Business School Press, 1986); G. Yip, "Global Strategy in a World of Nations," *Sloan Management Review* 31:1 (1989), 29–40.

5. R. Amit and P. J. H. Schoemaker, "Strategic Assets and Organizational Rent," *Strategic Management Journal* 14 (1993), 33–46; J. A. Vasconcellos and D. C. Hambrick, "Key Success Factors: Test of a General Framework in the Mature Industrial-Product Sector," *Strategic Management Journal* 10 (1989), 367–382.

6. "A Fruit Revolution," *Convenience Store News* 41:4 (2005), 20; J. Cioletti, "Flavoring the Market," *Beverage World* 124:3 (2005), 6; B. Bobala, "Water Wars," March 10, 2003 (accessed July 15, 2005), www.fool.com/news/commentary/2003/commentary030310bb.htm.

7. U.S. Census Bureau, "Economic Census: Concentration Ratios," *Economic Census 2002* (accessed April 15, 2007), www.census.gov/epcd/www/concentration.html.

8. Adapted from M. E. Porter, *Competitive Strategy: Techniques for Analyzing Industries and Competitors* (New York: Free Press, 1980).

9. M. Porter, *Competitive Strategy: Techniques for Analyzing Industries and Competitors* (New York: Free Press, 1980).

10. S. Leith, "Virgin Cola Returns—but More Quietly," *Atlanta Journal Constitution*, July 1, 2004, E1.

11. www.packersnews.com/archives/news/pack_10906648.shtml (accessed July 15, 2005).

12. A. Brandenburger and B. Nalebuff, *Co-Opetition* (New York: Currency Doubleday, 1996).

13. Much of this section is adapted from important studies in the field of game theory, and we'll return to the topic when we discuss strategic alliances and other cooperative strategies. At this point, we offer merely an overview. See A. Dixit and B. Nalebuff, *Thinking Strategically: The Competitive Edge in Business and Politics and Everyday Life* (New York: W. W. Norton, 1992); and A. Brandenburger and B. Nalebuff, *Co-Opetition*.

14. J. E. Ellis, "The Law of Gravity Doesn't Apply: Inefficiency, Overcapacity, Huge Debt . . . What Keeps U.S. Carriers Up in the Air?" *BusinessWeek*, September 26, 2005, p. 49; H. Tully, "Airlines: Why the Big Boys Won't Come Back," *Fortune*, June 14, 2004, p. 101.

15. W. C. Kim and R. Mauborgne, "Blue Ocean Strategy," *California Management Review* 47:3 (2005), 105–121; Wine Institute, "Strong Sales Growth in 2004 for California Wine as Shipments Reached New High," April 5, 2005 (accessed July 12, 2005), www.wineinstitute.org; www.elitewine.com/site/index.php?lang=en&cat=news&art=159.

16. R. Wiggins and T. Ruefli, "Competitive Advantage: Temporal Dynamics and the Incidence and Persistence of Superior Economic Performance," *Organization Science* 13 (2002), 82–105.

17. Adapted from M. E. Porter, *Competitive Strategy: Techniques for Analyzing Industries and Competitors* (New York: Free Press, 1980).

18. R. Stein, *The Automobile Book* (London: Paul Hamlyn Ltd, 1967).

19. Adapted from K. Rangan and G. Bowman, "Beating the Commodity Magnet," *Industrial Marketing Management* 21 (1992), 215–224; P. Kotler, "Managing Products Through Their Product Life Cycle," in *Marketing Management: Planning, Implementation, and Control*, 7th ed. (Upper Saddle River, NJ: Prentice Hall, 1991).

20. L. Argote, *Organizational Learning: Creating, Retaining, and Transferring Knowledge* (Boston: Kluwer Academic Publishers, 1999); A. S. Miner and P. Haunschild, "Population Level Learning," *Research in Organizational Behavior* 17 (1995), 115–166.

21. D. Pringle, "Slower Growth Hits Cellphone Services Overseas in EU, Japan, Saturation Leads to Some Contraction; Looking Beyond Voice," *Wall Street Journal*, May 23, 2005, A1.

22. See G. Moore, *Crossing the Chasm* (New York: Harper Business Essentials, 2002); C. Shapiro and H. R. Varian, *Information Rules: A Strategic Guide to the Network Economy* (Boston: Harvard Business School Press, 1998).

23. N. Rosenberg, *Technology and American Economic Growth* (New York, Harper & Row, 1986); M. L. Tushman and P. Anderson, "Technological Discontinuities and Organizational Environments," *Administrative Science Quarterly* 31 (1986), 439–465.

24. W. P. Barnett, "The Organizational Ecology of a Technological System," *Administrative Science Quarterly* 35 (1990), 31–60; R. M. Henderson and K. B. Clark, "Architectural Innovation: The Reconfiguration of Exist-

ing Product Technologies and the Failure of Established Firms," *Administrative Science Quarterly* 35 (1990), 9–30.

25. Tushman and Anderson, "Technological Discontinuities and Organizational Environments."

26. Tushman and Anderson, "Technological Discontinuities and Organizational Environments."

27. C. M. Christensen, *The Innovator's Dilemma* (Cambridge, MA: Harvard Business Press, 1997).

28. Christensen, *The Innovator's Dilemma*.

29. Christensen, *The Innovator's Dilemma*.

30. Christensen, *The Innovator's Dilemma*.

31. Consolidation may result from increased concentration when bigger players in an industry absorb the functions of suppliers, substitutes, complements, or customers (a process under way in the global media and entertainment industries). By getting bigger, these firms broaden the definition of their operations, but successfully managing all the components of a broader operation is a separate matter. Concentration often results in division when players that have grown too big can no longer give adequate attention to some segment of their market or some facet of their operations. Division also occurs when, because of increased concentration, a new market emerges to attract large firms.

5 Creating Business Strategies

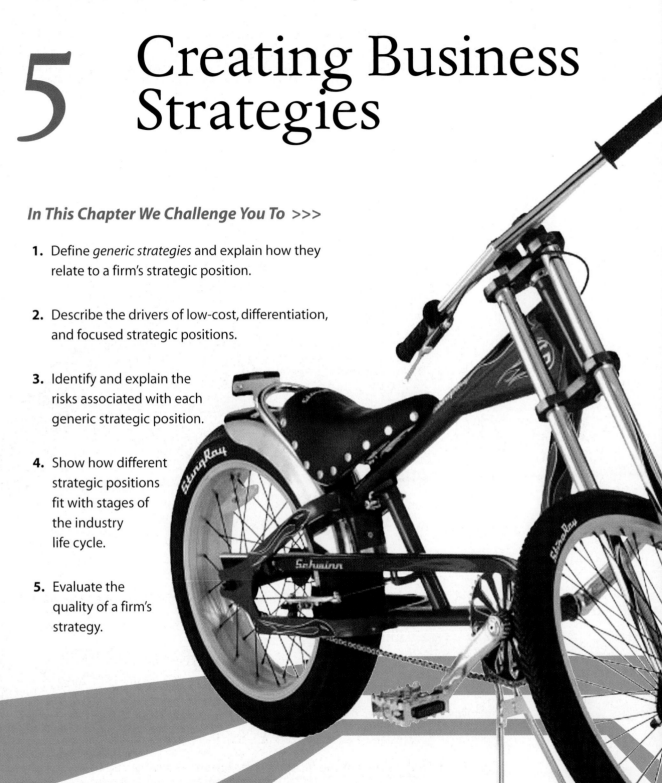

In This Chapter We Challenge You To >>>

1. Define *generic strategies* and explain how they relate to a firm's strategic position.

2. Describe the drivers of low-cost, differentiation, and focused strategic positions.

3. Identify and explain the risks associated with each generic strategic position.

4. Show how different strategic positions fit with stages of the industry life cycle.

5. Evaluate the quality of a firm's strategy.

A Tale of
Three Wheels
in the Bicycle
Industry

Chris Hornung, founder and first CEO of Pacific Cycle, grabbed the lion's share of the U.S. bicycle market by buying well-known brands and crafting big distribution deals with America's largest retailers. In 2005, over 19.8 million bicycles were sold in the U.S.[1] According to industry trade reports, the total retail value of bikes, parts, and accessories was more than $6 billion. Who sold all of these bicycles and bike-related products? There are literally hundreds of bicycle manufacturers in the U.S., but most are small, specialized firms.

Among them, one company—Pacific Cycle—sells more bicycles than any other company in North America. "We're interested in a high-volume business," said Hornung. "That's our business model." Pacific Cycle designs, markets, and imports a full range of bikes and recreation products under such familiar brand names as Schwinn, GT, Mongoose, Kustom Kruiser, Roadmaster, Pacific, Dyno, Powerlite, InSTEP, and Pacific Outdoors. Its powerful brand portfolio serves virtually all consumer demographics, price categories, and product categories (e.g., children's, mountain, and racing bikes).

Hornung started his company at age 22 as a modest bike import business. He pioneered the concept of sourcing bicycles from Asia for distribution in the U.S. While on a buying trip to Taiwan in 1983, Hornung met buyers from Target Corp. and Toys 'R' Us, which provided him an entryway into the mass market retailers.

Now, his company is one of the fastest-growing branded consumer-product companies in the U.S. Hornung has achieved this success by combining an aggressive acquisition of power brands with low-cost outsourcing, efficient supply-chain management, and multichannel retail distribution. In December 2000, Hornung acquired the bicycle division of Brunswick Corp. for $60 million, which included the Mongoose, Mongoose Pro, and Roadmaster brands. In the deal, Hornung got more than the brands of Brunswick, he got a very big customer. That purchase nearly doubled Pacific's sales, because Wal-Mart was Brunswick's biggest account, Hornung said. A year later, Hornung bought the assets of Schwinn/GT Corp. out of bankruptcy for $86 million, a move that added an American icon to the company portfolio.

Pacific Cycle's channels include leading mass-market retailers such as Wal-Mart, Target, and Toys 'R' Us; sporting goods chains such as Dick's, The Sports Authority, and Gart Sports; and independent dealers serving local markets. The company's brands appeal to the full spectrum of demographics, price preferences, and image and usage criteria that are critical to targeting the key consumer segments served by each channel. This broad-based marketing strategy enables Pacific to provide retailers with one-stop shopping and to respond efficiently to changes in the marketplace. For example, the Schwinn brand historically was only sold through specialty bike shops. But Hornung brought it into the mass market. "We didn't want to limit the Schwinn brand to just specialty dealers," Hornung said. "The major retailers were anxious to carry a brand that has 107 years of history behind it." The public wanted it, too: "Cycling is a family sport, and our move into the mass-market channel simply recognizes that Schwinn—the premium bike brand—must be available where most families shop today," Hornung said. Moving the brand into mass retailers broadened access to Schwinn bicycles to greater numbers of consumers and helped lower the price. The average price of a Schwinn at a mass retailer is $65, compared to $387 at a specialty store, according to the National Bicycle Dealers Association. Overall, the average retail price of bikes has declined steadily, at about 15 percent per year. That decline has made it important for Pacific to control costs, Hornung said. Hornung faces new challenges as well. Competition among distributors "is as tough now as I've ever seen it," Hornung said.

Hornung's strategy has been simple: Import quality bikes from Asia. Distribute them to mass merchants such as Wal-Mart. Keep payrolls to an absolute minimum. Since applying that strategy to Schwinn, Hornung has seen the brand lose the support of most independent dealers. But it's been a hit among mass merchants. Consumers now pay less for the new Sting Ray under Pacific's ownership. It may not be the engineering marvel that was the old Schwinn, but it retails at Wal-Mart for about a third of the original's price.

Pacific Cycle was recently acquired by Doral Inc., and now operates as an independent strategic business unit (SBU). It is now one of the most prolific bicycle suppliers in the world, selling products in more than 60 countries via more than 50 international distributors. In 2007, Pacific Cycle's President, Jeff Frehner, was promoted to President and Chief Executive Officer as Hornung ended his 30-year tenure at the company, leaving Pacific to launch NextTesting. Frehner will continue to build Pacific's international business and strengthen its brands across the globe.

Another successful bike maker, Trek Bicycle, has revenues similar to Pacific. Richard Burke and Bevill Hogg founded Trek in 1976. With $25,000 in seed money, Burke and Hogg started building bikes by hand in a Wisconsin barn. From the beginning, they targeted upper-end users, and success came quickly. Today, customers pay top dollar for smooth suspensions, custom paint jobs, and innovations in racing geometry. With annual sales of about $400 million, Trek is now the country's number-one maker of high-quality bikes and was perhaps the first U.S. bike maker to overcome European resistance to American-made cycles by focusing on quality and innovation, which have long been Trek's hallmarks. The company introduced its first mountain bike line in 1983, the first bonded-aluminum road bike in 1985, and a carbon-fiber road bike in 1986.

Although most of Trek's growth has been fueled by internally developed products, Trek has also made a few strategic acquisitions, including Gary Fisher Mountain Bike and two mountain bike competitors (Bontrager and Klein) in 1995. Trek now makes various types of bicycles, including mountain, road, children's, recumbent, police, and BMX bikes. Internationally, Trek bikes are sold through wholly owned subsidiaries in 7 countries and through distributors in 65 others. Trek designs all of its bikes at its Wisconsin headquarters and manufactures a quarter of them in this country. Finally, the company's sponsorship of seven-time Tour de France winner Lance Armstrong has given the company tremendous exposure and the centerpiece for a marketing plan that, as one Trek executive puts it, can be summed up as "Lance, Lance, Lance."

Whereas Pacific Cycle and Trek represent the larger players in the U.S. market, Montague fits the profile of a boutique-style bike firm. Frustration prompted Harry Montague, a Washington, D.C. architect and inventor, to develop the Montague line of high-performance, travel-friendly bicycles: He was unable to find anything but small-wheeled folding bikes, and they were both uncomfortable and inefficient for serious cyclists who wanted to take their bikes in the car or on public transportation. After much trial and error, Montague succeeded in developing a full-size high-performance folding bicycle that he then custom-built and sold out of his garage for D.C.-area riders.

Montague moved out of the garage after Harry's son David was required to create an extensive business plan for a course in entrepreneurship at the MIT Sloan School of Business. David designed a formal business plan around his father's bicycle, and as soon as David passed the course, he and his father formed the Montague Corp. to design and produce full-size bicycles that sacrifice little in performance while providing travel-friendly convenience for a targeted market of customers. Today, Montague is the world's leading manufacturer of folding bikes. All Montague bikes fold into a compact size in less than 30 seconds without the use of tools. They have been sold to the military for tactical use and to several car manufacturers for promotional packaging with SUVs.

Pacific Cycle, Trek, and Montague may be in the same industry, but each pursues a very different strategy in an attempt to meet the needs of customers. In this chapter, you will be introduced to the basics of business strategy—the tools and models that will help you formulate coherent strategies for competing within an industry context. **<<<**

An Introduction to Business Strategies

In this chapter, we build on Chapters 3 and 4 by discussing ways in which firms formulate business strategies that capitalize on their resources and capabilities to exploit opportunities in their competitive environments. At the same time, we set the stage for Chapter 6, which explores strategy in dynamic contexts. As we saw in Chapter 1, *business strategy* refers to the choices that a firm makes about its competitive posture within a particular line of business. These choices can be summarized by the *strategy diamond* and its *five elements of strategy.*

Economic Logic

As we saw in our opening vignette about three bicycle companies, there's more than one economic logic or way to compete in an industry. ◆ Pacific Cycle, for example, markets a product for virtually every segment, offers a range of quality in its product mix, and keeps costs down by outsourcing all of its production to China and Taiwan. Trek, meanwhile, though also a large company with a broad product mix, focuses on specialized and innovative product attributes to target specific customer segments and one channel—independent bike distributors. Montague is an entirely different company, marketing a highly specialized product targeted at a narrow range of potential customers.

As a rule, competitive positions can be established in many different ways, and the task of finding the best configuration of positions is the subject of this chapter. We'll start by introducing a well-established framework for strategic positioning developed by Michael Porter and then describe the conditions under which particular strategic positions are viable. We'll also examine ways in which alternative strategic positions are compatible with different stages of the industry life cycle. Finally, because a successful strategy must be consistent with both a firm's resources and the competitive environment, we'll conclude by describing a process for testing the quality of a strategy according to this criterion.

Types of Strategies—Finding a Position That Works

When you consider all the choices that can be made relative to the strategy diamond, there are almost endless potential strategies that a firm could choose. To simplify these possible choices for managers, in this section we introduce the generic strategy typology. This typology is useful to help select a starting strategic position. **Strategic positioning** refers to the ways managers situate a firm relative to its rivals along important competitive dimensions. The strategic positioning model that we present in this chapter is a classic framework in the field of strategic management—Michael Porter's *generic strategy model.* Recall that under the industry structure model that we introduced in Chapter 4, the key force in an industry—indeed, the force around which all others revolve—is rivalry among the firms in the industry. The purpose of strategic positioning is to reduce the effects of rivalry and thereby improve profitability, and the generic strategies that derive from the strategic positioning model are related to the industry structure model: They help managers stake out a position for their firm relative to rivals *in ways that reduce the effects of intense rivalry on profitability.*

strategic positioning   Means by which managers situate a firm relative to its rivals.

The concept of strategic positioning is a useful starting point in dealing with issues deriving from the strategy diamond model that we explored in Chapter 1. The generic strategy typology has managers start by identifying the intended *economic logic* of their strategy and the *arenas* in which they will compete. Underlying the choice of economic logic is also some idea as to what *differentiators* the firm might employ. First, the model asks strategists to decide if they will compete based on the logic of being a low cost leader (e.g., a competitor that will achieve higher margins due to a lower cost basis than rivals) or as a differentiator (e.g., a competitor that will achieve higher prices and margins because of superior quality). For instance, Trek attempts to position its brands as possessing superior quality, and therefore warranting higher prices, through endorsements by industry superstars such as Lance Armstrong and exclusive distribution through independent bike dealers. Secondly, the model asks strategists to decide whether they intend to serve the broad market or more specialized niches. An automobile manufacturer, for example, must decide whether to compete in all geographic markets and all product lines (say, everything from high-performance to economy-priced cars—as you might see when contrasting Porsche with Daimler).

This model also helps decision makers deal with questions about a firm's tactics for motivating customers to choose its products over those of competitors. Consider the market for luxury cars. Will customers buy from a firm because it offers the lowest-priced luxury sedan (such as the Buick Park Avenue), because it's known for its quality (say, Lexus), or because it offers the most valuable brand image (perhaps Mercedes Benz)?

A firm's choice of position should be primarily influenced by two important factors: (1) firm resources and capabilities and (2) industry structure. Formulating a strategy means using tools such as those that we introduced in Chapters 3 and 4 to make critical decisions about how and where to compete—that is, how to position a company relative to its rivals. In addition, if a firm hopes to exploit opportunities while withstanding competitive threats from within its industry, its strategy should be built on its unique resources and capabilities.

GENERIC STRATEGIES

In this section, we'll discuss one of the most durable concepts in the field of strategic management—Michael Porter's concept of the generic strategies by which firms develop defensible strategic positions. These positions are a function of two sets of choices—economic logic (low-cost leadership versus differentiation) and scope of arenas (broad versus niche market arenas). We'll explain the logic of the resulting four positions—*low-cost leadership, differentiation, focused cost leadership,* and *focused differentiation*—and show how a successfully implemented generic strategic position can reduce the negative effects of industry rivalry.

A simple two-by-two matrix, shown in Exhibit 5.1, helps you visualize the four alternative competitive positions; the alternative positions suggested by this model are what we mean by **generic strategies**.[2] The integrated position, shown in the middle of the exhibit, is discussed at the end of the section. Bear in mind that in order to be consistent with the overall model of strategy that we presented in Chapter 1 and avoid confusing Porter's categories with the more general concept of strategy, we'll refer to Porter's generic strategies as *strategic positions.* You can see that the strategic positions are not *strategies* in the way we define them using the strategy diamond. Rather, they are configurations of several elements of a firm's strategy. Consequently, understand that any one of these strategic positions still requires a carefully formulated set of choices regarding the five elements of the strategy diamond. However, selecting an intended generic strategic position first gives you a head start and guidance on making specific choices regarding the five elements of the strategy diamond.

generic strategies Strategic position designed to reduce the effects of rivalry, including *low-cost, differentiation, focused cost leadership, focused differentiation, and integrated positions.*

Cost or Differentiation
In 1980, Michael Porter introduced an integrated theory of strategy. Porter's model revised the concept of how firms achieve competitive advantage by going beyond the basic (and often wrong) notion that market share is the key to profitability. In part, Porter's theory considered the structure of an industry and its effect on the performance of firms within it (an idea that we introduced in Chapter 4). Porter also demonstrated the economic logic behind some prescriptions for choosing among viable means of gaining competitive advantage. As you see in Exhibit 5.1, the model hinges on two dimensions: the economic logic and the breadth of the target market.

According to Porter, there are two essential economic logics (or the source) of competitive advantage. These alternative sources of advantage are (1) having a lower cost structure than industry competitors or, (2) having a product or service that customers perceive as

Exhibit 5.1 The Strategic Positioning Model

The positioning model is adapted from M. E. Porter, Competitive Strategy *(New York: Free Press, 1980). The examples used in the model are the authors' analysis.*

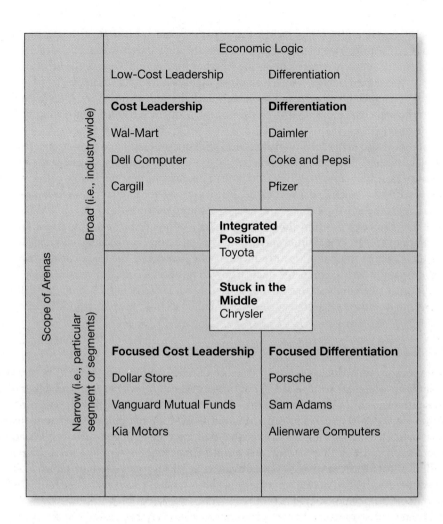

differentiated from other products in the industry—to the point that they will pay higher prices than what is charged for other products in the industry. In other words, a firm can gain a significant advantage over rivals in one of two ways:

- It can produce a product at a lower cost than its rivals.

- It can produce a differentiated product and charge sufficiently higher prices to more than offset the added costs of differentiation.

Along the horizontal dimension of Exhibit 5.1, firms choose the underlying economic logic by which they intend to establish a competitive advantage—that is, whether to compete on differentiation or cost. *Differentiation* refers to a general condition of perceived product "uniqueness" that causes customers to be willing to pay premium prices. When are customers willing to pay more for a product? Generally, premium prices for otherwise similar products are paid when a firm is able to uniquely satisfy a customer's needs. This satisfaction could be along the dimensions of quality, image, speed, access, or other identifiable dimensions of perceived need. However, firms can gain advantage in other ways as well. As shown on Exhibit 5.1, firms may decide to seek higher returns and a competitive advantage by keeping costs lower than those of competitors. This is typically done by offering a product that is good enough to meet the basic needs of many consumers, thereby allowing firms to cut down on production costs.

Scope of Arenas   Firms also make choices about the number and breadth of arenas in which they will compete when they decide how broadly they will compete for customers—a decision known as *scope of arenas*. In other words, firms make choices about which customers to pursue. Some firms compete broadly by trying to offer something for virtually everyone; others focus their efforts on narrower segments of the market. The vertical dimension in Exhibit 5.1 measures the scope of the market arenas in which a firm chooses to compete.

Importantly, even though a narrow market scope implies some form of market niche, this does not mean that every niche market is small. For example, Porsche is very focused on the high performance sports car market, a niche market in the auto industry, but Porsche still commands over $7 billion in revenues. Indeed, when you think of category killers like Staples (office supplies) or Lowe's (home and garden supplies), they have defined big and attractive market niches.

Four generic strategic positions result from the decisions measured by the model in Exhibit 5.1: *low-cost leadership, broad differentiation, focused (or niche) cost leadership,* and *focused (or niche) differentiation.* The primary classification criterion for the focused positions is that the firm targets one or a few related arenas or segments in an industry, as opposed to many industry segments. Let's look more closely at each of these positions.

Low-Cost Leadership   A strategic position that enables a firm to produce a good or offer a service while maintaining total costs that are lower than what it takes competitors to offer the same product or service is known as **low-cost leadership**. Not surprisingly, a firm that can produce substantially similar products at a lower cost has a significant competitive advantage. With a cost advantage, a firm can sell products for lower prices while still maintaining the same margins as rivals. In the process, of course, it will also gain market share. However, a low-cost leader does not necessarily pass all the cost savings onto the customer. Rather, the firm could keep its prices closer to those of competitors and reap higher margins than competitors. In this case, it will accumulate surplus resources that it can either distribute to shareholders or use to finance future strategic initiatives. Wal-Mart, for instance, attempts to share cost savings with customers—they offer lower prices than most mass merchants, but they retain a significant portion of the cost savings for their own benefit.

As a general rule, because taking a low-cost position requires sacrificing some features or services, firms that stake out this position try to satisfy basic rather than highly specialized customer needs.

The low-cost position works in many industries. In the bicycle industry, for instance, Pacific Cycle keeps manufacturing costs down by standardizing design and outsourcing production to low-cost labor markets. Unlike some low-cost leaders, Pacific also offers a wide array of products, many of which have strong brand equity, such as Schwinn and Mongoose—a strategic decision more often associated with a strategy of differentiation. Remember, however, that most of these brands came into Pacific's portfolio through acquisitions, and the company retained the brand names because they enjoy greater brand awareness than "Pacific Cycle." In the wine industry, Gallo Wines has achieved a low-cost leadership position by innovating cost-effective blending techniques, having lower costs due to scale of operations, developing efficiencies in the grape-procurement function, and generating scale economies in marketing and distribution.

In summary, with the low-cost position, firms attempt to deliver an acceptable product that satisfies basic needs at the lowest possible cost. In doing so, the firm attempts to create a sustainable cost gap over other firms. Successfully following this path results in above-industry-average profits. However, cost leaders must maintain parity or proximity in

low-cost leadership
Strategic position based on producing a good or offering a service while maintaining total costs that are lower than what it takes competitors to offer the same product or service.

To avoid head-to-head competition, Pacific Cycle positions itself differently than Trek. Pacific makes many different brands, selling them at various prices in numerous retail outlets. To keeps costs down, it manufactures its bikes exclusively in countries where costs are low.

satisfying the basic needs of buyers. Doing so is a challenge, because it generally requires tradeoffs—eliminating some features or services in order to drive costs down.

Some well-known companies, including Wal-Mart and Southwest Airlines, are successful low-cost leaders. Interestingly, both of these companies started out as a focused low-cost competitor but took up a more broad-based position as they grew.

Differentiation   If a firm markets products whose quality, reliability, or prestige is discernibly higher than its competitors', and if its customers are willing to pay for this uniqueness, the firm has a competitive advantage based on **differentiation**. Successful differentiation enables firms to do one of two things:

differentiation   Strategic position based on products or offers services with quality, reliability, or prestige that is discernibly higher than that of competitors and for which customers are willing to pay.

- Set prices at the industry average (and gain market share because consumers will choose higher quality at the same price).

- Raise prices over those of competitors (and reap the benefits of higher margins).

Coca-Cola and Pepsi—which spend billions to develop brand equity, sell in most markets, and strive to win customers through brand image—are also well-known differentiators. Or consider Mercedes Benz, perhaps the world's leading manufacturer of premium passenger cars. What differentiates Mercedes' products? A reputation for innovative engineering, safety, and comfort, along with product design aimed at buyers who will pay premium prices for the image that goes along with a Mercedes.[3] Interestingly, although most Americans regard Mercedes as a focused differentiator because only affluent customers can afford its products, Europeans have a different view. In Europe, Mercedes markets a wide line of products, ranging from the tiny SmartCar to more familiar luxury sedans.

In the motorcycle market, Honda, Yamaha, and Suzuki all have something for virtually every enthusiast. Honda's lineup, for instance, starts with the entry-level XR50R, which comes with semiautomatic gears to help youngsters learn off-road riding. Honda then proceeds to appeal to almost every other segment of the market with products ranging upward to the Gold Wing ST1300, a six-cylinder touring bike equipped with a sophisticated sport-type suspension, antilock brakes, and luxury touring features.

A successful differentiation position requires that a firm satisfy a few basic criteria. First, it must uniquely satisfy one or more needs that are valued by buyers and do so in a manner superior to that available from most competitors. However, doing so will *typically* result in higher costs in some value-chain activities. Thus, the second requirement that must be satisfied is that customers must be willing to pay higher prices for the added points of differentiation. Consequently, companies successful at a differentiation position pick cost-effective forms of differentiation. The results are above-average industry profits.

An example of a successful broad differentiator is Stouffers, the frozen-food company. Stouffers spends more on high-quality inputs than its competitors, it has developed a technology to make a superior sauce, and it offers innovative menus. Stouffers combines these features with high-quality packaging, the use of food brokers to get broad distribution, and advertising that creates the perception of quality. The price premium that Stouffers is able to generate exceeds the cost to improve frozen-food entrees above industry norms.

Focused Low-Cost Leadership

A strategic position that enables a firm to be a low-cost leader in a narrow segment of the market is known as **focused cost leadership**. JetBlue, a recent entry into the commercial airline market, is a focused low-cost competitor that serves a small subset of commercial travelers who are price sensitive. Using a variation on Southwest Airline's early business model, JetBlue managed during its first few years of operation to keep its operating costs per airline seat mile lower than even Southwest's. It was the most profitable commercial U.S. airline in 2002 and 2003 and second behind only Southwest in 2004. Fuel costs and weather-related operational difficulties hurt profits in 2005 and 2006; however, JetBlue still has the lowest operating costs of the major airlines.

focused cost leadership
Strategic position based on being a low-cost leader in a narrow market segment.

Focused Differentiation

When unique products are targeted to a particular market segment or arena, the positioning strategy is called **focused differentiation**. By definition, the greater the differentiation, the smaller the market segment to which a product will appeal: As quality is continually improved or luxury features added, fewer customers can afford the higher prices. In the bicycle industry, for example, Montague focuses on a small, specialized segment of the market that demands unique product features. Trek Bicycles also started as a focused differentiator. However, it now offers products in numerous segments and is moving toward a broad-based differentiator. Trek's products boast high quality and demand price premiums over products from Pacific Cycle, and, because it only sells products through independent bicycle dealers, are still classified as a focused differentiator. You also may be familiar with Cannondale, another focused differentiator that produces high-end mountain bikes. Unfortunately for Cannondale, however, the firm sought to leverage its reputation for quality mountain bikes in the motocross motorcycle market and went bankrupt as a result. It found that the resources and capabilities required to compete in mountain bikes, such as sturdy, high-performance frames, were very different than those required for gas-engined bikes—namely high-performance engines and drivetrains. Moreover, motorcycles are not typically sold by the same dealers that sell bikes.

Likewise, Mercedes Benz imports into the U.S. only its most expensive top-of-the-line models in each product category. In the U.S., therefore, Mercedes is a focused differentiator that markets only to the most affluent customers. Even more focused are such companies as Porsche and Ferrari. In the motorcycle industry, Harley-Davidson, which makes only larger models targeted at very specific segments of the market, is a more focused differentiator than Honda. Harley's lowest-priced motorcycle begins at about $6,500. Recently, other firms have entered this market space and have tried to out-focus Harley-Davidson. For instance, Orange County Choppers, which was made famous by the *American Chopper* TV series, sells only made-to-order motorcycles. Therefore, Orange County Choppers focuses on a very small segment of the overall motorcycle market.

focused differentiation
Strategic position based on targeting products to relatively small segments.

Harley-Davidson has successfully focused its business strategy on the large high-priced end of the motorcycle market. Other manufacturers, such as Orange County Choppers, have tried to muscle into Harley's well-defined market space with bikes such as the Fire Bike shown here.

Integrated Positions

It is very difficult for any firm to initially offer both a differentiated product demanding higher prices and still maintain a lower cost structure than competitors. In fact, firms that attempt to exploit both low-cost and differentiation strategies are often described as "stuck in the middle"—meaning they aim to do both but do neither very well. Chrysler, for instance, has suffered from attempting to lower costs while simultaneously trying to deliver differentiated products. The result in recent years has been a line up of cars that does not command premium prices (because of some of the quality problems associated with cost control initiatives) and higher than average costs (because of the increased costs of design efforts to differentiate the product). It is hard to escape the fact that the tradeoffs required to achieve a superior level on one dimension make it hard to succeed on the other. However, as firms perfect their initial position, the tradeoff choices may not be as stark. Some firms are eventually able to achieve an **integrated position**—one in which elements of one position support a strong standing in the other. And while it is typically unwise for a firm to aim to excel at both low cost and differentiation, the competitive reality is that if a firm excels on one dimension it still must be really good on the other dimension. For instance, a company that sells very unique products must also have good cost controls in place. Similarly, a firm that competes on price (or low cost), should also seek attributes that differentiate its products beyond price alone.

Some elements of a differentiation position can be adopted by low-cost competitors. Some low-cost companies, for instance, develop strong brand images even though branding typically supports a differentiation strategy. Heavy reliance on branding enables McDonald's to position itself as a reliable, high-quality provider of low-cost fast food. Whether the firm has achieved an integrated position, however, is judged by whether it achieves higher prices than its competitors for similar products. Toyota, for example, is an excellent example of a company that has achieved a successful integrated position. When Toyota first entered the U.S. market, it did so as a low-cost leader. Toy-

integrated position Strategic position in which elements of one position support strong standing in another.

ota was able to manufacture small cars at a much lower cost than U.S. automobile manufacturers. Over time, however, Toyota invested heavily in quality control, design, and marketing. Toyota's cars are now consistently rated as among the highest in customer and mechanic evaluations of quality. In addition, while Toyota used to have the cheapest cars available in the U.S., their models now command premium prices compared to their American competitors' models. Consequently, Toyota is now a model of both cost control and quality; they have lower costs than competitors and higher quality products, allowing them to charge higher prices for similar models and reap much larger margins than most automobile manufacturers.

Another example is IKEA Svenska AB, which manages to remain the world's largest home furnishings retailer while specializing in stylish but inexpensive furniture. IKEA's success can be traced to its vast experience in the retail market, where it practices both product differentiation and cost leadership. IKEA outlets are essentially warehouses stacked with boxes of unassembled furniture. The company operates under a fairly unique premise: namely, that value-conscious buyers will perform some of the tasks that other retailers normally perform for them, such as transporting and assembling their own furniture. By transferring these functions to the customer, IKEA can drive costs down and, therefore, offer prices low enough to fit most budgets. Thus, IKEA targets a rather large segment of the market, ranging from young low- to middle-income families. At the same time, the company has established a highly differentiated image with its enormous selection of self-assembly home furnishings and fun in-store experiences.

Firms that have integrated low-cost and differentiation positions can be found in most industries. So can firms whose products don't seem to fall into either category. As Exhibit 5.2 shows, integrated—and enviable—positions have in fact been forged in the auto industry. Note, for instance, that Toyota, a successful firm with an integrated position, generates better profit margins on comparable models than Chevrolet, Hyundai, or Ford. Chevrolet, at least in this model class, appears to be a successful low-cost leader.

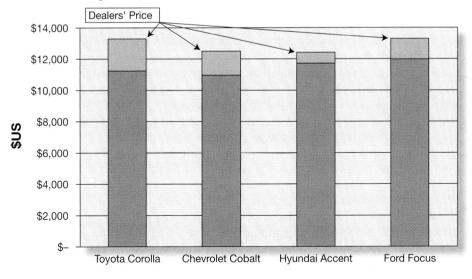

Comparative Cost and Profit of Automobile Manufacturers

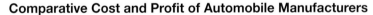

Exhibit 5.2   Integrated Positions: Low-Cost, Differentiation, Stuck-in-the-Middle

Exhibit 5.3 The Interplay Between Cost and Differentiation

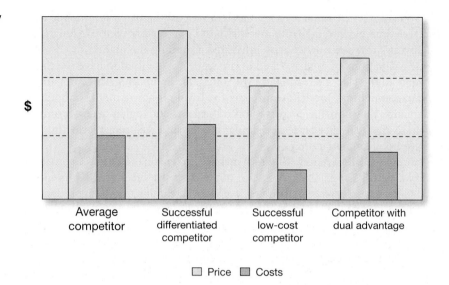

Ford is attempting to be a differentiator, yet their margins are significantly less than Toyota. Notice that Chevrolet's margins are even greater than Fords. Hyundai seems to be stuck in the middle. Their stated strategy is to be a low-cost leader. However, operational problems have resulted in costs greater than all but Ford in this example. Yet, the quality and image of the brand does not permit them to charge prices consistent with a differentiator.

The financial results of successful low-cost, differentiation, and integrated positions are illustrated in Exhibit 5.3. It is critical to remember that these successful positions are predicated on the effective implementation of the drivers of cost or differentiation advantage, or both. In the next section, we explore these drivers in detail.

Strategic Position, Firm Resources, and the Strategy Diamond   As we've seen, the appropriate strategic position for any firm depends on two factors: (1) its resources and capabilities and (2) the condition of its industry environment. A firm with strong innovative capabilities, for example, will generally favor differentiation strategies. Why? Because the ability to make product improvements, whether incremental or radical, enables a firm to offer newer and more unique products directed at specific customer needs. Intel favors heavy investment in product innovation so that it can remain on the leading edge of new-product introductions in the microprocessor industry. Notice, however, that Intel's differentiators (innovation and product development speed) are particularly valuable in the arenas where computer manufacturers like Dell want to be able to provide the latest and greatest technologies to their customers. This strategy enables Intel to charge higher prices during the early stages of the product life cycle, generating increased cash flows that it can, in turn, invest in building its brand and further differentiating its products.

Alternatively, capabilities in large-scale manufacturing and distribution generally favor low-cost strategies. Cooper Industries, for example, has developed skills in acquiring and consolidating companies in mature tool, hardware, or electrical-product industries, infusing them with modern manufacturing technology and increasing supplier power over critical customer segments. In particular, the ability to modernize manufacturing processes (the company calls it Cooperizing) gives the firm a cost advantage over many competitors. Thus, Cooper uses differentiators that are cost effective and give it an advantage in arenas where customers look at price as a key decision criterion. The point we are making here with the Intel and Cooper examples is that a strategic position is valuable to the extent that it helps the firm stake out turf in a desirable market.

Economic Drivers of Strategic Positioning

In order to fully understand the logic behind different strategic positions, we need to identify the different economic drivers that support and facilitate each strategic position and foster their success. In this section, we'll describe some of the key economic drivers of both low-cost and differentiation strategies. (Remember that because *focus* strategies are special variations on these two basic types of strategy, the same economic drivers apply to them.) In order to understand how firms might be able to achieve a competitive advantage as a result of their strategic position, we need to understand economic drivers and how they function.

DRIVERS OF LOW-COST ADVANTAGE

Firms have different production costs for several reasons. Some of the more common (and important) include economies of scale, learning, production technology, product design, and location advantages for sourcing inputs. In this section, we'll review some of these more important sources of potential cost advantage. A successful low-cost strategy requires that a firm is proficient at exploiting one or more of these drivers. Conversely, of course, firms that are unable to leverage these cost drivers either need to acquire the capabilities and resources to do so or to reevaluate their strategy.

Economies of Scale **Economies of scale** exist during a given period of time *if the average total cost for a unit of production is lower at higher levels of output*. To better understand the nature and importance of economies of scale, we need to review the various types of production costs:

economy of scale Condition under which average total cost for a unit of production is lower at higher levels of output.

- *Fixed costs* (such as rent and equipment) remain the same for different levels of production unless a firm expands the size of its production operations.

- *Variable costs* are the costs of variable inputs (such as raw materials and labor); they vary directly with output.

- *Marginal cost* is the cost of the last unit of production.

- *Total cost* is the sum of all production costs; it increases as output goes up.

- *Average cost* is the *mean* cost of total production (e.g., total costs/total # of units produced) during a given period (say, a year).

Economies of scale exist if *average costs* are lower at higher levels of production. Under what circumstances might it cost less to manufacture more products during one given time period than during another?

Economies of scale can result from a variety of efficiencies, all related to higher volumes of production relative to a given asset base: spreading fixed costs over greater volume, specializing in a specific production process, practicing superior inventory management, exercising purchasing power, or spending more effectively on advertising or R&D.

Economies of scale result primarily from the first reason—spreading fixed costs over greater levels of output. It stands to reason that within the feasible range of production at a given facility, increasing output will enable the firm to spread its fixed costs over greater levels of production. If, for example, R&D costs account for a significant portion of the firm's total cost, larger scale production enables the firm to cut average cost by spreading R&D costs over more units of production.

Often, greater economies of scale are only available if the firm expands its operations or consolidates several disparate operating facilities into a single, larger, and more efficient operation. For example, Coca-Cola bought back many bottling operations from individual franchisees during the 1980s and 1990s. These facilities were optimal for the exclusive geographic territory controlled by franchisees, but not as optimal as they could have been if they had served a larger area. But, individual franchisees had no incentive to expand their operation because they were limited by contract to being able to sell in a defined geographic territory. To solve this problem, Coca-Cola bought back many franchises, then consolidated into larger, more efficient geographic territories and built large and efficient bottling plants that had much greater economies of scale.

In addition, greater scale often encourages the use of more sophisticated inventory management systems. Some of these systems, though not cost-effective at lower volumes, bring significant rewards at sufficiently large scales of production. Audi, for instance, persuaded suppliers to locate operations in facilities adjacent to its newly centralized facilities in Ingoldstadt, Germany. In turn, the carmaker was able to implement just-in-time inventory techniques that didn't work when smaller-scale manufacturing operations were more widely dispersed.[4] Similarly, when numerous inputs are involved, the price depends, in part, on the volume purchased. That's why large buyers often have more leverage in negotiating price. Wal-Mart, for example, is renowned (even notorious) for exercising its buying power to hold down input costs.

If branding plays a key role in the firm's strategy, larger scale often provides a significant advertising advantage. In order to influence consumer decisions, advertising must first reach a certain "threshold" at which it creates awareness. If two firms of significantly different size allocate the same *proportion* of revenues to advertising, they'll achieve significantly different levels of awareness. Thus, large firms allocate more total dollars for advertising and reap the benefit of greater awareness. In addition, large firms can bargain for price discounts in various media that aren't extended to smaller accounts.

Diseconomies of Scale   Do not, however, make the mistake of assuming that size automatically ensures economies of scale. In reality, almost all operations processes are subject to the **diseconomies of scale** that occur when average total cost *increases* at higher levels of output.

Diseconomies of scale can result from bureaucracy, high labor costs, and differences in efficiency between interdependent operations. Moreover, a firm may have economies of scale in some value-chain activities that result in diseconomies of scale on other dimensions. For instance, consider the world of institutional fund management. The 20 largest fund managers control over 40 percent of professionally managed money in the world. According to research by a large consulting practice specializing in financial services, Mercer Oliver Wyman, fund management is a very scale-sensitive business. A fund manager with a $10,000,000 portfolio incurs the same costs as a manager with a $100,000,000 portfolio. The scale economies in the fund management industry are evidenced in the profitability of fund management companies. Profits for fund management companies are typically a function of scale—larger firms are more profitable. However, Mercer notes that while smaller firms are at a cost disadvantage, the funds that deliver the higher returns to investors in the fund (i.e., customers, not shareholders) tend to be smaller boutique firms.[5] They suggest that this might be due to some form of diseconomy of scale that manifests itself in fund performance, not firm profits.

Greater production volume may lead to greater sales revenues, but those added sales may have greater transportation or service costs or lower price structures. For instance, Microsoft is finding that it has saturated developed country markets with its Windows operating systems, and the entry into emerging economies like India and China will require very, very deep discounts on its traditional pricing. Large-scale operations can also lead to inflexibility—and increased costs—in the face of changing needs.[6] This is what happened to General Motors in the early 1990s. After spending billions to complement its massive scale with an appropriate level of automation, GM discovered that its technological upgrade didn't allow it to switch platforms fast enough to respond to shifts in the market. Inflexibility in the face of changing consumer preferences and new-model intro-

diseconomy of scale
Condition under which average total costs per unit of production increases at higher levels of input.

ductions by competitors actually caused costs at GM's newly automated plants to go up, not down.

Minimum Efficient Scale How, then, can a firm achieve optimal performance? Ultimately, the objective is to find the scale necessary to achieve the lowest possible average cost. Let's examine this concept in more detail.

As we've just seen, costs may decline at some ranges of production but increase at others. This fact suggests that *total average cost* can be represented by a *U*-shaped curve that has a minimum point. The output level that delivers the lowest possible costs is the **minimum efficient scale (MES)**. Often, firms operating below or above MES suffer from a cost disadvantage. Generally, there is a range of scale—or of output levels—at which costs will be minimized. MES is the smallest scale necessary to achieve maximum economies of scale. It's critical to decisions about a firm's scale of operations because it targets the level of production needed to enjoy all the benefits made possible by large scale. It also establishes the size that a new entrant must achieve in order to match the scale advantages enjoyed by incumbents. Exhibit 5.4 illustrates some possible relationships between economies of scale, diseconomies of scale, and minimum efficient scale, along with examples of these types of economies and diseconomies. Exhibit 5.5 gives you some examples of the ways in which scale may result in lower costs. Although MES understandably varies by industry and market segment, the exhibit generally conveys the idea that managers must take into account economy-of-scale tradeoffs when making investments in service or production capacity.

MES and Technology Not surprisingly, MES is also a function of technology. Obviously, an industry may employ more than one type of technology. In the steel industry, for example, some plants—so-called minimills—use electric-arc furnaces; whereas old-line integrated steel companies continue to use blast-arc furnaces. Minimills are designed to make steel in a simple three-stage process that starts with scrap metal; whereas integrated steel manufacturing requires investments in equipment that start earlier in the value chain with iron ore and coal. Consequently, the scale requirements of the two technologies are quite different, and minimills can achieve MES at roughly one-tenth the scale required for efficient operation at an integrated mill. However, the large integrated mills can have a cost advantage over the minimills when they are able to operate at full capacity.

minimum efficient scale (MES) The output level that delivers the lowest total average cost.

Exhibit 5.4 Scale and Cost

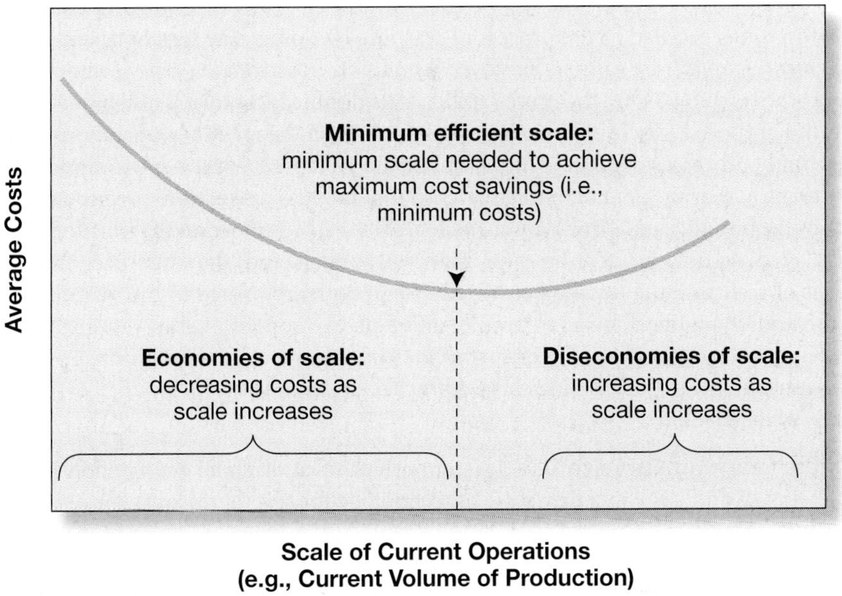

Exhibit 5.5   Examples of Scale Economies

Examples of Economies and Diseconomies of Scale	
Economies of Scale	**Diseconomies of Scale**
"Because we are producing and selling more, we can run our factories at full capacity." "Greater sales volume lets us deliver full truckloads instead of partial loads." "We have greater purchasing power with our suppliers." "Now our advertising costs in a region are spread over a larger number of retail outlets."	"Selling more products has required loosening production standards, which results in higher service and warranty work." "Higher production volumes has required more or larger suppliers of raw materials, who may be in a better bargaining position." "No distribution company is big enough to handle our increased volume, which means we have to build and manage the logistics capability ourselves." "Now that we are bigger, we have a bigger regulatory burden."

With some technologies, MES is reached only at relatively low levels of production, and although there's no scale advantage at higher levels, neither is there any disadvantage. Some technologies result quite quickly in a disadvantage at a scale larger than MES; whereas still others support wide ranges of scale without generating any real cost differences.

The Learning Curve   In addition to scale economies, other factors can contribute to lower operating costs. Two firms of the same size, for example, may have significantly different operating costs because one has progressed farther down the **learning curve**—in other words, it has excelled at the process of learning by doing. The basic principle holds that *incremental production costs decline at a constant rate as production experience is gained;* the steeper the learning curve, the more rapidly costs decline. This idea is attributed to T. P. Wright, who proposed a theory for basing cost estimates on the repetitive operations of airplane assembly processes in 1936.[7] (In the 1970s, the Defense Department commissioned research to refine learning-curve mathematics so that it could make more precise cost estimates.) See the box entitled "How Would *You* Do That? 5.1" for more on the learning curve.

Before reading any farther, be sure that you understand the difference between economies of scale and the learning curve. Although both are related to the quantity produced, the underlying mechanisms are quite different. Economies of scale reflect the scale of the operation *during any given period of time*—the volume of current production. Cost decreases attributable to the learning curve reflect *the cumulative level of production since the production of the first unit.*

Putting the Learning Curve to Use   It is important to understand the relationship between experience and costs in a firm's use of technology for several reasons. For one, managers can make more accurate total-cost forecasts when they're preparing bids for large projects. In addition, taking the learning curve into consideration may enable managers to make more aggressive pricing decisions. Japanese motorcycle and automobile manufacturers, for

learning curve Incremental production costs decline at a constant rate as production experience is gained; the steeper the learning curve, the more rapidly costs decline.

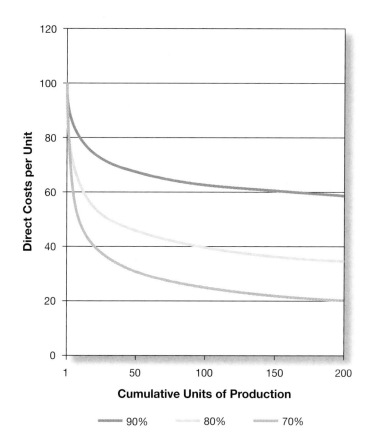

Exhibit 5.6 Pricing, Profitability, and the Learning Curve

example, considered the expected future costs savings associated with the learning curve when setting entry prices for the U.S. market. Although initial prices may actually have been below *current* production costs, they were set to reflect *future* cost estimates. The low prices also enabled the Japanese to make rapid gains in market share. Resulting higher volumes not only contributed to economies of scale, but also reduced costs due to learning. Later, Asian computer-chip manufacturers adopted the same strategy for entering the U.S. market.[8] This basic logic is summarized in Exhibit 5.6, where you can see how the price set for the product generates profits after a certain amount of cumulative volume-based learning has been accumulated. The intuition of the learning curve is that direct costs decline as a function of cumulative units of production. But different companies and different industries are likely to have different learning curves. So, in the second graph of Exhibit 5.6, you see three different learning curves compared. For instance, a 90% learning curve means that every time cumulative production doubles, direct costs are only 90% of what they were at prior levels. What else can you apply the learning curve to? Here are a few more questions that could help you answer:

- A new bank clerk needed an hour to encode his first 500 checks, 50 minutes for the second 500, and 42 for the fourth 500. When will he be able to work at the standard rate of 1,000 checks per hour?

- An electrical contracting firm wired a home in two hours. The same team took 90 minutes to wire an identical second home. The fourth home only took 70 minutes. How long will it take it to wire the tenth home?

How Would
YOU DO THAT? 5.1

How to Take the Learning Curve on Two Wheels

How can the learning curve actually help a company? To consider this question, let's review a problem faced by Montague, the maker of full-size, high performance bicycles that fold. Montague's latest innovation is the Paratrooper™ bike—a full-sized bike that is strong enough to drop from a plane, durable enough to traverse any terrain, and moves at high speeds with minimal maintenance. Montague actually developed this novel bike in partnership with the U.S. government's Defense Advanced Research Projects Agency (DARPA) to bridge the gap between heavy military vehicles and walking soldiers. Up to this point, the Paratrooper™ has only been in prototype form for evaluation by Montague and DARPA. However, after several tradeshows, it appears that there may be heavy commercial demand for the bike from military groups, emergency, police, and rescue patrols, and many civilians. Of course, now the challenge for Montague is to set a price for the Paratrooper ™ that customers are willing to pay, and at which it is likely to make a good profit. How can Montague take the principle of the learning curve into consideration in forecasting its cost and offering the most attractive price?

Let's assume that Montague has already made four prototypes and that it cost the firm $300 in direct costs to make the first bike, $270 for the second, and $243 for the last (fourth) bike made. (Fortunately, there were four prototypes; it's never wise to estimate trends with only two data points.) Using the concept of the learning curve, Montague can systematically use historical data to estimate future costs. Montague can do this in several ways. (Bear in mind, by the way, that we could measure either in terms of costs or hours; for the sake of simplicity, we'll use costs throughout this exercise.)

One way to estimate future costs is simply to calculate projected values using some basic math. To do this, we need to know a fundamental rule for quantifying the learning curve: For every *doubling* of *cumulative* production levels, costs decline at a constant rate. In our example, cumulative production has reached four bikes. In other words, it's doubled twice—once from one to two, and again from two to four. If we calculate the percentages for each doubling, we see that (conveniently enough) we have a 90-percent learning curve: The direct costs to make the second bike were 90 percent of the first, and the fourth was 90 percent of the second. Now we just repeat the process to estimate future costs: In other words, we take 90 percent of current production as our estimate for costs *once cumulative production doubles again,* repeating the process until we've reached our target level of production (100 bikes). Using this quick and dirty method, we see that the cost per bike falls to approximately $150 by the time we've reached 100 bikes. Our findings are summarized in Exhibit 5.7.

This procedure works fine for small batches, but it could become quite cumbersome for large production runs.

In more complicated situations, we need the actual *learning-curve formula*. With this formula and a good calculator or spreadsheet, we can project costs for a specific estimated number of units rather than having to interpolate from a table of values that increase at doubling rates.

Here's the formula for estimating learning curves:

$$y = ax^{-b}$$

where *y* is the cost per unit for the *xth* unit produced; *a* is the cost of the first unit produced; *x* is the cumulative number of products produced (or desired level if the rate of learning, *b*, is already determined); and *b* is the *rate* at which costs are reduced every time cumulative production doubles (always a negative number calculated from other known quantities). Using this formula and a spreadsheet, we can project future costs for any level of production and thus make a more informed decision about our costs. Our new findings are summarized in Exhibit 5.8.

If you're averse to math, you may prefer to resort to one of several aids. First, we could create a table in which we plug in the *rates* for several common learning curves (i.e., the figures needed to plug *b* into the previous formula). Then we can find our solutions by combining these rates with our spreadsheet capabilities, as shown in Exhibit 5.9.

If you want things even simpler, you could visit a NASA Web site that contains a "learning-curve calculator"

Number of Bikes Produced	Cost per Bike
1st	$300 actual
2nd	$270 actual
4th	$243 actual
8th	$218.70 estimate
16th	$196.83 estimate
32nd	$177.15 estimate
64th	$159.43 estimate
100th	$148.98 estimate
128th	$143.49 estimate

Exhibit 5.7 Cost per Bike and the Learning Curve

at www.jsc.nasa.gov/bu2/learn.html. Using this handy device, you can plug in a few basic data and wait for it to solve the problem for you. (*Hint:* Use the Crawford version of the calculator, which corresponds to the current formulation used in business.)

So, back to our question: At what price should Montague offer the Paratrooper™? Well, average gross margins (i.e., sales minus cost-of-goods-sold, as a percentage of sales) in the bike industry are 37 percent, and Montague aims to sell unique products,

so its margins should be better than this.[14] If Montague is confident that it can sell more than 100 Paratroopers™, then a price of $300 per bike would provide it with a $151.02 gross margin, or approximately 50 percent, per bike once it reaches the 100 unit sale mark.

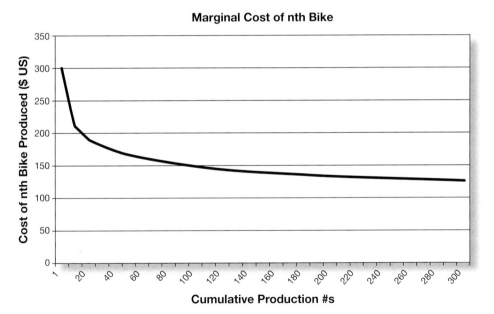

Marginal Cost of nth Bike

Exhibit 5.8 Marginal Costs for Montague

Learning Curve	80%	85%	90%	95%
Rate of Learning	–.322	–.234	–.152	–.074

Exhibit 5.9 Spreadsheet for Montague

- A fast-food trainee takes an hour to prepare her first 20 sandwiches, 45 minutes for the second 20, and her fourth batch of 20 sandwiches only took 34. What will her production rate be after 24 hours of experience?

- A custom boat builder built a prototype of a new sailboat. From past experience, he knows the learning curve rate for similar boats. What are the labor requirements for the second and third boats?

These questions may seem on the surface to be overly operational to be considered strategic. However, understanding the learning curve and how it works in your specific business helps a strategic manager forecast future costs, and develop an optimal strategic position for the firm given its cost structure. Cost structure is, after all, one of the key factors underlying your strategy's economic logic.

Multiunit Organizations and the Learning Curve A related effect of the learning curve occurs when a multiunit organization transfers learning from one unit to another.[9] Franchise systems, for instance, can codify their knowledge about the most effective way to operate a store. Technically, therefore, each new franchise doesn't have to start from scratch. Rather, every unit benefits from corporate training programs that give new franchisees a head start at tackling the learning curve. Because units can share new knowledge about effective practices, multiunit firms can make faster progress in mastering learning curves than single-unit operations.

Other Sources of Cost Advantage Other potential sources of cost advantage include *economies of scope, production technology,* and *product design.*

Economies of Scope As the term suggests, *economies of scope* are similar to economies of scale. They refer, however, to potential cost savings associated with *multiproduct* production. When a firm produces two or more products, it has greater scope of operations than a firm that produces only one. If such a firm can share a resource among one or more of its products—thereby lowering the costs of each product—it benefits from **economies of scope**.[10] We discuss this concept more fully in Chapter 7 because it's fundamental to diversification as a corporate strategy. Economies of scope, however, are available not only to large diversified firms but also to small privately held enterprises that are just beginning to expand their product offerings.

Here we offer a simple example to help you understand economies of scope.[11] The multipurpose table and furniture industry is made up of a fragmented group of about 60 major manufacturers who share a $1-billion market. One of these companies, Mity-Lite, was formed in 1987 by Gregory Wilson when he was in the institutional furniture business. The company's original product line consisted of folding tables targeted at such institutional users as schools, churches, civic organizations, and hospitals. From the outset, Mity-Lite used a heat- and vacuum-thermoforming process to mold engineering-grade plastics, and combined this process with durable folding-metal frames to build tables that are both much lighter and more durable than competing particleboard or plywood tables. As the company grew, it learned to implement a number of changes in both its manufacturing process and product designs—changes that have increased production volumes, improved quality, and lowered costs.

After a decade of successful market penetration, Mity-Lite developed a reputation as a leading designer, manufacturer, and marketer of folding-leg tables. With excess capacity in his Orem, Utah, plant, Wilson began to study possible growth options. Because customers of folding-leg tables often buy folding or stacking chairs at the same time, Wilson saw at least one opportunity to expand into complementary products. He soon discovered that the same technology he used to form durable tables could be used to manufacture chairs. Moreover, because expansion into chair production didn't require a new plant, the cost of the manufacturing facility could be shared in the production of both tables and chairs. These

economy of scope Condition under which lower total average costs result from sharing resources to produce more than one product or service.

cost savings reflect economies of scope. From its small beginnings as a supplier of church furniture, Mity-Lite has grown an average of 35 percent per year and has become an international player in the institutional furniture industry.

Production Technology   Naturally, different production technologies entail different costs. Often, a new entrant who wants to compete against industry incumbents with significant scale and experience advantages tries to match or beat incumbents' costs by introducing a production technology that's subject to different economics. JetBlue, for instance, has the lowest operating costs of all major U.S. airlines, and the source of its successful strategy—its production technology—compares quite favorably with the technologies used by other airlines.

Similarly, Nucor Steel originally entered an industry that wasn't particularly attractive from a traditional point of view. Profits were low, capital intensity was high, and the bargaining power of buyers was strong (i.e., steel is a commodity, which means that buyers make purchase decisions primarily on price if all other factors are equal). In addition, most incumbents had the advantage of a century's worth of experience. Nucor, however, didn't use the same technology as its incumbent competitors. Rather than building an integrated mill with blast-arc furnaces, Nucor opted for the lower-cost electric-arc technology favored by minimills.[12]

Product Design   Similarly, product design can sometimes be altered to lower a firm's production costs.[13] When Canon, for example, decided to enter the photocopier industry, incumbents such as Xerox had formidable advantages in scale and experience. Canon, however, redesigned the photocopier so that it required fewer parts and allowed for simpler assembly. The new design dropped Canon's costs below those of Xerox and enabled the new entrant to gain significant market share at Xerox's expense.

Finally, different sourcing practices result in different cost structures. Some firms try to attain lower production costs by locating their operations in cheaper labor markets. Others outsource manufacturing altogether. Pacific Cycle, for instance, makes bikes for less than Trek, whose operations are in the U.S., by outsourcing much of its production to China and Taiwan.

Drivers of Differentiation Advantages

In order to sell products at premium prices, firms must make their uniqueness and value apparent to customers. In this section, we'll review the economic logic and some of the common drivers of a successful differentiation strategy. While firms that pursue differentiation advantages must still be cost conscious and good at managing tangible aspects of their products and services, they must typically also excel at managing the intangibles. As a rule, differentiation involves one or more of the following differentiators among product offerings: *premium brand image, customization and convenience, unique styling, speed,* and *unusually high quality.* And though these differentiators have much about them that is intangible, these intangibles were nonetheless expressly managed and developed.

Premium Brand Image   When Toyota introduced its premium Lexus line in 1989, its strategy was based on extensive market analysis and product development efforts. Relying on its ability to manufacture high-quality automobiles, Toyota was confident that it could penetrate the highly profitable luxury car segment. In fact, managers regarded the whole idea as quite logical, given the brand image already enjoyed by Toyota. Consequently, the company launched and developed an entirely new brand with a separate dealer network. High quality was a Lexus trademark from the beginning, with the new luxury car winning its first J.D. Power and Associates number-one ranking in the 1990 Initial Quality Study. Being named one of *Car & Driver*'s 10 best and the Motoring Press Association's Best Imported Car of the Year also bolstered the Lexus image.

Bear in mind, however, that although quality earned a slew of technical awards for Lexus, targeted marketing created something even more important—customer awareness. In practice, a differentiation strategy means that marketers understand how to *segment* the market in which they intend to compete—a process known as *market segmentation*. They must identify specific subgroups of buyers who have distinguishable needs, select one or more of these unique buyer needs, and satisfy them in ways that competitors don't or can't.

Customization and Convenience   Curves International, for instance, saw a unique opportunity to segment the fitness-club industry by targeting women who desired a nonintimidating environment. Curves' equipment is different from that of competitors, not only because it's designed for women but because it uses hydraulic-resistance equipment that eliminates the need to worry about weight stacks. In addition, the Curves program features a convenient 30-minute exercise routine and small, local neighborhood gyms. Since its founding in 1992, Curves has opened more than 10,000 locations, and the company's success suggests that the segment it targeted was indeed overlooked or underserved by industry incumbents.

Similarly, customization and convenience are a theme evident at Swiss Colony. In case you have not heard of it before, Swiss Colony is a successful, privately-held direct-mail company with over $600 million in sales. If you have heard of it, you may think of this catalog sales company only as a purveyor of fine holiday cheese, sausage, and cracker gift baskets. However, then you would be overlooking the many other catalog brands that bring in the lion's share of the revenues per year for this profitable catalog and online retailer. Some of its many catalogs include Durdy Looks (apparel, furniture, and accessories), Room for Color (furnishings organized by color coordination), and Ashro Lifestyle (fashionable clothing for African American women).

Unique Styling   Some firms use style, fashion, and design as key ingredients in a differentiation advantage. Ironically, this can result in premium prices even when product quality is not particularly high. For instance, Harley-Davidson generates prices for motorcycles that exceed that of the competition even though its quality is measurably lower. Why would a potential motorcycle customer pay more for a Harley when it breaks down more often and requires more regular trips to the repair shop? Because many customers for large motorcycles are looking for the image that a Harley-Davidson motorcycle portrays. At a technical level, Honda motorcycles are superior and their quality is higher. Yet, for many enthusiasts, the styling, sound, and image offered by a Harley is worth every penny (or every $7,000–$20,000, as the case may be) that they cost.

Speed   You have probably heard of Moore's Law, the prediction attributed to Intel co-founder Gordon Moore that the number of transistors on an integrated circuit (a microchip) would double every 18 to 24 months. Although Moore's Law was initially made in the form of an observation and forecast, the more widely it became accepted, the more it served as a goal for an entire industry. This drove both marketing and engineering departments of semiconductor manufacturers to focus enormous energy aiming for the specified increase in processing power that it was presumed one or more of their competitors would soon actually attain. Intel is a great case in point. It uses its need for speed to remain in high demand among customers and well ahead of competitors. Ironically, not only are its products getting physically faster (i.e., the processing capacity and speed of its computer chips), but it is also getting faster at developing them and introducing them to the market. The strategic advantages created by Intel's speed are many. Most important perhaps is the fact that the people who buy computers also want to have very fast ones, which means that customers as well as suppliers are keeping fast chips in high demand. Moreover, since Intel is able to deliver on this promise of speed, its customers (like Dell and Apple) and related product developers (like Microsoft) are able to engineer their leading-edge products around Intel chips.

Unusually High Quality   Apple's computers cost, on average, ten percent more than comparably equipped Dell computers. There may be several reasons customers are willing to pay this premium, but the one most often cited by Apple users is the quality of the hardware and software. Apple's operating system is demonstrably more reliable and less susceptible to crashing than the Windows operating system included on Dell computers. In the fast food industry, it is easy to see that hamburgers (or any other genre of food) cost more at Red Robin or Fuddruckers than they do at McDonald's, Wendy's, or Burger King. The main reason a customer would pay four times more for a hamburger than they could at a more convenient location is because the product is of significantly higher quality.

Creating Value and Promoting Willingness to Pay   The goal of differentiation is to be able to demand a price sufficient to do two things: (1) recoup the added costs of delivering the value-added feature and (2) generate enough profit to make the strategy worthwhile. The point of differentiation is to drive up the customer's **willingness to pay**—that is, to induce customers to pay more for the firm's products or services than a competitors'. The producer wants to drive a wedge between what customers are willing to pay and the costs of producing the product or service.

willingness to pay   Principle of differentiation strategy by which customers are willing to pay more for certain product features.

Threats to Successful Competitive Positioning

For a firm using any of the generic strategies that we've discussed in this chapter, success hinges on a number of factors. Does the firm have the right resources, such as those that may accrue from scale or learning, for implementing a low-cost strategy? Will the marketplace reward a differentiation strategy? In some markets (those which, like steel, are more commodity-like), customers' purchase decisions are driven much more strongly by price than by product features, and in these cases there's not much that firms can do to justify higher prices. A summary of the common drivers of differentiation and low-cost advantage, along with the threats to those positions, is listed in Exhibit 5.10. Under most circumstances, a successful strategic position must satisfy two requirements: (1) It must be based on the firm's resources and capabilities, and (2) it must achieve some level of consistency with the conditions that prevail in the industry.

	Drivers	**Threats**
Low Cost	• Economies of scale • Learning • Economies of scope • Superior technology • Superior product design	• New technology • Inferior quality • Social, political, and economic risk of outsourcing
Differentiation	• Premium brand image • Customization • Unique styling • Speed • Convenient access • Unusually high quality	• Failing to increase buyers' willingness to pay higher prices • Underestimating costs of differentiation • Overfulfilling buyers' needs • Lower-cost imitation

Exhibit 5.10   Low Cost and Differentiation: Drivers and Threats

THREATS TO LOW-COST POSITIONS

In terms of these two critical requirements, let's look first at the numerous threats facing firms aiming for a low-cost competitive position. First, the firm may face threats on the technological front. In particular, the resource that makes it possible for a firm to compete on the basis of cost—often a certain technology—can be imitated. Efficient production and process technologies can move from firm to firm by any number of means, such as consultants with clients throughout the industry and the movement of key personnel from company to company.

Granted, even though an imitator may acquire comparable technology, the original firm may still enjoy the benefits of greater experience and the learning curve. A more serious threat to low-cost competitors is the possibility that another firm may introduce a new technology—one which, like minimill technology in the steel industry, supports a different scale and a more efficient learning process. In such cases, even small latecomers can establish cost positions significantly lower than those of larger, more experienced low-cost leaders.

Second, low-cost leadership means offering an acceptable combination of price and quality. A real threat to an intended low-cost position is the failure to offer sufficient quality to satisfy buyers' basic needs. Over the past decade, for example, Kmart's experiments in low-cost positioning have been thwarted not only by Wal-Mart's ability to stake out an even lower-cost position, but by Kmart's own inability to offer a retail experience of comparable quality (customers complain of empty shelves, uninviting environments, and less helpful staff).

Recently, another serious threat has arisen to low-cost competitors in labor-intensive industries: increased public awareness of questionable labor practices in developing countries. Struggling to keep wage costs as low as possible, many companies (some unwittingly) have entered into agreements with suppliers who enforce excessive work hours, deny basic employee services, employ children, and violate what, at least in the U.S., are considered acceptable working conditions. Watchdog groups regularly publicize such cases, and reforms push up costs.[15] Many multinational companies have established codes of ethical conduct for suppliers, but enforcing these standards—inspecting and auditing overseas suppliers—also increases costs. Managers must be certain that their foreign sourcing arrangements are in compliance with their corporate values.

THREATS TO DIFFERENTIATION POSITIONS

Needless to say, the intent to provide a differentiated product doesn't necessarily result in competitive advantage and enhanced profitability. A number of factors can sabotage a differentiation strategy. Obviously, a differentiating feature that buyers don't care about merely increases costs without increasing willingness to pay, which cuts into profit margins. Until recently, for example, Audi suffered from the fact that although its manufacturing costs were comparable to those of BMW and Mercedes, it couldn't get customers to pay comparable prices. In effect, Audi was either overfulfilling the needs of buyers who were in the market for well-made but more modestly priced cars or underfulfilling the needs of customers in the market for high-image, high-quality cars.

In addition, failing to understand the total costs entailed by differentiation can derail a differentiation position. The cost of differentiation has no direct effect on customers' willingness to pay, and in most industries, cost-plus pricing is not an option. Jaguar, for example, found itself in an apparently enviable position in the early 1980s: It had a highly differentiated product with good brand recognition and strong customer appeal, and unlike Audi's targeted customers, car buyers were willing to pay premium prices for Jaguars. Unfortunately, antiquated manufacturing processes drove costs so high that, even with products selling in the top price range, the company lost money. Many of its operations weren't even automated, but ironically, Jaguar took pride in its traditional hands-on methods—in part because managers believed that brand recognition and customer loyalty were tied to an appreciation of the individualized manufacturing process. Ford purchased Jaguar in 1990 and, after studying the company's operations, revamped assembly plants in an effort to combine the best aspects of both traditional and modern methods. Ford, for instance, retained the practice of installing hand-sewn leather interiors and natural wood inlays but significantly modernized the processes for assembling bodies and power trains.[16]

Two additional reasons differentiation can fail are overfulfillment and ease of imitation. When product features exceed buyer needs, the added costs to provide these unwanted features, coupled with customers' lack of willingness to pay for this differentiation, results in significantly lower margins. For instance, several years ago John Deere invested significant resources in the technologies that went into their farm equipment. The company was able to produce some of the most technologically sophisticated tractors on the market. Unfortunately, Deere's customers were unwilling to pay for them. They liked the technology, just not the price that went with the technology. Today, Deere gradually introduces new features at a pace that keeps them ahead of competitors, but only as quickly as customers demonstrate their willingness to pay. Finally, as the Deere example suggests, creating differentiation that competitors can emulate quickly or cheaply undermines any advantage that it might afford. Naturally, once competitors have matched a product's unique feature, it's no longer unique and will probably lose its ability to command premium prices. In some industries, patents provide short-term protection for innovative products. In others, companies must seek alternative means of protection. In the soft drink industry, where products are easily imitated (they are, after all, simple combinations of water, sugar, color, and flavoring), Coke and Pepsi discourage imitation by exercising power of scale over suppliers and buyers and conducting aggressive marketing campaigns to sustain brand image.

THREATS TO FOCUS POSITIONS

Although focused low-cost or focused differentiation positions are specialized cases of low-cost leadership and broad differentiation and thus subject to all the same threats as those just reviewed, they face one additional threat that deserves mention. Firms that implement focus positions face the threat of being out-focused by competitors. A firm relying on a focus strategy may lose its advantage by attempting to grow and consequently attempt to meet the needs of too many customers. If that happens, a competitor or new entrant may then more successfully target the needs of the original focused group of customers. As existing or new competitors identify new or previously unexploited needs of the segment, they may be in a better position to uniquely satisfy the needs of that segment. For instance, Harley-Davidson faces the threat that custom chopper shops will pull away customers because they can more uniquely satisfy the needs of a segment of Harley's market.

THREATS TO INTEGRATED POSITIONS

In his original analysis of generic strategic positions, Porter, arguing that they were mutually exclusive, warned against the temptation to straddle positions: Firms that try both to differentiate and to achieve a low-cost position will end up **straddling** two inconsistent positions.

All firms, Porter suggested, must make decisions about positioning their products and will consequently choose one strategy over the other. Developing a low-cost strategy means that a firm must forgo subsequent opportunities to enhance product uniqueness or quality (that is, to develop a position based on differentiation). In this respect, selected strategies and forgone opportunities must be regarded as tradeoffs. H&R Block, for example, can't enter the field of high-level estate and tax planning because such services require the kind of high-cost specialists that a low-cost competitor can't afford. Thus, Block trades off

straddling Unsuccessful attempt to integrate both low-cost and differentiation positions.

the advantages of high-margin services for the advantages of a low-cost tax preparation business. By the same token, a "pure" differentiator trades off the cost-saving advantages of producing standardized products for the advantages of satisfying a demand for customized products.

Although many firms have succeeded in pursuing integrated strategies, it's still critical for managers to understand the tradeoffs they make when they opt for one position over the other. Virtually no firm can succeed in being all things to all customers. For one, firms need to know exactly what opportunities they're forgoing.

Second, knowing what tradeoffs can be made in an industry helps managers recognize what competitors can and can't do in attempts to juggle strategies. Why, for instance, can't United, American, and Delta lower their costs to match those of Southwest Airlines? Many of the specific practices by which Southwest maintains its lower-cost position entail tradeoffs that the other carriers can't make. United, Delta, and American don't have the option of flying just one type of aircraft, even if it would save on training and maintenance costs. Nor can they abandon their expensive hub facilities, which are integral to the logistics of their flight systems, even though the hub system and its accompanying gate fees are much more costly than Southwest's reliance on secondary airports and smaller destination cities.

Strategy and Fit with Industry Conditions

In Chapter 1, we introduced the strategy-diamond model of strategy formulation. Recall that an important input into this model is a firm's objectives. Earlier in the chapter we detailed generic strategies *by type,* but in order to show how the strategy-diamond and generic-strategy models are compatible, we need to remind ourselves that when managers decide on generic competitive positions, they aren't deciding on strategies themselves: ◆ Rather, they're stating *objectives* with respect to several elements of their overall strategy—indicating precisely how they intend the firm to systematically deal with differentiators, economic logic, and certain aspects of arenas.

 Economic Logic

We know, too, that industry conditions have an important effect on strategy formulation. One way to illustrate this effect is to examine the threats and opportunities presented to a company during different phases of the industry life cycle. In this section, we'll treat each phase of the life cycle as if conditions are not likely to change in the short term. In other words, in order to show how alternative strategies function under different life-cycle conditions, we'll take advantage of the fact that industry analysis gives us a "snapshot" view of an industry at a particular point in its life cycle. In reality, of course, many industries are changing rapidly, and in Chapter 6, we'll turn our attention to strategies that take advantage of changes, such as the rapid and sometimes managed evolution of an industry from one stage in its life cycle to the next.

STRATEGIES FOR DIFFERENT INDUSTRY LIFE CYCLE CONDITIONS

Industry conditions should inform strategic leaders and have an influence on the strategies their firms formulate. Of course, not all firms will respond similarly to different industry conditions, but conditions at different phases of an industry life cycle provide differential opportunities and constraints. Consequently, firms' strategies tend to vary across these different phases. Exhibit 5.11 summarizes some of the more common effects of the industry life cycle on the elements of firms' strategies.

Embryonic Stage　During an industry's *embryonic* phase, when business models are unproven, no standardized technology has been established, capital needs generally outstrip the resources and capabilities of startups, and uncertainty is high. Early movers—those who

Exhibit 5.11 Strategies Tailored to Industry Life Cycle

Phase of Industry Life Cycle	Arenas	Vehicles	Differentiators	Staging	Economic Logic
Embryonic	Staying local	Internal development Alliances to secure missing inputs or distribution access	Target basic needs, minimal differentiation	Tactics to gain early footholds	Prices tend to be high Costs are high; focus is on securing additional capital to fund growth phase
Growth	Penetrating adjacent markets	Alliances for cooperation Acquisitions in targeted markets	Increase efforts toward differentiation Low-cost leaders emerge through experience and scale advantages	Integrated positions require choice of focusing first on cost or differentiation	Margins can improve rapidly because of experience and scale Price premiums accrue to successful differentiators
Mature	Globalizing Diversifying	Mergers and acquisitions for consolidation	More stable positions emerge across competitors	Choices of international markets and new industry diversification need rational sequencing	Consolidation results in fewer competitors (favoring higher margins), but declining growth demands cost containment and rationalization of operations
Decline	Abandoning some arenas if decline is severe Focusing on segments that provide the most profitability	Acquisitions for diversifying Divestitures enable some competitors to exit and others to consolidate larger shares of the market	Fewer competitors result in less pressure for differentiation, but declining sales results in greater pressure for cost savings	Timing of exit from selected segments or businesses	Rationalizing cost

succeed in establishing solid competitive positions during this stage—can set themselves up to be in a strong position during later phases of the industry life cycle.[17] Because primary demand is just being established and customers lack good information on the relative quality of products, successful tactics during this phase include getting a strong foothold and building capacity to meet growing demand.

Growth Stage As industries enter periods of rapid growth, incumbent firms increase market share by taking advantage of footholds established earlier. Rapid growth increases speed down the learning curve and presents leaders with an opportunity to establish low-cost positions that are difficult to imitate, at least in the short term. During this phase, however, technologies can change as new entrants learn from and improve on the work of early movers.

After introducing the PalmPilot, for example, Palm enjoyed an apparently formidable advantage in the PDA industry. The PalmPilot was hailed as the most successful consumer-product launch in history, reaching sales of 2 million units within three years and surpassing the adoption rates of camcorders, color TVs, VCRs, and cell phones.[18] Although it considered itself primarily a hardware device company, Palm developed its own operating system because it was dissatisfied with Microsoft's system for handheld devices. But as the PDA industry grew in size, it caught Microsoft's attention. Before long, Microsoft had renewed interest in its own operating system, and other new competitors, some of whom already had complementary relationships with Microsoft, entered the PDA software industry.[19] There's obviously an advantage in moving early, gaining a foothold that supports quick growth, and reaping cost advantages by moving quickly along the learning curve, but it doesn't necessarily constitute an impenetrable competitive barrier. New technologies and changing industry competitive structure remain threats.[20]

During the growth phase of an industry, firms make important decisions about how they intend to grow: They determine the strategic vehicles that they'll use to implement their preferred strategies. High-tech companies, for example, may seek alliances with established firms in adjacent industries, similar to the embryonic stage, in order to fill in gaps in their own range of competencies. Such is the case in the biotechnology industry; virtually all of the pure biotech companies have established alliances with large pharmaceutical companies in order to access clinical trial expertise and marketing capabilities.[21] During the growth stage, too, firms with desirable resources become attractive acquisition targets, both for incumbents wanting to grow rapidly and for firms in related industries seeking to enter the market.

Maturity Stage   As industries mature and growth slows, products become more familiar to the vast majority of potential customers. Product information is more widely available, and quality becomes a more important factor in consumer choice. A mature market, therefore, increases the ability of firms to reap premium prices from differentiation strategies.

Mature industries often undergo *consolidation*—the combination of competitors through merger or acquisition. Consolidation is often motivated by the twofold objective of exploiting economies of scale and increasing market power. The U.S. bicycle industry profiled through the examples of Pacific Cycle, Trek, and Montague, for instance, has experienced a virtual cascade of mergers and acquisitions for the better part of a decade. Although each new combination promises cost saving through greater economies of scale, evidence of significant savings remains inconclusive at best. Market power is a factor because many bicycle companies want to stay large enough to serve the needs of high-volume distribution channels such as Wal-Mart.

Decline Stage   In declining industries, products can take on the attributes of quasi commodities. Because price competition can be intense, containing costs is critical, and firms with low-cost positions have an advantage. Although customers don't entirely ignore differentiated products, declining sales discourage firms from investing in significant innovations.

During this stage, many firms consider the strategy of exiting the industry. Generally, the decision to exit means selling the company or certain divisions to competing firms. Because demand is declining, the industry probably suffers from overcapacity. Thus, reducing the number of competitors can enhance the profitability of those firms that remain. But this fact doesn't mean that exit signifies failure. In many cases, exit can be the best use of shareholders' resources.

A short case study about General Dynamics (GD) drawn from the defense industry demonstrates the potential benefits of exiting an industry during its decline stage.[22] GD was founded in 1899 as the Electric Boat Co. and a year later produced the first workable submarine, which it sold to the U.S. Navy. By the 1950s, GD was a full-fledged defense contractor, producing missiles, rockets, nuclear-powered submarines, and military air-craft. In the mid-1950s, due to the wide range of its defense-industry operations, the company changed its name to General Dynamics Corp. During the 1970s and 1980s, GD emerged as the only defense contractor to supply major systems to all branches of the U.S. military.

Despite many successful weapons programs, however, GD's profitability dropped during the late 1980s, largely because of changes in government procurement processes. In addition, the Cold War thawed rapidly in 1989 and 1990, with the Soviet withdrawal from Afghanistan, the fall of the Berlin Wall, and the collapse of Communist governments across Eastern Europe. Needless to say, the proliferation of arms treaties dampened the demand for weapons systems. GD was particularly hard-hit because it was the least diversified of all defense contractors, with a full 87 percent of its revenue tied to defense system sales.

In 1989, GD hired William Anders as chairman and CEO. His specific charge was to turn the floundering company around. Motivated by lucrative contracts that included generous incentives tied to stock-price performance, Anders and his top management team set about implementing a radical new strategy. Anders' team made immediate changes, cutting capital spending to 20 percent of the level just two years earlier (saving $337 million). They lost over $1 billion in sales and slashed R&D spending targets by 50 percent. Spending cuts were followed by massive layoffs. Anders was quite public in his pronouncements that the defense industry suffered from overcapacity, too many competitors, and dwindling demand. He publicly urged the industry to consolidate.

Over a two-year period beginning in late 1991, GD sold seven defense businesses for more than $3 billion, emerging as a much smaller and more focused company. Revenues for the new GD were a mere 34 percent of levels of two years earlier, but exiting from so many markets enabled GD to eliminate 94 percent of its outstanding debt, repurchase over 13 million shares of stock, increase dividends by 140 percent, and issue special dividends totaling $50 per share. At the end of this massive downsizing and business-exit campaign, GD had returned $3.4 billion to shareholders and debt holders. Moreover, despite the massive reduction in size, GD's market capitalization increased from about $1 billion in January 1991 to almost $2.9 billion by the end of 1993. Shareholders who held their stock during the three-year restructuring campaign realized a return of over 550 percent.

Testing the Quality of a Strategy

Now that you have command of an adequate repertory of strategy formulation tools—namely, the strategy diamond, VRINE, industry structure, and the strategic positioning models—you should be able to use them to test the quality of a firm's strategy. Clearly, developing a successful business strategy is a complex task. Although we've focused in this chapter on decisions regarding competitive position and strategic interactions, we must also stress that evaluating the effectiveness of a strategy requires that you apply all the tools and models that we've discussed in the first four chapters of this book. In this section, we'll lay out a simple five-step process that makes use of all of these tools and models to evaluate the quality of a firm's strategy. These steps are summarized in Exhibit 5.12.[23]

DOES YOUR STRATEGY EXPLOIT YOUR FIRM'S RESOURCES AND CAPABILITIES?

Your first step in testing the quality of a strategy is determining whether your strategy and competitive position exploit your firm's resources and capabilities. Low-cost strategic positions require manufacturing resources and capabilities that are likely to contribute to a cost

Exhibit 5.12 Testing the Quality of Your Strategy

Adapted from D. C. Hambrick and J. W. Fredrickson, "Are You Sure You Have a Strategy?" Academy of Management Executive 15:4 (2001), 48–59.

Key Evaluation Criteria	
1. Does your strategy exploit your key resources?	With your particular mix of resources, does this strategy give you an advantageous position relative to your competitors?
	Can you pursue this strategy more economically than your competitors?
	Do you have the capital and managerial talent to do all you plan to do?
	Are you spread too thin?
2. Does your strategy fit with current industry conditions?	Is there healthy profit potential where you're headed?
	Are you aligned with the key success factors of your industry?
3. Will your differentiators be sustainable?	Will competitors have difficulty imitating you?
	If imitation can't be foreclosed, does your strategy include a ceaseless regimen of innovation and opportunity creation to keep distance between you and the competition?
4. Are the elements of your strategy consistent and aligned with your strategic position?	Have you made choices of arenas, vehicles, differentiators, staging, and economic logic?
	Do they all fit and mutually reinforce each other?
5. Can your strategy be implemented?	Will your stakeholders allow you to pursue this strategy?
	Do you have the proper complement of implementation levers in place?
	Is the management team able and willing to lead the required changes?

advantage. For instance, Pacific Cycle is the lowest-cost bike distributor in the U.S. by virtue of its lean operations and the complete outsourcing of bike manufacturing to Taiwan and China. Likewise, a differentiation position depends on your ability to produce quality products and to project the necessary image of quality. In Trek's case, it has been careful to cultivate its high-performance image by sponsoring bike luminaries such as Lance Armstrong and selling only through the exclusive independent dealer channel. When two firms follow similar strategies, you must determine whether you can use your resources to implement your strategy more economically than your competitors can. Finally, you need to be sure that you have the capital resources—both financial and human—necessary to pull off your strategy.

DOES YOUR STRATEGY FIT WITH CURRENT INDUSTRY CONDITIONS?

Next, you must ask whether your strategy fits with the current conditions in your competitive environment. You need to know whether that environment is hostile, benign, or somewhere in between. Essentially, you want to be sure that you understand the profit *potential* of both your current position and the position toward which your strategy is taking you. Pacific Cycle viewed the big-box retailers and consolidation of the bike industry as opportunities for profitable growth. Ironically, Trek viewed the same environment with an eye toward shoring up relationships with independent bike dealers as a way to combat the influx of sales through low-cost, big-box retail channels. Thus, you need to determine whether your strategy aligns with the key success factors favored by your competitive environment.

ARE YOUR DIFFERENTIATORS SUSTAINABLE?

If competitors can imitate your differentiators, can you protect your current relationship with your customers? Imitation can erode competitive advantage, but some forms of imitation can reinforce brand loyalty to individual firms. Frequent flier programs, for example, are very easy to imitate, but customers who have accumulated many miles with one carrier are harder to steal than those who don't have very many miles. Ironically, then, imitation in this case actually serves to increase existing brand loyalty and, potentially, to benefit both firms. Frequent flier programs put up barriers to customer mobility, and without some kind of barrier that increases the cost of switching brands, a firm with easily imitated differentiators will have to rely on a continual stream of innovative offerings in order to sustain revenues.

ARE THE ELEMENTS OF YOUR STRATEGY CONSISTENT AND ALIGNED WITH YOUR STRATEGIC POSITION?

Your next step in testing the quality of a strategy is determining whether all of the elements of your strategy diamond are not only internally consistent but that they are also aligned with your strategic position, whether it is the one you occupy currently or the one toward which your strategy may direct you in the future. The challenge is to ensure that your choices of arenas, vehicles, differentiators, staging, and economic logic are mutually reinforcing and consistent with your objective, whether it's to be a low-cost leader, a differentiator, or a focused firm. For instance, to be poised for the growth phase, your strategy will need to accommodate rapid growth through the use of acquisitions or significant internal development of additional products and services. If you do not do so, your firm will be marginalized. This may be an acceptable outcome if the intended strategic position is one of focus. Alternatively, if your industry is approaching the end of the growth phase, have you implemented appropriate cost containment measures that will be required when additional price competition increases? The key is to make clear and explicit links between the vision of the firm, your strategy, and industry conditions. When these factors are aligned, the likelihood of achieving your objectives is maximized. When one of these features is not in alignment with the others, lack of coherence almost always causes the firm to slip behind competitors.

CAN YOUR STRATEGY BE IMPLEMENTED?

It does no good to concoct a brilliant strategy within the safe confines of your office at headquarters if your firm can't implement it. To test whether your strategy can be implemented, you need to make sure that it's aligned with the appropriate implementation levers. For instance, do you have the appropriate people, the necessary systems and processes, and incentives that are congruent with your objectives? If not, can you make these modifications within the organization in time to execute the strategy? Do you have the sufficient managerial talent and interest to pursue the strategy? One of the biggest obstacles to firm growth is insufficient managerial resources (e.g., time, people, interests) to focus on the details of execution. As a startup, for instance, JetBlue has set aggressive objectives for financial returns, growth, and a focused low-cost leadership position. Among other things, executing this strategy will mean continually hiring new employees who fit the company culture—people who share the core values of the firm. Otherwise, it will be vulnerable to the sort of labor problems that have beset other low-cost airlines. The most successful firms routinely discuss the integration of strategy and leadership. For instance, all discussions of new strategic initiatives will include answers to the question of "who exactly will get this done?" If there is no clear answer to this question, or if those individuals are likely to be spread too thin as a consequence, even attractive plans should not be given a green light.

Summary of Challenges

1. *Define* generic strategies *and explain how they relate to a firm's strategic position.* Strategic positioning is the concept of how executives situate or locate their firm relative to rivals along important competitive dimensions. The strategic positioning model—Porter's generic strategy model—is an enduring classic in the field of strategic management. Porter's strategy model uses two dimensions: the potential source of strategic advantage and the breadth of the strategic target market. The four generic strategies are low-cost leader, differentiation, focused low-cost, and focused differentiation.

2. *Describe the drivers of low-cost, differentiation, and focused strategic positions.* Low-cost leaders must have resources or capabilities that enable them to produce a product at a significantly lower cost than rivals. Successful low-cost leaders generally have superior economies of scale, are farther down the learning curve, or have superior production or process technologies than their rivals. However, to substantially reduce costs over rivals, low-cost leaders generally have to be willing to make tradeoffs—they cannot offer all the features, attributes, and quality that a successful differentiator can. Likewise, successful differentiators will normally have to accept higher costs than low-cost leaders. To make a differentiation strategy pay off, firms must segment the market so that customer needs are well understood, products are designed to uniquely satisfy those needs, and the products offered increase a customer's willingness to pay. Firms that attempt to straddle both positions generally do not perform well along either dimension. However, some firms have been successful at integrating basic features of both low-cost and differentiation. Those that do, typically perfect one set of economic drivers before trying to complement those with the seemingly inconsistent drivers associated with the other economic logic. A focused strategy is generally the application of a low-cost or differentiation approach to a narrowly defined arena.

3. *Identify and explain the risks associated with each generic strategic position.* Successful strategic positions are still vulner-

able. Threats to low-cost leadership include not having the resources necessary to implement the position, having low-cost drivers imitated by firms with better products, and not having sufficient quality to attract buyers. Threats to a differentiation strategy include increasing costs significantly to differentiate a product only to misperceive customer preferences, excessive cost to provide the targeted differentiation, and differentiating in ways that are easily imitated. A firm relying on a focus strategy risks growing too large, trying to meet too many needs, and then being outfocused by a more specialized company. An integrated position runs the risk of unsuccessfully straddling the logic of seemingly inconsistent economic drivers, resulting in neither a low cost position nor a differentiated one.

4. *Show how different strategic positions fit with stages of the industry life cycle.* During embryonic stages, primary demand is just beginning, and customers lack good information on the relative quality of products. Thus, building a strong foothold and the capacity to meet growing demand are more important than aggressively differentiating products. During growth stages, building on early footholds provides incumbents with an opportunity to gain market share and move down the learning curve and establish low-cost positions. Maturity stages bring lower levels of growth, and information is widely available to customers. Differentiation can reduce competitive threats and result in higher prices. During industry decline, price competition intensifies and cost containment becomes more important.

5. *Evaluate the quality of the firm's strategy.* The quality of a firm's strategy can be assessed by answering a few questions that can be answered by the basic tools of strategy, including the strategy diamond, VRINE, industry structure, and the strategic positioning models. First, you must determine whether the strategy and competitive position exploit the firm's resources and capabilities. Strategic positions such as low-cost leadership and differentiation have economic assumptions that cannot be satisfied in the absence of complementary resources and capabilities. Second, a quality strategy will also fit with the external environment—the current environment and the anticipated environment in dynamic contexts. Third, a firm's differentiators must be sustainable. Fourth, all of the elements of the strategy diamond must be inter-

nally consistent and aligned with the current or desired strategic position. Finally, a quality strategy is one that can be implemented by the firm. Brilliant plans are of little value if the firm is unable to execute them.

Review Questions

1. What do we mean by *generic strategies?*

2. What criteria must be met in order for differentiators and low-cost leaders to be successful?

3. What is the relationship between economies of scale and minimum efficient scale?

4. What are economies of scope?

5. How does the learning curve work?

6. What is market segmentation? What role does it play in strategic positioning?

7. What is willingness to pay? How does it relate to strategic positioning?

8. How does the industry life cycle affect business strategy?

9. What are the steps in testing the quality of a strategy?

Experiential Activities

Group Exercises

1. Review the opening vignette about the three bicycle manufacturers. Use the strategy-diamond and the generic strategy model to describe the positioning strategy of each firm. Based on what you know about the bicycle industry, can you identify any underserved (or overserved) segments?

2. Go back to Exhibit 4.1 in Chapter 4. Identify low-cost leaders from two of these industries. What seem to be the drivers of their cost-leadership positioning strategies? Are they the same? If not, why?

Ethical Debates

1. Among the global trends facing business, it is increasingly unclear who should provide basic social services (e.g., pensions, public health services, school infrastructure), regulate business and personal behavior (eg, self-regulation vs. government oversight), and be accountable for protecting rights, public goods, and resources. In developing a business strategy, where should a company's leaders draw the line between what is acceptable from a purely legal standpoint and what would be dictated by the ethics of different generations or demographic segments of consumers?

2. Environmental issues, including climate change, are increasingly discussed in the executive suite as it relates to strategy formulation and implementation. How "green" should a company be that is pursuing a low-cost strategy in an increasingly environmentally conscious society? And if following a differentiation strategy, would customers pay extra for being "green?" Is "green" a viable differentiator in either low cost or differentiation?

How Would YOU DO THAT?

1. Let's revisit the learning curve and change some of the assumptions made in the box entitled "How Would *You* Do That? 5.1." Assume that the first bike took 100 hours, the second 85, and the fourth 72.25. What would the incremental "cost" in hours be for the 16th bike? For the 124th? For the 1,000th? Try to find these numbers using both the formula presented in the feature and the learning curve calculator located at www.jsc.nasa.gov/bu2/learn.html.

2. Based on the information in the box entitled "How Would *You* Do That? 5.1," assume that you have determined that established leaders have such an experience advantage that you'll never catch their cost position. Devise a realistic strategy for entering and competing against an established player that has a significant low-cost leadership position.

Go on to see How Would You Do That at www.prenhall.com/carpenter&sanders

Endnotes

1. Personal interview with Trek executives, fall 2004; "Trek Bicycle Corporation Hoover's Company In-Depth Records," *Hoover's*, www.hoovers. com (accessed September 28, 2005); S. Silcoff, "Dorel Buys Biggest U.S. Cycle Maker: Gains 27% of U.S. Market Share with US$310M Purchase of Schwinn, GT Brands," *Financial Post*, January 14, 2004, p.1; www. montagueco.com/aboutusourhistory.html (accessed October 20, 2005). Statistics are from National Bicycle Dealers Association http://nbda. com/page.cfm?PageID=34 (accessed April 27, 2007); Becca Mader, "Shifting into High Gear," *The Business Journal of Milwaukee*, May 16, 2003; Becca Mader, "Firm to Launch Schwinn Line for Mass Retailers," *The Business Journal of Milwaukee*, August 7, 2002; Griff Witte, "Schwinn's Bard Bump in the Road," *The Washington Post*, December 9, 2004; http:// www.pacific-cycle.com/ourstory/timeline.php (accessed on April 27, 2007).

2. Exhibit adapted from M. E. Porter, *Competitive Strategy* (New York: Free Press, 1980).

3. http://www.autointell.net (accessed July 15, 2005).

4. Personal interview with Audi senior management, May 2003.

5. S. Targett, "U.S. Companies Win at the Scale Game," *Financial Times*, February 16, 2004, p. 9.

6. R. Sanchez, "Strategic Flexibility in Product Competition," *Strategic Management Journal* 16 (1995), 135–149.

7. See S. S. Liao, "The Learning Curve: Wright's Model vs. Crawford's Model," *Issues in Accounting Education* 3 (1988), 302–315.

8. A. S. Grove, *Only the Paranoid Survey: How to Exploit the Crisis Points That Challenge Every Company* (New York: Currency, 1996).

9. E. D. Darr, L. Argote, and D. Epple, "The Acquisition, Transfer, and Depreciation of Knowledge in Service Organizations: Productivity in Franchises," *Management Science* 41 (1995), 1750–1762.

10. D. Teece, "Economies of Scope and the Scope of the Enterprise," *Journal of Economic Behavior and Organization* 1 (1980), 223–247.

11. Interview with Mity-Lite corporate officers, November 2004. See also www.mity-lite.com.

12. C. Christensen, *The Innovator's Dilemma* (New York: Harper Business Press, 2000).

13. C. K. Prahalad and G. Hamel, "The Core Competence of the Corporation," *Harvard Business Review* 68:3 (1990), 79–91.

14. Estimates of margins from the National Bicycle Dealers Association, nbda.com.

15. See www.sweatshops.org/; www.uniteunion.org/sweatshops/sweatshop. html; and www.business-humanrights.org/home.

16. Personal interview with Jaguar executives, June 2003.

17. D. C. Hambrick, I. A. MacMillan, and D. L. Day, "Strategic Attributes and Performance in the BCG Matrix: A PIMS-Based Analysis of Industrial Product Businesses," *Academy of Management Journal* 25 (1982), 510–531.

18. D. B. Yoffie and M. Kwak, "Mastering Strategic Movement at Palm," *Sloan Management Review* 43:1 (2001), 55–63.

19. Yoffie and Kwak, "Mastering Strategic Movement at Palm."

20. Hambrick, MacMillan, and Day, "Strategic Attributes and Performance in the BCG Matrix."

21. F. T. Rothaermel and D. L. Deeds, "Exploration and Exploitation Alliances in Biotechnology: A System of New Product Development," *Strategic Management Journal* 25:3 (2004), 201–221.

22. J. Dial and K. B. Murphy, "Incentives, Downsizing, and Value Creation at General Dynamics," *Journal of Financial Economics* 37 (1990), 261–314; company annual reports, hoovers.com (accessed September 28, 2005).

23. This adapted exhibit and section draws heavily on D. C. Hambrick and J. W. Fredrickson, "Are You Sure You Have a Strategy?" *Academy of Management Executive* 15:4 (2001), 48–59.

6 Crafting Business Strategy for Dynamic Contexts

1. Distinguish the ways in which firms' strategies are related to dynamic contexts.

2. Identify, compare, and contrast the various routes to revolutionary strategies.

3. Evaluate the advantages and disadvantages of choosing a first-mover strategy.

4. Recognize when an incumbent is caught off guard by a revolutionary strategy and identify defensive tactics to reduce the effects of this competition.

5. Explain the difficulties and solutions to implementing revolutionary strategies.

Roxio *and the* Resurrection *of* Napster

"Napster concludes our fiscal year 2007 with over 830,000 paid subscribers, which we believe makes us the largest on demand music subscription service in the industry," said Chris Gorog, Napster's chairman and chief executive officer.[1] "We have a paid subscriber base that is both larger than Rhapsody, as well as larger than all of the remaining subscription competitors combined."

Napster was riding high again in April 2007, under the leadership of Chris Gorog, whose career spans virtually all aspects of the media and entertainment industry and its convergence with technology. In this dynamic industry, Gorog was the one to lead Napster, given his background. Gorog had been Chairman and CEO of Napster, the leader in CD recording and digital media, which he took public under the corporate name of Roxio in 2001. Before that, Gorog served as President of New Business Development and Executive Vice President of Group Operations for Universal Studios Recreations Group. Prior to Universal, Gorog was President and CEO of ITC Entertainment Group, a leading motion picture and television producer, and led a management buy-out of the group's global business. Before joining ITC, Gorog served as Vice President of Business Affairs for Motion Pictures and Television at The Walt Disney Company. Gorog was also a director of House of Blues, a leading North American concert producer and The Guitar Center, the nation's largest musical instrument retailer.

When someone draws up a conclusive list of the software that made the Internet what it is, somewhere among e-mail and Web browsers there will be a spot for Napster. Napster was really two pieces of software: freely available "client" software that ran on home computers, enabling individuals to copy music to their PCs and play it for free, and a central Napster-run server that dispensed information about music. When it arrived in late 1999, Napster showed how easily music could be distributed without a costly infrastructure (namely, recording-artist royalties, CD manufacturers, record distribution, and record stores). The timing was also right as consumer preferences were shifting to entertainment-on-demand, big players such as Sony and Samsung were providing stylish, miniaturized portable music systems, and there was little in terms of clear legal precedent against music sharing. By facilitating music sharing, Napster sent ripples of panic through the music industry, which depended on the traditional music-industry infrastructure to generate a considerable amount of revenue. In June 2002, after four years of legal battles with the Recording Industry Association of America (RIAA), which represents every major U.S. music label, Napster filed for bankruptcy. At the time, Napster had listed assets of $7.9 million and liabilities of more than $101 million.

Gorog led the acquisition of Napster after its bankruptcy through his software company, Roxio. This illustrates a common pattern in which a new CEO, such as Gorog, remakes his company to fit his prior experience. Under Gorog, with his media background, Roxio morphed from software company to a media company. In 2003, Gorog relaunched Napster as a legal download music provider site and took over as its CEO. Roxio itself had gone public in 2001 as a software-only firm specializing in the development and sale of CD-recording products to both original-equipment manufacturers (OEMs) of PCs and CD-recordable-drive manufacturers, integrators, and distributors. In preparation for the Napster launch, Roxio courted two tech-industry players once spurned by Napster—Microsoft and music producers. Why Microsoft? Roxio supplied the CD-burning software bundled with all new PCs operated by Microsoft XP. As for music producers, Roxio, unlike the original Napster, intended to keep them happy by abandoning the idea of free music sharing.

The question for Roxio was whether it would still be around in five years, after the online-music business had shaken out. It faced competition not only in its original software business, but in its new online-music business as well. Approaches to providing online music included the following:

■ The à la carte approach (employed by Roxio and Apple's iTunes). For 79 cents to $1.20, customers can buy any number of individual tracks (or albums for $9.99 and up). After downloading music onto their hard drives, they can burn it onto CDs, copy it to portable music players, or stream it through home-entertainment centers.

▣ The subscription model (used by emusic). Customers pay a monthly fee to download a specified number of songs. For $9.99 a month, emusic lets customers download 40 songs (65 for $14.99) and use them any way they want.

▣ The streaming model (favored by RealNetwork's Rhapsody). Music lovers pay a monthly fee to listen to as many songs as they can stand and, for a little extra (usually under a dollar a track), download their favorites.

The uncertainty created by the availability of competing technological standards was heightened by the fact that the idea of online-music consumption had only just begun to catch on.

Going forward, Roxio aimed to compete by keeping its hand in the turbulent online-music business while keeping a firm grip on its position as the number-one seller of CD- and DVD-burning software. This strategy meant that the company had to maintain strong ties with Microsoft as well as with other tech-industry heavyweights, such as RealNetworks, and the music industry—an array of stakeholders who view Roxio as everything from a partner to competitor. Moreover, Roxio would also need to keep close tabs on firms that manufacture CD and DVD burner/players. Why? Because they may enter the software business as a means of differentiating increasingly commoditized hardware products.

Perhaps the most telling factor in this story of dynamic strategy in dynamic contexts is the sale of Roxio's software business to competitor Sonic Solutions in January 2004 and the subsequent renaming of the surviving online-music company to Napster. This completed the remaking of the company to fit Gorog's background in media. In May 2005, Yahoo! entered the online-music fray with a service priced at half that of Napster's—now that's a dynamic context!

The dynamic nature of the Internet has made it challenging for Gorog to find a workable (that is, a legal and profitable) business model for Napster. Even as late as September 2006, Gorog was struggling. "Napster's still trying to find a working business model, which is bad from an operating standpoint," said Kit Spring, analyst with Stifel Nicolaus & Co Inc. Spring thought that Gorog would put Napster up for sale, based on Gorog's hints that "We do not have our heads in the sand regarding an M&A (merger and acquisition) transaction," In a call to analysts in September 2006, Gorog left all options on the table. "We continue to receive a lot of interest in the company. We will always carefully weigh any valuation alternative against the opportunity and risk associated with continuing as a stand-alone company," Gorog said.

In 2006, Napster was facing stiff competition from iTunes, which is not a subscription-based service. Gorog decided to go back to a model that had worked before: free. Gorog created a Web site where consumers could listen to as many as five tracks for free while watching ads. This time, though, the free music would be legal because Napster would pay the record labels from the ad revenues. New subscriber growth on Napster fell as Gorog focused on the new site, but Gorog believed that the new site would improve conversion from free users to paid users. In addition, Napster would get a new revenue stream from ads. Gorog's ad sales team worked with advertisers to create custom playlists to accompany the ads. Analysts remained skeptical, however. "It will be interesting to see how much revenue they can get from advertising," said Jupiter Research analyst David Card. "But they're still going to live and die by subscriptions."

Perhaps the greatest testimony to the competitiveness and dynamism of this market space is Napster's profitability: From the date of its spinoff from Adaptec through April 2007, Napster has never shown a profit. **<<<**

Strategy and Dynamic Contexts

In this chapter, we build on Chapter 5 by showing you how firms can develop competitive advantage in the face of dynamic competition. Although the notion of the industry life cycle you studied in Chapter 5 suggests that strategy should always be dynamic, because it must be externally oriented to be effective, the dynamic competition we refer to here requires that strategies also be dynamic by virtue of the rapid and sometimes unpredictable changes taking place in the firm's external environment. For most industries, certain features of the industry are dynamic. In some industries, these features are central to success in the largest and most lucrative parts of the industry. So, at a minimum, firms must know how to respond to dynamic competition. More important is figuring out how to be the instigator of successful and dynamic change; being an industry revolutionary can be the path to improved and dynamic competitive advantage. As you can see from our opening vignette about the on-line music business, dynamic strategies still require firms to make coherent tradeoffs between the economic logic of low cost and differentiation as the primary factors in any strategy for getting customers to buy their products. Dynamic competition, however, challenges a firm to improve its game continuously, and maybe even figure out how to rewrite the rules of competition.

This challenge is what differentiates the relatively stable context of strategy explored in Chapter 5—even for strategies that address one stage of the industry life cycle—from the *dynamic* context of strategy. Moreover, successful strategies increasingly require that they be revolutionary—that they change the rules of the game. These strategies, however, also necessitate the nearly seamless integration of formulation and implementation and tend to reward an appetite for experimentation and risk taking. This is why, after understanding what constitutes a dynamic context, you will also learn how to conceive of a revolutionary strategy and use tools designed to help formulate revolutionary strategies, such as the value-curve and real-options analysis.

Before introducing the strategies and tools for dealing with dynamic markets, let's start by reviewing the specific ways in which dynamic contexts can undermine competitive advantage.

THE CHALLENGES TO SUSTAINABLE COMPETITIVE ADVANTAGE

It's important to understand why dynamic conditions can undermine competitive advantage, whether with blinding speed or over an extended period of time. Indeed, as we saw in the opening vignette, even though it may seem that an industry has changed overnight, many of the seeds of that apparently dramatic change may have been sown and nourished over a fairly long period. For instance, changes in consumer preferences and portable music technologies evolved over an extended period of time. In addition, change often results from a combination of drivers, several of which you learned about in earlier chapters and which are reviewed further in this chapter.

Recall from prior chapters that competitive advantage is developed when a firm can create value in ways that rivals cannot. And the likelihood of developing a competitive advantage is facilitated by possessing resources and capabilities that fulfill the VRINE criteria. Firms with VRINE resources and capabilities are much more likely to be able to create strategic positions of low cost and differentiation than firms that lack such resources and capabilities. Challenges to sustained competitive advantage include anything that threatens VRINE resources and capabilities. Consequently, we need to examine the types of change that make valuable resources and capabilities lose their value; that make valuable and rare resources and capabilities become common; that make valuable and rare resources and capabilities easy to imitate or substitute; and that weaken a firm's ability to exploit resources and capabilities that satisfy the value, rarity, inimitability, and nonsubstitutability criteria of the VRINE model.

In addition, formulating strategies either to protect against threats from or to exploit the opportunities associated with dynamic environments generally encompass special cases of finding new ways to generate a low-cost or differentiation advantage. Because dynamic markets move at a much faster pace than stable markets, strategies for dealing with dynamic markets involve special attention to the *arenas* and *staging* elements of the strategy diamond.

Three dimensions of dynamic change are explored in this chapter: *Competitive interactions, industry evolution,* and *technological disruptions* (global issues, the other cause of dynamic contexts, will be discussed separately in Chapter 8). These categories are interrelated and are intended to help you think about the different facets of a changing competitive landscape. The relative speed of changes in these categories further complicates strategy in dynamic contexts.

Competitive Interaction

How do principles of dynamic context and change complement the principles of strategic decision making that we've already discussed in prior chapters? We know that managers can use tools such as the strategy diamond, the VRINE model, and industry structure analysis to formulate a strategy and hammer out a strategic position. We know, too, that the firm's strategy and strategic position should be consistent with its strengths and its ability to seize opportunities presented by its competitive environment. Finally, we know that strategic positioning decisions are supported by a wealth of tactical decisions made to implement and reinforce the firm's strategy.

Now consider the possible effects of all this decision making in a context of interactive competition. Competitive interactions are composed of two related factors: the interactions between incumbents and the interactions of new entrants and incumbents. The interactions caused by new entrants are a particularly severe source of dynamism when the entrants introduce a new business model—that is, a strategy that varies significantly from those used by incumbents. Research on competitive interaction has identified four underlying phases, summarized in Exhibit 6.1.[2]

To examine these phases, let's say that a regional title insurance company developed a strategy designed to help it grow into a premier national company. That strategy involves a sequence of activities: entry into adjacent regional markets, followed by increased focus on differentiators designed to build brand awareness, followed by more rapid expansion through acquisitions funded by an increasingly valuable stock price.[3] In its first phase, such an aggressive series of tactical moves may go unnoticed or ignored by competitors. Eventually, however, if customer reactions in phase 2 appear to be, or are anticipated to be, positive, then other firms will formulate responses to the first firm's competitive behavior, as shown in phase 3. In phase 4, competitors evaluate the results of their interactions, and the cycle may then recommence.

Competitive actions can generate a wide range of competitive responses.[4] *Competitive interaction theory* suggests that because competitive actions will generate reactions, a firm's managers should predict reactions to its actions and use that information to determine what would be the best course of action given competitors' likely reactions.[5] Competitive action can be initiated in phase 1 in essentially four ways: aggressiveness, complexity of the competitive action repertoire, unpredictability, and tactics that delay the leaders' competitive reaction. The responses to those various actions have been shown to play out differently in terms of the competitive advantage of the challenger and the challenged.

With regard to competitive aggressiveness, strategy research has shown that a challenger can erode the leadership position of another firm by rapidly launching many assaults on the leader in a short period of time. Such interaction explains how Nike overtook Reebok's dominant sports shoe position in the late 1980s and how, in 2005, SABMiller regained market-share-growth leadership from Anheuser Busch in the light beer segment. SABMiller did so through a combination of aggressive advertising that suggested that Anheuser Busch's beers lacked flavor and backed it up with consumer surveys saying that the SABMiller's beers had more and better taste.

Exhibit 6.1 Phases of Competitive Interaction

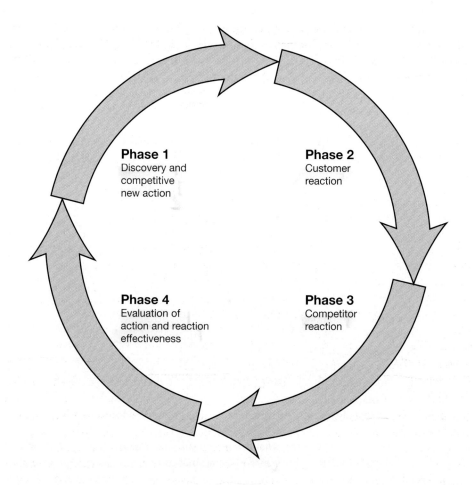

Phase 1
Discovery and competitive new action

Phase 2
Customer reaction

Phase 4
Evaluation of action and reaction effectiveness

Phase 3
Competitor reaction

Similarly, the more complexity and unpredictability inherent in these aggressive moves, the more likely the attacker will succeed in improving its market position. Complexity and unpredictability play to the attacker's advantage by confusing the industry leader and putting it on the defensive. As a result, the leader may also lose focus on the coherent execution of its strategy, as seen by the fragmentation of scarce resources to defending multiple competitive fronts. For example, Anheuser Busch was so thrown off by SABMiller's aggressive tactics that it responded by launching a new beer, Budweiser Select, and advertising it as a flavorful, high-quality beer. SABMiller turned around and pointed to the new product as further evidence that Anheuser Busch's products did not have taste.

Finally, to the extent that the challenger can engage in competitive moves that are difficult to respond to quickly or simply catch the leader unaware, the attacker can gain competitive market position. Strategy research has shown, for instance, that Nike's competitive success can be partially attributed to the fact that Nike initiated new competitive moves (e.g., promotions, new product launches, endorsements) and responded to Reebok's actions much faster than Reebok responded to Nike's.[6] This same research has shown such tactics to hold true in industries ranging from telecommunications and personal computers to airlines and brewing.

When leading companies face new competitors who utilize new business models that are disruptive—strategies that are both different from and in conflict with those of incumbents—they face vexing dilemmas. Should they respond to these new entrants with disruptive strategies and, if so, how? These types of innovations essentially result in a possible change in the rules of competition within the industry. Such disruptions have several common characteristics. First, compared to incumbents, these firms typically emphasize different product attributes. Second, they generally start out as rather low-margin businesses. Third, they can grow into significant companies that take away market share. However, because of tradeoffs with value-chain activities that are essential to the incumbents, these new firms' business models cannot be imitated in short order by incumbents. Examples of these types of disruptive entrants are found in many industries, such as rental cars (Enterprise), retailing (Amazon.com), retail brokerage (E*Trade and Charles Schwab), steel (Nucor), and airlines (Southwest, JetBlue, and RyanAir). Your opening vignette on the new Napster is another good example of a new business model. Devising appropriate strategies to deal with these types of competitive interactions is particularly difficult.

Industry Evolution Rivalry and the nature of competition, as we pointed out in Chapter 4, often change as a function of industry evolution—from differentiation to cost, or vice versa. Because a successful low-cost strategy requires different resources and capabilities than a differentiation strategy, a change in the basis of competitive advantage will cause advantage to shift over time from firms with the obsolete resources and capabilities to those favored by industry conditions. Because all industries evolve and mature, a firm's strategy must always anticipate the repercussions of change. Of course, the best case is where the firms can both be the cause of such change, and be positioned to benefit from it. As we saw in Chapter 5, for example, strategies may differ from one stage of the industry life cycle to another. The strategic management of industry evolution involves not only dealing with the industry life cycle but also strategies for changing arenas and strategies for responding to changes in a firm's environment. One particular challenge associated with industry evolution that goes beyond the industry life cycle challenges outlined in Chapter 5 is the pressures of commoditization.

The Pressures of Commoditization Managers must consider the pressure for change exerted by *commoditization*, which we defined in Chapter 4 as the process by which industry-wide sales come to depend less on unique product features and more on price. As industry products become perceived as undifferentiated, the ability of firms to generate premium pricing diminishes. Consequently, differentiation strategies are vulnerable to the pressures of commoditization.

Research suggests that firms can choose from among different tactics to deal with the pressures of commoditization.[7] The manager, however, must make difficult choices in terms of timing—for instance, if the firm changes its strategy too soon, it risks losing extra profits, but if it moves too late, it may never be able to regain the market lost to newcomers or incumbents who moved sooner. As you will see, all the tactics have clear implications for the five elements in the strategy diamond—namely, arenas, differentiators, vehicles, pacing, and economic logic.

Technological Change Chapter 4 introduced you to the concept of *technological disruptions*, which can cause leading firms to fall by the wayside. Industry decline is often forestalled by the introduction of a new technology that propels the industry into another growth phase. A *technological discontinuity* is an innovation that dramatically advances an industry's price-versus-performance frontier; it generally triggers a period of ferment that is closed by the emergence of a dominant design. A period of incremental technical change then follows, which is, in turn, broken by the next technological discontinuity.[8]

Keep in mind that *technology* is a very broad term. We tend to think of technology rather myopically, focusing only on pure technological innovations. However, technological disruptions may also be *process innovations* (such as Charles Schwab's migration to on-line trading or Toyota's adaptation of lean manufacturing), *application innovations* (such as GM's integration of Global Positioning Systems into vehicles through the OnStar system), and *business model innovations* (such as Amazon.com's move from online bookselling to becoming a logistics provider for countless retailers).[9]

Technological change is particularly disruptive when change is discontinuous, so that it does not sustain existing leaders' advantage. Additionally, technological change is particularly risky when it primarily affects business *processes*. The Progressive Direct on-line insurance market is an example of this. Progressive bypasses traditional and costly insurance agents and relies instead on direct sales through the Internet. In doing so, Progressive is able to offer some of the lowest-priced insurance products on the market. And to ensure that customers shop with Progressive first, the company provides quotes for competitors' policies, and will even sell them instead if a consumer prefers that. Progressive makes money both ways, through the sale of its own policies and through the commissions it receives from the sale of competitors' policies. Discontinuities that affect *product* technology often favor differentiation strategies. In the moderate to high-end segment of the photo industry, for instance, the current technological shift from chemical film to digital photography gives firms like Sony an opportunity to establish a competitive stronghold based on their electronic miniaturization capabilities in an industry that it might never have entered prior to the digital age. Similarly, Apple's pricey iPod portable music device takes advantage of the technological shift reviewed in the opening vignette on Napster.

If the new technology is introduced by an incumbent firm, it stands a good chance to continue its dominance. For instance, in the aircraft manufacture business, Boeing has long been an innovator in the development of new airframes and has persisted as a leading firm, though the technology of the most efficient design has changed numerous times. Some discontinuous technologies are introduced by new entrants, and because they change the face of the business landscape by altering who the leaders are, they are often referred to as *disruptive technologies*. When the new technology is developed by new entrants, incumbent firms face the very real possibility that they will be marginalized or eliminated. For instance, every leading firm in the minicomputer business was wiped out by firms that innovated and marketed the PC.

What can firms do to avoid or withstand a technological discontinuity? Research suggests that to withstand such technological changes, firms must either proactively create new opportunities for themselves or react defensively in ways to counteract the powerful forces of change.

Speed of Change   Over and above any particular change driver, the speed of change is a critical factor in keeping up with the basis of competition in an industry. Speed tends to compound the effects of every change driver, whether industry evolution, technological discontinuities, or other causes. As the pace of change increases, so, too, must a firm's ability to react swiftly to (and even anticipate) changes in the basis of competitive advantage. In many cases, the most profitable avenue is availed to firms that have the ability to *lead* industry change.[10] *Reacting to change* means detecting and responding quickly to unexpected customer demands, new government regulations, or competitor's actions. *Anticipating change* means foreseeing the appearance of global markets, the development of new market segments, and emergence of the complementary or conflicting technologies.

Then we'll discuss the development of revolutionary strategies designed to help firms thrive in dynamic environments. We then examine when and why firms would want to be firm movers in introducing new strategies. Finally, we conclude by applying the five elements of the strategy diamond to strategies in dynamic contexts. When you're finished with this chapter, you should be able to formulate a strategy for managing the dynamic context and prepare a plan for implementing it.

Revolutionary Strategies That Lead Industry Change

In Chapters 4 and 5 we needed to walk a bit of a pedagogical tightrope. We presented you with some fundamental theories and models of strategic management, like the model of industry structure and generic strategies. These tools are frequently used in industry and have enormous analytical power. However, if used naively, they present a static picture of the world and suggest that there is a strategic position that a firm can assume to assure high levels of profitability. If you correctly identify the factors affecting industry profitability, and zero in on the key success factors in the industry, you can then use your resources and capabilities to position your firm with a well-developed strategy that results in a cost or differentiation advantage. But, as we noted in those chapters, industry contexts are not usually stable; they are always changing (slowly or quickly, but inevitably) and this makes formulating a strategy that will have enduring profitable returns very problematic.

Consider a few industries that you are very familiar with; you will see several types of competitors. First, there are the large incumbents, usually some of the earliest and most successful entrants. Companies such as McDonald's in fast food, Hertz in rental cars, and Blockbuster in movie rentals are firms that originally established the "rules" of the industry; these "rules" are the norms that most firms follow in carving out their strategy. Each of these industries has a group of other firms that have imitated the leader and tried to carve out a subsistence through a similar, if somewhat differentiated, strategy. These are firms like Burger King, Avis, and Hollywood Video that all compete directly with the major leaders using strategies that are only slightly differentiated from their rival—they implicitly seem to follow the rules laid down by the market leaders. But, then there are the rule breakers. These are firms like Subway, Enterprise, and NetFlix. Each of these firms made fundamentally different assumptions about what consumers would pay for and introduced strategies that differed in some radical ways from the industry leaders.

In this section we outline five types of revolutionary strategies that can introduce dynamic change into an industry. Successfully implemented, such strategies can overturn an established industrial structure and rewrite the rules of competition. Research suggests that these five revolutionary strategies tend to fall into one of three categories: high-end disruptions, low-end disruptions, or hybrid.

High-End Disruption A new-market disruption that significantly changes the industry value curve by disrupting the expectations of customers by vastly improving product performance is referred to as **high-end disruption**. High-end disruption often results in huge new markets in which new players unseat the largest incumbents. Incumbents can also use new-market disruption strategies. To do so, they need to shift competitive focus from head-to-head competition to the task of redefining the business model for at least a part of the existing market. A new-market-creation strategy, for example, may enable a firm to avoid the pitfalls of commoditization and evolution, but pursuing it doesn't necessarily mean that the same firm will become, or even intends to become, the industry leader. Cirque du Soleil significantly disrupted the circus industry by incorporating many features more common in Broadway theater than in traditional circuses, generating significant new growth and higher profits than any other traditional circus.

high-end disruption Strategy that may result in huge new markets in which new players redefine industry rules to unseat the largest incumbents.

Low-End Disruption Recall the concept of *disruptive technologies*. Some disruptive technologies appear at the low end of industry offerings and are referred to as **low-end disruptions**. Incumbents tend to ignore such new entrants because they target the incumbents' least valuable customers. These low-end disruptions rarely offer features that satisfy the best customers in the industry. However, these low-end entrants often use such footholds as platforms to migrate into the more attractive space once their products or services improve. Indeed, by the time they do improve, these low-end disruptions often satisfy the needs of the center of the market better than incumbents' products do because incumbents have been busily making incremental improvements to satisfy their best clients' demands even while these improvements cause the firms to outshoot the needs of the center of the market. Southwest Airlines has been a very successful low-end disrupter, satisfying only the most basic travel needs and eliminating many services that had been taken for granted by established airlines.

low-end disruption Strategy that appears at the low end of industry offerings, targeting the least desirable of incumbents' customers.

Hybrid Disruption Strategies As you might expect, most newcomers adopt some combination of new-market and low-end disruption strategies. Today, it may look as if Amazon.com has pursued a single-minded low-end disruption strategy, but along the way, it also has created some new markets, mainly by bringing more buyers into the market for books. Many Amazon customers buy in the quantities they do because of the information that the Amazon site makes available. The strategies of such companies as JetBlue, Charles Schwab, and the University of Phoenix are also hybrids of new-market and low-cost disruption strategies.[11] JetBlue's focused low-cost strategy, for instance, has been able to achieve the lowest-cost position in the industry by eliminating many services (a business model it borrowed from Southwest) but also adding services that increased customer loyalty. In addition, they targeted overpriced but underserved markets, thereby stimulating new demand—both taking a portion of the existing market from incumbent competitors *and* creating a new market by attracting consumers who couldn't ordinarily afford air travel. Schwab pioneered discount brokerage as a new market but has since enticed legions of clients from full-service brokers such as Merrill-Lynch. The University of Phoenix is taking a strategic path much like the one blazed by Schwab.

We now turn to the five types of revolutionary strategies that can introduce major disruption into an industry by changing the rules of the game. In Exhibit 6.2, we categorize these five types as: *reconceiving a product/service, reconfiguring the value chain, redefining the arenas, rescaling the industry, and reconsidering the competitive mindset.*

Exhibit 6.2 Revolutionary Strategies

Type of Industry Disruption	Reconceiving a Product/Service	Reconfiguring the Value Chain	Redefining the Arenas	Rescaling the Industry	Reconsidering the Competitive Mindset
Definition	Breaking away from existing industry conceptions of what products and services look like	Changing elements of the industry value chain	Changing when and where you compete	Using a business model that relies on different economics relative to scale	Avoid direct competition
Example	• Creating a new value curve (e.g., Cirque du Soleil) • Separate function from form (e.g., electronic hotel keys)	• Use a new value chain (e.g., Amazon) • Compress the value chain (e.g., IKEA)	• Changing temporal and geographical availability (e.g., Redbox) • Total imagined market versus served market (e.g., disposable cameras)	• Increase scale for greater economies of scale (e.g., waste disposal) • Downscale in search of higher prices in niche markets (e.g., microbreweries)	• Look to make competitors complementors (e.g., American and Delta defraying costs from Boeing) • Avoid head-to-head competition by moving into areas where there is little competition (e.g., [yellow tail]®)

RECONCEIVE A PRODUCT OR SERVICE

Creating a New Value Curve   You are probably already familiar with Cirque du Soleil, a recent example of how a new value curve is created. Exhibit 6.3 summarizes Cirque's novelty. Cirque's value curve demonstrates that they dropped a number of features common in other circuses, but they added features completely unheard of before in the circus industry. Where did these ideas come from? They appear to have been borrowed from another form of entertainment—Broadway.

Most companies have no trouble focusing on their existing rivals and actively trying to match or beat their rivals' customer offerings. However, as a result of this focus on rivals' behaviors, strategies often converge. This convergence grows stronger according to the amount of conventional industry wisdom about how to compete. This type of convergence is often associated with incremental innovation. It will rarely result in breakthroughs that create new markets.

One way to create a revolutionary strategy that avoids the pitfall of strategic incrementalism is the creation of a new value curve (a model introduced in Chapter 4). Creating a new value curve requires a different approach and a different way of thinking about innovation. Instead of looking for the next incremental improvement, new markets are often created when managers create innovations that build on the best of the existing industry, import ideas from other industries, and eliminate some features that industry incumbents take for granted but that are not critical to key customers. This style of new-market creation has been shown to work in both fast-paced industries and those that are seemingly stagnant—both conditions that are ripe for significant changes. Fast-paced industries are dynamic by definition. Stagnant industries are often ripe for change—through new technologies that will send the industry on a new growth trajectory, or through shakeout, which is a dynamic process but usually in a very negative sense for many incumbents.

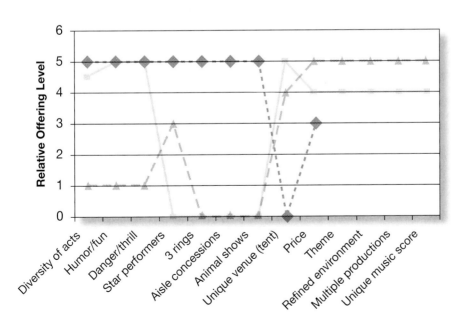

Exhibit 6.3   Cirque du Soleil at the Nexus of Circus and Broadway

The key to discovering a new-market space lies in asking four basic questions. These questions are illustrated in the Four-Actions Framework shown in Exhibit 6.4.[12] By answering these questions, you will be able to define a new value curve for an industry, or at least a segment of an industry.

First, what product or service attributes that rivals take for granted should be *reduced* well below the industry standard? Second, what factors that the industry has taken for granted should be *eliminated?* Third, what product or service attributes should be *raised* well above the industry standard? And fourth, are there any factors that the industry has never offered that should be *created?* By finding answers to these questions, managers could modify a firm's strategy either so that its products are further differentiated from competitors', so that its cost structure is driven significantly below that of competitors or, conceivably, both. In addition, by following this path, firms often generate new customers for the industry or industry segment; they actually grow the business by means other than, or in addition to, stealing customers from competitors. And while we introduce the four-actions framework in the context of new value curve creation, you will likely find that the framework translates well to all the revolutionary strategies covered in this section.

"How Would *You* Do That? 6.1" illustrates the application of the value-curve tool, in conjunction with the four-actions framework, to the wine industry using [yellow tail]®.[13] In Chapter 4 you learned how to apply the value curve to help map existing competitors. Here, the purpose of the tool is extended to reveal how a firm might create a new value curve in ways that separate its strategy from those of incumbents.

As you will recall from the earlier definition of strategic groups in Chapter 4, a strategic group is a cluster of firms that pursue similar strategies within an industry. The curve for each strategic group visually represents how those firms present their products to customers along key buying criteria. It conceptually represents the underlying logic incumbents use in positioning their products. Being able to visualize how competitors perform along these differentiators helps reveal the assumptions being made by the industry. It also helps you to determine which assumptions might be tested. Along these dimensions, question whether some levels of delivery on the key success factors can be reduced or eliminated; likewise, question whether some can be increased or whether new points of differentiation can be added. As a result of using the

Exhibit 6.4 The Four-Actions Framework of New Market Creation

value-curve tool, firms can develop strategies that challenge and change the rules of competition.

Separating Function and Form   Another way to create a revolutionary strategy is to look for ways to separate function and form. *Function* is the benefits of the product; *form* is the embodied product. Let's consider credit cards as an example. Credit cards first emerged at the beginning of the 20th century. Toward the end of the century, magnetic storage technology was used to make credit cards more secure and speed the payment to merchants by encoding cards with data about the customer and their account. When swiping the card through a reader, the transfer of funds from the purchaser to the merchant could be significantly accelerated.

So, let's think about the function and the form of the credit card. The function includes the identification of the cardholder and their account along with permission to charge a purchase. The form is a slim piece of plastic. How can permission and identification be used in ways other than the specific case of permission to make a charge at a merchant? Several uses have emerged: employment identification badges, which allow access to secured areas; hotel keys, which grant access to your hotel room but no others; student identification cards, which allow everything from library checkout privileges to payment for lunch; and membership and discount cards for establishments ranging from grocery stores to athletic gyms. In all of these cases, the credit card companies did not see the opportunity to apply the form of the encoded card to a new or related function—rather it was new entrants attempting to solve problems for customers that used existing technology from other industries to do so.

RECONFIGURE THE VALUE CHAIN

Recall that a value chain is the sequential steps of value-added activities that are necessary to create a product or service that is used by the end consumer. Some revolutionary strategies were created while reconfiguring the value chain in ways that others never thought of, or tried to do, before. Two related ways this can be done are to improve the customer's value equation by using a *new* value chain, and *compressing* the value chain.

Radically New Value Chain   Sometimes an industry can be revolutionized by making completely new assumptions about the value chain. When Jeff Bezos started Amazon.com as the world's largest bookstore, he actually started with the concept that the Internet would provide an opportunity to bring a radically new value chain to a number of industries. He settled on the book industry, but Amazon has now taken their radically new value chain into many products. Beyond eliminating the costly physical infrastructure of retail stores, the Amazon model also cuts other significant costs from the value chain. For instance, large book retailers return on average about 30 percent of their orders each year to wholesalers and publishers, but at Amazon, returns are a slim 3 percent.

Skype Technologies' popular Web-based phone service is another example of a radically new value chain. Indeed, there was virtually no overlap in Skype's value chain and that of traditional telephone companies. Skype uses software to allow users to make phone calls using the Internet. Initially, all calls had to be made PC-to-PC, but a new SkypeOut service allows PC-to-phone calling, and these calls are still at much lower rates than traditional phone service. After eBay purchased Skype in 2005, Skype added new services, including content distribution (users can send and receive pictures and ringtones, for example) and a call-forwarding service. To use Skype, customers download free software, and must have a PC with a microphone and speakers, or a USB phone. So, the only portion of the traditional telecommunications value chain that Skype kept was the local land line for customers who use dial-up Internet access.

Compress the Value Chain   A more conventional way to reconfigure the value chain is to simply compress it. Wal-Mart, Dell, and IKEA are all good examples of this. The typical compression involves eliminating a middle-man in the value chain. Often, the

[yellow tail]® Creates a New Value Curve in the Wine Industry[14]

You learned a bit about the intensely competitive wine industry in Chapter 4. When we mapped the industry in "How Would *You* Do That 4.1," based on the characteristics of the key players, you saw that the industry was comprised of two dominant strategic groups—wineries competing in the budget segment or high-price segments, or both.

So what is a new entrant to do? [yellow tail]® arrived at its new value curve through a process of strategic steps taken over many years. It all began back in the 1820s, when the first Casellas began crafting wine in Italy, then moved to Australia in 1951 to pursue their hopes and dreams of a better life. After years of growing and selling grapes to local wineries in 1969, the Casellas decided it was time to put their own winemaking skills to use, and the Casella winery was born. A new generation of Casellas entered the family business in 1994 and embarked on an ambitious

expansion to build a new winery with a vision of blending Old World heritage with New World technology. Today, Casella Wines is run by fifth- and sixth-generation Casella family members. In 2000, Casella Wines joined forces with another family-run company, W. J. Deutsch & Sons, to bring Casella wines and [yellow tail]® to the United States.

As shown in Exhibits 6.5 and 6.6, you can use the value-curve and four-actions framework to see how [yellow tail]® reconfigured the way it defined being a winery: offering wines at a moderate price; avoiding wine lingo; encouraging impulse purchases with its catchy labels; and targeting only two high-demand wines, Chardonnay and Shiraz. It also added new features that incumbents did not offer—easy drinking, ease of selection (again, only two varieties), and a spirit of fun and adventure.[15] [yellow tail]® used the four-actions framework to create a new value curve. It created alternatives instead of competing head-on with the

major players. It converted noncustomers to customers by luring traditional beer and cocktail drinkers with its catchy labels and easy-drinking wines. Sold around $7 a bottle, the [yellow tail]® Shiraz is the top-selling imported red wine in the U.S., while the [yellow tail]® Merlot and Chardonnay are both number two in their respective categories. This year, the Australian brand could sell 15 million cases in the U.S., and [yellow tail]® accounted for 39 percent of the total imported Australian wine market in the U.S. food store segment in 2006.

Ultimately, the choice between new-market and low-end disruption strategies depends on a firm's resources and capabilities, and the ability to then execute the chosen strategy. [yellow tail]® conceived of a new way to approach the wine industry, but it did so with the knowledge that it possessed the resources and capabilities to do so.

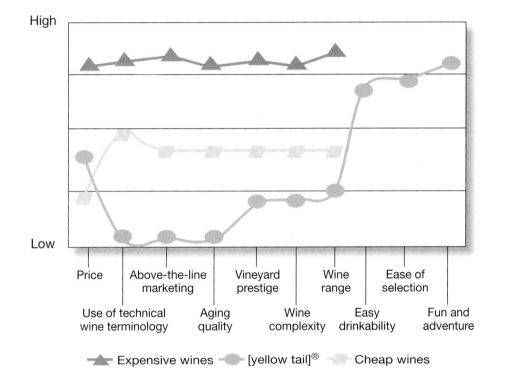

High

Low

Price

Use of technical
wine terminology

Above-the-line
marketing

Aging
quality

Vineyard
prestige

Wine
complexity

Wine
range

Easy
drinkability

Ease of
selection

Fun and
adventure

Expensive wines   [yellow tail]®   Cheap wines

Exhibit 6.5 A Value Curve for [yellowtail]®

Exhibit 6.6 The Four-Actions Framework and [yellowtail]®

Reduce	Eliminate	Create/Add	Raise
Wine complexity Wine range Vineyard prestige	Enological terminology and distinctions Aging qualities Above-the-line marketing	Easy drinking Ease of selection Fun and adventure	Price versus budget wines Retail store involvement

wholesaler or distributor is removed, though the compression need not be at this link in the value chain. Dell eliminated retail stores and manufacturing components (choosing to outsource all parts and simply oversee the assembly of computers). IKEA, one of the world's top furniture retailers, sells Scandinavian-style home furnishings and other housewares. IKEA lowers cost significantly by compressing several value chain activities. First, it cuts transportation costs by shipping unassembled furniture to its retail stores in flat packaging, allowing it to ship more product in much smaller spaces. But, it doesn't stop there; rather than incur the cost of assembly at the retail site, it shifts this step of the value chain to customers because customers buy the product in the box and assemble it at home. So, by designing furniture in pieces that can be easily assembled, it eliminates two costly steps from the value chain. This allows IKEA to pass some of the savings on to customers and keep some of the savings in the form of higher margins.

REDEFINE YOUR ARENAS

Managers generally have an idea of who their customers are and in what arenas they compete. Sometimes these conceptions act as blinders; they can obscure the vision of potential customers that don't traditionally purchase the company's products.

Changing the Temporal or Geographic Availability
New customers are often available at different times or places than those conventionally served. Fast food outlets inside large retailers like Wal-Mart and Target are obvious examples of finding new geographic availability without venturing into far-flung foreign markets. Similarly, most grocery stores now have bank branches located on the premises. Airlines, too, have a captive shopping audience during the flight. Of course, the Internet has opened up temporal and geographic accessibility for many businesses. McDonald's and Coinstar are partners in a radical innovation to the DVD rental industry by making DVDs available in vending machines located at McDonald's restaurants. After initial market tests were successful in the Denver market, the RedBox concept was quickly rolled out. Customers can select from a selection of recent releases and popular titles and rent a DVD for one night for one dollar. The concept was so popular, that it quickly expanded into other non-McDonald's locations such as grocery stores.

Imagining the Total Possible Market Rather than the Served Market
One way to redefine your arenas is to imagine the *possible* market rather than focusing on the *served* market. Consider the market for cameras. Today you can find inexpensive disposable cameras available at every grocery store checkout stand. These relatively new products opened up an entirely new market for filmmakers—children. Prior to these disposable cameras, no child was viewed as a likely customer for film.

New technologies can enable this reconceptualization of the total possible market as well. For instance, Copeland Corporation was considering the introduction of a new scroll compressor for residential air conditioning units. The compressor is to an air conditioner, what a computer processing chip is to a PC (the analogy would be "Intel Inside"). At low production volumes, this new and highly efficient and quiet scroll technology would cost too much for the average homeowner, and would therefore be attractive only to a small niche market. However, with higher production volumes, Copeland's costs for the scroll compressor dropped dramatically, to the point where it could actually be price-competitive with low-cost units. Copeland opted for the volume option, and actually helped move the technological standard in the industry to scroll.

Spearheading Industry Convergence
Industry convergence occurs when two distinct industries evolve toward a single point where old industry boundaries no longer exist. As you learned in Chapter 4, convergence examples are numerous. Computing and entertainment have come together in the TiVo video digital recorder, which allows users to

time-shift their TV viewing. The convergence of entertainment and communications have created a mobile music revolution—the distribution of digital music over wireless networks. Your cell phone is a tangible illustration of multiple industries converging in a single product; at one moment you use it as a phone, later you click a photograph, it serves as your music and video player, and it may also be your personal organizer all rolled into one. For example, the PlayStation 2 is not only a games console, but also a CD player, DVD player, and Internet connector. Broadband Internet access, television, telephone, and mobile phone service by firms that traditionally only offered one or two of these services, is another example of leading industry convergence.

Industries will converge over time. A revolutionary firm is one that discovers and leads convergence. Opportunities to create significant value are often found at the convergence of two or more industries. For instance, Napster and Swedish telecommunications company Ericsson teamed up to offer a new digital music service aimed at mobile phone customers around the world. Ericsson's long-established relationships with carriers could help Napster gain ground in what is new territory for a primarily PC-focused company. As this example illustrates, convergence can be the driver behind bundling multiple products into a single offering, or it may lay the groundwork for entirely new products.

RESCALE THE INDUSTRY

Significant economic opportunities can be found by exploring whether industry conventions about minimum efficient scale are correct. Revolutionary strategies can be created by searching for industries that have opportunities to benefit from increases in economies of scale. However, there are also many opportunities available to create value by downscaling.

Increase Scale   The financial services industry is currently in the middle of a major rescaling from local and regional, to national. Historically, regulation kept banks from seeking national economies of scale but deregulation opened the door for new business models. In this industry, rescaling has been accomplished mostly through mergers and acquisitions.

Service Corporation International (SCI) is a company whose strategy was almost entirely developed around the economic logic of seeking economies of scale through consolidating an industry. SCI is to death what McDonald's is to hamburgers; it is the largest funeral, cremation, and cemetery services company in the world. Historically, the funeral business was a local business with most operations owned and operated by local families. When SCI founder Robert Waltrip was 20 years old in the early 1950s, he inherited Houston's Heights Funeral Home, which his father and aunt founded in 1926. Waltrip noticed that national chains were emerging in several industries such as hotels (Holiday Inn) and fast food (McDonald's). As he examined the economics of running a funeral business, he determined that several of the cost drivers would indeed be sensitive to scale increases. Thus, Waltrip began his quest to achieve cost advantages through scale. SCI went public in 1969, and by 1975 it was the largest provider of funeral services in the United States.

Some revolutionary strategies used increases in scale that were unconventional at the time in their industries; examples include such disparate industries as waste management services and adult education. Many firms attempting to rescale an industry toward larger economies of scale do so through acquisitions (e.g., SCI, Waste Management), but others, such as the University of Phoenix in adult education, have done so primarily through internal growth.

Downscaling to Serve Narrow or Local Customers   In some industries, there is an opportunity to generate significant margins by downscaling. Downscaling necessarily implies going after a smaller segment of the market. But, rather than just going after a small market, downscaling also implies attempting to add significant value to a niche of the market that is underserved.

Take the example of local microbreweries. The minimum efficient scale for breweries necessitates broad-based, national marketing. However, significantly smaller scale can be efficient if the market is local and the quality offered justifies a significant price premium. Examples of successful microbreweries can be found in almost every major city. Bed and breakfast inns (B&Bs) are another example of how one can compete against large national chains in the lodging industry. Bed and breakfast inns typically have only a few to a dozen rooms. At one level of analysis, the cost structure would seem very inefficient compared to the scale economies available to national chains. However, because the level of service is so personal at B&Bs, and because the properties are generally very unique and charming, B&Bs can charge prices that far exceed that of the chain hotel.

RECONSIDERING THE COMPETITIVE MINDSET

Creating Complementors Out of Suppliers, Buyers, and Competitors

Recall that in Chapter 4 you learned about industry structure and Porter's Five-Forces model which suggests that the attractiveness of an industry is a function of the power of *suppliers, buyers,* and *substitutes,* the *barriers to entry,* and the degree of *rivalry.* In essence, each of these forces competes for a share of industry profitability.

We noted that a new factor is often added to that model, the idea of *complementors.* Rather than compete for industry profitability, a complementor helps to increase the total profits that can be made in an industry. How does the idea of complementors relate to reconsidering the competitive mindset? Research suggests that most managers tend to view the parties they interact with as competitive threats. As summarized in Exhibit 6.7, the value net model is a framework that represents all the players in the market and the interdependencies between them.[16] It will help you think about how the competitive mindset might be changed.

Here is how you use the value net. Identify a player as a complementor if customers value your product more when they have the other player's product than when they have your

Exhibit 6.7
The Value Net

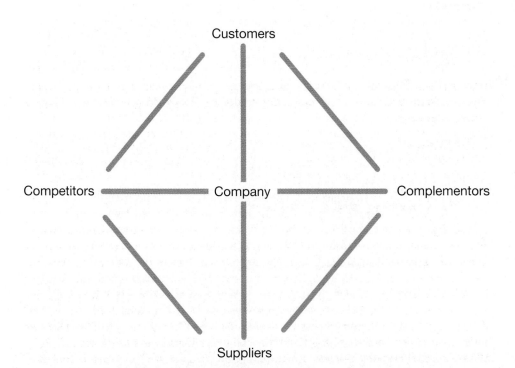

product alone. Alternatively, identify them as a competitor if customers value your product less when they have the other player's product than when they have your product alone. One complementor for GM would be any company providing auto loans. Most customers cannot afford to pay cash for a new car. Thus, more GM cars are sold when there are more firms involved in automobile financing. Similarly, FedEx and UPS are complementors for Land's End catalog. The ability to ship product quickly and reliably increases catalog sales, so they are complementors. Of course, novel software that is available to run on computers will increase PC sales.

An important insight from the value net model is that the same player might be a competitor in some interactions but a complementor in others. Let's illustrate this through a few simple relationships. Delta and American are fierce competitors in the airline business. Do Delta and American ever act as complementors? The answer is *yes*. Consider who the suppliers to Delta and American are. Both airlines buy many planes from Boeing, but they also have the option of buying from Airbus. In order for Boeing to make money on a new plane, they need many orders. If only Delta orders the new 787, Boeing's costs must all be passed on to Delta. Alternatively, if American also places an order for the 787, then Boeing can amortize its fixed costs of product development over a greater number of sales, which results in the ability to lower the price for both airlines. Boeing also will benefit from greater production scale economies, and some of the benefits of these economies will likely be passed on to buyers like Delta and American in the form of lower prices. Consequently, in trying to persuade travelers to fly on their airlines, Delta and American are competitors, but in dealing with one of their key suppliers, Delta and American are complementors.

This insight leads us to four observations about competitors and complementors.

- A firm is your *competitor* if customers value your product *less* when they have the other firm's product than when they have your product alone (e.g., Delta and American).

- A firm is your *complementor* if customers value your product *more* when they have the other firm's product than when they have your product alone (e.g., Delta and American Express).

- A firm is your *competitor* if it's *less* attractive for a supplier to provide resources to you when it's also supplying the other firm than when it's supplying you alone (e.g., Micron and Apple bidding for flash memory from Lexar when Lexar has capacity constraints).

- A firm is your *complementor* if it's *more* attractive for a supplier to provide resources to you when it's also supplying the other firm than when it's supplying you alone (e.g., Delta and American).

The opportunity to use this insight to create value, then, is to avoid the bias of looking at other players in your industry strictly from a competitive mindset; hunt for opportunities to cooperate as complementors as well. As the value net framework suggests, turning parties who compete with you for profits into partners who help you create value increases the size of the economic pie available in the industry.

A Shift in the Focus of Strategic Thinking

Several of the revolutionary strategies just reviewed suggest a shift in focus from conventional head-to-head rivalry to a different strategic mindset. Some of the fundamental differences in assumptions between viewing strategy as head-to-head competition and thinking instead about creating new markets through revolutionary strategies are summarized in Exhibit 6.8. Whereas the traditional view emphasizes actions and capabilities that are determined by competitors' moves, new-market creation emphasizes *actions and capabilities that eclipse the competition rather than meet it head-on* [yellow tail]®, the company discussed in the box entitled "How Would *You* Do That? 6.1," provides a nice example of such a strategy in dynamic contexts.

Exhibit 6.8 Creation of New Markets through Revolutionary Strategies

Dimensions of Competition	Head-to-Head Competition	New-Market Creation
Industry	Emphasizes rivalry	Emphasizes substitutes across industries
Strategic group and industry segments	Emphasizes competitive position within group and segments	Looks across groups and segments
Buyers	Emphasizes better buyer service	Emphasizes redefinition of the buyer and buyer's preferences
Product and service offerings	Emphasizes product or service value and offerings within industry definition	Emphasizes complementary products and services within and across industries and segments
Business model	Emphasizes efficient operation of the model	Emphasizes rethinking of the industry business model
Time	Emphasizes adaptation and capabilities that support competitive retaliation	Emphasizes strategic intent—seeking to shape the external environment over time

First Movers, Second Movers, and Fast Followers

First- versus second-mover categories are related to the principles of competitive interaction that we discussed in Chapter 5. In this chapter, we focus on the relative magnitude of the firm's actions. Specifically, here we are talking about the introduction of a new product or service that defines or redefines a new market segment; whereas in Chapter 5, competitive interaction involved actions taken within a preexisting market segment. In particular, we need to know how each approach to technological discontinuities depends on a firm's resources and capabilities. The principle of dynamic strategy suggests that firms consider the relative strength of their resources and capabilities when they determine whether to lead or to respond to change.

First movers are firms that choose to initiate a strategic action. This action may be the introduction of a new product or service or the development of a new process that improves quality, lowers price, or both. Consequently, you may see firms pursuing either differentiation or low-cost strategies here. **Second movers** are simply firms that aren't first movers, but their actions are important nonetheless.[17] A second mover, for instance, may simply imitate a first mover—that is, those aspects of its new product, service, or strategy that meet its needs—or it may introduce its own innovation.[18]

FIRST-MOVER STRATEGY AND THE INDUSTRY LIFE CYCLE

Being a second mover doesn't necessarily mean that a firm is a *late* mover; in fact, many effective second movers can legitimately be characterized as *fast followers*—even if the elapsed time between first and second moves is several years. Why isn't the lag necessarily detrimental? For one, new products don't always catch on right away. They may eventually generate rapid growth and huge sales increases, but this period—widely known as the

first mover The firm that is first to offer a new product or service in a market.

second mover (often *fast follower*) Second significant company to move into a market, quickly following the first mover.

takeoff period—starts, *on average*, at some point within six years of the new-product introduction.[19] Although the industry life cycle suggests that the drivers of industry demand evolve over time, it doesn't predict how *quickly* they'll evolve. Indeed, it may take some new products a decade or more to reach the growth stage, and only then will they attract competitors.

By the same token, of course, *habitually* late movers will eventually fall by the wayside. Typically, survivors are either first movers or relatively fast followers. Late movers usually survive only if they're protected by government regulation, monopolistic or oligopolistic industry positions, or extensive cash reserves. Increasingly, however, competitive advantage results from the ability to manage change and harness the resources and capabilities consistent with first- or second-mover strategies.

> **takeoff period** Period during which a new product generates rapid growth and huge sales increases.

THE PROS AND CONS OF FIRST-MOVER POSITIONING

Intuitively, we tend to think of first movers as having a distinct advantage: After all, many races are won by the first contestant out of the starting blocks. The history of the Internet offers a wealth of first-mover success stories. The market dominance of Amazon.com, for instance, reflects a first-mover advantage—namely, the firm's ability to charge higher prices for books. According to a recent study, a 1-percent price increase reduced Amazon.com sales by 0.5 percent; at BarnesandNoble.com, however, the same price hike cut sales by a relatively whopping 4 percent.[20]

However, if you take a close look at Exhibit 6.9, you'll see that first-movers don't always attain dominant positions.[21] For instance, you are probably familiar with the Microsoft XBox, the Palm Pilot PDA, and the Boeing 747, but did you know that the first electronic games, PDA, and commercial jets were released by Atari, Apple (the Newton in 1993), and deHaviland, respectively? In some cases, a first-mover strategy can even be a liability, and in many others, the first mover isn't necessarily in a position to exploit the advantages of being first.

A first-mover advantage is valuable only under certain conditions:

- A firm achieves an absolute cost advantage in terms of scale or scope.

- A firm's image and reputation advantages are hard to imitate at a later date.

- First-time customers are locked into a firm's products or services because of preferences or design characteristics.

- The scale of a firm's first move makes imitation unlikely.[22]

First movers also bear significant risks, including the costs not only of designing, producing, and distributing new products, but of educating customers about them. Let's say, for example, that you're a midsized consumer products company with a promising new product. When you stop to consider the immense power wielded by a certain member of your distribution channel—say, Wal-Mart—you'll recall how dependent you are on one giant retailer to help you attract a market large enough to make your product profitable. Meanwhile, certain second movers (say, Unilever or Procter & Gamble) may take the time to evaluate your new product and decide to compete with it only when it's developed some traction in the market (at some point during the takeoff period). Sometimes, a patient (and sufficiently powerful) second mover simply acquires the first mover; sometimes, a second mover introduces a similar product, perhaps of higher quality or with added features.

In short, first-mover advantages diminish—and fast-follower advantages increase—under a variety of conditions, including the following:

- Rapid technological advances enable a second mover to leapfrog a first mover's new product or service.

Exhibit 6.9 A Gallery of First Movers and Fast Followers

Product	Pioneer(s)	Imitators/Fast Followers	Comments
Automated teller machines (ATMs)	DeLaRue (1967) Docutel (1969)	Diebold (1971) IBM (1973) NCR (1974)	The first movers were small entrepreneurial upstarts that faced two types of competitors: (1) larger firms with experience selling to banks and (2) the computer giants. The first movers did not survive.
Ballpoint pens	Reynolds (1945) Eversharp (1946)	Parker (1954) Bic (1960)	The pioneers disappeared when the fad first ended in the late 1940s. Parker entered 8 years later. Bic entered last and sold pens as cheap disposables.
Commercial jets	deHaviland (1952)	Boeing (1958) Douglas (1958)	The pioneer rushed to market with a jet that crashed frequently. Boeing and Douglas (later known as McDonnel-Douglas) followed with safer, larger, and more powerful jets unsullied by tragic crashes.
Credit cards	Diners Club (1950)	Visa/Mastercard (1966) American Express (1968)	The first mover was undercapitalized in a business in which money is the key resource. American Express entered last with funds and name recognition from its traveler's check business.
Diet soda	Kirsch's No-Cal (1952) Royal Crown's Diet Rite Cola (1962)	Pepsi's Patio Cola (1963) Coke's Tab (1964) Diet Pepsi (1964) Diet Coke (1982)	The first mover could not match the distribution advantages of Coke and Pepsi. Nor did it have the money or marketing expertise needed for massive promotional campaigns.
Light beer	Rheingold's & Gablinger's (1968) Meister Brau Lite (1967)	Miller Lite (1975) Natural Light (1977) Coors Light (1978) Bud Light (1982)	The first movers entered 9 years before Miller and 16 years before Budweiser, but financial problems drove both out of business. Marketing and distribution determined the outcome. Costly legal battles, again requiring access to capital, were commonplace.
PC operating systems	CP/M (1974)	Microsoft DOS (1981) Microsoft Windows (1985)	The first mover set the early industry standard but did not upgrade for the IBM PC. Microsoft bought an imitative upgrade and became the new standard. Windows entered later and borrowed heavily from predecessors (and competitor Apple), then emerged as the leading interface.
Video games	Magnavox's Odyssey (1972) Atari's Pong (1972)	Nintendo (1985) Sega (1989) Microsoft (1998)	The market went from boom to bust to boom. The bust occurred when home computers seemed likely to make video games obsolete. Kids lost interest when games lacked challenge. Price competition ruled. Nintendo rekindled interest with better games and restored market order with managed competition. Microsoft entered with its Xbox when they perceived gaming to be a possible component of its wired world.

- The first mover's product or service strikes a positive chord but is flawed.
- The first mover lacks a key complement, such as channel access, that a fast follower possesses.
- The first mover's costs outweigh the benefits of its first-mover position. (Fast followers, for example, can often enter markets more cheaply because they don't face the initial costs incurred by the first mover.)

Status of Complementary Assets

Exhibit 6.10 First-Mover Dependencies

	Freely available or unimportant	Tightly held and important
Weak protection from imitation	It is difficult for anyone to make money: Industry incumbents may simply give new product or service away as part of its larger bundle of offerings	Value-creation opportunities favor the holder of complementary assets, who will probably pursue a fast-follower strategy
Strong protection from imitation	First mover can do well depending on the execution of its strategy	Value will go either to first mover or to party with the most bargaining power

(Left axis label: **Bases of First Mover Advantages**)

FIRST MOVERS AND COMPLEMENTARY ASSETS

An additional framework for assessing whether a firm should pursue a first-mover or fast-follower strategy incorporates the factor of *complementary assets*. Exhibit 6.10, for example, provides a framework that explains why a number of notable first movers fared poorly despite apparently advantageous positions one would expect them to extract by virtue of being a first mover.[23] What's the moral of the lessons collected in Exhibit 6.10? Basically, they remind us that any firm contemplating a first-mover strategy should consider the inimitability of its new product, the switching costs holding together current customer relationships, and the strength of its complementary assets. It should, for example, consider its distribution channels as important complementary assets. Industry key success factors are also complementary assets, as is access to capital.

Let's say, for instance, that a firm makes a critical breakthrough in cancer therapy. Before putting any product on the market, it will need to conduct a decade's worth of animal and clinical trials, and if it doesn't have hundreds of millions of dollars in the bank, it won't be able to pay for such extensive preliminary testing. New PC-software applications often depend on Microsoft because its operating system and bundled software constitute a whole set of complements—a product, a channel, and a potential competitor. As you can see from the illustrations in Exhibit 6.9, in the context of the framework summarized in Exhibit 6.10, first-movers tend to succeed if their initial advantages are unique and defensible *and* if they're in a position to exploit the complementary assets needed to bring a new product to market.

Defensive Strategies for Incumbents Caught Off-Guard

Incumbents, such as Anheuser Busch, deserve special attention because they are increasingly viewed as Goliaths in the many David-and-Goliath competitive interactions unfolding around the world. In the mid-1990s, the front pages of the business press were littered with stories decrying the demise of the brick-and-mortar business and the rise of e-commerce and the dot-com. Inasmuch as most firms currently occupied real estate rather than cyberspace, the trend—or at least warnings about its repercussions—threatened most of them with extinction. Some, of course, did disappear, but most did not. As a matter of fact, the Internet phenomenon—and especially the breakneck speed with which it became a regular feature of the cultural landscape—underscored a number of strategies that incumbents can adopt to respond to rapid changes in the environment of an industry. As usual, the success of these strategies depends on a given firm's strengths and weaknesses. They are, however, particularly attractive to incumbent firms because they depend on—and can even reinforce—a firm's basic strengths. Each seeks a resource-based competitive advantage—that is, a position in which the exploitation of a resource makes that resource stronger and more resilient. Hopefully, the firm is organized per the VRINE framework to realize value from the stronger and more resilient resource.

Competitor-response strategies can be thought about in a number of different ways. Incumbent firms can respond to sources of industry dynamism through any of the following strategies: (1) containment, (2) neutralization, (3) shaping, (4) absorption, or (5) annulment. These responses typically vary in terms of the ease with which the external threat can be controlled and the corresponding level of action taken in response. We'll discuss and provide examples of each strategy in the following sections.

CONTAINMENT

The containment strategy works well when the firm has identified the threat at an early stage. (You may detect facets of this strategy in the bundling or process-innovation strategies that we described in the context of industry evolution in Chapter 5.) Although firms sometimes select one of these strategies, they typically resort to a combination that aligns well with their particular resources and capabilities. American Airlines, for instance, can compete with Southwest not only by increasing the benefits of its frequent flier program but by using its bargaining power to secure more exclusive airport gates (thus effectively raising Southwest's distribution costs at airports where it used to share gates with American).

Similarly, a large consumer products company can release a copy-cat product that both leverages the new market created by a competitor and can be sold through its own existing channels. Consider, for example, the fact that retailers in industries from clothing to groceries typically charge *slotting fees*—fees that suppliers pay for access to retailers' shelf space. Because of this practice, any new product may bump an existing product from retail shelves, and if the one that gets bumped is a new entrant's only product, the containment strategy will have been highly effective.

NEUTRALIZATION

If containment does not work, then leaders will try to neutralize the threat. Incumbents who pursue a neutralization strategy aggressively often succeed in short-circuiting the moves of innovators or new entrants even *before* they make them—or at least in forcing them to seek out the incumbent as a partner or acquirer. Microsoft, for example, is so aggressive at adding free software features to its popular Windows platform that new software firms routinely include partnership with Microsoft as part of their entry strategies.

A more common neutralization tactic, however, is the threat or use of legal action. (Because such action is often taken in concert with partners, we'll revisit it as an aspect of cooperative strategy in Chapter 8.) Recall from our opening case that one reason for Napster's initial downfall was legal action taken by the recording industry. In fact, the Recording Industry Association of America (RIAA) launched such a fierce legal attack on Napster that it forced even smaller Napster-like firms to stay out of the fray.[24] The German media giant Bertelsmann AG later acquired the Napster name when it realized that the Internet upstart was trying to engage in a legitimate music-sharing business. (When Bertelsmann couldn't turn a profit in the music-sharing business, Roxio was later able to acquire Napster and its assets for only $5 million.) Meanwhile, the RIAA also attempted to neutralize the Napster model by setting up an industrywide sharing standard, but this initiative collapsed when the major record labels squabbled about intellectual property rights, technology, and pricing.

SHAPING

Sometimes, of course, it's simply not possible to contain or neutralize the growth of a new product, often due to antitrust laws. Moreover, in some cases, the new product may be attractive to the incumbent even if the incumbent can't gain full control of it. Today, for example, a state of peaceful coexistence prevails between the American Medical Association (AMA) and chiropractic medicine. For decades, however, the AMA characterized chiropractors as quacks. Eventually, the AMA used regulators and educators as part of a strategy to *shape* the evolution of chiropractic practice until chiropractics transformed itself into a complement to conventional healthcare, as defined by the AMA.

Large firms can also use funding to pursue shaping strategies. Intel, for example, maintains its Intel Capital unit as one of the world's largest corporate venture programs for investing in the technology segment. The concept is fairly simple: Each investment is aimed at helping businesses that, if successful, will need Intel products to grow. In many ways, then, Intel is not only creating future markets for its own products but discouraging demand for competing products and technology and co-opting potential future competitors at the same time.

ABSORPTION

The purpose of this strategy is to minimize the risks entailed by being either a first mover or an imitator. Sometimes, the approach is direct: The incumbent identifies and acquires the new entrant or establishes an alliance. In the late 1980s, for instance, Microsoft identified money-management software as a potentially attractive, high-growth market. It therefore entered into an agreement to acquire Intuit, the market leader, which offers such products as Quicken, QuickBooks, and TurboTax. However, antitrust action forced Microsoft to abandon the purchase, and it resorted to a containment strategy—namely, by developing its own product, Microsoft Money (although Intuit's Quicken still has an 80-percent market share). If it's difficult to acquire the new entrant, the incumbent may also try to leverage a buyout by taking control over industry suppliers or distribution channels.

ANNULMENT

Incumbents can annul the threat of new entrants by improving their own products. In many ways, for example, Kodak has so successfully improved the quality of film-based prints that they're superior to many digital-based alternatives. The annulment strategy, however, is less about quashing the competition than about making it irrelevant. Indeed, to excel at an annulment strategy a firm must often assume the role of first mover—a position that entails considerable risk. Kodak forestalled the advance of digital photography, but Kodak executives knew that in order to stay in the photo business, the company eventually had to shift to digital.[25] For this reason, firms usually resort to annulment only when the competition is otherwise unstoppable.

IBM provides another excellent example of a firm that annulled a competitive threat by sidestepping it.[26] In the early 1990s, IBM was faced with a flagging core business in PCs and minicomputers. Its first strategic shift catapulted IBM into second place behind Microsoft as a PC- and networking-software powerhouse. Its next move entrenched the company in the IT and Internet consulting markets, where it emerged as the largest firm among such competitors as Accenture. Next, IBM took on such companies as EDS to become the market leader in outsourcing IT and service solutions. Throughout this transition process, IBM leveraged its resources, capabilities, and dynamic capabilities in services and software. In many ways, IBM, though ostensibly on the defensive, was also wielding the tools of offensive strategy, effectively combining improvisation and experimentation with deft staging and pacing. As a result of this complex strategy, IBM not only emerged as a leader in information technology but, at the same time, avoided the commoditization pressures that affected PC firms such as HP-Compaq. Most recently, it has completely exited its core PC manufacturing business by spinning off this part of its operations to China-based Lenovo.

THE PITFALLS OF THE RETALIATORY MINDSET

A word of warning about the five strategies covered in this section. Although they are certainly viable strategies for dynamic markets, many of the strategies are nonetheless purely defensive. If you rely on them exclusively, you'll soon stumble over an important pitfall of purely defensive strategizing: *Any firm that invests in resources and capabilities that support retaliation to the exclusion of innovation and change may only be prolonging its inevitable demise.*

Here's a good example. Ralston Purina was long considered one of the most efficient and competitively aggressive pet-food companies in the world. Every time a competitor made a move or a new entrant set foot in the market, Ralston responded with a twofold defensive strategy: undermining prices in the competitor's stronghold markets while simultaneously attacking its weaker markets. Although its defensive posture secured Ralston's market leadership for over 20 years, it also ensured that the company lagged behind the industry in terms of innovation. In 2003, Ralston sold out to Nestlé, whose constant attention to innovative products had positioned it to take over Ralston's slot as industry leader.

Taking an Option on Revolutionary Strategies   Instead of retaliation, incumbent firms may strategically decide that waiting for uncertainty to clear is the best course of action. Rather than be an early mover in a new strategy, the firm might decide to make a small investment that will allow it to have an option on making a bolder move later. This type of investment is generally referred to as a **real option**. The idea behind real op-

For more than 20 years, Ralston Purina fiercely—and successfully—defended its position as top dog in the pet-food industry. Unfortunately, the company put so much energy into its defensive strategy that it had little left for innovation. Ralston sold out to Nestlé in 2003.

tions is to preserve flexibility so that the firm has an ability to be well-positioned in the future when the competitive environment shifts. A perfectly positioned firm can become ill-positioned as the industry evolves, as new competitors emerge, and as technology makes current core competencies obsolete. By making small investments that preserve the option of taking a new course of action in the future, a firm can maintain its advantage. As an example, Intel invests heavily in internal R&D; however, it determined that it was unlikely to be the source of most innovations that could change how processing technology is used. Consequently, Intel made a conscious decision to invest in startups. By being a partial owner of the startups, Intel would have inside information on many new technologies being developed elsewhere. Intel has no obligation to increase its investment in these operations or to buy the products or internalize these innovations. However, by making these small investments, it has the option of doing so in the future.

So, what are real options? Quite simply, a real option is *the opportunity (though by no means the obligation) to take action that will either maximize the upside or limit the downside of a capital investment.* Ironically, of course, the greater the uncertainty and flexibility in the project, the greater the potential value of having options in managing it. Increasingly, managers in industries characterized by large capital investments and high degrees of uncertainty and flexibility (such as oil and gas, mining, pharmaceuticals, and biotechnology) are beginning to think in terms of real options. These companies typically have plenty of the market and R&D data needed to make confident assumptions about uncertain outcomes. They also have the sort of engineering-oriented corporate culture that isn't averse to complex mathematical tools.

Although real-options analysis is not a cure-all for strategic uncertainty, the technique is getting much more attention not only in the fields of finance and strategic management but among other companies and industries as well. In addition to those industries cited earlier, the automotive, aerospace, consumer goods, industrial products, and high tech industries are also interested in real-options analysis. Intel, for example, now trains finance employees in real-options valuation and has used the technique to analyze a number of capital projects. As a starting point, we suggest that you introduce yourself to real options by considering the following five categories:[27]

- **Waiting-to-invest options.** The value of waiting to build a factory until better market information comes along may exceed the value of immediate expansion.

- **Growth options.** An entry investment may create opportunities to pursue valuable follow-up projects.

- **Flexibility options.** Serving markets on two continents by building two plants instead of one gives a firm the option of switching production from one plant to the other as conditions dictate.

- **Exit (or abandonment) options.** The option to walk away from a project in response to new information increases its value.

- **Learning options.** An initial investment may generate further information about a market opportunity and may help to determine whether the firm should add more capacity.

real-options Process of maximizing the upside or limiting the downside of an investment opportunity by uncovering and quantifying the options and discussion points embedded within it.

Formulating and Implementing Dynamic Strategies

In this final section we focus on the ways in which dynamic strategies should be reflected in your application of both the strategy diamond and the strategy implementation models. (Because we devote Chapter 11 to a more detailed discussion of implementation levers and organizational structure, our remarks in this section will provide just a basic introduction.)

The arenas and staging, in conjunction with the implementation levers, will be key decision areas as you move forward to put your strategy into place.

FOCUSING ON ARENAS AND STAGING

Let's look first at our model of strategy formulation, which is critical because it establishes a set of simple rules for describing the business and showing how it creates value. Of course, all five elements of strategy are important and must be managed in concert, but the *arenas* and *staging* diamonds are especially important. In addition to recognizing the need for dynamic capabilities, focusing on these facets of strategy is what differentiates a dynamic strategy from a strategy developed for more stable contexts.

Arenas

The Role of Arenas   Arenas designate your choice of customers to be served and the products to be provided.◆ In each section of this chapter on dynamic strategy—sections dealing with industry and product evolution, technological discontinuity, and turbulence—we've tried to emphasize that the strategist is always making important and reasoned choices about the firm's mix of customers, noncustomers, products, and services. The remaining four diamonds of strategy—vehicles, differentiators, staging, and economic logic, will tell the strategist whether the mix of arenas is consistent with what we called a *coherent* strategy in Chapter 2.

Moreover, the role of arenas in the firm's strategy will vary according to the factor of the dynamic environment being considered. In the context of *industry evolution,* for example, arenas must fit with a firm's resources, capabilities, and dynamic capabilities. With regard to *technological discontinuities,* the role of arenas, though overlapping with its role in low-end disruption strategies, was broadened to include noncustomers, particularly when the strategy is designed to create new markets. *Globalization,* introduced in Chapter 4, adds yet another dimension to the role of arenas: If a firm is going global, managers need to apply what they have learned about competing in one geographic arena to the task of competing in others. Finally, in navigating *turbulent and hypercompetitive markets,* managers need to think of arenas as laboratories—sites in which to conduct experiments or launch probes into the possible future of the firm and its strategy.

Staging & Pacing

The Role of Staging   Competing in turbulent environments requires finesse in addressing the staging element of the strategy diamond.◆ In many ways, strategies in this context require the regular deployment and testing of options—options with new growth initiatives, new businesses, and new ways of doing business. From the prior section you now have a sense of how you would evaluate these options, financially. In this section, we review the findings of recent research on how firms manage the staging of strategy in order to succeed in turbulent or hypercompetitive environments. Research on strategy in this particularly dynamic context is typically anchored in so-called *systems, chaos,* or *complexity theories.* They're peppered with such biological terms as *self-organizing systems* and *co-adaptation,* and they're concerned with the same phenomenon—adaptation to a changing external environment in which change may be rapid and its direction uncertain.[28] By and large, they all share a basic premise: Firms need some degree of ability to thrive in chaotic environments in order to survive. In one study of several firms competing on the edge of chaos, researchers encountered the following three levels of activity, summarized by the curves in Exhibit 6.11:[29]

- Activities designed to test today's competitive strategy (defending today's business)

- Activities designed to lead to tomorrow's competitive strategy (drive growth in emerging businesses)

- Activities designed to influence the pacing and timing of change (seeding options for future new businesses and growth initiatives)

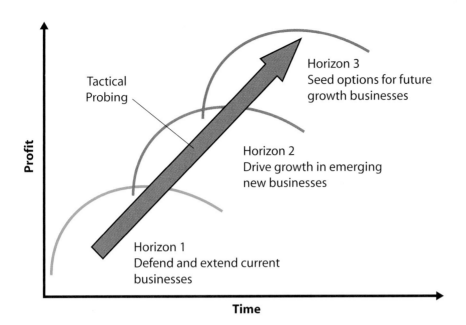

Exhibit 6.11   Creating Options for Future Competitive Advantage

The lower left-hand curve depicted in Exhibit 6.11 is the defense of existing businesses. The middle and upper right-hand curves represent activities focused on the future—the conditions toward which the change-oriented activities at the foundation of the strategy are aimed. At the same time, however, future products will embody indelible links to the past. In this model of business strategy, the bridge between past activities and future conditions is built on a substructure of experimentation and learning. For instance, S. C. Johnson found that one of its innovative home pesticide products in Europe could not pass U.S. regulatory hurdles, preventing its introduction in that country. However, through experimentation with its fragrances division, a key technology in the product was thought to be valuable and gave rise to the introduction of Glade PlugIns in 1993. S. C. Johnson effectively joined knowledge embedded in previously disconnected and geographically removed operating units (pesticides and fragrances divisions) to create an entirely new product category in the home air-freshener industry.

Successful new-business conditions are a reflection of those strategies that have been most successful. Ineffective strategies are jettisoned or marginalized as customers migrate toward firms with strategies that best meet their needs. Thus, managers use their understanding of the competitive environment to guide their selection and reconfiguration of portions of yesterday's business practices. Dell, for example, developed its direct-sales model for the consumer and small-business PC market, and when it entered the large-business computer-server market, it adapted its direct-sales model by providing on-site customer service. The model, however, had evolved: In this sector, while maintaining a very modest level of on-site staff for its largest corporate clients, most of Dell's consumer service is provided by a Web-based platform. With virtually a single stroke, Dell had changed the industry business model in a way that favored and further strengthened the model that had long been its fundamental source of competitive advantage. In other words, Dell's dynamic move forward into the server market was anchored in its past strengths in the PC market, and it has had a profound effect on the strategies of other firms as they've attempted to adapt to signals from the environment.

Tactical Probing A striking feature of this model of dynamic strategy is the close relationship between tactical moves and strategy evolution. A clear strategy enables the firm to excel in a given business, but it also gives rise to experimentation that leads to options on future businesses—horizons 2 and 3 in Exhibit 6.11. Often, we don't think of the operating decisions that we call tactics as *strategic* activities because, in and of themselves, they're fairly inconsequential in affecting cost or competitive impact. In dynamic markets, however, many tactical moves can be used as low-cost "probes" for experimentation—testing the current strategy and suggesting future changes.

Tactics, in other words, can be both tools for competing today and experiments in new ways of competing tomorrow. Consider the case of discount broker Charles Schwab. When the company found itself being squeezed on one side by deep-discount Internet startups such as E*Trade and discount initiatives by full-service brokers such as Merrill Lynch on the other, it experimented with new ways of reinforcing customer relationships and identifying new markets. In particular, Schwab developed futures-trading programs, simplified its mutual-fund offerings, and launched Internet-based products and services. Some of these probes, of course, went nowhere (Schwab aborted a line of credit cards and a foray into on-line mortgages). But those that did succeed enabled Schwab both to further differentiate itself from bare-bones discounters and to gain ground in markets dominated by full-service brokers.

Setting Pace and Rhythm   Finally, as managers move from one horizon to another they must concern themselves with the speed and pace of change. You're already familiar with this aspect of strategy because you're familiar with the staging diamond of the five-elements strategy model. Many managers, however, fail to appreciate fully the role played by time and timing in formulating and executing strategy. Consider, for example, the various approaches to staging and pacing described in Exhibit 6.12.[30] Obviously, attention to pacing and staging can prompt a company to think more seriously about the need for constant experimentation and probing. The concluding example of 3M may partially explain why that firm is consistently able to generate new and innovative products.

Exhibit 6.12   Staging and Pacing in the Real World

British Airways	"Five years is the maximum that you can go without refreshing the brand. . . We did it [relaunched Club Europe Service] because we wanted to stay ahead so that we could continue to win customers."
Emerson Electric	"In each of the last three years we've introduced more than 100 major new products, which is about 70 percent above our pace of the early 1990s. We plan to maintain this rate and, overall, have targeted increasing new products to [equal] 35 percent of total sales."
Intel	The inventor of Moore's Law stated that the power of the computer chip would double every 18 months. IBM builds a new manufacturing facility every nine months. "We build factories two years in advance of needing them, before we have the products to run in them, and before we know the industry is going to grow."
Gillette	Forty percent of Gillette's sales every five years must come from entirely new products (prior to its acquisition by P&G). Gillette raises prices at a pace set to match price increases in a basket of market goods (which includes items such as a newspaper, a candy bar, and a can of soda). Gillette prices are never raised faster than the price of the market basket.
3M	Thirty percent of sales must come from products that are fewer than four years old.

The Role of Implementation Levers   In terms of strategy implementation, the previous discussion provides you with some perspective on the type of strategy that needs to be implemented. In applying any implementation framework, the elements of the model must be balanced—in this case, a dynamic strategy should be reflected in organizational structures, systems, and processes that accommodate the strategic needs of firms in turbulent and hypercompetitive environments. One element of strategy formulation—staging— can also serve to bridge formulation and implementation because the staging component can specify how certain levers will be employed along the way.

Finally, both the strategic leadership of senior management and the culture of the organization that they foster should reflect a commitment to reasoned risk taking, learning, and responding to change. Indeed, it's hard to promote core values that support the strategy implementation in dynamic contexts if top management doesn't practice and champion them. That's just one reason why we studied strategic leadership in such detail in Chapter 2.

Summary of Challenges

1. *Distinguish the ways in which firms' strategies are related to dynamic contexts.* Dynamism can have dramatic effects on the quality of a firm's strategy and it can undermine competitive advantage—sometimes with blinding speed, but more typically over some extended period of time. Indeed, as noted in the opening vignette, although it may seem that the music industry has changed overnight, many of the seeds for that dramatic change were sown and nourished over an extended period of time. Technological discontinuities can alter the basis of competition and the requisite resources and capabilities for competitive advantage. The speed of change in an industry itself is a significant factor; it can either complement or compound the effects of industry evolution, technological discontinuities, and globalization.

2. *Identify, compare, and contrast the various routes to revolutionary strategies.* Revolutionary strategies are ones that do not take the existing rules of competition in the industry for granted but rather attempt to create value by approaching competition by violating some of these taken-for-granted rules. Reconceiving products and services, either by creating a new value curve or by separate function and form, can result in new offerings with high value-added for customers. Firms can also reconfigure the value chain, either by developing a new value chain or by compressing the existing value chain. Value can be created by redefining the arenas, either through focusing on the total possible market, rather than current customers served, or by spearheading industry convergence. Opportunities to increase margins are also found in rescaling the industry, either by consolidating the industry in search of greater economies of scale, or by downscaling the industry in search of profitable niche markets. Finally, revolutionary strategies can be found in reconsidering the competitive mindset, both by focusing on complementors and by shifting the competitive focus away from head-to-head competition and searching for areas where the competition has not yet ventured.

3. *Evaluate the advantages and disadvantages of choosing a first-mover strategy.* First movers are firms that initiate a strategic action before rivals, such as the introduction of a new product or service or a new process that provides a traditional product or service of dramatically higher quality or at a lower price, or both. Second movers are relatively early movers (because they are still not last-movers), but delayed enough to learn from first movers. Effective second movers are sometimes referred to as *fast followers*. They are distinguished from late movers, whose tardiness penalizes them when the market grows. First movers do not always have an advantage because there are significant risks associated with being the first to introduce new products, services, and business models.

4. *Recognize when an incumbent is caught off-guard by a revolutionary strategy and identify defensive tactics to reduce the effects of this competition.* As hard as they try, incumbents are not always successful in being the firm to revolutionize an industry and are caught off-guard by other incumbents or new entrants. In such cases, firms can resort to defensive tactics such as containment, neutralization, shaping, absorption, or annulment. They can also attempt to avoid surprise by taking out options on new businesses and technologies early in their life cycle (such as through investments in startups) that will give them the opportunity to acquire the new business at a later time on favorable terms should it prove to be a revolutionary idea.

5. *Explain the difficulties and solutions to implementing revolutionary strategies.* Vision is critical in that it serves as a set of simple rules that describe the business and how it creates value. Although all five elements of strategy are important and must be managed in concert, the arenas and staging diamonds are perhaps most important in dynamic markets. And, like the five elements of strategy, a balance among the implementation levers is critical.

These levers must accommodate environmental turbulence and hypercompetitive environments. The strategic flexibility demanded of these environments requires that organization structure and systems can be easily decoupled and recombined as circumstances change. Rigid bureaucracy is generally incompatible with turbulent environments. Strategic leadership must further support the firm's ability to identify the need for and undertake strategic change.

Review Questions

1. What are four sets of challenges to sustained competitive advantage outlined in this chapter?

2. What is the relationship between first and second movers?

3. What is industry commoditization? What are two strategies a firm may undertake to combat industry commoditization?

4. What is a new-market-creation strategy?

5. What is a low-end disruption strategy?

6. What are the three levels of activity that underlie strategies for turbulent and hypercompetitive markets?

7. What is the role of timing and pacing in revolutionary strategies?

8. What five defensive strategies might industry incumbents pursue in dynamic markets?

9. How might you apply real-options analysis, financially and conceptually, in the context of revolutionary strategies for turbulent and hypercompetitive markets?

10. What are the implications of dynamic strategies for strategy formulation and implementation?

Experiential Activities

Group Exercises

1. If you were the CEO of Napster (which started out as Roxio in the opening vignette), what material from this chapter would be most relevant to you? How would this material help you to formulate a strategy? What might key components of that strategy be? Now put yourself in Microsoft's shoes; would you see either Sonic Solutions or Napster as a threat? If so, what strategy would you formulate in response?

2. Review the list of first- and second-mover firms in Exhibit 6.9. What specific resources and capabilities do you think successful first movers must possess? What specific resources and capabilities do you think successful second movers and fast followers must possess? Do you think that a firm could be both a first mover and fast follower if it wanted to be?

Ethical Debates

1. Some firms manage disruptive strategy threats by investing in the firms that bring them to market, so that if the threat turns out to be wildly successful it can still benefit from it financially. Is this a purely business decision or are there ethical concerns as well?

2. You learned how incumbents can be blindsided by disruptive strategies. Litigation appears to be a prominent tool that incumbents can use to at least slow new entrants' growth. What might be some of your ethical concerns when using litigation to manage competition? Do you think that a firm's size will affect its ability to use this tactic? Does this matter?

How Would YOU DO THAT?

1. Pick an industry and use the box entitled "How Would *You* Do That? 6.1" as a template to map its value curve. What are the key success factors that define industry participation? Does there appear to be more than one strategic group in this industry operating with different value curves? Can you come up with a new value curve that would change the industry?

2. Identify a firm that you believe is pursuing a revolutionary strategy. How do its actions map onto the four-actions framework?

Go on to see How Would You Do That at www.prenhall.com/ carpenter&sanders

Endnotes

1. N. Wingfield and E. Smith, "With the Web Shaking Up Music, a Free-for-All in Online Songs," *Wall Street Journal,* November 19, 2003, A1; N. Wingfield and E. Smith, "Microsoft Plans to Sell Music over the Web," *Wall Street Journal,* November 17, 2003, A1; www.roxio.com (accessed June 28, 2005). "Napster Lives Again as Legal Distributor of Music on the Web," *The Wall Street Journal,* 25 February 2003, A10; N. Wingfield, "Roxio Agrees to Acquire Napster Assets," *The Wall Street Journal,* November 18, 2002, B4.

"Napster Achieves Number One Market Share in On Demand Music Subscriptions With Over 830,000 Subscribers and Will Exceed Fourth Quarter Guidance," *PR Newswire,* April 3, 2007; "Napster Subscriptions in Decline," *PC Magazine Online,* August 3, 2006; Emmanuel Legrand, "Napster: the Final Shutdown," *Music & Media,* September 14, 2002 p1(2); Gavin O'Malley, "Subscription Survivor?" *Advertising Age,* September 4, 2006 p6; "Market Commentary on Napster Inc." *M2 Presswire,* April 3, 2007.

2. Adapted from K. G. Smith, W. J. Ferrier, and C. M. Grimm, "King of the Hill: Dethroning the Industry Leader," *Academy of Management Executive* 15:2 (2001), 59–70.

3. D. C. Hambrick and J. W. Fredrickson, "Are You Sure You Have a Strategy?" *Academy of Management Executive* 15:4 (2001), 48–59.

4. M. Chen, "Competitor Analysis and Interfirm Rivalry: Toward a Theoretical Integration," *Academy of Management Review* 21 (1996), 100–134; M. Chen and D. C. Hambrick, "Speed, Stealth, and Selective Attack: How Small Firms Differ from Large Firms in Competitive Behavior," *Academy of Management Journal* 38 (1995), 453–482.

5. A. M. Brandenburger and B. J. Nalebuff, *Co-Opetition* (New York: Currency Doubleday, 1996).

6. K. G. Smith, W. J. Ferrier, and C. M. Grimm, "King of the Hill: Dethroning the Industry Leader," *Academy of Management Executive* 15:2 (2001), 59–70.

7. K. Rangan and G. Bowman, "Beating the Commodity Magnet," *Industrial Marketing Management* 21 (1992), 215–224; P. Kotler, "Managing Products through Their Product Life Cycle," in *Marketing Management: Planning, Implementation, and Control,* 7th ed. (Upper Saddle River, NJ: Prentice Hall, 1991); P. Kotler, "Product Life-Cycle Marketing Strategies," in *Marketing Management,* 11th ed. (Upper Saddle River, NJ: Prentice Hall, 2003), 328–339.

8. P. Anderson and M. L. Tushman, "Technological Discontinuities and Dominant Designs: A Cyclical Model of Technological Change," *Administrative Science Quarterly* 35 (1990), 604–633.

9. G. A. Moore, "Darwin and the Demon: Innovating within Established Enterprises" *Harvard Business Review* 82:7/8 (2004), 86–92.

10. S. Brown and K. Eisenhardt, *Competing on the Edge* (Boston: Harvard Business School Press, 1998).

11. These examples are drawn from an extensive and detailed list provided by C. Christensen and M. Raynor, *The Innovator's Solution* (Boston: Harvard Business School Press, 2003).

12. Adapted from W. C. Kim and R. Mauborgne, "Blue Ocean Strategy," *California Management Review* 47:3 (2005), 105–121.

13. W. C. Kim and R. Mauborgne, "Value Innovation: The Strategic Logic of High Growth," *Harvard Business Review* 75:1 (1997), 102–113; Kim and Mauborgne, "Charting Your Company's Future," *Harvard Business Review* 80:6 (2002), 76–82.

14. W. C. Kim and R. Mauborgne, "Blue Ocean Strategy," *California Management Review* 47:3 (2005), 105–121; Wine Institute, "Strong Sales Growth in 2004 for California Wine as Shipments Reached New High," April 5, 2005 (accessed July 12, 2005), www.wineinstitute.org; www.elitewine.com/site/index.php?lang=en&cat=news&art=159 (accessed July 12, 2005).

15. Adapted from W. C. Kim and R. Mauborgne, "Blue Ocean Strategy," *California Management Review* 47:3 (2005), 105–121.

16. The concept of the value net is common among game theorists, but was popularized by A. Brandenburger & B. Nalebuff in *Coopetition: A revolutionary mindset that combines competition and cooperation* (New York: Currency Doubleday, 1997).

17. M. E. Porter, *Competitive Strategy* (New York: Free Press, 1979), 232–233.

18. For a particularly rich discussion of these differences, see S. Schnaars, *Managing Imitation Strategies* (New York: Free Press, 1994), 12–14.

19. G. Tellis, S. Stremersch, and E. Yin, "The International Takeoff of New Products: Economics, Culture, and Country Innovativeness," *Marketing Science* 22:2 (2003), 161–187.

20. A. Goolsbee and J. Chevalier, "Price Competition Online: Amazon versus Barnes and Noble," *Quantitative Marketing and Economics* 1:2 (June, 2003), 203–222.

21. Adapted from S. Schnaars, *Managing Imitation Strategies* (New York Free Press, 1994), 37–43.

22. Schnaars, *Managing Imitation Strategies,* 37–43; J. Covin, D. Slevin, and M. Heeley, "Pioneers and Followers: Competitive Tactics, Environment, and Growth," *Journal of Business Venturing* 15:2 (1999), 175–210.

23. This framework is adapted from A. Afuah, *Innovation Management: Strategies, Implementation, and Profits,* 2nd ed. (New York: Oxford University Press, 2003). An earlier version appears in Schnaars, *Managing Imitation Strategies,* 12–14.

24. www.riaa.org (accessed July 28, 2005).

25. www.kodak.com (accessed July 15, 2005).

26. R. D'Aveni, "The Empire Strikes Back: Counterrevolutionary Strategies for Industry Leaders," *Harvard Business Review* 80:11 (November 2002), 5–12.

27. M. Amram and N. Kulatilaka, *Real Options: Managing Strategic Investment in an Uncertain World* (New York: Oxford University Press, 1998); E. Teach, "Will Real Options Take Root? Why Companies Have Been Slow to Adopt the Valuation Technique," *CFO Magazine,* July 1, 2003, 73.

28. See, for example, S. Kauffman, *At Home in the Universe: The Search for the Laws of Self-Organization and Complexity* (New York: Oxford University Press, 1995); M. Gell-Mann, *The Quark and the Jaguar* (New York: W. H. Freeman, 1994); J. Casti, *Complexification: Explaining a Paradoxical World through the Science of Surprise* (New York: HarperCollins, 1994); R. Lewin, *Complexity: Life at the Edge of Chaos* (New York: Macmillan, 1992).

29. Examples drawn from S. Brown and K. Eisenhardt, *Competing on the Edge: Strategy as Structured Chaos* (Boston: Harvard Business School Press, 1998).

30. Brown and Eisenhardt, *Competing on the Edge.*

7 Developing Corporate Strategy

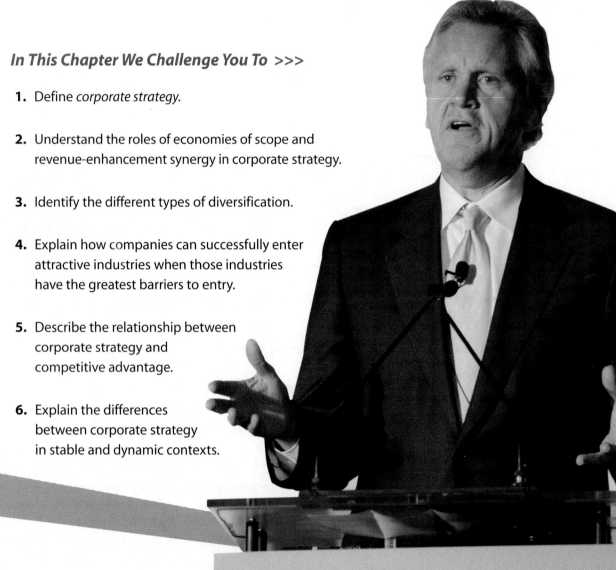

In This Chapter We Challenge You To >>>

1. Define *corporate strategy*.

2. Understand the roles of economies of scope and revenue-enhancement synergy in corporate strategy.

3. Identify the different types of diversification.

4. Explain how companies can successfully enter attractive industries when those industries have the greatest barriers to entry.

5. Describe the relationship between corporate strategy and competitive advantage.

6. Explain the differences between corporate strategy in stable and dynamic contexts.

Diversification at GE, 3M, and MITY Enterprises

*G*eneral Electric General Electric (GE) was established in 1892 as a merger between two manufacturers of electrical equipment, Thomson-Houston Electric Co. and Edison General Electric Co. (of which Thomas Edison was one of the directors).[1] GE's early products included such Edison inventions as lightbulbs, elevators, motors, and toasters. In 1896, GE was among the 12 original companies to be included in the newly created Dow Jones Industrial Average, and it's the only one that's still on the list.

By 1980, GE was earning $25 billion in revenues from such diverse businesses as plastics, consumer electronics, nuclear reactors, and jet engines. By 2007, its revenues were an astounding $163 billion and its businesses spanned consumer and commercial finance, health care, industrial, infrastructure, and news and entertainment. GE CEO Jeffrey Immelt described the range of GE: "We're not a monolithic company," Immelt said. "We have a $17 billion healthcare business that competes in a $4 trillion industry that's growing 8 percent a year. I can grow that business 8 percent. I've got a consumer-finance business in a $40 trillion global market growing 10 percent a year." How did GE evolve from an electronics company to an enormous conglomeration of many businesses? Over the years, GE developed some of the businesses through its own research and development (R&D) efforts. However, many of its current operations are the result of acquisitions. Indeed, GE is one of the most frequent acquirers of other businesses in the world. Between January 2000 and December 2004, GE acquired more than 250 different companies and spent more than $78 billion to do so. Despite its diversity of operations, GE stays competitive by following a vision that its CEO John F. (Jack) Welch formulated in 1981. Welch announced that GE would participate only in high-performing businesses in which it could be the number-one or number-two competitor. This gave GE a vision for growth as well as disciplined criteria for adding or divesting business lines. GE divested itself of many of its businesses, including air conditioning, housewares, and semiconductors, but it remains one of the most diversified companies in the U.S., if not the world. Today, the company's products and services include aircraft engines, locomotives and other transportation equipment, appliances (kitchen and laundry equipment), lighting, electric distribution and electric control equipment, generators and turbines, nuclear reactors, medical imaging equipment, commercial insurance, consumer finance, and network television (NBC).

Describing his strategy for the future, Immelt said in 2007, "We continue to execute on our strategy to invest in leadership businesses. Our focus remains on building faster growth, higher margin businesses. Since the beginning of the year, we have announced $15 billion of acquisitions in fast growth platforms in oil and gas, healthcare, and aviation. We continue to exit slower growth and more volatile businesses, and we are currently reviewing the potential disposition of our plastics business." The company's success has earned it the respect of the business community. In 2007, GE was named the top company on *Fortune* magazine's "America's Most Admired Companies" list, making 2007 the seventh year of the last ten in which GE was voted number one.

3M Minnesota Mining and Manufacturing (3M)—perhaps best known for its Post-it Notes and Scotch tape products—was originally founded in 1902 to sell corundum (an extremely hard mineral that is used as an abrasive) to grinding-wheel manufacturers. Within a couple of years, the fledgling company was specializing in sandpaper, but it wasn't until the 1920s, when it began focusing on technological innovation, that 3M hit its stride. Two products—Scotch-brand masking tape (introduced in 1925) and Scotch-brand cellophane tape (1930)—became so successful that they virtually guaranteed the company a long and prosperous future. Today, 3M has six operating units—industrial and transportation; display and graphics; health care; safety, security, and protection; electro and communications products; and consumer and office products. With nearly $23 billion in annual revenues, the company makes thousands of products, ranging from asthma inhalers to Scotchgard™ fabric coatings.

Coupled with enormous R&D spending (over $1 billion per year), 3M's policy of allowing scientists to dedicate 10 percent of their working time to experimentation has yielded a number of highly profitable innovations. Of course, not all divisions and innovations have been equally successful, and the company has spun off some divisions, including low-profit imaging and data storage ventures. 3M closed its audiotape and videotape businesses and got out of billboard advertising.

3M has entered most of its businesses through internal innovation, but it recently increased its pace of acquisitions. Between January 2000 and December 2004, 3M completed only 10 acquisitions and spent only a little more than $500 million on these deals in total. But in 2006 alone, the company completed 19 acquisitions and spent $900 million on them. The acquisitions ranged from a German firm that makes personalized passports to a Brazilian company that provides earplugs, eyewear, and hand cream. Despite the recent acquisitions, CEO George Buckley sees growth through external acquisitions as secondary to growth through internal invention. "We'll build first where 3M is strong, defend and expand market presence, and build size and scale," Buckley said. "We will also grow through continuous invention and reinvention in our core businesses—the marketplace manifestations of 3M imagination and 3M innovation." Beyond growing the core business, Buckley will look for acquisitions that expand 3M into adjacent markets. "Acquisitions will help us enter adjacent markets and build business in new spaces more quickly," Buckley said. 3M's healthy mix of businesses cushions the company from disruptions in any single market. "The unique nature of 3M's business model lends power unseen elsewhere," Buckley said. "At 3M, we have some real magic."

MITY Enterprises In contrast to corporate giants GE and 3M, MITY Enterprises is a small $55 million company founded just 20 years ago. MITY's first product was a lightweight, durable folding-leg table. Since then, the company has diversified into other product lines, including chairs and other low-cost furniture. The company looks for acquisitions, but for a company MITY's size, acquisition targets are not easy to find. Instead, MITY focuses on internal growth through innovation. "We believe that new product development will continue to propel our growth," said MITY CEO Bradley Nielson. "With that in mind, we are working on new chair lines, staging, dance floors, new healthcare chairs, and additional fencing and accessories."

Not all new product introductions work out. As Nielson said in 2006, "When we entered the year, we were just coming off a failed next-generation table experiment that was diluting our earnings base. However, rather than spending time licking our wounds, we quickly shifted gears and began executing a new plan." The new plan included taking the failed technology from the failed table experiment and applying it to a new area: fences. Like MITY's furniture, the fence panels are durable. "The panels are impact resistant, won't bow or sag in the sun, need no sanding, painting, or other kinds of maintenance, [and] are faster and easier to install than concrete or stone," Nielson said. The new product line is doing well, and MITY will continue developing innovative products. "Our growth is not dependent on making an acquisition," Nielson said. "We can do just fine going without."

As can be seen from these brief descriptions, many firms operate in more than one business. Some firms, like GE, participate in an incredible number of seemingly unrelated business operations. Others, like 3M, have grown into many businesses. Still others, like MITY Enterprises, are smaller companies, but they, too, seem to grow to a point where they venture out of their original businesses to experiment in other product lines. In this chapter, we will introduce you to the basic concepts necessary to understand and manage corporate strategy, including the diversification of firms. **<<<**

Corporate Strategy

Why would a firm that makes lightbulbs also make elevators? If you're in the table business, does it make sense to be in the chair business, too? If your core business activities result in innovative new products, should you retain ownership of these products and the units responsible for them, or does it make more sense to sell them? Questions such as these are fundamental to corporate strategy.

As we pointed out in Chapter 1 and have emphasized throughout this book, *corporate strategy* must address issues related to decisions about entering or exiting an industry. Specifically, effective corporate strategies must answer three interrelated questions:

- In which business *arenas* should our company compete?

- How can we, as a corporate parent, add value to our various lines of business?

- How will diversification or our entry into a new industry help us compete in our other businesses?

At the same time, however, corporate strategy also deals with issues affecting the overall management of a multibusiness enterprise, such as top-level efforts to orchestrate synergies across business units. **Synergy** occurs when the combined benefits of a firm's activities in two or more arenas are more than the simple sum of those benefits alone. After all, corporate-level strategy must maintain strategic coherence across business units and facilitate cooperation (or competition) among units in order to create value for shareholders. Thus, although fundamentally related to each other through the common goal of achieving competitive advantage, business strategy and corporate strategy have different objectives.

Most large and publicly traded firms are amalgamations of business units operating in multiple product, service, and geographic markets (often globally); they are rarely single-business operations. Obviously, companies approach corporate strategy in different ways, and as you can see from Exhibit 7.1, corporate portfolios can be built in a number of different ways. Although MITY Enterprises has diversified into new products, they're all related to the institutional furniture market niche. At the other end of the spectrum, GE not only makes everything from lightbulbs to locomotives, but offers financial services for virtually any business or consumer need. In between is 3M. This company's business units, though highly diversified, reflect common core competencies—the unique resources and knowledge that a company's management must consider when developing strategy—in innovation and adhesive technology.[2]

Recall that we introduced the important fact that most firms are multiproduct organizations in our earlier discussions of industry analysis, value chains, and market segmentation. That's why we're now going to discuss in some detail the ways in which managers can create (and squander) value through **diversification**. In this chapter, we'll focus on six key aspects of corporate strategy as it affects diversification decisions:

1. We'll review our understanding of corporate strategy and define *diversification*, and show how both concepts have changed over time.

2. We'll identify the potential sources of economic gain that make diversification attractive.

3. We'll describe alternative forms of diversification.

4. We'll present a rationale, or logic, for guiding corporate decisions about adding businesses.

5. We'll revisit the relationship between corporate strategy and competitive advantage.

6. We'll amplify our discussion of the roles of corporate strategy in dynamic contexts.

We will build our discussion around many of the elements of the strategy diamond. This framework is useful because it allows you to choose those elements of strategy formulation and implementation that are essential to developing a firm's corporate strategy under specific conditions. ◆ As was made apparent in the chapter's opening vignette, a firm's corporate strategy usually evolves over time. All three of our firms in the vignette have entered and/or exited business arenas. They have used the various major vehicles of strategy to facilitate these changes. The economic logic of diversification often incorporates such levers to achieve synergy and transfer

synergy Condition under which the combined benefits of activities in two or more arenas are greater than the simple sum of those benefits.

diversification Degree to which a firm conducts business in more than one arena.

 Economic Logic

Exhibit 7.1 Diversification Profiles

GE Product Scope

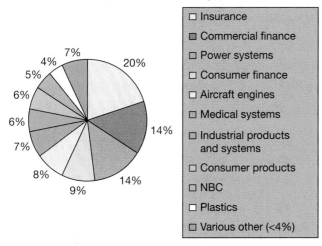

- Insurance
- Commercial finance
- Power systems
- Consumer finance
- Aircraft engines
- Medical systems
- Industrial products and systems
- Consumer products
- NBC
- Plastics
- Various other (<4%)

GE Geographic Scope

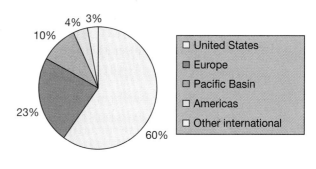

- United States
- Europe
- Pacific Basin
- Americas
- Other international

3M Product Scope

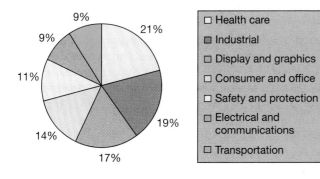

- Health care
- Industrial
- Display and graphics
- Consumer and office
- Safety and protection
- Electrical and communications
- Transportation

3M Geographic Scope

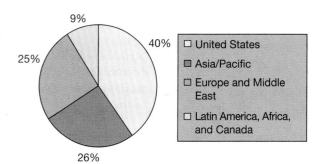

- United States
- Asia/Pacific
- Europe and Middle East
- Latin America, Africa, and Canada

MITY Enterprises Product Scope

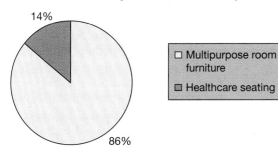

- Multipurpose room furniture
- Healthcare seating

MITY Enterprises Geographic Scope

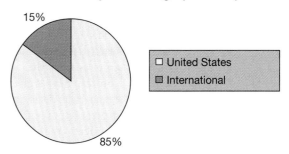

- United States
- International

knowledge between business units. The timing and pacing of such moves must be orchestrated in ways that do not negate the possible benefits of diversification.

THE EVOLUTION OF DIVERSIFICATION IN THE UNITED STATES

vertical integration
Diversification into upstream and/or downstream industries.

In the United States, the first form of organizational diversification was probably **vertical integration**. In order to secure needed resources, large firms often moved "upstream" in the industry value chain—that is, closer to the source of the raw materials they needed.[3] Early on, for example, General Motors began operating its own steel plants in order to supply its auto-frame and body factories. During the early phases of the industrialization of the U.S., many large firms also began investing in businesses that, though related to their operations, were not part of their original industry value chains. DuPont, for instance, started out making gunpowder and eventually applied the scientific discoveries generated by that business to enter new businesses, such as dynamite and nitroglycerin (1880), guncotton (1892), and smokeless powder (1894). Ultimately, DuPont controlled most of the U.S. explosives market. The company then diversified into paints, plastics, and dyes until antitrust action forced it to divest some of its explosive powder business.

In the late nineteenth century, the booming U.S. economy fostered a period of rapid consolidation. The Sherman Act of 1890 introduced federal antitrust law and led to the eventual breakup of many large monopolistic companies. In 1891, for instance, the courts ordered Rockefeller's Standard Oil to split into six separate companies. Similar rulings broke up other companies deemed to be anticompetitive.

By the 1960s, many large firms began expanding into areas unrelated to their core businesses, because this type of growth was generally exempt from antitrust restrictions. Unrelated diversification became a corporate strategy of choice, and soon a breed of corporations emerged that was characterized by curious mixes of operations. ITT's portfolio managed to accommodate telephones, donuts, hotels, and insurance. For a brief history of the diversification of ITT over time, see Exhibit 7.2.

conglomerate Corporation consisting of many companies in different businesses or industries.

Although it addressed certain problems entailed by antitrust constraints, the **conglomerate** model raised new issues of its own. How could a company manage a portfolio of far-flung enterprises? The need to address such questions fostered experiments in new management tools and models. One of the most popular of these tools was **portfolio planning**. Without knowing it, you are probably already familiar with the conglomerate version of portfolio planning (see Exhibit 7.3).

portfolio planning Practice of mapping diversified businesses or products based on their relative strengths and market attractiveness.

Portfolio planning was initially intended to help managers evaluate the diversified firm and achieve a balanced portfolio of large, stable businesses and high growth ones, such that resources could be channeled to fuel growth. Its basic purpose was to guide resource allocation among businesses, help make choices that achieve a balanced portfolio (in terms of growth, cash generation, cash needs, and so on), set performance hurdles and reward structure, and set business unit strategy. A key assumption of the portfolio planning approach was that firms were capital constrained—while this may or may not be a real constraint for a given firm, it is a pretty strong assumption that may unduly constrain managerial decision making. Regardless, the starting point in the portfolio planning process required the firm to analyze businesses in terms of their market share and growth prospects. With one variation of this tool, for instance, a company identified all of its businesses that were "dogs"—those businesses in which it didn't have a strong competitive position, typically based on low relative market share, and that were located in bad industries (i.e., mature or low-growth industries). Such businesses were then earmarked to be sold. Businesses that had very strong competitive positions but were in slow-growth industries were referred to as "cash cows." Portfolio planning dictated that cash cows should be maintained because the cash flow could be channeled into promising high-growth businesses ("stars").

Exhibit 7.2   A Brief History and Genealogy of a Conglomerate

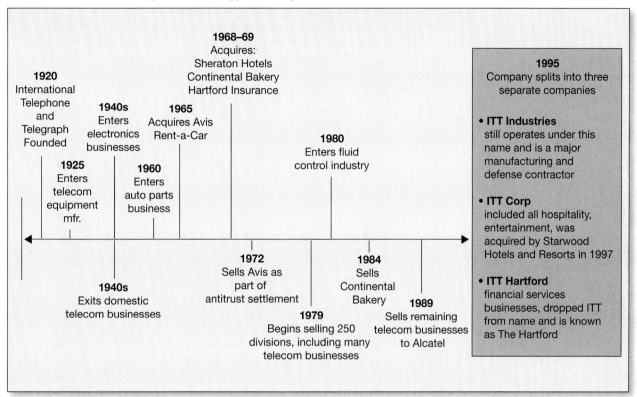

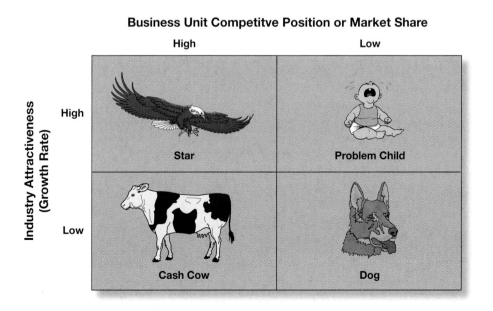

Business Unit Competitve Position or Market Share

Exhibit 7.3   A Portfolio Planning Lens on Diversification

Exhibit 7.4 shows the portfolio models for MITY, along with one for a highly diversified financial services company in 2007. In simple matrices, like that for MITY, you can use the size of the circle to represent the market share of that business in a particular industry. More elaborate versions of the matrix involve plotting out the size and profitability of each business. For instance, with the diversified financial services firm in Exhibit 7.4, the size of the

Exhibit 7.4 Portfolio Planning at Two Firms

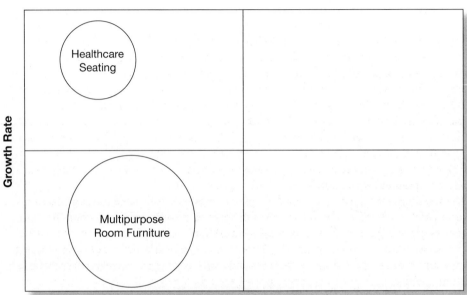

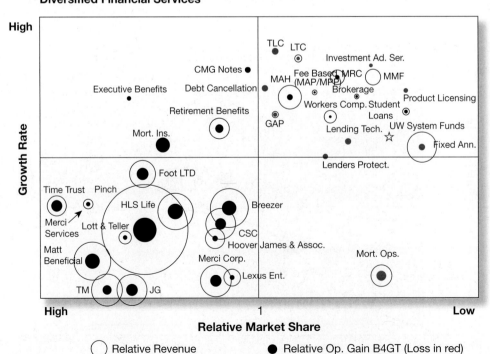

inner circle tells you the relative amount of revenue that business generates for the firm, while the color inside indicates whether or not it is profitable.

Several aspects of the more simplistic aspects of the portfolio planning approach have been debunked. The most basic reason is that it provides no fundamental competitive logic for which businesses should be entered and which should be maintained. Moreover, the sources of synergies among businesses—beyond the generation and usage of cash—are not recognized. Nor is there any accounting for the VRINE-based resources and capabilities that allow a firm to be successful in one business, but perhaps not another. Overly simplistic tools like this lead to questionable diversification moves such as a telecommunication company entering the hotel industry simply because the growth opportunities are attractive. Sears, for instance, used the model early in its history to diversify into growth industries like credit cards (Discovery), stock brokerage (Dean Witter), real estate brokerage (Coldwell-Banker), and insurance (Allstate). While Sears looked at these moves as logical, and aimed to develop a one-stop shopping strategy around what it perceived to be a mature retail business (Sears Department stores), these moves also led it to stop investing in the core retail business. Unfortunately for Sears, upstart Wal-Mart viewed retailing as a growth industry, and changed the rules of competition so dramatically in retailing that it almost put Sears out of business, and did lead to the demise of many retailers such as Kmart and others. Ironically, Wal-Mart is pursuing a similar one-stop shopping strategy (it has added groceries and is trying to enter the consumer banking industry), but Wal-Mart is still aggressively investing in its core retail business and making sure that it builds strong synergies among its portfolio of owned and partner businesses.

Despite the problems with the portfolio planning model, as demonstrated by Sears application of it, modified versions of the portfolio planning tool have been developed to help managers analyze the performance of single-industry and diversified companies as well as help them isolate performance problems. For instance, by plotting out businesses, managers can visually critique why and where there are or should be synergies between different business units, and identify those that might no longer fit the larger economic logic of the firm's corporate strategy. Similarly, managers can integrate what they know about product or industry life cycles with the portfolio visualization tool. As you can see in Exhibit 7.5, again using the example from the same diversified financial services firm portrayed in Exhibit 7.4,

Exhibit 7.5   A Portfolio Model that Accounts for the Life Cycle of Products

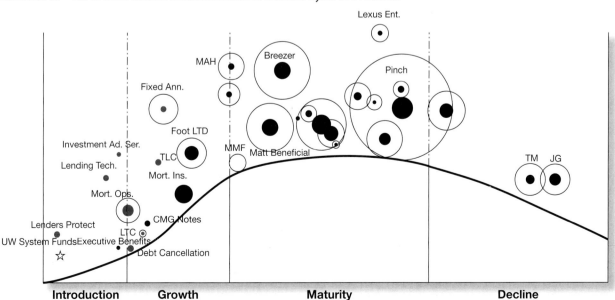

most of the firm's business activity is in relatively mature markets. This visual accounting of the businesses helped to motivate managers to invest more heavily in new product and service development. Beyond this modification, the portfolio management tool still helps managers communicate and align business unit managers' incentives and growth objectives. At a very basic level, particularly in firms with many business units, it provides a useful way to communicate and evaluate business unit strategies, and then relate them to corporate goals and objectives in changing environments. Since strategy is ultimately about making tradeoffs—what will the firm do and what won't it do—the portfolio approach clearly and visibly shows managers what the firm is doing, and what tradeoffs they are and are not making. We will introduce you to other portfolio models—ones that plot out industry characteristics or look at the intersection of industry characteristics and VRINE characteristics—that further incorporate aspects of dynamic strategy later in the chapter. You will have the opportunity to work with these portfolio-based tools in How Would *You* Do That? 7.1 and 7.2.

Shareholder dissatisfaction, especially on the part of institutional investors, coupled with the threat of hostile takeover opportunities, put pressure on conglomerates to reorganize in more manageable forms. Unwieldy portfolios of unrelated business units began to give way to more focused portfolios of related operations.[4] This move toward a more focused corporation can be seen in the more recent years of ITT, as illustrated in Exhibit 7.2.

Business history is littered with stories of failed growth and diversification strategies. The lesson taught by such cases is pretty clear: In and of itself, diversification not only doesn't necessarily create shareholder value but may in fact dissipate it. However, as we'll see later in the chapter, the logic behind *certain types* of diversification remains compelling. Indeed, substantial empirical evidence indicates that some forms of diversification can create significant shareholder wealth. Which types or forms of diversification are these? In the next part of the chapter, we'll identify and discuss the conditions necessary for value creation and the tools that can be used to increase its likelihood.

Economic Logic of Diversification: Synergy

Expanding the firm's scope—whether the addition of new vertical, horizontal, complementary, or geographic arenas—doesn't necessarily create value for shareholders. Strategists need to understand the sources of potential value creation from diversification, and they need to know how to determine whether a firm can leverage those sources. That's why we're going to turn to two concepts that are critical in evaluating opportunities for diversification and value creation: *economies of scope* and *revenue-enhancement*. Collectively, these are often referred to as *synergy*. However, they are two different economic logics for the possible profits from diversification. ◆

 Economic Logic

ECONOMY-OF-SCOPE SYNERGIES

economy of scope Condition under which lower total average costs result from sharing resources to produce more than one product or service.

We introduced the concept of **economy of scope** in Chapter 5, where we simply associated it with a firm's success in sharing a resource among two or more of its products. In this chapter, we'll provide a more complete definition and explain why economies of scope are one of the two key factors in determining whether a corporate strategy is adding value through the diversification of its business portfolio.

As you learned in Chapter 5, economies of scope are reductions in average costs that result from producing two or more products jointly instead of producing them separately. The concept of economies of scope can be represented by the following formula:

$$\text{Average costs (X, Y)} < \text{Average costs (X)} + \text{Average costs (Y)}$$

Economies of scope are possible when the company can leverage a resource or value chain activity across more than one product, service, or geographic arena. Although we focus on productive resources for the sake of presentation, you should recognize that economies of scope are possible in all value-chain activities, not simply production. For instance, comarketing of two products within one company may be less costly than marketing them separately in two companies (it may also help increase revenue-enhancement synergies, but we'll discuss that point later). For instance, it may have been less costly to market and distribute Sobe drinks within PepsiCo than it was to market it as a stand-alone product before PepsiCo purchased Sobe.

Sources of Economy-of-Scope Synergies   What tactics result in economies of scope? Economy-of-scope savings generally result when a firm uses common resources across business units. Or to put it another way: Whenever a common resource can be used across more than one business unit, the company has the *potential* to generate economies of scope. If, for instance, the cost of material that's common to two or more products is lower when purchased in greater quantity, then jointly producing two products may increase purchase volume and, therefore, cut costs. The ability to join the procurement function in this case and buy materials jointly creates an economy of scope.

Likewise, a manufacturing facility that achieves minimum efficient scale for one product may have excess capacity that it can put to use in producing other products. In this case, the total cost for both products will be lower because the cost of the common facility can be spread across two businesses. Sometimes the common resource is located farther down the firm's value chain. For instance, if a firm distributes products through a system with access to a large customer base, it may be able to add products to that system more cheaply than competitors launching similar new products that may need to create dedicated distribution networks from scratch. Coke and Pepsi enjoy such economies of scope in the markets for soft drinks, noncarbonated beverages, and bottled water.

REVENUE-ENHANCEMENT SYNERGIES

Another manifestation of synergy is revenue enhancement. **Revenue-enhancement synergy** exists when total sales are greater if two products are sold and distributed within one company than when they are owned by separate companies. Put another way, while economies of scope relate to cutting costs, revenue-enhancement synergies relate to growing revenues. In short, it's the difference between synergies that allow you to make more money by saving on expenses and those that allow you to grow the business! This can be represented by the following formula:

> **revenue-enhancement synergy**   When total sales are greater if two products are sold and distributed within one company than when they are owned by separate companies.

$$\text{Total revenues } (X, Y) > \text{Total revenues } (X) + \text{Total revenues } (Y)$$

Simply put, if two business units X and Y are able to generate more revenue because they're collectively owned by a single corporate parent than if they are in separate companies, the strategy of common ownership is synergistic.

Sources of Revenue-Enhancement Synergies   Revenue-enhancement synergy may result from a variety of tactics, such as bundling products that were previously sold separately, sharing complementary knowledge in the interest of new-product innovation, or increasing shared distribution opportunities.

Consider how Disney leverages its various resources to create revenue-enhancement synergies. The result of its web of collaborative activities is a consistent stream of new revenue sources that demonstrate a direct line between creativity in product design and financial acumen.[5] At the same time, Disney's collaborative context doesn't specify the forms that synergies must take; it merely reflects the principle that they should be profitable for all of the units involved. Two movies, for example, *The Little Mermaid* and *The Lion King*, became television shows. Another, *Toy Story*, was rolled out as a video game. Both *The Lion King* and another movie, *Beauty and the Beast*, became smash-hit Broadway musicals. The managers of Disney Tokyo share best practices with managers at Disney World in Orlando and Euro Disney outside Paris. Big Red Boat, a cruise line that specializes in Caribbean vacations, and Disney World, which offers vacation packages in Orlando on Florida's east coast, collaborate to build traffic in both venues. Characters from one animated series make cameos in others, and all shows are circulated through Disney's lineup of cable- and network-television channels, which include all or part of ABC, ESPN, A&E, E! Entertainment, and The History Channel. The voices of both live-action and animated characters circulate through Radio Disney.

Revenue-enhancement synergies generally arise from bundling and joint-selling opportunities. In recent years, for example, firms in the financial services industry have been actively acquiring or merging with firms in adjacent sectors in order to bundle products for current customers in different sectors.

A more specific example is found in the opening vignette. Founded in Orem, Utah, in 1987, MITY Enterprises originally made folding tables targeted at such institutional users as schools and churches. A decade later, when the company found itself with excess capacity in its Orem plant, managers began thinking about growth options. Because MITY's technology could be used to manufacture chairs and other types of furniture as well as tables, the company decided to expand into complementary products. MITY thus achieved synergy in two ways:

- Because expansion didn't require a new plant, the cost of the existing facility was spread across the various operations needed for different products.

- Because its manufacturing and distribution operations were geared toward multiple products, MITY's customers were more likely to buy more than one of its products, thus generating incremental sales that the firm could not otherwise have gained.

Similarly, firms in various sectors of the financial services industry have been actively acquiring and merging with firms in adjacent sectors in order to be able to bundle related products and cross-sell to existing customers.

ECONOMIC BENEFITS OF DIVERSIFICATION

Because mutual gains may be derived from either cost savings or revenue-enhancement synergies, a corporation that maintains ownership over multiple business units may have an advantage over competing businesses that are owned and managed separately. A company achieves this so-called "parenting advantage" when the joint cash flows of two or more collectively owned business units exceed the sum of the cash flows that they would generate independently.

When their collective market value exceeds the independent market values of a portfolio of business units, the financial markets will typically recognize the existence of a parenting advantage. Of course, the market doesn't compare business units by assigning both collective and independent value. Investors, however, can make reasonable estimates of a business unit's potential independent value. How? By using the market multiples (e.g., price earnings ratios or other similar multiples) of independent competitors in the industry within which its business units compete to compare the parent corporation's market value with the combined hypothetical values of its business units.

How and When to Seek Synergy   Two processes can generate synergy: sharing resources and transferring capabilities. We've discussed resource sharing extensively in our discussion of economies of scope. Transferring capabilities is actually a special case of resource sharing that can create both cost savings and revenue enhancement. Yum! Brands, for instance, can transfer knowledge about site location, franchise development, and internationalization from one restaurant brand to another. Black & Decker can share knowledge about small electric motors across its power tool and kitchen appliance units. Honda transfers knowledge gained about high-performance engines from its Formula 1 racing activities not only to its automobile division, but also to units that produce motorcycles and lawncare and recreational equipment.

LIMITS OF DIVERSIFICATION BENEFITS

Remember, however, that neither economies of scope nor revenue enhancement materialize simply because firms expand into new lines of business. In other words, it's not *necessarily* cheaper to produce two products jointly in a single firm than separately in distinct firms. Indeed, in many cases, diversification creates **diseconomies of scope**—average cost increases resulting from the joint output of two or more products within a single firm.

The critical question is *when economies of scope are likely to materialize.* Often, firms that can't demonstrate that diversification has generated economies of scope or revenue-enhancement synergies are forced to divest themselves of some units. During the 1990s, AT&T attempted to reap synergies across such businesses as long-distance telephone services, wireless cell phone service, and cable TV. However, it was never able to generate the cross-selling and synergistic outcomes it projected. Thus, in 2002 the company made the decision to split the company apart; some divisions were split off as separate companies, others were sold to competitors. The restructuring at AT&T reflects a failed diversification strategy; the sale of the surviving long-distance company to SBC Communications further testifies that AT&T's forays into new industries did not create the value and shareholder enthusiasm its leaders had hoped for. Ironically, SBC Communications changed their name to AT&T after acquiring the company. But, names can be deceiving; it is the shareholders and managers of SBC Communications that now own and manage the assets of the original AT&T long distance company. Of course, such divestitures are not always the result of failed diversification. Sometimes, a firm is quite successful but because of a change in strategy decides to divest itself of some successful businesses.

As the AT&T example illustrates, it often turns out that the collective value of a firm's portfolio is less than the total hypothetical value of the same businesses operated independently. In this case, the strategy of common ownership dissipates potential shareholder value. When investors—and corporate raiders, in particular—suspect the prospect of a significant diversification discount (i.e., the profits to be gained from buying the parent firm and selling off its portfolio piecemeal), a firm becomes a prime candidate for takeover and forced restructuring. Many investors have made huge profits by gaining control of an overly diversified company and selling various parts to firms in related areas—firms that are often willing to pay premium prices for operations related to their own.

Two things increase a firm's level of diversification: the number of separate businesses it operates and the degree of relatedness of those businesses. Relatedness is typically assessed by how similar the underlying industries are. The most diversified firms are those that own lots of businesses in very disparate industries; this is known as **unrelated diversification**. Firms that own many businesses clustered in a few industries are pursuing what is known as **related diversification**. Both forms of diversification can create management problems.

The harmful side effects of too much diversification include increased transaction and bureaucratic costs and burgeoning complexity. As firms become larger and multidivisional, corporate office functions tend to grow rapidly. If not held in check, these bureaucratic costs may exceed the benefits of diversification. Likewise, diverse firms may fall victim to doing too much internally and underutilize outside suppliers. Often the transaction costs of sourcing externally are sufficiently lower than the costs of organizing this activity internally. Finally, diversification increases firm complexity. For instance, the organization of a firm with ten businesses that span five industries is inherently more complex than a firm of the same size that operates only in one or a few industries. Complex firms are more difficult to manage than simple, focused firms. Research shows, for example, that diversified firms pay significantly higher compensation to attract and retain top management personnel than

diseconomies of scope
Condition under which the joint output of two or more products within a single firm results in increased average costs.

unrelated diversification
Form of diversification in which the business units that a firm operates are highly dissimilar.

related diversification Form of diversification in which the business units operated by a firm are highly related.

more focused firms of similar size.[6] Why? Because there are fewer top executives who are capable of managing complex firms. Bureaucratic costs, transaction costs, and complexity can all impede management's designs to create synergies.

If diversified firms are more difficult to manage—that is, if it's demonstrably harder to realize the benefits of diversification—then it stands to reason that there are real limits to those benefits. Indeed, research indicates that there's a point at which both the benefits of diversification and firm performance begin to decline. Exhibit 7.6 illustrates the relationship between diversification and two measures of firm performance—*return on assets* (ROA) and *total shareholder returns* (TSR).

In analyzing the data for the S&P 500 and S&P midcap firms over an eight-year period, we find that the relationship between diversification and performance takes the form of an inverted U (∩). At the median level of diversification, performance is much higher than at low levels of diversification (25th percentile) or high levels of diversification (75th percentile). These findings tell us that, on average, although diversification seems to benefit shareholders up to a point, it begins to dissipate value at high levels of diversification. Moderate values are typically achieved by firms which, like 3M, are active in several businesses that are somewhat related to each other.

When examining the relationship between diversification and performance reviewed in Exhibit 7.6, it is important to understand that there are exceptions to these averages. Some highly diversified firms perform quite well. For instance, GE is very diversified and over the long-term has performed very well, much better than most firms diversified at that level (and even single business firms). High levels of diversification, such as the conglomerate firm, can be very effective strategies in countries with developing capital markets. When capital markets are not as efficient as they are in developed countries, diversified firms can internally generate lower costs of capital than they can obtain in capital markets. Consequently, it can be efficient for firms to diversify and own more businesses than would be efficient in countries such as the United States, the United Kingdom, or Germany.

RESOURCE RELATEDNESS AND STRATEGIC SIMILARITY

To create economies of scope and revenue-enhancement synergies, a firm's resources should match its business activities. For this reason, whether they're thinking about en-

Exhibit 7.6

Diversification and Performance in S&P 500 and S&P Midcap Firms

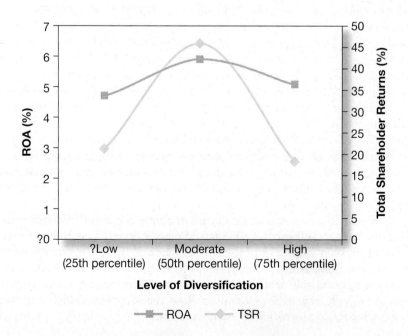

tering a new business arena or evaluating the suitability of a firm's portfolio for a proposed diversification move, strategists must assess the extent to which a firm's resources and capabilities match the needs of potential subsidiaries. One way to assess this match is in terms of how related the businesses are. When unrelated diversification is taken to the extreme—when there are many businesses and they are largely unrelated—firms are referred to as *conglomerates*. When there's a good match between the resource needs of parent and subsidiary—when diversification is related—it's more likely to create value. It's not critical, however, that both parent and subsidiary possess the *same* set of resources and capabilities. Indeed, in seeking to diversify, many firms are trying to acquire and bundle complementary resources and capabilities. The key issue is whether the match or fit between resources will help the parties compete more effectively.

Strategic Similarity Parent firms and their subsidiaries need to assess their fit on more than just the resources it takes to compete. In determining fit, we want to know if the strategies required to compete in the various businesses of the firm are similar. A firm's strategy affects the way in which managers view the firm's competitive activities and make critical resource allocation decisions. In general, it is easier to manage a firm that does not require dissimilar strategies across business units. For instance, the jobs of the top executives at 3M and GE are significantly more complex than at MITY Enterprises—and this would be the case even if MITY were as large as these other firms.

If the strategies of its businesses are similar, a firm's managers can respond more quickly and effectively to strategic issues. Conversely, when strategies differ significantly, managers will generally be slower and less decisive. Decision-making delays can be hazardous, especially in high-speed industries such as cell phones and computer peripherals; perhaps more important, dissimilarity in dominant logic increases the likelihood that when managers finally do make decisions they'll make bad ones.

Not surprisingly, the strategic characteristics of businesses in a diversified portfolio may vary widely. Two businesses, for instance, may depend on very different technologies, industry competitive structures, and customer-buying routines. Strategic dissimilarity, therefore, can make it much more difficult to manage the portfolio. The more similar the contexts across which its businesses compete, the easier it is to manage a firm's portfolio and to create value through economies of scope and revenue-enhancement synergy.

The maximum opportunities to exploit potential economies of scope and revenue enhancement synergies lie at the intersection of two dimensions: (1) the fit among parent–subsidiary resources and (2) the fit of parent–subsidiary strategies. Conversely, the least promising opportunity for creating synergies occurs when there's a misfit on both of these same dimensions. When there's a misfit, managers need to make organizational adjustments. Later in this chapter, we'll present two models that can help determine these adjustments.

ULTERIOR MOTIVES FOR DIVERSIFICATION

In addition to reducing costs and increasing revenue-enhancement opportunities, managers may have self-serving motives for diversification—motives that aren't necessarily in shareholders' best interests. Among these, we'll mention three: *risk reduction, empire building*, and *compensation*.

At first glance, risk reduction would seem to be a natural reason for diversifying. In fact, it's probably the reason cited most often by students who haven't yet been formally introduced to the pros and cons of corporate diversification. Why isn't the strategy of reducing risk by diversifying generally in shareholders' best interests? Because it's much cheaper for the shareholders themselves to diversify in other ways. They can, for example, diversify equity risk by building a diversified stock portfolio—a strategy that, compared to the cost of diversifying a corporate portfolio, is fairly inexpensive.

When executives embark on growth and diversification because they desire to manage a larger company, they are said to be engaging in empire building. Rarely will empire building result in shareholder value or higher margins. However, empire building almost always results in greater notoriety and prestige for top executives. Although some executives may pursue empire building simply because of hubris, there are opportunistic reasons why they would do so as well. This simple reason is that executives of larger companies are paid more than executives of smaller companies. The main determinant of how much CEOs are paid is company size. Therefore, growing and diversifying the company generally results in executives being paid more.

Types of Diversification

A firm that wants to expand the scope of its operations has several options. In this section, we'll show how a company can expand its arenas, the three dimensions of *vertical*, *horizontal*, and *geographic*.

VERTICAL SCOPE

vertical scope The extent to which a firm is vertically integrated.

Sometimes a firm expands its **vertical scope** out of economic necessity. Perhaps it must protect its supply of a critical input, or perhaps firms in the industry that supply certain inputs are reluctant to invest sufficiently to satisfy the unique or heavy needs of a single buyer. Beyond such reasons as these—which are defensive—firms expand vertically to take advantage of growth opportunities. Vertical expansion in scope is often a logical growth option because a company is familiar with the arena that it's entering.

In some cases, a firm can create value by moving into suppliers' or buyers' value chains if it can bundle complementary products. If, for instance, you were to buy a new home, you'd go through a series of steps in making your purchase decision. Now, most homebuilders concentrate on a fairly narrow aspect of the homebuilding value chain. Some, however, have found it profitable to expand vertically into the home financing business by

Homebuilders like Pulte and D.R. Horton have found a way to create value by moving down the home-buyer's value chain. Both companies now offer mortgage services, a complementor to the home building industry, making it easier for customers to buy their homes. Pulte and D.R. Horton benefit as well because they earn the revenues associated with mortgage financing.

offering mortgage brokerage services. Pulte Homes Inc., one of the largest homebuilders in the country, set up a wholly-owned subsidiary, Pulte Mortgage LLC, to help buyers get financing for new homes. This service not only simplifies the home buying process for many of Pulte's customers, but it also allows Pulte to reap profits in the home financing industry. Automakers and dealers have expanded into financing for similar reasons.

The Pitfalls of Increased Vertical Scope Although a firm's business segments lie adjacent along an industry's value chain, the structural features of the industries of these business segments (e.g., the industry five forces and complementors) may be fundamentally different. Thus, even though an adjacent segment is profitable, it doesn't follow that it's a good area for a firm to enter. Perhaps, for example, the firm doesn't have the resources needed to compete against established firms. Similarly, incumbents may enjoy significant cost advantages in performing the activities of their segment. Finally, the unwritten rules of competition in a segment, as well as the nature of strategic interactions, may be fundamentally different from those in a firm's base industry. A company should conduct thorough internal, industry, and competitor analyses before moving vertically into an adjacent segment of its industry value chain.

HORIZONTAL SCOPE

A firm increases its **horizontal scope** in one of two ways:

- By moving from an industry market segment into another, related segment; or

- By moving from one industry into another (unlike vertical-scope expansion, the movement here is into other industries not in the firm's existing value chain of activities).

The degree to which horizontal expansion is desirable depends on the degree to which the new industry is related to a firm's home industry. Industries can be related in a number of different ways. They may, for example, rely on similar types of human capital, engage in similar value-chain activities, or share customers with similar needs. Obviously, the more such factors that are present, the greater the degree of relatedness. When, for example, Coke and Pepsi expanded into the bottled water business, they were able to take advantage of the skill sets that they'd already developed in bottling and distribution. Moreover, because bottled water and soft drinks are substitutes for one another, both appeal to customers with similar demands.

However, when Pepsi expanded into snack foods, it was clearly moving into a business with a lesser degree of relatedness. Although the distribution channels for both businesses are similar (both sell products through grocery stores, convenience stores, delis, and so forth), the technology for producing their products are fundamentally different. In addition, although the two industries sell complementary products—they're often sold at the same time to the same customers—they aren't substitutes.

Cost Savings and Revenue Enhancement Opportunities Why is increased horizontal scope attractive? Primarily because it offers opportunities in two areas:

- The firm can reduce costs by exploiting possible economies of scope.

- The firm can increase revenues through synergies.

Because segments in closely related industries often use similar assets and resources, a firm can frequently achieve cost savings by sharing them among businesses in different segments. The fast food industry, for instance, has many segments—burgers, fried chicken, tacos, pizza, and so on. YUM! Brands Inc., which operates KFC, Pizza Hut, Taco Bell, A&W Restaurants, and Long John Silvers, has embarked on what the company calls

horizontal scope Extent to which firm participates in related market segments or industries outside its existing value-chain activities.

a "multibrand" store strategy. Rather than house all of its fast food restaurants in separate outlets, YUM! achieves economies of scope across its portfolio by bundling two outlets in a single facility. The strategy works, in part, because customer purchase decisions in horizontally related industries are often made simultaneously: In other words, two people walking into a bundled fast food outlet may desire different things to eat, but both want fast food, and both are going to eat at the same time. In addition, some of these combinations allow two food services that cater to purchases with different peak hours to share physical resources that would otherwise be largely unused during off-peak hours.

Profit Pools   One tool managers can use to evaluate adjacent market opportunities (whether vertical, horizontal, or complementary) is the **profit pool**. Beginning with a modified version of the firm and industry value chain, the profit pool can help you incorporate key complementary businesses near the point at which a firm is directly involved in customer transactions. The profit pool helps identify the size of value-chain segments (according to total sales) and the attractiveness of each segment (according to segment-by-segment profitability). Exhibit 7.7 illustrates the application of this tool to the auto industry in Europe and the global music industry.[7] Specifically, notice that sales volume for a segment is indicated visually by its width, while its profitability is shown by its height. As a map of the industry value chain, it reveals the breadth and depth of its alternative profit pools—each of the points along an industry's value chain at which total profits can be calculated.[8] The Western European profit pool is estimated to be approximately $62 billion, based on $885 billion in total revenues. In contrast, Exhibit 7.7 shows the United States' music industry profit pool to be about $10 billion, based on total industry revenues of $46 billion.

Some profit pools, of course, will be deeper (i.e., more profitable) than others. Moreover, depth may vary within a given value-chain segment. In the manufacturing segment of the PC industry, for instance, Dell enjoys much higher profit margins than Gateway. Segment profitability may also vary widely by product and customer group. Note that profit pools aren't stagnant; like industries in general, they change over time. Finally, and perhaps most importantly, the profit pool reminds us that *profit* concentration in an industry rarely occurs in the same place as *revenue* concentration.

Thinking in terms of profit pools also highlights a basic managerial mistake that's often made when developing corporate strategy. Firms often pursue strategies that focus on growth and market share on the assumption that profits automatically follow growth and size. *Profitable* growth, however, requires a clear understanding of an industry's profit pool. A profit-pool map, for example, will reveal the segments in which money is actually being made in an industry. More importantly, it may show where profits *could* be made. Consider, for instance, the consumer truck-rental business, in which U-Haul, Ryder, Hertz-Penske, and Budget are fierce competitors.[9] U-Haul, though the first entrant and largest player, faced significant disadvantages in the 1990s. Because its fleet was older, its maintenance expenses were considerably higher than those of competitors with newer fleets. U-Haul also charged lower prices than competitors. Lower revenues, coupled with higher expenses, generally result in lower margins. Indeed, U-Haul was barely breaking even on truck rentals. At the same time, however, U-Haul actually outperformed all of its competitors. Why? U-Haul beat its competitors because it went beyond its core business of truck rentals. It seized opportunities in complementary businesses that were relatively untapped, such as moving and storage accessories. By selling boxes, trailers, temporary storage space, tape, and other packing materials that truck renters needed, U-Haul squeezed out 10-percent operating margins in an industry in which the average was less than 3 percent. In How Would *You* Do That? 7.1, we walk you through the steps necessary to calculate the profit pool for a given industry.

profit pool   Analytical tool that enables managers to calculate profits at various points along an industry value chain.

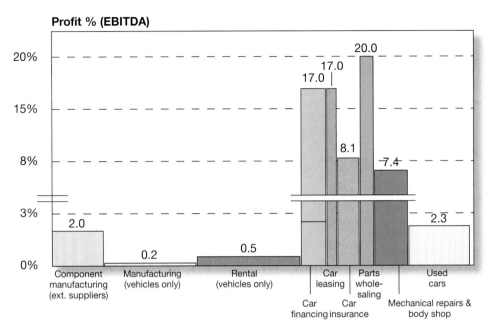

Exhibit 7.7a The European Auto Industry's Profit Pool

Exhibit 7.7b Global Music Industry's Profit Pool

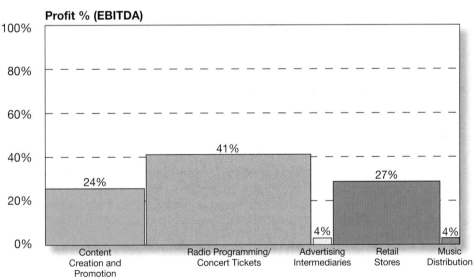

GEOGRAPHIC SCOPE

A firm typically increases **geographic scope** by moving into new geographic arenas without altering its business model. In its early growth period, for instance, a company may simply move into new locations in the same country. More often, however, increased geographic scope has come to mean *internationalization*—entering new markets in other parts of the world.

For a domestic firm whose operations are confined to its home country, the whole globe consists of potential arenas for expansion. Remember, however, that just as different industries can exhibit different degrees of relatedness, so, too, can different geographic markets, even those within the same industry. We can assess relatedness among different national

geographic scope Breadth and diversity of geographic arenas in which a firm operates.

Six Steps to a Profit Pool

The profit pool tool is an easy tool to understand. It also gives you a ready means for thinking about the boundaries of your focal industry where profits come from in a particular industry (or arena, in strategy diamond terms). Your profit pool analysis essentially follows six steps:

1. Define the profit pool in terms of its boundaries and the value-chain activities that are relevant to profit creation now and in the future. Think about the coffee industry, for example. For coffee, what are the key value chain inputs? You could go back as far as the farmers who grow the coffee beans, and even to specific coffee growing geographic arenas or arenas related to the variety or quality of coffee bean. Assuming that coffee growers are one end of the spectrum in this first step, you then want to identify the other end of the spectrum. So for coffee, does your interest in the industry stop at the coffee wholesalers (who sell bulk coffee to institutional and retail buyers), or do you move to institutional and retail buyers like Sysco Foods or Procter & Gamble, respectively, or all the way to consumer coffee purveyors like Starbucks or Dunkin Donuts, which sell ready-to-drink coffee products? Since you are already getting a good sense of what we mean by value chain activities in a given pool, you can see how those activities might vary by how

narrowly or broadly you define the beginning and end-points of the value chain. With this start and end-points in hand, now try to identify some of the intermediate value chain activities. Sticking with coffee, coffee-bean selection and roasting are important value chain activities in the larger coffee profit pool value chain since they determine the ultimate character of the final product.

2. Estimate the size of the profit pool. The size of the profit pool is the cumulative profits of all profit-pool activities for a given arena. One easy starting pointing in this step is to get figures on the total revenues and profits for all players in a given arena—this analysis has you starting at the top of the food chain since you want to know total revenues and profits for the finished product (though with coffee, recall that you could have been interested in wholesale product, product at the institutional or retail level, or the ultimate business to consumer level like a Starbucks coffee shop). In general, it is a good idea to think more broadly than narrowly about the scope of an industries value chain because, as in the case of coffee, if you stopped at wholesaling you would be missing pretty big pieces like institutional and retail sales, and ultimately the arena occupied by players like Starbucks (wouldn't you like to have been the

person who imagined that the coffee profit pool could become what Starbucks has achieved? 0). Taking Starbucks, or the business-to-consumer coffee arena as your profit pool, then in this step you would want to estimate the total sales and profitability of all players in this pool. While these data are hard to come by, market research companies like Mintel (often available through your library) can help you estimate market size and profitability, though typically on a country or regional basis. Investment bank reports, SEC documents, and data bases like Compustat will provide profitability and other data at a business unit level.

3. Estimate how profits are distributed among value chain activities. This is not as daunting of a task as it seems, when you remind yourself that every industry's cost-of-goods sold is the reflection of a downstream industry's total revenues and a determinant of that downstream industry's profitability. So where Step 2 has you aggregate revenues and profits for your focal profit pool, Step 3 has you disaggregate revenues and profits among the key value chain activities supporting the target profit pool. Keep in mind that this analysis is at an industry level so, in the case of the ready-to-drink coffee-consumer business, you would still want to

include coffee wholesalers, retailers, and roasters in your analysis (i.e., estimating their industry sales and profitability) even though you know that Starbucks has gone around them, roasts its own coffee, and works directly with coffee growers. Just like a good five-forces + complements industry analysis, your objective in profit pool analysis is to understand profit opportunities in an industry, now and in the future.

4. This is your reality-check step. Stand back and look at the value chain sales and profits across each of the activities and see how they reconcile with those of the focal profit pool. Try to reconcile inconsistencies by collecting additional data or doing further probing of the existing qualitative or quantitative data. Step 5 may give you some insights into why you are having difficulty reconciling the data in each value chain activity with the total revenue and profitability data you have compiled for the profit pool of interest.

5. Graph the profit pool. This fifth step is one reason why profit pool analysis is so powerful—because of the visual imagery it creates for you to explain industry profitability and the distribution and tradeoffs between sales and profitability across segments. The vertical axis on your profit pool grid, just as you see in the examples in Exhibit 7.7, should be industry profitability and the horizontal axis should be total industry revenues. You can play around with these, using percentages instead of absolute values, though the visual impression should be pretty similar across the two variants. The examples in 7.7 show percentages on the vertical access and actual dollars on the horizontal access. Just like a food chain, work from left to right where the first segment you plot on the left hand side is the first segment in the industry profit pool. So with coffee,

this would be the coffee bean growing industry (or different geographic, quality, or other (like organic, free-trade, etc.) segments of the coffee bean growing industry if they are relevant to your objectives. The height of each segment will reflect the segment's profitability, while the width will represent its sales. In the coffee profit pool, given that grocery stores are high volume but low profit businesses, you could imagine that segment of the profit pool to be very low (low profitability relative to other segments in the profit pool) but very wide in terms of sales volume.

6. You have probably learned a lot about the determinants of industry and firm profitability through the first five steps of your profit pool analysis. Though, the sixth and final step is the most interesting and creative. In this step you have the opportunity to do at least two things. First, you can step back and look at the value chain that comprises the profit pool and imagine the business potential were you to integrate some of these activities within a firm, or eliminate them altogether. You learned a bit about such strategies in Chapter 6 (revolutionary strategies), and step 5 of the profit pool tool is a great opportunity to do this. We've already given you the example of Starbucks, and how it bypassed the retail and wholesale channel, integrated roasting to provide distinctive coffee (ironically, they instruct their roasters to burn the beans more than other roasters!). IKEA would be an example of a firm that eliminated the value chain activity of furniture assembly, and actually outsourced it to you and me as consumers. Most recently, the T-shirt design house, ThreadFree, has eliminated fashion designers from its value chain cost structure. Through its web-site, thousands of customers submit T-shirt designs, its web-community picks one as the winner, and as a result 100% of the

new T-shirt design is sold out as quickly as it is produced (the design winner receives a $2000 design award).

Second, in this final step you can strive to identify *complements* and adjacent value chain arenas (sometimes called *adjacencies*) where additional value could be tapped or increased demand created. A traditional example of this is where General Motors has its own financial services arm (which is very profitable), and many car and recreational vehicle companies have found that they can sell more products when they also can provide on-the-spot financing. This is an example of a complementary business that has been integrated into the General Motor's corporate strategy. The European auto industry profit pool, shown in Exhibit 7.7a, shows this incorporation of financial services like insurance and financing into the industry profit pool. Complements like the iPod and SNOCAP (musician to consumer direct sales), are examples of complements that could be added to the music industry example in Exhibit 7.7b.

An adjacent business is somewhat different. The example of U-Haul presented earlier in the chapter is a great example of how U-Haul has exploited adjacencies. It makes much more profit on packaging material than it does on the rental of trucks. The use of adjacencies is not a new phenomenon. For instance, not long after Xerox introduced the photocopier (and actually created that industry), it found that it had a captive audience for copier paper sales, and had greater sales volume and profits on the sale of copy paper than on copiers! You have surely heard the saying that razor companies give away the handles to make money on the replacement razor blades.

markets by examining a number of factors, including laws, customs, cultures, consumer preferences, distances from home markets, common borders, language, socioeconomic development, and many others.

Economies of Scale and Scope   Geographic expansion can be motivated by economies of scale or economies of scope. R&D, for example, represents a significant, relatively fixed cost for firms in many industries, and when they move into new regions of a country or global arenas, they often find that they can spread their R&D costs over a larger market. For instance, the marginal cost for a pharmaceutical firm to enter a new geographic market is lower compared to the R&D and clinical trial costs involved in bringing a new drug into the U.S. market. Once the costs of development and entry are covered, entering new geographic markets not only brings in new revenues, but because fixed costs have been spread over the new, larger market, the average cost for all the firm's customers goes down. It should come as no surprise, then, that industries with relatively high R&D expenditures, such as pharmaceuticals and high-tech products, are among the most globalized.

Strategy and the Local Environment   Sometimes, firms expanding into new geographic markets find that they must adapt certain components of their strategies to accommodate local environments. In this country, for instance, Dell is famous for the business model that allows it to skip middlemen and go directly to suppliers and customers. In its early years, Dell experimented with a retail distribution strategy but quickly retrenched. As it has expanded into some international markets such as India and China, however, Dell has found that it must, even temporarily, delay the implementation of its direct model, at least for the consumer and small business markets, although it worked well for government and large business buyers. Why? Basically because it needs local intermediaries to help develop both a base of business and acceptable levels of awareness among those particular buyers. Once the market has been penetrated to a sufficient degree, the direct model is implemented and used to reach consumers and small businesses.

Although Dell provides a nice example of adaptation, most global firms tend to approach the subject of corporate strategy from the perspective of their domestic market—such an ap-

In the United States, Dell has traditionally sold its computers straight to consumers without going through intervening middlemen or retail stores. In Asia, however, this strategy works only with institutional buyers, such as governments, schools, and businesses. As a result, Dell had to change its distribution strategy there.

proach can be problematic. Microsoft is a case in point here. The respective regulatory authorities of the U.S. and the countries of the E.U. employ very different traditions and models of competition, which in turn means that strategies must vary across these important markets. Had you not been aware of these differences, you might think that Microsoft implemented an ideal resource-based corporate strategy in its diversification into Europe. It bundled its Windows operating system with the Explorer browser and other software to increase customers' perceptions of value and, therefore, willingness to pay. It also used its extensive experience with PC software and operating systems and applications to better penetrate the market for software and operating systems in the server market, where customers are primarily businesses. Finally, Microsoft also tried to lock out competitors by including its Media Player as a standard feature in both its server and home PC operating systems.

The E.U. took exception to this strategy.[10] The European Commission recently signaled it would keep up the pressure on Microsoft, saying the company's "illegal behavior is still ongoing." It also warned that it remains concerned about Microsoft's "general business model," saying that it "deters innovation and reduces consumer choice in any technologies which Microsoft could conceivably take an interest in and tie with Windows in the future." In addition to a fine of over $600 million, the E.U. gave Microsoft 90 days to release versions of its Windows operating systems for home PCs and servers without the Windows Media Player and begin providing rivals access to the details of the code underlying its proprietary server systems. This is not the first time such differences in regulatory environments have been ignored or underestimated by global firms. Just a few years earlier, the European Commission's ruling dealt a fatal blow to the all-but-done merger between Honeywell and GE.[11]

Strategies for Entering Attractive New Businesses

So, what new businesses should a firm enter if it is contemplating diversification? We've already mentioned that the business should require the same or related resources and that it should have strategic similarity. But, there are literally thousands of possible businesses that a firm might enter, how else might managers narrow down the search? Certainly, some businesses will be more attractive than others. Recall that Chapter 4 taught you how to analyze the attractiveness of an industry. Among other things, attractive industries tend to benefit from higher levels of profitability. So, a manager might target a high-profit business that requires related resources and that is strategically similar to the firm's core business. However, Chapter 4 should have also taught you that there are reasons that industries have higher average profits; one critical reason is that it likely has strong entry barriers. Consequently, the most attractive markets are generally the hardest to enter. There are three ways to solve this paradox. First, entry barriers can be circumvented by acquiring a company already in the industry. Chapter 10 will address mergers and acquisitions as a vehicle for entering a new market. Second, a firm can enter in a manner that incumbents don't initially take notice of your entry. Third, entry should exploit something that the new entrant can do with a cost advantage over incumbents and other new entrants. We outline three methods for accomplishing this that are based on concepts you have already learned earlier.[12] These methods are not mutually exclusive strategies; they are often used in combination to formulate robust entry moves into attractive industries.

FOCUS ON A NICHE

Recall that in Chapter 5 you learned the concept of generic strategic positions. These were low cost leadership, differentiation, focus cost leadership, and focus differentiation. Entering an attractive industry is difficult to do if making a direct assault on incumbents' strongholds.

One way to enter and not attract lots of attention and retaliatory behavior is to focus the entry on a niche in the market. One type of niche to look for is a segment of the market whose needs are currently underserved. Consider the soft drink market. Coca-Cola and PepsiCo enjoy gross margins of more than 60 percent and return on assets of over 17 percent.[13] Many firms have attempted to enter the industry, but few have succeeded in establishing competitive positions. A successful niche entry to consider is the case of Red Bull. Rather than enter into the heart of the market, Red Bull entered the niche market of energy drinks.

Red Bull markets its nonalcoholic and functional energy drink in more than 100 countries. The nonalcoholic drink contains the amino acid taurine, B-complex vitamins, caffeine, and carbohydrates. Austrian Dietrich Mateschitz discovered the drink while doing business in Thailand. He formed a joint venture with the Thai businessman and adapted the drink for Austrian tastes.

Red Bull entered the United States in 1997 with little fanfare but city by city introduced the product and targeted the young adult market. The drink's popularity grew quickly and eventually captured more than 70 percent of the U.S. market for energy drinks, and rapid growth industry in and of itself. Of course, even though this was a niche market, that kind of growth captured the attention of Coca-Cola and PepsiCo, and many other firms and entrepreneurs. Red Bull's market share has slipped into the 40s, but the market has grown significantly as well, so Red Bull's sales continue to climb.

USING A REVOLUTIONARY STRATEGY

Entering an attractive industry is risky because it will get the attention of incumbents. In our first example, we suggested that entering by targeting a niche would provide some protection because incumbents often ignore niche markets. Likewise, entering with a revolutionary strategy will afford some protection because such a strategy breaks with the convention of the incumbents. Because it is so different from the status quo, incumbents generally are predisposed to think such a strategy is inferior, unwise, or risky. It is only after such a strategy proves successful that incumbents will rally to try to protect their ground. By then, it is often too late.

As you learned in Chapter 6, there are several ways a strategy can be revolutionary. For illustrative purposes, we use reconfiguring the value chain as an example, but successful new-business entry could be accomplished with any revolutionary strategy. One of those strategies was to reconfigure the value chain. Recall the example of Skype. How did Skype enter the telecom services industry with established and well-financed incumbents? It used a completely new value chain. Rather than rely on the existing telecom infrastructure, Skype used Voice-over-Internet-Protocol (VOIP) that allowed their customers to utilize their PCs to place calls, thereby bypassing the entire value chain of incumbents and giving them a totally different (and lower) cost structure. The service was targeted to price sensitive customers, so initially it was able to avoid direct retaliation from incumbents.

Pixar, part of the Walt Disney Company since its acquisition in 2006, provides another example of diversification. You will see value-chain reconfiguration here, but facets of other revolutionary strategies as well. In 1986, Steve Jobs purchased the computer graphics division of Lucasfilm, Ltd. for $10 million and established an independent company named Pixar. With the new animation technologies that it developed and controlled, Pixar began to experiment with film shorts and commercials. The technology allowed Pixar to cast lifelike characters without the cost of their care and feeding. While you may not be familiar with Pixar as a technology company, you probably have heard about Toy Story—the breakthrough film launched as a joint Disney/Pixar production in 1995. At that time, Toy Story provided the most dramatic glimpse of the promise of this new animation technology for global media market. Pixar is an example of a technology company diversifying into commercial (i.e., advertising) and then consumer animation (i.e., short and long animated feature films). As a result of this value-chain configuration, the core technology of many animated films was drastically changed, to the point that Disney abandoned its traditional animation approach in 2005.

LEVERAGE EXISTING RESOURCES

Successful new entrants use resources they already control, and possibly supplement these with a partner's resources, to leapfrog entry barriers. Consider Wal-Mart's entry into the soft drink business in the early 1990s. What resources Wal-Mart could bring to the table were shelf space and a top-flight distribution network. However, it did not have any capability in formulating soft drinks or bottling them. So, it partnered with Cott Corporation from Canada to develop Sam's Choice. By leveraging its resources with those of Cott, Wal-Mart has been able to capture approximately 5 percent of the soft drink market since its entry into softdrinks.

Recall the opening vignette from Chapter 1 about Under Armour. Under Armour initially entered the performance apparel market and established a loyal customer base. Its reputation for manufacturing high-quality performance apparel, combined with its brand image, were combined to help it enter the football cleat market. Under Armour leveraged these resources and product design to such an extent that they were able to capture 20 percent of the football cleat market share overall, and an amazing 40 percent of the market for cleats priced over $70! But Under Armour didn't enter the football cleat market as an end-game strategy. They view it as a stepping stone to allow entry into the broader athletic footwear market in future years. They used the resources they had to develop an entry strategy for cleats, but they plan to accumulate the resources (e.g., experience, expertise, distribution channels) in this niche area of footware to allow easier entry into the broader market later.

COMBINATION STRATEGIES

You have probably noticed in the examples of the three entry strategies reviewed above that several of the examples actually have elements of two or more of the strategies. For instance, Skype combined its reconfigured value chain with a niche strategy; they specifically targeted price-sensitive customers who would tolerate inferior quality. Wal-Mart's entry into soft drinks was a combination of leveraging their existing resources (e.g., shelf space and distribution network) with a reconfigured value chain; they did not distribute through typical retailers, they make no attempt to secure fountain drink contracts, and they do not stock vending machines except at their own properties.

The key to entering an attractive business is to do so in an indirect way; an entry strategy that does not directly assault the incumbents and immediately threaten their profitability. Pursuing niche markets initially is often ignored by incumbents because they represent customers that the incumbents were previously serving. Reconfiguring the value chain and leveraging existing resources help protect firms entering attractive markets. A reconfigured value chain gives the entrant a cost advantage and leveraging existing resources gives the entrant something to build off of that incumbents and other possible new entrants are likely to lack.

Competitive Advantage and Corporate Strategy

At the business level, competitive advantage reflects the relative position of a firm compared to positions of industry rivals. At the corporate level, it reflects management's success in creating more value from the firm's business units than those units could create as standalone enterprises or subsidiaries. Our goal is to identify the conditions under which the strategy of owning a corporate portfolio of businesses creates value for shareholders.

You are already familiar with the element of arenas in business strategy. Sometimes a firm chooses a corporate strategy of competing in only one arena. However, the corporate strategy of many firms involves operating in more than one arena. Corporate strategy becomes more complicated if the competitive or operational characteristics of those arenas differ in some way, whether subtly or substantially. Ultimately, it is the combination of arenas, resources (i.e., VRINE), and implementation that determines whether the corporate strategy leads to competitive advantage.

ARENAS

 Arenas

Theoretically, a firm can compete in any combination of discrete business arenas. In practice, of course, firms rarely enter arenas randomly but rather select those that are logically connected to the arenas in which they already participate. ◆ The key to logical connection is *relatedness*. Businesses can be related along several different dimensions, including similarity in markets, use of identical resources, and reliance on comparable dominant logic.

Resources provide the basis for corporate competitive advantage. The nature of corporate resources varies along a continuum, and whether the resources are specialized or general dictates the limits of a firm's scope, the manner of organizational control and coordination, and the effectiveness of corporate headquarters. Although most firms maintain some degree of relatedness among the various businesses in which they participate, some combinations require greater relatedness than others. Finally, it's not always easy to determine the dimensions along which corporate businesses are related.

Some conglomerates are actually portfolios of strategic business units within which several related businesses are combined for management purposes. GE, for instance, participates in such far-flung enterprises as jet engines, elevators, light bulbs, appliances, and financial services. Each of these businesses, however, is located in a business unit with conceptually similar units.

RESOURCES

As we saw in Chapter 3, resources and capabilities are tangible or intangible, and their usefulness in creating a competitive advantage depends on five factors: (1) how valuable they are, (2) whether they're rare in the industry, (3) whether they're costly to imitate, (4) the availability of substitutes, and (5) whether the firm has complementary capabilities to exploit them. At this point, we need to remember that these factors apply to the usefulness of resources in creating competitive advantage at the *business* level. At the corporate level in the VRINE framework (e.g., valuable, rare, inimitable, nonsubstitutable, exploitable), they must be supplemented by an additional factor: namely, how *specialized* or *general* a firm's resources are.

specialized resources
Resource with a narrow range of applicability.

Specialized Resources   **Specialized resources** have a narrow range of applicability. Knowledge about fiber-optics, for example, is fairly specialized, whereas managerial know-how and skill are more general in nature. Granted, fiber-optics has many uses in multiple contexts (such as telecommunications, electronics, routing and switching equipment), but its utility is more limited than that of a general resource such as general managerial skill.

general resources   Resource that can be exploited across a wide range of activities.

General Resources   **General resources** can be exploited across a wide range of activities. For instance, expertise in efficient manufacturing and mass-marketing techniques can be exploited in any number of contexts. In fact, many companies have created significant shareholder value by leveraging these general resources across different businesses engaged in a variety of industries. General resources aren't confined to narrow applications, and the extent of resource specialization affects both a firm's scope and its organizational structure.

IMPLEMENTATION

As explained in Chapters 1 and 2 and will reaffirm in 11, *implementation levers* include organizational structure, systems and processes, and people and rewards. Strategic leaders use these levers to implement strategies. The success with which diversified firms are managed in accord with key organizational features has a significant effect on the level of value that can be created through their portfolios. Implementation levers that are critical for corporate strategy vary from firm to firm, but some of the more important levers to achieve successful diversification include knowledge-transfer mechanisms, coordination mechanisms, rewards, and corporate oversight.

Knowledge transfer enables a diversified firm to apply superior performance results observed in one organizational business unit to other units that are not performing as well. In practice, knowledge transfer is difficult because it may not be entirely clear what is causing the superior performance in the high-performing unit. Three mechanisms facilitate knowledge transfer. First, just the knowledge that superior results are being achieved in another business unit can be used to reset performance expectations for future performance in other units. In this case, no real knowledge of actual practices is transferred, but the superior performance is used to create stretch goals that motivate learning in other units. Second, underperforming units can study the operational practices of high-performing business units to determine the source of superior performance. Finally, knowledge transfer is perhaps best facilitated when members of lower-performing business units simply seek advice from the higher-performing units. It is often the case that high-performing business units have explicit routines and practices that can be detailed by key employees in those units.[14]

Coordination mechanisms are the management systems and processes that facilitate intrafirm activity. Coordination depends on a variety of structural mechanisms, including reporting relationships, informal meetings and exchanges, and detailed policies and procedures for such activities as intrafirm transfer pricing. Greater relatedness of businesses within a firm requires more intense coordination across business units. Why? Because resources in highly related diversified firms are often shared across business units. Illustratively, more cross-business coordination is needed at 3M than at GE. For instance, adhesive technology is used in multiple divisions in 3M, and this knowledge sharing requires coordination. Alternatively, knowledge transfer or resource sharing (other than cash) does not occur between GE's jet engine and consumer finance divisions. Consequently, 3M can generate more revenue-enhancement synergy between related units than GE can generate between unrelated businesses, but to reap these possible benefits requires that energy and resources be devoted to coordination efforts.

Successful diversification may require adjustments in how managers are compensated and rewarded. Generally speaking, a firm with a broad (highly diversified) portfolio should reward managers differently than a focused or related diversified firm.[15] Why? In a firm with a broad scope, division-level managers do not share resources and cooperate to implement their strategies. Consequently, it is more effective to reward managers for the performance of their divisions than to reward (and punish) them for the performance of divisions that they have no control of or influence over. Conversely, in a related diversified firm, managers of different divisions are generally required to share resources and cooperate to implement their strategies. As a result, it is more effective to reward managers for the firm's collective performance than to focus all rewards on division-level performance. For instance, when division-level profits drive bonuses, managers have little incentive to help other divisions.

When corporate-level management grows unwieldy, it can be a drag on corporate earnings. What factors should determine the size and organization of corporate-level management? Basically, two factors govern this decision: the firm's resources and the scope of its involvement in disparate arenas. When a firm's portfolio contains numerous unrelated units that aren't significantly interdependent, it doesn't need heavy corporate-level oversight;

there's not much that corporate-level management can do to add value on a day-to-day basis (a good example is Warren Buffet's Berkshire Hathaway Inc.). By contrast, when a firm's portfolio consists of highly interdependent businesses, more corporate-level control is needed to facilitate the sharing of resources and to oversee interbusiness transactions (e.g., S. C. Johnson, whose businesses include insect control, home cleaning, and plastic products).

Now that we've identified the ingredients of a good corporate strategy, we need to remind ourselves that it's the alignment of these ingredients in support of a firm's mission and vision that makes it possible for its managers to implement the firm's corporate strategy and create competitive advantage at the corporate level. Indeed, the configuration of these elements will determine whether a firm achieves corporate-level competitive advantage.

Corporate Strategy in Stable and Dynamic Contexts

By this point, you probably have a strong suspicion that corporate strategy is developed according to the relative dynamism of the context in which an organization operates. You are, of course, correct, and in this section we'll see how corporate strategy is designed to take dynamic context into account. Moreover, because alliances and acquisitions are vehicles for both business and corporate strategy, we'll elaborate on this theme in subsequent chapters as well. We'll see, for example, that, depending on whether a firm's context is stable or dynamic, different strategy vehicles are likely to play different roles. In particular, alliances and acquisitions have different implications for the allocation of a firm's resources and capabilities. We'll show that because certain issues arise in both stable and dynamic contexts, differences are often matters of emphasis. At the same time, however, we'll stress the point that even if the *content* of strategy is similar in both stable and dynamic contexts, the dynamism of the context will still have an effect on its *implementation*.

CORPORATE STRATEGY IN STABLE CONTEXTS

Many of the traditional notions of the relationship between diversification and corporate strategy are based on analyses of companies operating in relatively stable contexts. As we've seen, historically a firm may have diversified into a high-growth industry because growth prospects in its current industry were unattractive. That's why Kansas City Southern (KCS), a railroad, got into financial services in the late 1960s and soon owned almost 90 percent of the Janus Group of mutual funds. But recall, too, our observation that this form of unrelated diversification often fails. Indeed, due to an obvious lack of synergy between the rail industry and mutual funds—plus an increasing level of management conflict between its railroad and mutual-fund divisions—KCS divested Janus in 1999 (a move widely approved by the market).[16]

Stable Arenas and Formal Structures   As we've seen, creating synergies among its businesses is an important part of a corporation's strategy. Synergies can come from shared know-how, coordination of business-unit strategies, shared tangible resources, vertical integration, and pooled negotiating power.[17] In relatively stable environments, such synergies are typically conceived as functions of static business-unit arenas and the formal structural links among them. Corporate-strategy objectives focus primarily on synergies as means of achieving economies of scope and scale. In fact, corporate strategy explicitly defines the form and extent of the coordination and collaboration among business units. Thus, the managers of individual units are often compensated according to a combination of division- and corporate-level performance. Generally speaking, the overarching objective of corporate strategy in a stable environment is ensuring that the firm operates as a tightly interwoven whole.

The best example of such strategy in action is probably the related diversified firm. Masco Corporation, a multibillion-dollar manufacturer and distributor of plumbing fixtures and other home building and home repair supplies, is just such a firm. Starting with Delta Faucets in the early 1960s, Masco built a diversified portfolio of manufacturing businesses by acquiring well-run firms in a variety of industries. Today, Masco is one of the leading makers of home improvement and home building products and a powerhouse in the do-it-yourself industry dominated by such retail chains as Home Depot and Lowe's. We've summarized the breadth of Masco's holdings in Exhibit 7.8. Operating a tightly knit set of businesses is an effective corporate strategy for Masco. Why? Primarily because each business alone is unattractive, and by combining them under one corporate roof, Masco gives them greater selling and merchandising power in dealing with aggressive customers such as Home Depot. In addition, because its businesses are sufficiently related, Masco can leverage manufacturing, design, marketing, distribution, and merchandizing expertise across them.

CORPORATE STRATEGY IN DYNAMIC CONTEXTS

Masco's strategy would be problematic for firms competing in more dynamic contexts. Adaptec Inc., for instance, was once an integrated maker of both computer hardware and software. The strategy was logical because the firm could extract synergies from operations in such complementary businesses. Adaptec soon discovered, however, that rapid changes in technologies and advances by competitors were weakening its ability to maneuver well in both areas. In 1999, therefore, Adaptec spun off its software side as Roxio through an IPO.

Even a seemingly focused business like Palm, which makes PDAs, can find it difficult to perform well in both hardware (Palm Pilot PDAs) and software (the Palm operating system), accordingly, Palm actually split into two separate companies. Ironically, as late as 2000, 3Com, then a supplier of computer, communications, and compatibility (network-interfacing) products, spun off Palm as a separate business for similar reasons.[18] In turn, Palm used the proceeds from its own IPO to strengthen its position in the market for handheld devices and operating systems. 3Com now concentrates on its core networking business, along with research and development in emerging technologies.

Diversification in Dynamic Contexts   Despite the examples of Adaptec and 3Com, both of which have used divestitures to increase corporate focus, diversification can be a viable strategy in dynamic contexts. Bear in mind, however, that firms seeking to diversify in dynamic contexts usually need strong resources and capabilities in the areas of learning, knowledge transfer, and rapid responsiveness. If corporate ownership hinders nimbleness and response time in a dynamic environment, it's more likely to be an encumbrance than an advantage. It's hard enough to manage competitively in dynamic contexts without having to struggle under excess layers of corporate hierarchy.

Coevolution   The ebbs and flows of firms' corporate strategies in dynamic contexts are best described as a web of shifting linkages among evolving businesses—a process that some researchers call **coevolution**.[19] Borrowed from biology, the term *coevolution* describes successive changes among two or more ecologically interdependent species that adapt not only to their environment but also to each other. Business units coevolve when senior managers do not target specific synergies across business units but rather allow business-unit managers to determine which linkages do and don't work. As business-unit managers search for fresh opportunities for synergies and abandon deteriorating linkages, internal relationships tend to shift. As in the organic world, coevolution can result in competitive interdependence, with one unit eventually absorbing another or rendering it unnecessary. Coevolution means that cross-business synergies are usually temporary, and managers must learn to deal with the fundamental tension that results from the agility afforded by fewer linkages and the efficiency afforded by more. Finally, research suggests that in successful coevolving companies, managers, rather than trying to control, or even predict, cross-business-unit synergies, simply let them emerge in the "natural" course of corporate operations.[20]

coevolution   Process by which diversification causes two or more interdependent businesses to adapt not only to their environment, but to each other.

Exhibit 7.8 Masco: A Holding Company at a Glance

Domestic	International
Cabinet and Related Products	
d-Scan Inc.	AlmaKüchen, Germany
Diversified Cabinet Distributors	Alvic, Spain
KraftMaid	Aran Group, Italy
Merillat	Berglen Group, UK
Mill's Pride	Grumal, Spain
Texwood Industries	Moores Group Ltd., UK
Zenith	Tvilum-Scanbirk, Denmark
	Xey, Spain
Plumbing Products	
Aqua Glass	A & J Gummers, UK
Brass Craft	Breuer, Germany
Brasstech	Bristan Ltd., UK
Delta Faucet	Damixa, Denmark
H&H Tube	Glass Indromassaggio SpA, Italy
Mirolin	Hansgrohe AG, Germany
Peerless Faucet	Heritage, UK
Plumb Shop	Hüppe, Germany
Watkins Manufacturing	NewTeam Limited, UK
	Rubinetterie Mariani, Italy
	S.T.S.R., Italy
Decorative Architectural Products	
Behr	Avocet, UK
Franklin Brass (Bath Unlimited)	SKS Group, Germany
GAMCO (Bath Unlimited)	
Ginger	
Liberty Hardware	
Masterchem	
Melard (Bath Unlimited)	
Vapor Technologies	
Specialty Products	
Arrow Fastener	Alfred Reinecke, Germany
Cobra	Brugman, Holland
Computerized Security Systems (CSS)	Cambrian Windows Ltd., UK
Faucet Queens	Duraflex Ltd., UK
Gamco/Morgantown Products	Gebhardt, Germany
MediaLab	Griffin Windows, UK
Milgard Manufacturing	Jung Pumpen, Germany
PowerShot Tool Company	Missel, Germany
	Premier Manufacturing Ltd., UK
	Superia Radiatoren, Belgium
	Vasco, Belgium

Ironically, of course, coevolution means that units owned by the same corporation are potentially both collaborators and competitors. This paradoxical relationship is perhaps easiest to detect when a firm operates both traditional and e-business units. It's less obvious when it arises because new technologies have emerged to threaten established processes, but the costs of allowing a competitor—even one with which you share a corporate umbrella—to gain a technological advantage are often steep. In dynamic contexts, corporate strategy usually takes the form of temporary networks among businesses, and if strategic alliances are added into the mix, the network may include companies that the corporation doesn't own as well as those it does.

Divestitures and corporate spinoffs can be effective strategic vehicles for dealing with the sort of disruptive innovations that we discussed in Chapters 4 and 6, and they also figure frequently in stories of corporate coevolution.[21] Because disruptive technologies compete with established technologies, it may not be enough to simply reorganize them as new units under the same corporate umbrella. The resulting problems from retaining ownership of the disruptive part of the business range from the creation of messy internal politics to simply starving the new business of resources so that it eventually fails. We've summarized the key differences between corporate strategies in stable and dynamic contexts in Exhibit 7.9. The box entitled "How Would *You* Do That? 7.2," demonstrates how you might evaluate dynamic corporate strategy at Disney.

 Vehicles

Stable Contexts	Dynamic Contexts
Top management team emphasizes collaboration among the businesses and the form of that collaboration.	Top management team emphasizes the creation of a collaborative context that is rich in terms of content and linkages.
Collaboration is solidified through stable structural arrangement among wholly-owned businesses.	Collaboration is fluid, with networks being created, changed, and disassembled between combinations of owned and alliance businesses.
Key objectives are the pursuit of economies of scale and scope.	Key objectives are growth, maneuverability, and economies of scope.
The business units' roles are to execute their given strategies.	The business units' roles are to execute their strategies and seek new collaborative opportunities.
Business units' incentives combine business with corporate-level rewards to promote cooperation.	Business units' incentives emphasize business-level rewards to promote aggressive execution and collaborative-search objectives.
Balanced-scorecard objectives emphasize performance against budget and in comparison to within-firm peer unit.	Balanced-scorecard objectives gauge performance relative to competitors in terms of growth, market share, and profitability.

Exhibit 7.9 Comparison of Corporate Strategies in Stable and Dynamic Contexts

Evaluating Diversification at Disney

To evaluate Disney's corporate strategy, we can use an adapted portfolio analysis. You learned about the problems with the traditional use of portfolio analysis, but it is still widely used in the modified form we present in this example. Disney's vision is to be the industry leader in providing creative entertainment experiences. The arenas in which Disney participates are focused on family entertainment and include media networks (41 percent), theme parks and resorts (28 percent), studio entertainment (24 percent), and consumer products (7 percent). A few of the fundamental resources that Disney shares across these arenas are the Disney name and legacy, the library of films and Disney's cast of animated and real-life characters, capabilities in the creation and management of world-class entertainment, and service-management expertise (this is obviously an abbreviated list of resources and capabilities).

Implementation is the glue holding these arenas and resources together. Although the company appears to be diversified into related arenas, each business is treated as a profit center, and managers are compensated according to business-unit performance. To overcome the lack of cross-division cooperation that this might motivate, Disney has historically relied on special "synergy management" positions. Imagine the powerful scope economies that are created when Disney launches a hit character and then leverages the

fictional personality through every channel, from toy licensing to Disney Radio. Just as important, however, is the skill with which Disney pulls the right implementation levers to make this synergistic dynamo work.

We want to evaluate how well Disney is doing with its corporate strategy. To do so, we will use a portfolio analysis tool that incorporates VRINE and other key strategy concepts that you have already learned about. We want to map Disney's business units along four dimensions: the size of the divisions, the VRINE characteristics of the division, the industry's five forces score, and the profitability of the divisions relative to competitors in these businesses. This 4-D exercise will allow us to visualize how well Disney is performing, given the industry contexts of each business and the resources and capabilities possessed by the divisions.

In Exhibit 7.10, we have tabulated the data for Disney's divisions using the tools you have learned earlier. For the five forces analysis, we rank each industry in which Disney participates using the tool that you learned in "How Would *You* Do That? 4.1" in Chapter 4.

For the VRINE analysis, we gave each division a score of 1 to 5, depending on whether its resources satisfy the VRINE requirements (e.g., 1 point given if the resources are valuable; 2 points if they are valuable and rare; 3 points if they are valuable, rare, and difficult to imitate; 4 points if they are valuable, rare, difficult to

imitate, and non-substitutable; and 5 points if they meet the first four requirements and the firm is able to exploit the resources. We also report the size of each division, the business unit profit margin, the weighted average profit margin for other firms in those industries, and the industry adjusted performance for each of Disney's business units (e.g., business unit profit margin minus the weighted average industry profit margin).

We can use this data to create a bubble chart in an Excel worksheet, which will make the data easier to interpret and present to managers. Bubble charts can plot three values. We use the VRINE scores for the X axis (i.e., the horizontal axis), the five forces score for the Y axis (i.e., the vertical axis), and the business unit size for the size of the bubble. After the chart is plotted, we then add the profit margin for each division using the text box feature. Exhibit 7.11 illustrates what we have found.

What do we learn from this type of portfolio analysis? Quite simply, it allows us to see whether Disney is creating synergy across its business units. Recall that synergy either results in economies of scope (which should lead to lower costs than competitors) or revenue enhancement, which should give us greater revenue relative to costs compared to competitors. Thus, if we've truly created synergy we should perform better than average. Portfolio analysis also helps us analyze the performance of the portfolio as a whole. For instance, we can see how business

Exhibit 7.10   Comparison Portfolio Data for Disney

	Business Unit VRINE Score	Strength of Five Force Score	Business Unit Size ($ millions)	Business Unit Profit Margin	Industry Weighted Average Profit Margin	Industry Adjusted Business Unit Profit Margin
Parks and Resorts	5	3	9023	13%	19%	−5.88%
Media Networks	2	2	13207	21%	10%	10.81%
Studio Entertainment	2	4	7587	?	10%	−7.28%
Consumer Products	3	2	2215	23%	30%	−6.75%

units perform relative to each other, which helps managers determine where they need to focus their attention.

So, how is Disney doing? Not too well, actually. Only Media Networks is performing above industry averages. The industry was scored as rather favorable (i.e., a low score for the level of the five forces). However, this will help all firms perform well in the industry, not just Disney. Perhaps Media Networks is best exploiting the synergies of all the divisions, allowing it to perform better than its competitors. The other divisions are all under-performing their competitors.

We need to emphasize that we are using industry-adjusted performance to evaluate the portfolio. Why? A firm (or business unit) might perform at what appears to be a healthy clip. For instance, the consumer product division of Disney achieves 23 percent profit margins, which are among the highest in the company. However, Disney's competitors in consumer products average more than 30 percent. So, actually, it would be a mistake to conclude that Disney is doing well in that division.

Exhibit 7.11   Disney Portfolio

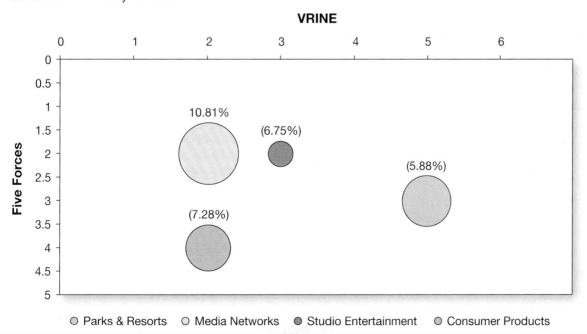

○ Parks & Resorts   ○ Media Networks   ● Studio Entertainment   ○ Consumer Products

Summary of Challenges

1. *Define* **corporate strategy.** Corporate strategy encompasses issues related to decisions about entering and exiting businesses. A fundamental part of corporate strategy is the decision about what business *arenas* to enter and exit. However, corporate strategy also encompasses the overall management of the multibusiness enterprise, such as corporate headquarters' efforts to orchestrate the cross-business-unit synergies. Corporate strategy deals with the logic for owning more than one business within a firm.

2. *Understand the roles of economies of scope and revenue-enhancement synergy in corporate strategy.* Expanding the scope of the firm, whether vertically, horizontally, or geographically, does not necessarily create value. Value is created by either lowering costs or increasing revenues through diversification. This can take place when economies of scope result from diversification, such as when two businesses are able to share the same resources. Revenue-enhancement synergies can also create value. For synergies to be present because of joint ownership, the combined revenues of two distinct businesses must be greater when owned jointly than when operated independently. These economic gains are more likely when there is resource similarity between businesses and when the dominant logics necessary to manage the businesses are similar.

3. *Identify the different types of diversification.* Firms have several options when expanding the scope of their operations beyond the original business definition. In this chapter, we discussed the concept of diversification along three trajectories of new business arenas: vertical, horizontal, and geographic (global). Vertical scope is ownership of business activities along the firm's vertical value chain. Horizontal scope, typically called diversification, is increased by owning businesses in different industry segments or different industries entirely. Geographic scope entails moving into new geographic areas, typically new countries.

4. *Explain how companies can be successfully enter attractive industries when those industries have the greatest barriers to entry.* In the evolution of firms over time, most decide to expand into new businesses. The industries that attract the most attempts for new entry are industries that are more profitable on average than others. However, entry barriers make it difficult for firms to enter these industries, as evidenced by the fact that most new entrants to such industries earn profits far below the average of the industry, and even below what entrants to unattractive industries earn. To successfully enter an attractive industry a firm needs to orchestrate an indirect assault, not attack the incumbents in their strongholds, such as by entering in a niche segment of the industry. In addition, successful entrants leverage their existing resources and enter with a fundamentally different value chain than incumbents.

5. *Describe the relationship between corporate strategy and competitive advantage.* Competitive advantage at the corporate level is a function of the fit among arenas, resources, and organizational systems, structures, and processes. When these are connected in a coherent fashion, the corporation is more likely to achieve its long-term objectives. When resources are specialized, the firm will likely find greater value creation opportunities in a narrow scope of business arenas. Conversely, general resources can be applied across a greater spectrum of businesses. Firms with a broad scope of business activities have different demands for organization structure, systems, and processes than firms that are narrowly focused on a specific set of business arenas.

6. *Explain the differences between corporate strategy in stable and dynamic contexts.* In relatively stable environments, synergies are typically achieved through static definitions of the business-unit arenas and formal structural links among them. Corporate strategy objectives are aimed primarily at using synergies to achieve economies of scope and scale and, in fact, the strategy explicitly defines the form and extent of business units' coordination and collaboration. Firms in dynamic contexts must usually have strong resources and capabilities in the areas of learning, knowledge transfer, and rapid responsiveness for diversification to yield benefits. Otherwise, the nimbleness and responsiveness required of business units in dynamic contexts is dampened as a consequence of corporate ownerships being more of an encumbrance than an advantage. In dynamic environments, allowing managers of business units to pursue a pattern of synergistic relationships that mimics biological coevolution is generally more advantageous than corporate-forced synergistic relationships.

Review Questions

1. How does corporate strategy differ from business strategy?

2. How has the practice of corporate strategy evolved over time?

3. What is a conglomerate?

4. How can managers decide whether they should diversify into a new business?

5. What are the types of diversification and how is value created by each type?

6. What is the difference between economies of scope and synergies?

7. What is the relationship between diversification and firm performance?

8. What factors tend to limit the attractiveness of diversification?

9. How does a dynamic industry context affect the possible benefits of diversification?

Experiential Activities

Group Exercises

1. Choose two firms that are well-known to your group members—perhaps firms that you've done case analyses on in the past. For each of these firms, identify their vertical, horizontal, and geographic scope. Having done that, evaluate the resources that are necessary for each business arena for the firms. How similar are the resource requirements? Identify the dominant logic in each of their main lines of business (if you picked a very diversified firm, just choose the largest two or three business segments). How similar are they across the business divisions?

2. Try to apply the profit pool tool to another industry. Where would you turn for data to do this? How "friendly" is that data for the purposes of using this tool? If you are having trouble being precise, make informed estimates for what you are missing. You will likely find some profit pools that are deeper than others. Why are there big differences between segments? Which firms in the value chain are best able to enter these attractive segments?

Ethical Debates

1. Textbook publishers face growing competition on numerous fronts, including new models of textbook delivery. One such model provides students with online textbook content for "free," on the condition that students provide personal information about themselves to vendors like credit card, student loan, and cell phone companies. For any publisher that is considering diversification into this new media space, what might be some of the ethical issues?

2. You can imagine that firms in the alcohol, tobacco, or firearms businesses may feel a need to diversify into less scrutinized or regulated businesses. How might ethical issues related to these core businesses affect their ability to enter, or costs of entry, into new businesses? How might these ethical issues affect their ability to exit, or costs of exiting, their traditional businesses?

How Would
YOU DO THAT?

1. The box entitled "How Would *You* Do That? 7.1" helps you see how a profit pool model is developed for a particular industry or geographic or product arena. You are given Starbucks and ready-to-drink coffee market as an example, but never shown a profit pool diagram for that industry. Using the resources you have available, try to map out the basic segment characteristics of this arena for the United States. Start with the narrow definition of the coffee business provided in the box. Finally, try to identify the complements or adjacencies that a company like Starbucks could exploit. Do you see new growth opportunities for Starbucks using all the steps of the profit pool tool?

2. "How Would *You* Do That? 7.2" applies a portfolio evaluation tool to Disney. Internally, Disney executives view one of their dynamic capabilities as that of being the best at creating world-class entertainment within financial constraints. What are your thoughts on this view? As you think about Disney and what you view as its resources and capabilities, and the insights you gain from evaluating Disney's portfolio of businesses, what arenas should it consider for future diversification or divestiture moves?

Go on to see How Would You Do That at www.prenhall.com/ carpenter&sanders

Endnotes

1. Corporate descriptions were compiled based on corporate histories on corporate Web sites (www.ge.com, www.3m.com, www.mityinc.com); business descriptions were compiled based on information available at www.hoovers.com (accessed July 15, 2005 and May 5, 2007); G. Colvin, "Q & A: On the Hot Seat," *Fortune*, November 27, 2006; "GE Reports Strong Fourth-Quarter and Full-Year Results for 2006," *Business Wire*, January 19, 2007; A. Fisher, "America's Most Admired Companies," *Fortune*, March 19, 2007, pp. 88–94; *MITY Enterprises Annual Report*, 2006; M. Moylan, "Whither 3M?" *Minnesota Public Radio*, February 28, 2007; "Economic Management," http://solutions.3m.com/wps/portal/3M/en_US/global/sustainability/s/governance-systems/management-systems/economic-management/ (accessed on May 4, 2007).

2. See especially C. K. Prahalad and G. Hamel, "The Core Competence of the Corporation," *Harvard Business Review* May–June (1990), 79–91; K. P. Coyne, S. Hall, J. D. Clifford, and P. Gorman, "Do You Really Have a Core Competency," *McKinsey Quarterly* 1 (1997), 40–54.

3. A. Chandler, *Strategy and Structure: Chapters in the History of the American Industrial Enterprise* (Boston: MIT Press, 1962).

4. G. F. Davis and S. K. Stout, "Organization Theory and the Market for Corporate Control: A Dynamic Analysis of Characteristics of Large Takeover Targets: 1980–1990," *Administrative Science Quarterly* 37 (1992), 605–633; G. F. Davis, K. A. Diekman, and C. H. Tinsley, "The Decline and Fall of the Conglomerate Firm in the 1980s: A Study in the Deinstitutionalization of an Organization Form," *American Sociological Review* 59 (1994), 547–570.

5. S. Wetlaufer, "Common Sense and Conflict: An Interview with Disney's Michael Eisner," *Harvard Business Review* 78:1 (2000), 44–48. See also K. Eisenhardt and C. Galunic, "Coevolving: At Last a Way to Make Synergies Work," *Harvard Business Review* (2000), 91–101.

6. A. D. Henderson and J. W. Fredrickson, "Information Processing Demands as a Determinant of CEO Compensation," *Academy of Management Journal* 39 (1996), 575–590; W. G. Sanders and M. A. Carpenter, "Internationalization and Firm Governance: The Roles of CEO Compensation, Top-Team Composition, and Board Structure," *Academy of Management Journal* 41 (1998), 158–178.

7. The concept of profit pools has been around for decades but this particular tool is adapted from O. Gadiesh and J. L. Gilbert, "Profit Pools: A Fresh Look at Strategy." *Harvard Business Review* 76:3 (1998), 139–147.

8. O. Gadiesh and J. L. Gilbert, "Profit Pools: A Fresh Look at Strategy," *Harvard Business Review* 76:3 (1998), 139–148.

9. For more details on this example and other examples, see Gadiesh and Gilbert, "Profit Pools."

10. J. Kanter, D. Clark, and J. R. Wilke, "EU Imposes Sanctions on Microsoft—Fine, Disclosure Penalties Aim to Undercut Dominance; Continued Pressure Signaled," *Wall Street Journal*, March 25, 2004, A2; M. Wingfield, "DOJ Calls EC's Record Fine of Microsoft 'Unfortunate,'" *Dow Jones Newswires*, March 25, 2004; B. Mitchener and J. Kanter, "Monti's Initiatives on Commerce Leave an Enduring Mark," *Wall Street Journal*, March 25, 2004, A2.

11. Y. Akbar, "Grabbing Victory from the Jaws of Defeat: Can the GE-Honeywell Merger Force International Competition Policy Cooperation?" *World Competition* 25:4 (2002), 26–31.

12. The ideas in this section draw heavily from the work of Bryce and Dyer. D. J. Bryce and J. H. Dyer, 2007. Strategies to Crack Well-Guarded Markets. *Harvard Business Review* 85(5): 84–92.

13. Based on the companies' 10K filings for 2006. The averages over the past decade are consistent with these figures.

14. G. Szulanski, R. Cappetta, and R. J. Jensen, "When and How Trustworthiness Matters: Knowledge Transfer and the Moderating Effect of Causal Ambiguity," *Organization Science* 15 (2004), 600–613.

15. C. W. L. Hill, M. A. Hitt, and R. E. Hoskisson, "Cooperative versus Competitive Structures in Related and Unrelated Diversified Firms," *Organization Science* 3 (1992), 501–521.

16. A. Stone, "Can Kansas City Southern Keep Its Janus Spin-Off on Track?" *Business Week*, August 31, 1999, 27.

17. M. Goold and A. Campbell, "Desperately Seeking Synergy," *Harvard Business Review* 76:5 (1998), 131–143.

18. L. Bransten and S. Thurm, "For Palm Computers, an IPO and Flashy Rival," *Wall Street Journal*, September 14, 1999, B1.

19. Eisenhardt and Galunic, "Coevolving"; S. Brown and K. Eisenhardt, *Competing on the Edge* (Boston: Harvard Business School Press, 1998).

20. Eisenhardt and Galunic, "Coevolving"; Brown and Eisenhardt, *Competing on the Edge.*

21. C. Christensen, *The Innovator's Dilemma* (New York: Harper Collins, 1997).

8 Looking at International Strategies

1. Define *international strategy* and identify its implications for the strategy diamond.

2. Understand why a firm would want to expand internationally and explain the relationship between international strategy and competitive advantage.

3. Use the CAGE framework to identify desirable international arenas.

4. Describe different vehicles for international expansion.

5. Apply different international strategy configurations.

6. Outline the international strategy implications of the static and dynamic perspectives.

Dell *goes* *to* China

"*T*oday there are one billion people on-line worldwide, and many of the world's second billion users are right here in China," said Michael Dell, chairman and chief executive of Dell Inc. "We intend to earn their confidence and their business." Mr. Dell was speaking in Shanghai in 2007. His company was the world's second-biggest PC maker and the third largest in China. The company had come a long way since 1999, when Mr. Dell first put plans for the company's expansion into China in motion.

In 1999, Dell had a negligible presence in many regions of the world, most notably China, where it ranked a distant seventh in PC sales. This lagging position bothered Dell executives because computer industry analysts were predicting that by 2002, China would become the second-largest PC market behind the

United States. Consequently, in 1999 Dell set the ambitious goal of achieving 10 percent of its global PC sales from China by 2002, which would amount to nearly 50 percent of PC sales for the entire Asian region.

"Faster sales growth in China could really give Dell a boost because of how big the market is and how much potential it has," said William Bao Bean, an analyst with Deutsche Securities in Hong Kong. According to Dell, only about seven in 100 people own PCs in China. About 25 million PCs were sold in China in 2006. What's more, China's economy grew 10.7 percent in 2006, the fastest rate in more than a decade. Increasing wealth is making electronic goods like computers more affordable to a larger section of the population. "Smaller cities and towns are really where the growth is in China because incomes are rising and people are shopping for their first computers," Bean added.

Dell's overall approach in China is to stay flexible. Its direct-selling model works well with commercial buyers. But to reach first-time computer consumers, the company is opening physical stores—called "experience stores"—in Nanjing, Chongqing, and Tianjin. The reason, as Bryan Ma, a research director at International Data Corp., explained, is that "Consumers are accustomed to buying things with cash, touching and feeling a product in a store and getting instant gratification, rather than calling into a call center or placing an order on-line and waiting a few days for the machine to arrive." Dell China says that its purpose for opening the stores is to have Chinese consumers able to get in touch with Dell's products and enjoy the unique advantages of these products. On August 4, 2006, Dell opened its first product experience store in China in Chongqing. Opening an experience store may be a surprising move for the king of direct-sell, but Michael Dell understands the importance of flexibility: "The thing I've been saying internally is the direct model is not a religion. It's a great strategy, [and it] works well; there are things we can do with it. But that's not the only thing we can do as a company."

Michael Dell is optimistic about Dell's future in China: "We have a lot of opportunity" in the consumer market, he says, "You'll see a lot more products" like the ones he unveiled in March 2007.

For many U.S. companies, China is attractive simply due to its size, but it is also a competitive environment fraught with many hazards—and it can turn potential profits into a cash-flow black hole. Sourcing components and products from China has proven successful for many global firms, although some companies such as Mattel have faced serious quality and safety problems. The Chinese consumer market appears to be an entirely different matter. By 1999, for example, Motorola and Kodak had already sunk many millions of dollars into China hoping for large domestic market share and commensurate profits but instead were reeling from enormous and continuing losses. Dell's management was not ignorant of these warning signals but viewed the situation as "if we're not in what will soon be the second-biggest PC market in the world, then how can Dell possibly be a global player?"

The Dell-in-China situation showcases all five elements of the strategy diamond. It also shows how a firm must engage these elements flexibly and entrepreneurially to do business in markets different from their home markets. That is, internationalizing firms face challenges as to how to be global yet local at the same time and to what extent they should be global or local. China is a relatively new geographic arena for Dell. Within this country arena, Dell is targeting certain market segments, or subarenas; it is also using different channels as part of its market segmentation strategy.

In terms of vehicles, and regardless of global location, Dell typically goes it alone in assembly and distribution, entering into alliances only for its inputs and raw materials. A key facet of Dell's competitive advantage is distribution via its Dell Direct model—an on-line PC assembly and sales-on-demand powerhouse. In China, however, Dell initially formed alliances with independent distributors for the consumer market, a channel it had learned to exploit in its earlier entry into India. This was a risky move for Dell but also one that showed that management recognized that it had to be flexible and act in a locally sensitive fashion in approaching new geographic markets. Dell initially planned to use Chinese distributors, as it had in India, and then migrate sales over a five-year period to the typical kiosk sales model it employs in other parts of the world, further allowing it to leverage its Dell Direct model. Dell was able to draw immediately on the model for the large multinational-firm market, with which it already had established customer relationships. It could also use the Dell Direct model for the government-users market. As in all of its other markets, Dell's intended strategy was based on a performance-for-value logic and its Dell Direct service model to maintain its solid relationships with corporate and government clients in China.

In terms of staging, Dell flipped its distribution model on its head. This is a third example of how the company flexibly adapted its historic strategic approach to enter into China. In the United States, Dell built its Dell Direct model through the direct-to-consumer market; it entered the corporate-customer market only after it had established a strong, profitable foothold with consumers. In China, however, the Dell Direct market was more commercially viable with corporate customers, who have both the cash and access to infrastructure to make the Dell Direct model work effectively. Although Dell initially worked through distributors in China for the consumer market, its staging plan was to migrate these consumers eventually to its Dell Direct model.

Finally, Dell's economic logic is one of both scale and scope economies. It can leverage its size to gain the best terms and prices for the best technologies for the products it sells. It can use this cost advantage to compete in China and at the same time further enhance the Dell Direct model's footprint on the global computer market. So far, it appears that Dell's global strategy, and its flexible approach to entering countries like China, is paying off. Michael Dell said the company's overall business in China was strong, growing, and profitable. Dell's revenue in China increased 26 percent in 2006. Dell's revenue share in China is about 20 percent, which is double its 10-percent share of product shipments, because the company also sells services and other products beyond PCs there.

Nonetheless, Dell is facing strong competition. On December 9, 2004, IBM announced the sale of its entire PC division to Lenovo, a Chinese multinational firm. This left Dell, Hewlett-Packard, and Lenovo as the world's top three PC makers. At the time, industry analysts were placing their bets on wildly efficient Dell to broaden its lead, both globally and in China, by the middle of 2007. Dell seemed invincible using the low-cost model. Now, however, other companies have figured out how to make and sell PCs as cheaply as Dell. Exhibit 8.1 shows the respective market positions of the top five desktop, notebook, and PC makers, with HP leading the pack.

To respond to the fierce competition in China, Dell will have to cut its costs. Just a few weeks after CEO Michael Dell's heralded trip to the Middle Kingdom, local Chinese media report that Dell China has formulated a plan to reduce staff at the end of April 2007. According to the plan, Dell China will reduce up to 13 percent of the staff in each of its departments. The reports say that it is urgent for Dell to reduce its staff because its operational expenditures increased remarkably over ten consecutive quarters, but its revenue per employee dropped to the lowest level in seven years. **<<<**

Exhibit 8.1 Global PC Industry Market Share Comparables

Company	Global Market Share	Annual Sales Growth
HP	17.4%	23.9%
Dell	13.9%	–8.7%
Lenovo	7.1%	9.3%
Acer	6.8%	33.1%
Toshiba	3.8%	24.5%
Rest of Market	51.0%	3.8%
Total Market	100.0%	7.4%

international strategy
Process by which a firm approaches its cross-border activities and those of competitors and plans to approach them in the future.

International Strategy

What is *international strategy?* When should managers consider such a strategy? A firm's **international strategy** is how it approaches the cross-border business activities of its own firm and competitors and how it contemplates doing so in the future. In the narrowest sense, a firm's managers need only think about international strategy when they conduct some aspect of their business across national borders. Some international activities are designed to augment a firm's business strategy, such as sourcing key factors of production to cheaper labor markets (i.e., attempts to become more competitive within a core business). Other international activities represent key elements of the firm's corporate strategy (i.e., entering new businesses or new markets). Whether expanding internationally to reinforce a particular business's strategy or as part of a corporate strategy, international expansion is a form of diversification because the firm has chosen to operate in a different market.

Throughout this text, you have been exposed to many organizations, including those focused on one primary geographic region and others that are very global in their operating scope. For some organizations, a global mindset pervades managerial thinking and is explicit in the firm's vision, mission, goals, objectives, and strategy. With other firms, international strategy may be very new. Regardless of the case, a firm must carefully prepare for an international strategy through the analysis of all the dimensions of the strategy diamond.

The preventative cure for domestic-strategy myopia, and surefire pathway to a global mindset, is a broad awareness of the international landscape. Exhibit 8.2 highlights some of the top global trends that executives consider relevant to the competitive fortunes of their businesses.[1]

These trends suggest new market opportunities, such as the growth of consumer demand in emerging markets. They also suggest new concerns and constraints, particularly those related to natural resources and the environment. We encourage you to learn about these broader trends, different countries, and national cultures and internalize a cosmopolitan view of international strategy. In the broadest sense, a firm needs to consider its international strategy when any single or potential competitor is not domestic or otherwise conducts business across borders. Increasingly, it is this latter context that makes it imperative that almost all firms think about the international dimensions of their business, even if they have no international operations whatsoever. Thus, international strategy essentially reflects

Exhibit 8.2   Global Trends to Watch

Trend	Examples
Shifting of economic activity between countries and regions	Growth in demand for energy and basic materials (such as steel and copper) is moving from developed countries to developing ones, predominantly in Asia. Demand for oil in China and India, for example, will nearly double from 2003 to 2020, to 15.4 million barrels a day. Asia's oil consumption will approach that of the United States—the world's largest consumer—by the end of that period.
Shifting of economic activity within countries and regions	The story is not simply the march to Asia. Shifts within regions are as significant as those occurring across regions. For example, by 2015 the Hispanic population in the United States will have spending power equivalent to that of 60 percent of all Chinese consumers.
Growing number of consumers in emerging economies	Economic growth in the developing world will usher nearly a billion new consumers into the global marketplace over the next decade, as household incomes reach the level (around $5,000) associated with discretionary spending. Although these consumers will have less spending power than do their counterparts in the developed world, they will have similar demands as well as access to global brands. Many industries, therefore, face polarized markets where premium and no-frills offerings are squeezing middle-of-the-road offerings.
Increasing availability of knowledge and the ability to exploit it	Knowledge is increasingly available and, at the same time, increasingly specialized. The most obvious manifestation of this trend is the rise of search engines (such as Google) and online marketplaces (such as eBay and Amazon) that make an almost infinite amount of information available instantaneously.
Increasing global labor and talent markets	Ongoing shifts in labor and talent will be far more profound than the widely observed migration of jobs to low-wage countries. The shift to knowledge-intensive industries highlights the importance and scarcity of well-trained talent. The increasing integration of global labor markets, however, is opening up vast new talent sources. The 33 million university-educated young professionals in developing countries is more than double the number in developed ones. For many companies and governments, global labor and talent strategies will become as important as global sourcing and manufacturing strategies. For instance, in India there are about 245,000 Indians answering phones from all over the world about credit card and cell phone offers, along with bill collection. This type of skill shift is repeated across areas from data-input to programming to copyediting.
Resource and environmental strains	As economic growth accelerates—particulary in emerging markets—demand for natural resources is growing at unprecedented rates. Oil demand is projected to grow by 50 percent in the next two decades, and without large new discoveries or radical innovations supply is unlikely to keep up. Similar surges in demand across a broad range of commodities are being seen as well. In China, for example, demand for copper, steel, and aluminum has nearly tripled in the past decade. Evidence is emerging that one of our scarcest natural resources—the atmosphere—will require dramatic shifts in human behavior to keep it from being depleted further.

the choices a firm's executives make with respect to sourcing and selling its goods in foreign markets, and dealing with foreign competitors who enter their markets.

It probably comes as no surprise to you that all of the world's largest corporations are global as well. A simple review of the top-20 firms among *Fortune*'s Global 500 provides you with a snapshot of these global behemoths each year, in terms of who is largest and who has the best global reputation. As you can see in Exhibit 8.3, some of these large firms, seen at the beginning of 2007, had revenues greater than many countries' GDP!

And, with the exceptions of Wal-Mart and GE, the mix of top firms is clearly clustered among the oil and gas, automotive, banking, and insurance industries.[2] Even among this special group, you can see that firms vary significantly in terms of their international presence. What may be surprising, however, is the increasing presence of arguably tiny firms that are global very early in their lives, such as Logitech (which started in Switzerland and California and was global from inception) and Skype (which started in Sweden and went global in a year, and was recently acquired by EBay).

As you work through this chapter, you will see how international strategy must be reflected in all facets of the strategy diamond. Exhibit 8.4 summarizes some of the key strategic questions that firms must answer about the strategy diamond, such as Dell did in the opening vignette, as they expand into international markets.

Exhibit 8.3   Top 20 Global Companies Based on Revenue

Rank	Company	Country/HQ	Industry	Revenues ($ millions)	Profits ($ millions)	% Foreign Sales
1	Exxon Mobil	USA	Oil and Gas	339,938.0	36,130.0	69.14%
2	Wal-Mart Stores	USA	Retail	315,654.0	11,231.0	22.35%
3	Royal Dutch Shell	UK/Netherlands	Oil and Gas	306,731.0	25,311.0	57.25%*
4	BP	UK	Oil and Gas	267,600.0	22,341.0	70.17%
5	General Motors	USA	Automotive	192,604.0	−10,567.0	37.77%
6	Chevron	USA	Oil and Gas	189,481.0	14,099.0	55.19%
7	DaimlerChrysler	Germany	Automotive	186,106.3	3,536.3	14.64%
8	Toyota Motor	Japan	Automotive	185,805.0	12,119.6	63.23%
9	Ford Motor	USA	Automotive	177,210.0	2,024.0	49.32%
10	ConocoPhillips	USA	Oil and Gas	166,683.0	13,529.0	30.37%
11	General Electric	USA	Diversified	157,153.0	16,353.0	45.45%
12	Total	France	Oil and Gas	152,360.7	15,250.0	76.01%
13	ING Group	Netherlands	Banking	138,235.3	8,958.9	77.12%
14	Citigroup	USA	Banking	131,045.0	24,589.0	32.38%
15	AXA	France	Insurance	129,839.2	5,186.5	17.00%
16	Allianz	Germany	Insurance	121,406.0	5,442.4	70.72%
17	Volkswagen	Germany	Automotive	118,376.6	1,391.7	72.80%*
18	Fortis	Belgium	Banking	112,351.4	4,896.3	15.94%
19	Crédit Agricole	France	Banking	110,764.6	7,434.3	43.0%
20	American Intl. Group	USA	Insurance	108,905.0	10,477.0	48.77%

*Royal Dutch Shell and Volkswagen report domestic sales as sales in Europe.

Exhibit 8.4 The Five Elements in International Strategy

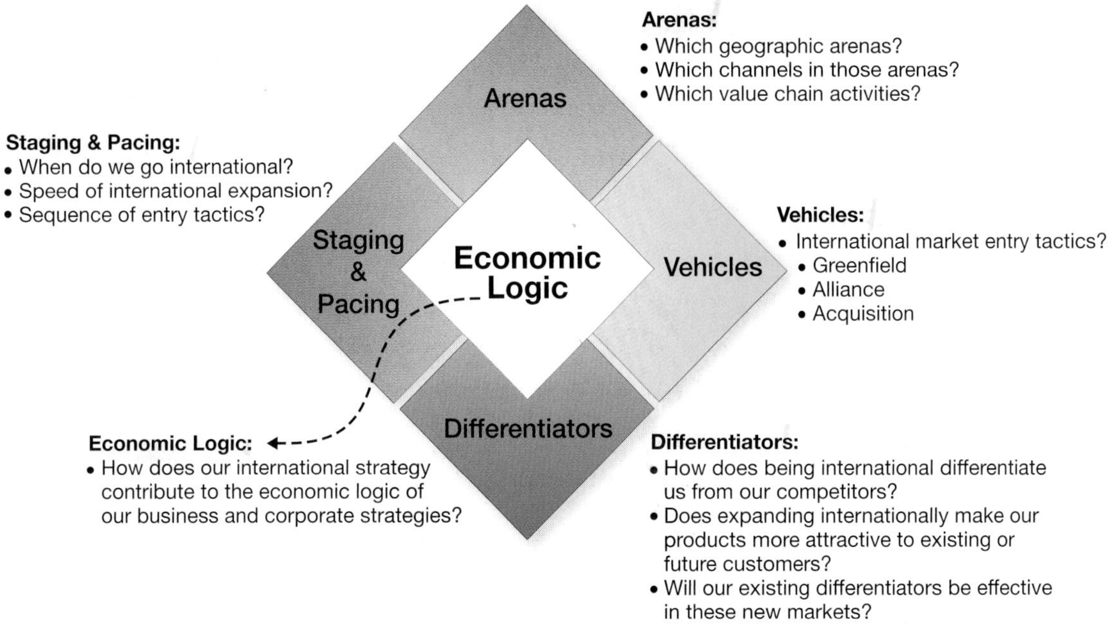

Arenas:
- Which geographic arenas?
- Which channels in those arenas?
- Which value chain activities?

Arenas

Staging & Pacing:
- When do we go international?
- Speed of international expansion?
- Sequence of entry tactics?

Staging & Pacing

Economic Logic

Vehicles

Vehicles:
- International market entry tactics?
  - Greenfield
  - Alliance
  - Acquisition

Differentiators

Economic Logic:
- How does our international strategy contribute to the economic logic of our business and corporate strategies?

Differentiators:
- How does being international differentiate us from our competitors?
- Does expanding internationally make our products more attractive to existing or future customers?
- Will our existing differentiators be effective in these new markets?

International Strategy and Competitive Advantage

Why, where, and how? Using the strategy diamond and another simple framework we refer to as the 1-2-3 Model, these are the three basic questions that international strategy must answer. While there is obviously a lot of analysis that must go into answering them, these three basic questions—summarized in Exhibit 8.5—will put you in a good position to determine the scale and scope of your international strategy.

Too often, executives make international strategy choices based on what competitors are doing, instead of starting with answers to fundamental strategy diamond questions like: (1) *Why* should we expand into another geographic arena (is the economic logic compelling and do our differentiators apply)?; (2) If so, *where*—which new geographic arena?; and (3) If this arena, then *how*—what vehicles will we use, and how should entry be staged and paced? Notice, for instance, that Dell identified the need to be a global player based on its growth objectives, customer needs, and opportunities to garner new customers. These needs fit with the economic logic of Dell's strategy. They also leveraged Dell's differentiators—relationships with customers and Dell's quality image. Dell then identified China as an important stepping stone—or stage—in its global growth aspirations. Finally, it chose an entry strategy—starting with an alliance with Indian distributors—for staging its efforts to do well in the new China market.

Given the complexities and risks of managing business activities across borders, it is imperative to understand why any firm would take on the often significant costs of doing so in terms of time, dollars, and managerial attention. One reason is simply necessity. Increasingly, many experts in the field of strategic management view global expansion as necessary for just about every medium and large corporation. This opinion is based on a few basic observations: (1) that capital markets and employees favor fast-growing firms, and many domestic markets in developed countries are becoming saturated; (2) that efficiencies in all value-chain activities are linked across borders, and the linkages and pressures for efficiency continue to escalate; (3) new market opportunities are present in developing economies; (4) that knowledge is not uniformly distributed around the world, and new ideas increasingly

Exhibit 8.5   Your 1-2-3 Model of Internationalization

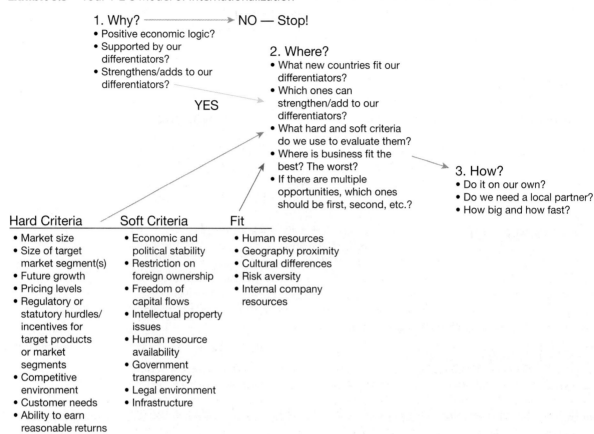

are coming from emerging economies; (5) that customers themselves are becoming global at both the organizational level in terms of the growth and proliferation of multinationals and at the individual level in terms of consumer preferences; and (6) that competitors are globalizing, even if your organization is not.[3]

THE PROS AND CONS OF INTERNATIONAL EXPANSION

International expansion is no panacea for corporate-growth needs, and it is inherently hazardous even when it promises revenue opportunities. For instance, at the beginning of the 1990s, PepsiCo established an ambitious goal to triple its international sales from $1.5 billion to $5 billion within just five years. PepsiCo aggressively pursued this growth, yet it failed to keep pace with the growth of international markets and actually lost ground to Coca-Cola. While Coke was reaping the benefits of the growth of soft drinks in international markets, Pepsi's international market share actually shrank.[4] Pepsi's experience demonstrates that simply participating in international markets does not equate to having a competitive advantage to exploit international opportunities. Indeed, if you consult *Fortune*'s list of the largest global firms, you will typically find Wal-Mart at the top of that list. Yet, Wal-Mart's non–U.S. operations do very poorly in comparison to its domestic business. Global expansion can just as easily contribute to profitability as it can detract from it. The key is to align international expansion with the firm's strategy in a way to exploit and further develop firm resources and capabilities.[5] Ultimately, the benefits must outweigh the costs, and more often than not, questions about a firm's nondomestic profitability take years to answer. The opening vignette on Dell demonstrates the ups and downs associated with international strategy and the necessary alignment of the elements of strategy and the firm's resources and capabilities. In addition to the possible benefits of international expansion, a firm incurs a number of costs when diversifying its business operations around the globe.[6] The costs of geographic diversification include the liabilities of newness and foreignness, and governance and coordination costs.

Liabilities of Newness and Foreignness

Liability of newness can be thought of as a disadvantage (cost disadvantage or other disadvantages) associated with being a new player in the market. For instance, a firm suffering from a liability of newness does not initially gain benefits from the learning curve. Likewise, *liability of foreignness* is the disadvantage a firm faces by not being a local player. This disadvantage may be cultural, in that the firm's managers do not understand local market conditions. It may also be political, such as when the firm does not understand local laws or have relationships in place to manage the local regulatory environment.

Firm managers contend with many challenges when establishing operations in a new country, including the logistics of purchasing and installing facilities, staffing, and establishing internal management systems and external business networks. Costs associated with establishing a new business can put a new foreign division in a disadvantageous position relative to local or more established foreign competitors. These types of disadvantages tend to dissipate with time as the division gains local experience, which in turn diminish the negative influence of liability of newness and foreignness.

Costs Associated with Governance and Coordination

Although the disadvantages of newness and foreignness typically decline over time, governance and coordination costs are disadvantages that tend to increase as international diversification increases. Some of the issues that increase governance and coordination costs include information distortion as it is transferred and translated across divisions and countries. Coordination difficulties and possible misalignment between headquarters and divisional managers in international firms increases as international diversification increases, much as in highly diversified domestic firms. Because every country has a relatively unique business environment, the more country environments a firm must deal with, the greater the difficulty and cost of coordinating operations across these diverse environments.

Offsetting Costs and Benefits

As shown in Exhibit 8.6, the costs associated with internationalization can offset the possible benefits of operating in multiple markets.[7] A firm's level of internationalization, shown on the horizontal axis, refers to the degree to which it has tapped foreign markets, particularly for product or service sales. The potential economic benefits of internationalization are modest at first, and then become quite significant before the marginal benefits level off. These potential increases in revenue must of course be balanced with the costs of internationalization. Costs are significant in early efforts to internationalize. After a presence is established, economies of scale and scope kick in, and the incremental costs of further expansion are minimal. However, bureaucratic and management costs can spike at extreme levels of internationalization. This increase in costs is similar to the notion of diseconomies of scale and scope introduced in earlier chapters. Consequently, research suggests that performance gains from internationalization come not at the early stages but at moderate to high levels; however, at very high levels of internationalization, firms tend to suffer performance declines.[8] The key for managers is to find a way to exploit the possible advantages of economies of scale and scope, location, and learning without having them offset by the excessive costs of internationalization. The tradeoff between costs and benefits of internationalization results in an S-curve relationship between internationalization and firm performance.

Exhibit 8.6   Costs and Benefits of Internationalization

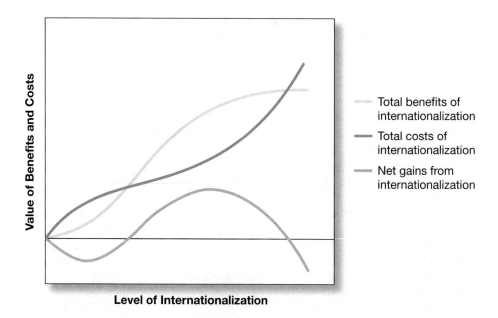

KEY FACTORS IN INTERNATIONAL EXPANSION

International strategy, particularly in the form of international expansion, can contribute to a firm's competitive advantage in a number of interrelated ways. The four most important aspects are *economies of scale and scope, location, multipoint competition,* and *learning.* While most of these aspects are directly related to the economic logic of a firm's strategy, they also can contribute to the differentiators. Firms must understand the specific benefits in one or more of these areas if they are to proceed with international expansion plans.

Global Economies of Scale and Scope   Referring back to the strategy diamond, international strategy affects a firm's economic logic through its implications for economies of scale and scope. ◆ Larger firms are not necessarily more efficient or more profitable, but in some industries, such as pharmaceuticals and aircraft manufacturing, the enormous costs of new-product development require that the firm be able to generate commensurate sales, and this increasingly requires firms to have a global presence.

For instance, R&D costs are skyrocketing in many industries. This requires that firms in those industries seek a larger revenue base, typically outside of their home countries. This re-lationship is demonstrated by strategy research showing that the performance benefits from R&D increase with a firm's degree of internationalization: Firms generate more profits out of their R&D investments if they are also highly global.[9] One reason for this is that there is a minimum threshold of R&D investment necessary to launch a new product. When the firm can amortize those costs across many markets, it can in effect lower its average cost per sale. It is interesting to note that, when graphed, the relationship between performance, R&D in-vestment, and internationalization further demonstrates the S-curve relationship between internationalization and firm performance discussed earlier in this chapter. Such economies of scale can also be realized for intangibles, such as a firm's brand, much as CitiGroup, McDonald's, and Coca-Cola leverage their brands in practically every country in the world.

Scale and Operating Efficiency   The larger scale that accompanies global expansion only creates competitive advantage if the firm translates scale into operating efficiency. As you learned in Chapter 5, cost savings are not axiomatic with larger scale. Larger scale must be managed to avoid diseconomies of scale. As with economies of scale in general, the poten-tial scale economies from global expansion include spreading fixed costs over a larger sales and asset base and increasing purchasing power.[10] Attempts to gain scale advantages must be focused on resources and activities that are scale sensitive, and it means that these resources and activities must be concentrated in just a few locations.[11] However, if these resources and activities are concentrated in a few locations, they can become isolated from key markets, which may lead to delayed responses to market changes. For instance, until Dell established a regional office and manufacturing facility in Brazil (Eldorado do Sul), its sales and service record in Brazil suffered.

Economies of Global Scope A specialized form of scope economies is available to firms as they expand globally. Recall that scope economies were defined as the ability to lower average costs by sharing a resource across different products. Numerous scope economies are available to firms that expand globally. For example, CitiGroup, McDonald's, and Coca-Cola profit from scope economies to the extent that the different country markets share the benefits of brand equity that these firms have built up over time. The opening vignette on Dell, too, provides several examples of scope as well as scale economies across different geographic and customer markets, starting with its ability to take advantage of its brand; its capability to leverage its Dell Direct sales model and related Internet sales and support technologies; its experience and relationships with distributors in India and then China; and its different geographic units' ability to pool their purchasing power for key components, such as CPUs, from powerful suppliers like Intel.

Consider how a supplier to McDonald's could exploit economies of global scope, which in turn provide it with economies of scale in production and other related value-chain activities. McDonald's needs the same ketchup products in Europe and South America as it does in the United States. A vendor with sufficient global scope to satisfy McDonald's worldwide demand for ketchup would be an attractive sourcing alternative to McDonald's compared with sourcing this supply from numerous local suppliers.[12] In this case, global scope gives a supplier an opportunity to generate revenue that it would be unable to generate in the absence of global scope. Of course, McDonalds' global scope also gives it access to more suppliers from around the globe, including local suppliers in many markets. Local suppliers may also have some advantages over global players in terms of being able to provide more immediate service and greater knowledge of local business practices. Thus, firms like McDonald's are in the enviable position of being able to source the lowest cost inputs and use lower local prices and service levels to force global suppliers to keep prices down and service levels high.

Attempts to gain economies of scope also face numerous hazards as well. Although economies of scope are possible as resources are shared across markets, strategy must still be executed at the national level.[13] In cases such as China, the United States, and Europe, where the "nation" is actually composed of distinctly different subgeographic markets (cantons in Switzerland, countries in other parts of Europe, states in the United States, and provinces in China), successful execution at the local level is further complicated. This can easily lead to tension between the need to identify and satisfy the local client contact and the aim of lowering costs by sharing resources and having actions coordinated across markets.

Location
National and regional geographic location has an impact on competitive advantage as well, because of its implications for input costs, competitors, demand conditions, and complements. A basic five-forces industry analysis can be used to determine the importance of a given location. The analysis of industry structure should include such features as barriers to entry, new entrants, substitutes, and existing competitors, both domestic and international. Related and supporting industries that are forward and backward in the value chain, as well as true complements, also need to be identified.

With such an analysis in hand, the value chain and five-forces analysis can be geographically segmented to consider how and why rivalry may play out differently in different geographic arenas. ◆ In terms of customers, for instance, an analysis of consumption trends among the top 25 countries in the global soft drink industry shows that India and China

 Arenas

Huge international chains, such as McDonald's, are able to achieve economies of scope, thereby lowering the costs of inputs they purchase both globally and in local markets.

exhibit fairly steady growth. A firm's managers can thus assess the desirability of investing in one market versus another, the competitive consequences of such an investment, and the value-chain activities needed to locate in each region. For instance, India and China may be prime locations to launch new growth initiatives for large players like Coca-Cola and Pepsi. Such an analysis should show how the firm's strategy has connected the dots, so to speak, in terms of linking resources, capabilities, and locations—and in this case, the choice of a new geographic arena should be consistent with the other facets of the firm's strategy, as seen in the strategy diamond.

Arbitrage Opportunities Beyond the five-forces and value-chain assessment, location differences also present an opportunity for arbitrage. Arbitrage represents the age-old practice of buying something in one market and selling it another market where it garners a higher price. Historically, the value added in such arbitrage was simply tracking down a desirable commodity, such as spice, tea, or silk, from a faraway land, and transporting it to a market that would pay a premium for it. Companies can improve performance and potentially build competitive advantage by optimizing the location of their value-chain activities. Significant cost differences for different types of value-chain activities exist around the globe. A firm that can optimize the intercountry cost differences better than its rivals will have a cost advantage. The caveat here is that arbitrage opportunities may be fleeting in that once they are identified, competitors who lack entry barriers can quickly realize them as well. Therefore, a firm that relies on arbitrage as a core part of its competitive strategy must possess greater capabilities in continually identifying new arbitrage opportunities as well as in increasing entry barriers for competitors trying to follow it.

Multipoint Competition Firms can develop competitive advantages through multipoint competition. **Multipoint competition** refers to the situation when a firm competes against another firm in multiple product markets or multiple geographic markets (or both). For instance, Proctor and Gamble and Unilever not only compete head to head in personal care products around the globe, they also compete in the soaps and detergents markets. When the firm competes in multiple international markets, as a special kind of multipoint

multipoint competition
When a firm competes against another firm in multiple product markets or multiple geographic markets (or both).

tactic, the stronghold assault becomes available. *Stronghold assault* refers to the competitive actions a firm takes in another firm's key markets, particularly when the attacking firm has little presence in that market. In the case of international strategy, stronghold assault refers to attacks on the geographic markets that are most important to a competitor's profitability and cash flow. A classic example of international stronghold assault is provided by the actions of French tire manufacturer Michelin and the U.S. tire company Goodyear in the 1970s.[14] Early on, both firms had negligible market presence in each other's respective domestic markets (Europe and the United States). Michelin became aware of Goodyear's intent to expand its presence in Europe, so it started selling its tires in the United States at or below its actual cost. Although these sales were a miniscule part of Michelin's overall sales, Michelin's sales tactic forced Goodyear to drop its prices in the United States, and hence lower the profitability of its largest market.

Such multipoint competitive tactics often initially benefit customers at the expense of competitors until a new market equilibrium is reached. Moreover, Michelin's low-price ploy earned it a larger share of the U.S. market, such that the lost profits in the United States began to take a toll on Michelin's overall profitability. In addition, nothing prevented Goodyear from doing the same thing in Michelin's home markets, further eroding both firms' profitability. Eventually, both firms ended up in the international courts charging each other with "dumping"—selling goods below cost in a foreign country.

Even today, stronghold assault is a motivation for global investment, but as the Michelin case highlights, it must be used with care and is typically not sustainable. Therefore, firms that employ this tactic should also have strategies in the staging component that take into account when and how the firm will shift from price competition to more sustainable bases of competition. For this reason, stronghold assault is used not only to underprice a competitor's products in its home market but also to simply eliminate the competitor's home market monopoly. Just as with the cola wars, the Michelin–Goodyear war left the industry landscape forever changed, and both firms had to adjust their strategies to survive in the new industry structure that resulted.

Learning and Knowledge Sharing   Learning is very important to the success of a firm's international strategy for a variety of reasons. At the very least, a firm with operations that cross borders must learn how to cope with different institutional, legal, and cultural environments. For the most successful firms, international expansion is used as a vehicle for innovation, improving existing products in existing markets, or coming up with new ideas for new markets. It is one thing to use such tools as the five-forces, value-chain, and other frameworks to identify profit or arbitrage opportunities, for instance, but it is quite another thing to exploit them successfully and profitably. For instance, Michelin initially shipped products to the United States and didn't care whether it made money on them because it viewed any losses as insignificant. But eventually that tactic caused the U.S. market to grow in importance as part of the French tire maker's overall global sales, and it had to reckon with making this part of its business profitable or admit defeat and abandon the U.S. market—one of the auto industry's largest and most profitable markets.

Similarly, Dell first used Indian then Chinese distributors in serving the consumer segment in China, but this is a much less profitable vehicle and differentiator than its core distribution and sales engine—the Dell Direct model. Dell's goal was to migrate from its Chinese distributors and eventually learn enough about the Chinese marketplace to use its direct-sales vehicle, which can be accessed through kiosks placed in busy foot-traffic locations. Like the product-diversified firm, the geographic-diversified firm must somehow learn how to ensure that the benefits of being international outweigh the added costs of the infrastructure necessary to support its nondomestic operations.

Learning and local adaptation appear to be particularly difficult for U.S. firms, even when they are very big firms that already have an international presence. For instance, with nearly a half-billion dollars in annual sales, Lincoln Electric completed its largest acquisition ever in 1991—the $70-million purchase of Germany's Messer Gresheim, a manufacturer of welding equipment, which was Lincoln's core business.[15] Although Lincoln maintained the bulk of its business in the United States, it had over 40 years of marketing and manufacturing experience in Canada, Australia, and France. Moreover, the company was in the process of aggressively ramping up manufacturing and sales operations in Japan, Venezuela, Brazil, the Netherlands, Norway, and the United Kingdom. With the acquisition of Gresheim, as with the other newly established international operations, Lincoln's management simply assumed that it could transplant its manufacturing approach, aggressive compensation and incentive systems (Lincoln pays employees only for what they produce), and culture—the three key success factors in the U.S. business—to the newly obtained German and other foreign operations. Within a year, the European operations were in disarray; losses were mounting in Japan and Latin America; and Lincoln reported a quarterly consolidated loss of $12 million—the first quarterly consolidated loss in the company's 97-year history.

Although Lincoln eventually recovered from the brink of disaster and ruin, it only did so after top management recognized and took steps to remedy the harsh reality that it had insufficient international experience, a dearth of experience in and knowledge about running a globally dispersed organization, and no understanding of how to manage foreign operations and foreign cultures. Part of its salvation involved scaling back many of the foreign operations it had acquired, giving the firm breathing room to develop its international operating and managerial capabilities. As a consequence of its learning from its failures abroad, Lincoln is now a global success story, as summarized in excerpts from its 2006 annual report shown in Exhibit 8.7.

Learning, Knowledge, Transfer, and Innovation Beyond the rather obvious aspects of learning shown in the Lincoln Electric case, a firm that has operations in different coun-

Exhibit 8.7 Global Strategy at Lincoln Electric

To Our Shareholders: During 2006, the continued strong worldwide demand for our products, combined with the effective execution of our global strategy, contributed to another year of excellent performance for Lincoln Electric. By maintaining our focus on the five key components for excellence—people development, customer service, operational efficiency, global expansion, and innovative products—we have been able to take advantage of many opportunities in rapidly growing markets around the world.

We are expanding our footprint, strengthening our global leadership position in the welding industry and taking advantage of significant growth opportunities. Our performance has been strong everywhere we operate—in North America, Europe, Asia, the Middle East and Latin America—and we have gained market share in each of these regions.

From a global perspective, we are strengthening our position in emerging markets while continuing to serve existing markets. In Asia, specifically China, which stands to be the largest market for welding products for the foreseeable future, we are significantly increasing our manufacturing capacity for flux cored wire. We also are constructing a new facility in India to begin production of consumables in 2007, and we have recently expanded capacity at our Indonesia consumables plant.

Economic development is advancing rapidly on a global scale, evidenced by huge investments in infrastructure, transportation, manufacturing, energy production and transmission, and construction. All of these require substantial welding, and Lincoln Electric is **POWERING UP** in key markets and locations around the world to meet this growing demand.

Source: Lincoln Electric Annual Report

tries has the opportunity to increase innovation and transfer knowledge from one geographic market to another. For example, SC Johnson's European operations learned about a product that involved the combination of household pesticides and a simple plug-in device. In Europe, this product was sold in stores to consumers who needed a cheap and efficient deterrent for mosquitoes and other annoying insects. SC Johnson demonstrated its ability to learn from its European operation by transferring the technology to its fragrance division in the United States, thus giving rise to a whole new category of air fresheners called Glade PlugIns.[16]

A second facet of this form of learning is to locate a firm or a particular aspect of its operations in a part of the world where competition is the fiercest. So, for example, a U.S. automaker might locate a product facility in Japan. Ironically, although one goal of such a move is actually to compete on Japan's own turf against incumbents Toyota and Honda, the learning objective is to try to emulate and learn from Japan's auto manufacturers' leading-edge production practices and transfer that advanced knowledge to the U.S. company's plants in other parts of the world, such as the United States, Canada, and Mexico. Similarly, because France and Italy are leaders in the high-fashion industry, companies such as DuPont and W. L. Gore & Associates, which aim to compete with leading-edge fabrics such as Lycra and Gore-Tex, place high value on those countries as production and marketing locations because of the learning opportunities about future customer preferences (e.g., touch, feel, color, etc.). In this view, the strategically most important markets will be those that feature not only intrinsic market attractiveness but an opportunity to learn and innovate in ways that can improve the organization's operations, products, and services around the globe.[17]

Sharing Knowledge Across Business Units Finally, large multinationals can exploit opportunities for inter-business-unit collaboration, which results in valuable knowledge sharing.[18] Sharing knowledge across business units has several tangible benefits. First, it enables firms to transfer best practices across national and business-unit boundaries. Because these best practices are proprietary—and probably tailored to the idiosyncrasies of the firm—they are more likely to result in competitive advantage than borrowing best practices from other firms. Why? Because all competitors have access to that information as well.

An example of this type of knowledge sharing is illustrated by a case study of British Petroleum (BP). A U.S. business unit that operates service stations was looking for novel ways to reduce costs in BP convenience stores. A manager borrowed ideas from colleagues in the Netherlands and the United Kingdom about how to reduce working-capital requirements. Copying these practices and implementing them in the United States resulted in a 20-percent reduction in working capital.

Sharing knowledge across business units can also uncover revenue-enhancement opportunities. The country manager of GlaxoSmithKline in the Philippines found a new drug therapy for tuberculosis in the company's R&D lab in India. Although this therapy was not widely known within the company because it represented a very small slice of the multinational firm's business, it represented a huge market opportunity in the Philippines and other developing countries, where tuberculosis is more widespread than it is in Europe and the United States.

Using CAGE to Choose Foreign Countries

Now that you have answered the *why* question of international strategy, you must move on to answer the *where* question. But the world is a big place, so where do you start? Some markets are growing so quickly that their sheer size merits consideration. Exhibit 8.8 presents the top ten countries in terms of population, in addition to information on GDP, and GDP growth.[19]

The European Union and the United States have the most global Fortune 500 firms, 172 and 114 respectively, as of the start of 2007. And, as you might expect, Brazil, Russia,

Exhibit 8.8   Comparative Country Information of the Top 10 Markets by Population

Country	Est. Population 2007	Labor Force	Internet Users	GDP (in $ millions)	Average GDP Real Growth Rate (%)
China	1,321,851,888	798,000,000	123,000,000	10,000,000	10.50
India	1,129,866,154	509,300,000	60,000,000	4,042,000	8.50
European Union	460,827,146	222,700,000	247,000,000	12,820,000	2.80
United States	301,139,947	151,400,000	205,327,000	12,980,000	3.40
Indonesia	234,693,997	108,200,000	16,000,000	935,000	5.40
Brazil	190,010,647	96,340,000	25,900,000	1,616,000	2.80
Pakistan	164,741,924	48,290,000	10,500,000	427,300	6.50
Bangladesh	150,448,339	68,000,000	300,000	330,800	6.10
Russia	141,377,752	73,880,000	23,700,000	1,723,000	6.60
Nigeria	135,031,164	48,990,000	5,000,000	188,500	5.30

India, and China (you will often see them referred to collectively as BRIC) figure greatly into the landscape of developing economies where there is great opportunity married with great risk. Moreover, these four particular markets are giving rise to a new breed of savvy global competitor. They are shaking up entire industries, from farm equipment and refrigerators to aircraft and telecom services, and changing the rules of global competition (see Exhibit 8.9 for one view of how they are shaking things up in strategy and competition).[20]

The CAGE Framework   Generally, the greater the distance covered and the greater the value differences between the disconnected markets, the greater the profit potential that arises from arbitrage. However, greater distance also tends to be accompanied by greater entry costs and risks.

Although most people tend to think of distance in geographic terms, in the area of international strategy distance can also be viewed in terms of culture, administrative heritage, and economics. As summarized in Exhibit 8.10, this broader **CAGE framework**—Culture, **A**dministrative, **G**eographic, and **E**conomic—provides you with another way of thinking about location and the opportunities and concomitant risks associated with global arbitrage.[21] CAGE-related risks would be most relevant in industries in which language or cultural identity are important factors, the government views the products as staples or as essential to national security, or income or input costs are key determinants of product demand or cost. You learned about these broader cultural and socioeconomic factors through your use of the PESTEL framework in Chapter 4. CAGE asks you to look at countries and regions, try to assess the degree to which they are different or similar along many of the PESTEL dimensions, and then try to estimate the implications of such differences for a firm that wishes to move into a new geographic market.

Application of the CAGE framework requires managers to identify attractive locations based on raw material costs, access to markets or consumers, or other key decision criteria. For instance, a firm may be most interested in markets with high consumer buying power, so it uses per capita income as the first sorting cue. This would result in some type of ranking. For example, one researcher examined the fast food industry and found that based on per capita income, countries such as Germany and Japan would be the most attractive markets for the expansion of a North American-based fast food company. However, when the analysis was adjusted for distance using the CAGE framework, the revised results showed that Mexico ranked as the second-most-attractive market for international expansion, far ahead of Germany and Japan.[22]

CAGE framework   Tool that considers the dimensions of culture, administration, geography, and economics to assess the distance created by global expansion.

Exhibit 8.9 The Emerging Market Boom

In the world of global strategy and competition, new contenders are hailing from seemingly unlikely places, developing nations such as Brazil, Russia, India, China, and even Egypt and South Africa. They are shaking up entire industries, from farm equipment and refrigerators to aircraft and telecom services, and changing the rules of global competition. These changes are consistent with those presaged by the trends you learned about in Exhibit 8.2.

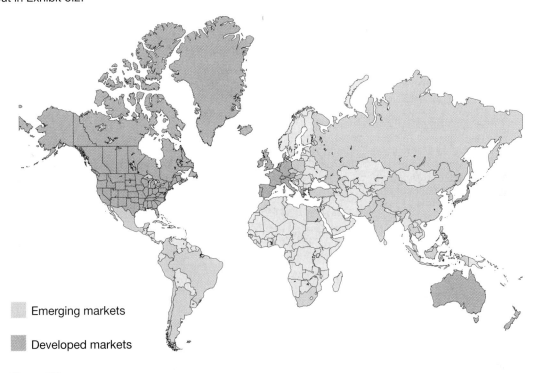

■ Emerging markets

■ Developed markets

Grey—Other

Unlike Japanese and Korean conglomerates, which benefited from protection and big profits at home before they took on the world, these emerging economy upstarts are mostly companies that have prevailed in brutally competitive domestic markets, where local companies have to duke it out with homegrown rivals and Western multinationals every day. As a result, these emerging champions must make profits at price levels unheard of in the United States or Europe. Indian generic drugmakers, for example, often charge customers in their home market as little as 1% to 2% of what people pay in the United States. Cellular outfits in North Africa, Brazil, and India offer phone service for pennies per minute. Yet these companies often thrive in such tough environments. Egyptian cellular operator Orascom boasts margins of 49%; Mahindra's pretax profit rose 81% in 2006.

Some already are marquee names. Lenovo Group, the Chinese computer maker, made waves in 2005 by buying IBM's $11 billion PC business. Indian software outfits Infosys, Tata Consultancy Services, and Wipro have revolutionized the $650 billion technology services industry. Johannesburg brewer SABMiller PLC is challenging Anheuser-Busch Cos.' leadership right in the United States.

These companies are just the first wave. The biggest international cellular provider? Soon it may be Mexico's América Móvil, which boasts more than 100 million Latin American subscribers and led BusinessWeeks's 2006 rankings of the world's top information technology companies. Never heard of Hong Kong's Techtronic Industries Ltd.? If you buy power tools at Home Depot Inc., where its products now fill the aisles, you probably know some of the brands it manufactures: Ryobi, Milwaukee, and RIDGID. Brazil's Embraer has surged past Canada's Bombardier as the world's No. 3 aircraft maker and is winning midsize-jet orders that otherwise

(continued)

Exhibit 8.9 Continued

would have gone to larger planes by Airbus and Boeing. Western telecom equipment leaders have long looked down on China's Huawei Technologies Co. as a mere copier of their designs. But in 2006, Huawei snared $8 billion in new orders, including contracts from British Telecommunications PLC for its $19 billion program to transform Britain's telecom network.

Many more companies are using their bases in the developing world as springboards to build global empires, such as Mexican cement giant Cemex, Indian drugmaker Ranbaxy, and Russia's Lukoil, which has hundreds of gas stations in New Jersey and Pennsylvania. Boston Consulting Group (BCG) recently published a report describing the amount of progress as "surprising," in view of the progress made by emerging-market companies in the last few years. BCG identified 100 emerging multinationals that appear positioned to radically transform industries and markets around the world. The 100 had combined $715 billion in revenue in 2005, $145 billion in operating profits, and a half-trillion dollars in assets. They have grown at a 24 percent annual clip in the past four years.

What makes these upstarts global contenders? Their key advantages are access to some of the world's most dynamic growth markets and immense pools of low-cost resources, be they production workers, engineers, land, petroleum, or iron ore. But these aspiring giants are about much more than low cost. The best of the pack are proving as innovative and expertly run as any in the business, astutely absorbing global consumer trends and technologies and getting new products to market faster than their rivals. Techtronic, for example, was the first to sell heavy-duty cordless tools powered by lightweight lithium ion batteries. Jetmaker Embraer's sleek EMB 190, which seats up to 118, has taken smaller commercial aircraft to a new level with the fuselage design that offers the legroom and overhead luggage space of much larger planes. Globalization and the Internet allow these emerging market firms to tap the same managerial talent, information, and capital as Western companies. In most industries, strategy and competition have clearly become a global game.

Any international expansion strategy would still need to be backed up by the specific resources and capabilities possessed by the firm, regardless of how rosy the CAGE analysis paints the picture. Think of international expansion as a movement along a continuum from known markets to less-known markets; a firm can move to more CAGE-proximate neighbors before venturing into markets that are portrayed as very different from a CAGE-framework perspective. Let's look at each dimension of CAGE.

Cultural Distance Culture happens to be the first facet of CAGE, in terms of the acronym, but it also can be the most practically perplexing facet for managers. Culture is sometimes referred to as the software of the mind, in that it has a sometimes invisible but indelible influence on people's values and behaviors. *Cultural distance,* then, has to do with the possible differences existing in relation to the way individuals from different countries observe certain values and behaviors.

A number of researchers have identified significant cultural differences among countries. Among these, for instance, Geert Hofstede drew together distinct cultural differences he observed around the following dimensions: power distance (the extent to which individuals accept the existence of inequalities between subordinates and superiors within a hierarchical structure); uncertainty avoidance (individuals' willingness to coexist with uncertainty about the future); individualism (how the individuals in a society value individualistic behaviors as opposed to collective ones); predominant values (regarding quantity or quality of life, that is, whether more importance is given to material aspects or a stronger emphasis is laid on interpersonal relationships); and long-term or short-term orientation (the focus on future rewards or the concern about the maintenance of the stability related to the past and the present).[23] A cross-section of these cultural dimensions for a sampling of developed and developing countries around the world are presented in Exhibit 8.11.

Exhibit 8.10   The CAGE Framework

Cultural Distance	Administrative Distance	Geographic Distance	Economic Distance
Attributes Creating Distance			
Different languages Different ethnicities: lack of connective ethnic or social networks Different religions Different social norms	Absence of colonial ties Absence of shared monetary or political association Political hostility Government policies Institutional weakness	Physical remoteness Lack of a common border Lack of sea or river access Size of country Weak transportation or communication links Differences in climates	Differences in consumer incomes Differences in costs and quality of: • natural resources • financial resources • human resources • infrastructure • intermediate inputs • information or knowledge
Industries or Products Affected by Distance			
Products have high linguistic content (TV) Products affect cultural or national identity of consumers (foods) Product features vary in terms of size (cars), standards (electrical appliances), or packaging Products carry country-specific quality associations (wines)	Government involvement is high in industries that are: • producers of staple goods (electricity) • producers of other "entitlements" (drugs) • large employers (farming) • large suppliers to government (mass transportation) • national champions (aerospace) • vital to national security (telecom) • exploiters of natural resources (oil, mining) • subject to high sunk costs (infrastructure)	Products have a low value-of-weight or bulk ratio (cement) Products are fragile or perishable (glass, fruit) Communications and connectivity are important (financial services) Local supervision and operational requirements are high (many services)	Nature of demand varies with income level (cars) Economies of standardization or scale are important (mobile phones) Labour and other factor cost differences are salient (garments) Distribution or business systems are different (insurance) Companies need to be responsive and agile (home appliances)

From Exhibit 8.11 you can see, for instance, that the United States has one of the lowest scores for uncertainty avoidance (i.e., a culture with a high tolerance for uncertainty), and one of the highest scores for individualism (i.e., a highly individualistic culture). These differences may influence the success of a strategic initiative due to the way a new product is perceived by consumers, or the effect they have on how a firm traditionally manages its operations. You have already been introduced to the global trials and successes of Lincoln Electric, for example. One of its key strategic weapons was the use of highly individualistic pay practices, which resonate well with its U.S. employee stakeholders. However, as you can see from Exhibit 8.11, the German culture is not as individualistic, and this offers a partial explanation for the initial failure of this management tool in Germany.

Administrative Distance   *Administrative distance* reflects the historical and present political and legal associations between trading partners; for example, colonial ties between trading partners, or participation in common trading blocs. This facet of CAGE asks you to examine whether there are historical or current political factors that might favor or impede a business relationship between a company and a new country market. NAFTA, for instance, decreased the administrative distance between U.S. firms and Mexico and Canada.

Exhibit 8.11   Cultural Differences Among Countries

Country	Power Distance	Individualism	Masculinity	Uncertainty Avoidance	Long-term Orientation
Arab World	80	38	52	68	na
Brazil	69	38	49	76	65
China	80	20	66	30	118
Germany	35	67	66	65	31
India	77	48	56	40	61
Japan	54	46	95	92	80
Philippines	94	32	64	44	19
South Korea	60	18	39	85	75
Sweden	31	71	5	29	33
United Kingdom	35	89	66	35	25
United States	40	91	62	46	29

*Hofstede estimated these values for the region comprised of Egypt, Iraq, Kuwait, Lebanon, Libya, Saudi Arabia, and United Arab Emirates. Long-term orientation was not included in his estimates.

Similarly, historical political hostilities between the United States and Cuba make it virtually impossible (and illegal) for most U.S. firms to do business there.

As you can imagine, trade practices between countries can be significantly affected by laws and regulations enacted at the national or international level. Because they affect fundamental business practices, they often affect the competitive position of firms as well. Some of the key legal considerations for U.S. firms include the following:

■ **Free Trade Agreements.** Since presidential Trade Promotion Authority (TPA) was restored in 2002, the United States has embarked on an unprecedented effort to open foreign markets to U.S. exports by expanding its network of free trade agreements (FTAs). In 2003 and 2004, negotiations for FTAs with Chile, Singapore, Australia, and Morocco were concluded and subsequently approved by Congress. The latter two came into force in 2005; the FTAs with Chile and Singapore are already generating impressive results. U.S. exports to Chile, for example, increased by 28 percent in the first year of the agreement's implementation.

■ **Import Laws.** Under longstanding U.S. law, harm to U.S. companies caused by dumped products can be offset by antidumping duties if U.S. government investigating agencies— the Commerce Department and the International Trade Commission—are satisfied that certain criteria are met. Similarly, these two agencies can impose countervailing duties on subsidized imports to offset harm caused to U.S. industries by those imports. And numerous other laws are designed to restrict imports on grounds ranging from public health and safety to national security to protection of intellectual property. Such laws are still on the books, even though the recently established World Trade Organization has as a mandate continuing efforts to reduce such practices worldwide.

■ **Foreign Corrupt Practices Act (FCPA).** This U.S. federal law, amended to include OECD antibribery conventions, requires firms to have adequate accounting controls in place, but is most commonly known for its antibribery provisions. The antibribery provisions of the FCPA make it unlawful for a U.S. person, and certain foreign issuers of securities, to make a payment to a foreign official for the purpose of obtaining or retaining business for or with, or directing business to, any person. Since 1998, they also apply to foreign firms and persons who take any action in furtherance of such a corrupt payment while in the United States. The definition of foreign official is broad. For example, an owner of a bank who is also the brother of the minister of finance would qualify as a foreign official according to the U.S. government. There is no materiality to this act, which makes it illegal to offer even a penny as a bribe. The government focuses on the intent of the bribery more than the amount of it.

■ **Intellectual Property Protection.** Patents and trademarks are territorial and must be filed in each country where protection is sought. A U.S. patent or trademark does not afford protection in another country. However, the Patent Cooperation Treaty (PCT) streamlines the process of filing patents in multiple countries. By filing one patent application with the U.S. Patent and Trademark Office (USPTO), U.S. applicants can concurrently seek protection in up to 127 countries. Notable exceptions to this process include China. Indeed, if a firm enters the China market with a product but does not register its mark at China's Trademark Office, one of the firm's competitors, distributors, or partners may be able to register the trademark before them and bar them from manufacturing or selling the products with their mark in China. Despite international attention to the importance of intellectual property rights, their protection remains problematic in many developing countries. At the www.stopfakes.gov website, maintained by the U.S. Department of Commerce, there are intellectual property protection toolkits for Brazil, China, Korea, Malaysia, Mexico, Peru, Russia, and Taiwan—countries identified as among the most problematic.

Geographic Distance How far apart are trading partners in physical terms: the size of the country, differences in climates, and nature of transportation and information networks? You can think of *geographic distance* as absolute, in terms of the miles or kilometers that separate a firm from another market or supplier. Technology, however, has shrunk distance in terms of transportation time, and now with digital products and services, almost entirely eliminated geographic distance as a constraint of trade between some markets.

One of the most dramatic changes in trade was facilitated by the shipping container, which in many cases moves seamlessly between one country, shipping channels, and another country. The most recent example, of course, where distance has been reduced is with the case of the Internet. W.W. Grainger, for example, a leader in the U.S. maintenance, repair, and overhaul (MRO) industry, found that the Internet provided it a ready sales vehicle into European markets. Prior to the Internet it could not justify an investment in a far-flung European brick-and-mortar presence. With the Internet, its storefront in Europe became virtual.

Economic Distance Finally, *economic distance* captures fundamental differences relating to income, the distribution of wealth, and the relative purchasing power of segments of a geographic market. This has been one of the biggest barriers, for instance, in the way of U.S. firms success selling products in emerging markets. In global terms, this is the four billion people who live on less than $2 per day. The phrase "bottom of the pyramid" is used in particular by people developing new models of doing business that deliberately target that market, typically using new technology. An example of a product that is designed with the needs of the very poor in mind is that of a shampoo that works best with cold water. Such a product is marketed by Hindustan Lever (part of the Unilever family of firms).

How would you calculate economic difference? You should have ready access to information on per capita income and relative purchasing power across countries. In the following "How Would *You* Do That? 8.1," you can see a sample per country per capita income difference for a cross-section of countries. This data will give you a sense of the income that individuals or companies may have to spend on a new product or service. At the same time, you should gain an understanding of the pricing for comparable products or services. This is why economic distance also includes the economics of supply for comparable or

How Would YOU DO THAT? 8.1

Putting CAGE to Work at Virgin Mobile

The starting point for your CAGE analysis is something called a country attractiveness portfolio (CAP). A CAP is created using data on a country or region's per capita income, along with data on some aspect of the market's desirability, such as market penetration or per capita spending on a focal product or service. With this information, you would have two reference points that you plot on a grid, for each country. For instance, if you were Virgin Mobile, a U.K.-based cell phone company with an interest in entering a new geographic arena outside of its home European Union market, you would want to collect information on the percentage of the population that uses cell phones in other countries, along with country per capita income. By looking at the CIA's 2006 World Factbook, which is summarized in Exhibit 8.12, you found

the following information (you also happened to collect information on each country's population, since that will give you an idea of the percentage of people who have cell phones, or the current market penetration for cell phones in each country).

Since you were smart enough to rank order the data by cell phones, you can see that China has the biggest actual market. In some markets you see that the number of cell phones in use actually exceeds the labor force, which means that kids and retired people must be using them as well. Your next step is to plot out some of this data on a grid, so you have a better visual image of the possible market arenas. This is where the population data come in. You simply plot each country's location on the grid using number of cell phones on the X axis, and per capita income on the

Y axis—then use the bubble size to give you a rough impression of the relative opportunity presented by each market, in terms of the actual population. We picked population because it maps well to the idea of the potential cell phone market, but you could use other aggregated indicators like gross domestic product, number of factories, and so on. The best dimension is one that can give you an idea of the country's market size for the particular product or service you are analyzing. Exhibit 8.13 shows you your CAP, using population as an indicator of market size.

Had you not been reading this chapter, you would have concluded that you were done with your analysis. Based solely on the information in Exhibit 8.13, what country would you have chosen for Virgin's expansion move? And sadly, this is why so many

Exhibit 8.12 Market Characteristics

Rank	Country	Cell Phones	Per Capita Income	Population
1	China	334,824,000	$7,600	1,321,851,888
2	European Union	314,644,700	$29,400	460,827,146
3	United States	194,479,364	$43,500	301,139,947
4	Japan	91,473,900	$33,100	127,433,494
5	Russia	74,420,000	$12,100	141,377,752
6	India	69,193,321	$3,700	1,129,866,154
7	Brazil	65,605,000	$8,600	190,010,647
8	Mexico	38,451,100	$10,600	108,700,891
9	South Korea	36,586,100	$24,200	49,044,790

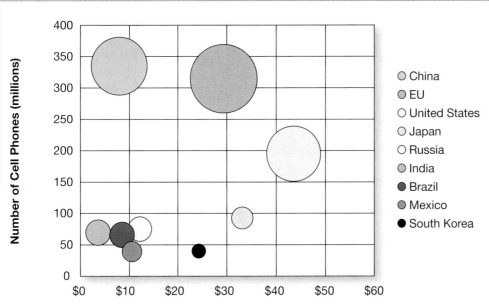

Exhibit 8.13 Country Attractiveness Portfolio

CAP's are fundamentally flawed. The information in Exhibit 8.13 does give you an idea of the relative attractiveness of each country market, and you can see their relative size related to per capita income, and so on. For a company like Virgin, they would probably like to enter a new country market where income is high, and the market is very big. They do fine in Europe, and as you can see from Exhibit 8.12 (and 8.13), that market is both big and relatively rich. However, these exhibits do not tell you how well Virgin is prepared to enter those markets—you only know that they are big, but will they be big (as in a homerun) for Virgin? The third and final step is to adjust the size of the bubbles upward or downward for CAGE-based differences along the dimensions of culture, administration, geography, and economics. This will tell you how attractive each country is, *after adjusting for the critical CAGE differences*. For instance, this would probably lead you to discount all the markets, other than the U.S. market, and you might adjust the U.S. market upward. A CAGE-adjusted CAP is shown in Exhibit 8.14.

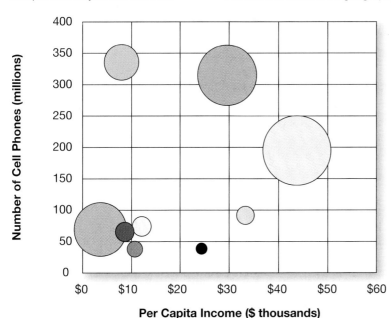

Exhibit 8.14 CAGE-Adjusted CAP for Virgin Mobile

substitute products in a market. For instance, processed cheese (like Velveeta) tends to cost less than fresh cheese in U.S. supermarkets, and low relative price is a key selling point for processed cheese. A recent U.S. entrant to the Brazilian cheese market assumed this same price relationship. After setting up their factory, however, they found that fresh cheese was very good *and* cheap in Brazilian supermarkets. The company wrongly assumed they would have a price advantage, when in fact the economics of cheese production in Brazil typically made processed cheese a higher-priced, and relatively less attractive, product.

Based on the CAGE-adjusted CAP you calculated for Virgin, for instance, you would probably recommend that Virgin Mobile should think about entering the U.S. market. Beyond this work, a full analysis could consider how a company's own characteristics operate to increase or reduce distance from foreign arenas. ◆ Companies with a large cadre of cosmopolitan managers, for instance, will be less affected by cultural differences than companies whose managers are all from the home country. Other company characteristics can help or hurt as well. In Virgin's case, consideration of company-specific features make the United States even more attractive. For instance, Virgin's parent company, Virgin Atlantic Airways, has a pretty sexy image in the United States, particularly in the demographic that would be the ideal target market for Virgin Mobile. Despite starting well behind companies like Orange or Vodafone in the United Kingdom, Virgin has become the fastest-growing cell phone provider in that country, with more than 700,000 customers added in its first 15 months of operation.

 Arenas

So what have we learned by using CAGE in the context of Dell and Virgin Mobile, and international expansion more generally? You should now see that the CAGE framework can be used to address the questions of where to expand internationally (which arena) and how to expand (by which vehicle). It can also help you map out the staging and pacing of your strategic international expansion moves so as to maximize the strategy's anchoring in the firm's VRINE-based resources and capabilities. You can see the CAGE-based logic at work in recent moves by Indian and Chinese competitors, for instance. Chinese technology-based companies like Lenovo are offering their products (laptops in Lenovo's case), but outsourcing the service side to English-speaking Indian firms. In contrast, a number of Indian companies have bought third- and fourth-tier U.S. or European manufacturers, and used their proximity to China to outsource production to China. Finally, a firm with an already large, but diverse, global presence can use CAGE to reevaluate which countries to stay in, and which ones to exit.

The opening vignette about Dell further demonstrates the usefulness of the CAGE framework. As you saw in the case of Dell, the vehicles it used to enter China were just as important in its China strategy as the choice of geographic arena it entered. For Dell's corporate clients in China, a CAGE framework would reveal relatively little distance on all four dimensions, even geographic, given the fact that many PC components are sourced from China. However, for the consumer segment, the distance is rather great, particularly on the dimensions of culture, administration, and economics. One outcome here could have been Dell's avoidance of the consumer market altogether. However, Dell opted to choose an alliance with distributors whose knowledge base and capabilities enabled it to better bridge the CAGE-framework distances until it was in a position to engage its Dell Direct model with consumers (staging and pacing).

Entry Vehicles into Foreign Countries

The strategy diamond says that a critical element of a firm's strategy is how it enters new markets. Now that you have answered questions about economic logic and desired geographic arena, your international strategy must answer the "how" question. How will you enter that new market? With international strategy, these new markets just happen to be in different countries, with different laws, infrastructure, cultures, and consumer preferences. The various entry mechanisms are referred to as *vehicles of strategy*. Consequently, a critical

Exhibit 8.15   Choice of Entry Vehicles

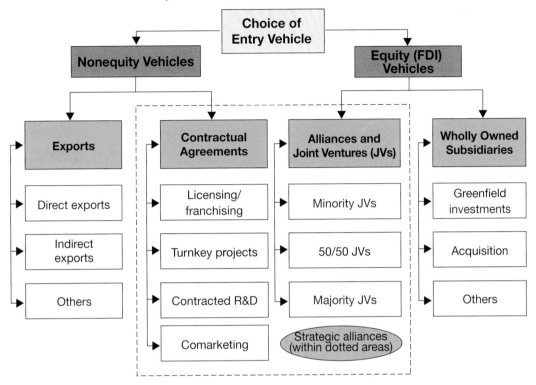

element of international expansion is determining which vehicles to use to enter new global markets. The first choice that managers must make is whether they will enter a foreign country with a vehicle that requires the firm to put some, or even considerable, capital at risk. As shown in Exhibit 8.15, firms can choose among a variety of nonequity and equity vehicles for entering a foreign country.[24] ◆ Exhibit 8.16 provides you with examples of the vehicles chosen by different firms around the world.[25]

 Vehicles

The second choice that managers must make is the type of the vehicle. Typically, each type of vehicle offers differing levels of ownership control and local presence. Although firms can expand internationally in a number of different ways, we present them to you under three overarching foreign-country entry vehicles: *exporting, contractual agreements* and *alliances,* and *foreign direct investment (FDI),* either through the acquisition of a company or simply starting one from scratch. At the end of this section, we will briefly discuss the use of importing as a foreign-country entry vehicle; it is somewhat of a stealth form of internationalization.

Foreign-country entry has been viewed historically as a staged process. Like the industry life cycle, the internationalization life cycle starts with a firm importing some of its raw materials or finished product for resale at home, followed perhaps by exporting products or raw materials abroad, and lastly ending in some type of partial or full ownership of plant, equipment, or other more extensive physical presence in a foreign country. These stages could be accomplished using vehicles ranging from simple contracts for purchases or sales on a transaction basis, through alliances, and perhaps even via mergers or wholesale acquisitions. Lincoln Electric, which was discussed in the previous section, offers an example of international growth through acquisition.

Over time, research has suggested that although some firms do follow such stages, they are better viewed as being more descriptive than predictive. Specifically, some firms follow the stages, starting with importing through foreign direct investment, whereas others jump right to the direct investment stage as their first internationalization effort.[26]

Exhibit 8.16 Vehicles for Entering Foreign Markets

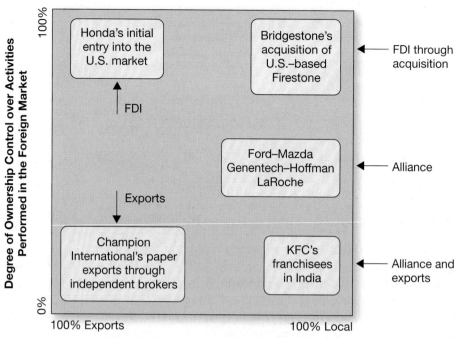

It is also helpful to note that the different entry vehicles have differing degrees of risk and control. For instance, a company that is only exporting its products abroad is typically risking its payment for the product, and perhaps its reputation if the product is not serviced well in the foreign locale. This also shows how little control the exporter has over the downstream activities once it has shipped the product. Although the exporter may have some legal or distribution agreement with local firms, this is very little control compared

South African Breweries, the maker of Castle Lager, successfully entered one of the largest beer markets in the world—the United States—by acquiring Miller Brewing Company in 2002. The combined corporation is known as SABMiller.

to ownership of local factories or distribution, or partial ownership through some form of alliance. In this section, we will walk you through these alternative entry vehicles.

EXPORTING

Exporting is exactly the opposite of importing; it can take the form of selling production or service inputs or actual products and services abroad. With the advent of the Internet and electronic banking, the physical entry barriers to becoming an exporter are lower than ever before. Although the importer is ultimately responsible for the issues relating to customs, packaging, and other trade requirements, the exporting firm will generally only be successful to the extent that it can deliver a product or service that meets customers' needs.

exporting   Foreign-country entry vehicle in which a firm uses an intermediary to perform most foreign marketing functions.

Costs of Exporting

Exporting is a popular internationalization vehicle with small firms because the costs of entering new markets are relatively minimal with this vehicle. Exporters generally use local representatives or distributors to sell their products in new international markets. The main costs associated with exporting are transportation and meeting the packaging and ingredient requirements of the target country. Consequently, exporting is most common to international markets that are relatively close to the domestic market or to markets in which competitors and substitutes for the firm's products are not readily available. A large percentage of the born-global firms discussed later in the chapter used exporting as a vehicle to go global quickly.[27]

Contractual Agreements

Contractual agreements are an entry vehicle where a firm typically relies on another to manage their market presence. The contract itself can take a variety of forms, from a verbal agreement to an extensive legal document, but often relates to one of the following four types of agreements.

contractual agreement   An exchange of promises or agreement between parties that is often enforceable by the law.

Licensing and Franchising

Exporting can take the form of shipping a product overseas and leaving marketing and distribution up to a foreign customer. It can also take the form of licensing or franchising, turnkey projects, R&D contracts, and comarketing. Due to some of the characteristics of these latter vehicles, as shown in Exhibit 8.15, such contractual arrangements are often considered a form of strategic alliance. Licensing and franchising provide a case in point. When a firm licenses its products or technologies in another country, it transfers the risk of actually implementing market entry to another firm, which pays the licensor a fee for the right to use its name in the local country. Franchising in a foreign country works similarly to franchising in a domestic market. A firm receives a sign-up fee and ongoing franchise royalties in exchange for teaching the franchisee how to open and operate the franchisor's business in the local market.

The risk, of course, to the licensor or franchisor is that the licensee or franchisee will violate the terms of the agreement, either to the detriment of the product or service itself, by refusing to pay agreed-upon fees or royalties or simply selling a copy of the product or service under another name (that is essentially stealing the intellectual property entirely). The primary risks to the franchisee or licensee are that the product or service will not perform as promised or that the licensor or franchisor will do something that diminishes the market attractiveness of the product or service.

Turnkey Projects, R&D Contracts, and Comarketing

The latter three forms—turnkey projects, R&D contracts, and comarketing—are specialized contractual agreements whereby a firm agrees to build a factory, conduct a specific R&D project, or comarket or cobrand a product such that the contracting firm has used it as a foreign-market entry vehicle. For example, the Norwegian firm Kvaerner A/S contracts to build paper mills and deep-sea oil rigs for Brazilian paper and petroleum companies; the German firm Bayer AG contracts a large R&D project to the U.S. firm Millennium pharmaceuticals with the work undertaken in both firms' respective countries; McDonald's in Japan packages its kids meals with characters that are familiar to Japanese children based on characters like Pokémon or Hello Kitty that are popular at the time.

ALLIANCES

Alliances are another common foreign-market entry vehicle. Because we devote an entire chapter to alliances later in the text, here we simply explain why alliances are so commonly used for international expansion. Often, alliances are chosen because of government regulations. For example, only recently did the Chinese government allow non-Chinese ownership of companies in China. As a result, firms could only enter China through various partnerships. Alliances may also be used as an international-strategy vehicle due to management's lack of familiarity with the local culture or institutions or because the complexity of operating internationally requires the firm to focus on the activities it does best and to outsource the rest. Some combination of these three factors—regulations, market familiarity, or operational complexity—typically explain why alliances are so often used by firms competing internationally. For instance, Virgin Mobile partnered with Sprint when it initially entered the U.S. market in 2002.

FOREIGN DIRECT INVESTMENT

foreign direct investment (FDI) Foreign-country entry vehicle by which a firm commits to the direct ownership of a foreign subsidiary or division.

greenfield investment Form of FDI in which a firm starts a new foreign business from the ground up.

Foreign direct investment (FDI), as the term implies, is an international entry strategy whereby a firm makes a financial investment in a foreign market to facilitate the startup of a new venture. FDI tends to be the most expensive international entry tactic because it requires the greatest commitment of a firm's time and resources. FDI can be implemented in several ways, such as through acquisitions or through a so-called greenfield alliance—the startup of a foreign entity from scratch. This latter form of FDI is called **greenfield investment**. In the previous section, we reviewed how alliances can be a vehicle to foreign market entry. As you will learn in Chapter 9, alliances do not require any equity investment. However, many alliances do involve equity investment, and when they do in the context of foreign market entry, it is a special case of greenfield investment. For instance, DaimlerChrysler and BMW each invested $250 million to start a new engine factory in Curitiba, Brazil.

Acquisitions and Equity Alliances Because greenfield investment usually involves the greatest risk, expense, and time, many firms pursue FDI through acquisitions or alliances (you will learn more about these particular strategy vehicles in Chapters 9 and 10). Acquisitions provide the firm with rapid entry because the firm purchases existing businesses that are already staffed and successfully operating. For instance, when the battery maker Rayovac entered Brazil in 2005, it did so by purchasing Microlite, the dominant battery maker in Brazil. Similarly, South African Breweries purchased Miller Brewing in 2002 to gain an instant presence and production capacity in one of the largest beer markets in the world, the United States.

After its horrendous experiences with rapid international expansion, Lincoln Electric amended its corporate policy on FDI: It now engages only in FDI through alliances with local players in order to maximize the knowledge needed about local market conditions, both in terms of production and market demand. Sometimes alliances are dictated by the necessity to have a certain proportion of local content in a product, such as a car or motorcycle, in order to sell the product into a nonlocal market. Brazil and China are two examples of countries that have stringent local-content laws. Minimum efficient scale is another explanation for the use of alliances as an FDI foreign-entry tactic.

For example, the DaimlerChrysler and BMW alliance mentioned earlier was necessary because neither company could justify the volume of production needed by the new plant to justify it economically. Therefore, the two firms joined forces to form Tritec, a state-of-the-art automotive engine factory that supplies parts for BMW's Mini Cooper assembly plant in the United Kingdom and DaimlerChyrsler's PT Cruiser assembly plants in Mexico, the United States, and South Africa.[28]

IMPORTING AND INTERNATIONAL STRATEGY

In many ways, **importing** is a stealth form of internationalization because firms will often claim they have no international operations and yet directly or indirectly base their production or services on inputs obtained from outside their home country. Firms that engage in importing must be knowledgeable about customs requirements and informed about compliance with customs regulations, entry of goods, invoices, classification and value, determination and assessment of duty, special requirements, fraud, marketing, trade finance and insurance, and foreign trade zones. Importing can take many forms, from the sourcing of components, machinery, and raw materials to the purchase of finished goods for domestic resale to outsourcing production or services to nondomestic providers.

importing Internationalization strategy by which a firm brings a good, service, or capital into the home country from abroad.

Outsourcing and Offshoring This latter activity, international outsourcing, has taken on the most visible role in business and corporate strategy in recent years. International outsourcing is not a new phenomenon. For instance, Nike has been designing shoes and other apparel for decades and manufacturing them abroad. Similarly, Pacific Cycle does not make a single Schwinn or Mongoose bicycle in the United States but instead imports them from Taiwanese and Chinese manufacturers. It just seems that international outsourcing is new because of the increasingly rapid pace with which businesses are sourcing services, components, and raw materials from developing countries such as China, Brazil, and India.

Information technologies (IT), such as telecommunications and the widespread diffusion of the Internet, have provided the impetus for the international outsourcing of services as well as factors of production. Such *business process outsourcing (BPO)* is the delegation of one or more IT-intensive business processes to an external nondomestic provider which, in turn, owns, administers, and manages the selected process based on defined and measurable performance criteria. Sometimes this is referred to as **offshoring** because the business processes (including production/manufacturing) are outsourced to a lower-cost location, usually overseas. Offshoring refers to taking advantage of lower-cost labor in another country. Although outsourced processes are handed off to third-party vendors, offshored processes may be handed off to third-party vendors or remain in-house. This definition of offshoring includes organizations that build dedicated captive centers of their own in remote, lower-cost locations. The many U.S. firms that have established *maquiladoras* (assembly plants) in Mexico are examples of offshoring without outsourcing.

offshoring Moving a value chain activity or set of activities to another country, typically where key costs are lower.

Firms in such service- and IT-intensive industries as insurance, banking, pharmaceuticals, telecommunications, automobiles, and airlines seem to be the early adopters of BPO. Of the industries just mentioned, insurance and banking are able to generate savings purely because of the large proportion of processes they can outsource, such as claim processing, loan processing, and client servicing through call centers. Among those countries housing BPO operations, India appears to be experiencing the most dramatic growth for services that require English-language skills and education. BPO operations have been growing 70 percent a year and are now a $1.6 billion industry, employing approximately 100,000 people. In India alone, BPO has to grow only 27 percent annually until 2008 to deliver $17 billion in revenues and employ a million people.[29]

More generally, foreign outsourcing and offshoring locations tend to be defined by how automated a production process or service can be made, the relative labor costs, and the transportation costs involved. When transportation costs and automation are both high, then the knowledge-worker component of the location calculation becomes less important. You can see how you might employ the CAGE framework to evaluate potential outsourcing locations. However, in some cases firms invest in both plant and equipment and the training and development of the local workforce. Brazil is but one case in point, with examples from Ford, BMW, Daimler-Benz, and Cargill. Each of these multinational organizations is making significant investments in the educational infrastructure of this enormous emerging economy.[30]

International Strategy Configurations

How a firm becomes involved in international markets—which appears to be increasingly important, if not obligatory, for many if not all firms—differs from how it configures the interactions between headquarters and country operations. It is important to note that international-strategy configuration is as much about strategy formulation as it is about implementation, because management is making choices about which value-chain components to centralize, where to centralize those operations geographically, and the degree to which those decentralized and centralized value-chain activities will be managed and coordinated. Remember, too, that strategy helps a firm manage important tradeoffs that differentiate it and its products from competitors.

RESOLVING THE TENSION BETWEEN LOCAL PREFERENCES AND GLOBAL STANDARDS

In this section, we discuss the underlying tensions created between a firm's attempts to be responsive to the local needs of diverse sets of customers and yet remain globally efficient. Meeting the ideal tradeoff between customizing for local needs and achieving cost efficiencies requires further tradeoffs with respect to the firm's value chain regarding which activities will be standardized and which will be locally tailored. These are the central tradeoffs a firm must wrestle with in designing and managing its international strategy.

Globalizing firms must reconcile the natural tension that exists between local preferences and global standards. The domination of local preferences over the search for global efficiencies, left unchecked, often leads to what strategy researchers describe as *market fragmentation*.[31] In addition, local adaptation of products and services is significantly more expensive than relying on global standards. Consequently, attempting to achieve high levels of local responsiveness will almost always lead to higher cost structure.[32] A product that is uniform across markets is highly efficient to produce because the firm can simply design a factory of the most efficient size in a location that most efficiently balances the costs of inputs with the transportation costs of getting outputs to the desired markets. If this product has the same brand around the world, then marketing and promotion efforts are similarly focused on that single brand. However, even products like Coca-Cola, which appear to be ubiquitous, have different flavorings, packaging, and promotion constraints in each market. Some of these constraints are a function of local regulatory pressures; others reflect underlying differences in consumers' tastes. Just as important, other constraints are a function of the competitive norms that have prevailed in the industry, either globally or locally. The variations of international strategy configurations that we cover in this section—making tradeoffs between local responsiveness and global efficiency—are summarized in Exhibit 8.17.[33]

We will also speak briefly about born-global firms in this section because more and more organizations appear to have operations that span national borders early in their existence. As you will see, born-global firms employ an amalgam of exporting and FDI, but do so much more rapidly than firms have in the past. In the strategy diamond, exporting and FDI are considered vehicles, and the timing and sequencing of the usage are viewed in the context of staging. Each of these vehicles provides a firm and its management with experience and knowledge about cross-border business practices.

Exhibit 8.17 International Strategy Configurations and Local/Global Tradeoffs

	Relatively Few Opportunities to Gain Global Efficiencies	Many Opportunities to Gain Global Efficiencies
Relatively High Local Responsiveness	**Multinational Vision** Build flexibility to respond to national differences through strong, resourceful, entrepreneurial, and somewhat independent national or regional operations. Requires decentralized and relatively self-sufficient units. **Example:** MTV initially adopted an international configuration (using only American programming in foreign markets) but then changed its strategy to a multinational one. It now tailors its Western European programming to each market, offering eight channels, each in a different language.	**Transnational Vision** Develop global efficiency, flexibility, and worldwide learning. Requires dispersed, interdependent, and specialized capabilities simultaneously. **Example:** Nestlé has taken steps to move in this direction, starting first with what might be described as a multinational configuration. Today, Nestlé aims to evolve from a decentralized, profit-center configuration to one that operates as a single, global company. Firms like Nestlé have taken lessons from leading consulting firms such as McKinsey and Company, which are globally dispersed but have a hard-driving, one-firm culture at their core.
Relatively Low Local Responsiveness	**International Vision** Exploit parent-company knowledge and capabilities through worldwide diffusion, local marketing, and adaptation. The most valuable resources and capabilities are centralized; others, such as local marketing and distribution, are decentralized. **Example:** When Wal-Mart initially set up its operations in Brazil, it used its U.S. stores as a model for international expansion.	**Global Vision** Build cost advantages through centralized, global-scale operations. Requires centralized and globally scaled resources and capabilities. **Example:** Companies such as Merck and Hewlett-Packard give particular subsidiaries a worldwide mandate to leverage and disseminate their unique capabilities and specialized knowledge worldwide.

Emphasize Local Responsiveness Each of the configurations identified in Exhibit 8.17 presents tradeoffs between global efficiency and local responsiveness. Recognize that in reality, most firms' international strategy configurations vary slightly or significantly from those shown in Exhibit 8.17. By definition, strategy must be internally consistent and externally oriented. However, management must make judgments as to what an external orientation means in terms of how the strategy takes competitive pressures and consumer preferences into account. At the same time, management must also make judgments about the firm's internal resources and capabilities to support a particular international-strategy configuration. This explains why firms with seemingly very different international-strategy configurations can coexist in the same industry.

When Lincoln Electric first embarked on becoming a global firm, it had relatively independent operations in many markets around the world. It used its strongest national

cross-subsidizing   Practice by which a firm uses profits from one aspect of a product, service, or region to support other aspects of competitive activity.

positions to **cross-subsidize** market-share battles or growth initiatives in other countries. Such an approach is essentially a portfolio of geographically removed business units that have devoted most of their resources and capabilities to maximizing local responsiveness and uniqueness. Firms which, like Lincoln Electric, employ this configuration have the objective to develop a global presence but may or may not use the same brand names in each market or consolidate their buying power or distribution capabilities.

Emphasize Global Efficiencies with Some Local Advantages

Another configuration centralizes some resources, such as global brand and distribution capabilities, in order to achieve costs savings; but decentralizes others, such as marketing, in order to achieve some level of localization. This strategy is common among firms that have created something in their home market that they wish to replicate in foreign markets, allowing them the economies of scale and scope necessary to create and exploit innovations on a worldwide basis. Heavy R&D companies such as Intel and Pfizer fit this mold: Even though the products that they produce are relatively standardized around the world, local marketing and distribution channels differ.

Emphasize Global Efficiencies

This configuration focuses only on global efficiency. A tradeoff is made between local responsiveness and the lower costs associated with global efficiency. With this configuration, production and sourcing decisions are designed to achieve the greatest economies of scale. Firms following this configuration potentially sacrifice the higher prices that follow customization, but they are counting on the likelihood that their products or services will meet enough needs to be demanded without finely tuned customization. Firms in commodity industries such as steel and copper, such as BHP-Billeton, fall into this category. Because end customers make purchase decisions based on price alone, the firm is organized to realize the lowest possible production costs.

Seek to Exploit Local Advantages and Global Efficiencies

The final international-strategy configuration that we discuss is one that attempts to capitalize on both local responsiveness and global efficiency. When successfully implemented, this approach enables firms to achieve global economies of scale, cross-subsidization across markets, and the ability to engage in retaliatory and responsive competition across markets. This configuration is available to companies with high degrees of internationalization. However, as with any other strategic tradeoff, it is extremely difficult to find the balance between cost efficiencies and the ability to customize to local tastes and standards. McDonald's is often used as an example of a firm that fits this configuration because it uses its purchasing power to get the best prices on the global commodities it uses for inputs, yet tries to tailor its menu offerings to fit local tastes and cultural preferences.

BORN-GLOBAL FIRMS

One reason that global strategy—and the four international strategy configurations—will become an increasingly important topic is the fact that more and more firms, even very small ones, have operations that bridge national borders very soon after their founding. Perhaps appropriate for the Internet age, this new breed of firms that emerged in the 1990s is being dubbed "born global" because their operations often span the globe early in their existence. A common characteristic of such firms is that their offerings complement the products or capabilities of other global players, take advantage of global IT infrastructure, or otherwise tap into a demand for a product or service that at its core is somewhat uniform across national geographic markets. Although many firms may fall into this category by virtue of their products, the operations and customers of born-global firms do actually span the globe. Born-global firms position themselves globally, exploiting a combination of exporting and FDI.

Logitech, the computer-mouse and peripherals company, is perhaps one of the best early examples of a successful born-global firm.[34] It was founded by two Italians and a Swiss, with operations and R&D initially split between California and Switzerland. Logitech's primary focus was on the PC mouse, and it rapidly expanded production to Ireland and Taiwan. With its stylish and ergonomic products, Logitech had captured 30 percent of the global mouse business by 1989, garnering the startup a healthy $140 million in revenues. Today, Logitech is an industry leader in the design and manufacture of computer-peripheral devices. It has manufacturing facilities in Asia and offices in major cities in North America, Europe, and Asia Pacific and employs more than 6,000 people worldwide.[35]

How to Succeed as a Global Startup   Successful global startups must complete two phases. In the first phase, managers ask, "Should my firm be a global startup?" If they can answer "yes" to all or most of the follow-up questions entailed by phase 1, then they need to be sure that they can quickly build the resources and capabilities identified in phase 2. Research has shown that those firms unable to connect the dots in phase 2 were forced to cease operations after short, albeit sometimes lively, adventures.[36]

During phase 1—*and before moving on to phase 2*—managers should consider questions that will help them determine whether the firm should be a global startup:

- Does the firm need human resources from other countries in order to succeed?

- Does the firm need financial capital from other countries in order to succeed?

- If the firm goes global, will target customers prefer its services over those of competitors?

- Can the firm put an international system in place more quickly than domestic competitors?

- Does the firm need global scale and scope to justify the financial and human capital investment in the venture?

- Will a purely domestic focus now make it harder for the firm to go global in the future?

If the answer to all or most of these questions is "yes," managers can commit to moving the firm into phase 2 and put together the tools they will need to move the firm into the global market:

- Strong management team with international experience

- Broad and deep international network among suppliers, customers, and complements

- Preemptive marketing or technology that will provide first-mover advantage with customers and lock out competitors from key suppliers and complements

- Strong intangible assets (Logitech has style, hipness, and mindshare via their brand)

- Ability to keep customers locked in by linking new products and services to the core business, while constantly innovating the core product or service

- Close worldwide coordination and communication among business units, suppliers, complements, and customers

So why do we introduce the concept of global startups at this point in the text? One reason is because of their increasing prevalence, which is driven, in part, by globalizing consumer preferences, mobile consumers, large global firms, and the pervasiveness of the Internet and its effects. The second reason, which should become clear after reading the next section, is that dynamic contexts typically give rise to the need for firms to strive for a global presence and to understand global markets early in their evolution.

International Strategy in Stable and Dynamic Contexts

Staging & Pacing

A recent McKinsey study suggests that the creativity that some companies have found in emerging economies, and that have resulted in inexpensive but high-quality products, will now compel incumbents to go down the same road.[37] This assertion gets at the heart—the question of urgency and timing—of how international strategy is approached in relatively stable versus dynamic contexts. ◆ Moreover, it also suggests that industries that might have been considered relatively stable will increasingly take on dynamic characteristics as a result of global competition. In many ways, what you have learned so far about business and corporate strategies in dynamic contexts is equally applicable in purely domestic and already globalizing organizations. The key difference, however—a difference that we hope is apparent after reading this chapter—is that cross-border business adds another level of complexity to both strategy formulation and execution and, that unfortunately, such complexity may be unavoidable for firms in dynamic contexts.

GLOBAL CONTEXT AND INDUSTRY LIFE CYCLE

Recall from earlier chapters that we differentiated between external- and internal-based views of strategy. The internal view emphasizes resources, capabilities, and activities as the source of competitive advantage; whereas the external view draws attention to how firms need to adapt or modify their competitive positions and strategies to the external environment to position themselves in a manner conducive to superior returns. These views have implications for the dynamic nature of international strategic action, as well. Taking the external perspective, for instance, typically draws managerial attention to the dynamic nature of the industry life cycle and how that drives decisions to internationalize. Specifically, as an industry matures, the international implications of industry structure—and therefore strategic choices and firm behavior—should change in fundamental ways.[38]

First-Mover Advantage   In the introductory stage of an industry's life cycle, the external perspective would expect firms to engage in few exports, largely because the market for the industry's products is still highly uncertain and there are few accepted quality, service, or technological standards. As you will see, the length of this stage may vary significantly by country. Firms should begin to export during the growth stage of industry life cycle because new firms enter the market and compete for existing customers. Early movers in the domestic market then have an opportunity to be early movers in foreign markets as well and to continue growth even as domestic competition heats up. As the industry matures, exports gain even more steam in the face of domestic market saturation, and firms start producing products abroad to satisfy foreign demand and to search for global efficiencies. Industry shakeout and consolidation also tend to follow industry maturity, and consolidation through acquisitions leads to a few large global companies.

Staging and Geographic Markets   Similarly, when discussing international strategy from an external perspective, the fact that geographic markets differ in many legal, cultural, and institutional ways—differences which, in turn, are likely to have implications for product demand—must also be taken into account. Indeed, demand characteristics of geographic markets have been shown to evolve at different rates. For example, the time from new-product introduction to the growth stage (sometimes called market takeoff) in Portugal may occur after a longer period of time than the same transition in Denmark. Indeed, although the average period of time between a new-product or new-service introduction and market takeoff is 6 years, a new product takes only about 4 years to take off in Denmark, Norway, and Sweden, compared to 9 years in Greece and Portugal (the United States averages 5.3 years).[39]

Role of Arenas in Global Strategies   Identification of arenas ensures that the most critical national markets are identified and brought into the plan. Similarly, even with thoughtful treatment of staging and arenas, structures, systems, and processes must be in complete alignment with the firm's vision and global intent. A firm that strives to execute the most complex global strategy—the transnational strategy—must have enormous investments in its ability to coordinate and integrate activities around the globe, complemented by customer characteristics that enable such a global strategy to create true value.

Resources and Global Strategy   The resource-based perspective has important implications for international strategy in dynamic contexts as well. It is here, too, that the questions of staging and geographic arenas from the strategy diamond model are critically important to effective international strategies. From the resource-based perspective, staging is important because the firm's global resources and capabilities do not materialize overnight. Lincoln Electric's experience is a case in point here. Lincoln's pace of international expansion exceeded its organizational capabilities to integrate foreign acquisitions, let alone manage them once they were integrated. Lincoln also attempted to internationalize almost exclusively through acquisitions. However, research on foreign expansion reveals that the firms most successful at internationalizing combine greenfield investments with acquisitions and alliances.[40] Simply expanding through greenfield investment can lead to inertia and lack of learning. Acquisitions help broaden a firm's knowledge base. However, exclusive reliance on acquisitions is not only costly but makes knowledge transfer and learning more difficult. Firms that balance greenfield investments and acquisitions seem to transfer more knowledge and create more value than firms that rely on either process exclusively.

Capabilities and Global Strategy   One of the fundamental ideas of having a dynamic view of strategy is to continuously build and renew firm capabilities. Many born-global firms fall into this dynamic-context category nearly from inception. By continuously evolving its stock of resources and capabilities, a firm maximizes its chances of adapting to changing environmental conditions. Thus, when a firm decides to enter a particular new foreign market, it must also embark on developing the resources necessary to make that market-entry decision a success. At the same time, what it learns in those new geographic markets should be evaluated for application or adaptation to existing market positions.

In addition, as a firm internationalizes and becomes more dependent on a particular foreign location, the need for high-level capabilities to perform the local activities increases commensurately.[41] For instance, as Ikea expands around the globe, its ability to understand local furniture markets increases. However, these needs are greatest in markets where it faces the most exposure; Ikea's early missteps in the United States have been attributed to lack of market intelligence.[42] This leads us to our closing section on global strategy in dynamic contexts.

DEVELOPING A MINDSET FOR GLOBAL DYNAMIC COMPETITIVENESS

Given the emphasis on the importance of leadership skills throughout this text, it should come as no surprise that what may make or break the effectiveness of a firm's international strategy is the internationally related capabilities and global mindset of the firm's executives, particularly in dynamic markets. Moreover, such capabilities and mindset may enable one firm to change a once relatively stable competitive context into a dynamic and vibrant one.

Global Perspective   The global mindset has two distinct but related dimensions. The first dimension is something that strategy researchers simply refer to as global perspective.[43] Executives with a global perspective require a combination of specific knowledge and skills. In terms of knowledge, executives with a global mindset have an appreciation for the fact that countries and their peoples differ culturally, socioeconomically, and sociopolitically; view those differences as potential opportunities as opposed to threats; and can link such differences to necessary adaptations in business operations. In addition, they also recognize that the management processes guiding those business operations must also be adapted to cultural, socioeconomic, and sociopolitical differences.

As opposed to conventional and routine cross-country transfers, companies are exposing managers to problem-solving situations in different business environments. An interesting example in this context is Dell Computer. Traditionally, Dell's practice has been to use local managers to run its outfits in different parts of the world. For important functions, Dell uses teams of specialists who move around the world providing expertise in specific areas. One such team which picked up design expertise while setting up Dell's manufacturing facilities in Texas, has been spending time in countries such as Ireland, Malaysia, China, and Brazil to set up plants there. In each of these countries, the team spends typically six months to one year.

Learning on a Worldwide Scale   In many ways, the second dimension of a global mindset requires the first dimension as a foundation. The second dimension is the capacity to learn from participation in one geographic market and transfer that knowledge to other operations elsewhere in the world. This means that the firm not only has globally savvy executives, but that these executives form an effective network of communication throughout the organization on a worldwide scale. You can tell that a firm and its managers possess this second dimension when the firm is routinely able to take knowledge gained in one market and apply it elsewhere, as was demonstrated in the case of SC Johnson's transfer of a plug-in household insect repellent product from Europe to the development of a new category of air-freshener products in the United States—Glade PlugIns.

Ironically, many global firms, and even more so with less global ones, are not very effective at retaining their managers once they return from an international assignment. These managers are either *expatriates*—someone from the home country who has moved abroad temporarily—or, increasingly, *inpatriates*—a manager recruited from the "local" market for their local business savvy. This apparent disconnect between a need for globally-seasoned executives and their retention by the firms that need them most can be explained by two factors. First, when the managers accept an international work assignment they often lose contact with the elements of the organization where strategy is formulated, such as corporate headquarters. In the case of inpatriates, they may never have had an opportunity to establish a strong network and power base at headquarters. Second, the expatriates' or inpatriates' firms do not have a repatriation plan in place to take advantage of their expertise. Because they have been-out-of-sight-and-out-of-mind, there is no ready way to plug them into the top management team.

Obviously, the development of a global mindset is more easily said than done. Our hope is that, given the fact that there are very few industries or markets untouched by global competition (just look around your classroom, for instance, and you will likely see at least one person from another country), you will take it upon yourself to start investing in your own global mindset.

Summary of Challenges

1. *Define* international strategy *and identify its implications for the strategy diamond.*   A firm's international strategy is how it approaches the cross-border business activities of its own firm and competitors and how it contemplates doing so in the future. International strategy essentially reflects the choices a firm's executives make with respect to sourcing and selling its goods in foreign markets. A firm's international activities affect both its business strategy and its corporate strategy. Each component of the strategy diamond may be affected by international activities.

2. *Understand why a firm would want to expand internationally and explain the relationship between international strategy and* *competitive advantage.* Firms often expand internationally to fuel growth; however, international expansion does not guarantee profitable growth and should be pursued to help a firm build or exploit a competitive advantage. International expansion can exploit four principle drivers of competitive advantage: economies of scale and scope, location, multipoint competition, and learning. However, these benefits can be offset by the costs of international expansion, such as the liabilities of newness and foreignness, and governance and coordination costs.

3. *Use the CAGE framework to identify international arenas.* CAGE stands for *c*ultural distance, *a*dministrative distance, *g*eographic distance, and *e*conomic distance and is a tool to help you better understand the firm-specific implication of a country attractiveness portfolio (CAP). You learned how to identify a portfolio of geographic markets and rank them on their relative attractiveness. The first step involved gathering data on personal income and market performance for a particular segment or industry. The second step involved creating a CAP by plotting the data on a grid to observe relative differences in attractiveness across countries. The third step asked you to make judgments about relevant CAGE dimensions and apply them to your CAP.

4. *Describe different vehicles for international expansion.* Foreign-country entry vehicles include exporting, alliances, and foreign direct investment (FDI). Exporters generally use local representatives or distributors to sell their products in new international markets. Two specialized forms of exporting are licensing and franchising. Alliances involve partnering with another firm to enter a foreign market or undertake an aspect of the value chain in that market. FDI can facilitate entry into a new foreign market and can be accomplished by greenfield investment or acquisition.

Although importing is not technically a form of international expansion, it does provide firms with knowledge, experience, and relationships on which future international expansion choices and activities can be based.

5. *Apply different international strategy configurations.* The different forms that international strategies may take are driven by tradeoffs in attempts to customize for local needs and to pursue global cost efficiencies. The first configuration seeks to achieve high levels of local responsiveness while downplaying the search for global efficiencies. The second configuration seeks relatively few global efficiencies and markets relatively standard products across different markets. The third configuration seeks to exploit global economies and efficiencies and accepts less local customer responsiveness (i.e., more standardized products). The fourth configuration attempts to simultaneously achieve global efficiencies and a high degree of local product specialization.

6. *Outline the international strategy implications of the stable and dynamic perspectives.* Cross-border business adds another level of complexity to both strategy formulation and execution, and unfortunately such complexity may be unavoidable for firms in dynamic contexts. As products mature, firms' international strategies evolve, often moving from little global involvement during the introductory phase to high degrees of internationalization in mature markets. Resources need to be renewed more rapidly in dynamic markets. Thus, when a firm enters a new foreign market, it must also embark on developing the resources necessary to make that market-entry decision a success. In addition, what is learned in new markets can be leveraged for application in existing markets. Obviously, these objectives can be best achieved when managers with an international mindset are in place.

Review Questions

1. What is meant by *international strategy?*

2. Which aspects of the strategy diamond are related to international strategy?

3. What are the four most important ways a firm's international strategy can be related to its competitive advantage?

4. What three foreign-country entry vehicles are emphasized in this chapter?

5. What is typically the most cost- and time-intensive entry vehicle?

6. What are characteristics of firms that fit the four international strategy configurations discussed in this chapter?

7. On what two dimensions do the four international strategy configurations differ?

8. What does the external perspective tell you about international strategy in dynamic contexts?

9. What does the resource-and-capabilities-based perspective tell you about international strategy in dynamic contexts?

10. What role do managers play in effective international strategies, particularly in dynamic contexts?

Experiential Activities

Group Exercises

1. Why have firms typically followed an international strategy path that started with importing or exporting, followed by alliances, and then FDI? What risks do born-global firms face in trying to do all of these at once? What resources and capabilities must they possess to do all of these effectively?

2. Are all Internet firms global by definition? What opportunities and barriers does the Internet present to firm internationalization?

Ethical Debates

1. You have successfully grown your local pasta company and while traveling in other countries you found that you might be able to produce and sell your product profitably there as well. In exploring these opportunities further, you were surprised to find that one of these countries has much stricter ingredients labeling and contents laws, while the other country much looser ones (in comparison to those of your home country, which you considered to be pretty strict to begin with). All three opportunities look to be profitable, regardless of the differences in regulations. Which regulations do you abide by in each country? The strictest ones, or the respective country standards, even if they are different?

2. As you learned in the section exploring CAGE, the Foreign Corrupt Practices Act is a U.S. federal law that makes it illegal for a citizen or corporation of the United States or a person or corporation acting within the United States to influence, bribe, or seek an advantage from a public official of another country. You, as an employee of a U.S. firm, are bidding for a contract in a foreign country where you understand that bribery is a common practice. Does the U.S. law put your firm at a competitive disadvantage? What should you do?

How Would YOU DO THAT?

1. Refer to the box entitled "How Would *You* Do That? 8.1." Pick another industry that is of interest to you. What did you identify as your indicator of potential market size? What market performance indicator did you use (for instance, in the example we used current cell phone usage)? How different were your CAP and CAGE-adjusted CAPs?

Go on to see How Would You Do That at www.prenhall.com/carpenter&sanders

Endnotes

1. "Acting on Global Trends: A McKinsey Global Survey," *The McKinsey Quarterly*, 7, May 2007, www.McKinsey.com.

2. Information provided on companies' respective websites. General information on the global Fortune 500 can be found at www.Fortune.com.

3. The imperatives are summarized in A. Gupta and V. Govindarajan, "Managing Global Expansion: A Conceptual Framework," *Business Horizons* 43:2 (2000), 45–54.

4. R. Tomkins, "Battered PepsiCo Licks Its Wounds," *The Financial Times*, May 30, 1997, 26.

5. A. K. Gupta and V. Govindarajan, "Converting Global Presence into Global Competitive Advantage," *Academy of Management Executive* 15 (2001), 45–56.

6. J. W. Lu and P. W. Beamish, "International Diversification and Firm Performance: The S-Curve Hypothesis," *Academy of Management Journal* 47 (2004), 598–609.

7. J. W. Lu and P. W. Beamish, "International Diversification and Firm Performance: The S-Curve Hypothesis," *Academy of Management Journal* 47 (2004), 598–609.

8. Lu and Beamish, "International Diversification and Firm Performance."

9. Lu and Beamish, "International Diversification and Firm Performance."

10. A. D. Chandler, *Scale and Scope: The Dynamics of Industrial Capitalism* (Cambridge, MA: Harvard University Press, 1990).

11. Gupta and Govindarajan, "Converting Global Presence into Global Competitive Advantage."

12. Gupta and Govindarajan, "Converting Global Presence into Global Competitive Advantage."

13. Gupta and Govindarajan, "Converting Global Presence into Global Competitive Advantage."

14. K. Ito and E. L. Rose, "Foreign Direct Investment Location Strategies in the Tire Industry," *Journal of International Business Studies* 33:3 (2002), 593–602.

15. This anecdote is based on an interview with Lincoln Electric's chairman emeritus in D. Hastings, "Lincoln Electric's Harsh Lessons from International Expansion," *Harvard Business Review* 77:3 (1999), 163–174.

16. Based on information from a personal interview with Sam Johnson.

17. Adapted from A. Gupta and V. Govindarajan, "Managing Global Expansion: A Conceptual Framework," *Business Horizons* 43:2 (2000), 45–54.

18. The points in this paragraph draw heavily on the work of M. T. Hansen and N. Nohria, "See How to Build a Collaborative Advantage," *Sloan Management Review* Fall (2004), 22–30.

19. CIA World Factbook, www.cia.gov.

20. Based on surveys reported in *Business Week* and Grant Thornton LLP. See *2007 Grant Thornton International Business Report* at www.gti.org, and "Emerging Giants Multinationals from China, India, Brazil, Russia, and even Egypt are coming on strong. They're hungry—and want your customers. They're changing the global game," *BusinessWeek,* July 31, 2006, Cover Story.

21. P. Ghemawat, "The Forgotten Strategy," *Harvard Business Review* 81:11 (2003), 76–84. Recreated from www.business-standard.com/general/pdf/113004_01.pdf.

22. P. Ghemawat, "Distance Still Matters," *Harvard Business Review* 79:8 (2001), 1–11.

23. G. Hofstede, *Culture's Consequences. International Differences in Work-Related Values* (Newbury Park, CA: Sage Publications, 1980); G. Hofstede, *Culture's and Organizations. Software of the Mind* (London: McGraw-Hill, 1991).

24. Adapted from Y. Pan and D. Tse, "The Hierarchical Model of Market Entry Modes," *Journal of International Business Studies* 31 (2000), 535–554.

25. Examples drawn from A. Gupta and V. Govindarajan, "Managing Global Expansion: A Conceptual Framework," *Business Horizons,* March/April 2002, 45–54.

26. J. Johanson and J. Vahlne, "The Internationalization Process of the Firm," *Journal of International Business Studies* 8 (1977), 23–32; F. Weidershiem-Paul, H. Olson, and L. Welch, "Pre-Export Activity: The First Step in Internationalization," *Journal of International Business Studies* 9 (1978), 47–58; A. Millington and B. Bayliss, "The Process of Internationalization: UK Companies in the EC," *Management International Review* 30 (1990), 151–161; B. Oviatt and P. McDougall, "Toward a Theory of International New Ventures," *Journal of International Business Studies* 25 (1994), 45–64.

27. O. Moen, "The Born Globals: A New Generation of Small European Exporters," *International Marketing Review* 19 (2002), 156–175.

28. www.tritecmotors.com.br

29. Gupta and Govindarajan, "Managing Global Expansion."

30. www.fordfound.org, www.tritecmotors.com.br, and www.cargill.com.br.

31. G. Hamel and C. K. Prahalad, "Do You Really Have a Global Strategy?" *Harvard Business Review* 63:4 (1985), 139–148.

32. Gupta and Govindarajan, "Converting Global Presence into Global Competitive Advantage."

33. Adapted from C. Bartlett, S. Ghoshal, and J. Birkenshaw, *Transnational Management* (New York: Irwin, 2004). Note that Bartlett and Ghoshal distinguish among international, multinational, global, and transnational strategies. We have found these distinctions are difficult for students to apply and have chosen to use the underlying dimensions of local responsiveness and global efficiency as the tradeoffs that international strategy emphasizes.

34. B. Oviatt and P. McDougall, "Global Start-Ups: Entrepreneurs on a Worldwide Stage," *Academy of Management Executive* 9:2 (1995), 30–44.

35. www.logitech.com.

36. Summarized from Oviatt and McDougall, "Global Start-Ups."

37. J. S. Brown and J. Hagel, "Innovation Blowback: Disruptive Management Practices from Asia," *McKinsey Quarterly* January (2005).

38. M. Porter, *Competitive Advantage* (New York: Free Press, 1998).

39. G. Tellis, S. Stremersch, and E. Yin. "The International Takeoff of New Products: Economics, Culture and Country Innovativeness," *Marketing Science* 22:2 (2003), 161–187.

40. F. Vermeulen and H. Barkema, "Learning Through Acquisitions," *Academy of Management Journal* 44 (2001), 457–476; M. A. Hitt, M. T. Dacin, E. Levitas, and J. Arregle, "Partner Selection in Emerging and Developed Market Contexts: Resource-Based and Organizational Learning Perspectives," *Academy of Management Journal* 43 (2000), 449–467.

41. Gupta and Govindarajan, "Converting Global Presence into Global Competitive Advantage."

42. "Furnishing the World," *The Economist,* November 19, 1994, 79–80.

43. B. Kedia and A. Mukherji, "Global Managers: Developing a Mindset for Global Competitiveness," *Journal of World Business* 34:3 (1999), 230–251.

9 Understanding Alliances and Cooperative Strategies

In This Chapter We Challenge You To >>>

1. Explain why strategic alliances are important strategy vehicles.

2. Identify the motivations behind alliances and show how they've changed over time.

3. Compare and contrast the various forms and structures of strategic alliances.

4. Explain alliances as both business- and corporate-level strategy vehicles.

5. Understand the characteristics of alliances in stable and dynamic competitive contexts.

6. Summarize the criteria for successful alliances.

An Alliance *that* Fits Like *a* Glove[1]

*P*rocter & Gamble's Mr. Clean brand, launched in 1958 with a muscle-man sailor as the mascot, had become a 98-pound weakling in the liquid cleaner segment by the 1990s. Jeffrey Weedman, P&G Vice President of External Business Development, saw the problem. "Mr. Clean is a singleproduct line and we aren't focusing enough on it," he told Nancy Bailey of Nancy Bailey & Associates. "Nancy, why don't you take the Mr. Clean brand and see what you can do with it." Bailey & Associates specializes in brand extension licensing, and Bailey went right to work finding an alliance partner who could help revitalize the Mr. Clean brand. Bailey found Jordan Glatt, President of Magla, a $30 million unbranded manufacturer of household gloves. Magla excelled at making high-quality products, but gloves are a commodity product, which, if undifferentiated and unbranded, can't command a premium price. Mr. Clean, on the other hand, was a well-known brand looking to expand beyond its core liquid-cleaner line. An alliance between the two companies could help both. In just 60 days, P&G and Magla signed an agreement to market a line of Magla household gloves under the Mr. Clean name. Glatt was "excited about the prospects of producing upscale household gloves under the Mr. Clean brand name and developing creative packaging and promotions to further distinguish our products," he said. Magla would use the Mr. Clean trademark and pay P&G royalties, but Magla would remain separate from P&G and would sell directly to the big retailers. The deal brought a strategic line extension for Mr. Clean while expanding the customer base and distribution channels for Magla. Describing the agreement, Glatt said, "A partnership with P&G provides Magla with a great niche-marketing opportunity. Mr. Clean has widespread name recognition." Similarly, Scott Lazarczyk, Brand Manager of Mr. Clean, explained the benefit to P&G: "This licensing agreement is a great example of how we're leveraging the Mr. Clean brand across product categories that add to our current offerings."

In an age of speed, alliances make sense. If done right, they can help a company grow faster, introduce new products faster, or expand into new areas less expensively. As Glatt said, "An added benefit from working with P&G is that we could hook in to their national FSCIs [free-standing coupon inserts] that appear in newspapers, which make the P&G and Magla products look like a seamless Mr. Clean product line. A company our size could never afford this type of investment." What's more, the alliance helped Magla expand overseas. Mr. Clean is known overseas as Mr. Proper in mainland Europe, Don Limpio in Spain (*limpiar* is the Spanish verb for "to clean") and Mastro Lindo ("Master Clean") in Italy. Glatt said, "The Mr. Clean brand provides us with a wonderful opportunity to enter the European market with a leading brand with high awareness and an exceptional reputation."

Pursuing an alliance is an important strategic consideration for growth. Indeed, Glatt initially came up with the idea of using alliances long before the Mr. Clean opportunity presented itself. In the 1990s, Glatt was debating with his top managers about whether to launch a line of work gloves. Magla already made gloves for household chores, so adding a line of work gloves made strategic sense. But Glatt and his team realized that pursuing such an expansion strategy would be risky because Glatt knew that Magla had neither the brand name nor the retail connections to enter the home improvement market. Glatt worried that a big player like Stanley Works (a company known for its hardware and tools) could easily get into the market. Glatt decided to circumvent the potential problems of expansion and potential competition through an alliance with Stanley. He signed a licensing deal for Magla to make and sell work gloves under the Stanley name. In 2005, Glatt continued with his alliance strategy, this time entering into an agreement with the American Red Cross to market a complete line of branded medical gloves. The partnership was the first of its kind for the American Red Cross, with a portion of the proceeds from the sale of each retail package going directly to benefit the organization's relief efforts. The alliance strategy has paid off for Glatt—by 2006, his company's revenues had more than tripled to $100 million. Said Glatt: "Partnerships have turned us into a new company."

For its part, giant P&G is likewise benefiting from its alliances. P&G expanded the Mr. Clean brand even further through alliances with other companies. Its alliance with automotive and chemical supplier Old World Industries yielded a Mr. Clean Premium Windshield Wash. Even better, P&G's strategic alliance with Old World covers other P&G brands beyond Mr. Clean. For example, Old World is producing a specialty automotive version of P&G's Febreze air fresheners and Swiffer dusters that bring these two brands out of the home and into the car. For the Febreze auto line, Old World tailored Febreze into a lightly scented formula made specifically to eliminate odors in car interiors.

Successful alliances have led P&G's Jeff Weedman to coin "Weedman's Corollary": The second deal takes one-half of the time of the first deal. The third deal takes one-third of the time, and so on. And that law appears to have worked well for P&G, Magla, and Stanley. The subsequent deals are not only faster, but they also tend to be more profitable. Weedman's corollary means that P&G looks for ways to extend its alliances with good partners. P&G benefits from sustained collaborations and discovers new value creation opportunities that it previously did not know about. Small businesses can bring the giant company ideas it needs. As Jeff Weedman says, "This isn't a revolutionary idea. It's just smart business." <<<

Strategic Alliances

Why do firms enter alliances? Are most alliances successful? Was the agreement between P&G and Magla typical? How long do typical alliances last? Are alliances really a form of courting prior to the acquisition of one party by another? Or, does one party use the alliance to gain knowledge at the expense of the other party? By the end of this chapter, you should be able to answer these and many other questions about the formation, implementation, and termination of strategic alliances. Like most relationships, alliances have a beginning and an end. As you work through the chapter, you'll see that the opening vignette on P&G and Magla features many of the characteristics of strategic alliances. Alliances often enable participants to share in investments and rewards while reducing the risk and uncertainty that each firm would otherwise face on its own. In addition, shared activities enable each organization to focus its resources on what it does best. Finally, alliances foster economies of scale and scope—both within the partner firms and between partners and the alliance vehicle—that companies wouldn't otherwise be able to achieve, at least not in the same cost-effective manner.

Studies have shown that companies that participate most actively in alliances outperform the least-active firms by 5 to 7 percent.[2] And most alliances average seven years in duration before they are dissolved, or one of the parties to the alliance buys out the other. Some might argue that this 5 to 7 percent performance premium results from the fact that better-run firms are also simply better at initiating and managing alliances. In the early 1990s, for instance, BMW and DaimlerChrysler determined jointly that the minimum efficient economic scale of a small automobile engine facility would be a plant capable of producing 400,000 engines annually. Separately, however, each firm had internal demand for only 200,000 engines per year. The solution? An alliance through which they shared the cost of building a new plant large enough to turn out 400,000 engines. BMW uses the motors in its line of Mini Coopers, and DaimlerChrysler uses them in both its Neon and PT Cruiser lines.

Remember, however, that alliances are not strategies in and of themselves. Rather, as you will recall from the strategy diamond, which represents the five elements of the strategy diamond, an alliance is simply one *vehicle* for realizing a strategy. ◆ In addition, an effective alliance must be consistent with the economic logic of the strategy. The firm must also have the managerial capabilities to create economic value through cooperative arrangements, not simply the actions that are internal to the firm. In this chapter, we'll review the critical features that firms must master if they're going to use alliances effectively and in a manner that's consistent with the economic logic underpinning their overall strategies.

 Vehicles

Exhibit 9.1 The Value Chain

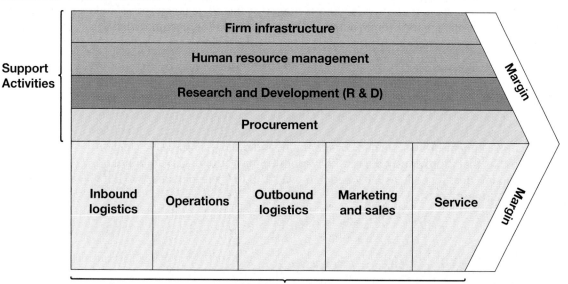

strategic alliance Relationship in which two or more firms combine resources and capabilities in order to enhance the competitive advantage of all parties.

A **strategic alliance** is a partnership in which two or more firms combine resources and capabilities with the goal of creating mutual competitive advantage. An alliance may involve sharing resources related to only one key activity in the partners' value chain, such as R&D. Recall the value chain you studied in Chapter 3 (see Exhibit 9.1 for a generic reproduction of the value chain model).

As shown in Exhibit 9.2, however, an alliance may involve coordination across many value chain activities. For example, the partners may work together to develop new products via shared R&D and also cooperate on the production and marketing of the new products. Indeed, the number and combinations of linkages is practically endless.

Note, too, that an alliance may be strategic to one firm and only tactical or operational to the other. This distinction is typically a function of the relative size of the alliance partners, and the truly unique character of the alliance function. Wal-Mart, for example, has long sought to reduce the number of its suppliers through a variety of so-called *sole-sourcing* and *just-in-time supply agreements*. Both types of agreements mean that a buyer has chosen only one or a few suppliers for its raw materials, and with the just-in-time arrangement, it expects that the supplier will provide the buyer with those materials at the exact point in time that they are needed in the production or sales cycle. In terms of investment in distribution infrastructure, sales volume, and concentration of sales to one buyer, such agreements may be strategic for the supplier but not necessarily to Wal-Mart, which is rarely dependent on any one supplier. In 1994, for instance, when Rubbermaid sought to raise its prices to Wal-Mart, its single largest customer, the giant retailer responded by dropping Rubbermaid products from every one of its stores.[3] Only after Rubbermaid was acquired by Newell in 1999 was it restored to Wal-Mart's good graces.

GROWTH OF ALLIANCES

Given its attractive features—as well as increasing competitive intensity in most industries—it shouldn't be surprising that the use of alliances as a strategy vehicle has grown dramatically in the last few decades. As a percentage of revenues, alliances ballooned from 2 to nearly 16 percent between 1980 through 1995. In particular, as of 2007, it is believed that large multinational corporations will have over 20 percent of their total assets tied up in al-

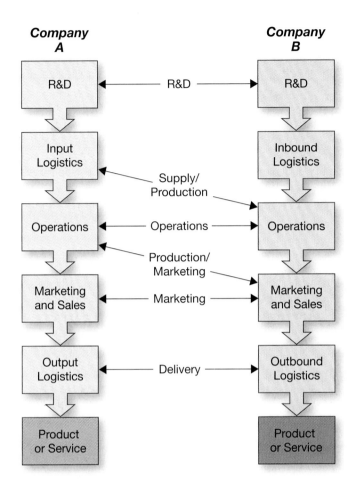

Exhibit 9.2 Possible Points of Value Chain Coordination in an Alliance

liances.[4] If outsourcing arrangements were factored into this calculation, then the percentage of assets related to alliances would surely be much higher. For U.S. firms, alliance partners are largely, and not surprisingly, concentrated in Asia and Europe.

FAILURE RATES

Note, however, that despite their apparent popular use, the failure rate for alliances is about 50 percent (and nearly 70 percent in some cases). An alliance can be deemed a failure when one or more of the partners did not achieve its objectives and, in more dismal cases, when one partner benefited but the other partner was left worse off competitively. Clearly, alliances can be high-risk as well as high-return vehicles for realizing a firm's strategy.[5]

Interestingly, however, such a high failure rate doesn't surprise economists and many other experts. Why? Most economic theories assume that, left to their own devices, individual entities will behave in their own *self-interest*. The success of an alliance, of course, depends on the willingness of partners to subordinate their own interests to those of the alliance, but even when partners start out by suspending self-interest, circumstances can change dramatically over time, compromising even the best of intentions.

In the remaining sections of this chapter, we'll examine the various forms that alliances can take, and we'll show how the objectives underlying them have evolved over time. We'll discuss alliances as strategy vehicles and explain the risks to which they're prone. We'll also focus on the ways in which both the objectives and structures of alliances vary in stable versus dynamic contexts. Finally, because so many alliance failures are due to faulty implementation, we'll conclude by discussing four specific ways to improve the probability of alliance success.

Why Alliances?

Not surprisingly, firms participating in effective alliances can improve their competitive position and gain competitive advantage. Remember that one alternative to an alliance is a purchase contract. However, there are significant limits as to what can and cannot be contracted, particularly in dynamic contexts. Put bluntly, contracts alone are not always sufficient to coordinate and control partners' behaviors. In this section, we review how the use of alliances is related to competitive advantage and how the motivation for using alliances has evolved over time.

ALLIANCES AND COMPETITIVE ADVANTAGE

Alliances can help firms achieve their objectives in several ways. Alliances not only spread the risk of business ventures by sharing that risk with other firms; they also give firms access to knowledge, resources, and capabilities that the firm might otherwise lack. Alliances achieve these potential building blocks of competitive advantage in four ways: *joint investment*, *knowledge sharing*, *complementary resources*, and *effective management*.[6]

Joint Investment   Alliances can help to increase returns by motivating firms to make investments that they'd be unwilling to make outside a formal alliance relationship. This advantage is particularly important in light of the fact that productivity gains are possible when activities linked in the value chain are supported with transaction-specific investments.

In many situations, a supplier won't make an investment pertaining specifically to an exchange with one buyer. Why? Because the investment would tie the supplier too closely to one buyer and expose it to too much risk, the greatest risk being that the buyer reneges on its commitment to buy the supplier's products or services or grinds the supplier down on price due to its dependence on the single buyer.[7] For instance, if you invested $10 million in a piece of equipment that made products that could be sold only by Wal-Mart, you would be very dependent on Wal-Mart because of the asset specificity of such an investment. A buyer, therefore, often integrates backward vertically in the value chain, making the necessary investment to internalize the supply. The supplier's hesitancy, however, can be overcome if the buyer is willing to enter a formal arrangement that reduces the supplier's risk. Both supplier and buyer can benefit not only from gains in efficiency but also from savings in the bureaucratic costs entailed by vertical integration.

Knowledge Sharing   One common reason of entering into alliances is to learn from partners. Learning, however, requires partners to cooperate in transferring knowledge. Although partners may not be equally capable of absorbing knowledge, two factors can help to facilitate the transfer of knowledge: (1) mutual trust and familiarity between partners; and (2) consistent information-sharing routines, such as that obtained through higher-level executive contact, integrated information systems, and employee swapping and cross-company career paths. As an example of the latter, John Deere regularly exchanges key employees with alliance partner Hitachi in certain product segments.

Complementary Resources   In Chapter 3, we saw that a firm's resources and capabilities are the primary sources of competitive advantage. When partners combine resources and capabilities, they may be able to create a stock of resources that's unavailable to other competitors in the industry. If that stock combines complementary resources and capabilities, then the alliance may be able to generate a shared advantage. Finally, if the combination of resources and capabilities is valuable and rare, the alliance may be able to generate greater profits than the sum of the partners' individual profits. Thus, when Nestlé and Coke combined resources to offer canned tea and coffee products, the alliance offered a vehicle that was more attractive than going it alone due to complementarities between the parties.[8]

Effective Management   One way to judge the appropriateness and effectiveness of an alliance is through comparing its costs with the alternatives of an arm's-length transaction or formal internal integration (providing the activity internally or buying a company that can provide the activity). The second way to judge whether an alliance is effective is if it helps build a competitive advantage. This evaluation process is referred to as a *buy or make* decision, with alliances lying somewhere in between the two extremes—this is sometimes called make, buy, or ally.

Look at the principle from the following perspective: A potential problem in any alliance is that one partner may take advantage of another. To minimize this risk, many alliances call for formal protection mechanisms, such as equity investments (which should align incentives) or formal contracts (which should outline expected behavior and remedies for violations). Although such mechanisms are costly, they may still be cheaper than formal integration of activities within one firm. However, some experts argue that the true cost savings of alliances comes to those firms that can rely on less formal managerial control over their partners' behavior and instead depend on self-enforcement and informal agreements. Informal arrangements, of course, require a great deal of trust, which is likely to develop only after multiple dealings between partners.[9] We'll address the subjects of learning and trust more fully in the concluding section of this chapter.

Recall from the VRINE framework that resources and capabilities are the basis of competitive advantage only when they satisfy certain criteria: They must be valuable, rare, difficult to imitate, and supported by organizational arrangements. If an alliance (or network of alliances) is a vehicle that helps the firm's strategy satisfy these criteria, it has probably developed a collaborative advantage that helps one or more of the member firms achieve a competitive advantage over rivals outside the alliance.

ALLIANCE MOTIVATION OVER TIME

Although the overarching motivation behind alliances—the pursuit of competitive advantage—hasn't changed, the ways in which alliances contribute to such advantage have. This is one reason why it is so critical for you to understand strategic management from a dynamic perspective. In the late 1980s, in an effort to better understand why alliances were becoming increasingly common, the consulting firm Booz-Allen began studying the alliance practices of 1,000 U.S. firms. Among other things, the study revealed dramatic changes in the motivations that impelled firms to enter alliances over the course of several decades.[10] Note, these drivers represent *cumulative* needs.

As shown in Exhibit 9.3, alliances formed during the 1970s emphasized product and service performance.[11] The alliance strategy of Corning Glass Works (now called Corning) exemplifies this focus. Its alliance with Dow (Dow-Corning) allowed Corning to leverage its advanced glass-making capabilities in new products and new markets, and creating scale and scope economies, both at home and abroad. In the 1980s, firms tended to stress the building and reinforcing of market position. Microsoft and Intel, for example, joined to informally establish the Wintel alliance. Microsoft's Windows family of operating systems functioned best on PCs with Intel's chips, and as long as Microsoft kept increasing processing-speed requirements, Intel could count on consistent product demand. In some ways, P&G's alliance with Magla is a position alliance, since P&G can leverage Magla's strengths in gloves with its own brands to enter new markets or reinforce existing market positions.

Exhibit 9.3 Cumulative Motivation of Alliances Over Time

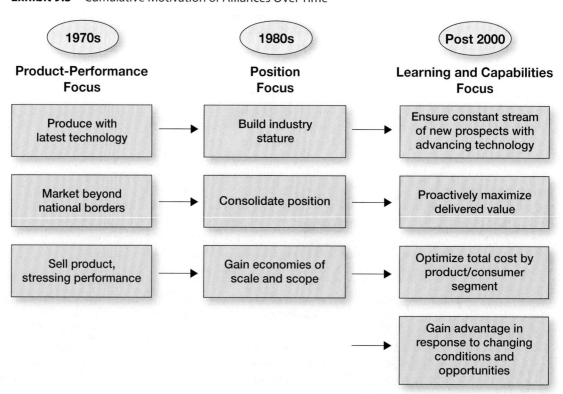

More recently, corporations have begun to emphasize more complex benefits, such as organizational learning and the development and accumulation of valuable resources and capabilities. In this vein, we can look at the case of the bicycle distributor Pacific Cycle. Recall that Pacific is sort of the Nike of bikes—it designs and distributes its bikes, but outsources production entirely to overseas factories in China. While Pacific does have its own design team in the United States, it relies heavily on its suppliers for new product ideas. In fact, these suppliers have the capability of rapidly building prototypes of new bikes that Pacific can then quickly test market in its major venues. As a reward for such innovativeness, Pacific will often grant the production contract for the new bike to the factory that invented it. Thus, Pacific and its suppliers have a shared gain in any successful products that are brought to market.

Form and Structure of Alliances

Note that we've been using the term *strategic alliances* as a catchall term. In reality, cooperative arrangements can take a number of forms. Exhibit 9.4 summarizes the vast continuum of forms that cooperative arrangements, including strategic alliances, may take. As you can see, the two primary dimensions on which alliances can be categorized are the nature of the *time commitment* (e.g., timeframe and resources) and respective *investment commitment* of the alliance and inputs into the alliance (ranging from cash to people to technology).

Whether or not a particular alliance is deemed as strategic will depend on the degree to which one or both parties' survival or competitive advantage depends on the alliance. For instance, a contract to supply coffee to a company's offices might be important, but there is no shared equity involved (no cross investment), and the relationship can probably be easily replaced by another provider. However, a contractual relationship between an enterprise software provider like SAP and its client, while perhaps not strategic for SAP, is mission critical for SAP's customer because such software is likely to be the lifeblood of their operations.

Exhibit 9.4 Degrees of Alliance Intensity

Time ↑	No Linkages Beyond Transaction	Information Sharing	Asset, Resource, and Capability Sharing	Cross-Equity (partners take ownership in one party or each other)	Shared Equity
Long-term				*Keiretsu* in Japan or *chaebols* in South Korea	Caltrex, which was jointly owned by Chevron and Texaco prior to their merger
	Outsourcing	Many technology standards consortia	Examples include technology collaborations such as the PowerPC chip between Motorola, IBM, and Apple	Anheuser-Busch's cross-ownership with Kirin in Japan and Modelo in Mexico	Standalone joint ventures such as Dow-Corning
	Purchase agreements that are renewable annually or every several years	Agreements to distribute products or services	Cross-licensing such as that between Disney and Pixar or R&D partnerships as between Millennium Pharmaceuticals and some of its smaller partners		
Transactional	Simple purchase order for commodities, sometimes called a spot transaction	Short-term agreements on functions such as advertising or manufacturing to achieve efficiencies—for example, contract brewing of Miller Beer by Anheuser-Busch			

Nonequity Alliances — Equity Alliances

Level of Commitment ↑ — Time Commitment — Financial Commitment →

JOINT VENTURES AND OTHER EQUITY ALLIANCES

The form of an alliance depends on such factors as legal structure and the number and objectives of participants. In a **joint venture**, for instance, two companies make equity investments in the creation of a third, which exists as an independent legal entity. This is the case with Dow-Corning, which, as the name suggests, is a joint venture between Dow and Corning; if mapped to Exhibit 9.3, it would fall under the shared-equity category. Many joint ventures are 50/50 splits in ownership and control, but they need not be equal partnerships. As you can probably imagine, each partner typically wants 51% ownership, so that they have technical control over the alliance. In reality, partners usually identify the specific aspects of the alliance that they are most interested in, so the respective ownership question becomes less of a stumbling block.

It isn't necessary, however, for an alliance to create a separate legal entity or share equal ownership. In many cases, **equity alliances** involve unequal partners. This may be the case when one partner owns a greater percentage of the alliance's equity than another partner; when a separate legal entity is not established, and one partner instead takes partial ownership of the other partner; or when contracts are used to govern the sharing and respective rights regarding contributed assets, resources, or capabilities. Millennium Pharmaceuticals, for example, prefers arrangements in which larger partners take a percentage ownership not only in Millennium itself, but also a minority-percentage interest in any alliance with a separate legal structure. (It also manages several strategic alliances with traditional 50/50 splits.[12])

joint venture Alliance in which two firms make equity investments in a third legal entity.

equity alliance Alliance in which one or more partners assumes a greater ownership interest in either the alliance or another partner.

Dow Corning Corporation, the Michigan-based silicon-products maker, is a joint venture between Dow and Corning, as its name suggests. In joint ventures, partners often invest on an equal basis and split corporate ownership and control down the middle.

NONEQUITY ALLIANCES

The most common form of strategic alliance involves neither equity interest nor separate organizations. Arrangements such as *sole-sourcing, just-in-time supply agreements, licensing, cobranding,* and *franchising* often fall under the heading of *nonequity alliances.* The coffee company example provided earlier fits this category.

nonequity alliance Alliance that involves neither the assumption of equity interest nor the creation of separate organizations.

Nonequity alliances are typically contracts that call for one firm to supply, produce, market, or distribute another's goods or services over an extended period of time, but without substantial ownership investments in the alliance. Starbucks, for instance, has extended the presence of its brand into a number of customer-contact locations through alliances with such companies as Barnes & Noble (bookstore cafés), United Airlines (in-flight coffee service), Dreyer's (coffee ice cream), Pepsi (Frappuccino ready-to-drink coffee), and Kraft (ground and whole coffee beans distributed through grocery stores). The various strategic roles that these nonequity alliances play for Starbucks are shown in Exhibit 9.5.[13]

MULTIPARTY ALLIANCES

consortia Association of several companies and/or governments for some definite strategic purpose.

Thus far, we've described alliances involving two partners. Other types of alliances, such as **consortia,** usually involve many participants, perhaps even governments. The primary contribution to these cooperative arrangements is information, though there may be some cost sharing as well. Perhaps the most complex multifirm alliances are those in the technology arena. SEMATECH, for example, is a consortium of semiconductor manufacturers established in the mid-1980s to prop up the U.S. semiconductor industry, which at the time was considered to be of strategic importance to national defense. To some extent, SEMATECH's cooperative structure was modeled after joint projects by which Japanese semiconductor producers were responsible for advancing their collective technological competencies in the late 1970s.[14] The consortium has since evolved to include both U.S. and non–U.S. firms, and a related venture called SEMI/SEMATECH (or SEMI) is an alliance of suppliers to the semiconductor industry.[15]

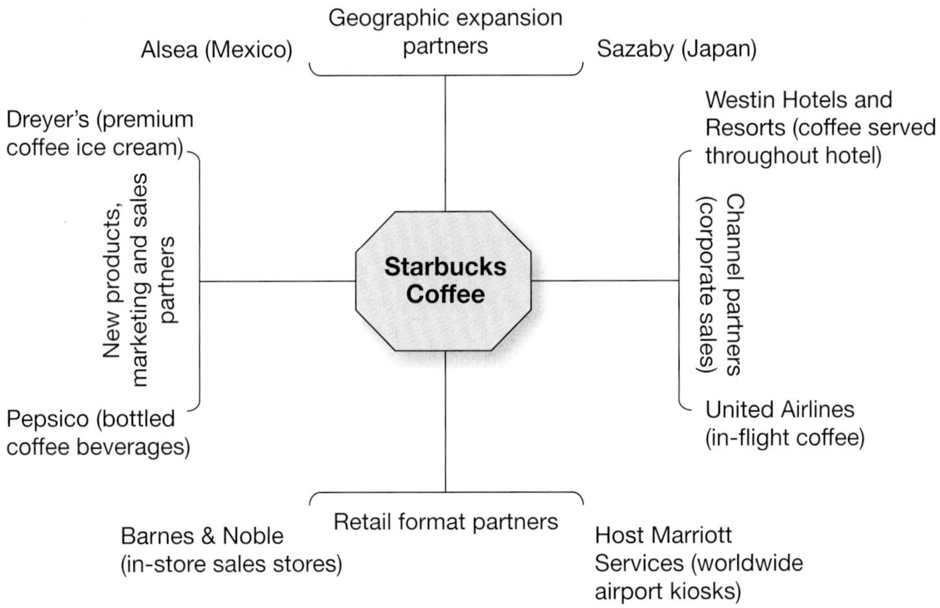

Exhibit 9.5 Starbuck's Universe of Alliances

Alliances as Strategy Vehicles

You probably are beginning to realize this, but almost any organization is a potential alliance partner, and deciding with whom to partner is a matter of a firm's business and corporate strategies. The challenge is to, first, determine if you are going to use alliances as a strategy vehicle and then, second, begin to identify potential partners.

ALLIANCES AND BUSINESS STRATEGY

Let's start by considering factors related to business strategy—strategy that determines how a firm competes in a chosen industry. A quick review of the five-forces model and related complementors of industry structure that we introduced in Chapter 4 reinforces the number and variety of a firm's potential partners. Who might these allies be?

■ **Rivals.** Are there opportunities to partner with rivals? Although there are certainly legal prohibitions against cooperative arrangements among competitors that harm consumers, rivals will often engage in strategic alliances. The various airline alliances, such as One World and Star, are a case in point. Sometimes a company may partner with a competitor to manage surplus production demand or to help it manage excess capacity. Beer companies collaborate in production and distribution for instance—if a truck can deliver two breweries' products to the same market then both companies benefit from the cost sharing. Similarly, breweries often contract with competitors to brew their beer when their demand outstrips capacity. This has been one of the secrets of success for Sam Adams. Sam Adams creates the beer recipes but then has the beer produced by Anheuser-Busch, Miller Beer, and others.

■ **New entrants.** Industry incumbents can ally with new entrants to diversify or to co-opt a future potential rival. Wal-Mart's alliance with the Mexican retailer Cifra is a good example of this. If you know a new competitor has an interest in your market, one firm can take the initiative to work together with the other, usually with the end-game strategy of merging the two entities.

■ **Suppliers.** Increasingly, firms are developing alliances with key suppliers. These can take on the form of sole-sourcing and just-in-time arrangements or include more complex forms, such as Tritec, in which the supplier is formed by two rivals. This alliance approach can take several forms. For instance, SC Johnson sells many of its products in Wal-Mart. However, since SC Johnson is so good at merchandising its products, Wal-Mart has designated SC Johnson as the category manager for several lines of products. What this means is that SC Johnson is responsible for stocking its own goods on Wal-Mart's shelves, but also for coordinating and merchandising all the other producers' products in, say, the category of household cleansers. As a result, SC Johnson is in a much stronger position, and can improve its merchandising skills, and Wal-Mart benefits by having the best in the business managing this part of its in-store merchandising.

■ **Customers.** The customer-incumbent relationship is the flip side of the incumbent-supplier relationship. This is most often seen in business-to-business relationships. For instance, when Copeland Corporation developed a new line of air conditioning units, it partnered with its customers to provide that part, while the end-user like Trane or Rheem manufactured the rest of the air conditioning unit. This situation is very analogous to the Intel inside story. Intel makes the chips, but its alliances with Apple and Dell and others ensures that they are the leading edge processor in those machines.

■ **Substitutes.** These products and services pose a threat to the incumbent. Through an alliance, this threat can actually be exploited. For instance, soy milk is a clear substitute for dairy milk. Instead of actively competing against the growing market for soy milk, Dean Foods established a joint venture with, and then acquired, industry leader Silk. You can see how you can employ this same logic with any substitute. If there is an opportunity to collaborate, and offer consumers broader choices, then perhaps both parties will gain through the alliance.

■ **Complementors.** Recall that complements are those products or services that, when bundled together, create greater value than when acquired separately. An alliance between an industry incumbent and a complement can lock out competitors. As a case in point, most major fast-food chains provide Coke or Pepsi products, not both. We elaborate further on this aspect of managing alliance strategy below.

The Value Net Model and Co-opetition One way to think about all of the players identified in the industry structure model in a manner that highlight possible alliance possibilities is to rearrange the players into the **value net model**. You were introduced to this model in Chapter 6, and it is reproduced for you here in Exhibit 9.6.[16] Notice that in this model we place the firm of interest in the center and link it to all possible exchange partners. In allowing them to identify opportunities for cooperative relationships among all possible exchange partners and even competitors, the value net model helps managers find alternatives to conventional win-lose business scenarios.

How might a firm establish a cooperative relationship with a competitor? Consider a firm like Motorola, which may in some business situations be a competitor to Intel, such as in the sale of microprocessors. In other situations, it may be in a partnership with Intel, such as in the development of a new technology. Still in other situations, Motorola might be a customer of Intel, sourcing key components for a particular product.

Co-opetition The term **co-opetition** refers to a situation in which firms are both competitors and cooperative partners. The purpose of co-opetition is to find ways of increasing the total value created by parties in the value net, not just determining how to compete for

value net model Map of a firm's existing and potential exchange relationships.

co-opetition Situation in which firms are simultaneously competitors in one market and collaborators in another.

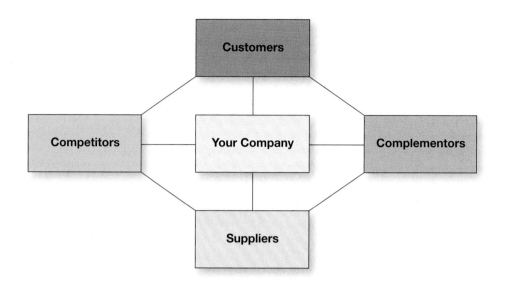

Exhibit 9.6 The Value Net

industry profits. The value net helps managers find potential partners; in other words, it helps them to identify those parties that are possible complementors rather than just competitors. In the following two sections we illustrate how the value net can be applied to various types of alliances.

Alliances can figure into most aspects of business strategy, but they generally provide a means of managing competitive pressures, uncertainty, or both. Business-strategy alliances tend to fall into two major categories: *vertical alliances* or *horizontal alliances*.

Vertical Alliances   A **vertical alliance** is formed when a firm partners with one or more of its suppliers or customers (typically, the latter only occurs in business-to-business relationships). This is exactly the type of alliance we referred to in the section about supplier and customer alliances earlier. The purpose of a vertical alliance is to leverage partners' resources and capabilities in order to meet two goals: (1) to create more value for the end customer and (2) to lower total production costs along the value chain. In a sense, the vertical alliance is an alternative for vertical integration, the *corporate* strategy whereby a firm takes ownership of downstream supply or upstream distribution or other marketing functions.

Jeffrey H. Dyer, a prominent strategy professor who specializes in the study of strategic alliances, has found that vertical alliances can create lean value chains by reducing total supply-chain costs in four areas: transaction, quality, product-development, and logistics costs:[17]

- *Transaction costs* are often lower among alliance partners than among firms in third-party arm's-length transactions.

- Because quality is often improved, *quality-related costs*—those associated with defects, returns, and warranty work—go down.

- When partners share knowledge and human capital and focus their efforts on improving product design and quality, vertical alliances can control *product-development costs.*

- Reduced warehousing and transportation costs not only reduce inbound *logistics costs* but result in lower inventory costs as well.

vertical alliance   Alliance involving a focal firm and a supplier or customer.

Exhibit 9.7 An Example of Co-opetition

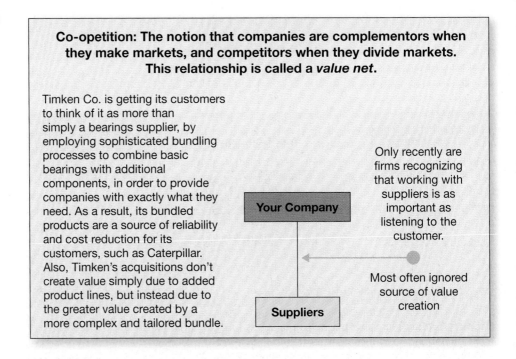

Co-opetition: The notion that companies are complementors when they make markets, and competitors when they divide markets. This relationship is called a *value net*.

Timken Co. is getting its customers to think of it as more than simply a bearings supplier, by employing sophisticated bundling processes to combine basic bearings with additional components, in order to provide companies with exactly what they need. As a result, its bundled products are a source of reliability and cost reduction for its customers, such as Caterpillar. Also, Timken's acquisitions don't create value simply due to added product lines, but instead due to the greater value created by a more complex and tailored bundle.

Your Company

Suppliers

Only recently are firms recognizing that working with suppliers is as important as listening to the customer.

Most often ignored source of value creation

Vertical alliances also improve value to the customer by making it possible for alliance partners to increase speed to market, improve quality, introduce newer technologies and features, and respond more quickly to market changes. Exhibit 9.7 shows how Timken applies the net value to vertical integration alliances by bundling its product offerings.

horizontal alliance Alliance involving a focal firm and another firm in the same industry.

Horizontal Alliances Horizontal alliances are partnerships between firms in the same industry. These types of alliances enable competitors, or potential competitors, to gain a presence in multiple segments of an industry. As a component of a firm's value net, a horizontal alliance, which gives a company access to multiple segments of an industry, can create value in a number of ways. First, it can reduce risk. For instance, when two oil exploration firms enter into a joint venture, they spread the risk entailed by the costs of drilling. Likewise, Kraft's alliance with Starbucks gives it a super-premium coffee brand that it can distribute through the grocery channel to complement not only its Maxwell House and Yuban brands in the same channel but also its Gevalia brand in the direct-marketing and business-to-business channels. Mondavi's various alliances with top wine producers in Chile, Italy, Argentina, and France give it access to a broader range of high-quality wines than it could support if it had to rely solely on its own resources.

Horizontal alliances can also help partners achieve greater efficiency. Thus, when McDonald's and Disney cooperate in promotions, each leverages its advertising expenditures. In addition, although Disney benefits from McDonald's promotion of Disney characters and programming, McDonald's benefits from the popular appeal of Disney characters, which appear as toys in products aimed at kids.

Finally, horizontal alliances foster learning in the development and innovation of new products. SEMATECH and the Automotive and Composites Consortium (launched by GM, Ford, and Chrysler) are good examples of learning alliances. In the case of SEMATECH, for instance, all U.S.–based semiconductor manufacturers pooled their knowledge to improve the production process and were collectively able to turn the competitive tide against the rising dominance of Japanese firms. The Apple–Sony partnership that developed the PowerBook is a good example of firms using horizontal alliances to access complementary skills. Finally, horizontal alliances can help firms overcome political obstacles. In China, for example, the Otis Elevator–Tianjin joint venture enabled Otis to enter an attractive and growing market that at the time was inaccessible without a local partner.

Let's return for a moment to the concept of co-opetition, which is based on the principle that firms must often cooperate and compete simultaneously. Because horizontal alliances make allies of competitors, it's crucial that all parties understand the conditions that favor success in such ventures. First, they're potentially beneficial when partners' strategic goals converge and competitive goals diverge. When, for instance, Philips and DuPont collaborated to make compact discs (CDs), neither firm was invading the other's markets for other products. In addition, horizontal alliances are more likely to succeed when the partners are chasing industry leaders, as when Asian semiconductor-chip makers collaborated in making memory chips in an effort to cut into Intel's market share. Finally, in successful horizontal alliances, all partners acknowledge the fact that, though each must be willing to share knowledge, each can and must protect proprietary skills. For example, the Fuji Photo–Xerox alliance, established in 1962, allows the two makers of copiers and printers to collaborate in the Japanese and Pacific Rim markets. In return for access to these markets, Fuji is entitled to a 75-percent share in the joint profits. Fuji agreed to the arrangement because it believed that it could protect its film business in these markets; Xerox, meanwhile, believed that the venture would not endanger its copier business elsewhere in the world.

CORPORATE AND INTERNATIONAL STRATEGIC ALLIANCES

Although alliances are typical business strategy vehicles, they can also be vehicles for corporate and international strategy. In the first case, the alliance facilitates product or service diversification within an existing market, while in the second case the alliance facilitates entry and competition in another geographic market. ◆

Arenas

Alliances and Corporate Strategy
As we saw in Chapter 7, corporate strategy is largely concerned with two activities:

- Determining the right mix of businesses in the corporate portfolio

- Ensuring that this mix creates shareholder value

Let's consider each of these activities in terms of decisions about alliances. As for portfolio mix, alliances are vehicles for exploring and implementing diversification options. Through its office-copier business, for instance, a company like Xerox may have developed a set of technologies that may provide access into the intensely competitive desktop-copier and computer-printer businesses. In an alliance with a strong partner like Fuji Photo of Japan, it can share the risk and development costs related to an uncertain diversification move. Similarly, through its alliance with Magla, P&G diversified into household gloves and Magla diversified into branded consumer products.

Corporations can also use alliances to create value across a portfolio of individual businesses. At first glance, for example, you might think of venture capitalists (VCs) and their various investments as independent entities. They do, however, represent strategic alliances. How so? Whereas the VC provides capital and managerial expertise, the entrepreneurial firm provides an opportunity for new products. From a corporate-strategy perspective, the VC firm can create more value for its investments by identifying key individuals in one firm who could help create value for its other units. The VC firm Softbank, for example, leverages its investments in broadband-application and broadband-provider companies by circulating its best and brightest managers and technologists among its wholly owned companies as well as those in which it has investments.[18] Likewise, a diversified firm can also broker relationships among its portfolio businesses.

Alliances and International Strategy   Finally, as shown in the example of the international partnership between Dell Computer and the Asian distributors in the opening vignette in Chapter 8, a firm's international strategy should issue from its business- and corporate-strategy objectives. Many of the alliances that we've described in this chapter are international in nature: either they involve partners from different countries or the alliance itself is headquartered in a country different from those of the partners. Cross-border alliances differ from domestic alliances in that governments, public policies, and national cultures often play significant roles. Also important, of course, are differences in workplace regulations and socioeconomic conditions.

In some cases, a firm can only do business in another country through an alliance. For instance, a U.S. firm that wishes to do business in Saudi Arabia can only do so if it has a partner with a local firm. In fact, the partner has to be a member of the Saudi Royal family. Alliances are not just a vehicle used by U.S. firms. Many Chinese companies are buying U.S. and European high-technology firms, and then partnering with Indian companies for the customer service component. Similarly, Indian firms are buying large manufacturing firms in Latin America, the United States, and Europe, and then through alliances outsourcing production to more efficient facilities in China.

Not surprisingly, in international contexts, decisions about internal and external vehicles through which to execute a firm's strategy are much more complex than in domestic contexts. Multinational corporations, for instance, may be better than alliances in facilitating the flow of knowledge across borders. Analysis of patent citations by semiconductor companies suggests that multinationals are better than both alliances and market forces in fostering cross-border knowledge transfer, primarily because they can use multiple mechanisms for transferring knowledge and are more flexible in moving, integrating, and developing technical knowledge.[19]

ALLIANCE NETWORKS

Related to the study of the strategic functions of alliances is the concept that alliances are taking on characteristics of networks. Network theory has two implications for organizational practice. First, as alliances become a larger component of a firm's strategy, the strategy discussion will shift from particular alliances as a vehicle to networks of alliances as a vehicle. In this sense, the firm is operating as a hub, or node, in a complex array of owned, partially owned, and nonowned businesses. Looking back at the value net portrayed in Exhibit 9.6, you can imagine how multiple alliances among complementors, competitors, suppliers, and customers might easily come to resemble a web of complex network relationships.

Second, as networks themselves take on the characteristics of organizations, competition among networks should arise both within and across industries. Exhibit 9.8 lists several alliance networks formed in the past, some of which have been dissolved or restructured as the nature of the partners' relationships or the competitive environment has evolved. The clearest current example of network competition can probably be found in the airline industry, where three alliances—Star, One World, and Sky Team—are battling for air passengers. [20]

Perhaps more dramatic still are the alliance networks that are battling over emerging technological standards. As you can see in Exhibit 9.9, Sun, HP, IBM, and MIPS, are all plac-

Business or Industry	Selective Rival Constellations
Hardware and Software for Interactive TV	▶ Motorola, Scientific Atlanta, Kaleida ▶ Time Warner, Silicon Graphics ▶ Intel, Microsoft, General Instruments ▶ H.P., TV Answer
Video CDs	▶ Sony and Philips ▶ Toshiba, Time Warner, Matsushita, others
Global Telecommunications	▶ AT&T Worldpartners (includes 12 partners) ▶ British Telecom and MCI ▶ Sprint, Deutsche Telekom, France Telecom
Automobiles and Trucks	▶ G.M., Toyota, Isuzu, Suzuki, Volvo ▶ Ford, Mazda, Kia, Nissan, Fiat, VW ▶ Chrysler, Mitsubishi, Daimler-Benz
Biotechnology Research	▶ Genentech network ▶ Centocor network
Pharmaceutical Marketing (United States)	▶ Merck and Medco (merger) ▶ SmithKline and DPS (merger) ▶ Eli Lilly and PCS (merger) ▶ Pfizer and Value Health ▶ Pfizer, Rhône-Poulenc, Caremark, others
Global Airline Services	▶ Delta, Swissair, Singapore Airlines, SAS ▶ KLM and Northwest ▶ British Airways and USAir
Global Comercial Real Estate Services	▶ Colliers International (44 companies) ▶ International Commercial (23 companies) ▶ Oncore International (36 companies) ▶ New America Network (150 companies) ▶ Cushman & Wakefield (52 alliances) ▶ CB Commercial (70 affiliates) ▶ Grubb & Ellis (six affiliates)

Exhibit 9.8 Different Alliance Networks

ing bets on certain technological standards, and they have a vast array of partners helping them to battle their respective parts of the fray.[21]

Importantly, the fortunes of the many small firms in the network are dependent upon the success of the larger group. Just as beta and VHS battled it out, with VHS being the eventual winner, so too will this battle have its winners and losers. What is clear, however, is that the loser is typically not a single firm, but instead many of the smaller players aligned with the network core. If one of these battles is lost, it means less to SUN, HP, IBM, or MIPS, but it can make or break the fortunes of a much smaller firm.

Finally, there is another variation of alliance networks where a focal firm sets itself out as the hub of an enormous wheel of alliance relationships. The most dramatic example of the new organization form is P&G, and it has dubbed this aspect of its strategy as "Connect +

Exhibit 9.9 Alliance Networks of Sun, HP, IBM, and MIPS

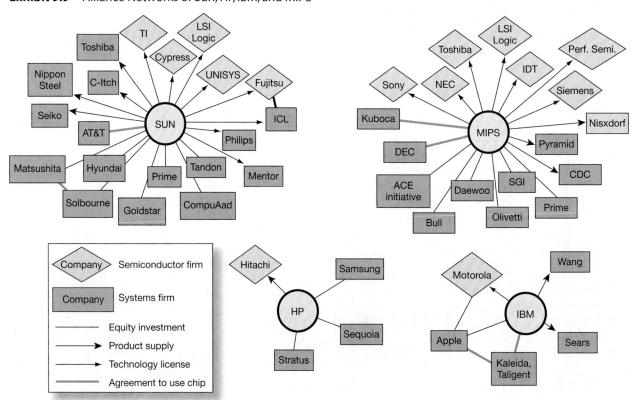

Develop," instead of the traditional notion of research and development. Exhibit 9.10 summarizes P&G's view, and in particular, how it comes from the CEO himself.

P&G even maintains a Connect + Develop (C+D) website that invites new potential partners. While P&G is no slacker when it comes to investment in new products—2006 R&D spending amounted to about $2 billion across 150 science areas—by the company's own calculations, its C&D activities with just its top 15 suppliers provides it access to more than 10,000 new products, and an estimated combined R&D staff of 50,000! P&G's goal is to have over 50 percent of its new products originated through the C&D process by 2010.

RISKS ARISING FROM ALLIANCES

As we mentioned in the introduction to this chapter, one of the potential benefits of an alliance is the reduction of risk or uncertainty borne by any one party. With that said, however, we must point out that cooperative ventures can be risky. There are six potential alliance risks:

■ **Poor Contract Development** This problem is relatively self-explanatory. Typically, the hardest part of drawing up good alliance contracts is negotiating rights, particularly those pertaining to termination prior to the intended maturity date.

■ **Misrepresentation of Resources and Capabilities** This issue arises when a partner *misrepresents*, intentionally or unintentionally, the quality or quantity of a resource or capability—say, a crucial technology or the availability of staff with particular skill sets— that its partners deem critical to the success of the venture.

Exhibit 9.10   Welcome to P&G's Connect + Develop Website

Connecting with the world's most inspired minds. Developing products that improve consumers' lives.

We've collaborated with outside partners for generations—but the importance of these alliances to P&G has never been greater.

Our vision is simple. We want P&G to be known as the company that collaborates—inside and out—better than any other company in the world.

I want us to be the absolute best at spotting, developing and leveraging relationships with best-in-class partners in every part of our business. In fact, I want P&G to be a magnet for the best-in-class. The company you most want to work with because you know a partnership with P&G will be more rewarding than any other option available to you.

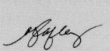

A. G. Lafley

Chairman of the Board,

President and Chief Executive

The Procter & Gamble Company

Source: The Procter & Gamble Company http://pg.t2h.yet2.com/t2h/page/homepage

■ **Misappropriation of Resources and Capabilities** *Misappropriation* occurs when one partner takes something of value, whether to the partner itself, to the alliance, or to both. Sometimes misappropriation is so endemic that would-be partners garner reputations for misappropriation. China, for example, has a notoriously poor reputation when it comes to protecting intellectual and trademark property rights.

■ **Failure to Make Complementary Resources Available** Related to the risk of misappropriation is the risk that a partner may fail to make available a promised complementary resource, such as a valuable technology or the people with the skills needed to implement or design new products or processes.

- **Being Held Hostage Through Specific Investments** Sometimes, even when such resources are made available, the firm that needs them may become so dependent on the alliance that it's virtually held hostage. Resources can range from a proprietary technology that the partnership controls or simply a production capability controlled by one of the partners. Trek Bicycles, for example, outsources much of its production to an Asian manufacturer called Giant. The alliance allows Trek to focus on the design, marketing, and distribution of high-quality bikes. In turn, Giant enjoys economies of scale in production. Giant, however, is also a competitor of Trek and, given Trek's dependence on Giant's production capabilities, Giant could conceivably raise its prices to Trek in order to gain price advantage over Trek in the latter's primary markets. Or consider the arrangement by which Rayovac (Spectrum) licenses its core battery technology from Matsushita, on whom it was dependent for a key technology.

- **Misunderstanding a Partner's Strategic Intent** The Trek and Rayovac examples provide a jumping off point for exploring another alliance risk. Both Trek and Rayovac are not only dependent on their partners for a critical resource, but they're much smaller than their partners and much weaker financially. It would be relatively easy for Giant to exploit and weaken Trek—perhaps eventually buy it out for relatively little investment. Likewise, Matsushita could raise licensing fees for its battery technology or even suspend Rayovac's access to it altogether. In addition, although Matsushita sells consumer electronics products (under the Panasonic label), its share of the U.S. battery market is quite small. Conceivably, one way of increasing it would be to weaken Rayovac, undermining its U.S. competitor to the point at which it would become an easy acquisition target. In each case, then, it's crucial for the vulnerable partner to have a strong sense of whether its larger partner is interested in a co-opetition strategy or a winner-take-all strategy.

Alliances in Stable and Dynamic Contexts

Another factor in determining whether an alliance is a suitable strategic vehicle is the level of stability or dynamism of a firm's competitive context. Relative dynamism of an industry context may affect an alliance decision in two ways:

- From a practical standpoint, relatively stable environments are much more forgiving of mistakes, such as poor choices in partners or alliance structures.

- Because they make maintenance and management easier, stable environments allow firms to participate in more alliances. Likewise, although wasted time, effort, and resources are undesirable in any situation, relatively stable contexts provide firms with the luxury of learning from their mistakes and regrouping.

Consider, for example, an alliance between Nestlé and Mars that allows Nestlé to put Mars-brand M&Ms in its ice creams. The success or failure of this alliance is not going to make or break either company. As we'll soon see, however, in dynamic contexts, competitive stakes are typically much higher, and any distraction of a firm's resources or managerial time and attention can have serious consequences. Particularly when dynamism is coupled with technological intensity. If, for instance, Millennium Pharmaceuticals chooses an unsuitable partner, it will lose time and money, and it also risks the possibility that while it's busy trying to manage the alliance, a competitor will make some advance in product or technology that gives it a significant advantage. Such risks place tremendous pressure on firms not only to choose the

Nestlé and Mars share an alliance whereby Nestlé is allowed to put Mars' M&Ms in its ice creams. Because the companies compete in a relatively stable competitive environment, however, the success or failure of the alliance isn't likely to make or break either firm.

right partners (and the right number of partners), but to structure alliances so that they contribute to the development and enhanced value of its resources and capabilities.

RELATIVE STABILITY AND ALLIANCE MOTIVATION

Relative environmental stability of a firm's external context also affects the objectives that partners set for an alliance. In many ways, relative stability has played a role in the evolution of alliance motivation that we discussed previously. In relatively stable environments, for example, partners are typically seeking access to production technologies or markets. Their objective is essentially to consolidate market positions and generate economies of scope and scale.[22] These objectives also motivate firms in dynamic contexts, but under such conditions, firms are also motivated to use alliances as means of identifying new market threats and opportunities and of providing dynamic capabilities with which to respond to changes (and perhaps even to drive changes) in the competitive landscape.

RELATIVE STABILITY AND THE COEVOLUTION MODEL OF CORPORATE STRATEGY

Focusing on relative stability will also help us to better understand the coevolution model of corporate strategy that we outlined in Chapter 7. Recall that *coevolution* means orchestrating a web of shifting linkages among evolving businesses. In making alliances, a firm opts to develop vertical, horizontal, or complementary linkages with other firms instead of seeking them solely among wholly owned businesses. The use of alliances in such a web enables a firm to develop its specific dynamic capabilities in concert with the best resources and capabilities available. Just as important, alliances sustain a specific focused strategy. Periodically, for instance, certain alliances can be abandoned and others added. Thus, if a firm is pursuing, say, a growth strategy, the coevolution approach suggests that it drop alliances developed around commoditized products and add those with partners who are active on the technology frontier or in other forward-looking strategies for enhancing competitive advantage.[23]

What Makes an Alliance Successful?

Given the prevalence of alliances as a critical and valuable strategy vehicle, it is imperative for managers to understand the ingredients that make them successful, as well as the factors that can derail them. Professor Ben Gomes-Casseres, one of the world's leading experts in alliances, identifies ten features that separate successful alliances from unsuccessful ones. These are summarized in Exhibit 9.11.[24]

But how do you put these features into place? Strategy research has considered the ten features identified in Exhibit 9.11, and distilled out of them five particular areas where organizations can increase the probability of alliance success. As you will see in the final section of this chapter, some of these areas are related to relationships between the partners, while others relate to the experience and supporting structures put into place in a focal firm. These five areas are:

■ Understanding the determinants of trust

■ Being able to manage knowledge and learning

■ Understanding alliance evolution

■ Knowing how to measure alliance performance

■ Creating a dedicated alliance function

The first four apply readily to firms of all sizes, both domestic and international. The last usually pertains to larger firms and those that otherwise use alliances as a key vehicle for strategy execution. Understanding what's involved in all five areas puts managers in a better position to design alliances that will contribute to a firm's competitive advantage.

Exhibit 9.11 Features of Successful Alliances

1. The alliance has a clear strategic purpose—alliances are never an end in or of themselves, they provide tools to achieve a business strategy
2. Good partner fit—a partner with compatible goals and complementary capabilities
3. Specialized partner roles—allocate tasks and responsibilities in the alliances in a way that enables each party to do what they do best
4. Create incentives for cooperation—working together never happens automatically, particularly when partners were former rivals
5. Minimize conflicts between partners—the scope of alliance and of partners' roles should avoid pitting one against the other in the market
6. Share information—continual communication develops trust and keeps joint projects on target
7. Exchange personnel—regardless of the form of the alliance, personal contact and site visits are essential for maintaining communication and trust
8. Operate with long time-horizons—mutual forbearance in solving short-run conflicts is enhanced by the expectation of long-term gains
9. Develop multiple joint projects—successful cooperation on one project can help partners weather the storm in less successful joint projects
10. Be flexible—alliances are open-ended and dynamic relationships that need to evolve in pace with their environment and in pursuit of new opportunities

UNDERSTANDING THE DETERMINANTS OF TRUST

It may be stating the obvious to say that alliances perform better when partners trust each other. Research suggests that a network of trustworthy partners can itself be a competitive advantage, as can be a reputation for trustworthiness.[25] Unfortunately, because not all partners are equally trustworthy, parties in alliances often must rely on a variety of mechanisms to safeguard their interests. Formal mechanisms, such as long-term contracts, stock ownership, and collateral bonds, can signal credible long-term commitments to alliance partners. They do not, however, ensure information sharing, which is critical to alliance success. Partners foster interorganizational trust by using understandable and predictable processes. Informal mechanisms, such as firm reputation and personal trust among managers and officers, are also keys to creating long-term value.

Mutual trust generates several benefits. It results in conditions that increase the value of the alliance and, therefore, the probability that it will contribute to competitive advantage.[26] As you might expect, trust leads to a greater willingness to make investments in assets customized to the alliance. When such partnership-specific investments raise the potential for hold-up, they're also more likely to yield the economies of scope and scale that make such partnerships pay off economically. The investment in Tritec by BMW and DaimlerChrysler is a good example, because both firms invested considerable time and dollars in the plant and it is delivering some of the most dependable and efficiently produced four-cylinder car engines in the industry.

Besides increasing learning by encouraging investment in mechanisms that promote greater information sharing, trust reduces the costs of monitoring and maintaining an alliance. Savings can result from such simple gestures as foregoing new legal agreements for small changes in the arrangement or from such critical decisions as an agreement to rely on a simple management structure rather than a more complicated structure requiring a board of directors.

Relational Quality

Because trust is so important to alliance performance, firms need to focus on the areas that affect it most. One approach to identifying these areas is called **relational quality**, which identifies four key elements in establishing and maintaining interorganizational trust.[27] You'll probably find one or more of these elements to be intuitively obvious, but research suggests that organizations don't do a good or consistent job of paying attention to them.

> **relational quality** Principle identifying four key elements (initial conditions, negotiation process, reciprocal experiences, outside behavior) in establishing and maintaining interorganizational trust.

Initial Conditions The first element refers to the mutual attitudes of the parties before negotiations begin. Attitudes may be based on prior experiences or on reputation. Sometimes they reflect a larger set of political and economic circumstances. As we noted earlier, for example, China's reputation for condoning property-rights abuses would probably make a prospective partner wary of allying with a Chinese firm.

The Negotiation Process Prior experience with the process can influence the attitudes that any party brings to the negotiating table. Initial conditions provide a foundation for the development and upgrading of resources and capabilities, but the social interactions that characterize the negotiations process will determine whether any promise in the negotiations is eventually realized. Your own relationships provide a relevant example here. When you meet someone, for instance, you may feel positive about that person due to his or her behaviors or prior reputation. However, your interaction with that person after the initial meeting will determine whether a friendship and otherwise productive relationship develops.

Reciprocal Experiences   Once some level of interorganizational trust is established, stock and flow reflect the partners' reciprocal experiences. Do they, for instance, share information openly, disclose potential problems, or behave in other ways that add to the stock of existing interorganizational trust?

Outside Behavior   Trust is also a function of the reputation the organization develops as a consequence of its interactions with other organizations outside of the alliance. When Wal-Mart dropped Rubbermaid as a supplier, other suppliers undoubtedly became concerned about the degree to which the retailer could be trusted as a partner.

MANAGING KNOWLEDGE AND LEARNING

For many firms, learning from alliance partners is one of the primary objectives of entering an alliance. In addition to reflecting trust, the ability of a partner to learn increases the collective benefits derived by every partner in the alliance. However, wanting to learn, though obviously important, isn't enough to make learning take place.[28] Learning is enhanced if a firm develops specific processes for managing knowledge exchange. Some explicit activities enable firms to learn from alliances.

Learning and Supplier Support at Toyota

Toyota is one of the most successful firms at managing learning through alliance networks and provides a helpful example of knowledge management best practices. Research by Jeffrey H. Dyer highlights Toyota's success in managing its alliances so that knowledge and productivity gains accrue to all alliance members.[29] In studying Toyota's U.S. alliance networks, Dyer found that Toyota's U.S. suppliers were able to achieve efficiency gains in manufacturing that suppliers for GM and Ford couldn't match. In fact, Toyota's suppliers outperformed the other automakers' suppliers despite the disadvantage of being newer and at an earlier stage of the learning curve. Performance *improvements* far outpaced those of other suppliers, and *absolute* performance rapidly surpassed that of suppliers to American firms. Dyer suggests that these efficiency gains resulted from concentrated efforts to ensure that learning flowed both ways and that suppliers learned from each other, not just from Toyota. The strategy depends on the carmaker's Toyota Supplier Support Center (TSSC), which has twenty consultants working with U.S. suppliers.

Let's look at the process a little more closely. Toyota divides its suppliers into groups of six to twelve, with direct competitors assigned to separate groups. To keep interactions fresh, group composition changes every three years. Each group meets with Toyota consultants to decide on a theme for the year, such as styling, demographic fit, supplier relations, and so on. Representatives from each group visit each supplier's plant over a four-month period, examining operations and offering suggestions for improvement. Finally, Toyota hosts an annual meeting at which each group reports on the results of the year's learning activities.

The results have been impressive—an average improvement of 124 percent in labor productivity and inventory reductions of 75 percent. The lesson is quite clear: Alliances result in significant productivity gains when learning is facilitated by coordinated efforts to exchange knowledge and disseminate best practices within the network. Note, too, that such a high level of learning is made possible by an overarching commitment to mutual trust.

UNDERSTANDING ALLIANCE EVOLUTION

At the outset of this chapter, we asked whether you thought the outcome of Magla's alliance with P&G was a common one. You may not be surprised to learn that what starts out as an alliance may eventually become an acquisition.[30] In fact, one study found that nearly 80 percent of equity joint ventures end in the sale of one partner to another.[31] The researchers suggested that managers who don't look out for this twist in the road may run head-on into an unplanned divestiture or acquisition. Although some alliances are actually structured to terminate in the eventual transfer of ownership, most are not, and unplanned sales may erode shareholder value.

Of course, a sale that's well managed and planned in advance can be to a firm's advantage. The same study indicated that alliances can advance a firm's long-term strategy by providing companies with a low-cost, low-risk means of previewing possible acquisitions.

At the same time, it should come as no surprise that relationships between partners may change over time. Indeed, if one partner is aggressively pursuing a coevolution strategy that involves alliances, these changes should be monitored closely and included in the ongoing strategy of both the alliance and its partners. The box entitled Exhibit 9.12 provides a good example of well-managed coevolution through the Fuji-Xerox alliance.[32]

MEASURING ALLIANCE PERFORMANCE

Ironically, one reason for the high failure rate of alliances is the fact that few firms have effective systems for monitoring alliance performance.[33] In the short term, a lack of monitoring systems means that managers who are responsible for the alliance must rely more on intuition than on good information. The long-term consequences are even more serious: When problems do surface, it's much more expensive to fix them. Moreover, performance may have declined so drastically that one or more of the partners starts looking for ways to exit the alliance—an event that often starts a downward spiral toward more performance problems and eventual termination.

Although it may, therefore, seem eminently logical for firms to put monitoring systems in place, there are at least three barriers to getting it done:

■ Partner firms often have different information and reporting systems. DaimlerChrysler and BMW, for instance, have quite different quality, production, and financial reporting systems. The systems at their alliance firm, Tritec, differ from those of both partners. The two carmakers have recently decided that, despite the expense in time and money, Tritec will "translate" its performance data into information that can be accessed through both DaimlerChrysler's and BMW's systems.

■ Even when firms go to great lengths to gauge performance, the inputs that the alliance receives from its corporate parents can be difficult to track and account for. For example, say a manager from DaimlerChrysler joins a Tritec team and that team develops a novel new manufacturing approach. Very often it is difficult to determine whether it was the specific team member or the larger team that came up with the new idea.

■ Similarly, it's also difficult to put a precise value on alliance outputs. What price or value, for example, would you attach to the alliance-based knowledge that a partner uses to improve operations in other parts of the organization?

DEDICATED ALLIANCE FUNCTION

Recent research indicates that cooperative strategies are more likely to succeed when a firm has a dedicated alliance function.[34] A dedicated alliance function may simply be one manager who is responsible for setting up, tracking, and dissolving the firm's alliances; however, typically this function is managed by a group of individuals working together as a team. In many ways, such a function is a structural solution to the need to manage trust, learning, evolution, and performance in a systematic fashion. Although some firms can't afford this added management function, the benefits make it worth looking for a way to fill this role. A

Exhibit 9.12
Coevolution in the
Fuji-Xerox Alliance

Some of the best examples of coevolution reinforce the important roles played by time and investments. Take the case of Fuji-Xerox, which provides some insight into the resources and capabilities acquired through alliances. This alliance between Fuji Photo and Xerox also provided fertile ground for the successful turnaround of Xerox itself by Anne Mulcahy, which you read about in the opening vignette to Chapter 2.

The Fuji-Xerox alliance had been in place for several years, but it was not until early 1970 that it began to bear fruit as a source of competitive capabilities and knowledge for both the alliance and the partners. Xerox was in dire financial straits at the time, having positioned its products against then high-powered rivals such as Eastman Kodak and IBM but being undermined at the same time by low-cost Japanese manufacturers. The first transition was the transfer of Fuji Photo's manufacturing plants in 1970 to the Fuji-Xerox alliance and the resulting development of low-cost manufacturing capabilities by the venture. Following the development of these capabilities, from 1976 to 1978, Xerox initiated R&D and technology-reimbursement agreements between itself and Fuji-Xerox. This transfer agreement fostered the design and fabrication of copy machines for distribution in Europe and the United States.

Over the next decade, Fuji-Xerox continued to upgrade its resources and capabilities in low-end copiers and printers, and Xerox aggressively absorbed these advantages as they grew in importance in the global marketplace. For instance, following an agreement to allow Fuji-Xerox control over its own R&D, Fuji-Xerox began to internalize Japanese total-quality-control manufacturing processes. Xerox, in turn, adopted these processes, and at the same time used the Fuji-Xerox alliance as a platform to expand its own products' presence in Japan.

Ironically, the success and rapid growth for the Fuji-Xerox alliance was a function of the autonomy granted to it by its parents. By 1991, those parents established a new alliance, Xerox International Partners, to market the Fuji-Xerox printer mechanism outside of Japan to companies such as Hewlett-Packard, which were largely captive to the industry leader, Canon. At the same time, this same mechanism satisfied the majority of Xerox and Rank Xerox (another alliance) low-end copier sales. Although the alliances were largely autonomous, top executives at Xerox and Fuji-Xerox were careful to hold top-executive "summits" twice a year, exchange key personnel, and fund joint research programs to avoid redundant and wasteful R&D efforts.

It was on this platform of global success that Anne Mulcahy made a case for the acquisition of the color-printer division of Tektronix by Xerox in 2000. These color-printer capabilities were shared, not surprisingly, with Fuji-Xerox, which flourishes to this day, with Xerox owning 25 percent and Fuji Photo owning 75 percent. As for Xerox? Well, you know much of the rest of that story from the vignette in Chapter 2.

firm might, for example, assign a chief alliance officer, whose responsibilities are outlined in Exhibit 9.13.[35]

The first two roles in the components of a dedicated-alliance-function process are often the most critical. Regardless of the levels of trust, learning, and capabilities that an alliance boasts, it won't be productive under either of the two following situations:

- When there isn't a strong business case for the alliance as a vehicle

- When assessment fails and there simply isn't a good fit between partners

Exhibit 9.13 A Dedicated Alliance Function

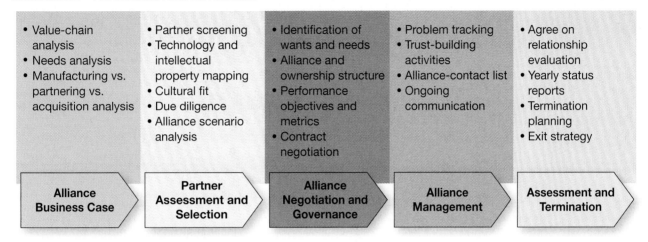

Good intentions alone do not make alliances work. Nothing can replace a good strategy that spells out the role of alliances in a firm's strategy and partner fit.

WHEN DO PARTNERS FIT?

The issue of fit isn't easy to resolve, and to do so, firms must be able to answer yes to the following questions:

- *Strategic fit:* Are the partners' objectives compatible? For how long?

- *Resource and financial fit:* Are the partners willing and able to contribute the resources and competencies?

- *Cultural fit:* Can the partners understand each other? Do they share the same business logic and commitment?

- *Structure, systems, and processes fit:* Can the decision-making and control mechanisms be aligned?

- *Additional fit criteria:* What other key questions should be on the table, such as timing, other alliances, alliance alternatives, environmental context, and competitive pressures?

Because we're interested in alliances as a strategy vehicle, the first question pertains to *strategic fit.* Researchers at the consulting firm of McKinsey and Company have identified lack of strategic fit as a common starting point for those alliances that eventually failed.[36] In many ways, the opening vignette on Magla provides an example of an alliance where strategic fit was good because Magla needed better access to the mass-market channels and capital than it could attain on its own. Sometimes, alliances between weaker and stronger firms even lead the weaker firm to a position of strength, in which case the alliance is usually dissolved, or in other cases in which the stronger partner acquires the weaker one. Partnerships among complementary equals tend to be the strongest and longest lasting. In some cases, competitive tensions and industry conditions may lead one partner to acquire the other, usually after about seven years. In other cases, the partners remain strong and independent. Some alliances, such as Fuji-Xerox, exemplify true co-evolution and are most likely to survive for much longer than seven years. In the case of Fuji-Xerox, the alliance has lasted several decades and has spawned additional complementary alliances.

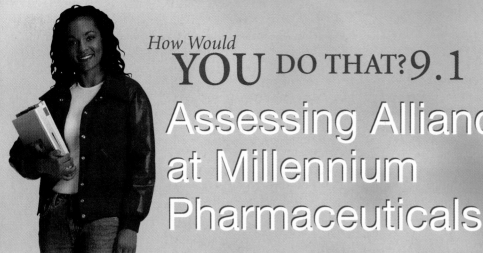

How Would YOU DO THAT? 9.1

Assessing Alliance Fit at Millennium Pharmaceuticals

Evaluating alliance opportunities is not simple, but you do have the advantage of a framework that helps you start the process. The first step is to develop a grid, shown in Exhibit 9.14 that lays out how well the potential partner fits with your firm.

Note that you should always include alternative potential partners, since you may be more likely to enter a bad deal when you have nothing to compare it to. This may sound silly, but many CEOs say that some of the most important alliance or acquisition decisions they have made, are the decisions not to do them! In this example, Millennium Pharmaceuticals was faced with a huge alliance opportunity with German firm Lundberg—it involved lots of cash and a savvy global partner with a great deal of experience. Why, then, would Millennium turn such a deal down? Using the following alliance-fit framework, and setting up Abbott Labs as the comparison alliance, Millennium decided that it was best to pass on the Lundberg alliance (though it turns out that the Abbott alliance was in the works):

- *Strategic fit?* In general, the strategic fit was good. However, Millennium had recently put together a very similar large alliance with Monsanto, and it was not clear how another deal would move Millennium's strategy forward.
- *Resource fit?* Other than money, the Lundberg did not bring much to the table in terms of new resources and capabilities. In fact, Millennium would

be putting most of its unique capabilities to work, which in turn could stretch its technical and research staff with no benefit other than additional cash in the bank. At the time, Millennium was strong financially.

- *Cultural fit?* The potential partner was a large, private agribusiness firm, whereas Millennium was a relatively small, public biotech firm. In initial meetings, there was some indication with the potential partner that top management was keen on an alliance but that lower-level managers were out of the loop. Cultural misfit often arises when line managers are not involved in the alliance-building process from the very start.
- *Structural fit?* This, too, was a big question mark. Millennium's management had the impression that the partner would not grant it the autonomy or flexibility that it desired in its alliances. Thus, the structure appeared too rigid from Millennium's perspective.
- *Other questions?* Because Millennium was still contemplating other options and partnerships, it was not as if this was the only opportunity in the market. Finally, the top-management team determined that it was not excited about the alliance beyond the fact that the partner had a great reputation and brought lots of cash to the relationship.

So, you are probably asking what happened to Millennium after it passed up such a lucrative deal. Shortly thereafter, Millennium and Abbott formed a five-year alliance primarily for collaborative research and development in the area of metabolic diseases. The companies agreed to share equally the cost of developing, manufacturing, and marketing products on a worldwide basis. The arrangement with Abbott also includes an equity investment by Abbott in Millennium, amounting in total to $250 million over several years, and a technology exchange and development agreement. Moreover, Millennium and Aventis expanded their existing joint development pipeline to include an aggregate of eleven additional discovery projects that were previously pursued outside the joint collaboration by Millennium or Aventis. These new assets included chemokine receptors, kinases, and integrins, which are important as potential drug-development target classes in inflammatory disease research. As a result of this expansion, that alliance yielded approximately fifty jointly funded discovery projects. Soon, Millennium had created more than twenty alliances with leading pharmaceutical and biotechnology companies—close to $2 billion of committed funding. You can learn more about why Millennium sees such a network of alliances as a central vehicle in its strategy—to eventually become a full-fledged pharmaceutical firm—through its R&D page at www.millennium.com.

Exhibit 9.14 Comparing Alliance Opportunities

	Partner A—Lundberg	Partner B—Abbott Labs
Strategic Fit?	Good, but no new learning opportunities	Good and ample learning and growth opportunities
Resource Fit?	Cash resources, but cash is generic	Cash and technology resources, and technology is unique
Cultural Fit?	Likely to be poor	Good
Structural Fit?	Unknown	Good
Other Key Questions? • Capital market demands—who drives strategy here? • Timing—are capital markets hot or cold? • Timing—do we need another deal like this? • Timing—how plentiful and attractive are other alliance options? • Does "no" here mean no more options? • Again, other criteria? • What other key questions should be on the table?	Management was not excited about the deal	Management was excited about the deal—high level of motivation

The second question concerns *resource and financial fit.* This question deals with either the availability of a resource or the willingness and ability of a partner to make that resource available. Questions of *cultural fit* typically relate to the cultural characteristics of the organizations themselves. In the early years of SEMATECH, for instance, Intel's participation was problematic because Intel's highly competitive culture clashed with the cooperative culture being fostered by the consortium.[37] Though *structural fit* can be a simple matter of making financial reporting systems compatible, conflicts may arise over arrangements of authority and decision making.

Finally, in determining fit, a company should take situation-specific factors into consideration. Is the firm, for example, already involved in too many alliances? Is the timing right? Do competitive conditions currently favor alliances as a strategy vehicle? The box entitled "How Would *You* Do That? 9.1" shows what happened when Millennium Pharmaceuticals applied a checklist for assessing partner fit in determining whether to enter into an alliance with a potential partner. The answer, as you can see, was no.

Dyer's research shows that it's difficult to develop the rich alliance capabilities that will satisfy a checklist like Millennium's. At the same time, however, Dyer notes that firms that succeed in developing the requisite capabilities may be better competitors as a result. Not only may such capabilities contribute to near-term performance and competitive position, but they may also enhance the reputation of a company as a preferred partner. Wal-Mart, for example, though known as a very aggressive competitor, has established a solid reputation in Latin America as a dependable partner. As noted earlier, Wal-Mart is now leveraging these alliance skills and the reputation built through local partnerships to fuel its growth in China and Japan.

Summary of Challenges

1. *Explain why strategic alliances are important strategy vehicles.* Alliances enable participants to share in investments and rewards, while reducing the risk and uncertainty that each firm must bear on its own. Such sharing also enables firms to focus their efforts on what they do best, while benefiting from the similarly focused efforts of their partner firms. In economic terms, alliances may lead to higher firm performance by enabling firms to realize economies of scope and scale that would otherwise not be realized if they had to operate on their own.

2. *Describe the motivations behind alliances and show how they've changed over time.* Although firms seek economies of scope and scale from alliances, their ultimate objective is that the alliance contributes to their competitive advantage. The VRINE framework can be applied to alliances. If the alliance creates something of value, has benefits that are both rare and difficult to imitate (including less costly imitation by a simple market purchase agreement or wholly owned business), and the partners are able to extract value from the alliance (i.e., the resources and

capabilities in the alliance are supported by features of the organization), then a firm can reap competitive advantages. Over time, the basis for alliance advantage has shifted from simple efficiencies and economies of scope and scale to a vehicle for organizational learning and innovation.

3. *Identify the various forms and structures of strategic alliances.* Alliances can take many forms. A joint venture is the most complex form because it results in the establishment of a third, independent entity. Joint ventures, in which partners contribute cash and other resources to the partnership, fall into the broader category of equity alliances. Nonequity alliances are the most common form of alliance. These typically take the form of contracts to supply, produce, market, or distribute a firm's goods or services. Sole-sourcing, just-in-time supply agreements, licensing, and cobranding are examples of nonequity alliances. Equity and nonequity alliances may involve many participants. Such alliances are sometimes called *industry associations, cooperatives,* or *consortia.*

4. *Compare and contrast alliances as business- and corporate-level strategy vehicles.* The five-forces model and value net are good tools for both identifying potential partners and reaffirming that just about any firm related to the business can be considered a potential partner. Business strategy alliances fall into two categories: vertical and horizontal. Vertical alliances link a focal firm to downstream raw materials and other critical inputs; upstream they link that same firm to marketing, arenas, and other channels of distribution. Horizontal alliances enable firms in one segment of the industry to partner with firms in other segments. Strategic alliances are also a useful vehicle for a firm's corporate and international strategies. Cross-border alliances differ from domestic-only alliances in that government, public policies, and national culture often play a more visible role. Alliances can also take on the characteristic of a network when clusters of companies compete against each other for customers or new technology standards. Finally, cutting across all these alliances are six risks that contribute to their failure or lackluster performance. These risks range from poor contract development to the misinterpretation of a partner's strategic intent.

5. *Understand the characteristics of alliances in stable and dynamic competitive contexts.* Just as strategies may vary according to context, so, too, should the expectations and design features of alliances as a strategy vehicle. Stable contexts afford firms the luxury of managing many alliances. Although the choice of alliance partners is always important, any one alliance failure is unlikely to break the company. However, in dynamic contexts the stakes are much higher. Such heightened stakes can take the simple form of greater dollar investments in new technological platforms but typically are manifest in a rapidly evolv-

ing environment where being in the wrong partnership today could mean the ultimate demise of the firm later. The use and design of alliances in dynamic contexts fits well with the coevolution model introduced in Chapter 7. That is, alliances are included in the firm's orchestration of a web of shifting linkages among evolving businesses.

6. *Summarize the criteria for successful alliances.* Five interrelated criteria for effective alliance implementation were emphasized in this chapter. First, firms must understand the determinants and benefits of trust. Alliances that are based on trust benefit from lower transaction costs, greater economies of scope and scale, and greater learning and knowledge management. Second, firms must be good at managing knowledge and knowledge flows. This means that they should establish learning objectives for each alliance and mechanisms for realizing them. The third criterion is the need to understand alliance evolution. Alliances may follow different pathways depending on their initial conditions and partner relations, and an understanding of both the role of initial conditions and the potential pathways will inform the establishment of an alliance and its management once it is in place. Linking the alliance to a performance management system is the fourth criterion. Such tracking will help to ensure both near-term benefits and the avoidance of problems that may fester for lack of attention. Finally, firms should consider the establishment of some systematic and coherent structural response to the unique and complex management challenges that alliances give rise to. This structure can take the form of an individual with the title of chief alliance officer or, where appropriate and financially feasible, the establishment of a dedicated alliance function.

Review Questions

1. What is a strategic alliance?

2. Do most strategic alliances succeed?

3. What forms can strategic alliances take?

4. What is the difference between an equity and a nonequity strategic alliance?

5. Provide an example of a nonequity strategic alliance.

6. Why do firms enter into alliances?

7. What are the three forms of strategic alliance that support business strategy?

8. What do the value net and industry structure models tell you about potential alliance partners?

9. How do alliances serve as a vehicle for corporate strategy?

10. What risks do alliances pose to partner firms?

11. How do alliances differ in stable and dynamic contexts?

12. What are the five critical criteria for successful alliances (hint: don't confuse these with the ten observations made about alliances in Exhibit 9.11)?

Experiential Activities

Group Exercises

1. Increasingly, firms such as P&G, Corning (www.corning.com) and Millennium Pharmaceuticals (www.millennium.com) claim to have a core competency and competitive advantage based on their ability to manage alliances. Develop statements that both defend and critique this proposition. Identify risks that firms run when their strategy is essentially a network of alliances.

2. Identify a firm and document its alliance activity over the past five to ten years (visit the Web site of a public firm, particularly the "history" page). Examine the list of officers at the company (these are always detailed in the annual report and often on the firm's Web site). Do they appear to have a dedicated alliance function? What kinds of changes would they have to make if they were to follow the recommendations on implementation levers necessary to achieve an effective dedicated alliance function? What would be the costs and benefits of such a change?

Ethical Debates

1. One of the biggest barriers for firms entering into alliances with foreign partners, and even domestic ones, are issues of trust. Does a well-crafted legal agreement prevent breaches of ethics by either party to the agreement?

2. You have seen many reports in the press about Adidas or Nike and how the working conditions of the foreign partners and suppliers are sometimes abysmal. Is this just a cost of doing business through foreign alliances or can firms do something to manage these situations?

How Would YOU DO THAT?

1. The box entitled "How Would *You* Do That? 9.1" shows how Millennium Pharmaceuticals evaluated a potential alliance partner. Apply the Millennium fit framework to the alliances of another firm you are familiar with. Do these appear to be good alliances? Do any of the alliances suggest that your focal firm is on a pathway to acquire its partner or be acquired by it?

Go on to see How Would You Do That at www.prenhall.com/carpenter&sanders

Endnotes

1. "Growth: Hand In Glove," *Business Week*, Fall 2006, (accessed August 15, 2007), at http://www.businessweek.com/magazine/content/06_38/b4001838.htm; D. G. Thomson, *Blueprint to a Billion: 7 Essentials to Achieve Exponential Growth* (New York: Wiley, 2005); "Mr. Clean Expands Licensing Program Internationally," *PR Newswire*, January 10, 2002; "Magla Plans to Sell Household Gloves Under Procter & Gamble Mr. Clean Brand Name," *Business Wire*, January 16, 2000; *Magla Company Story* (accessed on April 25, 2007) at http://www.magla.com/geninfo/Type.cfm?Type=About&Level=General&Width=1878; "Magla Signs Licensing Agreement to Sell Disposable Exam Gloves Under the American Red Cross Brand Name," Press Release, February 23, 2006, accessed June 21, 2007; "Inspirational Consumers," *Brand Strategy*, July 12, 2005, p. 24; "Driving with Mr. Clean." *Grocery Headquarters*, January 2006, p. 96; "P&G Keeps Expanding Its Far-flung Empire," *Household & Personal Products Industry*, January 2007, p. 100; H. Chesbrough and K. Schwartz, "Innovating Business Models with Co-Development Partnerships," *Research-Technology Management*, January–February 2007, p. 55(5).

2. J. Harbison and P. Pekar, *Smart Alliances: A Practical Guide to Repeatable Success* (San Francisco: Jossey-Bass, 1998).

3. C. Wolf, "Rubbermaid Struggles to Put Lid on Problems: Company's Earnings Tumble after Price Increase Backfires," *Cincinnati Enquirer*, April 8, 1996, D1.

4. J. Cook, T. Halevy, and B. Hastie, "Alliances in Consumer Packaged Goods," *McKinsey on Finance*, Autumn 2003, 16–20.

5. J. Bleeke and D. Ernst, *Collaborating to Compete* (New York: John Wiley & Sons, 1993); D. Ernst and T. Halevy, "When to Think Alliance," *McKinsey Quarterly* 4 (2000), 46–55.

6. J. H. Dyer and H. Singh, "The Relational View: Cooperative Strategies and Sources of Interorganizational Competitive Advantage," *Academy of Management Review* 23 (1998), 660–679.

7. O. E. Williamson, *The Economic Institutions of Capitalism* (New York: Free Press, 1985).

8. G. Hamel and C. K. Prahalad, *Competing for the Future* (Boston: Harvard Business School Press, 1994).

9. J. B. Barney and M. H. Hansen, "Trustworthiness as a Source of Competitive Advantage," *Strategic Management Journal* 15 (1995), 175–190; Dyer and Singh, "The Relational View."

10. Harbison and Pekar, *Smart Alliances.*

11. Adapted from J. Harbison and P. Pekar, *Smart Alliances: A Practical Guide to Repeatable Success* (San Francisco: Jossey-Bass, 1998).

12. www.mlnm.com/media/strategy/index.asp (accessed July 15, 2005).

13. Adapted from J. D. Bamford, B. Gomes-Casseres, and M. S. Robinson, *Mastering Alliance Strategy: A Comprehensive Guide to Design, Management, and Organization* (San Francisco: John Wiley & Sons, 2003), p. 22.

14. For detailed discussions of the Japanese projects, see K. Flamm, *Mismanaged Trade? Strategic Policy and the Semiconductor Industry* (Washington, D.C.: Brookings Institution, 1996), 39–126; J. Sigurdson, *Industry and State Partnership in Japan: The Very Large Scale Integrated Circuits (VLSI) Project* (Lund, Sweden: Research Policy Institute, 1986). For a dissenting assessment, see M. Fransman, *The Market and Beyond: Cooperation and Competition in Information Technology Development in the Japanese System* (Cambridge: Cambridge University Press, 1992).

15. Semiconductor Equipment and Materials International, About Us (accessed June 6, 2005), at http://wps2a.semi.org/wps/portal/_pagr/103/_pa.103/259.

16. Adapted from A. Brandendburger and B. Nalebuff, *Co-Opetition* (New York: Doubleday, 1996).

17. J. H. Dyer, *Collaborative Advantage: Winning through Extended Enterprise Supplier Networks* (New York: Oxford University Press, 2000).

18. www.softbank.co.jp (accessed August 12, 2005).

19. P. Almeida, J. Song, and R. M. Grant, "Are Firms Superior to Alliances and Markets? An Empirical Test of Cross-Border Knowledge Building," *Organization Science* 14 (2002), 157–171.

20. Adapted from B. Gomes-Casseres, "Competing in Constellations: The Case of Fuji-Xerox," *Strategy and Business* First Quarter (1997), 4–16; www.fujixerox.co.jp/eng/company/history (accessed July 15, 2005) and the Xerox Fact Book (2005–2006), at www.xerox.com (accessed November 8, 2005).

21. Adapted from B. Gomes-Casseres, "Alliance Strategies of Small Firms," *Small Business Economics* 9 (1997), 33–44.

22. Harbison and Pekar, *Smart Alliances;* E. Bailey and W. Shan, "Sustainable Competitive Advantage Through Alliances," in E. Bowman and B. Kogut, eds., *Redesigning the Firm* (New York: Oxford University Press, 1995).

23. S. Brown and K. Eisenhardt, *Competing on the Edge* (Boston: Harvard Business School Press, 1997).

24. Adapted from B. Gomes-Casseres, "Critical Eye," www.criticaleye.net, June–August, 2004. See http://www.alliancestrategy.com/, for more alliance resources.

25. Barney and Hansen, "Trustworthiness as a Source of Competitive Advantage."

26. Dyer, *Collaborative Advantage.*

27. A. Arino, J. de la Torre, P. S. Ring, "Relational Quality: Managing Trust in Corporate Alliances," *California Management Review* 44:1 (2001), 109–134.

28. G. Probst, "Practical Knowledge Management: A Model That Works," *Prism* (Arthur D. Little Consultants), Second Quarter (1998), 17–29.

29. Information in this section is drawn from J. H. Dyer, *Collaborative Advantage.*

30. J. Bleeke and D. Ernst, *Collaborating to Compete* (New York: Wiley, 1993).

31. Bleeke and Ernst, *Collaborating to Compete.*

32. Adapted from B. Gomes-Casseres, "Competing in Constellations: The Case of Fuji-Xerox," *Strategy and Business* First Quarter (1997), 4–16; www.fujixerox.co.jp/eng/company/history (accessed July 15, 2005) and the Xerox Fact Book (2005– 2006), at www.xerox.com (accessed November 8, 2005).

33. J. H. Dyer, P. Kale, and H. Singh, "How to Make Strategic Alliances Work," *Sloan Management Review* 42 (2001), 121–136. According to the authors, 51 percent of the alliances surveyed had no performance monitoring systems, and only 11 percent believed that they had good systems in place.

34. Dyer, Kale, and Singh, "How to Make Strategic Alliances Work."

35. Adapted from J. H. Dyer, P. Kale, and H. Singh, "How to Make Strategic Alliances Work," *Sloan Management Review* 42:4 (2001), 121–136.

36. J. Bleeke and D. Ernst, "Is Your Strategic Alliance Really a Sale?" *Harvard Business Review* 73:1 (1995), 97–102.

37. L. D. Browning, J. M. Beyer, and J. C. Shetler, "Building Cooperation in a Competitive Industry: SEMATECH," *Academy of Management Journal* 38:1 (1995), 113–151.

10 Studying Mergers and Acquisitions

In This Chapter We Challenge You To >>>

1. Explain the motivations behind acquisitions and show how they've changed over time.

2. Explain why mergers and acquisitions are important to strategy.

3. Identify the various types of acquisitions.

4. Understand how the pricing of acquisitions affects the realization of synergies.

5. Outline the alternative ways to integrate acquisitions and explain the implementation process.

6. Discuss the characteristics of acquisitions in different industry contexts.

eBay + Paypal + Skype
How to Acquire Customers

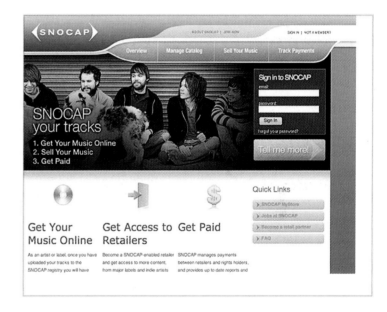

*S*trategy is important at every firm, but Meg Whitman, CEO of eBay, says that on the Internet "the landscape changes quarterly," which elevates strategy to a mission-critical task.[1] eBay, as most people know, is an Internet-based auction and marketplace site on which some 233 million registered customers buy and sell tens of thousands of products ranging from Beanie Babies to used cars. The company generates revenues through advertising and by charging listing and selling fees. For the 2007 year, eBay expected revenues between $7.2 billion and $7.45 billion.

eBay has grown fast, and acquisitions are part of Whitman's toolkit. Some acquisitions, like the purchase of Butterfields (a 140-year-old auctioneer of high-end merchandise) didn't work well and Butterfields was sold off three years later. Others, like eBay's purchase of PayPal in 2002, were greeted skeptically but have paid off. Whitman said she thought the PayPal acquisition was "one of the all-time great acquisitions, even though at the time people about had a heart attack that we paid $1.5 billion for PayPal. I mean, I got creamed in the press.' The woman is crazy. I cannot believe she paid $1.5 billion dollars for this, you know, stupid little company.'"

Indeed, PayPal didn't come cheap. The sale entailed a 100-percent stock transaction, and the price—about $1.5 billion—represented a 20-percent premium over PayPal's stock value prior to the announced acquisition. Thus, eBay paid a premium of about $250 million, and on the day that the sale was announced the market discounted eBay's stock price by 7 percent. After successfully negotiating and closing this transaction, Whitman was left with the reality of trying to make it work. She either had to identify significant cost savings or find new revenue-enhancement opportunities (i.e., synergies) in order to recoup the capital that was necessary to snag PayPal. Whitman's approach was to look for synergies. "The magic is, what opportunities do various combinations of our two assets open up?" As Whitman sees it, "eBay and PayPal was one of the most remarkable combinations because they made each business stronger on their own, and then created a whole new opportunity called merchant services." Most payment companies faced the problem that they couldn't get enough buyers to use the payment system and therefore couldn't get merchants to accept the payment form. But eBay provided PayPal with ready-made droves of customers. "PayPal became the *de facto* payment standard on the biggest locus of small business in the world, and as a result was able to extend off that market place," Whitman said. At the end of March 2007, PayPal had 143 million total accounts. Those accounts helped drive record TPV (total payment volume) of $11.36 billion the first three months of 2007 alone.

Let's take a closer look at the synergies between PayPal and eBay: PayPal's network builds on the existing financial infrastructure of bank accounts and credit cards to create a global payment system. Its revenue comes from the float in the personal accounts and fees charged for Premier and Business Accounts. Float can mean many things in finance, but in this case it refers to the fact that eBay has buyers' money, via PayPal, for a period of time and can invest those monies for profit between the time it receives the money and the time it pays it out to sellers. eBay management viewed PayPal's strategy as complementary to its own. Both business models, shown in Exhibit 10.1, for example, relied on transaction-based revenue sources. Neither required inventory or warehousing of merchandise, and neither maintained any sales force to speak of. Finally, both strategies called for high operating leverage and low capital requirements.

Just because there are synergies between two companies, however, doesn't mean that executing the acquisition plan is easy. For example, when eBay first bought PayPal, eBay executives debated whether to rename the company something like "eBay Payments" rather than PayPal. "In fact," Whitman admitted, "for a while on the website, it was called 'eBay Payments.' We were a little confused." Ultimately, however, the team decided that if PayPal was to grow as a system used by merchants beyond the eBay space, it had to retain its own brand identity. "We decided that eBay stands for e-commerce, it stands for connecting buyers and sellers. PayPal stands for payments," Whitman said. Had eBay called it eBay Payments, Whitman continued, "I don't think we'd have a merchant services business, because I'm not sure Dell.com would necessarily want eBay Payments as a payment module."

One of Whitman's latest acquisitions was of the Internet phone service startup Skype, which eBay bought in 2005 for as much as $4.1 billion (depending on how Skype performs). Whitman made the acquisition for several reasons: "We loved the Skype viral effect of how it had grown its user base—it looked a lot like eBay. You know, in the earliest

eBay Business Model

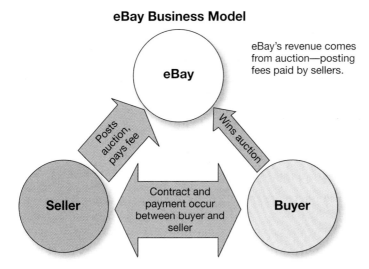

eBay's revenue comes from auction—posting fees paid by sellers.

PayPal Business Model

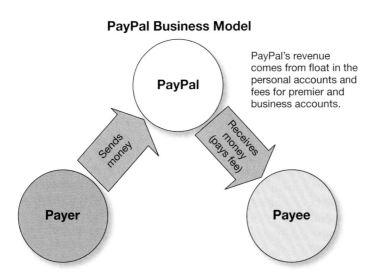

PayPal's revenue comes from float in the personal accounts and fees for premier and business accounts.

Exhibit 10.1   eBay and PayPal Business Models

days, [it had] even more rapid adoption. So it was very clear to me that something quite unique was going on at Skype—it was pioneering a whole new technology, but building a thriving ecosystem of users, developers, hardware manufacturers, and chipset manufacturers."

Most of all, however, Skype added to synergies with Paypal and eBay. "In the case of eBay, [there is] communication synergy. And with PayPal, this whole notion of PayPal being the wallet on Skype, and every new Skype user getting a PayPal account and vice versa," Whitman said. "That's why we were so excited when we saw Skype—there's something here that will unlock the Skype business, and will enable each business to grow on its own," Whitman said. Skype had grown to 196 million registered users at the end of March 2007, representing a 107 percent increase from the 95 million users at the end of March 2006.

In short, Whitman's strategy boils down to three critical synergies among eBay's properties: that eBay buyers and sellers will talk using Skype (generating ad revenue for eBay);

that Skype callers will use PayPal to pay for their calls (the ones that aren't free, that is); and that Skype will encourage PayPal's expanding cross-border remittance business. This economic logic of eBay's strategy is summarized by Whitman: "We want to build the synergies between these businesses," Whitman said at a shareholder conference in 2006, "so that one plus one plus one equals a lot more than three." The jury is still out on the actual synergies and other benefits to be gained by eBay through the high-profile Skype acquisition, but as you will see later in the chapter, it appears that the PayPal leg of the trio is paying off handsomely in eBay's strategy. **<<<**

Motives for Mergers and Acquisitions

Why do firms acquire companies rather than entering new businesses on their own or through alliances? Was eBay's acquisition of PayPal a typical acquisition? Are most acquisitions successful? Why do companies often pay huge costs, such as the 20-percent premium that eBay paid for PayPal, to acquire another firm? By the end of this chapter, you should be able to answer these and other questions about mergers and acquisitions (M&As). Indeed, as you work through the chapter, you'll see that our opening vignette on eBay and PayPal introduces many of the features common to acquisitions.

DIFFERENCES BETWEEN ACQUISITIONS AND MERGERS

Although it is regular practice to use the terms *mergers* and *acquisitions* together, and sometimes interchangeably, they aren't the same thing. The differences can be subtle, and depending on who's using the terms and in what country, each term tends to have different meanings. Disputes over differences in legal definitions can end up in court. For instance, Chrysler investor Kirk Kerkorian sued DaimlerChrysler in 2001 for billions based on the argument that the marriage of Daimler with Chrysler in 1997 was actually an acquisition by Daimler and not a merger. What was Kerkorian's interest in the transaction being labeled an acquisition? An acquisition would result in much more money being paid to Chrysler shareholders, including Kerkorian.[2]

Technically, the term **acquisition** means that a transfer of ownership has taken place—that one firm has bought another. A **merger** is the consolidation or combination of one firm with another.[3] When the term *merger* is used, it often refers to a class of mergers known as *mergers of equals*. These mergers are typically between firms of relatively equal size and influence that fuse together to form one new larger firm. Although there are many technical, legal, and detailed differences between mergers and acquisitions, for our purposes in understanding how they serve as vehicles of strategy, they are more similar than dissimilar. Consequently, we will focus on how firms use M&As to pursue their objectives.

We will emphasize the motives for M&As and the strategic implications of those motives. The motives behind M&As fall into three basic categories: *managerial self-interest*, *hubris*, and *synergy*. In this section, we'll review these three types of motives and assess the effects of M&As undertaken in pursuit of each of them. Because the first two motives usually don't reflect shareholders' best interests, the rest of the chapter will focus on M&As undertaken in pursuit of synergy.

MANAGERIAL SELF-INTEREST

Sometimes senior managers make decisions based on personal self-interest rather than the best interests of shareholders. We call this behavior **managerialism**. Conceivably, managers can make acquisitions—and even willingly overpay in M&As—in order to maximize their own interests at the expense of shareholder wealth. Executive compensation, for instance,

acquisition Strategy by which one firm acquires another through stock purchase or exchange.

merger Consolidation or combination of two or more firms.

managerialism Tendency of managers to make decisions based on personal self-interest rather than the best interests of shareholders.

tends to be linked to firm size. Managers might, therefore, enhance their paychecks by making acquisitions that accomplish nothing more than enlarging the firm.[4] As you have learned, getting bigger, in and of itself, does not create shareholder wealth.

Likewise, because year-end bonuses (and job security) are often tied to the firm's earnings, some managers might pursue diversification through M&A in order to stabilize annual earnings. Managers could, therefore, make acquisitions in order to boost earnings by diversifying the firm's revenue stream.[5] Certainly, organic growth could achieve the same goal but not as quickly. In any case, diversification of a firm's revenue stream creates little value for shareholders. Why? Because, as we've seen, they can diversify their personal securities portfolios much more cheaply.

HUBRIS

In the mid-1980s, economist Richard Roll proposed what he called the *hubris hypothesis* to explain, at least in part, why acquisition premiums are so large and yet acquisitions remain so common.[6]

As we've already pointed out, when a publicly traded firm is acquired by another firm, the purchase price almost always exceeds the target firm's market value. The average premium—the amount received by the target firm's shareholders in excess of the value of their stock—was between 30 and 45 percent during the 15-year period between 1989 and 2004. Why would anyone pay such a generous premium? After all, the target firm's market value prior to the acquisition bid was the market's best estimate of the present value of target firm's future cash flows.

According to Roll, managers not only make mistaken valuations but often have unwarranted confidence both in their valuations and in their ability to create value. This attitude, says Roll, reflects **hubris**—a Greek term denoting excessive pride, overconfidence, or arrogance. Hubristic managers may overestimate their own abilities to implement potential synergies.

A final word: Although we're going to focus on synergy as a motivation for acquisitions, you shouldn't ignore the other two motivations—managerialism and managerial hubris—when you're evaluating M&As. When managerialism and hubris are kept in check, acquiring firms are more likely to realize synergies and positive performance benefits.

hubris Exaggerated self-confidence that can result in managers' overestimating the value of a potential acquisition, having unrealistic assumptions about the ability to create synergies, and a willingness to pay too much for a transaction.

SYNERGY

When M&As are undertaken in pursuit of synergy, managers are guided by the belief that the value of two firms combined can be greater than the sum value of the two firms independently. This category includes all forms of M&As that are motivated by value creation. Synergy may derive from a number of sources, including reduced threats from suppliers, increased market power, potential cost savings, superior financial strength, economies of scope and scale, and the sharing and leveraging of capabilities.

Reducing Threats   As was noted in Chapter 7, sometimes a supplier cannot or will not make an investment that's specific to an exchange with one buyer. Why might this situation arise? Perhaps the investment would tie the company too closely to one buyer, expose it to too much risk, or overtax its financial means. In such cases firms may need to integrate vertically, backward into the supply chain.[7] The quickest way to do this is through an acquisition. Some of Cisco Systems' acquisitions of network switch technology companies are examples of this type of backward integration.

Increasing Market Power and Access   If a company improves its competitive position by means of a merger or acquisition, it may be possible to derive potential market power from the deal. Firms have market power when they can influence prices, and price competition is reduced significantly when rivalry is reduced. In the banking industry, for example, some mergers—especially those involving two moderate-sized banks—seem to have been motivated by a desire to improve market power. Thus, when First Union purchased Wachovia, the combined company vaulted into the number-four slot among U.S. banks. When Daimler merged with Chrysler in an effort to exploit potential synergies, its share in the global automotive market increased significantly. And the merger was designed to improve market access for both companies in geographic arenas where they were weak but their merger partner was strong. Another example of improved access is provided by PepsiCo. In 1992, for example, when PepsiCo still owned Pizza Hut, Taco Bell, and Kentucky Fried Chicken, it purchased Carts of Colorado (CC), a small food cart (e.g., kiosk) manufacturer, for $7 million, seeing it as the ideal means of installing new restaurants quickly and cheaply. Not only did the purchase give PepsiCo access to new cart technology, but it also provided it with an inexpensive means for quickly establishing fast food outlets in high-traffic locations. One of PepsiCo's first successful cart locations was in the Moscow metro system.

Realizing Cost Savings   Cost savings are the most common synergy and the easiest to estimate. Financial markets tend to understand and accept cost savings as a rationale and are more likely to reward savings-motivated M&As with higher stock prices than other forms of synergy. Revenue-enhancement opportunities, such as increasing total sales through cross-selling and enhanced distribution, also represent a significant upside in many M&As. It's more difficult, however, to calculate and implement revenue enhancement synergies (sometimes called *soft synergies*) than cost-saving synergies.

Increasing Financial Strength   Other synergies can be created by various forms of financial engineering. An acquisition, for instance, can lower the financing costs of the target firm when the two firms' respective credit ratings are markedly different and significant debt is involved. Such would be the case if a company with AAA-rated debt were to buy a B-rated company. Various tax benefits also provide unique financial synergies. If, for example, the target company has operating loss carry-forwards (i.e., financial losses that the IRS allows firms to apply to future years' earnings) that can't be fully utilized, the acquiring company can use them to reduce the tax bill of the combined firm.

Sharing and Leveraging Capabilities   Transferring best practices and core competencies can create value. This form of synergy is important in the resource-based view of competitive advantage. According to this view, one reason for acquiring another firm would be to absorb and assimilate the target's resource, knowledge, and capabilities—all of which, as we saw in Chapter 3, may be primary sources of competitive advantage. When firms combine resources and capabilities through M&As, they may be able to create a bundle of resources that is unavailable to competitors. If the combined resources and capabilities are complementary, the competitive advantage may be long-term. If the combination is valuable and rare, the acquiring firm may be able to generate profits greater than the sum of the two firms' individual profits. Bear in mind, however, that transferring resources, knowledge, or capabilities can create long-term competitive advantage only if the cost of the acquisition doesn't exceed the cost to other firms of accumulating comparable resource stocks.

Mergers, Acquisitions, and Strategy

Three points need to be kept in mind when considering acquisitions as a part of a firm's corporate strategy. First, as with other elements of strategy, managers need to be clear about the economic logic: How does the acquisition help the firm earn profits? Second, managers need to consider alternatives to the acquisition, such as developing the new business internally rather than buying it. Third, acquisitions are fraught with hazards that can end up ruining the projected returns, and managers need to know what these hazards are and how to navigate around them.

THE VEHICLE AND ITS ECONOMIC LOGIC

Acquisitions enable firms to enter new businesses quickly, reduce the time and risks entailed by the process of starting new businesses internally, and rapidly reach minimum efficient scale. Research shows, however, that M&As come with significant risks and uncertainties of their own. Although some acquisitions succeed, such as eBay's acquisition of PayPal, others fail to produce anticipated synergies, resulting in small losses, and some fail miserably, resulting in huge losses. eBay, for instance, was forced to sell Butterfields at a significant loss in terms of both dollars and managerial time and attention. In this chapter, we'll discuss some of the keys to making acquisitions serve as an effective vehicle for growth and, at the same time, avoiding common potential pitfalls.

What we said of alliances in Chapter 9 also holds true for mergers and acquisitions: They are not strategies in and of themselves; rather, as we're reminded in the strategy diamond shown in Exhibit 10.2, M&As simply represent one element of a strategy. Specifically, they are *vehicles* for realizing a strategy—that is, for entering or exiting a business.[8]

However, acquisitions have significant implications for other elements of strategy. Acquisitions take firms into new arenas. Acquisitions that result in diversification are used in the staging of corporate strategies. And finally, acquisitions have implications for the financial success of strategies—for the realization of the anticipated economic logic of the strategy.

Perhaps because they enable companies to accelerate their strategies, acquisitions are quite popular. The number of acquisitions over the past few decades suggests that they constitute a fundamental element of many firms' strategies. Exhibit 10.3 shows that M&A is not a new strategy vehicle, but its usage has grown dramatically in recent years.[9] The graph of aggregate M&A activity clearly displays a wave-like behavior with several notable peaks. The most intense quarter of M&A activity in Exhibit 10.3 is 1899:1, while the least intense quarter occurred during the Great Depression (1932:1). However, current M&A activity, as you will see in later exhibits, dwarfs these early peaks in both dollar volume and number of deals.

Research suggests that firms average about one acquisition per year, but of course, there's tremendous variance in firms' propensity for using acquisitions as a growth vehicle.[10] Not

M&A and the Strategy Diamond.
While mergers and acquisitions are explicitly vehicles of strategy, they have major implications for arenas, staging, and economic logic as well.

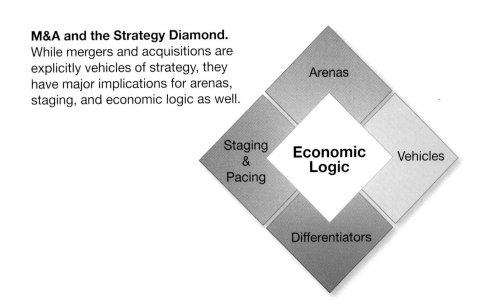

Exhibit 10.2 The Place of Acquisitions in the Strategy Diamond

Exhibit 10.3 Long-term View of M&A Activity (Relative Frequency of Deals)

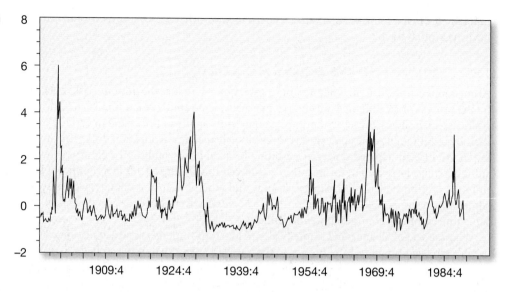

surprisingly, the financial success of any given acquisition depends on a number of factors and has a significant effect on the overall economic logic of a firm's strategy. As you can see in Exhibit 10.4, which summarizes acquisition activity involving U.S. firms between 1995 and 2006, the value of acquisitions involving U.S. firms demonstrates that acquisitions represent a major economic activity.[11]

Also, as shown in Exhibit 10.5, the frequency of cross-border M&A is on the rise.[12] Across all deals, over 40 percent of transactions were valued in excess of $1 billion; about 30 percent were in the $100 million to $500 billion range.

As you can also see from Exhibit 10.5, recent acquisition activity peaked near the turn of the century. That wave coincided with the tremendous bull market when firms used their inflated stock prices as currency to purchase other firms.

Exhibit 10.4 Recent M&A Activity

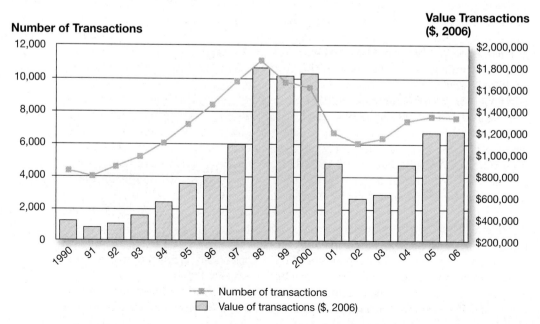

Exhibit 10.5   Global M&A Activity

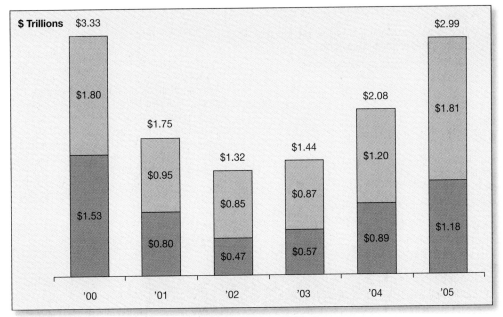

Despite—and because of—their economic consequences, M&As get a lot of bad press and receive criticism from scholars and consultants as well. We can attribute this criticism—at least in part—to the high visibility of many spectacular acquisition mistakes. Notable acquisition "mistakes" include AT&T's acquisition of NCR, Quaker's acquisition of Snapple, and AOL's acquisition of Time Warner. As is the case of so many acquisitions, the managers who made these deals seemed to be unable to make them work.

Quaker, for instance, purchased Snapple thinking that it could create profitable synergies between Snapple and its own Gatorade.[13] Apparently, however, Quaker failed to do its preacquisition homework, particularly when it came to the differences in the distribution networks of the two products. There were troublesome delays in implementing key aspects of the acquisition, and Snapple's market position in relation to newer brands was seriously eroded. The pressure from analysts and shareholders grew so intense that just two years after acquiring Snapple, Quaker pulled the plug on the acquisition and sold it for $300 million—a hefty $1.5 billion less than it paid for it. After just three years of repositioning Snapple, the new owner, Triarc, sold the brand for $1.45 billion to Cadbury Schweppes PLC, where it's now successfully positioned in a portfolio of brands run by a company with the capabilities necessary to build the Snapple brand. Snapple's financial-market roller coaster ride, which is illustrated in Exhibit 10.6, provides a good lesson in the combination of risks and opportunities that often accompany acquisitions as a strategy vehicle.

And while you might think that firms would learn from others' M&A mistakes, Daimler's recent sale of Chrysler for $7.4 billion, after having paid $36 billion for it in 1998, is striking evidence that hubris is alive and well in the world of M&A.

From what we've seen so far, it's clear that **divestiture**—the selling off of a business and the flip side of acquisition—is also a key strategic vehicle. eBay, AT&T, and Quaker all exited businesses by selling business units to competitors. In this chapter, we focus primarily on acquisitions as vehicles for entering or expanding businesses, but remember that closely related types of transactions enable firms to exit businesses as well.

When deciding to enter a new business, companies have alternative vehicles from which to choose, including *internal development*, *alliances*, and *acquisition*. Here, we'll explain why the

divestiture   Strategy whereby a company sells off a business or division.

Exhibit 10.6 Ups and Downs at Snapple

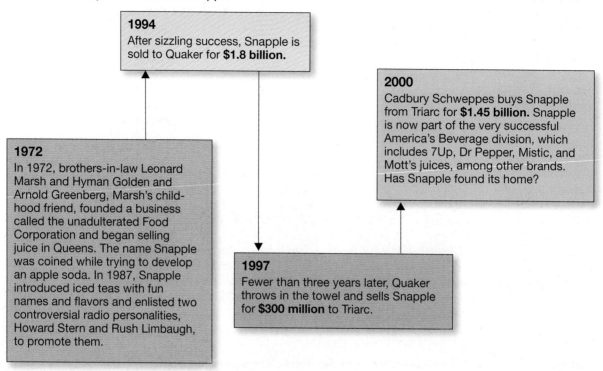

1994
After sizzling success, Snapple is sold to Quaker for **$1.8 billion.**

2000
Cadbury Schweppes buys Snapple from Triarc for **$1.45 billion.** Snapple is now part of the very successful America's Beverage division, which includes 7Up, Dr Pepper, Mistic, and Mott's juices, among other brands. Has Snapple found its home?

1972
In 1972, brothers-in-law Leonard Marsh and Hyman Golden and Arnold Greenberg, Marsh's childhood friend, founded a business called the unadulterated Food Corporation and began selling juice in Queens. The name Snapple was coined while trying to develop an apple soda. In 1987, Snapple introduced iced teas with fun names and flavors and enlisted two controversial radio personalities, Howard Stern and Rush Limbaugh, to promote them.

1997
Fewer than three years later, Quaker throws in the towel and sells Snapple for **$300 million** to Triarc.

tradeoffs between internal development and acquisition—make or buy decisions—are important considerations when deciding whether to enter a new business through acquisition.

BENEFITS OF ACQUISITION OVER INTERNAL DEVELOPMENT

One of the primary advantages of acquisition over internal development is *speed*. Although an acquisition quickly establishes a foothold in a new business, internal development can take years. A corollary benefit is critical mass. An acquisition ensures that a firm enters a new business with sufficient size and viable competitive strength. The acquiring firm, for example, can be assured of entering at minimum efficient scale for cost purposes. As another advantage, acquisitions can provide access to complementary assets and resources. In developing a new business, a firm invests its existing stock of resources and capabilities, and although it may develop new resources and capabilities in the process, there's always the chance that it may simply expend existing resources. With an acquisition, new resources and capabilities can be integrated with those of the buyer, who may actually improve its competitive position in other businesses as well. Finally, entry by acquisition may foster a less competitive environment. By acquiring an existing firm in a new business, the buyer eliminates a competitor that would otherwise remain in the market.

DRAWBACKS OF ACQUISITION OVER INTERNAL DEVELOPMENT

Conversely, firms may find it preferable for several reasons to enter new businesses by means of internal development. First, acquisitions can be more expensive than internal development. Buyers often pay steep premiums for existing companies. In many cases, these premiums outweigh any potential benefits of the acquisition, and in some cases, they make it economically more viable either to enter through internal development or to avoid entry altogether. In short, firms may decide against entering new businesses because they aren't likely to generate sufficient return on capital to justify the premium cost. In addition, the acquiring firm will often inherit several unnecessary adjunct businesses. As an acquirer, you must either be willing to run these unwanted businesses or go through the administrative hassle of spinning them off.

Second, although acquisitions represent a major one-time commitment of resources, internal development entails incremental investment over time. The internal development process, therefore, allows for many points at which the project can be assessed and reevaluated before further investment is made. If, for example, economic circumstances change, a firm can pull the plug. Acquisitions, on the other hand, are typically all-or-nothing propositions.

Finally, organizational conflict may emerge as a potential problem; the eruption of *cultural clashes* can impede the integration of two firms. The process of integration requires significant effort, and firms may encounter setbacks or even failure. Because integration is such a major factor in making M&As work, we'll discuss it in greater detail later in the chapter.

As you can see, many potential roadblocks can make it difficult for firms to realize economic gains from acquisitions. And the greater the cost in capital and time required for integration, the more synergies managers will have to squeeze out of the deal.

Types of Mergers and Acquisitions

There are many types of M&As, and each has a particular purpose—a specific rationale for creating synergies. In this section, we'll survey the different forms of M&As and link the economic logic of each form to firm strategy.[14] Because the logic behind each form varies, so, too, do the criteria for their success.

TYPES OF ACQUISITIONS

Acquisitions can figure into most aspects of business strategy, but they're generally regarded as a means of managing competitive pressures, uncertainty, or both. Thus, business-strategy acquisitions, like business-strategy alliances, tend to be fundamentally related to the firm's core business through *vertical, horizontal,* or *complementary relationships.*

A vertical acquisition has three purposes:

- To secure a reliable supply

- To leverage the resources and capabilities of upstream activities in order to create more value for the end customer

- To reduce total production costs across the value chain

Coca-Cola and Pepsi each have engaged in several vertical acquisitions over the years as they have purchased independent bottling operations. These acquisitions are downstream vertical acquisitions. Recall from the opening vignette in Chapter 4 that Coke and Pepsi sell most of their core product (concentrate) to bottlers who then mix the concentrate with other ingredients, bottle the product, and distribute it to retail outlets. Coke and Pepsi were able to reduce some threats that were beginning to emerge from large bottlers, as well as infuse more efficiency into these downstream activities, by consolidating bottling operations into more efficient regional operations.

In contrast, horizontal acquisitions help expand the company's product offerings. The Cadbury Schweppes purchase of Snapple was a horizontal acquisition that helped expand the buyer's beverage portfolio, particularly in the growing juice and tea segment.

Best Buy's 2002 acquisition of the Geek Squad, a Twin Cities computer-support service, was a product-market extension.

A complementary acquisition involves a complementary business—one that increases the sale of another product. Best Buy's recent acquisition of the Geek Squad, a computer-support service, is a complementary acquisition: When computer-service capability is bundled with retail computer sales, each business potentially increases sales of the other's product.

A Complete Classification   Because this simple breakdown of acquisitions into vertical, horizontal, and complementary relationships is a little oversimplified, let's take a look at the typology proposed by Harvard professor Joseph Bower, illustrated in Exhibit 10.7. It will give us a better understanding of the strategic logic behind five more commonly employed forms of acquisition.[15]

Though developed through a study of extremely large acquisitions (over $500 million), this schema provides a useful way of thinking generally about M&As.

Product and Market Extension   In a *product-extension acquisition*, the acquiring company expands its product line by purchasing another company. Basically, the buyer has decided that it can reap higher rewards by buying a company with an existing product than by developing a competitive product internally. In a *market-extension acquisition*, one company buys another that offers essentially the same products as the buyer but has a platform in a geographic market in which the buyer has no presence.

The journey of Snapple that we described earlier in this chapter is an interesting example of two different companies using the same acquired firm for the purpose of product extension. Conceivably, Quaker Oats could have developed its own line of fruit juices, lemonades, and teas. At the time, however, Quaker management believed that an internally developed line would lag too far behind those of incumbent firms in the market segment. Likewise, Cadbury Schweppes certainly has the capability to develop new drinks internally but chose to cultivate expertise in extending product offerings through the acquisition of established brands.

Geographic Roll-Ups   A **geographic roll-up** occurs when a firm acquires several firms that are in the same *industry* segment but in many different *geographic* arenas. It's not the same strategy as market extension. With a roll-up, the acquiring company is trying to change the nature of industry competition in a fundamental way; it seeks to become a large

geographic roll-up   Strategy whereby a firm acquires many other firms in the same industry segment but in different geographic arenas in an attempt to create significant scale and scope advantages.

Exhibit 10.7 Bower's Classification of Acquisitions

	Product/Market Extension	Roll-up M&A	M&A as R&D	Overcapacity M&A	Industry Convergence
Example	Pepsi's acquisition of Gatorade	Service Corporation International's more than 100 acquisitions of funeral homes	Intel's dozens of acquisitions of small high-tech companies	DaimlerChrysler merger	AOL's acquisition of TimeWarner
Objectives	Synergy of similar but expanded product lines or geographic markets	Efficiency of larger operations (e.g., economies of scale, superior management)	Short cut innovation by buying it from small companies	Eliminating capacity, gaining market share, and increasing efficiency	Anticipation of new industry emerging; culling resources from firms in multiple industries whose boundaries are eroding
Percent of All M&A Deals	36%	9%	1%	37%	4%

regional, national, or international player in what's probably been a fragmented industry. The purpose of a roll-up is to achieve economies of scale and scope. Prior to its merger with First Chicago, for example, Banc One had grown from a small regional bank in Ohio to a large national bank by buying smaller local and regional banks around the country. (The merged company is called Bank One.) In a roll-up, the acquiring company usually retains the resources and management of acquired companies but imposes its processes on them.

Entrepreneur Bradley Jacobs made a fortune deploying the roll-up strategy to build two extremely successful companies in two different industries. In the waste-management business, Jacobs used United Waste Systems as a roll-up company to buy small trash-hauling firms in a fragmented industry. He later sold the company to USA Waste Services (now Waste Management) and used the proceeds to launch another startup—one that would use the same roll-up strategy to consolidate the equipment rental industry. He launched United Rentals by purchasing six heavy-equipment leasing firms and then proceeded to buy equipment rental companies all across the country. Through a series of more than sixty acquisitions in seven years, it has become the largest equipment rental company in the United States.

What's the rationale behind a roll-up strategy? Basically it's that a large regional or national player can achieve economies of scale that smaller local firms can't. Centralized management, for example, may improve overall operational effectiveness through large volume supply discounts. In addition, a national firm may have the resources to win customer accounts that smaller local firms don't have. United Rentals, for instance, may be able to win equipment rental contracts with large customers who want a single national provider for all of their heavy equipment needs.

M&As as R&D Some firms use acquisitions in lieu of or in addition to internal R&D. Usually, the acquiring firm buys another company in order to gain ownership of its technology. The strategy is common in industries in which technology advances rapidly and in which no single company can do all the innovating that it needs to continue competing effectively.

Exhibit 10.8 M&A
as R&D

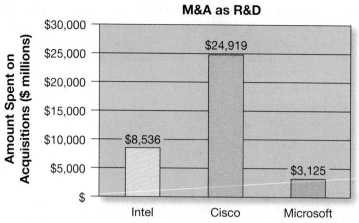

In the telecommunications equipment and computer industries, this strategy has been used to good effect by such firms as Cisco, Microsoft, and Intel. Exhibit 10.8 indicates how important acquisitions are to these companies as R&D vehicles.

First of all, bear in mind that the average U.S. company engages in approximately one acquisition per year. In the five-year period between 1999 and 2003, each of these three companies averaged more than ten acquisitions per year. All three companies allocate money for internal R&D, but each also spends considerable sums to acquire new technologies by buying startups that have made promising innovations. The strategy, of course, represents a tradeoff.

To get a better idea of what this tradeoff entails, consider the acquisition expenses of Intel and AMD. Both firms devote significant capital to traditional internal R&D projects. However, Intel made dozens of acquisitions during the past several years, whereas AMD made only three. This suggests that these two firms in the same industry have very different approaches to R&D. Intel apparently uses acquisitions as an opportunity to acquire potential future innovations from small startup companies with promising technologies.

Overcapacity M&As The purpose of an *overcapacity acquisition* is to reduce the number of competitors in a mature industry in which capacity exceeds decreasing demand. In essence, parties to an overcapacity acquisition are trying to consolidate the industry. Such is the case, for instance, when two companies in the same industry merge (or one acquires another) in order to rationalize the industry and reduce overcapacity. Overcapacity mergers are often explained as attempts to create economies of scale, but in many cases both companies are already large enough to be operating at a minimum efficient scale. Improved efficiencies come from reducing redundant operations and trimming the size of combined units. This was the rationale behind Daimler's acquisition of Chrysler (Daimler's recent sale of Chrysler for a significant loss is evidence of the difficulty implementing large acquisitions). The banking industry, in which firms are jockeying for market position and trying to create greater economies of scale, has experienced extensive overcapacity-M&A volume in the past decade.

Industry Convergence M&As When two industries start to overlap and become highly complementary, they begin to *converge*. When this happens, we see an increase in the level of M&As involving firms in the converging industries. In the media and entertainment industries, for example, Time Inc. had an extensive print media business and some cable operations (as well as HBO). Warner Brothers Inc. had a bigger presence in cable operations and a huge library of movies. In 1990, the two companies combined through Time's acquisition of Warner to form Time Warner (which acquired Turner Broadcasting in 1996 and which was later acquired by AOL in 2001) in order to consolidate media content and distribution. In response to the AOL–Time Warner combination, Viacom, whose core business was cable TV production and distribution, bought Paramount, a movie and TV producer (1993); Blockbuster, a chain of video outlets (1994); and the TV network CBS (2000). In

1996, Disney, already a media conglomerate, bought ABC, including cable broadcaster ESPN (1996). The entertainment industry's landscape continues to shift as firms try to find the right mix of businesses to compete effectively in converging industries.

The logic behind M&As in converging industries holds that such calculated investments will put firms in a better competitive position if and when industry boundaries erode. One can also view acquisitions in this environment as attempts by companies to acquire resources that, although less valuable in the present competitive environment, will be critical in projected new industry contexts.

Investor/Holding Company M&As Although we won't discuss this category in much detail, investor holding company M&A represents a significant portion of total acquisition activity. In investor/holding company transactions, independent investors or holding companies purchase existing firms. Such might be the case when an investment fund engages in a leveraged buyout of a company. Rather than merge the purchased company with other firms in its portfolio, the buyer tries to bring some management, operating, and financial discipline to the company, intending to sell it later at a profit. In other cases, investors (such as Warren Buffett's Berkshire Hathaway) purchase companies for long-term ownership and management.

International Acquisitions Bower's classification doesn't provide a specific category for international M&As, but in Exhibit 10.5 you learned that they are fairly prevalent. Our analysis of data compiled by Thompson Financial Services reveals that since 1990, cross-border M&As have accounted for an increasing percentage of all M&A activity. However, the issues confronting firms during international acquisitions are significant and you may need to examine the issues of differing cultures, laws, and competitors very closely before executing an international acquisition. An international acquisition can be of any of the types reviewed (e.g., R&D, product/market extension, roll-up, convergence, overcapacity, holding company). Obviously, the use of acquisitions as a strategy vehicle by any firm wanting to enter a new international arena should flow from its business- and corporate-strategy objectives, but firms must be aware that the international context introduces significant complexity into M&A transactions.

Pricing and Premiums

In this section, we'll review some of the basic financial issues relating to potential M&A success. These issues include pricing, premiums, and the benefits of establishing a walk-away price.

PRICING

What is the right price to pay for an acquisition? You might imagine such an assignment from a future boss (or a finance professor on an exam!); however, in the real world there really is no single correct price for an acquisition or merger. Why? Simply because the value of a target depends on how well it fits with the acquiring company. A potential acquisition will have a different value for different buyers. The ultimate purchase price will depend on a number of specific factors, including the target's current market value, its intrinsic value, and the value to be gained from any potential synergies between the target and buyer. Intrinsic value and the value of potential synergies cannot be known with certainty; these values are estimated by managers of the acquiring firm, investment bankers, and outside analysts. The firm contemplating an acquisition can consider a number of factors when determining its offer price for another firm.

Market and Intrinsic Value Of course, one of the first (and easiest) things to consider when evaluating a possible acquisition is the target's current market value. As the term suggests, **market value** is the current market capitalization of a firm, which is typically

market value Current market capitalization of a firm.

intrinsic value Present value of a company's future cash flows from existing assets and businesses.

purchase price Final price actually paid to the target firm's shareholders of an acquired company.

acquisition premium Difference between current market value of a target firm and purchase price paid to induce its shareholders to turn its control over to new owners.

calculated by multiplying the number of shares outstanding by the firm's stock price. This value is theoretically the market's estimates of the current value of the firm's future cash flows. A firm's **intrinsic value**, however, is the present value of a company's future cash flows from existing assets and businesses for a particular owner or buyer. It can be higher or lower than a company's market value, with the difference reflecting a number of factors. Markets make important adjustments in the valuation of a firm, evaluating future growth opportunities that will result in products and generate additional cash flows, assessing discounts for bad management or excessive diversification, or awarding premiums to firms that are likely to become the targets of bidding wars themselves.

The **purchase price** is the value actually paid to the target firm's shareholders. Like market price, it may be either higher or lower than intrinsic value, but it's almost always greater than current market value. The only exception to this rule involves target firms that are in dire financial condition (e.g., Daimler recently had to pay a buyer to take Chrysler off its hands).

Why would a potential acquirer offer to pay more than a firm's market price in an acquisition? Recall that synergy is the economic value created by being able to reduce costs or increase revenues by operating in two or more businesses instead of a single business. Synergy is essentially another way of saying that two or more combined entities create economies of scope and scale. If a buyer perceives that an acquisition will offer synergy potential, it may rationally pay more than the current market value for another firm. When synergies exist, they have the effect of increasing the intrinsic value of a target firm for that buyer.

Because synergy is a function of the *strategic fit* of the acquiring and the target firms, each bidding firm may value the target differently. In addition, the market may react differently in evaluating different bidding firms. When, for instance, Vodafone and Bell Atlantic both made bids for AirTouch, Bell Atlantic's stock price dropped while Vodafone's price went up—even though Vodafone entered the bidding with a higher offer. Why? The market believed that Vodafone and AirTouch could achieve greater synergies than Bell Atlantic and AirTouch.

PREMIUMS

The difference between current market value and the final purchase price is called the **acquisition premium**. A premium is what induces shareholders of the target to sell their shares to new owners. Our analysis of the acquisitions tracked by Thompson Financial Services finds that in the United States, average acquisition premiums have ranged between 30 and 45 percent during each of the past fifteen years. For instance, a firm with a market value of $100 million would normally sell for a purchase price of between $130 and $145 million.

Paying premiums for acquisitions, however, presents a basic problem for managers of would-be acquirers. When the managers of an acquiring firm agree to pay a premium for a target firm, they must expect that they will be able to generate better returns by combining the firms than the firms would achieve independently. In other words, to justify paying a premium of 30 to 45 percent, managers will need to generate more net income from the combined companies than the market assumed would be realized before the announcement of the acquisition. Where is this increase in return supposed to come from? Apparently it is from the synergies achieved by the combined firms. Synergies, however, are not guaranteed and there are several managerial traps that can make synergies difficult to achieve. Some of the managerial problems will be discussed in more detail later in the chapter. First, let's consider the practical implication of premiums.

The Synergy Trap In a study of acquisition premiums, Mark Sirower of the Boston Consulting Group (BCG) discussed what he called the "synergy trap."[16] He argued that premiums present two problems for managers:

1. Premiums increase the level of returns that must be extracted from the combined businesses.

2. Because of the time value of money, the longer it takes to implement performance improvements, the lower the likelihood that the acquisition will be successful. Consequently, any delays in implementing and extracting synergies increase the ante on required performance improvements.

Not surprisingly, paying too much for an acquisition can not only jeopardize the success of an acquisition, but it can also cause irreparable damage to the acquiring firm. Regularly in his letters to shareholders, Warren Buffett has reminded shareholders of Berkshire Hathaway that paying too much for a company can lead to disastrous effects. The box entitled "How Would *You* Do That? 10.1" goes into more depth on the issue of premiums and their effects on acquisition success and helps you gain confidence in calculating the required performance improvements associated with a particular acquisition premium. **Required performance improvements** are the annual increases in cash flow that are necessary to justify the level of premium paid. Calculating required performance improvements utilizes simple principles from discounted cash flow analysis that you've learned in your finance classes. The tools we provide you with in "How Would *You* Do That? 10.1" make the calculations even easier.

required performance improvements The increases in combined cash flow of the acquiror and target that are necessary to justify the acquisition premium.

Reaching a Walk-away Price

Given what you now know about the synergy trap (and perhaps about Warren Buffett's shrewdness as a strategic investor), it shouldn't surprise you to learn that in 2000, when Coke CEO Douglas Daft tried to buy Quaker Oats in order to add Gatorade to the company's product line, board member Buffett opposed the idea. Buffett argued that the bidding by Coke and Pepsi had driven the premium too high and Coke should walk away from the negotiations. (The board sided with Buffett and withdrew from the bidding.) Similarly, in 2004, cable operator Comcast made a tender offer for Disney of 0.78 share of Comcast Class A stock for each Disney share. The stock market wasn't overly thrilled with the proposed deal and Comcast's share price dropped while Disney's increased. Comcast was forced to withdraw the offer, however, because the value of its stock subsequently dropped too far: There came a point at which Comcast would have to pay out too many shares to reach the offered value. In effect, that point was Comcast's "walk-away price."

Escalation of Commitment and the Winner's Curse

Establishing a walk-away price is relatively easy; sticking to it is not. One reason for this is that executives escalate the commitment to their initiative as they proceed through a transaction. This—coupled with excessive fear of failure—means that bidders are sometimes seduced into making questionable decisions. Bidders who allow their prices to get carried away (or allow themselves to get carried away with their bidding) often suffer from the so-called **winner's curse**. Although the bidders win the "prize," they're saddled with the consequences of having paid too much.

winner's curse Situation in which a winning M&A bidder must live with the consequences of paying too much for the target.

The Acquisition Process

So far we've focused mostly on the technical side of M&As: what they are and how they're used as strategy vehicles, along with the roles of pricing and premiums. The success of M&As as a strategy vehicle, however, depends on much more than the choice of a good target and paying the right price. The process by which M&As are completed and targeted firms are integrated into acquiring firms can have a significant bearing on success or failure. Indeed, some experts say that the acquisition process is the single largest factor.[17]

The Impact of Premiums on Required Synergies

Assume that you worked for eBay prior to its acquisition of PayPal. You have learned from your division manager that PayPal will be folded into your division after the acquisition. Your boss, in a moment of pause from the hysteria surrounding the deal, has suddenly realized that she will be held responsible for integrating the acquisition and generating the synergies that Meg Whitman has been touting in discussions with Wall Street analysts. She turns to you and asks you to calculate just how much synergy she will have to deliver to make the deal a success. How would you translate the premium paid in this acquisition into actionable division budgets for the coming years?

This is not an entirely hypothetical question. Every time an acquisition is completed, it affects how division managers operate. Indeed, it often affects the targets that the CEO imposes upon them in terms of revenue targets and expense containment. To illustrate how this happens, let's go back to eBay's acquisition of PayPal. The opening vignette noted that eBay paid a premium of $250 million (a 20-percent premium over PayPal's market value prior to the acquisition).

Let's start with our objective: We need to know the synergy required to make the deal a success. Let's call this *required performance improvement*, or RPI for short. Understanding how to

calculate RPI is a useful managerial tool here. The RPI to justify a premium paid can be calculated with various degrees of sophistication, including the use of discounted uneven cash flows and probability statistics. But that level of sophistication isn't necessary to get in the ballpark.

We have simplified the various formulas and created a simple table of factors in Exhibit 10.9 that will help you understand the concept. The three factors that you'll need to know are (1) the premium expected to be paid, (2) the number of years before you expect synergies to be implemented (on the vertical axis) and (3) the cost of capital of the firm (on the vertical axis). Together, these are the factors that can be used to determine the annual synergies required to make the acquisition a success. The synergy trap calculation also assumes synergies are captured over a 10-year period, so if synergies start in year 1, that amount would need to be captured in each of the remaining 9 years as well. If they start in year 9, then they would need to be captured in 9 and 10, and so on.

Locate the intersection of the years assumed to make the synergies materialize and the cost of capital. Then multiply that factor by the premium paid to determine just how much synergy must be generated *each year* over the 10-year synergy period, depending upon when the synergies start, through the

combination of annual cost savings and new revenue improvements. If we assume that synergies will materialize immediately after the acquisition, then the amount of synergy that must be achieved is determined by simply multiplying the cost of capital by the premium. However, as you can see, as the years increase before synergies are implemented, or as the cost of capital increases, the amount of synergy that must be generated increases very quickly (the amount of synergy required is reflected in the yellow area of the exhibit).

In the case of eBay's acquisition of PayPal, the premium was approximately $250,000,000. So if the company thought that it would take two years to implement the synergies and it knew that their cost of capital was 15 percent, then the operational synergies required could be estimated by multiplying the premium by the factor as follows: $250,000,000 × 0.198 = $49,500,000. What does this number represent? It is the amount of additional net income that is needed *each* of the eight remaining years in a 10-year period. The acquisition of PayPal over and above the existing net income of both companies combined. eBay would have to find almost an additional $50 million in synergies just to pay for the premium.

Recall that synergies can take the form of increased revenues or reduced

Years Until Synergies Are Implemented	Cost of Capital		
	10%	15%	20%
0	0.100	0.150	0.200
1	0.110	0.173	0.240
2	0.121	0.198	0.288
3	0.133	0.228	0.346
4	0.146	0.262	0.415
5	0.161	0.302	0.498

Exhibit 10.9 Synergies Required to Justify a $10 Million Premium

costs for the combined firm, or both an increase in revenues and reduction of costs. Synergies can also be found in specific parts of the business such that one unit can grow faster or have a better cost position than it had previously. Ultimately, if it is considered a successful acquisition, the acquisition must leave the acquired and the acquiror better off than had the acquisition not been consummated.

While it is too early to tell how the Skype acquisition will turn out, and it is less obvious where the synergies from that deal might come from, we can at least provide a post-mortem on the PayPal deal. Here are the facts:

- eBay launches BillPoint in 1999 for online payments (though took a year to launch, and when finally up and running, PayPal had registered its millionth user)

- By mid-2001, eBay is losing $10–15 million yearly on BillPoint

- eBay buys PayPal in July 2002 for $1.5 billion, and eBay's cost of capital at the time was 15 percent

- eBay integrated PayPal in *one year*, with 74 percent of all eBay transactions by 2004, and 9 percent of U.S. e-commerce (5 percent globally)

- Experts point to the availability of PayPal as partial explanation for the exponential growth of eBay's total revenues, beyond those garnered by PayPal. While it is hard to point to the PayPal acquisition as the single source of eBay's growth, all indicators suggest that PayPal is a great example of a complement obtained through acquisition!

In summary, the synergy trap tool will help you evaluate what must be done with an acquisition if it takes place and considering some basic financial assumptions. Ironically, CEOs will comment that the best acquisitions are sometimes the ones they did not make, and the synergy trap tool lets the managers who must eventually integrate and make good on the purchase wrestle with whether or not the numbers made sense. Recall from our opening vignette that the business press considered the PayPal acquisition to be more hubristic than synergistic, but that in the end the deal proved a home run for eBay. You can bet though, as is the case in most acquisitions, that had the strategy not worked, many a critic would have said "I told you so!"

STAGES OF THE ACQUISITION PROCESS

Exhibit 10.10 summarizes the four major stages in an acquisition: *idea generation, justification* (including due diligence and negotiation), *integration*, and *results*. As the exhibit suggests, the M&A process really begins with the strategy because management has identified and prepared for M&A as a strategy vehicle, understands what strategic differentiators the firm will gain, bolster, or develop as a result of M&A, and has accounted for all the acquisition process stages in the staging and pacing facet of its strategy.

Problems at any of the first three stages can sow the seeds of failure.[18] This model identifies two types of problems: *decision-making problems* and *implementation* or *integration problems*. Decision-making problems can arise during the idea-generation, justification, and integration stages, whereas implementation problems occur during the integration stage. However, these integration problems could have their roots in an earlier stage of the process.

Idea Integration starts with the strategy itself, since the strategy will have foreseen M&A as a critical vehicle for success. But once M&A is part of the strategy, then the *idea* is the impetus for the acquisition. Some firms have well-articulated strategies that state the conditions under which acquisitions will be the vehicle of choice for implementing strategic plans. Recall, for instance, the case of United Rentals' roll-up strategy: Acquisitions were a key vehicle in the firm's strategy. Conversely, Quaker Oats' purchase of Snapple was an opportunistic (and ill-considered) move. Whereas some firms have well-defined strategies, in terms of the role of M&A as strategy vehicles, others don't. Firms that do have clear concepts about the role of M&A in their strategy, and have the requisite M&A capabilities, can be more opportunistic in the use of acquisitions.[19]

Justification, Due Diligence, and Negotiation The major analytical stage of an acquisition includes the processes that a firm goes through to develop the internal and external logic for the acquisition. Researchers Philippe Haspeslagh and David Jemison contend that several critical decisions must be made at this stage: strategic assessment, devel-

Exhibit 10.10
Acquisition Process Stages

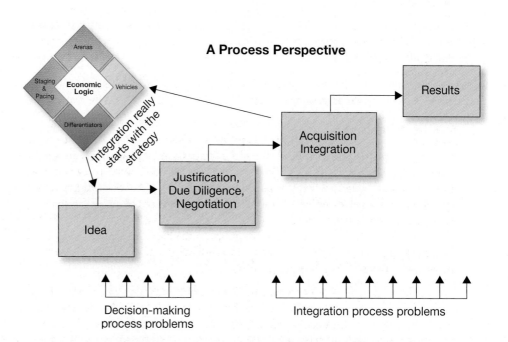

oping a widely shared view, a degree of specificity, organizational conditions, implementation timing, and a walk-away price.

■ *Strategic assessment* is the process of determining how an acquisition will contribute to overall strategy and competitive position. It should do more than analyze the target: It should address the issue of how the acquisition will affect the acquiring firm's pursuit of its core objectives. Managers should also make sure that their assessment isn't too static: It should consider the firm's future needs as its industry evolves.

■ Because many people will be involved in implementing an acquisition and integrating the target firm into the parent, it's important that the purpose and strategic logic of the acquisition be widely understood by members of the organization. The following is a list of eight questions that managers should ask at this stage of an acquisition:[20]

1. What is the strategic logic behind this acquisition? Does it correspond with the firm's strategy? Why this company?

2. Is the target industry attractive? What are the key segments? What is the prognosis about industry evolution?

3. If this is an international acquisition, what are the key differences between this country and our experience? Do these differences have performance implications?

4. Does an analysis of the target company (products and services, market position, customers, suppliers, distribution channels, costs, etc.) suggest that it is healthy and viable in the long term?

5. How well does this company fit with ours? What are the expected benefits, and what might impinge on the realization of those benefits?

6. How will the acquisition be integrated? Who will lead this process? How will we be organized?

7. Have alternative *scenarios* been considered? What is the outcome given reasonable, optimistic, baseline, and pessimistic assumptions?

8. Is the valuation reasonable? Is this acquisition priced at a premium or distress—priced? What do alternative valuation methods conclude (accounting-based, market-based, NPV, option)?

■ Managers should be as specific as possible in identifying the possible benefits and problems of an acquisition throughout the organization. This step is important for two reasons:

1. If operational managers aren't aware of the potential sources of synergies identified by upper management and the acquisition team, they'll have a hard time determining what's expected of them. Moreover, if they understand that synergies are needed but have little idea about how to gain them, the task is just as daunting. Let's go back to Quaker Oats' purchase of Snapple. Perhaps some acquisition managers understood Snapple's operations but no one seemed to understand fully the differences between the two industries' distribution systems. Operating-level managers were thus left to discover and deal with them through trial and error. A good deal of time and effort was wasted in trying to implement the acquisition in ways that simply were not in sync with Quaker Oats' business model.

2. Although identifying possible problems is also important, some acquisition teams tend to understate them, usually because they're afraid of causing key decision makers to shy away from the deal.[21] All in all, it's much better for all parties to know what

the potential roadblocks are; they can be dealt with more effectively if the acquisition team provides some suggested solutions.

Understand the Conditions Required for Creating Synergies Managers must understand the organizational factors on which key synergies hinge and the organizational conditions necessary to implement desired synergies. Synergies in a cross-border acquisition, for example, may depend on the transfer of a functional skill from one company to another. If so, executives at the acquiring firm must identify the managers and key employees who are critical to the transfer. Even when the numbers look good, more and more firms are scuttling acquisitions because of a lack of organizational fit—which can undermine possible synergies. Cisco Systems is one of the most successful high-technology acquirers; their screening criteria and means of achieving these criteria are summarized in Exhibit 10.11. Cisco regularly uses acquisitions to supplement internal R&D. However, Cisco discovered that the ability to realize synergies was to manage the entire process actively, from screening possible acquisitions to diligently managing the integration process.

Control the Timing of Implementation and Integration Timing is critical in most acquisitions. It's important because of the time value of money. In addition, stock markets can be volatile, which is important when a firm is paying for an acquisition with its own stock. Moreover, timing is critical because acquisitions cause major disruptions in both the target and acquiring firms. Many organizational problems arise from disruption in the lives of affected employees who may be impacted by the acquisition; such problems can be lessened if implementation and integration are achieved quickly. As you learned from the synergy trap tool, the more quickly that synergies can be realized through implementation and integration measures, the greater the premium a firm can afford to pay for the acquisition.

Establish a Walk-away Price Finally, managers should settle on the maximum price that they're willing to pay for the target firm. As we've already seen, it's wise to set a walk-away price early in the process, before rival bidders succumb to *escalation of commitment* and overestimate the value that they believe will be derived from the acquisition. Potential synergies are often uncertain and ambiguous, and they'll vary from one prospective buyer to

Exhibit 10.11
Organizational-Fit Acquisitions Screening by Cisco Systems

Screening Criteria	Means of Achieving Criteria
Offer both short- and long-term win-wins for Cisco and acquired company	• Have complementary technology that fills a need in Cisco's core product space • Have a technology that can be delivered through Cisco's existing distribution channels • Have a technology and products that can be supported by Cisco's support organization • Is able to leverage Cisco's existing infrastructure and resource base to increase its overall value
Share a common vision and chemistry with Cisco	• Have a similar understanding and vision of the market • Have a similar culture • Have a similar risk-taking style
Be located (preferably) in Silicon Valley or near one of Cisco's remote sites	• Have a company headquarters and most manufacturing facilities close to one of Cisco's main sites

the next. Problems arise when managers mistake a rival's higher bid as a signal that they've overlooked some attractive feature of the deal; in responding with a more competitive offer, they're often overpaying.

Integration Many acquisitions fail during the integration stage. The best means of integrating an acquisition varies from case to case, and failure to identify it can cancel any potential synergies that may have been derived from the deal. Determining the best process for implementing and integrating an acquisition means understanding potential interactions between the target and the acquiring firm. Because this stage is so important, we'll devote the next section to presenting a model for dealing with integration problems.

Integrating and Implementing an Acquisition

When one company acquires another it has several options for how the acquired company will be integrated into the firm. At one extreme, the acquired company may be granted near-complete autonomy. Warren Buffett's Berkshire Hathaway often treats its acquired companies this way. Alternatively, the acquiring company may attempt to fully integrate the acquired firm into its operations so that the two firms are melded into one.

How should managers decide whether an acquisition should be treated in a rather hands-off approach or be tightly integrated? Two concepts should be considered in making this decision—the strategic interdependence of the businesses and the need for organizational autonomy of the acquired business.

STRATEGIC INTERDEPENDENCE

Let's go back to one of the basic principles identified in this chapter: The primary purpose of M&As is to create synergies—value that can be created by combining two firms that isn't available to them as standalone firms. To what extent should the target firm and acquiring firm remain strategically interdependent? It depends on the types of resource sharing and skill transfers anticipated by the two firms. When the logic of the acquisition requires that they share tangible and intangible resources, the success of the deal usually requires a relatively high level of interdependence. Likewise, when the logic of the deal calls for transferring people with different functional skills in order to share knowledge, it entails more interdependence between the two organizational units than if it called simply for a transfer of general management skills. Alternatively, when the resources being transferred are primarily financial (say, borrowing power or excess cash), very little interdependence is required. Thus the first factor that determines how integration should be handled is the level of strategic interdependence between the acquiring firm and the acquired firm.

NEED FOR AUTONOMY

The second factor that should be considered is the target's need for autonomy. The value of some acquisitions lies largely in the retention of key people and transfers of capabilities. Key people, however, often leave once their firm has been acquired—especially when the acquisition disrupts their operating procedures and their autonomy in conducting them. Just how much autonomy should be granted an acquired firm? There's no single answer, of course, but the following is a good rule of thumb: The appropriate amount of autonomy depends on whether it is necessary to create value. Granted, even this response is a little too simple. Perhaps, for example, autonomy is necessary only in certain facets of the acquired firm's operations, whereas others can be easily assimilated.

When Swiss giant Nestlé set out to purchase British candy maker Rowntree York (makers of such candies as Kit Kat and Rolo) in order to extend its reach in chocolates and confectionary markets, it found that it could not, in accord with its usual policy, fully integrate its latest acquisition. Rather, to get the deal approved by Rowntree, Nestlé had to allow Rowntree executives to remain in the United Kingdom and run the strategic office in charge of all confectionary businesses. Thus, in this case, autonomy was needed simply to get the managers of the target firm to support the acquisition and agree to the buyout. Cisco, the network company, has used acquisitions extensively as part of its strategy. Generally, they try to integrate the target as soon after the closing as possible. For instance, they attempt to have the target's products in its sales peoples' catalogues the moment the acquisition closes. In order to achieve this, they need the target firms to adopt all of Cisco's systems and be fully integrated. However, periodically, Cisco acquires a target that resists some aspect of Cisco integration. They claim that to be innovative, they need some organizational autonomy, and that their engineers want to work for a small and dynamic company, not a big, "bureaucratic" Cisco. Consequently, in a few cases, Cisco has deviated from their normal integration policy in order to complete a transaction that they deem is of strategic imperative.

THE IMPLEMENTATION PROCESS

No matter what approach managers take—fostering interdependence, autonomy, or some combination of these—they will be well served by reminding themselves that acquisition integration is a *process* and not an *event*. By analogy, think of acquisition integration as a comma in a sentence, not a period. To this end we can learn some lessons from so-called **serial acquirers**—companies that engage in frequent acquisitions—that will be useful in understanding how the process can be handled smoothly and effectively.

It's a Continual Process, Not an Event
The best serial acquirers start the integration process during initial screening interviews and negotiations, well before closing the deal. M&A is already designed into the arenas, differentiators, vehicles, staging and pacing, and economic facets of their strategy (notice these comprise *all* five facets of the strategy diamond). During this process, called **due diligence**, executives and lower-level managers at both companies begin to plan for the postdeal structure of the combined firm. Although some pretransaction discussions can be awkward, they're essential in identifying both potential obstacles and additional opportunities. Once the deal is closed, specific decisions must be executed and prearranged organizational structures implemented. The lesson, in short, is that it's better to make tough decisions early rather than delaying them. Firms such as GE Capital and Cisco, which have successfully integrated many acquisitions (and some not so successfully), have found that initiating and pursuing a comprehensive integration and communications process is the lynchpin for success.

Integration Management Is a Full-time Job
Many firms make the mistake of assuming that people at all levels in both organizations will work together to make the acquisition as seamless as possible. Unfortunately, so many organizational issues are involved in integrating an acquired company that line managers often can't oversee operations *and* manage the integration process. Many successful acquirers, therefore, appoint an *integration manager*. Ideally, this person will be someone from the due-diligence team who understands both companies. Having met many line managers in both organizations, the integration manager spearheads integration efforts, guiding newly acquired managers through the maze of the new organizational hierarchy.

At GE Capital, for instance, integration managers introduce both executives and employees of the acquired firm to the business requirements and organizational standards of the new parent company. They also deal with a number of seemingly mundane issues that have been found to hamper integration efforts, such as communicating information about benefits and human resources policies. They educate new employees about such idiosyn-

serial acquirers Company that engages in frequent acquisitions.

due diligence Initial pre-closing screening, analysis, and negotiations for an acquisition.

cratic features of the firm as culture, business customs, and even acronyms. Finally, in order to prevent unnecessary overload and redundant activities, they channel information requests from the parent company to both new managers and those who are veterans of the original organization.

GE Capital has found that individuals with strong personal and technical skills make the best integration managers and typically draws candidates from one of two pools. First, the company recruits "high-potential individuals"—people with strong functional-area management credentials and leadership potential. These people function best as integration managers when the integration is highly structured and relatively uncomplicated. For more complex integrations, GE Capital relies on seasoned veterans who know the company well. Experience has shown that these individuals can be drawn from every functional area.

Key Decisions Should Be Made Swiftly

As we've already seen, speed is of the essence in the acquisition process simply because of the cost and the time value of money. Certain organizational factors also dictate swift integration. For one, employees—both those of the target firm and those of the acquiring firm—are naturally concerned about the impact of the acquisition on their jobs. As much as executives and managers would like everyone to feel like a team player with a secure place in the organizational lineup, when they're worried about their jobs, people succumb to distractions. Successful acquirers have found that it's best not to prolong the suspense: Decisions about management structure, key roles, reporting relationships, layoffs, restructuring, cost-cutting, and other career-affecting aspects of the acquisition should be announced as soon as possible—even within days of the acquisition announcement. Telling employees that everything will be "business as usual" is almost never being honest and will probably hamper the integration process. In addition, swift implementation of the integration process allows the firm to get on with its primary task—creating value. Because sluggish integration makes it more difficult to focus on this task, it weakens the value-creation process.

Integration Should Address Technical and Cultural Issues

When integrating acquisitions, most managers tend to focus on technical issues. At Cisco, for example, a key technical issue is the rapid integration of the target's products into the Cisco system so that sales representatives can begin selling the new product line. Successful integration means identifying and addressing such issues as early as possible.

Issues related to corporate culture should also be addressed immediately. Some of these issues are as simple as meeting and greeting new employees. The cultures of any two firms are bound to be different, and the faster managers and employees can meld the two organizations, the more smoothly the integration will proceed. Even when two organizations seem to have a lot in common, profound cultural differences may exist that could threaten successful integration. When, for instance, Franklin Quest merged with Covey, many observers expected cultural integration to be smooth. After all, the two businesses were highly complementary, and because both firms were located in Utah, they had similar employee bases. In addition, the two CEOs were well acquainted with one another. Surprisingly, however, the two cultures were highly dissimilar. For instance, Franklin Quest was built on a culture of efficiency, whereas Covey eschewed efficiency for effectiveness. Everything from products to company vision statements were tied to these critical underlying philosophies. During the acquisition process, executives dismissed these differences as semantics, but discovered during the integration phase that these were rather incongruent philosophies. In addition, more functional things, such as incompatible accounting systems, also impeded quick integration. Successful acquirers identify cultural clashes early; in fact, they may walk away from deals when the potential clashes are too severe.

Acquisitions in Different Industry Contexts

Not surprisingly, M&A activity varies across industries. It is determined largely by the development phase in which a given industry finds itself and by the extent of industry dynamism. In addition, competitive conditions will determine whether acquisition is a suitable strategy vehicle for a firm in a given industry and what the most viable type of acquisition may be. In this section, we'll discuss the role of M&As and industry context in terms of the industry life cycle and the level of industry-wide turbulence.

M&AS AND INDUSTRY LIFE CYCLE

Recall the model of industry life cycle and industry dynamics that we presented in Chapter 4. In this section, we'll use this model to illustrate how different types of acquisitions play different roles in each stage.

Introduction
During the introduction stage, acquisitions tend to involve the purchase of startup firms by well-established firms in related but more mature industry segments. Many partial acquisitions may occur, with established companies making equity investments in startups but not acquiring them outright. Thus, at this stage M&As tend to be R&D and product- and market-extension acquisitions.

Growth
During this phase, we see several types of acquisitions. Established companies from one industry segment may start entering other segments with greater frequency, looking mostly for proven and growing targets. Although some M&A activity may be for R&D, most of it is likely to be for the purpose of acquiring products that are proven and gaining customer acceptance. The geographic roll-up also becomes more common, especially at the end of the growth stage and through the maturity stage. In high-velocity industries, industry-convergence acquisitions appear and continue into the maturity stage.

Maturity
At this point, we begin to see overcapacity acquisitions. Why? During the growth stage, the industry witnessed the entry of new firms and aggressive expansion, with numerous competitors jockeying for competitive position. Capacity built during this period often exceeds the long-term needs of the segment, and as demand starts to flatten, companies see consolidation as a way to rationalize the industry. Overcapacity M&A activity continues throughout the decline stage of the cycle.

M&AS IN DYNAMIC CONTEXTS

Dynamic contexts are often home to firms that engage in acquisitions at a frantic pace. What is it about dynamic contexts that makes acquisitions such popular strategy vehicles? In Chapter 4, we discussed factors that can alter an industry landscape, particularly discontinuities and globalization. These factors tend to accelerate acquisitions. Note that within these two broad categories, many factors can affect the attractiveness of acquisitions as strategy vehicles. We'll focus on *technological change, demographic change, geopolitical change, trade liberalization,* and *deregulation.*[22]

Technological Change
In high-velocity industries, technological change and innovation can transpire at lightning speed, and some firms respond with aggressive acquisition campaigns. Both Cisco and Microsoft, for example, use acquisitions to ensure that innovation and technological change among competitors don't contribute to the erosion of their strong competitive positions.

Demographic Change   Demographic changes, such as the aging of the population and mass emigration, may alter customer profiles significantly. Spanish-language speakers, for instance, are an increasingly important market segment for U.S. media companies. Thus, when the Tribune Company merged with Times-Mirror in 2000, it acquired *Hoy*, the leading Spanish-language daily in New York and one of the fastest-growing publications of its kind. The Tribune Company has recently launched editions in Chicago and Los Angeles.

Geopolitical Change   Such events as the fall of the Iron Curtain, the emergence of the European Union, the opening of China, and conflict in the Middle East all have significant effects on the operations of global companies. In some cases, changes enhance opportunities for acquiring established companies in new locations. In others, they foster divestiture. For example, IBM was able to divest its personal computer division to the Chinese firm Lenova in 2005 largely because of the rapid growth and commercialization of the domestic Chinese marketplace, which was fostered by the loosening of some government interventions.

Trade Liberalization   Trade liberalization also opens new opportunities for doing business. In the wake of the European Union and the North American Free Trade Agreement (NAFTA), for example, cross-border acquisition activity increased in industries conducting business in those regions. Wal-Mart's acquisition of the successful Mexican retailing giant, Cifra, is a case in point. Geographic proximity and NAFTA make it cost-effective for Wal-Mart to stock its shelves in the United States with goods assembled in Mexico as well as provide otherwise more expensive U.S.–made goods to Mexican consumers through Cifra's outlets. Wal-Mart gained improved economies of scope and scale as a result of NAFTA.

Deregulation   Finally, deregulation has had a major impact on the volume of M&A activity in a number of industries. Prior to deregulation, for instance, the wave of M&As that swept the banking industry would not have been possible. Regulation and deregulation have also affected acquisitions and divestitures in the telecommunications industry. AT&T, for example, was allowed to exist as a virtual monopoly until 1984, when antitrust action forced its breakup. The seven so-called Baby Bells divided up local service, leaving the parent company, AT&T, with long-distance and telecom equipment businesses. Following subsequent deregulation, M&A activity has put the industry in a state of almost constant change.

M&AS AND COEVOLUTION

As with alliances, the use of acquisitions in dynamic contexts fits into the coevolution model of corporate strategy. Recall our definition of coevolution as the orchestration of a web of shifting linkages among evolving businesses. In the case of acquisitions, acquisitions can enable a firm to absorb the capabilities of their targets in order to develop specific dynamic capabilities in concert with the best resources and capabilities available on the market. Just as important, acquisitions (at least well-conceived ones) support a specific, focused strategy. Consequently, in keeping with this strategy, certain businesses are periodically pared off through divestitures and others added through acquisitions. If, for instance, the firm is pursuing a growth strategy, the coevolution perspective would suggest that it divest slow-growth businesses and products and acquire firms that are operating on the technology frontier or that offer some other basis for future competitive advantage.[23]

Summary of Challenges

1. *Explain the motivations behind acquisitions and show how they've changed over time.* The three basic motivations for acquisitions are synergy, manager self-interest, and hubris. Synergy is the primary motivation for acquisitions, and it can be generated in many different ways. Synergies can come from cost savings, revenue enhancements, improved competitive position, financial engineering, and the transfer of resources, best practices, and core competencies between targets and acquiring firms. Manager self-interest can motivate some acquisitions because many managers find it attractive to lead larger organizations, size and diversification can help smooth earnings, and compensation is higher for managers of large firms. This motive is known as *managerialism.* Hubris is exaggerated self-confidence, and it can result in managers overestimating the value of a potential acquisition, having unrealistic assumptions about the ability of an acquisition to create synergies, and being too willing to pay too much for a transaction. Thus, hubris results in more acquisitions than would be the case if it were kept in check.

2. *Explain why mergers and acquisitions are important to strategy.* Acquisitions enable firms to enter new businesses quickly. One of the key benefits of an acquisition over internal development of a new business is that the time and risks associated with business startup are reduced significantly. For instance, if the acquisition is of a firm of sufficient size, minimum efficient scale is achieved immediately. In addition, proven products are already in distribution. Acquisitions can also put firms in a position to achieve significant synergies—they can create value when the two firms combined are more valuable than when owned separately.

3. *Identify the various types of acquisitions.* Several types of acquisitions are possible, and each has a specific purpose. A product- or market-extension acquisition has the aim of expanding the products offered or markets served. A geographic roll-up is a series of acquisitions of firms in the same industry segment but in different geographic segments. A R&D acquisition is the purchase of another company for the purpose of acquiring its technology. An overcapacity, or consolidation, acquisition is the combination of two large firms in a mature industry that has excess capacity for slowing demand. An industry-convergence acquisition occurs when the boundaries between two industries start to fade and firms need to participate increasingly in both industries to be competitive; firms often use acquisitions to enter the converging industry. Finally, a significant portion of acquisitions are transactions by investors or holding companies (not an existing operating company) that are purchasing a company as an investment.

4. *Understand how the pricing of acquisitions affects the realization of synergies.* The pricing of an acquisition is critical to its success. The price of an acquisition normally exceeds its current market value by a significant premium. And although there is no one correct price for an acquisition target, managers of each potential acquiring firm can estimate the potential synergies between their company and the target. The price a firm is willing to pay for a target should be based on these synergies. Using Sirower's formula for acquisition premiums, managers can calculate the maximum premium they should be willing to pay. Likewise, if the price that is needed to make the acquisition is known first (such as in bidding situations), managers can easily estimate the required performance improvements that would be necessary. The greater the premium paid, the more synergies that must be extracted from the deal to make it economical. Likewise, the greater the premium, the more important it is to realize the synergies quickly.

5. *Outline the alternative ways to integrate an acquisition and explain the implementation process.* How an acquisition is integrated should be a function of the target firm's need for autonomy and the strategic interdependence between the target and the acquired company. Successful implementation requires recognition that acquisition integration is a continual process, that dedicated managers are required to oversee the process, that the process is enhanced by swift decisions, and that it focuses on both technical and cultural issues.

6. *Discuss the characteristics of acquisitions in different industry contexts.* Different types of acquisitions are seen with greater frequency at different stages of the industry life cycle. During the introduction stage, acquisitions tend to be by firms in related segments acquiring technology (R&D acquisitions) or products of startups (product extensions). During the growth phase of the industry life cycle, several types of acquisitions are common. Some R&D acquisitions of a now-proven technology by later-moving established companies from related industry segments still take place. But given that in the growth phase, products have achieved more accepted status, many more product-extension acquisitions are seen. The geographic roll-up tends to appear at the waning stages of the growth phase. In high-velocity industries, industry-convergence acquisitions also start to appear. During the maturity stage, overcapacity acquisitions start to emerge, and roll-ups and product-extension acquisitions continue. Overcapacity acquisitions continue throughout industry decline. Industry turbulence, such as technological change, demographic change, geopolitical change, trade liberalization, and deregulation are all forms of industry shock that tend to increase acquisition activity because they change the competitive landscape.

Review Questions

1. What is an acquisition?

2. Why would firms use acquisitions rather than create a new business internally?

3. What are the possible motives for acquisitions?

4. What are the ways in which synergies can be created in acquisitions?

5. How easy or difficult is it to achieve the alternative types of synergies?

6. What are the various types of acquisitions?

7. How do market-extension acquisitions and geographic roll-ups differ?

8. Give examples of product extension, overcapacity, and R&D acquisitions.

9. What is an acquisition premium?

10. How can you calculate the synergies that must be extracted from an acquisition with a given premium?

11. How do acquisitions tend to be used in different stages of the industry life cycle?

Experiential Activities

Group Exercises

1. Pick a firm of interest to your group. Identify potential acquisition candidates. Explain why these companies would make sense as an acquisition target. Evaluate and describe possible implementation barriers to this acquisition.

2. Pick a firm of interest and peruse its annual reports over a 5- to 10-year period. Assess the information presented on M&As in the annual reports. Do you see any explicit mention of the link between strategy formulation and implementation with respect to the acquisition mentioned in the annual reports? (As a starting place, see the chairman's letter to the shareholders.) What are the before-and-after scenarios that you find regarding the M&As?

Ethical Debates

1. During the due diligence phase of a pharmaceutical company's acquisition, you discover that an executive of the po-tential target may have funneled payments to government regulators overseeing the company's drug approval process. The case in question only represents a minor drug in the target's portfolio of therapies. What should you do?

2. While negotiating a possible buyout with the management of a firm, the CEO of the target starts to play hardball. He continues to add contingencies to the deal. In addition, he has recently raised the issue of a golden parachute for himself if he can convince the largest shareholder to agree to the deal. The CFO of the target pulls you aside and indicates that he can persuade the largest shareholder to sell and that he can do it for much less than the CEO is asking for in his golden parachute. What should you do?

How Would
YOU DO THAT?

1. Identify a company that has recently announced an acquisition. Study the terms of the deal and identify to the extent possible the market value of the target, its intrinsic value, and the acquisition price. What was the acquisition premium? Using the synergy trap formula presented in the box entitled "How Would *You* Do That? 10.1," determine the performance improvements required to justify this acquisition premium. Calculate the required performance improvements with different assumptions as to how long it will take to implement them in, say, one, three, and five years. What is the difference in these required performance improvements if the acquisition premium is 50 percent lower than what was paid? What if it is 50 percent higher?

Go on to see How Would You Do That at www.prenhall.com/ carpenter&sanders

Endnotes

1. N. Wingfield and J. Sapsford, "eBay to Buy PayPal for $1.4 Billion," *Wall Street Journal*, July 9, 2002, A6; N. Wingfield, "eBay Completes PayPal Deal, Gaining Web-Payments Heft," *Wall Street Journal*, October 4, 2002, B8; N. Wingfield, "eBay's Profit More Than Triples as Transaction Revenue Surges," *Wall Street Journal*, October 18, 2002, B4; Adam Lashinsky, "Building eBay 2.0," *Fortune*, October 5, 2006; "Interview Transcript: Meg Whitman, eBay," *Financial Times*, June 18, 2006; "Analysis: eBay's Growth To Come From Community" *InformationWeek*, June 19, 2006; "eBay Inc. Announces Financial Results for First Quarter 2007," *M2 Presswire*, April 19, 2007; "eBay Quarterly Net Beats Expectations, Raises Outlook," *eWeek*, April 18, 2007.

2. "Kerkorian Files Briefs in Lawsuit Alleging Deception by Daimler," *Wall Street Journal*, June 19, 2001, A4.

3. See R. F. Bruner, *Applied Mergers and Acquisitions* (Hoboken, NJ: John Wiley & Sons, 2004).

4. P. Wright, M. Kroll, and D. Elenkov, "Acquisition Returns, Increase in Firm Size, and Chief Executive Officer Compensation: The Moderating Role of Monitoring," *Academy of Management Journal* 45 (2002), 599–608.

5. Y. Amihud and B. Lev, "Risk Reduction as a Managerial Motive for Conglomerate Acquisitions," *The Bell Journal of Economics* 12 (1983), 605–617.

6. R. Roll, "The Hubris Hypothesis of Corporate Takeovers," *Journal of Business* 59 (1986), 197–216.

7. O. E. Williamson, *The Economic Institutions of Capitalism* (New York: Free Press, 1985).

8. Adapted from Hambrick and Fredrickson, "Are You Sure You Have a Strategy?" *Academy of Management Executive* 15:4 (2001), 48–59.

9. Data drawn from U.S. Department of Commerce sources.

10. P. Haunschild, "How Much Is That Company Worth?: Interorganizational Relationships, Uncertainty, and Acquisition Premiums," *Administrative Science Quarterly* 39 (1994), 391–411; W. G. Sanders, "Behavioral Responses of CEOs to Stock Ownership and Stock Option Pay," *Academy of Management Journal* 44 (2001), 477–492.

11. Data compiled from SDC Platinum, a product of Thompson Financial.

12. Data compiled from SDC Platinum, a product of Thompson Financial.

13. R. F. Bruner, *Deals from Hell: M&A Deals That Rise Above the Ashes* (New York: Wiley, 2005).

14. Figure is adapted. This typology was developed by J. T. Bower, "Not All M&As Are Alike—and That Matters," *Harvard Business Review* 79:3 (2001), 92–101.

15. Bower, "Not All M&As Are Alike."

16. M. L. Sirower, *The Synergy Trap: How Companies Lose at the Acquisition Game* (New York: Free Press, 1997).

17. Haspeslagh and Jemison, *Managing Acquisitions*; D. B. Jemison and S. B. Sitkin, "Corporate Acquisitions: A Process Perspective," *Academy of Management Review* 11:1 (1986), 145–163.

18. Brunner, *Applied Mergers and Acquisitions*; Haspeslagh and Jemison, *Managing Acquisitions*.

19. Haspeslagh and Jemison, *Managing Acquisitions*, 42.

20. Haspeslagh and Jemison, *Managing Acquisitions*.

21. Haspeslagh and Jemison, *Managing Acquisitions*.

22. Brunner, *Applied Mergers and Acquisitions*, 88.

23. S. L. Brown and K. M. Eisenhardt, *Competing on the Edge: Strategy as Structured Chaos* (Boston: Harvard Business School Press, 1998).

11 Organizational Structure, Systems, and Processes

In This Chapter We Challenge You To >>>

1. Outline the interdependence between strategy formulation and implementation.

2. Demonstrate how to use organizational structure as a strategy implementation lever.

3. Illustrate the use of systems and processes as strategy implementation levers.

4. Identify the roles of people and rewards as implementation levers.

5. Explain the dual roles that strategic leadership plays in strategy implementation.

6. Describe how global and dynamic contexts affect the use of implementation levers.

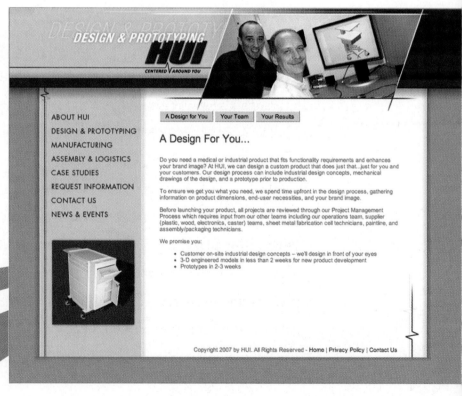

The "Leaning" of HUI

Success *as a* Journey, *not a* Destinations

*T*he notion of "Lean" manufacturing (commonly referred to simply as *Lean*) is typically associated with the enduring success stories of Toyota Motors of Japan or Danaher Corp. in the United States. Lean is a generic process management philosophy derived mostly from the Toyota Production System (TPS) but also from other sources. It is renowned for its focus on reduction of the original Toyota 'seven wastes' in order to improve overall customer value (you will learn more about lean throughout the chapter). However, when the CEO of a small metal fabricator—HUI—successfully rebuilds his business based on Lean principles, it points out the far-reaching strategic implications of the Lean revolution well beyond the context of global, large-scale manufacturers.

HUI (previously known as Household Utilities, Inc.) has been in the Kiel, Wisconsin area since 1933, and was originally founded as a metal fabrication business by Albert Deibele Sr., a German immigrant to the Kiel area. Metal fabrication involves the stamping, bending, coating, and finishing of sheet metal and other raw material to form product parts to trays and rolling carts used in hospitals. You should also know that metal fabrication is a cutthroat business—the barriers to entry are trivial, amounting to $800,000 and three people, and any single firm faces 100–300 competitors that are just a speed-dial number away. In 1996, Kurt Bell, who had been Operations Manager at HUI, accepted the position of President/CEO and purchased a majority ownership position in 2002. Prior to joining HUI, Kurt had been a CPA with one of the large global consulting and accounting firms. Under Kurt's guidance, HUI has grown and prospered, both in revenue growth and, more importantly, in employee development. Today, the company is 135-people strong, and garners a profitable $20 million in annual revenues. HUI has reinvented itself from a traditional family business, with limited sharing of information and authority, to an open-book managed company with defined roles and responsibilities and authority spread throughout the company.

This reinvention required HUI to create alignment between its revamped strategy and key pieces like marketing, organizational structure, employee evaluation methodology and pay systems, decision-making processes, performance metrics, and group dynamics. Lean principles provided the catalyst for bringing the pieces together.

In the CEO's Message, posted on the firm's website, Kurt Bell tells of HUI's Lean story like this:[1]

> HUI embarked on the Lean journey in September of 1998. At that time it was done for all the normal reasons: decrease lead-times, reduce costs, better satisfy our customers and improve profitability.
>
> Although those are good reasons to start with they are not what we've discovered to be the compelling factors that keep us going. Those have proven to be quite a bit loftier and more comprehensive.
>
> HUI aspires to be "The Company of Choice in all that we do today and tomorrow." Pretty inspirational and we may never get there but the journey is proving to be worthwhile and very rewarding.
>
> What is the role of Lean in all this? Lean is being utilized company-wide and does many things for HUI, our customers, and our suppliers. Above all, Lean increases our speed and adulthood.
>
> In today's world there are two types of companies, the quick and the dead. In order to play, HUI has to produce the right part at the right time, at the right price, the right way. All of this must be done quicker than the customer expects and quicker than last time. This is the world we live in.
>
> Lean increases our speed. It allows us to reduce the roadblocks and speed bumps that get in the way of our ability to quickly add value. This is accomplished with set-up reduction, standardized work, adhering to a process, visual systems, cross-trained teammates and quality at the source. The list goes on and on. These tools and principles are being used company-wide at HUI, from the front door to the back door. By doing these things well we will constantly increase our ability to deliver value quicker.
>
> Lean increases our degree of adulthood. As an adult you should be able to know what is expected, know what to do, know when to do it, know how you are doing, and know what to do to improve performance, all without being told. In other words, Lean helps to create an environment where people can be adults at work. Many of the same tools that deliver measurable waste reductions also put people in a position to act as adults. A good visual

system increases the likelihood that people can decide for themselves what needs to be done and how things are going. Being on a well functioning, self-directed work team leads to greater accountability, responsibility and personal growth.

So why we started is pretty normal, why we keep going is NOT NORMAL to most companies. For us at HUI, it's a way of life. Each day we strive to be faster and more adult like than yesterday.

This is not an easy journey, but the road to greatness rarely is.

Kurt Bell, CEO

The move to Lean by HUI also meant that it would embrace cellular manufacturing. This involves significant organizational changes, but also has big benefits. With cellular manufacturing, you make one product at a time immediately—the opposite of the mass-batch method, where products are processed and set aside for assembly. Exhibit 11.1 shows the way that the traditional manufacturing line is converted to a U-shaped work cell.

An obvious reward is that errors are detected quickly because a welded product, for instance, won't sit around for days waiting for the next step. If the welding isn't right, production is stopped immediately and the error is fixed, which enhances productivity and creates less waste. More benefits include scheduling flexibility, reduced lead-time and decreased inventory. Finally, in the best cases—as is the case at HUI—these cells are self-managing, so that there is no need for a supervisor to oversee the traditional line. Members of the cell coordinate activities collectively, instead of following the direction of the line manager. A full layer of management, and the time and cost associated with it, is thus eliminated.

The Lean revolution at HUI, however, did not stop with manufacturing. Bell restructured his back office to a cellular structure as well, and created cells comprised of sales, customer service, engineering, purchasing, and accounting staff, organized by customer. The restructuring process started with viewing the back office as a factory, and asking questions like: What will my customers (external and internal) pay me to do? What are our products? And, what are the flows required to produce those products? For instance, "products" were identified such as project quotes, engineering designs, and shop-floor routing instructions. Like manufacturing at HUI, this U-shaped customer-business-development cell is self-directed. Moreover, it is responsible for its own sales.

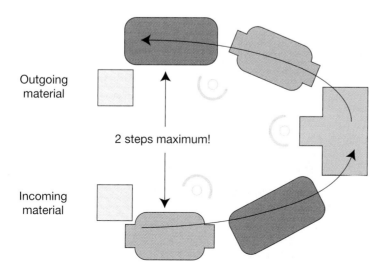

Outgoing material

Incoming material

2 steps maximum!

Exhibit 11.1 The U-Shaped Work Cell in Lean

For Lean to work well, experts say that the organization's culture must change in significant ways—and Bell saw that this type of change had to start with him—particularly the need to shift operating control from "management" to the employees. From a command-and-control culture, which is typically associated with efficiency, HUI moved to a culture of customer and process ownership by employees, with a team-based structure, and a broader orientation toward learning and individual growth. Where employees had deep knowledge of specialized areas in the old model, the Lean model asked them to cross-train each other, and complement depth with breadth so that they could better coordinate activities to benefit the customer and lower costs. This deep cultural change took a decade to build, resulted in the departure of many employees who could not adapt to the aggressively cooperative and performance-demanding climate, but also created a more enduring source of competitive advantage for HUI. This advantage can be seen in the firm's agility, creativity, product quality, and production efficiency. Ironically, CEO Bell sees Lean as a table stake in future battles for market share, though it is clear that the culture that enables it is not easily duplicated. **<<<**

Interdependence of Strategy Formulation and Implementation

By now, you should have a very good idea of what makes a good strategy: Good strategies enable an organization to achieve its objectives. You've also learned how to describe and evaluate business and corporate strategy formulation according to the strategy diamond. You know that *strategy formulation* is *deciding what to do* and that *strategy implementation* is the process of *executing what you've planned to do*.[2] You understand that neither formulation nor implementation can succeed without the other, and you're aware that the most successful firms often adjust strategies and execution according to feedback from the implementation process itself. That's why the processes of formulation and implementation are iterative and interdependent, with the objective being a consistent and coherent set of strategy elements and implementation levers. As Exhibit 11.2 reminds us, the overarching model of strategy hinges on the integral relationship among *formulation* (the process of aligning the five elements of the strategy diamond), *implementation levers*, and *strategic leadership*.

Exhibit 11.2 Formulation and Implementation

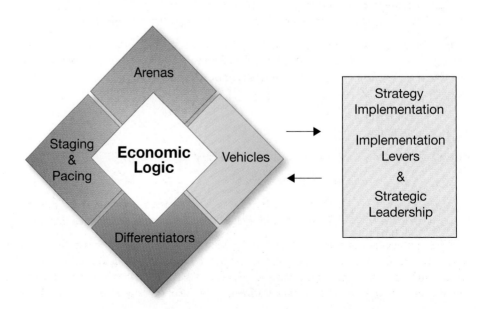

In this chapter, we'll focus on issues concerning strategy implementation—specifically, such implementation levers as organization structure, systems, and processes, and the aspects of strategic leadership that facilitate successful implementation.

When a firm is experiencing difficulties, it's always good to ask three questions:

- Is the strategy flawed?

- Is the implementation of the strategy flawed?

- Are both the strategy and implementation flawed?

It shouldn't come as any surprise that, more often than not, implementation problems are the source of performance problems.[3] Obviously, no strategy can be effective if it's implemented poorly. By the same token, although we tend to attribute success to effective strategies, some of the most stellar performers achieve competitive advantage because of *how* they execute their strategies.

A MODEL COMPANY

The opening vignette on HUI describes a company whose strategy implementation integrates all of the key elements of the overarching implementation model outlined in Exhibit 11.2 (and indeed, it hits on all the points of the more detailed implementation framework we will review later in the chapter):

- HUI's implementation levers function in unison to support a focused strategy of growth through innovative new products.

- The lack of formal titles, hierarchy, and bureaucracy reflect a flat organizational structure that facilitates both the flow of information and quick decision making (though this presents a challenge to coordination and rapid change at an organizational level).

- Systems are in place to identify new-product opportunities, to ensure that they have product champions, and to reward employees for their contributions to both product lines and the company's overall profitability.

- Because the selection and retention of people, in terms of both necessary skills and personal fit with the organization, are a critical factor in HUI's success, these functions are rigorously managed. Attention to human resources also reinforces a deep culture that values leading-edge innovation, and top management reiterates the importance of the firm's "core values."

By the end of this chapter, you should be able to identify the implementation levers and strategic leadership functions that drive successful strategies. You should be able to identify levers that are in need of repair and propose a plan for using certain levers to implement a strategy more effectively.

THE KNOWING-DOING GAP

Let's go back to a couple of admonitions that we cited in Chapter 1:

- "A strategy . . . is only as good as its execution."[4]

- "The important decisions, the decisions that really matter, are strategic. . . . [But] more important and more difficult is to make effective the course of action decided upon."[5]

These principles apply to our focus in this chapter as well: By and large, firms find it much more difficult to implement good ideas than to generate new ideas and knowledge. A recent study, for instance, found that 46 percent of large companies surveyed regarded themselves as good or excellent at generating new knowledge; only 14 percent of the same

knowing-doing gap
Phenomenon whereby firms tend to be better at generating new knowledge than at creating new products based on that knowledge.

firms reported having launched new products based on the application of new knowledge.[6] This difference between what firms *know* and what they *do* has been dubbed the **knowing-doing gap**.[7] Let's look a little more closely at this phenomenon.

What Causes the Knowing-Doing Gap?

One explanation of the knowing-doing gap is the fact that the strategy formulation process itself isn't shared with those stakeholders, including lower-level managers, who will be integral in rolling out the strategy. Other observers argue that, even if all the right stakeholders are included in the strategy formulation process, management often fails either to determine whether the proper implementation levers are in place or to take appropriate strategic leadership actions.

Obstacles, External and Internal Some experts believe that strategy implementation failures result from management's inability to assess potential implementation obstacles. Some obstacles reside in the external environment. Prior to its merger with Hewlett-Packard, for example, Compaq's attempts to mimic Dell's direct-sales model met with stiff resistance from its existing retail base, including such outlets as CompUSA and Best Buy. Of course, obstacles also exist inside the firm—a fact that we've already touched on by emphasizing the importance of assessing existing resources, implementation levers, and management action plans. In diversified firms, the parent company itself may be an internal obstacle, particularly if one business unit is proposing a strategy that puts it in direct competition with another.

culture Core organizational values widely held and shared by an organization's members.

The Impact of Culture One of the most critical, and yet most overlooked, internal implementation factor is a firm's *culture*. Exhibit 11.3 sums up Lou Gerstner's view of culture as he came on board to revive a dying IBM.[8]

Ironically, Gerstner's challenge was not to change the IBM culture, but instead to harness and direct the aspects of that culture that had previously made IBM great. Culture sometimes presents management with a persistent challenge: It's both difficult and time-consuming to change, and it can be a source of competitive advantage.[9] **Culture** consists of the core organizational values that are widely held and shared by organizational members (including employees, managers, and owners). Recent studies have found evidence confirming the theory that firms with strong shared values are better at implementing strategies and achieving higher levels of performance than firms with weaker values. Across industries, for example, firms with strong cultures generally achieve higher average levels of return on investment, net income growth, and change in share price.[10] In addition, firms

Exhibit 11.3 Lou Gerstner's View on the Role of Culture

"Along the way, something happened—something that quite frankly surprised me. I fell in love with IBM. I came to see, in my decade at IBM, that culture isn't just one aspect of the game—it is the game. We changed almost every process in this company, but none of those changes would have gotten done if we didn't convince the IBM team that a whole new set of values and behaviors had to emerge. And interestingly many of them were a return to IBM's true values, not the grotesque misalignment of those values that had emerged during the bad years. Once IBM was reminded of its core culture, it helped rally the company, bind it together in ways that had been absent for years."

with strong cultures seem to be less variable in their performance outcomes.[11] Finally, these positive effects of shared values on performance appear to be even stronger in highly competitive markets.[12] Why? Perhaps because effective strategy implementation is even more important in highly competitive industries, where there's less room for error. The opening example on HUI shows how important the shared culture was to the successful implementation of Lean processes.

Sometimes, company culture reflects the values of the CEO and other top managers, whereas at others, leaders steward and protect existing values. Shared values are typically few in number, deeply embedded in the organization, give meaning and identity to the firm's members, and state the purpose of the firm's work. The shared values of HUI may be one of the reasons why it thrives despite having a structure that seems too chaotic for a firm of its size. HUI's values can be summed up as fairness, freedom, commitment, and consultation. Associates, for instance, are expected to treat one another fairly. They're given the freedom to grow in knowledge, skill, and scope of responsibility. Finally, although everyone is empowered to make decisions, any management decision that may affect the firm's image or performance must be run past other associates.

In short, a firm's strategy must be consistent with its shared values if it's to be implemented successfully. Thus, it's crucial that strategists understand what's really important to members of the organization. First, of course, they need to ask whether employees have any shared values. If the answer is no, top management may have to spend some time developing and communicating a core set of values, starting with the vision and mission statements, and getting organizational members to buy into them.

Mismatches Not surprisingly, mismatches between strategy and implementation levers or between strategy and strategic leadership actions are easy to recognize in hindsight. Of course, they're much more difficult to catch in real time. Executives who are responsible for formulating strategy are often prone to making overly optimistic projections and downplaying the obstacles to execution. Consider, for instance, the number of hardware and software firms that have attempted to become IT solution providers by adding a consulting arm to their existing business. Most have failed, usually because they lacked the organization to execute the strategy.[13] SAP provides a good example of this.

As a provider of ERP software, SAP grew quickly at first because of demand for its unique product. In its zeal for growth, however, the firm neglected to focus on structure, employee retention, and balance between rewards for sales and rewards for profitability. SAP eventually recovered (as you will see in Exhibit 11.4), but only after a new CEO dramatically revamped the firm's infrastructure, cost controls, and human resource policies.[14]

As the SAP example in Exhibit 11.4 shows, implementation levers tend to be interrelated, which means that a change in one will probably require a change in all or some of the others.[15]

We'll deal with further examples of these interrelationships in the following sections, but at this point we suggest that you use the following statement to guide you in your study of the material in this chapter:

> [T]he strategist will not be able to nail down every action step when the strategy is first crafted, nor should this even be attempted. However, he or she must have the ability to look ahead at the major implementation obstacles and ask, "Is this strategy workable? Can I make it happen?"[16]

By the end of this chapter, you'll be able not only to answer questions such as these, but also offer recommendations for employing implementation levers and taking strategic leadership actions. These two facets of strategy implementation—levers and leadership—are summarized in Exhibit 11.5.[17]

Exhibit 11.4   Picking Up the Pieces at SAP

The enterprise software company SAP dodged a bullet, but just barely. It did so not by overhauling its strategy but rather by dramatically changing its leadership and implementation approach. We will focus on SAP America, one of the largest subsidiaries of the German firm SAP, because it characterizes much of what took place globally in this firm. From 1992 through most of 1996, SAP America's revenues grew at an astounding triple-digit annual rate, from $49 million to an annualized $818 million. The number of employees over that same period grew from 284 to 1,621. This rapid growth was spurred by two things. First, SAP had what many U.S. multinationals perceived to be the best ERP product on the market. The product was highly profitable due to its relatively standardized design and high market demand. Second, SAP was a fairly decentralized organization, with functional emphasis primarily in sales and on an incentive system that rewarded sales and sales growth. Career paths were unclear and focused on regions, but because the compensation was so lucrative, employees could earn huge salaries based on sales and then jump ship to a firm where their career and mobility might be more clearly laid out. As a result, SAP America was built for speed (though not efficiency), and its rocket-like sales growth reflected the levers and leadership that were in place.

Coming into late 1995, however, the rocket seemed to be running out of fuel. The combination of growing competition from the likes of Oracle and Siebel systems, market saturation, and a lack of organizational accountability that was a by-product of the growth focus was beginning to undermine SAP's profitability, customer service, and reputation. SAP Germany's kick in the pants to SAP America started with the promotion of then-CFO Kevin McKay to the position of CEO (and the departure of the old CEO, Paul Wahl, to competitor Siebel Systems). McKay moved quickly to increase cultural sensitivity to costs and cost management, implement an administrative structure to bolster the organization's overall professionalism, and formalize human resource policies. This latter step took the form of hiring an HR director (no one had held that role at SAP America before, despite all of the hiring that had gone on) who put a formal HR system in place. These decisions were complemented by increased R&D funding to explore the Internet applications of SAP software, a platform that the software giant had ignored up to that point. At the same time, McKay subtly shifted SAP's strategy from one of pure growth through new accounts to account "farming"—an increased focus on garnering a greater share of each existing customer's IS business needs, coupled with the modification of the firm's reward system to reward such behaviors.

While these changes caused many people to leave SAP, this loss was more than offset by the hiring of new executives and workers who bought into the new organizational arrangements and SAP's vision. By 2000, the firm had successfully launched a Web-based version of its software, called MySAP, and regained its position of industry leadership.

Exhibit 11.5   Key Facets of Strategy Implementation

Implementation Levers

- Organizational structure
- Systems and processes
- People and rewards

Intended Strategy

Realized Strategy

Strategic Leadership

- Lever and resource allocation decisions
- Support among stakeholders

Implementation Levers

We have been using the term *implementation lever* without providing a precise definition. Before we explore the concept in detail, therefore, it may be useful to make clear that **implementation levers** are mechanisms that a strategic leader has at his or her disposal to help execute a strategy. Although anything that enables an executive to get leverage to execute change can be considered an implementation lever, we categorize the major levers as *structure, systems and processes,* and *people and rewards.* In this section, we will go into some depth on each of these.

implementation levers
Mechanisms used by strategic leaders to help execute a firm's strategy.

STRUCTURE

Because structure is the implementation lever that usually gets the most attention in an organization, we'll start with it. Alfred Chandler's classic research on the interdependence of strategy and structure based on studies of General Motors, DuPont, and Sears raised the topic to prominence in the 1960s.[18] Today, practically every issue of the *Wall Street Journal* announces that some firm is busy "restructuring" or reporting decreased earnings due to "restructuring charges." Most firms develop *organizational charts,* which are static representations of their structure. But what is *structure* itself? We'll define **organizational structure** as the relatively stable arrangement and division of responsibilities, tasks, and people within an organization. Organizations are composed of people who are assigned to certain divisions and who perform certain delegated and specialized tasks. The *structure* of an *organization,* therefore, is the framework that management has devised to divide tasks, deploy resources, and coordinate departments.[19] Structure provides a way for information to flow efficiently from the people and departments who generate it to those who need it. Structure also spells out *decision rights*—policies that tell individuals who's responsible for generating particular information and who's authorized to act on it.

organizational structure
Relatively stable arrangement of responsibilities, tasks, and people within an organization.

Control and Coordination   Briefly, structure includes a firm's authority hierarchy, its organizational units and divisions, and its mechanisms for coordinating internal activities. Organizational structure performs two essential functions:

▪ It ensures control.

▪ It coordinates information, decisions, and the activities of employees at all levels.

As both functions become more complex, firms generally modify their structure accordingly. Structure should be consistent with the firm's strategy. The more diversified the firm, the more the structure that will have to be designed to accommodate coordination. After all, if a firm is participating in related businesses, it is probably trying to exploit synergies—a task that, as we saw in our chapters on corporate and international strategy, often requires sharing information and resources across product or geographic divisions. Conversely, the more focused the firm is on a single business (or even on each of multiple unrelated businesses), the more its structure should be designed to emphasize control. As we'll see, the popular means of organizing firm structure include the *functional, multidivisional, matrix,* and *network* forms.[20]

Traditionally, both scholars and managers have thought of structure as being determined by a firm's strategy,[21] and in most cases, this assumption is valid. We'll soon see, however, that structure can result in new or modified strategies. In fact, the way in which tasks are delegated and resources deployed can produce rather dramatic changes in a firm's strategy.

With respect to structure, a key question is whether the firm's current structure facilitates the implementation of its strategy and provides the information it needs to revise its existing strategy. At all times, a firm's structure should seek a balance between the control needed to achieve efficiency and unity of direction and the delegation of authority required to make timely decisions in a competitive environment. Let's examine two cases in which new structure resulted directly in changes in strategy.

How Structure Influences Strategy (I) After developing an innovative process for economically producing industrial gas onsite at customers' factories, the French firm Air Liquide (translated as *liquid air*) began locating personnel at client sites. This restructuring gave employees at customer sites more decision-making autonomy. Before long, on-site employees discovered a host of new services that Air Liquide could offer its clients, such as handling hazardous materials, troubleshooting quality-control systems, and managing inventory. The result, of course, was a wealth of new business opportunities—most of which offered higher margins than the company's core gas production and distribution business. Such services now account for 25 percent of Air Liquide's revenues, as opposed to just 7 percent before the restructuring.[22]

How Structure Influences Strategy (II) Part of this next story was presented in the opening vignette to Chapter 3. In the early 1980s, Intel derived more than 90 percent of its revenue from the manufacture of memory chips. A feature of its organizational structure is credited with being the key to its transformation into a maker of PC microprocessors in a span of less than two years. Although they appear similar, the capabilities underlying effective competition in memory versus microprocessors differ. Originally, Intel's structure permitted production managers to make production decisions based on a set of established rules. Among other things, these rules stipulated that managers allocate production capacity based on margins per square inch of silicon wafer. In response to this requirement, production managers started shifting manufacturing capacity from memory chips to microprocessors (previously just a small side business), because the margins were much greater. Interestingly, this shift wasn't dictated or orchestrated by senior management. In fact, Intel's senior management didn't ratify the decision to become a microprocessor manufacturer until well after microprocessors had come to account for about 90 percent of companywide output.[23]

FORMS OF ORGANIZATIONAL STRUCTURE

In this section, we'll review four basic forms of organizational structure: *functional, multidivisional, matrix,* and *network.* We also briefly describe partnerships and franchises. Consider these structures to be "pure" forms. In reality, they're just basic models on which many variations have been played. Later in the chapter, we'll show how they've been modified to accommodate global and dynamic contexts.

functional structure Form of organization revolving around specific value-chain functions.

Functional Structure A **functional structure** organizes activities according to the specific functions that a company performs. As shown in Exhibit 11.6, common units include finance, sales and marketing, production, and R&D. From a practical standpoint, any of the functions in a firm's value chain can be organized as a unit in a functional structure.

Functional structures tend to work best in smaller firms and those with few products or services. Platypus Technologies, for instance, is a small nanotechnology firm with thirty em-

Exhibit 11.6 Functional Structure

ployees,[24] most of whom are R&D scientists working in the lab. Obviously, however, Platypus also has small departments dedicated to finance, marketing, and human resources.

Functional organization helps managers of smaller firms improve efficiency and quality by fostering professionalism in the performance of specialized tasks. Bear in mind, however, that as firms grow and become more complex (perhaps by venturing into multiple lines), a functional firm can become downright dysfunctional. Often, problems arise if each functional unit begins to focus too narrowly on its own goals and operations, thus losing sight not only of other functional activities but also of customer needs and corporate objectives. This phenomenon has given rise to the term *functional silos.*

The functional organizational model may also exacerbate problems in multiproduct, multimarket firms. Expansion, whether into product or geographic markets, can become problematic if the strategy that's appropriate in one market doesn't work very well in another. The types of products, for example, that enjoy dominant domestic share may not meet the needs of foreign consumers. Similarly, a firm involved in two different product markets may find that the same competitive methods don't work equally well in both or that different markets call for different sales channels. When a functional structure is used in contexts characterized by varying market demands and sales characteristics, functionally structured organizations may be sluggish in responding to changing customer demands and in accessing potential new customers.

Multidivisional Structure   One solution to the problems of managing activities in multiple markets is the **multidivisional structure**, illustrated in Exhibit 11.7 for the Walt Disney Company. Divisions can be organized around geographic markets, products, or groups of related businesses, with division heads being responsible for the strategy of a coherent group of businesses or markets. Such strategic specialization means that strategic decisions are more likely to be appropriate and timely. It also enables firms to design compensation systems that reward performance at the business-unit, versus functional, level.

One of the first companies to adopt a multidivisional structure, GM is mostly organized according to product divisions (GM Trucks, Chevrolet, Buick, Cadillac, Saturn, and so forth). Each division maintains a finance function, a marketing function, and so on. Multidivisional structure makes it possible to implement division-specific incentives and performance accountability standards, and because each division has ready access to key resources, multidivisional structure also fosters speedier reactions to opportunities and challenges.

multidivisional structure
Form of organization in which divisions are organized around product or geographic markets and are often self-sufficient in terms of functional expertise.

Exhibit 11.7   Multidivisional Structure at Disney

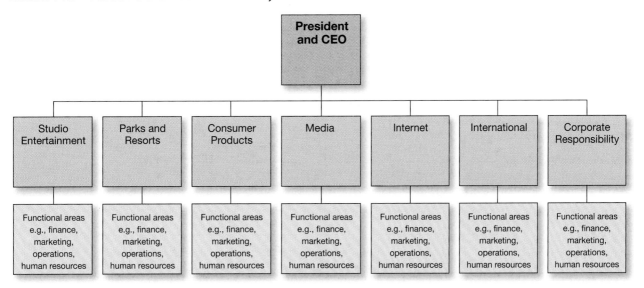

Multidivisional structure is also effective in coordinating diverse economic activities. Headquarters, for example, plans, coordinates, and evaluates all operating divisions, allocating the personnel, facilities, funds, and other resources needed to execute divisional strategies. Divisional managers, meanwhile, are in charge of most of the functions revolving around major product lines and, as such, are typically responsible for divisional financial performance.

For instance, Emageon, a 225-employee provider of advanced visualization tools to hospitals and other medical organizations, has two divisions.[25] One offers electronic hardware, and its sales force works with executives who are responsible for IT decisions at target customers. The second division specializes in software for X-rays and CAT scans, and because physicians usually make the software purchase recommendations, Emageon's software sales force focuses on them. Together, the two divisions provide a complete solution for firms in Emageon's target industry, and as it so happens, each can cross-sell the other's products.

Of course, multidivisional structure is not without drawbacks. It can, for instance, foster undesirable competition between divisions. Emageon doesn't have this problem, but it's not hard to see how GM's higher-end Buicks bump up against its lower-priced Cadillacs.

In addition, when each division is functionally self-contained, there may be costly duplications of staff functions that could be handled more efficiently under some other form of organization. Finally, coordination across divisions can be difficult if cooperation is in the best interests of one division but not those of another.

Matrix Structure   The matrix structure, which is represented in Exhibit 11.8, is a hybrid between the functional and multidivisional structures.

Exhibit 11.8   Matrix Structure

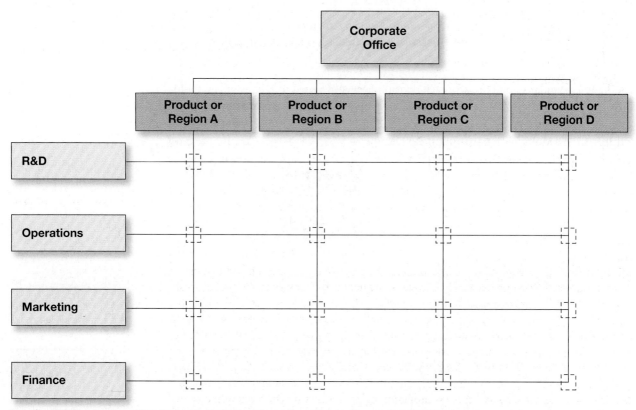

E. Prewitt, "GM's Matrix Reloads," CIO, September 1, 2003. http://www.cio.com/archive/090103/hs_reload.html

A **matrix structure** is designed to take advantage of the benefits of both basic forms—namely, functional specialization and divisional autonomy. As you can see in Exhibit 11.8, two reporting channels exist simultaneously. In our hypothetical company, for instance, there are functional divisions for finance and marketing, but personnel from both divisions are assigned to specific product or geographic divisions. A finance specialist, therefore, reports simultaneously to a finance executive and an executive in one or another of the product or geographic divisions.

The Swiss–Swedish technology giant Asea Brown Boveri (ABB) furnishes perhaps the most dramatic example of the matrix structure in action. In the early 1990s, the firm was composed of more than 900 matrix units. Any structure that sets up so many loci of authority is going to have problems with conflicts over authority and accountability. At ABB, however, managers in one matrix unit rarely exercise direct authority over their counterparts in other units. (Dealings between units, therefore, often depend on managers' skills in the arts of negotiation and persuasion.) Moreover, the matrix provides flexibility by making it possible to organize teams around specific projects, products, or markets.

The utility of a matrix structure increases when the pressures facing a firm are unpredictable and require both high degrees of control and extensive coordination of resources. Many firms find it difficult to implement the matrix structure because it calls for high levels of resource sharing across divisions; in fact, it's generally feasible only when strong culture and shared values support cross-division collaboration. As it turns out, even though ABB enjoyed a strong culture, the company eventually realized that coordinating 900 matrix units was far too complex. Massive restructuring began in early 2000, and today, though ABB is still operating under a matrix structure, it has reduced the number of its operating units by about half.

One word of caution here to those firms that may view a matrix structure as a panacea to organizational problems: While the matrix is great for collaboration, particularly when it is focused around customer needs, it also requires a very different managerial skill set. For instance, in the functional and multidivisional structures, each employee typically reports to one or several bosses. In a matrix, the reporting structure is much more of an adhocracy, and managers with the best power bases and negotiating skills get their agendas accomplished. In general, this means that a shift to a matrix structure, while perhaps desirable, also requires attention to the negotiation and communication skill-sets of the managers tasked with making the matrix work. This is another example of how implementation levers—in this case structure, people, and skills—need to be orchestrated in concert.

Network Structure

A more recent development in organization design, the **network structure** consists of small, semi-autonomous, and potentially temporary groups that are brought together for specific purposes—a team, for example, that's been assembled to work on a new product idea. A network structure also includes external linkages with such groups as suppliers and customers. Sometimes these external linkages take the form of strategic alliances, which you learned about in Chapter 9. Authority is based on the control of resources, knowledge, and expertise, rather than on hierarchical rank, and because it's highly flexible, a firm can reconfigure staff and resources rapidly enough to exploit rich but fleeting bubbles of opportunity. Drawbacks include the potential for confusion and ambiguity.

Gore Industries provides a good example of the network structure in action. You probably know about Gore through its popular GORE-TEX fabrics. Although difficult to diagram here, imagine what an organizational structure would look like for Gore, with its approximately 7,400 associates working in more than forty-five plants and sales locations worldwide. Sales and customer service sites are located in Argentina, Australia, Austria, Brazil, China, Finland, France, Germany, Greece, Hong Kong, India, Italy, Japan, Korea, Malaysia, the Netherlands, New Zealand, Poland, Russia, Scotland, Singapore, Spain, Sweden, Taiwan, and the United States. Manufacturing operations are clustered in the United States, Germany, Scotland, Japan, and China. Gore separates its products into ten categories:

matrix structure Form of organization in which specialists from functional departments are assigned to work for one or more product or geographic units.

network structure Form of organization in which small, semiautonomous, and potentially temporary groups are brought together for specific purposes.

aerospace, automotive, chemical processing, computers/telecommunications/ electronics, energy, environment, industrial/manufacturing, medical/healthcare, military, and textiles. As with the typical network organization, Gore employees work in small teams and are encouraged to participate in direct one-on-one communication with other Gore associates, customers, and suppliers. So, Gore employees do not report through the normal hierarchical structure, but through shifting project teams.

The Real Network　You have likely heard the saying that it's not *what* you know, but *who* you know, that matters. Increasingly, organizations are recognizing that it is the informal networks, and not the formal reporting relationships in the organization chart, that matter most. These informal networks operate beyond the boundaries of the formal structure and actually help the firm evolve in positive ways that the fixed organizational structure might otherwise prevent. Research on social networks has shown that the most productive firms are those that identify "brokers"—individuals who are successful and effective at linking otherwise unconnected parts of the organization. They also identify and promote "central connectors"—individuals whom others frequently consult for information, decision-making help, or expertise. Regardless of the actual formal structure, firms that foster these fluid and living network relationships are more likely to see achievement of desired results.[26]

Partnerships and Franchises

Before leaving this section, we should mention two additional forms of organization structure—the professional partnership and the franchise system. Although both are as much forms of legal ownership as they are organizational structures, they offer a few unique structural characteristics that can impact persistent organizational problems. In addition, because both are common fixtures on the business landscape, it's important that you understand their role in the national economy.

Professional Partnerships　In several industries, the professional partnership is the structural form of choice. In a professional partnership, the company is organized as a group of partners who own shares or units in the company. Generally, the partners vote on a managing partner who will act as a supervisor, but this person serves at their pleasure. Consequently, a senior partner has significant authority and prestige but perhaps not nearly the power that a CEO of a large firm has over subordinates. Partnerships are pyramid-shaped structures, with each partner having a number of associates (of various levels). Industries in which the partnership form is common include legal offices, accounting firms, consulting firms, advertising agencies, and real estate companies. Until recently, investment banking firms were structured as partnerships, but most have converted to publicly held corporations. The management structure of investment banking firms has remained relatively the same, but the change to a corporate form has enabled firms to increase their capitalization.

Franchise Structure　The franchise system not only transfers ownership of local facilities to a franchisee, it likewise shifts all local management responsibility to the franchisee. One purpose of using a franchise model is that it enables a firm to grow rapidly because much of the capital costs are picked up by the franchisees. However, the franchise model fundamentally changes the organizational structure of the firm. A franchisee assumes all management responsibility for individual business locations. For the right to the franchisor's business model and brand name, the franchisee pays a royalty percentage and other fees to the franchisor.

SYSTEMS AND PROCESSES

When asked to think about the systems and processes needed to manage an organization, people usually mention information systems (IS). In reality, an IS is just one type of vital system. Systems and processes make it possible to manage budgeting, quality control, planning, distribution, and resource allocation in complex contemporary organizations. However, two particular systems are taking root in American firms and it is important that you are at least familiar with them. These are the balanced scorecard and Lean process improvement. You learned a little about Lean through the opening vignette on HUI, and before talking more about it, we will give you a primer on the balance scorecard.

In Chapter 2, we pointed out that ambitious vision and mission statements don't automatically translate into higher levels of financial performance.[27] Conversely, of course, a myopic focus on financial accounting results, such as return on equity or return on sales, may cause managers to lose sight of long-term strategic initiatives and divert their attention from other key stakeholders.[28] For this reason, many firms are developing performance-measurement and management systems that enable them to balance the need to report short-term financial returns with the need to pursue longer-term (and often intangible) objectives. Various approaches can be used to gauge the success with which implementation levers are aligned with strategic objectives; the most common term for these performance management systems is the *balanced scorecard.*

The Balanced Scorecard

For the firms that utilize this practice best, the **balanced scorecard** has evolved into what might just as well be called a *strategy scorecard*. It's a strategic management support system devised to help managers measure vision and strategy against business- and operating-unit-level performance along several critical dimensions.[29] It provides balance because it requires managers to reconcile priorities across functions, over time, and across initiatives. It is important to note that the balanced scorecard and strategy map are not strategies in and of themselves. Instead, they serve to (1) translate the strategy into operational terms, (2) align the organization with the strategy, (3) make strategy everyone's job, (4) make strategy a continual process, and (5) mobilize change through executive leadership. The cascading nature of vision through the balanced scorecard and strategy map is summarized in Exhibit 11.9.[30]

> **balanced scorecard**
> Strategic management support system for measuring vision and strategy against business- and operating-unit-level performance.

What this diagram should make clear, is that the balanced scorecard and strategy map are the means for achieving the strategy—particularly the staging and pacing components of the strategy diamond—too often firms go through the expensive exercise of formulating a strategy, and then leaving it in a three-ring binder on a shelf. The scorecard and mapping process pushes the company to act on what it said it was going to do in terms of strategy. It provides a coherent mechanism for managing tradeoffs, since the scorecard is driven by the staging and pacing of the strategy itself.

Beyond these larger issues, the balanced scorecard approach teaches three fundamental lessons:

1. Translate strategy into tangible and intangible performance metrics (recall the summary of financial and nonfinancial performance measures summarized in Exhibit 2.10 of Chapter 2).

2. Use a *strategy map* to align metrics with strategy.

3. Make strategy a continuous and dynamic process.[31]

Let's look a little more closely at each of these principles.

Relying on a Range of Metrics Managers should pay attention to a variety of performance metrics, not just to short-term financial performance indicators. Granted, financial performance is the easiest metric to apply, but other indicators are just as critical in diagnosing and maintaining the long-term health of an organization. The balanced scorecard prevents managers from relying solely on short-term financial or other outcome measures and forces them to focus instead on those measures, both tangible and intangible, that are relevant to the elements of value being delivered to key stakeholders.

Exhibit 11.9 Cascading Nature of the Balanced Scorecard

Leading proponents of this approach advise managers to consider four perspectives on performance: *financial, external, internal business process,* and *learning and growth:*

1. The *financial perspective* involves strategy for growth, profitability, and risk when viewed from the shareholder's or owner's perspective.

2. The *external relations perspective* pertains to strategy for creating value and differentiation from the perspective of the customer.

3. The *internal business process perspective* reflects strategic priorities among processes according to their contributions to customer and shareholder satisfaction.

4. The *learning and growth perspective* focuses on the organization's priorities for fostering change, innovation, and growth.

Exhibit 11.10 illustrates the links among these four perspectives and a firm's vision and strategy. It can also serve as a worksheet for identifying a performance metric, its target level, and the specific initiatives aimed at achieving the target.

Recall that the overarching strategic management process introduced in Chapter 1 flows from vision to goals and objectives and then to the strategy diamond, which sets out how those goals and objectives are to be achieved. You can think of the balanced scorecard as an elaborate summary of the goals and objectives in the strategic management process. Essentially, management must distill tangible and intangible strategic objectives for each area down into specific measures that will be used to gauge those

Exhibit 11.10 The Balanced Scorecard System

External			
"To achieve our vision, how should we appear to our customers?"	Objectives	Measures	Targets	Initiatives

Financial			
"To succeed financially, how should we appear to our shareholders?"	Objectives	Measures	Targets	Initiatives

Vision and Strategy

Internal Business Process			
"To satisfy our shareholders and customers, what business processes must we excel at?"	Objectives	Measures	Targets	Initiatives

Learning and Growth			
"To achieve our vision, how will we sustain our ability to change and improve?"	Objectives	Measures	Targets	Initiatives

objectives. Are our goals growth goals, profitability goals, market share goals, or some combination of these? The balanced scorecard communicates these perspectives clearly and coherently; since strategy tells managers what they should do and what they should not do, this visual aspect of the balanced scorecard becomes very powerful. Targets are then set for those measures and initiatives that are launched to reach the desired targets. Ideally, these measures will have leading, pacing, and lagging characteristics such that management can tell if they are moving forward, how well and quickly they are doing so, and when initiatives are drawing to a successful conclusion. For instance, GE uses a very simple leading indicator to determine if business is growing or slowing: sales people ask their customer if they would refer them to another prospective client. GE has found this to be a very reliable indicator of future business. The beauty of the balanced scorecard process is, with this type of knowledge, GE can direct resources to the types of actions that lead to more customer referrals. Previously, it was investing in many different marketing approaches with no idea as to which marketing approach generated the greatest yields.

Developing a Strategy Map Exhibit 11.10 shows how managers can begin the strategy-mapping process.[32] This is not an easy process, and requires that managers talk through their interests, share information about their functions and businesses, and reconcile their priorities. Through this process, the most important objectives are identified, measures are assigned to those objectives (again, leading, lagging, and pacing indicators), and then specific targets are designed. ◆

The purpose of the targets is to help the firm understand if the staging and pacing of the strategy is on track. Specific initiatives are then designed to achieve the desired targets, and so on. The benefit of this visual tool is that managers now understand what other initiatives

Staging & Pacing

are being invested in across the business. In some cases this prevents duplication of effort, and in other cases lets parts of the firm pool their resources to realize greater or quicker gains.

The next, and most critical, step of the process is to develop a *strategy map* wherein managers link all performance metrics to the firm's strategy. Many managers begin mapping systems and processes by diagramming activities across the four perspectives that we've already developed: (1) financial, (2) external relations, (3) internal business processes, and (4) learning and growth. An example of this cause-and-effect approach to strategy mapping is shown in Exhibit 11.11.[33]

The strategy map states objectives—in terms of business processes, cycle time, productivity, and other important internal processes—to guide key activities. It is important to note that the bubbles you see in the chart are not generic, but instead are agreed upon by the management team as those most relevant to the respective perspectives. When mapping learning-and-growth objectives, managers should indicate what must be done—in terms of people and product and process development—if learning-and-growth processes are to be developed and sustained.

The two remaining perspectives shown in Exhibit 11.11—customer and financial—state objectives that reflect the desired outcomes. How, for instance, does the firm want customers, partners, and other external stakeholders to perceive it? How will planned activities ultimately translate into financial results and economic value? The arrows that connect the various boxes and bubbles are important, in that they should demonstrate expected cause and effect relationships. Just as importantly, if a bubble or box does not have an arrow coming from or to it, then it either means that activity is not important or that there is nothing in place to achieve it.

As the box entitled "How Would *You* Do That? 11.1" demonstrates, a balanced scorecard can smooth the process of strategy implementation—for all of the reasons described so far. Linking objectives in this way helps managers articulate causality between objectives—a key factor in linking strategy to relevant performance measures.[34]

Making Strategy a Continuous and Dynamic Process   To ensure that a strategy remains continuous and dynamic, managers must succeed at two tasks:

1. Disseminating the key features of a strategy and stipulating responsibilities for executing it throughout the organization

2. Linking the strategy with the financial budget

In one important sense, the balanced scorecard can serve as a tool for communicating vision, mission, and strategy throughout an organization—a theme which we'll return to later in the chapter when we discuss the roles of strategic leadership in strategy implementation. Employees who've participated in developing and revising a balanced scorecard should have a fairly in-depth understanding of a firm's strategy and of the ways in which underlying maps come together to support it. During the process, they should also develop a good sense of whether the organization's culture will support the strategy. Finally, beyond simple communication, the dissemination process can foster broader support for the strategy among stakeholders, improve understanding of how the balanced scorecard works to ensure that the strategy is effectively implemented, and furnish a mechanism for receiving feedback.

To be sure, in the form of operational budgets, the process of financial budgeting not only provides a feedback tool, but also helps to determine resource allocation. However, operational budgets impose a form of outcome control that, by its very nature, tends to constrain managers and hamper investment in new capabilities and products.

In contrast, a *strategic* budget focuses on identifying and acquiring new customers, new capabilities, new operations, and new products. The balanced scorecard is important in de-

Exhibit 11.11   The Strategy Map Basis for the Balanced Scorecard

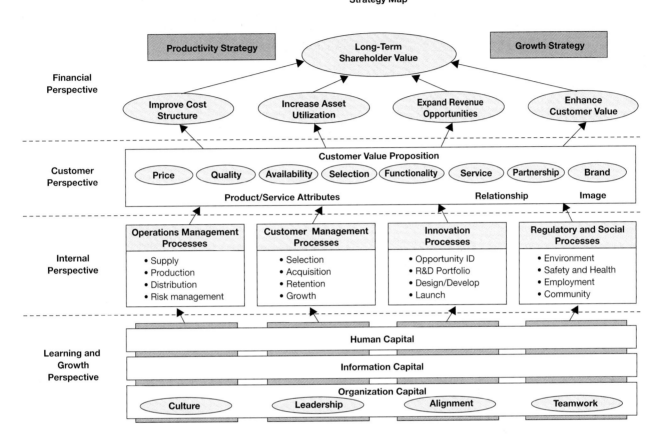

termining the mix and amount of spending in the strategic budget. The relationship between strategic priorities and the scorecard is further reinforced when compensation is tied to financial and nonfinancial measures. Microsoft, for instance, now ties the compensation of its top 600 officers to customer satisfaction scores, a critical nonfinancial performance measure in the company's balanced scorecard.[35]

What Is Lean?   Beyond the balanced scorecard, another profound process change in manufacturing and service operations is the adoption of lean practices. As you learned in the opening vignette on HUI, Lean is a generic process management philosophy derived mostly from the Toyota Production System (TPS) but also from other sources. It is renowned for its focus on reduction of the original Toyota 'seven wastes' in order to improve overall customer value. Lean is often linked with Six Sigma because of that methodology's emphasis on reduction of process variation (or its converse, smoothness). Toyota's steady growth from a small player to the most valuable and the biggest car company in the world has focused attention upon how it has achieved this, making "Lean" a hot topic in management science in the first decade of the twenty-first century. The opening vignette on HUI, and its success through its adoption of lean initiatives, should tell you that Lean would likely be a necessary part of any future leader's vocabulary.

For many, Lean is the set of TPS "tools" that assist in the identification and then steady elimination of waste (*muda*), quality improvement, and production time and cost reductions. While the use of Japanese terms may appear distracting at first, you will quickly find

Developing a Balanced Scorecard for the NUWC

Exhibit 11.12 shows the first steps in the mapping process at the U.S. Naval Undersea Warfare Center (NUWC), the Navy's full-spectrum research, testing, and engineering center for submarines, autonomous underwater systems, and weapons systems associated with undersea warfare.[36]

As a result of the strategic-mapping process, which involved communication among managers in all parts and levels of the organization in addition to external stakeholders, three organizational themes emerged—innovation, affordability, and putting the customer first. In turn, these themes led to the development of a system of performance metrics that is aligned with the clearly articulated strategic direction of NUWC. (This example, by the way, shows that the concept of the balanced scorecard can be applied to both nonprofit and for-profit organizations.)

The next step (for NUWC or any other organization) is to develop objectives, measures, targets, and initiatives for each of the key perspectives. These perspectives should then be used to develop the overarching strategy map. If there are inconsistencies between pieces in the map, then the relevant stakeholders

Exhibit 11.12   Balanced Scorecard Development at the Naval Undersea Warfare Center (NUWC)

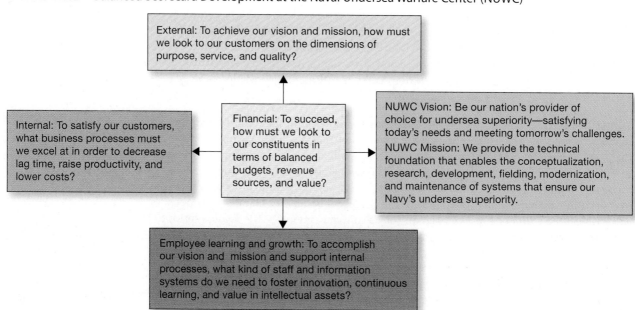

External: To achieve our vision and mission, how must we look to our customers on the dimensions of purpose, service, and quality?

Internal: To satisfy our customers, what business processes must we excel at in order to decrease lag time, raise productivity, and lower costs?

Financial: To succeed, how must we look to our constituents in terms of balanced budgets, revenue sources, and value?

NUWC Vision: Be our nation's provider of choice for undersea superiority—satisfying today's needs and meeting tomorrow's challenges.
NUWC Mission: We provide the technical foundation that enables the conceptualization, research, development, fielding, modernization, and maintenance of systems that ensure our Navy's undersea superiority.

Employee learning and growth: To accomplish our vision and mission and support internal processes, what kind of staff and information systems do we need to foster innovation, continuous learning, and value in intellectual assets?

can use this information as an opportunity to refine the implementation of the strategy, including revision of the objectives, measures, targets, and initiatives. Because the perspectives and their underlying objectives are related to strategic priorities, the system goes well beyond a mere listing of things to do or key performance indicators. By means of the mapping process, all metrics are related to strategic objectives.

The next step in the process for NUWC would be to create the strategy map. For this scenario, a simple strategy map like the one shown in Exhibit 11.13 will do.

You can see that we have further simplified the form to let you identify the relationships among financial, external, internal, and learning perspectives, alongside the measures, targets, and initiatives you would align with those perspectives. When you are done with the mapping process, you can imagine that you will have a good idea what it will take to implement the strategy you have outlined with your strategy diamond, as well as what activities are not mission-critical. Given what you know in general about NUWC or perhaps what you can glean from the web, take a stab at filling out this map for NUWC.

Exhibit 11.13   Strategy Map Worksheet

Overarching Themes	Measurement	Target	Initiative
Financial Quality Balance Revenue			
External			
Internal			
Learning			

Exhibit 11.14   Elimination of Waste as the Soul of Lean

Muda 無駄 is a Japanese term for activity that is wasteful and doesn't add value. It is also a key concept in the Toyota Production System and is one of the three types of waste (Muda, Mura, Muri) that it identifies. Waste reduction is an effective way to increase profitability. Following are the seven deadly wastes, along with their definitions:

1. Defects Quality defects prevent the customer from accepting the product produced. The effort to create these defects is wasted. New waste management processes must be added in an effort to reclaim some value for the otherwise scrap product.

2. Overproduction Overproduction is the production or acquisition of items before they are actually required. It is the most dangerous waste of the company, because it hides the production problems. Overproduction must be stored, managed, and protected.

3. Transportation Each time a product is moved it stands the risk of being damaged, lost, delayed, etc. as well as being a cost for no added value. Transportation does not make any transformation to the product that the consumer is willing to pay for.

4. Waiting Refers to both the time spent by the workers waiting for resources to arrive, the queue for their products to empty as well as the capital sunk in goods and services that are not yet delivered to the customer. It is often the case that there are processes to manage this waiting.

5. Inventory Inventory—be it in the form of raw materials, work-in-progress (WIP), or finished goods—represent a capital outlay that has not yet produced an income either by the producer or for the consumer. Waste occurs when any of these three items are not actively processed to add value.

6. Motion As compared to transportation, motion refers to the producer or worker or equipment. This has significance to damage, wear, or safety. It also includes the fixed assets and expenses incurred in the production process.

7. Overprocessing Using a more expensive or otherwise valuable resource than is needed for the task or adding features that are unneeded by the customer. There is a particular problem with this item with regard to people. People may need to perform tasks that they are overqualified for so as to maintain their competency. This training cost can be used to offset the waste associated with overprocessing.

that it is the common vocabulary surrounding Lean thinking. You have a brief introduction to these seven wastes in Exhibit 11.14. To solve the problem of waste, Lean has several "tools" at its disposal. These include continuous process improvement (*kaizen*), the "5 Whys," and mistake-proofing (*poka-yoke*).

There is a second approach to Lean promoted by Toyota in which the focus is upon implementing the "flow" or smoothness of work (*mura*) through the system and not upon "waste reduction" per se. Techniques to improve flow include production leveling, "pull" production (by means of *kanban*), and the Heijunka box. The implementation of smooth flow exposes quality problems that always existed and thus waste reduction naturally happens as a consequence. The advantage of this approach is that it naturally takes a system-wide perspective, whereas a "waste" focus assumes this perspective.

Lean was originally developed and applied in a manufacturing context, but is now seen as relevant to service firms, and all value chain aspects of the firm. Sales, human resources, and customer service, for instance, all can provide a context for the application of Lean principles. As you began to see in the introductory vignette on HUI, key Lean principles are:

■ Perfect first-time quality through quest for zero defects, revealing and solving problems at their ultimate source, achieving higher quality and productivity simultaneously, teamwork, and worker empowerment

- Waste minimization by removing all non-value-added activities, making the most efficient use of scarce resources (capital, people, space), just-in-time inventory, and eliminating any safety nets

- Continuous improvement (reducing costs, improving quality, increasing productivity) through dynamic process of change, simultaneous and integrated product/process development, rapid cycle time and time-to-market, and openness and information sharing

- Flexibility in producing different mixes or greater diversity of products quickly, without sacrificing efficiency at lower volumes of production, through rapid set-up and manufacturing at small lot sizes

- Long-term relationships between suppliers and primary producers (assemblers, system integrators) through collaborative risk-sharing, cost-sharing, and information-sharing arrangements

PEOPLE AND REWARDS

This next subset of implementation levers draws attention to the importance of people and the rewards that can be used to align their energies and actions with the organization's objectives. We'll treat people and rewards together because inappropriate incentives and controls can frustrate the efforts of even the best people. Let's go back to our earlier example of the impact of inadequate compensation policies on SAP's strategy. One problem was that the company's compensation system rewarded people for generating new sales regardless of whether SAP product packages were priced to yield a profit for the firm. In terms of sales, the firm grew quickly, but SAP eventually realized that, over time, many of its customer relationships were costing it more money than it was making.

People Employees are sometimes called a firm's *human capital* in order to distinguish them from fixed assets and financial capital. Individually, people are a critical component in strategy formulation and implementation. Collectively, people comprise the firm's culture, and such culture contributes strongly to a firm's dynamic capabilities and competitive advantage. Barclay's Global Investors (BGI) provides a good case in point of how a firm's culture of action orientation and self-reliance can and must be aggressively nurtured and protected:

> One of the things we discovered was that there are certain basic things—values, vision, the culture of the firm—that are not up for discussion. You can discuss it in the sense of explaining it and understanding it, but it's not something that is going to be changed. It's important for people to understand that. When you become part of BGI, this is what you are signing up for. And quite frankly, we've still got a small hard-core group of our managing directors that still are questioning it. So we are at the point of saying to them, "Well, maybe it's best that you go someplace else, because these things aren't up for discussion."[37]

As we've indicated on several occasions, a strategy will succeed only if a firm has the right people with the right experience and competencies. As the BGI example demonstrates, this also includes people who share and steward the corporate culture. Thus, recruitment, selection, and training with an eye to competencies and values are critical to strategy implementation. In a recent study, management researcher Jim Collins examined eleven firms that went from good to excellent performance and sustained it over a 15-year period. He then compared these firms with peer companies that had similar prestudy performance but never reached the level of great performance. In all eleven cases of good-to-great companies, making sure they had the right people working was a major priority for CEOs early in their tenures. Collins reports that many executives believe the people lever to be the most crucial to the successful implementation of strategy. Successful CEOs, according to Collins, "attended to people first [and] strategy second. They got the right people on the bus, moved the wrong people off, ushered the right people to the right seats—and then they figured out where to drive it."[38] In BGI's case, for example, management's clarity on the requisite values and principles each employee should hold enabled managers to identify quickly those individuals who fit the desired BGI culture.

So how do people influence firm performance? In many organizations, of course, the skills of their people make it possible for them to do what they do best.[39] That's why the VRINE framework regards such expertise as an important part of a firm's bundle of strategic capabilities. Some consultants and scholars think that these bundles of skills, all the way down to the level of those possessed by teams and even specific individuals, are the key factor in a firm's long-term viability and its ability to innovate new products.[40] People decisions are critical to performance because decisions about which and how many people to employ hinge on the desire either to improve efficiency or generate new revenues.[41]

Because human resources are generally a firm's largest operating cost, many managers focus on reducing this cost. Moreover, the stock market tends to react positively to downsizing.[42] Ironically, however, research shows that although downsizing results in a short-term stock-price improvement, it's often followed by productivity declines that can take several years to correct.[43] These results are consistent with research showing that when a firm's HR policies focus on enhancing its human capital, there are positive effects on several dimensions of operational performance (such as employee productivity, machine efficiency, and the alignment of product and service capabilities with customers' needs).[44]

The continued success of highly profitable growth companies results largely from skill in recruiting people who fit the organization, adhere to its values, and work toward common goals. Both JetBlue and Southwest Airlines, for example, expend considerable effort making sure that new hires will fit the firm.

Many companies focus on staffing cuts because employees represent their largest expense. Although Wall Street usually reacts positively to such moves, firms that downsize often experience long-term performance declines.

Regardless of the specifics of the strategy, at the end of the day, success depends on hiring the right people and developing and training them in ways that support a firm's strategy. Competitive advantage, therefore, is inextricably bound up in a firm's human capital.[45] Unfortunately, many firms don't seem to appreciate fully the role of people in developing and sustaining a competitive advantage. One study found that only 50 percent of managers in firms today believe that human capital matters; only about half of those actually launch human-resource initiatives, and only about half of those stick to those initiatives.[46] Not surprisingly, the remaining one-eighth includes such world-class companies as Southwest Airlines, General Electric, and Microsoft. According to the authors of another recent study, few leaders seem to understand that their "most important asset walks out the door every night."[47]

The importance of having the right people is accentuated in human-capital-intensive industries. If, for instance, a key resource in a firm's industry is access to oilfields, it doesn't have the same concern about human resources as a firm whose key resource is access to scientific knowledge. Oil fields can't quit and jump to a competitor, demand higher wages, reject authority, lose motivation, or become dissatisfied with management and coworkers.[48] Consequently, firms in human-capital-intensive industries must develop strategies to reduce the risk of losing the human capital. Besides fostering job satisfaction, companies can develop firm-specific knowledge that's less transferable to other firms. Profit-sharing initiatives encourage valuable people to stay with an employer because they have a stake in any value that they help to create. Adjusting organization structure to eliminate authoritative and mechanistic processes and to accommodate more egalitarian and participative models reduces turnover.[49]

Rewards

Although rewards are technically the function of a system, we discuss them in this section because of their obvious relationship to people. An old management adage is *you get what you measure.* In reality, however, this proposition may need to be altered slightly: In the real workplace, it seems that what gets done is that which is rewarded.[50] Some experts grant that although organizational culture may be difficult to change, **reward systems**, which determine the compensation and promotion of an organization's employees, express and reinforce the values and expectations embedded in its culture.[51] Thus, any strategist who wants to get things done must think and act flexibly with regard to compensation and align rewards not only with strategy, but also with other implementation levers.

reward system   Bases on which employees are compensated and promoted.

The Components of the Reward System   Reward systems have two components:

1. Performance evaluation and feedback

2. Compensation, which can consist of salary, bonuses, stock, stock options, promotions, and even such perquisites as cars and coveted office spaces

Single-business firms usually have one reward system, although the compensation component will probably vary by functional area. Salespeople, for instance, will have incentives based on sales growth, particularly profitable sales growth; whereas employees in production and procurement will have incentives based on quality, cost control, and customer service. Again, rewards are designed to encourage achievement of the organization's strategic objectives, and neither rewards nor penalties apply to performance that's unrelated to those objectives.

Rewards as a Form of Control   Like structure, systems, and processes, rewards also serve as a form of control. Rewards necessarily require that performance and behavior targets be stipulated, but their control function can take one of two forms: outcome controls or behavioral controls.

Outcome Controls   **Outcome controls** monitor and reward individuals and groups based on whether a measurable goal has been achieved. Such controls are generally preferable when just one or two performance measures (say, return on investment or return on assets) are good gauges of a business's health. Outcome controls are effective when there's little external interference between managerial decision-making and business performance. It also helps if little or no coordination with other business units is required, because each unit's people will be seeking to maximize their performance on the targeted measure. Because of this, outcome controls often provide a disincentive for cross-unit collaboration.

outcome controls   Practice of tying rewards to narrowly defined financial criteria.

Behavioral Controls   **Behavioral controls** involve the direct evaluation of managerial decision-making, not of the results of managerial decisions. Behavioral controls tie rewards to a broader range of criteria, such as those identified in the balanced scorecard. Behavioral controls and commensurate rewards are typically more appropriate when many external and internal factors can affect the relationship between a manager's decisions and organizational performance. They're also appropriate when managers must coordinate resources and capabilities across different business units.

behavioral controls   Practice of tying rewards to criteria other than simply financial performance, such as those broadly identified in the balanced scorecard.

Compensation in the Diversified Firm   Although diversified firms may rely on a single reward system for all business units, reward systems usually vary in order to reflect both overall corporate strategy and the competitive environment and strategy of each business unit. A diversified company like GE, which owns several unrelated businesses, achieves the best results by linking the pay of division managers to the performance of the units that they manage. On the business-unit level, therefore, outcome-based controls and reward systems are aligned with both corporate strategy and organization structure.

However, in a diversified firm that expects divisions to share resources and otherwise cross-subsidize each other, the same sort of compensation would provide *disincentives* for resource sharing. Division managers who are paid solely on the basis of business-unit performance, for instance, might reasonably conclude that it's not in their best interest to subsidize other divisions because doing so may jeopardize their own units' performance and, therefore, their pay.

Conversely, a diversified firm that's trying to generate synergies across business units can increase the likelihood of desired outcomes by linking unit managers' rewards to actual decisions and other balanced-scorecard criteria rather than to individual unit performance.[52] To encourage managers to recognize their own stakes in organizational prospects, rewards often include stock-based incentives or bonuses based on firmwide performance.

To further illustrate how reward systems can affect strategy implementation, let's consider the ways in which incentive systems can impact the realization of postmerger synergies. Many mergers are driven by the belief that two companies can generate net new revenue if they're combined in one firm. But what if compensation systems don't reward employees for sharing knowledge and resources? Obviously, synergies probably won't materialize. Mergers between commercial and investment banks, for instance, are often hampered by incongruent incentive systems.[53] Key employees of commercial banks are typically rewarded for managing relationships, whereas investment bankers are rewarded for doing deals. Paying bankers to do deals is generally at odds with the need for commercial banks to minimize risk and retain customers. Alternatively, investment bankers generally earn bigger bonuses on larger and higher-risk deals.

Contingency Framework for Analyzing Pay People are an essential element in strategy execution, but the employment relationship with them can vary by context, which is typically a function of firm strategy. Some organizations view their relationships with employees as passive and transactional, while others view them as enduring or family-like. On a second dimension, the employees themselves may have a weak or highly committed relationship with their employer. Taken together, these factors have been shown to play out in different compensation profiles, as summarized in Exhibit 11.15.[54]

These characterizations are intended to give you an idea of how compensation can take on different flavors, depending on the employer-employee relationships. Obviously, there will be many exceptions to the examples in this typology but it at least gives you a way to

Exhibit 11.15 Employer/Employee Relationship Matrix

High — Employer transactional relationship	High Pay—Low Commitment • Hired Guns—Investment Bankers	High Pay—High Commitment • Cultlike—Google
Low	Low Pay—Low Commitment • Workers as Commodity • Employers of Migrant Laborers	Low Pay—High Commitment • Family—Starbucks
	Low High	

Employee Relations

Exhibit 11.16   Pay Philosophies at Medtronic and AES

Stated Pay Objectives at Medtronic and AES	
Medtronic	**AES**
<ul><li>Support objectives and increased complexity of business</li><li>Minimize increases in fixed costs</li><li>Emphasize performance through variable pay and stock</li><li>Competitiveness aligned with financial performance: 50th percentile performance paid at 50th percentile of market, 75th percentile performance paid at 75th percentile of market</li></ul>	<ul><li>Our guiding principles are to act with integrity, treat people fairly, have fun, and be involved in projects that provide social benefits. This means that we will:</li><li>Help AES attract self-motivated, dependable people who want to keep learning new things</li><li>Hire people who really like the place and believe in the AES system</li><li>Pay what others are paid both inside and outside AES, but hire people who are willing to take less to join AES</li><li>Use teams of employees and managers to manage the compensation system</li><li>Make all employees stockholders</li></ul>

think about the employee-employer relationships, as it relates to compensation. The best way to see how these objectives play out is to look at examples of statements of pay practices by such firms as Medtronic, a medical device manufacturer, and AES, a global energy company, shown in Exhibit 11.16. [55]

Rewarding A, While Hoping for B   We can't conclude this discussion of rewards without reminding you of the classic article by Steven Kerr titled "On the folly of rewarding A, while hoping for B."[56] This section is more of a reminder than a toolkit item for you, but we hope that you take it to heart. The essential message is that organizations often have a strategy to achieve certain objectives, but then set out a reward system and incentivize behaviors that work at odds to that strategy. The balanced scorecard, by the way, is one tool that can help firms avoid these all-too-common problems. Some of the common management follies are summarized in Exhibit 11.17.[57]

Exhibit 11.17   Common Management Follies with Regard to Reward Systems

We Hope For . . .	But We Reward For . . .
Long-term growth; environmental responsibility	Quarterly earnings
Teamwork	Individual effort
Setting challenging "stretch" objectives	Achieving goals; "making the numbers"
Downsizing; rightsizing; delayering; restructuring	Adding staff; adding budget; adding Hay points
Commitment to total quality	Shipping on schedule, even with defects
Candor; surfacing bad news early	Reporting good news, whether it's true or not; agreeing with the boss, whether or not (s)he's right

Strategic Leadership and Strategy Implementation

Strategic leadership plays two critical roles in successful strategy implementation. We're going to highlight them here so that you can incorporate them into your assessment of a strategy's feasibility and include them in your implementation plans. Specifically, strategic leadership is responsible for:

- Making substantive implementation lever and resource-allocation decisions
- Communicating the strategy to key stakeholders

Let's take a closer look at both of these roles.

DECISIONS ABOUT LEVERS

We hope that it is obvious to you that the choices about which levers to employ and when to employ them do not appear out of thin air as a result of executive action (and sometimes inaction or neglect). The examples you have seen in this chapter, and in other parts of the text, have emphasized the importance of aligning strategy with the appropriate implementation levers. For instance, the executives at HUI are very careful to preserve the organization's deep culture of innovation and the unique levers that reinforce this culture and, ultimately, the firm's strategy and competitive advantage. New ventures by HUI are also launched with all of these key supporting implementation levers in place.

Like strategy-formulation decisions, decisions about levers involve important tradeoffs regarding what the firm will and will not do. Misalignment between the levers and the strategy can arise because management has made poor choices about which levers to employ, is employing too simple or too complex a repertoire of levers for the given situation, or the organization or its competitive environment has changed such that the levers need to be changed but have not been. For example, a firm that is small, experiencing the growth stage of its respective arena, and facing little direct competition may be well served by a functional structure, relatively little bureaucracy, and an incentive system that emphasizes growth and innovation. However, as the firm grows, its operations typically become more complex, including diversification into new product and geographic markets. Similarly, it is likely that it will face growing competition and cost pressures. Top management should probably be in the process of changing the implementation levers to favor some form of multibusiness or matrix structure and a compensation system that rewards financial accountability and not just growth. Absent such important management choices about which levers to employ, the firm may lose its once-strong competitive foothold.

DECISIONS ABOUT RESOURCE ALLOCATION

A good strategy guides managers in making decisions about the allocation of resources. Again, a good strategy tells managers what the firm should and shouldn't be doing, and thus helps them decide on important tradeoffs—an extremely important function because an organization that tries to be all things to all people by investing equally in every value-chain activity is doomed to mediocrity at best. Top managers must allocate resources in ways that are consistent with the firm's strategy and make the tradeoffs that this entails. Unfortunately, internal interests—whether political, self-serving, or misguided—can sabotage effective resource allocation decisions and undermine even well-crafted strategies.

Both the misallocation of resources and the failure to make hard investment choices often result from a firm basing its resource allocation on that of its competitors. As a result, not only does the firm become less distinctive from a competitive standpoint, but many of the key players in an industry start to look like clones of one another.

Let's look at the ways in which different carriers in the airline industry manage—and don't manage—certain tradeoffs.[58] Exhibit 11.18 summarizes the key areas in which commercial airlines make strategic resource allocation decisions (if you look back at the example of [yellow tail] wine in Chapter 6, you will see a similar picture of the importance of resource allocation tradeoff choices in the wine industry).[59]

As you can see, in the airline industry, the key resource allocation choices are numerous and range from price for tickets to frequent departure times. Recall that these lines are not meant to depict trends but rather the different patterns of resource allocation choices made by the respective parties. What's striking is the fact that most major airlines seem to be mimicking each other's resource allocation decisions. Two exceptions are Southwest and JetBlue, which, as you can tell from their resource allocation decisions, are following decidedly different strategies. Some have even suggested that for Southwest, with its extensive network of short routes and frequent departures, the greatest competition actually comes from customers' automobiles! JetBlue's management committed itself to allocation decisions that would support the airline's overarching strategy, even when tempted with less expensive options. As a low-cost airline, for instance, JetBlue decided that it needed a modern fleet of new, fuel-efficient aircraft. Used aircraft would have been significantly cheaper (but only in the short run), and management could have rationalized the savings of precious startup capital. Such a shortcut, however, would have been inconsistent with the specific low-cost economic logic of the firm's strategy.

The point to be made here—and which we've made throughout this book—is that competitive advantage goes to those firms who develop unique advantages. Most of the time, such firms develop unique advantages because they make independent resource allocation decisions instead of mimicking those of everybody else in the industry. Remember, too, that resources and capabilities—especially those that are likely to distinguish a firm from its competitors—are usually scarce. Scarcity takes many forms; a firm, for example, may have a team of brilliant researchers who can only work on so many projects for so many hours in a week. Managers, therefore, must revisit their strategy diamond and make at least two

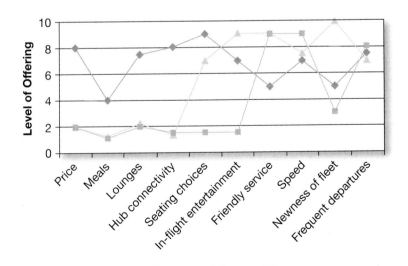

Exhibit 11.18 Resource Allocation Decisions in the Airline Industry

difficult decisions when allocating the firm's resources and capabilities: (1) what to direct at each arena and (2) what to direct to each differentiator.

One additional point bears mention here. You are already aware, from earlier chapters, of how well Intel reoriented its resource allocation to favor a much more profitable and successful computer chip—one that essentially wrote the winning ticket for Intel. What you might not know is that it took another year for Intel to figure out that it was still spending over a billion dollars of R&D investment on the discontinued product! This is a poignant reminder that if strategy is about what you do and don't do, you still need the systems and processes in place to stop doing the things you should not be doing.

COMMUNICATING WITH KEY STAKEHOLDERS ABOUT STRATEGY

From the outset, we've emphasized the interdependence of strategy formulation and implementation. In many ways, because suppliers, customers, and an organization's own managers will ultimately contribute to the strategy's success or failure, the process of communicating with stakeholders about strategy begins in the strategy formulation process itself. It is, therefore, a strategic leadership function.

In performing this strategic leadership role, managers must evaluate both the need and the necessary tactics for persuasively communicating a strategy in four different directions: *upward*, *downward*, *across*, and *outward*.[60]

Communicating Upward
Increasingly, firms rely on bottom-up innovation processes that encourage and empower middle-level and division managers to take ownership of strategy formulation and propose new strategies. Such is particularly the case at highly diversified firms, but even fairly focused firms such as HUI endorse bottom-up processes. Communicating upward means that someone or some group has championed the strategy internally and has succeeded in convincing top management of its merits and feasibility.

Communicating Downward
Communicating downward means enlisting the support of the people who'll be needed to implement the strategy. Too often, managers undertake this task only after a strategy has been set in stone, thereby running the risk of undermining both the strategy and any culture of trust and cooperation that may have existed previously. Starting on the communication process early is the best way to identify and surmount obstacles, and it usually ensures that a management team is working with a common purpose and intensity that will be important when it's time to implement the strategy.

Communicating Across and Outward
The need to communicate across and outward reflects the fact that implementation of a strategy will probably require cooperation from other units of the firm (*across*) and from key external stakeholders, such as material and capital providers, complementors, and customers (*outward*). Internally, for example, the strategy may call for raw materials or services to be provided by another subsidiary; perhaps it depends on sales leads from other units. Recall, for instance, our earlier example of Emageon. Emageon couldn't get hospitals to adopt the leading-edge visualization software that was produced and sold by one subsidiary until its hardware division started cross-selling the software as well. This internal coordination required a champion from the software side to convince managers on the hardware side of the need and benefits of working together.

External constituencies play a comparable role, and a strategy must similarly be communicated to them. Managers can use stakeholder analysis to identify these key players and determine whether suppliers, customers, complementors, and relevant regulatory agencies support the firm's strategy. In the early 1990s, for instance, when IBM first launched its ThinkPad, the product was an unexpected hit with customers. The launch,

however, was so successful that IBM's key component suppliers couldn't keep up with IBM's demand, thus costing the company sales on what should have been an even more profitable rollout.

The Three Cs of Strategy Communication

Just as communicating the strategy to stakeholders is a key factor in successful strategy implementation, so, too, is having the right people in place to communicate it. As one researcher puts it, "The strategy champion must have three Cs—contacts, cultural understanding, and credibility."[61]

Contacts Contacts are key because implementing a strategy—particularly one that's dynamic and innovative—often entails some back-channel maneuvering. 3M's PostIt notes, for instance, made it to market only because an enterprising manager convinced internal people to supply clerical and other support staff with experimental versions of the product as a means of demonstrating that there was actually a market.

Cultural Understanding Cultural understanding refers to the fact that the people communicating the strategy need to have a rich familiarity with the organization's culture, policies, and procedures. In an earlier example on BGI, you saw how culture provides a screen for recruitment, retention, and promotion. It may also provide strategy communicators with insights into internal and external network dependencies that may not be obvious but that nonetheless will be essential to the effort to sell across and outward.

Credibility Needless to say, it helps if strategy communicators are respected by management, peers, and staff, all of whom expect them to present ideas with a good chance of success. Credibility is based on perceptions of trustworthiness, reliability, and integrity. Yet studies indicate that many employees just don't believe or trust their organizational leaders. According to Bruce Katcher, president of Discovery Surveys, a Massachusetts–based firm specializing in employee opinion and customer satisfaction surveys and focus groups, just 53 percent "of employees believe the information they receive from senior management."[62] He bases the figure on a review of the company's database of 30,000 respondents from forty-four international companies. Closing the credibility gap can be helped by developing regular—at least annual—processes to gauge real employee perceptions about their managers' level of leadership as well as other issues, including morale, obstacles to higher performance, pet peeves, or key irritants. Managers must then pay attention to the findings and demonstrate real commitment to act on them. When actions speak louder than words, employees will have more reason to trust those above them.

Implementation Levers in Global Firms and Dynamic Contexts

As we've observed throughout this text, firms are increasingly facing challenges that are both global and dynamic in nature. In this section, we'll show how implementation levers can be adapted to these particularly important contingencies. We'll also link strategy implementation explicitly to strategy formulation through the staging component of the strategy diamond model.

IMPLEMENTATION SOLUTIONS FOR GLOBAL FIRMS

As you learned in Chapter 8, two critical needs confront firms in implementing global strategies: the need for *efficiency* and the need for *local responsiveness*.[63] In this section, we want to stress their role in terms of implementation levers and their function in executing globalization strategies. Paralleling the strategy research on global strategy, research has found that firms deeply involved in international business adopt one of four structural forms in the effort to manage the tension between the need for efficiency and the need for local responsiveness.[64] As we'll see, most of these forms place more emphasis on one or the other of these two competing forces and build on the general understanding of structure you have amassed thus far from this chapter. These four structural solutions accommodate the four international strategy configurations discussed in Chapter 8.

Emphasize Local Responsiveness
This structural solution resembles a decentralized federation, much like the relationship between the U.S. federal government and the fifty state governments. Assets and resources are decentralized, and foreign offices are given the authority to respond to local needs when they differ from those of the home market. Control and coordination are managed primarily through the interactions of home-office corporate executives and overseas executives, who are usually home-country managers who've been dispatched to run foreign offices.

From the perspective of top management, the corporation is a portfolio of relatively independent businesses located around the globe. SAP, for example, adhered to this model for much of the 1990s, until it determined that it fostered costly duplications of effort across markets and inadequate coordination among units across borders. Indeed, because SAP's customers were global firms with better coordination and integration than SAP itself, many of them managed to get SAP to compete against itself for new system sales. Nestlé, for instance, would get bids from SAP U.S. and SAP U.K. without informing either party that they were actually bidding against one another.

Emphasize Global Efficiencies with Some Local Advantages
The structure supporting this tradeoff reveals an organization that is a coordinated group of federations over which more administrative control is exerted by home-country headquarters. For reasons of both efficiency and strategy, firms like SAP typically evolve into this structure. SAP itself, for example, adopted it at the end of the 1990s when it realized that its customers were taking advantage of its Balkans-like structure.

Under this model, although resources, assets, and responsibilities are delegated to foreign offices, additional control—usually in the form of more formal management systems, such as centralized planning and budgeting—is exercised centrally. This control facilitates global account management, so that the quality and price of services provided to global clients can be made uniform. As a rule, top management regards overseas operations as appendages to the domestic firm. Local units, therefore, are highly dependent on home-office coordination of resource allocation, knowledge sharing, and decision approval.

Emphasize Global Efficiencies

Ideally, firms adopting this configuration have a structure that is based on the centralization of assets, resources, and responsibilities. Foreign offices are used to access customers, but demand is filled by centralized production. This form of organization was pioneered by firms such as Ford, which exported standardized products around the globe, and was popular among Japanese companies undertaking globalization in the 1970s and 1980s. The global configuration affords much less autonomy to foreign offices or subsidiaries than the two preceding models. Operational control is tight and most decisions centralized. Top management views foreign operations as pipelines for distributing products to a global, but homogeneous, marketplace.

Seek to Exploit Local Advantages and Global Efficiencies

Each of the three preceding organizational models responds in a different strategic fashion to the challenge of balancing the two fundamental demands of managing across borders. The global efficiencies configuration, for example, is clearly designed to achieve maximum efficiencies, largely through scale economies derived from centralized production. Because decisions and resources are controlled locally, the first form is well-suited to respond to local needs. The second model attempts to meet local needs while retaining central control. This fourth configuration is designed to accommodate both demands.

This configuration was designed to achieve not only efficiency and local responsiveness but innovation, as well. Its structural characteristics enable firms—at least those that are able to manage it—to achieve multidimensional strategic objectives. The key functions in this multidimensional strategy are *dispersion, specialization,* and *interdependence.* Resources and capabilities are dispersed to local units, and a networked control system is designed to achieve both coordination and cooperation. Because geographically dispersed organizational units are strategically interdependent, large flows of products, resources, and personnel, as well as value-chain activities, are channeled through the structure. To some extent, McDonald's, which features both standard and locally tailored menu items at outlets around the globe, depends on this structure. The structure fits with McDonald's transnational strategy and affords the global food company greater flexibility in adapting to local tastes while enabling it at the same time to exploit the global economies of scale that it enjoys by virtue of its size and geographic breadth.

People and Rewards Solutions in Global Firms

As firms expand globally, they face the critical issue of how to find and reward managers. On the one hand, using local managers can enhance a firm's understanding of local markets. On the other hand, using home-country managers strengthens the relationship between the foreign subsidiary and the parent company.

Naturally, operating subsidiaries in culturally distant locations gives rise to a great deal of uncertainty. Research suggests that a company's policy for finding and rewarding foreign managerial staff can have a significant bearing on its performance. For instance, multinationals that use overseas management positions as a training ground for future executives of the parent significantly outperform those that allow senior managers to ascend to the top ranks without spending time in overseas posts.[65]

The performance of foreign subsidiaries may be affected when parent-country nationals, or expatriates, are sent to manage them. When multinationals have subsidiaries in culturally distant locations (as opposed to those that are just geographically distant), costs and risks increase because of a so-called *information asymmetry* problem: Onsite overseas information may not be readily available to the parent company.[66] When a multinational relies more on parent-country nationals than local managers, the information asymmetry problem gradually diminishes: As subsidiaries gain experience in conducting transactions with home-country nationals, there's less need for deploying expatriates. Indeed, research shows that when a multinational firm staffs a culturally distant foreign subsidiary with parent-country managers, it improves subsidiary performance, largely because it's easier to exercise cultural control and enhances the transfer of firm-specific resources from the parent to the subsidiary.[67]

Apparently, however, this positive effect decreases over time because host-country nationals not only acquire knowledge and skills from expatriate managers, but also adopt the shared values of the parent company. Not surprisingly, given the high cost of managing an expatriate workforce (not to mention the high expatriate failure rate), reliance on expatriates is declining.

IMPLEMENTATION LEVERS IN DYNAMIC CONTEXTS

We observed early in this text that, because competitive pressures are compounded in dynamic, "high-velocity" industries, companies' strategies necessarily grow more complex. Moreover, the difficulties in *implementing* strategies in such industries are an order of magnitude more challenging than those of implementing strategies in relatively stable industries. As we've also seen, the task is becoming even more complex and difficult because dynamic markets are increasingly becoming global markets as well. Consider, for instance, the threat to a firm in a global industry that needs to develop or adopt a radically new technology in order to survive industry evolution. In Chapter 4 we described a special problem known as the innovator's dilemma—a situation where new entrants innovate in low-end, unattractive segments of the market that leaders tend to overlook because margins are apparently lower there, only to have those new entrants migrate into the more profitable segments with lower cost structures and increasingly popular products.[68] Firms have developed several structural adaptations to deal with the problems of implementing strategies in dynamic contexts, and in this section, we'll examine two of the most effective adaptations: the *ambidextrous organization* and the use of *patching* among diversified firms.

The Ambidextrous Organization
Even a firm that's successful at executing a strategy can face a problem as its industry becomes well-established: In particular, it's difficult to retain market leadership when a new disruptive technology (product or process) is pioneered and introduced by another firm. The incumbent also faces a disadvantage because it invests in order to sustain an advantage, not (like the new entrant) to destroy one.

Incremental Change Versus Radical Innovation: Revisiting the Innovator's Dilemma
This is the essence of the innovator's dilemma, and despite leaders who are perfectly capable of recognizing the problem, it often persists because of structural deficiencies among many organizations. When, for example, one division of a leading incumbent tries to pioneer its own version of disruptive technology, the rest of the organization may resist. Why? Perhaps because the status quo is perceived to be in the best interests of managers and employees. Or perhaps submerged but strong facets of the organizational culture favor the continued influence of large, established divisions.

Granted, many firms are skilled at introducing refinements into their current product lines. Usually such organizations don't resist moderate innovation because it's perceived as a means of sustaining or improving current competitive positions. At the same time, however, the same firms may face monumental obstacles when they try to introduce *radical* changes or offer products that require disruptive technologies. In that case, of course, they're faced with a paradoxical problem: To flourish in the long run, they must exploit existing advantages and explore innovations that will probably alter the industry significantly in the future. In other words, if a firm wants to sustain long-term competitiveness in a dynamic context (and most, of course, do), it must learn to integrate both incremental changes and radical innovations.

The **ambidextrous structure** is one response to this problem.[69] In fact, the idea evolved from studies of how firms dealt with the problem of simultaneously integrating two types of innovations:

ambidextrous structure
Organizational structure for dynamic contexts in which project teams are organized as structurally independent units and encouraged to develop their own structures, systems, and processes.

- *Incremental innovations* are those that make small improvements in existing products and operations and that are aimed at existing customers.

- *Discontinuous innovations* are those that make radical advances that may alter the basis of competition in an industry and that are aimed at new customers.[70]

Four Structures for Handling Innovation Researchers identified four basic forms of organization among the companies studied:

- A functional form in which innovation efforts are completely integrated into an existing organization structure.

- A cross-functional or matrix-style form in which groups of people from established organizational divisions are formed to work outside the functional hierarchy.

- A form in which teams or units, though nominally independent and working outside the established hierarchy, are limited in their independence and relatively unsupported by the organizational hierarchy.

- An "ambidextrous" form in which project teams focusing on radical improvements are organized as structurally independent units and encouraged to develop their own structures, systems, and processes. As you can see in Exhibit 11.19, these semiautonomous units may be integrated into the organizational hierarchy only at the senior-management level.[71]

Researchers found that the ambidextrous structure was quite effective in facilitating the integration of radical innovations; 93 percent of radical innovations were launched by firms characterized as ambidextrous. Firms that pursued radical innovation through autonomous units bound to the organizational hierarchy only through senior management had very high success rates for launching new products or operations. Conversely, firms trying to achieve radical innovation within the existing corporate hierarchy found that their efforts were often stymied. Finally, the ambidextrous form also fostered innovations that were initiated under some other organizational form and only later moved into an ambidextrous structure.

Among other things, these findings reveal just how difficult it is for firms to compete in dynamic industry environments that require not only constant incremental innovations, but periodic radical innovations as well. Ambidexterity allows for the simultaneous maintenance of the status quo (incremental business improvements made through conventional organizational units) and proactive preparation for future industry-wide alterations (radical innovation made through units that are unencumbered by existing organizational practices and allowed to implement strategies consistent with the requirements of competitive conditions).

Diversified Firms in Dynamic Markets: Patching A multidivisional firm operating in diverse product markets can create new synergies by actively managing the structure of its corporate portfolio through a process known as *patching*. **Patching** is the process of regularly remapping businesses in accordance with changing market conditions

patching Process of remapping businesses in accordance with changing market conditions and restitches them into new internal business structures.

Exhibit 11.19   The Ambidextrous Organization

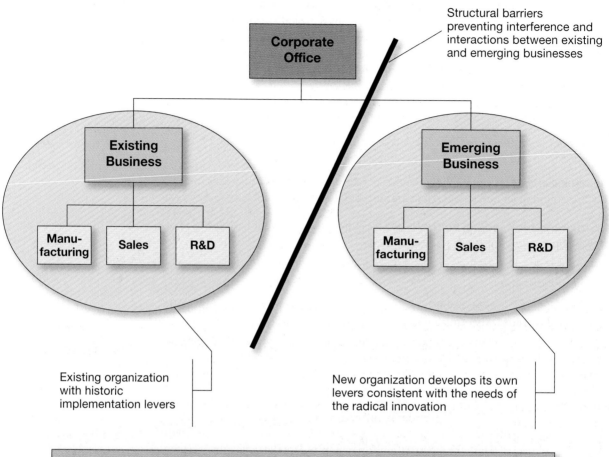

Structural barriers preventing interference and interactions between existing and emerging businesses

Corporate Office

Existing Business

Emerging Business

Manu-facturing   Sales   R&D

Manu-facturing   Sales   R&D

Existing organization with historic implementation levers

New organization develops its own levers consistent with the needs of the radical innovation

Ambidextrous organizations establish units that are structurally independent from all other units. The emerging business units are to develop their own structures, processes, systems, cultures, strategies, etc. They are only integrated into the mother organization at the level of senior management.

and restitching them into new internal business structures.[72] It can mean combining, splitting, or transferring units or exiting businesses or adding new ones. Patching is particularly effective in dynamic markets because it enables managers to exploit the best business opportunities while bypassing less promising ones. However, as you can imagine, patching is very complex to manage and requires a culture and workforce that is action-oriented and flexible, such as the one described at BGI.

Here's an example of patching at work. Originally, Hewlett-Packard's laser-printing business was a small startup operation with only modest growth expectations. Shortly after launch, however, sales climbed to ten times the expected level (100,000 units per month instead of the forecasted 10,000). As new applications for related technologies, such as the ink-jet printer, emerged, management stripped them away from the laser-printer business and patched them onto other business units. This technique of patching units not only allowed managers in the laser-printer unit to focus on their core growth business but ensconced the ink-jet business in a unit where it could get the support it needed to get off the ground, develop into a growth business, and become a major source of cash flow. In this case, patching required the transfer not only of a business but of related resources and personnel as well.

With patching, therefore, structure is intentionally altered so that managers can better maintain focus on core and growth businesses while seeding and protecting new opportunities. Because it requires managers to view organizational structure as flexible and contingent, they tend not to fret about getting a new structure exactly right. In addition, although patching is a proactive tool, it usually involves relatively small and incremental changes. Change, however, is ongoing, as managers constantly search for new combinations. To make patching work, firms need to adjust internal systems so that when a business is detached from one division and restitched elsewhere, companywide systems don't require extensive modification. Compensation systems, for instance, need to be fairly consistent across organizational borders.

Finally, we should note some key differences between patching and the ambidextrous organizational structure. Patching is a tool that helps diversified firms operate in multiple product or geographic markets. It doesn't involve radical technologies, but rather leverages either existing businesses or new but related businesses. It works when systems are consistent across the organization. In contrast, the ambidextrous organization is designed to enable radically new businesses to develop unencumbered by existing structures and processes.

LINKING STRATEGY IMPLEMENTATION TO STAGING

Before wrapping up this chapter, we'd like to underscore the relationship between implementation levers and a specific facet of strategy formulation. Recall that the staging element of the strategy diamond refers to the timing and pacing of strategic moves. ◆ Staging decisions typically depend on available resources—resources that include structures, systems and processes, and people and rewards. From the opening vignette on HUI, you gained some insight into how the firm coupled a unique resource base—its knowledge and intellectual property relating to Teflon—with the implementation levers necessary to launch new and highly innovative ventures. Thus, management of the implementation process should anticipate the staging objectives of the strategy.

 Staging & Pacing

More generally, it would be a rare case in which a change in strategy did not have implications for implementation. Consider, for instance, a firm that's considering expansion into foreign markets. It can achieve this strategic goal through a variety of vehicles, including exporting, alliances or acquisitions, and the establishment of foreign offices from which to conduct value-chain activities. If international staging is an explicit component of the firm's strategy, then managers must start modifying other implementation levers. In other words, they must determine whether the firm has the appropriate structure, systems, human capital, expertise, and culture to support its evolution into a global competitor. If, for example, the vehicle of choice calls for alliances or acquisitions, then the related skills and capabilities must be acquired as well. If the vehicle is exporting, the firm will need to acquire people who understand customer demands and distribution channels in foreign markets.

Summary of Challenges

1. *Outline the interdependence between strategy formulation and implementation.* Strategy formulation and implementation are interrelated. The introductory section of the chapter showed you the various ways in which formulation and implementation are interrelated and provided you with an overarching model for thinking about how to translate an abstract strategy into concrete action. You also learned that the relationship between formulation and implementation is not necessarily a linear one. In some cases, the iterative evolution of strategy is advantageous and desirable. The section closed with a discussion of why implementation efforts can and often do fail. Organizational culture can be one barrier to (or facilitator of) effective strategy execution and strategic change.

2. *Demonstrate how to use organizational structure as a strategy implementation lever.* Organizational structure exists to perform two essential functions within the organization: ensuring control and coordinating the efforts of managers and employees. As control and coordination become more difficult, firms generally modify their structure to improve control and coordination. Popular forms of organizing firm structure include the functional, divisional, matrix, and network forms. The structure chosen should be consistent with the firm's strategy. For instance, the more diversified the firm, the more the structure will need to accommodate coordination. The more focused the firm is in a single business, or in several unrelated businesses, the more the structure should emphasize control.

3. *Illustrate the use of systems and processes as strategy implementation levers.* Formal processes and procedures used by a firm should support the execution of strategy. Information systems are the most common systems, but all systems should be considered for their alignment with strategy (and other implementation levers). For instance, management control, performance and rewards, budgeting, quality, planning, distribution, client management, and resource allocation are all managed by systems. Systems can affect what people pay attention to and what information they have access to.

4. *Identify the roles of people and rewards as implementation levers.* For a strategy to succeed, a firm needs the right people with the right experiences and competencies. As a result, recruitment, selection, and training are critical to strategy implementation. Because human resources, or staffing issues, are often large sources of operating costs, too much focus may be placed on reducing the staffing costs. Investments in human resource systems have positive effects on multiple dimensions of firm performance. The importance of people is even more important in high-human-capital industries. Rewards are an important implementation lever. They reflect the degree to which a firm employs outcome versus behavioral controls. Rewards are composed of both performance evaluation and feedback and incentives, such as compensation and promotion. Ultimately, rewards enable the firm to get the right people to do the right things for the firm, such that it can achieve its goals and objectives.

5. *Explain the dual roles that strategic leadership plays in strategy implementation.* This section showed you that strategy implementation is much more than simply putting the right levers into place. The levers are important, but they must also be complemented by strategic leadership actions. The two actions we emphasized were decisions about resource allocation and levers and communicating the strategy to stakeholders. The resources and capabilities that differentiate a firm from its competitors are by definition scarce. Strategic leadership shows its mettle by making difficult tradeoffs in terms of the levers chosen and when and where not to deploy scarce resources. Communicating the strategy to stakeholders requires that managers promote and get strategic buy-in from top management, lower-level workers, other key organizational units; and external stakeholders, such as suppliers, customers, and complementors.

6. *Describe how global and dynamic contexts affect the use of implementation levers.* As a firm becomes more global, it faces contradictory needs for efficiency and local responsiveness. Depending on the primacy of these two demands, four configurations are possible. The most complex configuration aims to simultaneously achieve global efficiency and maximum local responsiveness. As in global contexts, coordination and control are made more difficult in dynamic contexts. In addition, being able to protect potentially radical innovations can be accommodated through the ambidextrous structure. Diversified firms in high-velocity environments can increase the likelihood of synergies by using patching techniques, which essentially assumes that the organizational structure is flexible and allows for the constant reconfiguration of business units. This enables managers to remain focused on high-volume businesses by placing high-potential-growth businesses in units that can better exploit these opportunities. This section closed by showing you how to link formulation and implementation through the staging component of the strategy diamond.

Review Questions

1. What is strategy implementation?

2. How are formulation and implementation related?

3. What are the basic forms of organizational structure? When is each appropriate?

4. What are some common systems and processes that are relevant to strategy implementation?

5. How are people relevant to strategy formulation and implementation?

6. How can rewards affect strategy?

7. What are the roles of strategic leadership in successful strategy implementation?

8. How does globalization affect organization structure?

9. What are organizational solutions to the problems caused by dynamic environments?

10. What component of the strategy diamond maps most closely to issues related to strategy implementation?

Experiential Activities

Group Exercises

1. Apply the concepts of strategy formulation and implementation to your college experience. What was your objective in going to college? When did your strategy for achieving this objective emerge? Has it ever changed? How would you adapt the implementation levers and strategic leadership roles to evaluate how well you have implemented your strategy? What is your overall personal evaluation?

2. Refer to the opening case on HUI. Assume that, for reasons of estate planning, the owners decided to take the company public through an IPO. What would be the effect on the firm's strategy and implementation practices if this were to happen? What, if anything, would need to change?

Ethical Debates

1. As part of a corporate restructuring, your analysis helps you conclude that you have rather extensive redundancy in corporate finance and accounting positions. Management concludes that through consolidation, cross training, and other shifts in responsibility, you could do the same work with 30 percent fewer staff. How do you downsize these jobs in the next twelve months without damaging morale of the surviving employees and while trying to treat the terminated employees in a fair manner?

2. Your company acquires another company in China. When you start to transform the organizational structure to that commonly used by your company at home and in other countries, you encounter significant resistance from local management. They claim that this new structure will never work in China. What do you do?

How Would YOU DO THAT?

1. In the box entitled "How Would *You* Do That? 11.1," you learned how SAP America responded to performance problems primarily through changes in strategy implementation. Find one or two firms that were once high flyers but that have recently fallen on hard times. Are these hard times primarily a function of a flawed strategy, flawed strategy implementation, or both? Using SAP as an example, what changes would you suggest in terms of implementation?

2. The example of the NUWC in the box entitled "How Would *You* Do That? 11.1" demonstrated the strategy mapping process and how to develop a balanced scorecard. Review Exhibits 11.12 and 11.13 and generate suggestions for specific objectives, measures, targets, and initiatives that would complete NUWC's use of the scorecard. If you prefer using the scorecard with a for-profit firm then apply the framework from scratch to a firm of your choosing.

Go on to see How Would You Do That at http://www.prenhall.com/ carpenter&sanders

Endnotes

1. http://www.huimfg.com/aboutus_president.html

2. K. R. Andrews, *The Concept of Corporate Strategy* (Homewood, IL: Irwin, 1987); *The Strategy Execution Imperative: Leading Practices for Implementing Strategic Initiatives* (Corporate Executive Board, 2001); C. M. Christensen, "Making Strategy: Learning by Doing," *Harvard Business Review* 75:6 (1997), 141–156.

3. D. Hambrick and A. Cannella, "Strategy Implementation as Substance and Selling," *Academy of Management Executive* 3:4 (1989), 278–285.

4. M. Porter, "Know Your Place: How to Assess the Attractiveness of Your Industry and Your Company's Position in It," *Inc.*, September 1991, 90.

5. P. F. Drucker, *The Practice of Management* (New York: HarperCollins, 1954), 352–353.

6. R. Ruggles, "The State of the Notion: Knowledge Management in Practice," *California Management Review* 40 (1998), 82–83.

7. J. Pfeffer and R. I. Sutton, *The Knowing-Doing Gap* (Boston: Harvard Business School Press, 2000).

8. L. Gerstner, *Who Says Elephants Can't Dance?* (New York: Harper-Business, 2002).

9. J. R. Kotter and J. L. Heskett, *Corporate Culture and Performance* (New York: Free Press, 1992); C. A. O'Reilly and J. A. Chatman, "Culture as Social Control: Corporations, Culture and Commitment," in B. M. Staw and L. L. Cummings, eds., *Research in Organizational Behavior* 18 (Greenwich, CT: JAI Press, 1996), 157–200; J. B. Sønrensen, "The Strength of Corporate Culture and the Reliability of Firm Performance," *Administrative Science Quarterly* 47 (2002), 70–91.

10. Kotter and Heskett, *Corporate Culture and Performance.*

11. Sønrensen, "The Strength of Corporate Culture and the Reliability of Firm Performance."

12. R. S. Burt, S. M. Gabbay, G. Holt, and P. Moran, "Contingent Organization as a Network Theory: The Culture Performance Contingency Function," *Acta Sociologica* 37 (1994), 345–370; Sønrensen, "The Strength of Corporate Culture and the Reliability of Firm Performance."

13. A. Slywotzky and D. Nadler, "The Strategy Is the Structure," *Harvard Business Review* 82:2 (2004), 16.

14. SAP Harvard Business School Case, SAP America 9-397-067, December 3, 1996.

15. SAP Annual General Shareholders' Meeting, Mannheim, Germany, May 3, 1997; SAP 1997–2003 Financial Reports (accessed on July 15, 2005),www.sap.com/company/investor/reports/pastfinancials/index.epx; Harvard Business School Case 9-397-067, SAP America, December 3, 1996; N. Boudette, "How a German Software Titan Missed the Internet Revolution," *Wall Street Journal,* January 18, 2000, A1.

16. Hambrick and Cannella, "Strategy Implementation as Substance and Selling," 278.

17. Hambrick and Cannella, "Strategy Implementation as Substance and Selling," 278.

18. A. Chandler, *Strategy and Structure* (Cambridge, MA: MIT Press, 1962).

19. R. L. Daft, *Management*, 6th ed. (New York: Southwestern, 2003).

20. L. G. Hrebiniak and W. Joyce, *Implementing Strategy* (New York: MacMillan, 1984).

21. Chandler, *Strategy and Structure.*

22. Slywotzky and Nadler, "The Strategy Is the Structure," 16.

23. R. A. Burgelman, "Fading Memories: A Process Theory of Strategic Business Exit in Dynamic Environments," *Administrative Science Quarterly* 39 (1994), 24–56.

24. www.platypustech.com (accessed July 15, 2005).

25. www.emageon.com (accessed July 15, 2005).

26. R. Cross, "The role of networks in organizational change," *McKinsey Quarterly*, Web Exclusive, April 2007; J. McGregor, "The office chart that really counts," *Business Week,* February 27, 2006, 48.

27. C. K. Bart and M. C. Baetz, "The Relationship Between Mission Statements and Firm Performance: An Exploratory Study," *Journal of Management Studies* 35:6 (1998), 823–853.

28. W. G. Sanders and M. A. Carpenter, "Strategic Satisficing? A Behavioral-Agency Perspective on Stock Repurchase Announcements," *Academy of Management Journal* 46 (2003), 160–178.

29. G. Reilly and R. Reilly, "Using a Measure Network to Understand and Deliver Value," *Journal of Cost Management* 14:6 (2000), 5–14; R. Kaplan and D. Norton, *The Strategy-Focused Organization* (Watertown, MA: Harvard Business School Press, 2001).

30. Adapted from R. Kaplan and D. Norton, *The Strategy-Focused Organization.*

31. "The Balanced Scorecard's Lessons for Managers," *Harvard Management Update*, October 2000, 4–5.

32. Adapted from R. Kaplan and D. Norton, *The Strategy-Focused Organization.*

33. Adapted from R. Kaplan and D. Norton, *The Strategy-Focused Organization.*

34. R. Simons, *Levers of Control: How Managers Use Innovative Control Systems* (Boston: Harvard Business School Press, 1995); M. J. Epstein and J. F. Manzoni, "The Balanced Scorecard & Tableau de Bord: A Global Perspective on Translating Strategy into Action," INSEAD Working Paper 97/63/ AC/SM (1997).

35. E. Schonfeld, "Baby Bills," *Business 2.0* 4:9 (2003), 76–84.

36. Adapted from G. Harrigan and R. Miller, "Managing Change Through an Aligned and Cascading Balanced Scorecard," *Perform* 2:2 (2003), 20–26.

37. Quote from BGI's head of human resources, Garret Bouton, in J. Pfeffer and R. I. Sutton, *The Knowing-Doing Gap*, 227.

38. J. Collins, "Level 5 Leadership," *Harvard Business Review* July–August (2001), 66–76.

39. J. Bradach, *Organizational Alignment: The 7-S Model* (Boston: Harvard Business School Publishing, 1996).

40. C. K. Prahalad and G. Hamel, "The Core Competence of the Corporation," *Harvard Business Review* 79:1 (1990), 1–14; R. Nelson and S. Winter, *An Evolutionary Theory of Economic Change* (Cambridge, MA: Harvard University Press, 1982); D. J. Teece, G. Pisano, and A. Shuen, "Dynamic Capabilities and Strategic Management," *Strategic Management Journal* 18 (1997), 509–534; K. M. Eisenhardt and J. A. Martin, "Dynamic Capabilities: What Are They?" *Strategic Management Journal* 21 (2000), 1105–1121.

41. B. Becker and B. Gerhart, "The Impact of Human Resource Management on Organizational Performance: Progress and Prospects," *Academy of Management Journal* 39 (1996), 779–802.

42. W. N. Davidson III, D. L. Worrell, and J. B. Fox, "Early Retirement Programs and Firm Performance," *Academy of Management Journal* 39 (1996), 970–985.

43. C. Chadwick, L. W. Hunter, and S. M. Walston, "The Effects of Downsizing Practices on Hospital Performance," *Strategic Management Journal* 25:5 (2004), 405–428.

44. M. A. Youndt, S. A. Snell, J. W. Dean Jr., and D. P. Lepak, "Human Resource Management, Manufacturing Strategy, and Firm Performance," *Academy of Management Journal* 39 (1996), 836–866.

45. See J. B. Barney and P. M. Wright, "On Becoming a Strategic Partner: The Role of Human Resources in Gaining Competitive Advantage," *Human Resource Management* 37 (1998), 31–46; J. Pfeffer, *Competitive Advantage Through People* (Boston: Harvard Business School Press, 1994).

46. J. Pfeffer, *The Human Equation* (Boston: Harvard Business School Press, 1998).

47. F. Luthans and C. M. Youssef, "Human, Social, and Now Positive Psychological Capital Management: Investing in People for Competitive Advantage," *Organization Dynamics* 33:2 (2004), 143–160.

48. R. W. Coff, "Human Assets and Management Dilemmas: Coping with Hazards on the Road to Resource-Based Theory," *Academy of Management Review* 22 (1997), 374–402.

49. See Coff, "Human Assets and Management Dilemmas."

50. B. Gerhart and S. Rynes, *Compensation* (Beverly Hills, CA: Sage Publications, 2003).

51. J. Kerr and J. Slocum, "Managing Corporate Culture Through Reward Systems," *Academy of Management Executive* 1:2 (1987), 99–108.

52. C. W. L. Hill, M. A. Hitt, and R. E. Hoskisson, "Cooperative Versus Competitive Structures in Related and Unrelated Diversified Firms," *Organization Science* 3 (1992), 501–521.

53. CIBC Corporate and Investment Banking (A). Harvard Business School Publishing, 1999.

54. For an extensive review see Milkovich & Newman, *Compensation*, 8th Edition (New York, McGraw-Hill, 2004).

55. For an extensive review see Milkovich & Newman, *Compensation*, 8th Edition.

56. S. Kerr, "On the Folly of **Rewarding for A** while Hoping for B." *Academy of Management Journal*, December 1975, 18(4), pp. 769–83.

57. S. Kerr, "On the Folly of **Rewarding for A** while Hoping for B."

58. Adapted from W. C. Kim and R. Mauborgne, "Charting Your Company's Future," *Harvard Business Review* 80:6 (2002), 76–82.

59. Adapted from W. C. Kim and R. Mauborgne, "Charting Your Company's Future," *Harvard Business Review* 80:6 (2002), 76–82.

60. Hambrick and Cannella, "Strategy Implementation as Substance and Selling," 278–285.

61. N. Wreden, "Executive Champions: The Vital Link Between Strategy Formulation and Implementation," *Harvard Management Update* 7:9 (2002), 3–5.

62. www.clemmer.net/excerpts/pf_credibility.html (accessed October 25, 2005).

63. The information in this section draws heavily upon the work of Christopher Bartlett and Sumantra Ghoshal, *Managing Across Borders: The Transnational Solution* (Boston: Harvard Business School Press, 1989).

64. Bartlett and Ghoshal, *Managing Across Borders.*

65. M. A. Carpenter, W. G. Sanders, and H. B. Gregersen, "Bundling Human Capital with Organizational Context: The Impact of International Assignment Experience on Multinational Firm Performance and CEO Pay," *Academy of Management Journal* 44 (2001), 493–511.

66. Y. Gong, "Subsidiary Staffing in Multinational Enterprises: Agency, Resources, and Performance," *Academy of Management Journal* 46 (2003), 728–739.

67. Gong, "Subsidiary Staffing in Multinational Enterprises."

68. C. Christensen, *The Innovator's Dilemma* (Boston: Harvard Business School Press, 1997).

69. C. A. O'Reilly and M. L. Tushman, "The Ambidextrous Organization," *Harvard Business Review* 82:4 May–June 2004), 74–81.

70. For details of this study, see O'Reilly and Tushman, "The Ambidextrous Organization."

71. Adapted from C. A. O'Reilly and M. L. Tushman, "The Ambidextrous Organization," *Harvard Business Review* 82:4 (2004), 74–81.

72. This section draws heavily on K. M. Eisenhardt and S. L. Brown, "Patching: Restitching Business Portfolios in Dynamic Markets," *Harvard Business Review* 77:3 (1999), 72–82.

12 Considering New Ventures *and* Corporate Renewal

In This Chapter We Challenge You To >>>

1. Define *new ventures*, *initial public offerings (IPOs)*, and *corporate renewal* and explain how they are related to strategic management.

2. Understand entrepreneurship and the entrepreneurial process.

3. Describe the steps involved in new-venture creation and corporate new-venturing.

4. Map out the stages leading up to an initial public offering (IPO).

5. Understand the external and internal causes of organizational failure.

6. Outline an action plan for strategic change and corporate renewal.

From Napster *to* Snocap: Shawn Fanning *as* Serial Entrepreneur

I f you want to download new music today, you can buy it from a centralized site like iTunes, or Rhapsody, or you can get it directly from the artist's website or MySpace page. Snocap, however, is the company that is helping artists and copyright owners sell their music directly to their fans.

Snocap's founding team includes Shawn Fanning, the brain behind the original Napster. In 1999 Napster rocked the foundations of the music industry by making it easy to share music **"peer-to-peer,"** directly from one fan to another. With the advent of peer-to-peer music sharing services, music lovers no longer had to depend on radio stations or music stores, or even recording labels, to hear about new music. The only problem was that file sharing cut out any compensation for the artists who make the music.

peer-to-peer Where individual network members can engage in exchange with any other member of the network.

long-tail When the selling of individual products that each have low sales volume add up to huge revenues.

With Snocap, Fanning's goal was to keep the "many-to-many" or "granular" concept of Napster, but this time to extend it directly from artists to their audiences. The business model is based on the idea of the **"long tail"**—a concept coined by Chris Anderson, the Editor and Chief of Wired Magazine, that selling many individual products that each have low sales volume can add up to huge revenues. In essence, forget squeezing millions from a few megahits at the top of the charts. The future of entertainment is in the millions of niche markets at the shallow end of the bitstream. Anderson argued that products that are in low demand or have low sales volume can collectively make up a market share that rivals or exceeds the relatively few current bestsellers and blockbusters, if the store or distribution channel is large enough. Anderson cites earlier research that described the relationship between Amazon sales and Amazon sales ranking and found that a large proportion of Amazon.com's book sales come from obscure books that are not available in brick-and-mortar stores. The long tail is a potential market and, as the examples illustrate, the distribution and sales channel opportunities created by the Internet often enable businesses to tap into that market successfully. On the artists' side, a band may make only pocket change for the sale of each song, but when the music is available to millions of listeners, that change can add up quickly. And if a company like Snocap is the middleman on the transactions, then that could add up to lots of profits. The basic economics of the long tail are summarized in Exhibit 12.1.[1]

While Shawn Fanning is truly a creative genius—he invented Napster when he was 19—he also knew that he needed the best in the business when it came to directing a highly dynamic business in a fluid industry. Rusty Reuff was the perfect guy for the job, and joined Snocap as CEO in 2005. He had spent seven years in the videogame industry, as Executive VP of Human Resources at Electronic Arts. Reuff joined Snocap at a difficult time. Everyone

Exhibit 12.1 The Economics of the Long Tail

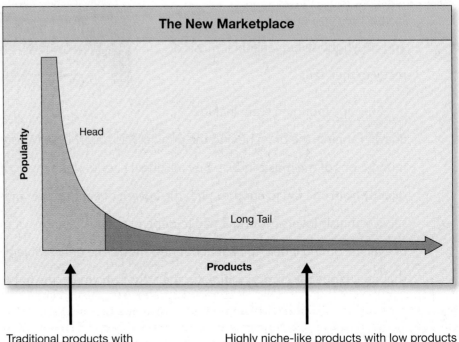

knew the old business models for selling music were disintegrating, but there were, and still are, many new ventures claiming to have the best model to replace it. Artists and labels were not jumping on SNOCAP's bandwagon as fast as they had hoped.

After careful examination of the external environment, Reuff and his team noted the similarities between peer-to-peer music sharing and the new **social networking** sites like FaceBook, Friendster, and MySpace. In 2006 they announced the creation of a partnership to offer digital music through MySpace pages.

social network The collection of ties between people and the strength of those ties.

Snocap's differentiators are based on two elements: rights protection and commerce. The first involves software that digitally fingerprints the songs to protect the copyright, and tracks the sales so copyright owners can be paid monthly. Artists (or content owners) can choose which songs they want to sell, and set the price themselves. To help with the commerce side, Snocap provides a ready-made "storefront," that can be added to a MySpace page or any webpage. Songs can also be sold through a list of "Snocap powered retailers" to expand distribution.

Snocap is betting that both music lovers and creators will see the potential of the Internet for sharing and supporting their music. There are about three million songs available for download through iTunes. But estimates are that there are ten times as many available in the marketplace as a whole. And music is only the beginning: one day Snocap hopes to bring the same tools to writers, videographers, and any creative artist who can sell their work on the Internet.

Perhaps the complete irony of this story is that whereas Fanning created Napster, a bootleg software engine that could virtually doom the entire music business as we know it, Snocap's business model is built around the total protection of artists' rights to the music they create. Snocap hopes that by targeting the long tail of the music industry it can carve out a competitive advantage. **<<<**

From New-Venture Creation to Corporate Renewal

Why are we going to discuss entrepreneurship and turnaround management (otherwise known as *corporate renewal*) in the same chapter? Throughout this text, we've described companies of various ages, sizes, and competitive positions. In this chapter, we want to focus on three particularly important phases or stages that can punctuate the life cycle of a firm:

- The birth of new ventures
- The transition from new venture to a more established firm, either as a public company via an initial public offering (IPO) or the incorporation of more professional management
- The rescue of established but struggling ventures

Not surprisingly, strategic management is critical to firms in all three of these phases. At first glance, it may seem that these three stages are far removed from one another, but by the end of this chapter, we will show that the entrepreneurial process is an important common thread that runs through all of them. Managers of startups, for example, must learn firsthand what it takes to develop and grow a business, whereas managers of distressed firms must recover the entrepreneurial orientation from which the firm originally emerged. This approach will demonstrate why what you've learned about strategy is equally applicable to both small and large firms as well as new and old ones.

If we've underscored any one concept in this book, it's that *strategies provide solutions to problems.* It just so happens that today new ventures face problems whose solutions involve not only the identification of new opportunities but the development of organizational resources and capabilities to operate profitably in that domain. The IPO, meanwhile, enables a firm not only to capitalize (literally as well as figuratively) on its initial success but to gain access to the financial resources needed to fuel future growth. Some firms do not need to resort to an IPO to support their growth, but they do at least make a transition from a visionary leadership style to one that increasingly incorporates aspects of professional management practices. While SNOCAP is not a public firm yet, if they succeed, an IPO would be one of the logical steps in their development path. In established firms, such entrepreneurial behavior faces the same growth management problems as those faced by startup firms. (An established firm, of course, must also deal with problems arising from its history and prior activities.) Finally, the five elements of a strategy are critical to any firm—established or new—that is engaged in entrepreneurial activity. Indeed, all of the tools of strategic management can be applied to problems arising from both new-venture creation and corporate renewal.

NEW-VENTURE CREATION VERSUS CORPORATE RENEWAL

new-venture creation Entrepreneurship and the creation of a new business from scratch.

corporate renewal Outcome of successful strategic change in the context of an established business.

initial public offering (IPO) First sale of a company's stock to the public market.

Note that in emphasizing new ventures, IPOs, and turnarounds, we're presenting a slightly simplified view of the organizational life cycle, **New-venture creation** refers to entrepreneurship and the creation of a new business from scratch, whereas **corporate renewal** refers to successful strategic change. **Initial public offerings (IPOs)** and/or the institutionalization of professional management often occur in the relatively early stages of a firm's life cycle. All firms start somewhere, and some firms go public. In addition, nearly all firms experience distress at some point, and corporate renewal prevents established firms—and sometimes even new and newly public ones as well—from vanishing from the face of the competitive landscape. As we already noted, because all three involve the creation of something new, all three stages in the organizational life cycle can engage in the entrepreneurial process. Indeed, a firm's success gives it a lot of options: It may remain independent, seek savvy private investors with deep pockets (as did SNOCAP), go public, or merge with an established firm seeking to enhance its future prospects.

In the sections that follow, you'll get a better idea of what entrepreneurship is and how the entrepreneurial process works. You'll also see how the same process may either lead to an IPO and professional management or provide an impetus for corporate renewal. By the end of the chapter, you'll understand the range of strategic ventures from startup to turnaround and see how strategic management is relevant to new enterprises. You'll also be able to identify the warning signs of organizational trouble and outline a resource-based turnaround plan for a struggling organization.

Entrepreneurship and the Entrepreneurial Process

Because of stories like the one in our opening vignette, you probably think of lone, self-reliant individuals like Shawn Fanning when you think about entrepreneurship and the creation of new ventures. Research shows, however, that no matter how important one individual is to an organization, its ultimate success depends as much on the entrepreneurial team as on the lead entrepreneur.[2] Dell, for instance, would have gone bankrupt in the early 1990s had it not recruited talented executives from IBM and Apple.

WHAT IS ENTREPRENEURSHIP?

Beyond the common misconception of entrepreneurship as an individual enterprise, people tend to associate it with a variety of images, from garage inventors to rogue executives who leave established employers to form their own companies. Such images have some validity, and throughout this chapter, you'll encounter certain behaviors that tend to characterize successful entrepreneurs. With this fact in mind, let's define **entrepreneurship** as the consequence of actions based on the identification and exploration of opportunity in the absence of obviously available resources. The **entrepreneurial process**, then, is the set of activities leading up to and driving the entrepreneurial venture.

Successful entrepreneurs, whether those who start new firms or who work within companies, are often those who challenge orthodoxy. *Orthodoxies* are the deeply held and broadly shared beliefs about what drives success within "the industry." Orthodoxies are not necessarily incorrect conceptualizations of the current market. Indeed, orthodoxies achieve their status because they do represent the status quo. However, orthodoxies also create blind spots to the recognition of new opportunities. Most industries have orthodoxies along several dimensions:

- Who the customer or end user is

- The type of interface and interaction with the customer or end user

- How benefit is defined and value is delivered

- How product/service functionality is defined

- What form the product/service should take

- How processes are structured and managed

- The "ideal" cost and pricing structure

Consider the examples reviewed in Exhibit 12.2 of a few notable business ideas and the orthodoxies they had to surmount to see the light of day.[3] Consider how the fortunes of some companies may have been different had they been able to overcome the orthodoxy internally and capitalize on the ideas and opportunities these innovations represent.

entrepreneurship Recognition of opportunities and the use of resources and capabilities to implement innovative ideas for new ventures.

entrepreneurial process
Integration of opportunity recognition, key resources and capabilities, and an entrepreneur and entrepreneurial team to create a new venture.

- "This 'telephone' has too many shortcomings to be seriously considered as a means of communication. The device is inherently of no value to us."
  —Western Union internal memo, 1876
- "The wireless music box has no imaginable commercial value. Who would pay for a message sent to nobody in particular?"—David Sarnhoff's associates in response to his urgings for investment in the radio in the 1920s
- "There is no reason anyone would want a computer in their home."—Ken Olson, President, Chairman and Founder of Digital Equipment Corp., 1977
- "The concept is interesting and well-formed, but in order to earn better than a 'C,' the idea must be feasible."—A Yale University management professor in response to Fred Smith's paper proposing reliable overnight delivery service. Smith went on to found Federal Express Corp.
- "A cookie store is a bad idea. Besides, the market research reports say America likes crispy cookies, not soft and chewy cookies like you make." —Response to Debbi Fields' idea of starting Mrs. Fields' Cookies
- "There will never be a market in selling stock over the Internet." —David Komansky, Merrill Lynch Chairman & CEO, 1999

Exhibit 12.2
Orthodoxies That Have Created Entrepreneurial Blind Spots

THE ENTREPRENEURIAL PROCESS

In this section, we'll elaborate on the entrepreneurial process, which, as you can see in Exhibit 12.3, integrates and coordinates three elements:

1. Opportunity

2. Key resources and capabilities

3. The entrepreneur and the entrepreneurial team

Because it emphasizes a need for balance and symmetry among its elements, this process model fits well with most of the theories that we've discussed throughout this book. It's also consistent with emerging research that considers entrepreneurship a function in most firms, regardless of their age or size.[4] For that reason alone, you'll see strong affinities with the resource- and dynamic-capabilities-based perspectives that we've described throughout the book.

The Starting Point: Opportunity SNOCAP is an example of an entrepreneurial starting point. Fanning identified a need to (1) protect the property rights of individual musicians and (2) connect individual musicians with individual consumers. Perhaps the biggest difference between strategy in existing firms and new ventures is the starting point. Most researchers agree that the starting point for new ventures is opportunity, whereas the strategy for existing firms typically begins with an assessment of the firm's underlying resources and capabilities.[5] You might be surprised to learn that you already possess some of the tools that may help you unearth a valuable business opportunity. Recall our discussion of revolutionary strategies in Chapter 6: All the revolutionary strategies provide a solid basis for identifying market opportunities. For instance, new market-creation strategies are designed to eliminate, reduce, create, or raise some previously assumed dimension of product/market supply and demand. For instance, new market-disruption strategies are an entrepreneur's dream because they're designed to enable a firm that's created a new market to grow into a dominant player in a new but

Exhibit 12.3 The Entrepreneurial Process

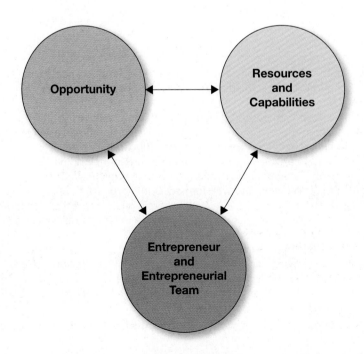

potentially huge industry. Google is a good example of this. Just a scant six years before it went public in 2004, a firm that now has more than $10 billion in revenue was bringing in less than $100,000 in a virtually nonexistent industry.[6] Low-end-disruption strategies involve identifying a business that will let a firm shift customers from a high-cost-to-serve to a low-cost-to-serve business model.

Like Fanning at SNOCAP, an entrepreneur identifies an opportunity and then seeks to cobble together the resources and capabilities to exploit it. Opportunities also can be identified by individuals who have close contact with scientific breakthroughs. In fact, scientific, technological, or process discoveries often inspire people to seek market opportunities. This is one reason why universities are increasing investments to support research faculty in the protection of intellectual property and identification of commercial opportunities. Universities like Stanford and the University of Wisconsin-Madison, for instance, maintain Offices of Corporate Relations that, among other services, assists individual researchers in the creation of new ventures. After all, faculty and staff members who create an early stage technology are often in the best position to develop it. Not only do they possess unsurpassed technical knowledge about their discoveries, they're often in a position to appreciate the promise that they hold.

Resources, Capabilities, and the Entrepreneurial Team   So far, we've focused on the element of opportunity in the entrepreneurial process. Our context, however—the intersection of technology and entrepreneurship—already suggests ways in which other elements—namely, resources and capabilities and people (the entrepreneur and entrepreneurial team)—are involved in the process. We discussed resources and capabilities in Chapter 3, and the VRINE framework that we presented there is as relevant in an entrepreneurial setting as it is in that of an established firm. Within the entrepreneurial firm, however, there's likely to be significant overlap between the people element and the resource-and-capabilities element. Why? Sometimes, the new opportunity is based in a technology whose benefits are recognizable only when it's complemented by the specific technical knowledge and experience of the people who created it. Similarly, if

Six years before going public in 2004, Google, founded by Sergey Brin and Larry Page, was bringing in less than $100,000 a year. Today Google Inc.'s annual revenues exceed $4 billion.

the opportunity is revealed by a "good idea," the entrepreneur and entrepreneurial team must often rely on their own personal resources, experience, and persuasiveness to acquire the needed resources and capabilities, including financial capital. In the case of SNOCAP, the firm has propriety technology to protect the property rights of the musicians, connect musicians with customers, and process and track payments for music purchased. In SNOCAP's lingo, "uploading and registering your music with SNOCAP enables you to sell tracks through your own SNOCAP MyStore and multiple retailers—all from one interface. It's non-exclusive and you keep all the rights to your music. Set licensing terms in the SNOCAP Digital Registry so SNOCAP-powered online retailers can sell your music. You determine the price, format, and digital rights (DRM) restrictions."

Although there is no litmus test for determining the characteristics of successful entrepreneurs and the people who make the best members of an entrepreneurial team, it's clear that without them, a new venture will never get off the ground. Sometimes, as we've already

Exhibit 12.4 The Google Management Team and Their Management Philosophy

"We run Google as a triumvirate. Sergey and I have worked closely together for the last eight years, five at Google. Eric, our CEO, joined Google three years ago. The three of us run the company collaboratively with Sergey and me as Presidents. The structure is unconventional, but we have worked successfully in this way.

To facilitate timely decisions, Eric, Sergey, and I meet daily to update each other on the business and to focus our collaborative thinking on the most important and immediate issues. Decisions are often made by one of us, with the other being briefed later. This works because we have tremendous trust and respect for each other and we generally think alike. Because of our intense, long-term working relationship, we can often predict differences of opinion among the three of us. We know that when we disagree, the correct decision is far from obvious. For important decisions, we discuss the issue with a larger team appropriate to the task. Differences are resolved through discussion and analysis and by reaching consensus. Eric, Sergey, and I run the company without any significant internal conflict, but with healthy debate. As different topics come up, we often delegate decision-making responsibility to one of us.

We hired Eric as a more experienced complement to Sergey and me to help us run the business. Eric was CTO of Sun Microsystems. He was also CEO of Novell and has a Ph.D. in computer science, a very unusual and important combination for Google given our scientific and technical culture. This partnership among the three of us has worked very well and we expect it to continue. The shared judgments and extra energy available from all three of us has significantly benefited Google.

Eric has the legal responsibilities of the CEO and focuses on management of our vice presidents and the sales organization. Sergey focuses on engineering and business deals. I focus on engineering and product management. All three of us devote considerable time to overall management of the company and other fluctuating needs. We also have a distinguished board of directors to oversee the management of Google. We have a talented executive staff that manages day-to-day operations in areas such as finance, sales, engineering, human resources, public relations, legal and product management. We are extremely fortunate to have talented management that has grown the company to where it is today—they operate the company and deserve the credit."
—Larry Page

seen, key people are among the intangible resources and capabilities that distinguish the potential new venture as an opportunity rather than just another good idea. For instance, Shawn Fanning is the creative genius behind SNOCAP, and Rusty Reuff is the innovative leader who connects the dots between the leading edge SNOCAP technology and the creative types who not only buy and sell through SNOCAP, but also work there. As a practical matter, it's the entrepreneur who drives the entrepreneurial process and ensures that all three elements—opportunity, resources and capabilities, and people—are in place and balanced. Because individuals have limits, team members are often selected because they bring skills that complement those of the lead entrepreneur and will ensure that the firm has the necessary human capital to achieve the objectives that it has set. This is why the positive chemistry between Fanning and Reuff is so important.

While the interplay among key team members is not always obvious, the letter to shareholders issued by Google in its 2004 IPO provides a rare and intriguing glimpse into this incredibly important context. Recall that Google was founded by Larry Page and Sergey Brin, and they soon brought in Dr. Eric Schmidt to serve as Chairman of the Board and CEO. Exhibit 12.4 summarizes their special, if not unique, relationship.

New-Venture Creation and Corporate New-Venturing

Entrepreneurship, which is the outcome of the entrepreneurial process, is embodied in the launch of a new venture. As we've already explained, the first step in new-venture creation is identifying an opportunity. Unfortunately, there's no rule of thumb for deciding on the next step. All we can say is that, typically, entrepreneurs begin a process of experimentation involving the confluence of several activities over time.

NEW-VENTURE SCENARIOS

Exhibit 12.5 summarizes these activities. As you can imagine, the traditional view of new-venture creation calls for the entrepreneur to exploit an opportunity by drawing up a business plan, obtaining external financing, and then launching the new product.[7]

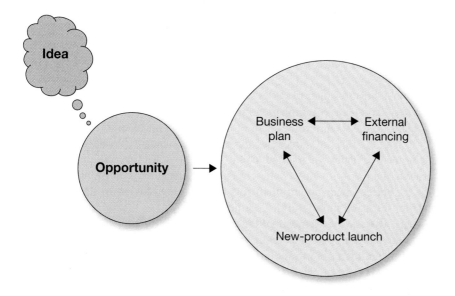

Exhibit 12.5 Activities in New-Venture Creation

A more realistic view allows for an alternative sequence of events that begins when the entrepreneur uses his or her own resources to launch a product and then seeks financing to stay in the game. The business plan often comes after the launch because its purpose is to obtain financing or to generate market interest (in the form of additional financing or purchase of the business) by explaining the venture's history and prospects.

Financing the New Venture   Commercializing a new venture requires capital for startup needs. The financing activity of the new venture can take many forms, with sources ranging from credit cards to venture capitalists to banks. You might expect most successful ventures to have access to adequate capital, but you'd be surprised. In fact, many successful entrepreneurs (and their investors) suspect that too much money, too early, produces more damage than good.[8] How, you're probably asking yourself, can excess cash possibly be a problem? Remember, first of all, that financing rarely comes without strings attached. Thus, entrepreneurs who depend on significant cash flow from loans or investor capital often find their flexibility considerably reduced. Second, ample funding can obscure potential problems until their consequences become irreversible. Finally, deep financial pockets shelter the new firm from the need to innovate in all aspects of its business. For instance, if you look at SNOCAP's website you will notice that they have venture capital financing from Ron Conway. Ron, besides being one of SNOCAP's founders, is a seasoned angel investor whose company, Angel Investors LLC, was an early investor in Napster. SNOCAP is also supported by Morgenthaler Ventures, WaldenVC, and Court Square Ventures. Nevertheless, without adequate startup financing, a new venture has difficulty getting off the ground.

bootstrapping   Process of finding creative ways to support a startup business financially until it turns profitable.

   Bootstrapping means exploiting a new business opportunity with limited funds. Many new ventures are bootstrapped: A study of about 100 of *Inc.* magazine's list of the 500 fastest-growing small companies in the United States found median startup capital to be around $22,000 in real terms.[9] Ironically, the fastest-growing firms typically require the most money because they have to support increases in inventories, accounts receivable, staffing, and production and service facilities.

The Business Plan   Once the new product has been launched and startup financing secured, many entrepreneurs draw up a formal business plan that brings all the elements of the new venture together for a specific purpose: namely, to assure key stakeholders that the firm has a well-considered strategy and managerial acumen. Even if such a plan isn't necessary for communicating with external stakeholders, preparing one is still a good idea. At the very least, it will help the entrepreneur to reexamine the five elements of strategy and look for ways of bringing them together to create a viable and profitable firm.

   In addition, a business plan provides the entrepreneur with a vehicle for sharing goals and objectives—and plans for implementing them—with members of the entrepreneurial team. Focusing on the staging component of the five elements of strategy, for example, is a good way to set milestones and time lines and otherwise manage the scale and pace of a new company's growth. Finally, when it does come time to seek external funding to support the firm's growth, the plan provides a coherent basis for engaging professionals who can not only help the entrepreneur obtain financing, but also offer advice on strengthening customer relationships and finding strategic suppliers.

   Familiarity with the five elements of the strategy diamond, implementation levers, and frameworks for analyzing external organizational context is helpful with drawing up a business plan. Although there are variations in form, the content of most plans covers the same topics. A multitude of examples—as well as software packages for creating a detailed and professional-looking document—are available on the Web.[10] Exhibit 12.6 provides a sum-

Exhibit 12.6 Table of Contents of a Typical Business Plan

1. **Executive summary.** One to three pages highlighting all key points in a way that captures the interest of the reader. Stress the business concept here, notthe numbers. It is the unique value proposition and business model that reallymatter.

2. **Company description.** Provide a brief description of the company's business,organization, structure and strategy. Provide a summary of how thecompany's patents or licenses to patents are connected with the developmentand introduction of products.

3. **Products and services.** Include a layman's overview of how the company's technology and patents relate to its products and services. Describe the products or services the company will sell, including a discussion of why people will want them, what problems they solve, and how much customers are likely to pay for them (i.e., the willingness to pay criteria).

4. **Market analysis.** Identify the need for the product, the extent of that need,who the customers will be, and why they will buy your product. This sectionshould also include a discussion of competitors or potential competitors andwhy the product will have a competitive advantage over their offerings.Include considerations of barriers to entry in this market.

5. **Proprietary position.** If the new venture's market position will rely on patentsor licenses to patents, discuss how these patents will contribute to thecompany's competitive position and whether other patents (competitors orotherwise) might limit the company's ability to market its products. If similarproducts do not already exist, discuss the alternative means by whichcustomers are likely to meet the needs the product addresses.

6. **Marketing and sales plan.** Show how the company plans to attract and maintain customers. Discuss product pricing, promotion, and positioning strategy.

7. **Management team.** Describe the management team with special emphasis onits track record at accomplishing tasks similar to those it will face in makingthe company successful. Investors place major emphasis on the managementteam, viewing it as the critical ingredient in catalyzing the growth of thecompany and responding to the unexpected.

8. **Operations plan.** Describe how the day-to-day operations of the company willbe organized and carried out to produce the products and services describedabove.

9. **Finances.** Identify the capital that will be required to build the business and how it will be used. Include projections of revenues and expenses that show investors how they will get their money back and what return they can expecton their investment.

mary of what is normally contained in a comprehensive business plan. It is important to keep in mind that the process of systematically thinking through the nine steps in the exhibit is probably more important than the business plan document itself.

Finally, a word of warning. All too often, would-be entrepreneurs tend to equate a good business plan with the probability of success in running a business. Needless to say, however, a well-crafted plan does not ensure a successful business. At this point in the process, the probability of success depends more heavily on the strength of the three elements that were present at the start of the process—a good opportunity (including the right timing), the right entrepreneurial team, and the necessary resources and capabilities. A business plan is no more a substitute for strategy and strong execution than a clear vision and mission or even such strategic vehicles as alliances and acquisitions. That's why consultants often suggest that entrepreneurs think of the business plan not only as a helpful and necessary starting point but as a continuous work in progress.[11]

CORPORATE NEW-VENTURING

The previous section discussed new-venturing as a process engaged in by entrepreneurs. However, many successful innovations and new ventures are sponsored by existing organizations. What you have learned about entrepreneurial new-venturing applies equally well to the process of **corporate new-venturing**—the creation of new businesses by established firms. In addition, your knowledge of co-opetition and coevolution should give you a pretty good idea of some of the challenges and opportunities encountered during the process of corporate new-venturing. However, the resources and capabilities of established firms and the corporate environment in which they do business differ. These factors often kill corporate new ventures before they get off the ground (or at least keep performance below levels that firms might have achieved through other investments or even by simply buying a portfolio of market stocks).[12] The stellar innovation track records of firms such as Merck, 3M, Motorola, Rubbermaid, Johnson & Johnson, Corning, General Electric, Raychem, Hewlett-Packard, Wal-Mart, and many others demonstrate that bigness is not in itself antithetical to new-venturing. At the same time, however, these are but a few of the thousands of large firms around the world.[13] Understanding the obstacles to entrepreneurship in large, established firms will put you on firmer ground when it comes time to translate what you know about entrepreneurship into the process of corporate new-venturing. Corporate new-venturing can take on one or a combination of two forms: establishing a new business or creating a new-ventures division.

Establishing a New Business

A firm may seek to develop a new business around some valuable process or technological breakthrough. Typically, an executive or group of executives will champion the innovation, and the process will proceed when the business concept has been tentatively validated and many of the major uncertainties resolved or reduced.[14] Attention then shifts from opportunity validation to the process of bringing the new business to life. Efforts are directed at assembling resources and capabilities, meeting production and sales goals, and solidifying organization. Interestingly, researchers note that creating a business climate supportive of entrepreneurial activity is the most difficult task faced by a large company trying to integrate an innovative new business.[15]

As a general rule, new-venture activities are less predictable and are, therefore, riskier than those in which a firm traditionally engages. In particular, such activities face three obstacles:

1. Although false starts and failures can sometimes be important learning mechanisms, most large firms naturally try to mitigate them by improving efficiency.

2. Moreover, new ventures often meet resistance because they challenge long-established assumptions, work practices, and employee skills. After all, by definition *new* means *different*.

3. Ironically—and most importantly—large organizations often lavish *too many resources*, including cash, on new ventures. How can this practice be a problem? To be successful at corporate new-venturing, large firms must learn to be simultaneously patient and tolerant of risk on the one hand, and stingy on the other. The need for stinginess comes from the observation by strategy researchers that corporate new ventures tend to thrive when their managers must face new markets on the same realistic terms that startups typically do outside the corporate bureaucracy.

New-Venture Division

The second form of corporate new-venturing, in which the firm sets up an internal new-venture division, is actually a structural solution to these obstacles. In many ways, this division acts like a venture capitalist or business incubator, working to provide expertise and resources and impart structure to the process of developing the new opportunity.

---

corporate new-venturing
New-venture creation by established firms.

In this case, too, the opportunity may revolve around some proprietary process, product, or technological breakthrough. This approach is designed to achieve one of two possible objectives:

1. The creation and retention of a new business that will fuel growth and perhaps foster corporate renewal

2. The creation of a high-growth new venture that the firm can sell off through an IPO at a significant profit

The advantage of the structural approach is that it provides a system for investing in a team that's assigned specifically to new-venture creation. If the system is managed properly, new-venture divisions can function like the best venture-capital operations—that is, they can be cost conscious while still encouraging risk taking, experimentation, and novel, market-oriented solutions. A new-venture division—for that matter, new-venturing in any form—is a form of diversification, with the firm betting that it has the resources and capabilities to do something new.

The structural approach first became popular in the late 1960s, when 25 percent of the *Fortune* 500 maintained internal venture divisions.[16] The next wave came in the late 1970s and early 1980s, when large players such as Gillette, IBM, Levi Strauss, and Xerox launched internal new-venture groups.[17] Next came the Internet boom, when many firms set up divisions to run e-commerce operations that mirrored their traditional brick-and-mortar operations.

The success of new-venture divisions can be measured in several ways. Using an internal rate of return metric, many of these divisions perform quite well. However, the performances of these divisions are generally not up to the levels of those achieved by private equity venture capital firms.[18] Why? Although a firm may have proprietary access to a valuable technology, it probably doesn't possess the necessary venture-capitalist managerial skills and experience. In addition, when it's in the hands of a new-venture division, the new business is isolated from the rest of the organization. This separation is often necessary to protect the new venture, as you saw with the discussion of the ambidextrous organizational structure in Chapter 11. However, if the loose linkages with the parent company, which are necessary to secure resources and transfer information, are severe or dysfunctional, then the parent firm is insulated from the new business and thus less likely to learn from its successes and failures. In addition, the new venture risks being starved for resources and capabilities possessed by the parent firm.

Is corporate new-venturing, then, doomed to failure? Of course not. Firms must, however, be careful to balance the requirements of entrepreneurial ventures—such as a supportive entrepreneurial climate—with the benefits of sustained linkage to the parent firm. The natural tension and potential dysfunction created by the need for separateness yet connectedness must be carefully managed. Entrepreneurship Professor David Garvin of Harvard Business School recently reviewed the history of corporate new-venturing. He suggested that corporate new ventures are more likely to succeed when they:[19]

- Are developed and validated in firms with supportive, entrepreneurial climates

- Have senior executive sponsorship

- Are based on related, rather than radically different, products and services

- Appeal to an emerging subset or current set of customers

- Employ market-experienced personnel

- Test concepts and business models directly with potential users

- Experiment, probe, and prototype repeatedly during early development

■ Balance demands for early profitability with realistic time lines

■ Introduce required systems and processes in time, but not earlier than the new venture's evolution required

■ Combine disciplined oversight and stinginess with entrepreneurial autonomy

Professor Garvin's guidelines for successful corporate venturing suggest that there are other inherent tensions in the decision-making process as well. Many of the guidelines in this list call for incorporating a resource-based approach into the new-venturing process. Even when a firm succeeds in creating a climate that's supportive of entrepreneurship, the evolving characteristics of the new venture may result in a unit that's more distinctive from—than complementary to—the core businesses. In that case, it might be wise for the parent firm to allow the new business to function independently—physically and legally. In part, the increase in new-venture public offerings can be attributed to the willingness of firms to take this advice. With this fact in mind, we turn in the next section to a discussion of initial public offerings (IPOs).

Initial Public Offerings and Managerial Professionalism

As firms grow, they face the need to transition to a more complex organizational form. Sometimes this form is dictated by the need for access to additional capital and professional management or managerial professionalism alone. Increasingly, experts are starting to view the IPO as a pivotal point in a firm's transition from small and entrepreneurial to large and established. An IPO takes place when a firm offers ownership shares through a public stock market.[20] In 2000, for instance, Krispy Kreme was a highly successful private company that decided to facilitate expansion by issuing an IPO. Typically, investment bankers (underwriters) and stockbrokers value the firm and place the stock with investors. Of course, a number of different transition vehicles are possible—alliances, mergers, sales, outright failure (the most common exit route). Given their recent visibility and rise to virtual holy-grail status among entrepreneurs, it's important to understand the workings of IPOs in greater detail.

HOW DOES AN IPO WORK?

How does an organization orchestrate an IPO? Once it's decided to make a securities offering, the company establishes a market value in the private sector. This value is estimated by an investment-banking institution, which will also sell the firm's shares to public investors. During this process, the company files an **S-1 statement**, which states its value proposition and financial prospects, with the Securities and Exchange Commission (SEC) and various state securities commissions. It is a good idea for you to track down the S-1 of recently IPO'd firms like TomoTherapy just to see the impressive amount of information that is provided about the firm, its strategy, competition, operating risks, and financial prospects. It also provides detailed information about the backgrounds of the management team and board of directors, as well as the schedule of their compensation. The front page of one of these statements is shown in Exhibit 12.7. Finally, the company and its brokerage firm "time" the offering to get maximum value from the sale of its stock.

One thing that companies are required to discuss at length is the challenges they face that could adversely affect shareholders. Google, for example, discloses in its S-1 prospectus that "We face significant competition from Microsoft and Yahoo."

Usually, the *prospectus* describes the perceived business opportunity, outlines the firm's strategy for exploiting it, and details its current products and activities, generally in the con-

S-1 statement Legal document outlining a firm's financial position in preparation for an initial public stock offering.

```
As filed with the Securities and Exchange Commission on February 12, 2007
                                                          Registration No. 333


                 SECURITIES AND EXCHANGE COMMISSION
                              Washington, D.C. 20549


                                  Form S-1
                          REGISTRATION STATEMENT
                                    UNDER
                        THE SECURITIES ACT OF 1933

                     TomoTherapy Incorporated
                    (Exact Name of Registrant as Specified in its Charter)

    Wisconsin                        3845                      39-1914727
(State or Other Jurisdiction of  (Primary Standard Industrial    (I.R.S. Employer
Incorporation or Organization)   Classification Code Number)  Identification Number)

                              1240 Deming Way
                          Madison, Wisconsin 53717
                                (608) 824-2800
                    (Address, including zip code, and telephone number,
                  including area code, of registrar's principal executive offices)


                             Stephen C. Hathaway
                       Chief Financial Officer and Treasurer
                              1240 Deming Way
                          Madison, Wisconsin 53717
                                (608) 824-2800
                   (Name, address, including zip code and telephone number,
                        including area code, of agent for service)


                                  Copies to:

  Gregory J. Lynch, Esq.          Shawn Guse, Esq.           Colin J. Diamond, Esq.
  Geoffrey R. Morgan, Esq.   Vice President, General Counsel and    White & Case LLP
 Michael Best & Friedrich LLP         Secretary          1155 Avenue of the Americas
  100 East Wisconsin Avenue    TomoTherapy Incorporated       New York, NY 10036
        Suite 3300                 1240 Deming Way      Telephone: (212) 819-8200
  Milwaukee, Wisconsin 53202  Madison, Wisconsin 53717  Facsimile: (212) 354-8113
  Telephone: (414) 225-2752   Telephone: (608) 824-2800
  Facsimile: (414) 277-0656   Facsimile: (608) 824-2996


 Approximate date of commencement of proposed sale to the public: As soon as practicable after the
 effective date of this registration statement.
```

Exhibit 12.7 Opening Page of TomoTherapy's S-1 Statement

text of the company's overall expansion strategy. The firm must clearly define its vision and describe its mission, business initiatives, and objectives. As we observed earlier in this chapter, the business plan should also spell out the firm's approach to the five elements of strategy and the implementation levers necessary for executing its strategy, and it should do so in a way that's clear and compelling for potential investors. Because investors will want to know what goals the firm has set for itself, treatment of staging is especially important.

COST OF AN IPO

When preparing a securities offering, consider the old saying that you need money to make money. While exact figures will vary by transaction level and complexity, the IPO process could easily require $400,000 in professional fees alone. Investment bankers exact a heavy toll for shepherding a firm through an IPO. A normal 6.5-percent commission would skim $1,625,000 off the top of a $25-million offering! As an illustration, Exhibit 12.8 breaks out the underlying IPO costs for a $25-million offering.[21] Some of the line items, such as the "road show," are discussed further in the next section.

Financial and Legal Requirements   The firm will have to pass certain financial tests. An independent SEC-approved CPA firm, for example, must audit the firm's financial statements for the previous three years. If the firm hasn't been audited over that period, the process may take months. If the company has been around for more than five years, it will have to include financial information from previous years in the (S-1) registration and prospectus statement.[22]

An SEC-approved CPA will require that all legal work be done and be done properly. If the firm doesn't pass the CPA's audit tests, it won't be issued an *unqualified opinion* on its financial statements. Instead, it will receive a *qualified opinion*—a statement of the auditor's

Exhibit 12.8   Minimum Costs of Going Public to Raise $25 Million

Source: P. Downing, 1998. IPO launch fraught with perils. The Ottawa Citizen, High Tech Report, October 12, 1998.

Pre-IPO costs over two years,		
1. Upgrading accounting and MIS	$150,000	
2. New personnel and board members	150,000	
3. Management/administrative time	100,000	
Minimum Pre-IPO Costs		**$400,000**
IPO-Process costs 90 days,		
6.5% underwriter commission		
$25 million IPO		$1,625,000
IPO professional fees		
1. Legal fees	$ 150,000	
2. Preliminary/final prospectus printing	100,000	
3. Translation	30,000	
4. Investors relations	40,000	
5. Accounting	50,000	
6. Road show and preparations	50,000	
7. Initial stock exchange listing fee	10,000	
Minimum IPO professional fees		430,000
Minimum IPO-Process Costs		**$2,055,000**
Post-IPO costs every year thereafter,		
1. Investor relations and Web site	100,000	
2. Directors' fees, travel costs, etc.	100,000	
3. Directors' liability insurance	50,000	
4. Corporate image, public relations	50,000	
5. Annual stock exchange fee	5,000	
6. Management/administration costs	100,000	
Minimum Annual Post IPO-Costs		**$405,000**
Total Minimum Cost of a $25 million IPO		**$2,860,000**

opinion that the audit reflects certain limitations, such as financial irregularities, lack of controls, and so forth. That's not good: In the securities world, an unqualified opinion is sometimes called the "blue screen of death," and it's particularly grave for the IPO.

The "Road Show"   Once the firm has met the financial and legal requirements, it enters the pre-IPO period and launches a **road show**, which is a series of presentations in which members of the top-management team, particularly the CEO, promote the company to interested investors and analysts. Depending on the quality of the road show, the firm may even get commitments from investors to buy shares of its stock. However, bear in mind that there are restrictions on the people to whom managers can talk and what they can talk about, and what's more, these rules change frequently. Obviously, top executives need to know the rules before they hit the road.

As pressure for financial transparency increases, the SEC may eventually require companies to open road-show presentations, which are now restricted to analysts and institutional investors, to individual investors, not only to expand the audience for promotional activities but to level the playing field in terms of access to information. The SEC hasn't yet worked out the logistics, but one way to give individuals access to road shows would be to broadcast them on the Internet. Road-show meetings with stock analysts, which must be open to the public, are often broadcast over the Internet.

Once the road show is over, the firm's brokers will want to time the offering so that shares become available under the most favorable market conditions.[23] For example, a high-tech company wouldn't want its stock brought to market during a sell-off in technology stocks. The firm's brokers may prefer things to be uneventful so that the IPO can make news. They might try to time the firm's offering to coincide with other attractive IPOs, taking advantage of a window during which investors feel eager to get in the game.

> **road show** Series of presentations in which top management promotes an IPO to interested investors and analysts.

AN IPO OR A MORE FORMAL ORGANIZATION?

Given the complexities and costs of an IPO, it is no surprise that not all growing firms go public. Recall that an IPO is part of the growth path of a firm because it provides access to additional capital as well as the opportunity and motivation to put more professional management in place. Professional management may take the form of executives experienced with running larger firms, rapidly growing firms, or those that require management of significant organizational change. The need to shift from purely entrepreneurial management to more formal or professional management was initially discovered by Professor Daryl Wyckoff in his study of the trucking industry.[24] Wyckoff coined the term the *Bermuda Triangle of Management* to describe the region where firms are faced with the need to cross over from entrepreneurial to formal management. The Bermuda Triangle is an infamous area in the Atlantic Ocean where legend has it that ships and planes enter but never escape; Wyckoff argued that firms face a similar scenario and that those trucking firms that never completed the shift from informal to formal, professional management is apt to fail and disappear from the scene.

Part of the explanation for the Bermuda Triangle effect is economic. Wyckoff found that the operating ratio (expenses as a percentage of revenues) in the trucking industry varied by firm size; large and small companies were generally more profitable than midsized companies (those ostensibly stuck in or trying to get through the Bermuda Triangle). Part of the effect was managerial. Wyckoff noted that small firms were informally managed and large firms were professionally managed.

What does formal, professional management entail? Based on his work with the trucking industry, Wyckoff concluded that formal management includes delegation of authority; detailed and frequent measurement systems; formalized, performance-based reward systems; formal ground rules, procedures, and resource-allocation systems; and separation of ownership and management. Although Wyckoff's work dates from the 1970s, more recent examples are easy to find. Recall the saga of SAP in the late 1990s, which struggled as it grew but ultimately succeeded by successfully transitioning from an informal to a formal management system.

Why Do Organizations Fail?

The new-venture process, whether undertaken by a new firm or within an existing firm, represents the beginning of a new organization. However, successful new ventures do not ensure long-term prosperity. Firms often must make major changes in order to survive, and the Bermuda Triangle phenomenon aptly demonstrates this. Before considering how firms can change to return to prosperity, it may be useful to review the broader set of explanations as to why organizations fail. Knowing the causes of failure will help us better understand what is needed to guide a firm through a strategic change to correct problems and avoid complete failure.[25]

Both public and private firms may experience distress at any point in their life cycle, and research indicates that a set of common factors underlies business failure. To be fair, it's usually much easier to determine the cause of organizational failure after the failure rather than before, but understanding and learning from the mistakes of other management teams is the responsibility of everyone charged with leading a business.

In the United States, publicly traded firms are required to disclose known risks that could lead to business failure. These risks are disclosed in the firm's annual 10-K filings and in S-1 filings when the firm first goes public. For instance, Google lists a number of risks that could affect the viability of its business. Some of these risks are summarized in Exhibit 12.9.

As you can see from reviewing the risks that have been identified by the managers (or more likely the investment bankers and attorneys) of Google, most of the risks identified as sources of potential business failure fall into two broad categories: *external* and *internal*. In the next section, we look at both categories in some detail.

EXTERNAL CAUSES OF ORGANIZATIONAL FAILURE

You will recall that there are two major contexts facing firms that determine the success of their strategies: in Chapter 3 you were introduced to the internal context of strategy and in Chapter 4 you learned about the external context. Just as these factors affect the success of strategies, it should not be surprising that causes of failure can also be categorized similarly. External causes of organizational failure reflect trends and events that strike at the core of a company's business. Some of these changes, such as population trends in peacetime, occur slowly and predictably. Others, such as natural disasters and wars, occur suddenly and with a severity that may change the shape of much more than the business world. Failure to foresee the possibility of such events and to consider their implications is an invitation to trouble. Remarkably enough, a recent study of fifty-one failed organizations found that not one of the failures was the result of unforeseeable events.[26] In each case, managers observed, discussed, and then disregarded the relevant change in the external environment.

External change may take one of four forms: *economic, competitive, social,* and *technological.*

Economic Change Managers are often heard to say that "the trend is your friend." A boom can cover many sins, and good economic times often mask organizational problems. A bust, however, can turn many small glitches into big problems. A list of economic problems includes (but is certainly not limited to) slackening overall demand, currency devaluation, international monetary crises, interest-rate hikes, and credit squeezes. Common sense would suggest that when economic activity levels off or declines, the number of failures will increase and vice versa. As a matter of fact, that's exactly how it works out.

Exhibit 12.9   Some of Google's Risk Listed in S-1

RISK FACTORS

An investment in Google involves significant risks. You should read these risk factors carefully before deciding whether to invest in our company. The following is a description of what we consider our key challenges and risks.

Risks Related to Our Business and Industry

We face significant competition from Microsoft and Yahoo.

We face competition from other Internet companies, including web search providers, Internet advertising companies and destination web sites that may also bundle their services with Internet access.

We face competition from traditional media companies, and we may not be included in the advertising budgets of large advertisers, which could harm our operating results.

We expect our growth rates to decline and anticipate downward pressure on our operating margin in the future.

Our operating results may fluctuate.

If we do not continue to innovate and provide products and services that are useful to users, we may not remain competitive, and our revenues and operating results could suffer.

We generate our revenue almost entirely from advertising, and the reduction in spending by or loss of advertisers could seriously harm our business.

We rely on our Google Network members for a significant portion of our net revenues, and otherwise benefit from our association with them, and the loss of these members could adversely affect our business.

Our business and operations are experiencing rapid growth. If we fail to manage our growth, our business and operating results could be harmed.

If we fail to maintain an effective system of internal controls, we may not be able to accurately report our financial results or prevent fraud. As a result, current and potential stockholders could lose confidence in our financial reporting, which would harm our business and the trading price of our stock.

Our business depends on a strong brand, and if we are not able to maintain and enhance our brand, our business and operating results would be harmed.

Proprietary document formats may limit the effectiveness of our search technology by excluding the content of documents in such formats.

New technologies could block our ads, which would harm our business.

Our corporate culture has contributed to our success, and if we cannot maintain this culture as we grow, our business may be harmed.

Our intellectual property rights are valuable, and any inability to protect them could reduce the value of our products, services and brand.

(continued)

Exhibit 12.9   Continued

We are, and may in the future be, subject to intellectual property rights claims, which are costly to defend, could require us to pay damages and could limit our ability to use certain technologies in the future.

Expansion into international markets is important to our long-term success, and our inexperience in the operation of our business outside the U.S. increases the risk that our international expansion efforts will not be successful.

We compete internationally with local information providers and with U.S. competitors who are currently more successful than we are in various markets.

Our business may be adversely affected by malicious third-party applications that interfere with the Google experience.

If we fail to detect click-through fraud, we could lose the confidence of our advertisers, thereby causing our business to suffer.

We are susceptible to index spammers who could harm the integrity of our web search results.

Our ability to offer our products and services may be affected by a variety of U.S. and foreign laws.

If we were to lose the services of Eric, Larry, Sergey or our senior management team, we may not be able to execute our business strategy.

The initial option grants to many of our senior management and key employees are fully vested. Therefore, these employees may not have sufficient financial incentive to stay with us.

If we are unable to retain or motivate key personnel or hire qualified personnel, we may not be able to grow effectively.

Our CEO and our two founders run the business and affairs of the company collectively, which may harm their ability to manage effectively.

We have a short operating history and a relatively new business model in an emerging and rapidly evolving market. This makes it difficult to evaluate our future prospects and may increase the risk of your investment.

At the same time, however, although economic change does indeed contribute to decline and failure, we should keep its role in proper perspective. According to one study, only 9 percent of all failures are caused chiefly by economic factors. The same study also found that during any economic cycle, good performers outperformed laggards by astonishing rates: While good performers' earnings per share grew at 33 percent annually, those of poor performers declined by 23 percent.[27] Can we draw any conclusions from these findings? One conclusion is perhaps that good management can offset poor economic conditions.

Competitive Change   Because so many events can drastically change the competitive landscape—the emergence of low-cost foreign competitors, the entry of new companies in an industry, the merger of two competitors—most companies operate in a world of constantly shifting competition. Thirty-five percent of all business failures are related to competitive change (i.e., the emergence of competition plus loss of market).[28] Usually, competitive change takes the form of price competition, as competitors lower prices in order to introduce products into new markets (a trend that's particularly common during economic downturns). In response, incumbents often try to keep factories at near-capacity production despite decreased demand.

A more sudden and less predictable type of competition comes from foreign countries or the appearance of a new technology. Foreign competition has been a fact of life for many years now, and in the United States, it's had a particularly devastating impact on clothing (shoes and textiles), consumer electronics, and steel. Failures in these industries highlight the importance of monitoring the external competitive environment.

Social Change   Because it generally takes a fairly long time for a society to accommodate significant changes, social change is usually less abrupt and less obvious than other forms of external change. The first signs of changes in Americans' attitudes toward work, such as the balance of men and women professionals and an aging workforce, have been evident for decades, but many companies still don't fully understand how the shift affects them.

Although such trends are hard to quantify, companies must realize that failure to recognize and respond to social changes can be extremely costly. Numerous companies have lost touch with markets or customers because they failed to observe or react to such social trends as changes in lifestyles, in the composition of given populations, or in attitudes toward such issues as pollution and personal health. Krispy Kreme, for example, the acclaimed purveyor of fried donuts, blamed a slowdown in business on the changing dietary habits of carbohydrate-conscious consumers. Apparently taken by surprise, the company issued its first profit warning since going public, thereby adding fuel to investor worries about its growth prospects.[29] Companies can even lose touch with their own employees, and the consequences may range from declining productivity to work stoppages.

Again, however, we should repeat that changes such as these tend to occur slowly, over long periods of time, and in one recent survey, CEOs agreed that in most industries reasonably astute management should be able to keep up with them.[30]

Technological Change   It's not overstating the case to say that global markets are what they are today because today's technologies make it possible to move information, products, and people quite easily. Technological change is a result of advances in information transportation technology.

Information Technology   The absolute amount of knowledge in the world has been growing at an increasing rate. Between 1965 and 1980, for example, the number of scientific articles published per day rose from 3,000 to 8,000, and because knowledge feeds on itself, this pattern isn't likely to change. In any case, even if the rate of increase were to diminish, the existing knowledge base would still be so large that the absolute increase in units of knowledge per unit of time would remain large throughout at least the first half of the next century.

Just as important, the growing number of advanced communications technologies will greatly increase the availability of all knowledge that is produced. Combined with the rate at which new knowledge is being generated, technology has also increased the *availability* of information substantially.

Transportation Technology   Transportation technology has increased the number of markets to which a business has access and the speed with which they can be accessed. Moreover, we now know a lot more about markets to which we've long had access, and not surprisingly, the effects of changes in information and transportation technology are closely related. The decline in U.S. manufacturing employment, for example, is a direct consequence of automation (information technology) and importation (manufacturing and transportation technologies).

The increasing availability and complexity of information make the task of focusing on relevant information more daunting than ever. This fact is especially important. As we said at the beginning of this section, organizational failure is rarely a consequence of unforeseen events. Rather, it very often results from management's failure to make the best use of relevant information.

INTERNAL CAUSES OF ORGANIZATIONAL FAILURE

It's nearly impossible to say exactly what percentage of business failures result from internal causes, but most experts agree that internal causes of failure are more common than external ones. Failure is generally the result of a bad strategy, poor executive judgment, or financial mismanagement.

Strategy Failure   By now it should be clear that a good strategy is preferable to a poor one and that expert implementation will always outperform poor implementation. Also, recall that a quality strategy exploits opportunities in the marketplace. It also enables the firm to fit with the current competitive environment and adapt to changes so that it will be well-positioned when the competitive environment changes. When a firm's strategy is poorly adapted to the current environment or a change in the environment results in a major misalignment, quick decline may result.

Management Failure   Why does poor management lead to failure? A recent study addressed the common assumption that failures are due to inept or incompetent CEOs or senior executives. After interviewing executives from over fifty failed firms, the researcher concluded that people who become CEOs of large corporations are almost always remarkably intelligent.[31] That's not surprising: They reach the top because they are regarded as the most capable, and are repeatedly chosen for positions over their fellow managers. So, how do smart managers lead organizations to failure? Some of these concepts were reviewed in Chapter 2, but we revisit a few of them here.

Dictatorial management styles, for instance, can be problematic. In a dictatorship, leaders ignore input from others, who soon stop offering it. Dictatorial managers tend to be-

Economic changes, such as rising crude oil and gasoline prices, can certainly contribute to business failures, but research shows they aren't the main cause. If anything, downturns "magnify" a company's shortcomings and put managers and their strategies to the test.

come either averse to change or unable to implement it effectively because they lack information they need.

A related problem is *lack of managerial depth*, which is often a by-product of dictatorial leadership. It arises when a strong leader refuses to be surrounded by equally strong people. When this problem sets in, it tends to compound itself. Lack of managerial depth has been cited as a contributing factor to the failure of several organizations. CEO Roger Smith of GM was notorious for getting rid of fellow executives who regularly disagreed with him, either firing them or exiling them to relatively desolate corners of the organization. As a result, the organization lost touch with a changing marketplace and saw its market share decline precipitously.

Another effect of flawed leadership is the tendency of top management to become unbalanced. A management team is unbalanced when experience in one product or functional area dominates the team, the board of directors, or both. Let's say, for example, that the CEO and the board of directors are executives with financial backgrounds. Once they reach a financial decision, it's not likely to be questioned, even by other top managers with financial experience.

Finally, although individual dishonesty and fraud are not as common as we might be led to believe by such cases as Enron, WorldCom, and Tyco, they can and do cause severe damage to organizations. They're especially dangerous when they involve systemic failures in a company's accounting and auditing functions. WorldCom, for example, admitted that in order to meet Wall Street expectations, it had inflated its profits by $3.8 billion between January 2001 and March 2002. Only *systemic* financial failure could lead to such a mammoth collapse.

A weak finance function can have a devastating impact on an organization, in part because it's ultimately a reflection of larger management problems. It may present itself in the form of an unbalanced executive team with little financial knowledge or experience or as a more general organizational defect that fosters inadequate financial controls, a weak auditing function, or both. One of the greatest dangers of a weak financial function—*creative accounting*—emerges during economic downturns. Fudging earnings or sales is a great temptation during a downturn, but it's a less attractive option in a firm with a strong financial function.

Warning Signals of Organizational Decline   At this point, you undoubtedly realize that organizations are complex and that a lot can go wrong with them. You may also be wondering if there are any early warning signals that would prompt someone to start questioning a firm's strategy or its execution, or simply the reliability or competency of its leaders. You can rely on certain indicators that reflect a variety of factors. The tools presented in Chapter 4—PESTEL, industry structure, and value-chain analysis tools—can be good *qualitative* indicators. Regular evaluation of the quality of a firm's strategy is another qualitative indicator. A strategy that does not fit with current external environmental conditions or the near-term environment will lead to organizational decline.

Not surprisingly, financial indicators are a common signal of the potential for decline. For instance, unexpected declines in earnings or revenues are always a red flag. So are declining customer satisfaction scores. WorldCom's rapid demise was foreshadowed by several quarters of record-breaking numbers of customer complaints about service quality. Sometimes incipient problems can be discovered by assessing financial ratios (profitability, operating, liquidity, and debt ratios are a good start) in terms of historical or industry data. In addition to the signals provided by operating leverage and sustainable growth rate, discussed later in the chapter, you can also use a combination of ratios to predict financial problems. Several of these tools are showcased in the box entitled "How Would *You* Do That? 12.1."

Are Ford's Numbers Fizzy or Flat?

Here we will use the 2005 and 2006 annual results from Ford Motor Company to walk you through a handful of financial analysis tools that you can use quickly to get a sense of a firm's financial strength. The breadth of Ford's activities once spanned the traditional Ford, Lincoln, and Mercury brands, plus import brands like Aston Martin, Jaguar, Volvo, Land Rover, and an equity interest in Mazda. Recently however, Ford sold off Aston Martin, and many auto industry experts speculate that Jaguar, Volvo, and Land Rover are on the auction block as well (and may have another home by the time you read this). This provides a good example given the recent press about their financial troubles, and we can use quantitative tools to see if there is substance behind the rumors. These tools are most often used to gauge the financial health and prospects of large firms, but they can be used to assess any new venture. These types of analyses can be used to determine whether the economic logic underlying the firm's strategy is actually paying off and to suggest implementation levers that may need to be pulled in case problems are discovered or predicted.

Z-SCORE MODEL

Let's start with the Z-Score model, the brainchild of Edward I. Altman, who is considered to be the dean of insolvency predictors. Altman was the first person to develop a highly accurate prediction model. A recent test of Altman's Z-Score found that it was 95-percent accurate in classifying companies. Altman's model takes the following form:

$$Z = 1.2A + 1.4B + 3.3C + 0.6D + .99E$$

where

A = Working capital/total assets
B = Retained earnings/total assets
C = Earnings before interest and taxes/total assets
D = Market value of equity/book value of total debt
E = Sales/total assets

If Z is less than 1.8, then the firm is classified as "high likelihood of failure." Although the model was developed to analyze manufacturing companies, it can also be applied to nonmanufacturing organizations by modifying the formula. The formula is modified by omitting the fifth component (E). The adjusted formula seems to provide equally valid predictive results. Applying the model to Ford's 2006 annual report, the numbers summarized in Exhibit 12.10, you would find:

$$Z = 1.2(.0038) + 1.4(-.0001) + 3.3(-.0250) + .6(.09147) + .99(.5517) = .52$$

Because Z is less than 1.8, it suggests that Ford is at great risk of failure.

SUSTAINABLE GROWTH

Another useful model for evaluating a firm's financial health is the sustainable growth rate. The value obtained from this analysis is the rate of growth the company can sustain with its current capital structure. Inasmuch as many firms get into trouble because they simply "grow broke," the sustainable growth rate is a useful tool.

To calculate the sustainable growth rate for a company, you need to know how profitable the company is as determined by its return on equity (ROE). You also need to know what percentage of a company's earnings per share is paid out in dividends, which is called the dividend-payout ratio. From there, multiply the company's ROE by its plowback ratio, which is equal to 1 minus the dividend-payout ratio.

Sustainable-growth rate = ROE × (1 − dividend-payout ratio)

Let's go through another example using Ford. Ford's ROE is a negative number (since they lost money in 2006) percent and yet dividends are still paid out of its earnings. Based on the formula, Ford has no sustainable growth, unless it finances that growth through new debt or equity. In fact, given its losses, it is using debt to finance dividend payments! So you should expect the next big step in any Ford turnaround to be the discontinuation of dividend payments (which Ford announced at the end of 2006). Now that we know Ford's sustainable-growth rate is basically zero (given current profitability or lack thereof), we should be concerned if the company promises that it can sustain a

Exhibit 12.10 Key Numbers at Ford Motor Company

	2005 (in U.S. millions)	2006 (in U.S. millions)
Working Capital (Current Assets—Current Liabilities)	$(5,072)	$1090
Total Assets	275,936	290,217
Retained Earnings	13,064	(17)
Earnings Before Interest and Taxes	8,276	(7,263)
Market Value of Equity	15,000	14,500
Total Liabilities	153,777	158,575
Revenues	176,896	160,123
Net Cash Flow	20,387	9,609
Liquidation Value We use current Assets minus all debt because that gives a value that might reasonably be achieved if the company had to be sold	(107,296)	(101,250)
Gross Profit Margin	18%	7%
Net Profit Margin	1%	(8%)
Return on Equity	10.7%	(na) Ford had negative equity of ($3,465) and an operating loss of ($12,613)
Dividend Payout Rate	.52	(na) lost $6.72 per share and paid out $.25 per share dividend

growth rate of well above that from now until eternity. From 2005 to 2006, Ford's sales actually declined by $16 billion. If you had calculated Ford's sustainable growth rate in 2005, you would have come up with 5.13 percent. This means that Ford was continually growing faster than the growth it can support using the existing debt and equity. To maintain this or a higher growth rate, Ford would have to become more profitable (which would boost its ROE), pay out fewer dividends as a percentage of earnings (which would reduce the dividend-payout ratio, but that is already at zero), or obtain more money through borrowing or the equity markets (as it did with the additional equity acquired in 2003).

OPERATING LEVERAGE

Finally, operating leverage can give you an idea how sensitive a firm's profits are to small increases or decreases in revenues. If scenario planning shows that many able competitors are liable to jump into the fray or that the firm's revenues will likely go down in the future for other reasons, this metric can be used to determine if fixed costs need to be cut immediately, before profitability suffers.

Operating leverage can be calculated simply by dividing *gross margin* (sometimes called *gross profit*) by *net profit margin*. The beauty of this indicator is that it shows very quickly the extent to which a percentage-profit decrease will be reflected in a percentage decrease in profitability. In

2005, for instance, Ford had a gross margin of 18 percent and a net profit margin of 1 percent. If you do the math, you'll find that Ford had an operating leverage of 18. What does this number mean? It means that a 1-percent decrease in revenues would result in an 18-percent decrease in profits (unless some element of the firm's fixed-cost structure was dramatically reduced). From this exercise, you should conclude that Ford is reasonably unhealthy, at least in financial terms. However, given that most of its competitors, such as GM and Toyota, are huge, many financial changes would need to be made for it to regain its historical financial strength.

Strategic Change and Organizational Renewal

Not surprisingly, strategic management—particularly in dynamic contexts—is a process for dealing with strategic change and organizational renewal. As was discussed in Chapter 11, implementing a change in strategy involves transforming the firm from its current state to a different one through the use of implementation levers and strategic leadership. In many ways, therefore, you already have a good foundation for understanding the processes of change and renewal in certain situations—namely, in firms that aren't yet facing crises.

A key premise is that all business environments are in a state of change. To remain successful, firms must take one of two actions: stay aligned with changes in their environments by responding quickly or actively anticipate changes in customer demographics, future technologies, and potential new products/services, and thereby recreate their industries.

Strategic change can be defined as significant changes in resource-allocation choices or business activities that align the firm's strategy with its vision. Strategic change could also encompass changes that are undertaken to inform the firm what its new vision should be. Strategic change is difficult. Consider the problem of orthodoxies reviewed earlier in the chapter. When a firm explicitly or tacitly adheres to orthodoxies to the point that it creates rigidities in the way management thinks about the firm and its environment or rigidities in internal practices, the difficulty of strategic change is compounded. The most traditional types of change processes involve some combination of cost reduction, asset reduction or redeployment, or restructuring.

strategic change Significant changes in resource allocation choices in the business and implementation activities that align the firm's strategy with its vision, or in its vision.

Cost Reduction   This tactic is as straightforward as it sounds. Sometimes this requires short-term reduction in staffing, or the elimination of expenses that don't clearly affect the quality or attractiveness of a product or service. One common consulting trick to control costs is to take stock of all the inputs that a firm uses, identify those that are high volume inputs but purchased in a decentralized fashion, then centralize the purchase of these key inputs to gain lower costs through larger average orders.

Asset Reduction or Redeployment   This tactic typically asks managers to identify assets that may be undervalued on the books (like real estate) and then sold to realize their true market value. Another variation is to use a piece of equipment on higher margin products, instead of wasting its productive capacity on lower margin products. For instance, a brewery can make much more money on craft beers than low-priced beers, but both essentially use the same fixed assets for the beers production. A common consulting trick here is to look at the portfolio of a firm's products and services and identify those that seem to command the highest margins, and then focus productive and sales resources on those products. This may sound silly, but firms often have a large inventory of product or service offerings, even though only a few of these offerings account for the lion's share of profitability.

Restructuring   Whereas cost and asset restructuring are typically narrowly defined tactics, restructuring is typically defined by a major change in the composition of a firm's assets combined with a major change in its business or corporate strategy. It usually involves selling off (or liquidating) businesses in multidivisional firms, either voluntarily through spin-offs or involuntarily through hostile takeovers. Restructuring also can occur once a leveraged buyout (LBO) of a firm has been completed. Thus, you should view restructuring as more than the simple divestiture of a single business unit, or reduction of assets or costs.

THE CHANGE PROCESS

Although change is rarely a linear process, it can be helpful to think of the elements of change in such a fashion in order to appreciate the magnitude of the effort. Using the principles you've already learned about the strategic management process, let's consider all that must happen in order to implement a strategic change successfully. The best place to start is with a broader understanding of the steps that lead to positive organizational transformation. Exhibit 12.11 provides you with this broader picture of what it takes to get change going.[32] This model was pioneered by John Kotter of the Harvard Business School, a professor long recognized as the guru of organizational transformation.

Exhibit 12.11 Essential Transformation Steps

Eight Steps to Transforming Your Organization

1 Establishing a Sense of Urgency
Examining market and competitive realities
Identifying and discussing crises, potential crises, or major opportunities

2 Forming a Powerful Guiding Coalition
Assembling a group with enough power to lead the change effort
Encouraging the group to work together as a team

3 Creating a Vision
Creating a vision to help direct the change effort
Developing strategies for achieving that vision

4 Communicating the Vision
Using every vehicle possible to communicate the new vision
    and strategies
Teaching new behaviors by the example of the guiding coalition

5 Empowering Others to Act on the Vision
Getting rid of obstacles to change
Changing systems or structures that seriously undermine the vision
Encouraging risk taking and nontraditional ideas, activities, and actions

6 Planning for and Creating Short-Term Wins
Planning for visible performance improvements
Creating those improvements
Recognizing and rewarding employees involved in the improvements

7 Consolidating Improvements and Producing Still More Change
Using increased credibility to change systems, structures, and
    policies that don't fit the vision
Hiring, promoting, and developing employees who can implement
    the vision
Reinvigorating the process with new projects, themes, and change agents

8 Institutionalizing New Approaches
Articulating the connections between the new behaviors and
    corporate success
Developing the means to ensure leadership development and succession

The first step, establishing a sense of urgency, is sometimes referred to as the "burning platform." A "burning platform" is a term used to describe an extremely urgent or compelling business situation in order to convey, in the strongest terms, the need for change. Using this process, you can get people's attention and build awareness of the need for change very quickly. The second part, a guiding coalition, is in essence a group of missionaries who believe in the need for change, are in positions of power where they can see that it is effected, work well as a team, and are good communicators of the vision. Often, some members of the coalition have been with the firm for a long time, so have deep respect from their colleagues in addition to good knowledge of the company's deep culture. The vision component you already know well. It is the first part of the strategy framework that you were introduced to in Exhibit 1.3 from Chapter 1. Without a clear and compelling vision, the change effort has no direction. We have already mentioned the fact that the guiding coalition needs to be comprised of good communicators, and this fourth transformation step means that they act on those abilities—there probably cannot be too much communication when so much is at stake in big transformation efforts.

While the guiding coalition is critical, they cannot accomplish transformation alone. Through their communication and empowerment of others, the transformation movement can take on a life of its own. This is why it is designated separately as a fifth step. Planning for and creating short-term wins is the essential sixth step. These successes need to be celebrated and shared so the firm sees that it is making progress with the transformation. An example of an early win was SAP's signing of Exxon as a client for its enterprise resource package software. This win signified that the SAP strategy was paying off, and suggested that better things were sure to come. Step 6 maps well to the staging facet of your strategy diamond. ◆ This is the point where the guiding coalition, and those that they have empowered, take stock of their successes and begin to map out the next staging and pacing of the transformation effort. Recall that strategy is about tradeoffs and choices, and through the consolidation process you are able to make choices about what should no longer be done, and what activities need added attention or additional direction. Finally, the accumulation of the activities undertaken to accomplish or work through steps 1 through 7, will have likely changed the culture in such a profound way that the transformational change is institutionalized. The term *institutionalization* is widely used in social theory to denote the process of making something (for example a concept, a social role, particular values and norms, or modes of behavior) become embedded within an organization as an established custom or norm within that system. In essence, what may have been considered novel, difficult, or even revolutionary at the beginning of the change process now becomes almost taken for granted, and new hires to the organization will often assume that the firm always operated that way.

Whereas Exhibit 12.11 gives you the larger agenda, Exhibit 12.12 lays out the nuts and bolts necessary for the change to be achieved, along with the possible repercussions if any particular nut or bolt is neglected.

Specifically, it illustrates this process and the possible outcomes if any of the elements of the change effort are missing. Consultants love this tool for this very reason—it is prescriptive, predictive, and diagnostic. The model should also reinforce your understanding of the interdependence of strategy formulation and implementation. There are some necessary and obvious areas of overlap between the two frameworks. For instance, a clear vision and the ability to communicate it clearly are identified as desirable and essential in both frameworks. Beyond this specific point of overlap, Exhibit 12.12 actually guides you in prescribing interventions that would lead to positive strategic change.[33] The upper path in the model, where all the conditions are present—from vision to an execution plan—suggests that strategic change is most likely to be effective (assuming the correct implementation of the components). However, when any individual component is weak or missing, then you can see that negative consequences are likely to occur. Let's talk through each of the scenarios, working with the boxes from left to right.

Staging
&
Pacing

Exhibit 12.12 The Levers of Organizational Transformation

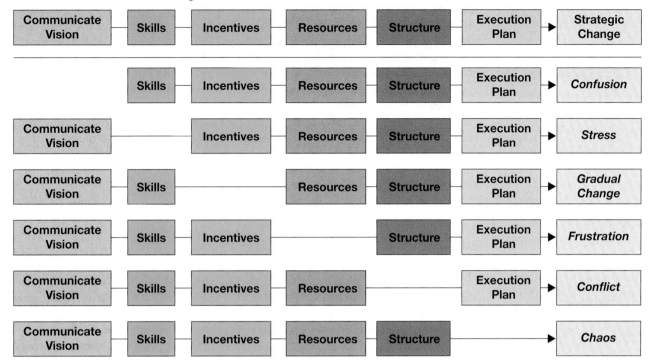

Vision First, in order to change, the firm must have a new vision of the desired end state. This was pretty clear in the framework discussed in Exhibit 12.11, just as it is here. This new vision must be communicated to those who will effect the change. As we have noted numerous times, because a vision is not a strategy, the new vision will require an executive plan—a strategy—that will serve as a map of the strategic-change process.

Skills Executing strategy is a task of all managers, indeed all employees, not just the work of those who dream up new strategies. Consequently, the change effort requires skills embodied in the people of the organization.

Incentives However, what tasks people spend their time on is heavily influenced by incentives. To get people to change their behaviors, as is often needed when an organization is trying to change its strategy, the firm will have to provide incentives.

Resources Next, it is critical to recognize that talented people with proper incentives will find it much easier to work toward the new vision if the organization allocates the resources necessary to accommodate the desired changes. These resources can be evaluated using the VRINE framework to gain a richer understanding of the unique opportunities or challenges faced by a particular change effort.

Structure An effective strategy, and in this case a strategic change, often requires modification, or at least clarification, of organizational structure. Finally, a plan that connects the dots in the change process must be put into place and widely communicated.

When all of these pieces of the change process are in place, a firm is likely to manage successfully the shift from one strategy to another—and the outcome is likely to be successful strategic change. Yet if any single step is missing, it undermines the entire change effort. Note that each missing step has different potential consequences for the change effort. Consider a few possible outcomes should we remove any one of the steps of strategic change.

First, if there is no guiding vision, organization members are likely to be extremely confused about why all these efforts are to be undertaken. If the organization does not have the right people who possess the skills necessary to carry out the efforts, extreme levels of stress will probably result among those who are left to shoulder the burden they are ill-equipped to carry.

Should the wrong incentives be in place, the organization is likely to change much slower than it could, or worse, actually pursue an unintended pathway because that is what is actually rewarded. If resources are not allocated, extreme levels of frustration are likely to emerge because managers and employees feel that they have been given a difficult goal without any institutional support. If the organizational structure does not accommodate the intended change, then there will be confusion and conflict over reporting and cooperative relationships. Finally, if there is no execution plan, a chaotic state is likely to emerge, with various managers pursuing different pathways to the desired end state.

TURNAROUND MANAGEMENT

The strategic-change process as just described is difficult work. However, all change is not created equal. Sometimes, there comes a point when a firm's future prospects seem hopeless, and this section is about strategy from that point forward. When an organization is going downhill fast, what can be done to turn it around? When the word *turnaround* comes into play, managers typically do not have the luxury of time, and the strategic-change framework presented in the previous section, though relevant, is also time-consuming. U.S. automakers Ford and GM are examples of historically strong firms facing current dire straits. Remembering that causes of failure are rooted in strategy, management, and financial mismanagement, we will now walk through five stages of the turnaround-management process summarized in Exhibit 12.13.[34]

We identify five distinct stages, but before we proceed, here are five caveats that you should bear in mind in thinking about these stages:

1. Because every turnaround is unique, each stage is not necessarily distinguishable in every turnaround.

2. The number of stages involved in each turnaround stage will depend on the seriousness of the financial crisis facing a given company: The more dire the trouble, the more stages the turnaround process is likely to involve.

3. The importance of each stage will vary from case to case. Sometimes, for instance, analysis will be more important than action, whereas the opposite will be true in other cases.

4. A company can find itself involved in more than one stage at a time. Stages can overlap, and some tasks may affect more than one stage.

5. The length of time required to address each stage is not only fluid but can vary greatly. The major factors in determining the amount of time entailed by each stage include the size of the company and the severity of its financial straits. Addressing every stage in the process may take 12 to 36 months.

The following stage-by-stage description of the turnaround process can be used as a template for designing a change-management program for a company in financial trouble. Exhibit 12.14 shows you how all these pieces work together in the successful turnaround of ISH, a German cable company.[35]

Stage 1: Changing Management   Changing management means one of two things: either changing the way management approaches organizational problems or changing the personnel at the top of the organization, which is more often the case. Most

Exhibit 12.13   Stages in the Turnaround Process

Stages	Management Change	Evaluation	Emergency	Stabilization	Return-to-Normal
Objectives and Action Items	1. Select new top-managementteam. 2. Weed out impediments.	1. Can it survive? 2. Identify strategy.	1. Survival. 2. Positive cash flow through cost reduction, asset reduction and restructuring.	1. Enhance profitability. 2. Restructure business toincrease ROI.	1. Seek profitable growth. 2. Build competitive strengths.
	3. Select a turnaround manager.	3. Develop plan. 4. Determine nature of turnaround.	3. Raise cash. 4. Take charge. 5. Get control of cash.		

CEOs and other officers will not relinquish power easily. Often egos make it difficult for them to admit that a downturn is really happening or that they're incapable of pulling the company out of its nosedive. The first step, therefore, is setting up a top-management team to lead the turnaround effort. In some cases, the board of directors may recruit turnaround specialists; bankers and corporate attorneys are also usually involved. As outsiders, turnaround specialists come aboard unfettered by obligations to the incumbent management team or the firm's current strategy. During this stage, the turnaround team will weed out and replace any top officials who may impede the turnaround effort. In general, it is believed that the benefits of the leadership capabilities that outsiders bring far outweigh their lack of organizational or industry experience.[36]

Stage 2: Analyzing the Situation   Before making any major changes, turnaround leaders must determine the chances of the firm's survival, identify appropriate strategies for turning it around, and develop a preliminary action plan. The first days, therefore, are devoted to fact finding and diagnosing the scope and severity of the problems at hand.

In the meantime, the team must deal with various stakeholder groups. The first group often consists of angry creditors who may have been kept in the dark about the company's financial status. Employees are confused and nervous. Customers, vendors, and suppliers are wary about the firm's future. It's essential that the turnaround team be open and frank with all of these groups.

Once the major problems have been identified, the team develops a strategic plan with specific goals and detailed functional actions. To keep the process moving and to make sure that priorities are adhered to, goals should be sequenced to correspond directly with the staging facet of the strategy diamond. Then the team must sell its plan to the key members of the organization, including the board of directors, the management team, and employees. Presenting the plan to key external parties—bankers, major creditors, and vendors—goes a long way toward regaining their confidence and financial support.

Exhibit 12.14   A Successful Turnaround at ISH

How exactly would you implement the turnaround steps shown in Exhibit 12.13? Here we illustrate the turnaround process for ISH GmbH, one of Europe's largest and most successful cable companies. Formerly part of Deutsche Telekom, in April 2002 this supplier of cable services to approximately four million homes in the German state of North Rhine Westphalia (NRW) was in a state of total business failure—bleeding cash, losing money, and in default on nearly €2.7 billion (€ is the symbol for euros) in debt. This is the story of ISH's resurrection from the organizational graveyard.

Stage 1: Changing Management

In April 2002, ISH's management brought in the strategy-consulting and turnaround firm AlixPartners to help it analyze its books and cash flow. AlixPartners is a professional turnaround firm recently credited with profit improvement at beleaguered Kmart. Nearly 120 days later, ISH shareholders appointed Jim Bonsall to fill the role of CEO. Bonsall is a principal with AlixPartners and has 25 years of experience working with European and multinational public and private companies.

Stage 2: Situation Analysis

Ironically, when AlixPartners was brought in, ISH management was completely unaware of the depth of the firm's problems. Although this may sound surprising, a management team may lose track of the need for change when its members are too heavily invested in the status quo. Initial analyses revealed that, although the firm had recorded current liabilities of €7 million, the actual number was €500 million! Management was also unaware that ISH was in default on many of its secured-debt facilities. These amounted to nearly €2.5 billion; thus, its total liabilities were approximately €3 billion.

Stage 3: Emergency Action

The complexities of Germany's insolvency code nearly always result in the total liquidation of a firm's assets. Once difficulties are discovered, a troubled firm has 21 days to resolve relationships with creditors prior to being declared insolvent. To take advantage of this three-week window of opportunity, AlixPartners worked quickly to gain 120 days of additional short-term bank financing and assigned teams of AlixPartners professionals to ISH's 17 largest vendors. Teams met weekly, and the objective was to educate bankers and vendors on the balance sheet and operating strengths of ISH while preventing a premature declaration of insolvency. By the end of the 120-day period, not only had insolvency been avoided, but the firm had reached agreement among the major creditors on an operating plan for going forward.

Stage 4: Restructuring ISH

Shareholders officially appointed Bonsall as CEO of ISH in late 2002. However, restructuring had actually started in the emergency-action stage in April of that year. Bonsall's early agenda for his tenure as CEO included establishing core organizational values, improving the company's image, solving problems using a team approach, and achieving profitability and industry leadership. He sought to do this by institutionalizing a balanced-scorecard system and tying a reward system to it that supported his objective of transforming the firm into a customer- and data-driven organization. Bonsall achieved these objectives the hard way: by achieving results and restoring trust and confidence in the company's goals. One of the biggest early restructuring tasks was to reorient ISH away from the Internet and back to its cable-television business. The company had put the vast majority of its time, money, and effort on building up its Internet subscriber base and had only 5,000 Internet subscribers to show for these efforts (versus its core, but neglected, resource of 4 million cable subscribers).

Stage 5: Normalcy and ISH's Return to Industry Leadership

Bonsall's management team agreed that the best way to grow the cable business would be to offer more selection and technical innovation through a digital-program offering in the key cities of Cologne, Düsseldorf, Bochum, and Neuss. All this would have to be achieved in the first year following the restructuring, starting in December 2003. ISH overcame numerous institutional and technical complications to achieve the digitalization objectives.

Signs that the ISH turnaround was succeeding was the fact that by January 2004, cable outages had become a thing of the past and customer satisfaction was increasing. ISH saw itself as a company that provided its four million customers with entertainment. Soon, the company would launch a showcase with up to 50 additional channels and Near Video on Demand. Bonsall expected a standard offering for the whole of Germany to be marketed jointly by all cable regions. ISH continued to offer high-speed Internet—with download speeds of 2 MB and upload speeds of 512 KB, leaving the competition behind in the residential customer segment.

Stage 3: Implementing an Emergency Action Plan   When the firm's condition is critical, the team's plan is usually both drastic and simple. Emergency surgery is performed to stop the bleeding and improve the organization's chances of pulling through. At this time, as employees are laid off or entire departments eliminated, emotions tend to run high. Such cuts should be made thoughtfully and objectively, but swiftly.

The turnaround team must also turn its attention to cash, which is the lifeblood of the business. It must establish a positive operating cash flow as quickly as possible, and it must make sure that there's enough cash to implement its turnaround strategies. Unprofitable divisions or units are often unloaded, sometimes after some quick, corrective surgery. As we mentioned in our opening comments on strategic change, the fundamental leverage points are cost reduction, asset reduction, and restructuring.

Stage 4: Stabilization   Once the bleeding has stopped, losing divisions sold off, and administrative costs cut, the turnaround team directs its efforts toward making current operations effective and efficient. Increasing profits and return on assets and equity usually means restructuring. In many ways, this stage is the most difficult: Cutting losses is one thing, but achieving an acceptable return on investment is another. In the new, leaner company, some facilities may be closed; the company may even withdraw from certain markets or target its products toward different markets.

Finally, as the company restructures for competitive effectiveness, the right mix of people becomes quite important. Reward and compensation systems, another implementation lever, are changed to reinforce the turnaround effort and to get people thinking "profits" and "return on investment." Everyone who still has a job must remember that survival, not tradition, is the number-one priority in reshaping the business.

Stage 5: Returning to Normal   In the final stage of the turnaround process, the company slowly returns to profitability. At earlier stages, the turnaround team focused on correcting problems. Now, however, it focuses on institutionalizing an emphasis on profitability, return on equity, and enhancing economic value. At this point, for example, the company may initiate new marketing programs to broaden its business base and increase market penetration. Financially, the firm shifts its emphasis from generating cash flow to maintaining a strong balance sheet, finding long-term financing, and setting up strategic accounting and control systems. Return to normalcy also entails a psychological shift: Rebuilding momentum and morale is almost as important as restoring ROI. Corporate culture must be renewed and reshaped, and negative attitudes must be transformed into positive attitudes.

Summary of Challenges

1. *Define new ventures, initial public offerings (IPOs), and corporate renewal and explain how they are related to strategic management.* New-venture creation is the creation of a new business from scratch. Young entrepreneurial firms often use initial public offerings (IPOs) to access the world's stock markets for capital. Corporate renewal is the outcome of actions and processes that return a failing or potentially failing firm to firm financial footing and resumption of profitable growth. All three activities require good strategies and solid execution.

2. *Understand entrepreneurship and the entrepreneurial process.* Entrepreneurship is the consequence of actions taken based on the perception and exploration of opportunity in the absence of obviously available resources. The entrepreneurial process leads to entrepreneurship and consists of the coordination of opportunity, key resources and capabilities, and the entrepreneur and entrepreneurial team.

3. *Describe the steps involved in new-venture creation and corporate new-venturing.* Entrepreneurial firms and established large firms follow the same steps in the new-venture creation process. The biggest difference between entrepreneurial new-venturing and corporate new-venturing is that the new venture in the latter context must overcome the fact that most large organizations are driven by the need to protect and optimize the use of existing resources and capabilities and discourage entrepreneurship and the pursuit of opportunity. New-venture creation starts with the identification of an opportunity. Opportunities can be distinguished from ideas in that they pass tests relating to market demand, market structure and size, and potential profitability. The remaining steps in new-venture creation are the drafting of a business plan, obtaining financing, and launching the new product or service. The order of these final three steps will vary significantly.

4. *Map out the stages leading up to an IPO.* Once a firm has validated a good opportunity and has some amount of prior success, its owners may seek to access capital through an IPO. First, the firm undergoes the legal and accounting preparation for a securities offering. Second, the firm contracts with an investment banker

to establish a value for the firm and eventually sell its shares. During this process, the firm files a registration document called an S-1 statement with the appropriate legal authorities. Finally, the firm and its investment bankers time the offering to coincide with a market that will likely provide the highest initial bids for the company's stock. An IPO typically provides access to capital and motivation to install more formal and professional management processes. If the firm does not have the capital needs, it may bypass the IPO and install professional management directly.

5. *Understand the external and internal causes of organizational failure.* The four main sources of external change that may lead to organizational failure are economic change, competitive change, social change, and technological change. Although there are many possible internal causes of organizational failure, most can be traced back to either management problems or an ineffective finance function. However, an ineffective finance function is essentially a reflection of larger management problems.

6. *Outline a plan of action for strategic change and corporate renewal.* Successful strategic-change efforts require communicating a new vision, defining an executive plan, having the right people and skills, getting incentives right, allocating needed resources, and altering the organizational structure if necessary. However, if the firm's financial condition has deteriorated to the point of near failure, a turnaround plan is necessary. The first stage of a turnaround plan is a change of management. It may also mean that the existing team must be replaced with executives who are able to assess the situation quickly and develop a plan to remedy the firm's woes. During the second stage, the management team determines the business' chances of survival, identifies appropriate strategies, and develops a preliminary action plan. The third stage is not required in all firms. The third stage is the implementation of an emergency-action plan when an assessment in the previous stage has determined that the firm is in critical condition. Oftentimes, assets are sold and parts of the business shuttered to avoid further crisis. The fourth stage is the actual restructuring of the business to align the organizational structure with the five elements of the strategy diamond. If all has gone as planned, the firm enters the fifth stage, during which it returns to normalcy and profitable growth.

Review Questions

1. What is entrepreneurship?

2. What is the entrepreneurial process?

3. How is the entrepreneurial process related to strategy?

4. What steps are involved in new-venture creation?

5. What is a business plan?

6. How do entrepreneurial new-venture creation and corporate new-venture creation differ?

7. What must organizations do to prepare for an IPO?

8. What are some of the external causes of organizational failure?

9. What are some of the internal causes of organizational failure?

10. What are the stages of a turnaround plan?

11. How do you know that a turnaround has been successful?

Experiential Activities

Group Exercises

1. Entrepreneurship starts with an idea. Without being critical or judgmental, brainstorm a set of 10 ideas that could lead to the startup of a new business. Screen your ideas and select those that would enjoy the greatest market demand, the most attractive market structure and size, and the best profit margins. Which of these screens caused most of the ideas to be discarded? What additional information would you need to seek out to answer all the screening questions?

2. This second exercise relates to turnaround and change management. Identify a company that is in dire financial straits. What are the financial symptoms of this distress? Do you think the cause of this distress is a bad strategy, bad implementation, or both? Again, using the brainstorming skills you applied with activity 1, flesh out a new product and strategy proposal that might put the firm on better financial and strategic footing.

Ethical Debates

1. You are the cofounder and president of a new venture, manufacturing products for the recreational market. Five months after launching the business, one of your key suppliers informs you it can no longer supply you with a critical raw material since you are not a large-quantity user. Without the raw material the business cannot continue. There is a 50/50 chance that your new product may take off, which would let you provide the supplier with a demand estimate that could lead the supplier to think you are a larger prospect, and therefore worth investing in as a large-quantity purchaser. What do you do?

2. Your small manufacturing company is in serious financial difficulty. A large order of your products is ready to be delivered to a key customer, when you discover that the product is simply not right. It will not meet all performance specifications, will cause problems for your customer, and will require rework in the field; but this, you know, will not become evident until after the customer has received and paid for the order. If you do not ship the order and receive the payment as expected, your business may be forced into bankruptcy. And if you delay the shipment or inform the customer of these problems, you may lose the order and also go bankrupt. What do you do?

How Would YOU DO THAT?

1. The box entitled "How Would *You* Do That? 12.1" introduced a number of financial tools for predicting a firm's financial troubles. Pick a public company that has recently announced financial woes and run these analyses on its financial results for the past three years. Do any of the indicators seem to detect looming problems? What might be the limits of these financial tools?

2. Exhibit 12.14 presented the successful turnaround of ISH GmbH. Identify another company in the business press that you believe to be in the turnaround process. Based on Exhibit 12.13, which stages has it entered and what have managers chosen to do in those stages? What stages remain? What do you think are the key challenges facing management in returning this firm to normalcy?

Go on to see How Would You Do That at www.prenhall.com/ carpenter&sanders

Endnotes

1. Adapted from C. Anderson, *The Long Tail* (London: Hyperion, 2006).

2. W. Bygrave and J. Timmons, *Venture Capital at the Crossroads* (Boston: Harvard Business School Press, 1992).

3. Adapted from G. Hamel and C. K. Prahalad, *Competing for the Future* (Boston: Harvard Business School Press, 1994).

4. For a comprehensive discussion, see J. Timmons, *New Venture Creation* (New York: Irwin-McGraw-Hill, 1999).

5. J. Eckhardt and S. Shane, "Opportunities and Entrepreneurship," *Journal of Management* 29:3 (2003), 333–349; J. Eckhardt and S. Shane, "The Individual-Opportunity Nexus: A New Perspective on Entrepreneurship," in Z. Acs and D. Audretsch, eds., *The Handbook of Entrepreneurship Research* (Boston: Kluwer, 2003), 161–191.

6. From Google, S-1 statement, 2004.

7. Adapted from J. Timmons, *New Venture Creation* (New York: Irwin-McGraw-Hill, 1999).

8. Timmons, *New Venture Creation*; A. Bhide, "Bootstrap Finance," *Harvard Business Review* 70:6 (1992), 109–117.

9. Bhide, "Bootstrap Finance."

10. Among other sites, try www.bplans.com, www.sba.gov/starting/ businessplan.html, www.morebusiness.com, and www.businessplans.org.

11. Timmons, *New Venture Creation*.

12. H. Chesbrough, "Designing Corporate Ventures in the Shadow of Private Venture Capital," *California Management Review* 42:3 (2000), 31–49.

13. Z. Block and I. MacMillan, *Corporate Venturing* (Boston: Harvard Business School Press, 1995).

14. D. Day, "Raising Radicals: Different Processes for Championing Innovative Corporate Ventures," *Organization Science* 9 (1994), 148–172.

15. D. Garvin, *A Note on Corporate Venturing and New Business Creation* (Boston: Harvard Business School, 1997).

16. N. Fast, *The Rise and Fall of Corporate New Venture Divisions* (Ann Arbor: UMI, 1978).

17. R. Gee, "Finding and Commercializing New Business," *Research-Technology Management* 37:1 (1994), 49–56.

18. Chesbrough, "Designing Corporate Ventures."

19. D. A. Garvin, "What Every CEO Should Know About Creating New Businesses," *Harvard Business Review* 82:7–8 (July–August 2004).

20. M. Pagano, F. Panetta, and L. Zingales, "Why Do Companies Go Public? An Empirical Analysis," *Journal of Finance* 53:1 (1998), 27–64.

21. Adapted from P. Downing, "IPO Launch Fraught with Perils," *The Ottawa Citizen*, High-Tech Report, October 12, 1998.

22. Because the regulations on IPOs are constantly changing, you may find it interesting to consult the source of these changes at www.sec.gov/ index.htm.

23. R. Rajan and H. Servaes, "Analyst Following of Initial Public Offerings," *Journal of Finance* 52:2 (1997), 507–529; J. Ritter and I. Welch, "A Review of IPO Activity, Pricing, and Allocation," *Journal of Finance* 57:4 (2002), 1795–1828.

24. D. Wyckoff, *Organizational Formality and Performance in the Motor Carrier Industry* (Lexington, MA: Lexington Books, 1973).

25. Much of this material is drawn from M. A. Carpenter, *A Primer on Turnarounds* (Chicago: Association of Certified Turnaround Professionals, 2004).

26. S. Finkelstein, *Why Smart Executives Fail* (New York: Portfolio Press, 2003).

27. D. B. Bibeault, *Corporate Turnaround: How Managers Turn Losers Into Winners!* (New York: Beard Books, 2001).

28. Bibeault, *Corporate Turnaround*.

29. C. Terhune, "Krispy Kreme Issues Profit Warning—After 1st Forecast Reduction Since IPO, Stock Falls 29%; Low-Carb Fervor Is Blamed," *Wall Street Journal*, May 10, 2004, A8.

30. Finkelstein, *Why Smart Executives Fail.*

31. Finkelstein, *Why Smart Executives Fail.*

32. Adapted from J. Kotter, "Why transformation efforts fail," *Harvard Business Review.* March–April, 1995: 59–67.

33. Adapted from A. Marcus, *Management Strategy* (New York: McGraw-Hill, 2004).

34. Thomas D. Hays, III, CTP, Certified Turnaround Professional, Nachman Hays Brownstein, Chicago, IL.

35. This turnaround summary was compiled from information available from www.turnaround.org, www.ish.com, www.alixpartners.com, and a summary of the turnaround in J. Bonsall, "Inside a German Turnaround," *Turnaround Management* Spring (2004). For information on Kmart, see K. Dybis, "Kmart Rings Up $200 Million Profit: Stock Soars as Embattled Retailer Reports Upswing for Nov., Dec., Its First Since 2000," *The Detroit News,* January 6, 2004, A1. Tecumseh Announces Performance Improvement Program, www.alixpartners.com/EN/pr_tecumseh.html, accessed December 16, 2005.

36. P. Tourtellot, "Turnarounds: How Outsiders Find the Inside Track," *Turnaround Management,* Spring (2004).

13 Corporate Governance *in the* Twenty-First Century

In This Chapter We Challenge You To >>>

1. Describe what *corporate governance* means and understand its basic principles and practices.

2. Explain how corporate governance relates to competitive advantage.

3. Identify the roles of owners and different types of ownership profiles in corporate governance.

4. Show how boards of directors are structured and explain the roles they play in corporate governance.

5. Analyze and design executive incentives as a corporate governance device.

6. Illustrate how the market for corporate control is related to corporate governance.

7. Compare and contrast corporate governance practices around the world.

Corporate Governance *in* Action *at* Hewlett-Packard

*B*ill Hewlett and David Packard started Hewlett-Packard (HP) in Palo Alto, California in 1938. Packard was the business operations partner and Hewlett was known as the one with the big ideas. The first product ended up being an audio oscillator. An audio oscillator is an instrument that generates one pure tone or frequency at a time. Through the years, HP oscillators were used to design, produce, and maintain telephones, stereos, radios, and other audio equipment. According to HP's corporate history, Bill and Dave made the first of these oscillators in the garage behind Dave's house and baked the paint on the panels in Lucile Packard's oven. Lucile claimed the roast beef never tasted right after Bill and Dave started using the oven as HP's first paint-baking facility.

Test and measurement devices were HP's first products. Its first product was an audio oscillator—a device used to test sound equipment—introduced in 1938. In later years, HP continued as a leader in this category, making instruments for measurement, medical technology and chemical analysis.

From those modest beginnings, the company went on to become the largest manufacturer of electronic instruments in the world. Along the way, HP became known for its prowess in innovation.

The company is credited with making the world's first handheld scientific calculator, one of the first PCs, the first desktop mainframe, and the LaserJet printer. Its initial PCs were known for their rugged build, tailored for factory operations. HP's early PCs were targeted for industrial uses, such as in factory operations. Consequently, they were ruggedly built but not suited as well for personal or office use and did not enjoy strong sales.

In 1999, HP recruited its first outsider as CEO, Carly Fiorina, a flashy telecommunications executive. HP and Ms. Fiorina bet their future on the controversial and strongly contested 2002 takeover of Compaq Computer Corp. Ironically, the contest wasn't with Compaq shareholders, but with HP's. The families of Hewlett and Packard were dead set against the deal. However, shareholders finally approved the deal, valued at $19 billion.

The Compaq merger was so large and complex that it took several years to integrate. Debate over the wisdom of the merger continued in its wake and continued to hound Fiorina in the years following the closing of the deal. HP management claimed that operating synergies amounted to about $3 billion and that they were realized within about 2 years of the closing. HP's market share in the PC business did increase and recently they passed Dell as the number-one manufacturer of PCs in the world. However, HP's stock price continued to languish. And Fiorina's leadership was now being questioned in the boardroom.

Ms. Fiorina's relationship with the board became strained in 2004. Stakeholders were questioning the acquisition of Compaq, the stock price was languishing, and board politics became problematic. Fiorina became very upset when confidential board discussions were leaked to the press. She confronted the board, which collectively supported her in maintaining that all conversations as a board were confidential. Fiorina was concerned that details of strategic plans were being fed to the press by one or more board members. She used legal counsel to interview each board member in an attempt to identify the leak.

Before the issue could be settled, the board asked Ms. Fiorina to step down. In public statements, the board and succeeding management indicated that the reason for Fiorina's dismissal had to do with personal leadership style and not strategy. The questions and problems were execution and not formulation. In the summer before her dismissal, Fiorina herself dismissed several top executives. Some suggested that this was a last-ditch scapegoating effort in an attempt to solidify her leadership.

Fiorina's dismissal left two holes at HP, the job of the CEO and that of the Chairman of the Board. The board quickly asked Patricia Dunn to step in as Chairman and appointed one of Fiorina's top executives, Mark Hurd, as CEO. In Hurd's early interviews with the press, he maintained that he would not be changing the strategy, just trying to fix the execution.

Ironically, Dunn took up two important issues. First, she thought the board needed some new heavy weight directors. Second, she carried on with Fiorina's quest to get to the bottom of the board leaks. She personally interviewed all directors and felt she had a mandate to plug the leaks.

In looking for new directors, Dunn proposed to the board that they recruit established CEOs from large U.S. firms. Because she felt that the business of HP was so complex, she maintained that they needed directors who had experience with large, diverse firms. She ran into resistance with some directors, particularly Tom Perkins, the famous Silicon Valley venture capitalist. He maintained that HP needed directors from high-tech companies who had experience in "fast cycle" industries. He claimed that some of the CEOs Dunn was recruiting had never dealt with products that change every year and that this experience was crucial to proper governance of HP.

On the issue of board leaks, rather than relying just on in-house counsel, Ms. Dunn authorized a more daring strategy: outside private investigators were hired to track down the truth. As a result of this investigation, the term "pretexting" is now part of the business vocabulary. Investigators felt sure that some directors were lying. So, they approached phone companies pretending to be a director seeking copies of their billing records (i.e., approaching a company under the pretext of being someone else).

Examination of these records revealed that long-time director George Keyworth had placed phone calls to the reporter at CNet.com who printed the detailed information about the HP board's contemplations. The *Wall Street Journal* estimates that HP private investigators spent more than $350,000 to finger Mr. Keyworth.

The HP scandal didn't end there; in fact, it was just getting warmed up. When Dunn convened the board and confronted Mr. Keyworth without prior notice, Tom Perkins, abruptly quit. He argued that the methods used to entrap Keyworth were unethical. In addition, he maintained that the information that was leaked was inconsequential. After his departure, Perkins was furious because in HP's filings with the SEC about his departure, they did not disclose his reasons for leaving. So, Perkins took matters into his own hands and contacted the SEC and the press on his own.

In the ensuing months, HP was regularly on the front page of the *Wall Street Journal* and the *New York Times* as they and other media outlets competed in a race to uncover what really happened at HP. Dunn and HP maintained that their methods were legal and ethical. When they were pressed on the practice of pretexting, they maintained that they were not in control of the methods used by the investigators. Later examination of internal emails revealed that Dunn and other executives were aware of the methods being used and had acquiesced because the issue of leaks was of so much importance.

The Hewlett-Packard board scandal resulted in hearings before congress and charges in California courts against the company and specific officers and directors. Eventually, HP agreed to pay a $14.5 million settlement and adopt corporate reforms to clean up its "pretexting" scandal. HP also fired Ms. Dunn and agreed to pay $650,000 in civil penalties and $350,000 to cover the cost of the attorney general's investigation. The 12-page injunction also requires the tech company to adopt a series of corporate governance reforms. HP will bolster its code of conduct; appoint a new, independent director to serve as the compliance watchdog for the board of directors; and expand the oversight of the company's privacy officer. In addition, HP's ethics and compliance officer will report to the board's audit committee as well as Chairman and CEO Mark Hurd. "We are pleased to settle this matter with the attorney general and are committed to ensuring that HP regains its standing as a global leader in corporate ethics and responsibility," Hurd said in a written statement. <<<

What Is Corporate Governance?

This chapter brings the strategy dialogue full circle. As the opening vignette illustrates, shareholders, employees, and other stakeholders run the risk that managers will engage in practices detrimental to the value, health, and vitality of the firm. As you learned in Chapters 1 and 2, the CEO and members of the top management team set and guide the vision for the firm and its stakeholders and are responsible for formulating and implementing the strategy that realizes that vision. Carly Fiorina was a rising corporate star when she was hired at HP in 1999. She was hired as HP's new CEO to help formulate a strategy that would restore HP to a dominant position. Six years later she was dismissed, as performance problems led to lack of confidence in her leadership.

Once shareholders invest in a firm, they have relatively little direct control over what happens within the firm. This separation of the ownership of the capital necessary to fund a business enterprise from the day-to-day operational management of business affairs is the crux of what is known as the **agency problem**. From shareholders' perspectives, the solution to the agency problem is to find ways to ensure that corporate resources and profits are not squandered, that executives will not make choices that benefit themselves at shareholders' expense, and that shareholders will receive a positive return on their investment.[1] The means and mechanisms used to ensure that managers act in accordance with investors' best interests are the topics of this chapter.

It should also be noted that whether a company resides in a country with a strong orientation toward shareholders' rights, such as the United States or the United Kingdom, or is located in a country with relatively weak shareholders' rights and stronger protection for other stakeholders, such as Germany or France, all companies have a corporate governance system. The differences across these national contexts are discussed later in the chapter.

Corporate governance is the system by which organizations, particularly business corporations, are directed and controlled by their owners. However, all organizations—public,

agency problem Separation of its ownership from managerial control of a firm.

corporate governance The system by which owners of firms direct and control the affairs of the firm.

private, and nonprofit—have some form of governance in place. Corporate governance addresses the distribution of rights and responsibilities among different participants in the organization, such as the board, managers, shareholders, and other stakeholders, and spells out the rules and procedures for making decisions on corporate affairs. By doing this, governance also provides the structure through which the company's objectives are set and the means of attaining those objectives and monitoring performance.[2] A broader stakeholder view of governance is that the firm, as a function of its governance, has the responsibility to benefit other stakeholders beyond shareholders. This is sometimes called the "triple bottom line" in the corporate world, because a firm's strategy and related investments have financial performance objectives and social and environmental objectives as well. In this chapter, we introduce you to the language and principles of corporate governance.

Corporate Governance and Competitive Advantage

Before considering specific governance mechanisms that can protect shareholders, consider the following overarching question: *What effect does corporate governance have on firm survival, performance, and competitive advantage?* Although the answer to this question is actually very complex and the governance mechanisms themselves required by regulators and peer pressure are very costly to implement and maintain, strong evidence suggests that shareholders favor good governance and that it can help firms outperform those with poor governance.

EVIDENCE THAT GOVERNANCE WORKS

Germany provides a case in point with respect to an important governance mechanism—stock-based incentive plans. Prior to 1998, German law did not permit firms to issue U.S.- and U.K.-styled stock-option pay to executives. A few firms found creative ways around this legal roadblock and implemented pay schemes that mimicked stock options. This led the German legislature to reconsider the prohibition. By 1998, the law had been rewritten to allow limited forms of stock-based compensation. Once the legal obstacle was removed, about half of Germany's largest firms quickly adopted stock-based incentive plans. Early adopters of such plans were rewarded by the stock market with higher share prices; however, these incentives also seemed to lead to new strategies in these firms; many started to restructure by divesting non-core business operations.[3]

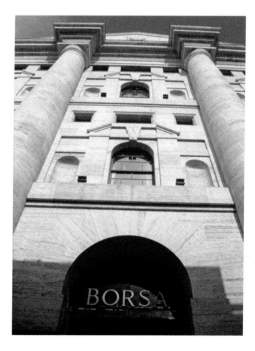

Small- and midsized Italian firms typically have been poorly governed. To encourage investment in these companies, the Italian Stock Exchange, called the Mercato Italiano di Borsa, started a new exchange for them called STAR. Companies listed on STAR adhere to strict corporate governance rules. As a group, these companies consistently outperform those listed on the Borsa.

Similar effects for governance mechanisms have been illustrated among Italian firms. In Italy, large investors have traditionally shied away from small and midsize companies because of concerns about liquidity and poor standards of corporate governance. To alleviate these concerns and help attract capital to this important economic segment, the Italian stock exchange, the Mercato Italiano di Borsa, started a new exchange called STAR. It was designed to be a separate market for small and midsize companies that follow strict governance prescriptions. Some of these prescriptions include provisions that the board must include a minimum number of independent directors and use performance-based compensation to reward both management and members of the board. Comparing the results of this index of well-governed firms with the general index of other small and midsized firms that do not adhere to these governance profiles illustrates the potential value of good governance. Even taking into consideration the possibility that better-managed firms are more likely to join the new STAR exchange, the companies on the STAR exchange have consistently outperformed their counterparts on the Borsa; during 2004, STAR firms achieved 24.5-percent greater returns than their counterparts.[4]

Consider the effect of governance mechanisms on the survival and market capitalization of Internet-based companies launched in the United States. These companies were risky for investors because they used new business models and lacked objective operating data that investors could analyze. This created significant uncertainty in the valuation of these new firms. Because of the lack of traditional indicators of quality that would enable analysts to value the firms objectively, the markets seemed to turn to secondary information sources as indicators of the underlying quality of these risky firms. Market valuations of these firms have been tightly linked to the firms' corporate governance characteristics (e.g., executive and director stock-based incentives, institutional and large-block stock ownership, board structure, and venture capital participation). Indeed, these governance factors were much stronger predictors of firm valuation and survival than things such as firm sales and profits.[5] The market seems to put more faith in risky new firms with good governance characteristics than in their counterparts with loose oversight by rewarding firms perceived to have good governance with significantly higher valuations.

Finally, consider the recent cases of corporate fraud and malfeasance in the United States. Corporate scandals have shaken the foundations of American business. In a short period, investors watched billions of dollars of wealth evaporate and dozens of individual managers and employees suddenly found themselves on the street or, worse, incarcerated. As it turns out, firms that engaged in the most egregious scandals exhibited several warning signs, as evidenced in the nature of how the corporate governance was structured. Sometimes effective governance may not prevent executive fraud, but it enables the firm to recover from its consequences. In summary, corporate governance has a strong bearing on the ability of firms to create a competitive advantage and exploit that advantage for the benefit of shareholders.

The Case of Krispy Kreme Some of these warning signals, as shown in the case of Krispy Kreme in Exhibit 13.1, were actually detected by organizations such as Governance Metrics International (GMI), which rates the quality of a firm's governance practices.[6]

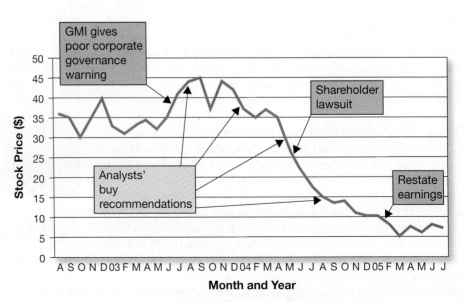

Exhibit 13.1 Early Warning Signals of Problems with Krispy Kreme from GMI

Could careful attention to corporate governance issues have saved Krispy Kreme investors lots of money? In other words, is corporate governance some kind of expensive window dressing, or does it actually impact the bottom line? Analysis of Krispy Kreme's stock price performance, analysts' recommendations, and the warnings of a GMI suggest that good governance has a positive impact on firm performance.

On January 4, 2005, Krispy Kreme Doughnuts Inc. announced that it was filing a financial restatement; its stock had fallen 73 percent over the previous 12 months. How did Krispy Kreme lose so much of its value in such a short period of time? GMI, which had begun evaluating firms in 2002, first rated Krispy Kreme in June 2003, and compared to all other U.S. companies, Krispy Kreme scored a below-average 4.0 for its corporate governance practices. (On the GMI 10-point scale, an average company earns about 6 points.) Among other things, GMI cited a relatively large number of nonindependent directors and related-party transactions and a lack of disclosure about ethical codes of conduct. In short, GMI concluded that the company did not have a strong overall governance record. Seven months later, in January 2004, GMI rerated the company, and its score had dropped to 2.5. At this stage, none of Krispy Kreme's financial woes had been discovered or announced, but the declining GMI scores clearly pointed to risk. Five months later, in May 2004, a shareholder suit was initiated, and in July, an SEC investigation was announced.

However, over this same period, several Wall Street firms were recommending the stock. On August 22, 2003, one had an outperform rating on the stock (even though it was a downgrade from a top pick), and as of January 2005, Krispy Kreme still had an outperform rating. On December 17, 2003, another Wall Street firm initiated coverage with a buy recommendation, as did another on March 30, 2004. Another initiated coverage on September 13, 2004, with a hold recommendation, and yet another issued a strong buy on September 28, 2004.

GMI is the first to admit that governance should not be the only screen in stock selection, but with this kind of downward move in ratings, one would think that financial analysts would have tempered their enthusiasm. Some analysts now believe that corporate governance attributes can have a strong influence on the quality of earnings. Further evidence of this belief is the recent action of Morningstar, one of the most respected investment advisory firms, to grade firms on an *A*-through-*F* scale based on the degree to which companies align their corporate governance practices with shareholders' interests.[7]

CORPORATE GOVERNANCE AND STRATEGY

Corporate governance is related to strategy formulation and implementation in several ways. The most visible roles are in establishing controls and incentives. Boards should ensure that the firm's vision and mission are reflected in its strategy, monitor the way that strategy is executed, and ensure that the top executives reap appropriate career and financial consequences in cases of failure or success.

The risk that managers will deviate from an organization's stated purpose and its guiding documents increases when managers are not the owners of the firm.[8] For instance, when the founders of a company raise capital through an IPO, they generally exchange a significant portion of the firm's stock for the financial capital needed to fund the operations and growth of the firm. After going public, the founders of an IPO firm dilute their ownership, often become minority owners of the firm, and instantly accept accountability for their actions to independent outside shareholders. Likewise, executives of older or large publicly held firms are generally owners of very small percentages of the firm.[9] For instance, research shows that the median level of executive ownership is 0.06 percent of outstanding shares.[10]

How do shareholders hold executives accountable for their actions and ensure that the firm is operated in a manner consistent with the firm's mission? What recourse do shareholders have if they find executives formulating strategies that lack coherence or fail to create value or, worse, engaging in unethical or illegal practices? A number of corporate governance mechanisms help shareholders avoid losing control of the corporation to unscrupulous or incompetent management.

THE MAJOR PARTIES IN CORPORATE GOVERNANCE

agent Party, such as a manager, who acts on behalf of another party.

principal Party, such as a shareholder, who hires an agent to act on his or her behalf.

An agency relationship exists when one party, the **agent**, acts on behalf of another party, the **principal**. In corporations like Hewlett-Packard, shareholders are viewed as principals, and key executives like Fiorina are viewed as agents.[11] Generally, a few assumptions can be made about principals and agents that highlight the potential problems in an agency relationship.

First, let's consider the interests of agents and principals in a corporation. What is it that each party wants from the relationship? Most theoretical treatments of the agency relationship in a modern corporation assume that both shareholders and executives are self-interested decision makers. This does not mean that they have no interest in the well-being of the other party; it simply means that they will generally make decisions that are in their own best interests. When the interests of shareholders and executives are virtually identical—when their goals are in alignment—then the agency problem is small. In this situation, executives will do what shareholders want them to do because it serves their own interests as well as those of the firm's shareholders.

However, in most situations, the interests of principals and agents do not naturally overlap completely; some things that would be in shareholders' best interests may be detrimental to those of executives and vice versa. For example, high executive salaries logically reduce corporate profits, which may be reflected in lower relative earnings per share if the higher pay has not led to higher firm performance in the first place. Similarly, executives may choose to diversify the firm to smooth earnings and reduce their own employment (or unemployment) risk without actually improving the competitive position of the firm. Thus, the key for shareholders is either to find a way to align the interests of executives with their own or to closely monitor and control what executives do so that shareholders' interests are protected.

CODES OF GOVERNANCE

codes of governance Ideal governance standards formulated by regulatory, market, and government institutions.

Many markets and investor groups around the globe have formulated **codes of governance**—ideal governance standards to which firms should adhere. Some of these are followed voluntarily; others are formalized by law. Codes of governance are aimed at four main issues: shareholder equality—upholding all shareholder rights; accountability by the board and management; disclosure and transparency through accurate and timely financial and nonfinancial reporting; and independence (audits and oversight; directors).

The Cadbury Code Following a series of corporate scandals in the United Kingdom and the United States, Sir Adrian Cadbury, former chairman of Cadbury Schweppes, raised the public's awareness and stimulated debate on corporate governance. His most celebrated achievement is the Cadbury Code of Best Practice, his namesake and a code of prescribed practices that has served as a model for reform around the world.

What is the Cadbury Code's history? In 1991, the Cadbury Commission was established in the United Kingdom to help raise corporate governance standards and increase the level of confidence in financial reporting and auditing by clarifying the respective responsibilities and obligations of relevant entities. In 1992, the Cadbury Committee issued a report with suggestions for corporate governance reform among U.K. companies. The report made nineteen recommendations for better firm governance. Since that time, similar codes have been crafted in many countries around the world, including Brazil, the Netherlands, Oman, the Philippines, Russia, Switzerland, Canada, France, Germany, Italy, and the United States. In all, more than fifty countries have adopted their own codes (see Exhibit 13.2 for examples of several of these codes). The burden placed on firms by these codes varies across the globe. However, all of these new codes significantly increased the stringency of recommended governance standards within their respective countries.

Some codes impose a comply-or-explain burden on firms. For instance, the SEC now requires companies to disclose whether they have financial experts on their audit committees and, if not, to explain why. As indicated in Exhibit 13.2, although all of the codes do not impose the same requirements, their aims and recommendations overlap considerably.

The Sarbanes-Oxley Act   Perhaps the most far-reaching governance reforms in the United States—at least from the standpoint that they are legal requirements—are seen in the Sarbanes-Oxley Act of 2002. What was the motivation for these new requirements? Just a few household names: Adelphia, Enron, Arthur Andersen, WorldCom, and Tyco. When corporate names like these synonymous with scandal and greed, public confidence in stock as a secure investment wavers. The Sarbanes-Oxley Act was signed into law on July 30, 2002, in response to these corporate scandals. Now, all companies are required to file periodic reports with the SEC. Noncompliance comes with significant penalties. The essential components of Sarbanes-Oxley deal with accounting oversight,

Exhibit 13.2   Examples of Codes of Governance

Country	What Is the Recommendation on Director Independence?	Can the Same Executive Be Both CEO and Chairperson?	Is Auditor Rotation Required?	Is Disclosure Required If the Company Does Not Comply with the Recommendations?
Brazil CVM Code (2002)	As many as possible	Split recommended	Not addressed	No
Russia CG Code (2002)	At least one-quarter	Split required by law	Not addressed	No
Singapore CG Committee (2001)	At least one-third	Split recommended	Not addressed	Yes
United Kingdom Cadbury Code[1] (1992)	Majority	Split recommended	Periodic rotation of lead auditor	Yes
United States Conference Board and CalPers (2003)[2]	Substantial majority	Separation is one of three acceptable alternatives	Recommended[3]	No

[1] In 2003, a Combined Code made further additions to the code, but these basic principles remain.
[2] Just one of several codes in existence in the United States.
[3] The Sarbanes-Oxley Act requires that the lead audit partner be rotated every 5 years changing audit firms either after 10 years of continual relationship or if former audit partner is employed by the company.

auditor independence, disclosure, analysts' conflicts of interests, accountability for fraud, and attorney's responsibilities.[12]

Public Company Accounting Oversight Board Sarbanes-Oxley resulted in the creation of the Public Company Accounting Oversight Board to oversee the audits of public companies. This board sets standards and rules for audit reports. All accounting firms that audit public companies must register with the oversight board. This board also inspects, investigates, and enforces compliance by these registered firms. A few of the new governance compliance rules that resulted from Sarbanes-Oxley include:

- Auditors must list the nonaudit services they are unable to perform during an audit.

- Audit-firm employees who leave an accounting firm must wait 1 year to become an executive for a former client.

- Transactions and relationships that are off the balance sheet but that may affect financial status must now be disclosed.

- Personal loans from a corporation to its executives are now largely prohibited.

- Research analysts for securities firms must now file conflict-of-interest disclosures. For instance, analysts must report whether they hold any securities in a company or have received corporate compensation.

- Brokers and dealers must disclose if the public company is a client.

- Altering, destroying, concealing, or falsifying records or documents with the intent to influence a federal investigation or bankruptcy case is subject to fines and up to 20 years of imprisonment.

Securities laws like Sarbanes-Oxley are complicated and confusing. For these reasons, there are a number of government initiatives underway to simplify these overwhelming and highly costly regulations. Regardless, failing to follow the Act's new restrictions and procedures can result in severe penalties.

Whether legal or voluntary, all governance guidelines appear to have four agency control mechanisms in common. These relate to (1) ownership concentration and power, (2) boards of directors, (3) incentive compensation, and (4) the market for corporate control. Each of these mechanisms, reviewed in the following sections, can work to decrease the likelihood that managers will act in ways detrimental to shareholders.

Ownership and the Roles of Owners

The ownership of for-profit firms can be subdivided into different ownership types, such as public and private firms (although the definition of public versus private varies from the U.S. definition in different parts of the world). A private firm is one in which the owner(s) has not listed shares of the firm on a public exchange; shares are typically owned largely by the founding families or by an investment group, such as a leveraged-buyout firm or venture capitalist. A public firm has sold shares to the general investing public, but how those publicly traded shares are dispersed or concentrated varies significantly and leads to another way to categorize public firms.

Dispersion of Ownership Some firms have a few select owners who control significant stakes in the firm. Consequently, these parties have so much voting power that they can have significant influence and control over the firm's strategy and governance. Sometimes they use that influence to determine who stays in power as CEO or chair of the board. An example of an owner-controlled firm is Nike; founder Philip Knight resigned as CEO, but he still owns

92 percent of the firm's class A stock and remains chair of the board of directors. Other firms have highly dispersed ownership, and managers also own small percentages of the firm's stock.

The dispersion of stock ownership affects the type and magnitude of agency problems that investors face. However, the presence of a powerful owner does not remove all forms of agency problems. One specific type of problem arises when a single powerful owner uses that power to extract private benefits from the company at the expense of other, less powerful owners. The fraud case against Adelphia alleges just such behavior. Members of the Rigas family were convicted of using their ownership power and board control to enable them to use corporate assets as collateral for personal and family loans, ultimately squandering the company's fortunes.[13]

Even when ownership is dispersed and no shareholder's ownership approaches a majority interest, some shareholders are in a position to influence corporate policies. In the United States, the SEC considers an ownership position of 5 percent sufficient to wield significant influence. Owners who control 5 percent or more of a firm's shares are referred to as *blockholders,* and this level of ownership or control must be publicly disclosed. Blockholders are considered powerful because voting blocks that large can sway boards of directors on important votes.

Exhibit 13.3 demonstrates a few different ownership profiles. The nature of executive/shareholder relationships varies across the firms in the exhibit. At Coca-Cola for instance, managers are very cognizant that over 13 percent of the company's stock is controlled by two individuals: Warren Buffet and James Williams. Both of these investors are members of the board of directors as a result of their sizeable investments. Contrast that profile with that of Dell, where the only major individual investor is founder Michael Dell.

Institutional Owners   FedEx has another type of powerful owner to deal with. Vanguard, Barclays, and Capital Research and Management Company each owned more than 5 percent of the company in 2004. Investors such as Vanguard are known as **institutional investors**; the money they control is capital invested in mutual funds and pension funds controlled by the company. Sometimes these institutional investors own large blocks of

institutional investors
Pension or mutual fund that manages large sums of money for third-party investors.

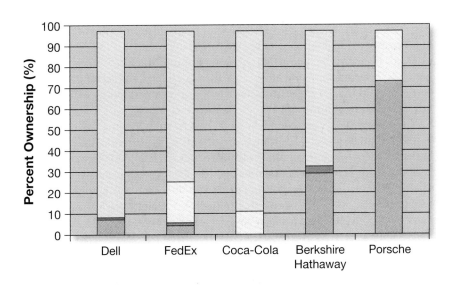

Exhibit 13.3 Ownership Structure Comparison

☐ Other shareholders (mutual funds, individuals, etc.)
☐ Blockholders (any ownership position >5%)
■ Management team
▨ Founder and family

individual companies. Most institutional investors are relatively passive investors: They essentially vote with their feet by purchasing or selling a stock based on their outlook for the firm's performance, and therefore the potential performance of the firm's stock. But they can also become quite active should the need arise, and some institutional investors, such as CalPers (the California Public Employees' Retirement System) and SWIB (State of Wisconsin Investment Board), are by their charter activist investors.[14]

Different types of institutional investors seem to have preferences for firms with different strategies. For instance, recent research has found that the managers of public pension funds prefer to invest in firms that follow strategies that attempt to exploit internal innovation, whereas investments made by managers of professional investment funds revealed preferences for firms that attempt to acquire innovations externally through acquisitions.[15] For sure, managers of these two types of institutional funds do not limit their investments to these types of firms, but their portfolios demonstrate non-random preferences.

Perhaps the most important lesson in this observation for managers of firms is the idea that owners do not have a unified voice. Economic theories make assumptions about shareholders and their preferences, but in reality different types of shareholders have different preferences. For instance, examine the types of owners that control Porsche, the German sports car manufacturer. It is unlikely that the family who owns most of Porsche would vote the same way on many corporate issues that independent mutual-fund managers would because the issues that are important to each are not always the same. Indeed, as you examine the marketing material for different mutual funds, you will notice that many of them have different objectives. The implication for managers is that they must understand who owns the company and what their interests are.

The Board of Directors

board of directors Group of individuals that formally represents the firm's shareholders and oversees the work of top executives.

One of the chief monitoring devices available to shareholders is the board of directors. All publicly held companies are required to have a **board of directors**. A board of directors—a group of individuals who formally represents the firm's shareholders—is charged with overseeing the work of top executives. The legal roles of the board include hiring and firing top executives, monitoring management, ensuring that shareholders' interests are protected, establishing executive compensation, and reviewing and approving the firm's strategy. Informal roles played by boards include acting as conduits of information from external sources, providing leads for acquisition and alliance partner candidates, influencing important external parties such as industry regulators and foreign government policy makers, and providing advice and counsel for the CEO and other top executives.

Although corporate laws vary around the globe, which results in some differences in board practices, the general responsibility of the board of directors is to ensure that executives are acting in shareholders' best interests. In the United States, shareholders elect members of the board of directors. In the wake of numerous high-profile financial scandals in recent years, boards have been under increasing pressure to exercise their monitoring responsibility with greater vigilance.[16] Part of this pressure comes from the U.S. Congress, which has created laws that require public firms to put particular governance reforms into place.[17]

INSIDERS VERSUS OUTSIDERS

A board of directors is typically composed of several very experienced individuals. Most of these individuals are generally not officers of the company but, rather, are employed by other companies. Executives of the firm who also serve on the board are often referred to as *insiders;* those on the board who are not employed by the firm otherwise are known as *outsiders.* Outsiders can typically be more independent in fulfilling their board responsibilities, but being an outsider does not necessarily make a director independent. For instance, the independent judgement of a director who has another business relationship with the company may be compromised.

Most institutional investors and watchdog groups prefer a large majority of independent directors. This helps to avoid conflicts of interests in carrying out fundamental responsibilities. As a result, there is a strong movement to increase the percentage of board members who are independent outsiders. However, insiders, although not independent, have access to more critical knowledge of the business and its environment and have the potential to add critical insight to board deliberations.[18]

Boards in the United States are typically comprised of a majority of outside directors, along with one or more senior executives of the firm. Although there is the presumption that outside directors make for a more vigilant board, this is not always the case. First, outside directors may not be independent; they may have business dealings with the firm or friendship ties to the CEO. Similarly, by virtue of their position, CEOs have considerable control over outside directors, which may make it difficult for them to be truly independent. These relationships can affect how they monitor and advise management. Although watchdog groups seem to clamor for more independent outsiders on boards, research reveals that in some circumstances, increasing the number of insiders (i.e., executives) on the board can increase the board's effectiveness. For instance, when the firm operates in highly technical areas, insiders can provide better information than can many independent outsiders.[19]

What to Do About the CEO Chair   In approximately 70 percent of U.S. public firms, the CEO also serves as the chair of the board of directors. Debate continues as to the wisdom of an "independent chair" structure in American corporate culture. As evidenced by the prevalence of dual CEO/chairs in the United States, corporations are generally resistant to the idea of separating the two positions. Although separating the roles of CEO and board chair is more common in European corporations[20] (and is one of the Cadbury guidelines in the United Kingdom), it remains the exception in the United States. However, the two roles are actually quite distinct, and there is a movement to separate the two jobs. In other countries, norms and laws lead to other configurations. In Germany, because such duality is prohibited, the CEO and the board chair are always different people. When the roles are split, it is critical that the board chair not take operational roles, just as the CEO shouldn't attempt to run the board.

The logic for combining the posts includes the need for specialized information that an outsider could not have, and a lack of qualified candidates. The logic for splitting is the need for monitoring: One cannot effectively serve as referee and player at the same time. Many critics of U.S. corporate governance practices believe, however, that true board independence may ultimately—within the next decade—require a serious reexamination of this historic combination of powers.[21] Consequently, pressure is increasing to separate these two positions so that the board can more effectively monitor top executives. Some large U.S. companies that have recently transitioned from a combined chair/CEO to a split model include Boeing, Walt Disney, and Oracle.

THE BOARD'S ACTIVITIES AND THE COMPANY'S STRATEGY

Boards generally are organized into several committees, with key board responsibilities being assigned to different committees. For instance, all companies listed on the New York Stock Exchange (NYSE) must have an audit committee, which is responsible for selecting the independent auditor and reviewing the reports provided by that outside auditor. Because independent audits of books and records is critical to effective monitoring, the NYSE requires that the audit committee be composed only of outsiders; insiders may not be responsible for ensuring the independence of the audit. In addition, boards have compensation committees that are charged with setting the level of executive compensation.

Exhibit 13.4   Board Roles and Actions

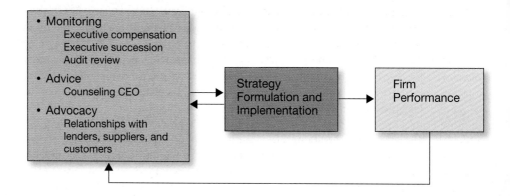

The relationship between the board and firm strategy and performance is illustrated in Exhibit 13.4. Let's review each of these mechanisms and discuss how managers can utilize the board to further the purposes of the firm.

Monitoring   One of the key roles of the board of directors is to monitor the performance of top executives and potentially replace management when necessary. **Monitoring** is the process of the board acting in its legal and fiduciary responsibility to oversee executives' behaviors and performance and to take action when necessary to replace management. The opening vignette on HP provides an example of this role. Some of the most important decisions made by the board are hiring and firing the CEO and other senior executives. Effective boards make sure that they have an executive succession plan that keeps the firm prepared in the event that a new CEO is needed. Some forms of succession, such as retirement, are easier to plan for than others. Orderly succession seems to have better results than sudden termination and turning to a new outsider to fix the firm's problems. A recent study of CEO successions in U.S. companies illustrates this point (see Exhibit 13.5).[22] Indeed the left-hand graph shows that firm's generally performed more poorly two years after an incumbent CEO was dismissed, while the right-hand graph demonstrates that firms with an orderly CEO succession process improved their stock-market and accounting-based performance.

Firing is a drastic monitoring device that should be used judiciously. More routine monitoring mechanisms include meeting regularly as a board, hiring competent external auditors, and diligently reviewing financial and operating results. Evidence suggests that when a CEO is fired for firm-performance reasons, it is more likely that the board will recruit an

monitoring   Functioning of the board in exercising its legal and fiduciary responsibility to oversee executives' behavior and performance and to take action when it's necessary to replace management.

Exhibit 13.5
CEO Firing

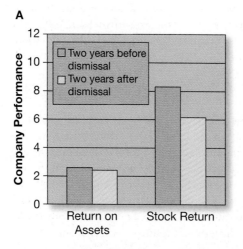

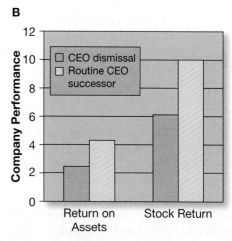

outsider as a replacement. Although outsiders do bring a fresh perspective, research shows that they are more likely than not to deploy strategies that lead their firms to underperform, not outperform, their competition. Indeed, the best-performing firms, following the forced replacement of the CEO, appear to be those run by executives who already have experience at the company they are leading.[23] Perhaps the best case-in-point here is the placement of Jack Welch, a GE manager, into the CEO role. Welch dramatically changed the firm's strategy and created the diversified powerhouse we know today.

Advising Managers   Although increasing emphasis is being placed on the monitoring roles of boards, recent research has shown that just as much, if not more, value is to be had by tapping into the expertise and contacts of the board and using board members as confidants and information sources. On the other hand, many critics of corporate governance argue that CEOs who have social ties and friendships with board members could put shareholders at risk because these relationships may make the board less likely to monitor the CEO effectively.

Research indicates that social ties typically fail to reduce the level of board-monitoring activity and that, in fact, such social ties improve the ability of the CEO to tap board members for advice and counsel on strategic issues. This suggests that social ties between CEOs and board members may increase board involvement rather than decrease it.[24] The same research found that CEOs were more willing to turn to board members for advice when they had social ties to these members—when they considered the relationship to be friendship-based, not solely monitoring-based. This suggests that when CEOs perceive they have a loyal board, they will involve the board more in strategic decision-making.

Finally, the research also demonstrated that firms in which CEOs collaborate with board members on strategic issues outside of board meetings perform significantly better than firms that limit CEO/board interactions to purely monitoring roles. The trend is to encourage board members to be more actively involved, as opposed to passively involved (i.e., simply a rubber stamp on the executive team's recommendations). For instance, General Electric now requires that its board members spend time at its various facilities around the world in addition to the regular boardroom meetings.

Because more advice and counsel interactions between board members and executives leads to improved firm performance, managers and board members alike are interested in how these interactions can be exploited for shareholders' benefit. How can the board be structured to maximize the positive strategic counsel that can take place between the board and the CEO? Simply adding more directors to the board is not an effective method for increasing these interactions; increasing the number of board members who can provide CEOs with appropriate strategic knowledge does increase board–CEO involvement.[25] Research shows that positive CEO–board interactions are maximized when the selection of outside board members matches the competitive environment facing the firm. When firms are in relatively stable competitive environments, the advice and monitoring of board members is enhanced when outside board members are drawn from other firms that are strategically related to the firm. In these stable environments, the knowledge and experience that board members gain in their own firm translates well to the firm they monitor.

However, when the firm is located in a very unstable competitive environment, board involvement is most effective when outside board members are drawn from strategically dissimilar firms. This is probably due to the fact that in unstable environments, boards need to tap into multiple experiential backgrounds to help make sense of the firm's competitive environment. Given the increasingly active role that directors play in strategy and the greater demands of the job, it should come as no surprise that the complexion of the boardroom is changing. Boards today are typically larger and more diverse, and members are more highly paid, than in years past.[26]

Using the Board as a Lever of Power and Influence Finally, boards also provide access to external resources, and it is not uncommon for a director to sit on multiple boards (a characteristic called a *board interlock*). These resources can range from access to capital, to new knowledge, to the ability to influence other external stakeholders, such as investors, banks, and regulators. CEOs often sit on the boards of other firms as well, though, given their time constraints, they often sit on only one or two others at the most. When asked why they would invest the required time and effort in another firm's success, they often respond that it is the learning component that drives their choice. They report that they learn from the CEO and executives of the other firm and benefit from the knowledge and contacts possessed by their peer directors.[27]

Beyond the straightforward fact that a board position may provide access to resources and be a lever of power or influence over other important stakeholders, some believe that such influence and power can get out of hand. One aspect of this perspective is CEOcentric from the standpoint that CEOs may be tempted to seek out other CEOs to sit on their boards if those potential board members are highly paid at their home firms. Landing highly paid CEOs as directors will probably lead to a board that will be supportive of paying high wages for CEOs. For instance, critics of corporate excess, such as the Conference Board or Institutional Shareholders Services, point to research showing that the CEOs of the boards of companies on which Home Depot's former CEO Bob Nardelli sat were overpaid relative to their peers and that Nardelli himself was overpaid.[28]

As you learned in the opening paragraph of this section, it is not unusual for directors to sit on multiple boards or for companies to be interconnected via their directors. For instance, PepsiCo director Robert E. Allen also sits on the board of Bristol-Myers Squibb. Ironically, Coca-Cola director James D. Robinson III, also sits on the board of Bristol-Myers Squibb, leaving you to wonder how the Cola Wars play out in the Bristol-Myers' boardroom. Debate continues as to whether such board interlocks help firms perform better by virtue of their access to better information or simply allow corporations to collude at the expense of the public at large. Although there is no evidence that consumers are generally harmed by such interrelationships at the board level, strategy research has shown that directors themselves may be more effective as monitors if they are linked to certain firms given the competitive standing and environmental turbulence facing the focal firms.[29] It has also been shown that common board ties can influence many other important factors, ranging from the choice of CEO to a firm's strategy in the face of failing performance.[30]

Executive Compensation

One of the fundamental conditions that leads to a potential agency problem in publicly held companies is the separation of firm ownership from company management. When professional managers, rather than the owners themselves, run the operations of a firm, situations can arise in which there may be conflicts of interest—where what is best for shareholders is not necessarily what is best for management. For instance, consider a situation in which the company could receive an attractive buyout proposal from a competitor. Shareholders might be interested in pursuing this buyout if the premium they are being offered for their shares is attractive. However, management may not be as interested in the buyout if their employment is threatened. Incentives are sometimes used to alleviate this potential conflict. Of course, it is also true that sometimes incentives can unwittingly exacerbate conflicts of interest. This is why it is important to understand how incentives work, including how people tend to respond to different types of incentives.

One possible solution to these potential conflicts of interest is to structure incentive arrangements so that managers are rewarded for doing what is in shareholders' best interests. **Incentive alignment** can be used to solve the agency problem. For instance, to avoid managers' hesitancy to examine acquisition-buyout options, boards can include "golden parachute" provisions in managers' compensation packages, which offer significant bonuses when loss of employment is a consequence of an acquisition with an acceptable premium.

incentive alignment Use of incentives to align managerial self-interest with shareholders'.

In practice, it is impossible to structure executive compensation to completely overcome all possible conflicts of interest. A number of mechanisms are frequently used to increase the incentive alignment between shareholders and executives. We review some of these common mechanisms in this section, but we also point out how each mechanism has its limitations.

EXECUTIVE OWNERSHIP

Perhaps the most direct way to align incentives is to require that executives own stock in the firm. The theory here is rather obvious: If you are an owner of the company you should behave more like an owner and less like a hired hand. In recent years, many firms have established ownership guidelines for senior executives. Consider the case of Dendrite International, which is discussed in Exhibit 13.6.[31] However, the ownership requirement may backfire. Executives cannot diversify their risk exposure as well as large shareholders.

Exhibit 13.6 Establishing Executive-Ownership Requirements at Dendrite International

As an illustration of a recent adopter of an executive stock-ownership plan, consider Dendrite. Dendrite (DRTE), a leading supplier of specialized software to the global pharmaceutical industry that was founded in Australia in 1986 and is now headquartered in Bedmaster, New Jersey, implemented a formal stock-ownership plan for its twenty senior-most executives and all of its nonemployee directors. The new program mandates ownership of Dendrite stock, ranging from 15,000 to 100,000 shares, depending on the executive's position.

The ownership requirements set by Dendrite are based on owned common stock, not stock options. Ownership of the predetermined number of shares must be achieved within 5 years, with an initial number attained in three years. Restrictions have been placed on the receipt of additional equity-based compensation and sale of Dendrite shares until ownership commitments are attained. The executive participants may obtain shares through purchase on the open market, receiving incentive compensation in shares or exercising options and holding shares.

In addition to instituting share-ownership requirements, Dendrite also made changes to its executive compensation program. Executives may now elect to receive incentive compensation in stock instead of cash. If the executive elects to receive stock, these shares are restricted from sale for 1 year, and the executive will receive a number of options equal to the number of restricted shares. Replacement options will be granted for shares used to exercise vested options.

By the start of 2005, Dendrite's executive stock ownership plan was fully in place. In addition, all of Dendrite's directors—executive and independent—owned at least some Dendrite stock, further aligning the board, top manager, and shareholder interests. While Dendrite is in a highly competitive and dynamic industry, it is notable that since beginning the implementation of the executive stock ownership plan in 2000, the firm has managed to garner shareholders a strong return. For instance, as of the end of 2005 shareholders had earned a 3-year average return of 28 percent, versus the S&P 1500 return of 12 percent. Standard and Poor also ranked the firm among the top tier of its peers, in terms of overall performance and outlook.

Is an executive stock ownership plan an easy pathway to competitive advantage? Probably not, but at least it is an important lever in a firm's corporate governance repertoire to provide executives and directors an incentive to see that the right strategy is being executed well.

Shareholders can spread their risks across many firms, but an individual executive who is required to invest heavily in the company is likely to have a very unbalanced investment portfolio.

In addition, executives risk their human capital—that is, their reputation and future job opportunities—through the employment relationship. For U.S. firms in particular, the Sarbanes-Oxley governance reforms now require that the CEO and CFO certify that the firm's financial statements are accurate, and they can be jailed if the statements are proven to be fraudulent or misrepresentative of the facts. This increases the pressures of top executives' jobs, one indication of which is the fact that CFO turnover has increased by about 23 percent over the last three years.[32] Consequently, executives suffer heavy exposure to firm-specific risk. This type of risk exposure could lead some executives to become very risk averse. Consequently, boards need to be very careful in structuring executive compensation so that they understand just what types of behaviors they are encouraging through the economic incentives they provide.

Stock-Ownership Policies   As mentioned earlier, many firms have established executive stock ownership policies. How prevalent are these programs, how are they put into place, and what do they require of executives? Based on research by F. W. Cook, a large executive compensation consulting firm, the prevalence of executive and director stock ownership guidelines has increased and is expected to continue to increase over the next several years because of the perception that it is one of the best forms of governance (see Exhibit 13.7).[33]

Ownership guidelines are generally grouped into two types: traditional and retention programs. Traditional stock ownership guidelines establish ownership levels through a multiple-of-salary approach. Retention programs express ownership as a percentage of the gains resulting from the exercise of stock options and other equity-based incentives, such as restricted stock. These two types of stock ownership are sometimes used together. For example, some firms may require that executives retain their shares (or some percentage of their shares) acquired through stock options until they own five times their salary in company stock.

Stock ownership requirements vary among firms that have such plans. For instance, among firms that have multiple-of-salary plans, the median value of stock ownership required is about $5 million, but it ranges from a mere $100,000 to over $20 million. The median multiple is five times the executive's salary; the highest requirement is at Mellon Financial Corporation, where the CEO is required to have twenty-five times the executive's salary.

Implementing a stock ownership plan requires time. Most CEOs do not have sufficient liquid assets to immediately buy the needed shares when a plan is implemented. Consequently, firms often allow CEOs several years to acquire the required shares (most companies allow 5 years). Alternatively, if companies use the retention method, no time requirement is necessary because they are only concerned with what is retained from granted options.

Exhibit 13.7   Comparison Executive Stock Ownership

	Largest 250 Companies with Stock Ownership Guidelines		
	Number of Companies	**Percent of Companies**	**Percent Increase from 2001 to 2004**
Executives	142	57	58
Directors	123	49	127

As noted in Exhibit 13.6, firms are increasingly requiring that their members of the board also own stock. The level of required ownership is much lower than for CEOs. The median level of required ownership among firms that have such requirements is either five times their annual director retainer or 5,000 shares. These levels equate to approximately $200,000.

INCENTIVE COMPENSATION

Firms use various forms of incentive compensation to reward executives and align the interests of their top-management team with those of shareholders. The two most common incentives are annual bonus plans and stock options. In recent years, firms have been increasing their reliance on newer forms of pay, such as restricted stock grants and long-term accounting-based incentive plans. Exhibit 13.8 illustrates how different firms in the food industry emphasize various incentive mechanisms when paying their CEOs.

Bonus Plans   Perhaps the oldest form of incentive pay is the bonus plan. The idea behind bonus plans is that the board can subjectively evaluate executives' performance on multiple dimensions and allocate a year-end cash award as appropriate. In theory, bonus plans should be linked to firm performance indicators. The bonus-plan incentive has two principle drawbacks. First, when bonuses are tied to accounting indicators of performance, executives may be motivated to make accounting decisions that maximize their possible bonus payout. For instance, research has found that firms are more likely to increase income deferrals when senior executives have reached the maximum payout under terms of their bonus plan.[34] Second, linking pay to annual firm performance can have the unintended consequence of short-term bias and inattention to long-term strategic needs. For instance, some research shows that bonus plans can lead to the underfunding of R&D initiatives.[35] To get around this problem, many firms are now tying bonus payouts to long-term performance, rather than annual performance. (These are often called Long-term Incentive Plans, or LTIPS, because incentives are based on firm performance over a period longer than one

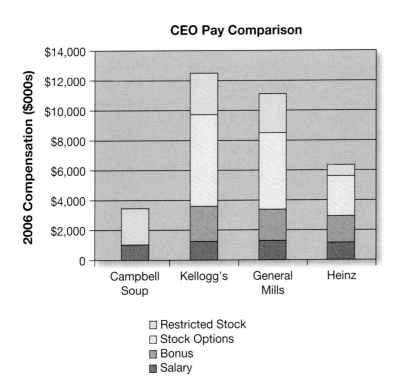

Exhibit 13.8   Comparison of Incentive Pay Usage in the Food Industry

year, but excludes other long-term incentives like restricted stock, stock options or stock appreciation rights plans.) Options and restricted stock are discussed in the next section.

However, bonuses do have some appealing characteristics. For instance, the board can tie them to multiple desired outcomes, including both financial performance and other important outcomes such as customer satisfaction and quality. In addition, the board can more easily revoke or withhold bonuses than it can other long-term incentives that it loses control of once they are granted. The effectiveness of annual bonus programs really comes down to how well the board links them to the achievement of desired objectives.

Stock Options
One of the most popular incentive devices of the past 20 years has been the executive stock option plan. The idea behind stock options is to simulate stock ownership for executives who do not or cannot buy lots of stock.

When a company grants a stock option, the executive's cash pay does not increase in the year the option is granted. Rather, a **stock option** gives an employee the right to buy a share of company stock at a later date for a predetermined price. Usually, stock option plans impose a vesting period, generally 3 years. After that period of time, the executive can redeem the option. If the company's stock price has increased, then the executive can buy the stock at a discount, sometimes a very significant discount. In addition, many companies do not require the executive to actually buy the stock, they sometimes allow them to receive the difference between the stock price and the option price as compensation at that future date. The rationale for the use of stock options is that they motivate executives to act like owners and take reasonable risks that will result in the company's stock price increasing. Advocates of stock options like their supposed win–win attributes: If executives do not create shareholder value in the form of higher stock prices, the options will be worthless.

Like most incentive plans, options do have their downside. Although used to simulate stock ownership, in reality they do not always achieve this objective. This is because options do not make executives bear any financial risk like stock ownership does. When executives own stock, they win if the stock price increases and they lose actual wealth if the stock price declines. With stock options, only the upside potential is conveyed. The only cost to executives is an opportunity cost.

Decision makers, such as executives, behave quite differently when they have something to lose. Indeed, upside potential and downside risks seem to motivate different behaviors. Research shows that stock options may increase excessive risk taking beyond the level of risk desired by shareholders.[36] For instance, executives with large proportions of their pay package derived from stock options tend to pursue aggressive acquisition and divestiture strategies; buying and selling divisions frequently is a key part of their corporate strategy. For instance, GE has historically used stock options heavily, and it may be no coincidence that it is one of the most prolific acquirers of other companies in the world. Likewise, in the opening vignette, Carly Fiorina was quick to use acquisitions to solve her company's revenue problems rather than exercising patience with internal development programs. Conversely, firms run by executives with high levels of stock ownership are much less likely to pursue acquisitions and divestitures and focus more on internally developed strategies.[37]

Restricted Stock
Restricted stock is a rather recent compensation initiative that is designed to help avoid the potential problems associated with annual bonus plans and stock options. To tie executives' financial rewards to shareholder value while avoiding the lack of downside risk associated with stock options (recall that executive's make money through options when the stock price goes up, but since they don't actually own any stock, they do not lose money if the stock price falls), companies can grant actual stock shares to executives. These shares are generally referred to as a *restricted stock grant* because the

grants have restrictions built in to ensure that managers do not sell the stock to convert it to cash (and thus lose the incentive power of stock ownership). The restrictions usually entail vesting over a period of 3 to 5 years and prohibitions on the sale of the stock for some extended period of time. The popularity of restricted stock has grown significantly in the past several years because of the wave of bad press associated with stock option abuses. With restricted stock grants, the executive has upside incentive associated with the stock, but they are also exposed to the downside risk. When the stock price drops, the value of the executives restricted stock declines as well. And because restricted stock has real value when granted (i.e., the value of the stock) and not only potential value like stock options, some boards think they are better at truly aligning the incentives of managers with those of shareholders.

Unions, shareholder watchdog groups, and other interested stakeholders often criticize the level of pay that CEOs are able to make, claiming that their rewards are excessive and that they sometimes achieve these high levels of pay without achieving stellar performance. How do some CEOs achieve high levels of pay without high levels of performance? Usually because they were given lots of stock options. Executives can make a great deal of money from options because any increase in the firm's stock price results in money for the CEO even if the firm's stock price gains are far outpaced by competitors. Exhibit 13.9 illustrates that star compensation can attract attention because it is so grandiose. You can see from the exhibit the average level of CEO pay among large U.S. companies and the two highest-paid executives in the United States as well as the two highest-paid female CEOs in the world. It is no wonder that CEO pay createsheadlines every year in the business press. CEO pay is very high relative to that of almost everyone else. (except perhaps movie stars and star athletes!).

The Well-Designed Incentive Plan   Notwithstanding recent abuses, if firms are careful about how they use incentives, monetary rewards are powerful tools that can be used to increase the likelihood that executives act in shareholders' interests. Proper use of incentives tied to long-term performance metrics (as opposed to the current stock price) increases the likelihood that executives will make necessary capital investments.[38] For instance, facing intense competition, cutbacks in military spending, and years of

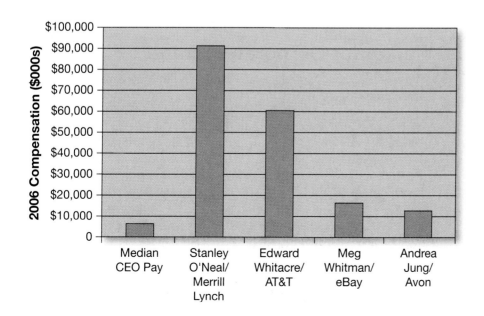

Exhibit 13.9   Variation Among CEOs' Pay

underperformance, in 1991 the board of directors of General Dynamics hired a new management team and charged it with formulating a strategy to create shareholder wealth. The company established strong links between shareholder wealth and managerial compensation through a combination of bonuses, options, and restricted stock. This pay-for-performance plan is largely credited with providing the incentive to devise a strategy that was politically unpopular but economically successful. The new management team downsized, restructured, and exited some of its businesses by selling divisions to competitors but in the process, it created gains for shareholders of approximately $4.5 billion. Scholars documenting this case suggest that such a dramatic and successful strategy would have been unlikely without these financial incentives.[39] The key to using incentives is to find the appropriate performance metrics (i.e., those identified in the balanced scorecard) and to link executive pay to these outcomes.

Options can be a part of a well-designed incentive package, but evidence suggests that option pay should be used in moderation and balanced with other types of incentives, such as annual bonus plans and stock ownership. In addition, research suggests that too much focus has been placed on keeping the CEO's pay level in line with market forces and not enough focus has been placed on the incentives of other key executives. For instance, the best-performing firms tend to compensate their second-level managers (i.e., CFO, COO, etc.) at levels more closely related to the pay of the CEO rather than have a star system where the CEO's pay significantly outpaces that of other top managers. This is probably due to the fact that strategic management is inherently a team function, and huge gaps in pay between the CEO and other officers creates an unhealthy social context in which to operate as an effective team.[40]

Firms that have large gaps in pay across top managerial ranks suffer negative effects. For instance, firms with large pay gaps seem to undermine their ability to develop managerial talent because manager turnover increases significantly when pay gaps are large.[41] Thus, to maximize performance, firms need to adjust both absolute and relative pay levels to achieve the proper fit with their strategic context.

The box entitled "How Would *You* Do That? 13.1" examines some of the factors that firms should consider when structuring CEO compensation. When establishing CEO pay and aligning it with a firm's intended strategy, recognize that boards of directors are often criticized but rarely praised for how they structure CEO incentives.

The Market for Corporate Control

market for corporate control Control over public corporations is traded, and this theoretically puts some pressure on managers to perform, otherwise their corporation can be taken over.

The final corporate governance mechanism we review is not a mechanism that the board puts in place to protect shareholders, but rather is a reflection of national and global institutions and their effect on the relative ease or difficulty of an individual or company simply taking full or partial control of another company. The **market for corporate control** is the idea that every public company is theoretically for sale. To explain this concept, let's take the phrase in its parts. The "market" is the sum of all the possible buyers of corporate stock and the individual shareholders of the company (who might be "sellers" in this market). The term "control" refers to what can be bought and sold in this market. Control of what? Control of corporations. Don't confuse this market with the stock market where you can go buy lots of shares. The stock market is merely the mechanism that the market for corporate control uses to allow one party to take control away from another. Several types of battles for the control of large corporations can take place. For instance, the problems HP faced during the Carly Fiorina's period were tied to her strategy to acquire Compaq. The acquisition and integration of Compaq's assets and product lines into HP was the outcome of an active market for corporate control.

Doing Some Repairs at Home Depot

Hiring (and firing) and compensating the CEO are some of the chief responsibilities of the board of directors. After all, the CEO is expected to foster the formulation of a leading-edge strategy and champion it. Ultimately, the CEO is held accountable for the strategy's successful execution. When Home Depot and Bob Nardelli parted ways in 2006 because of poor performance, the board decided that the best candidate was Frank Blake, a senior executive of the firm. By deciding to hire an insider, the Home Depot board in some ways simplified their job because they would not have to offer a big carrot to recruit an executive from another firm to come to Home Depot. When a board goes outside the firm to hire a CEO, they usually pay a premium because they need to lure an executive from another position. But, deciding what, and how, to pay the CEO is still a major challenge for the board. The

board's objective is to offer a compensation package that will result in incentives consistent with Home Depot's objectives—incentives that will motivate the CEO to formulate a strategy that achieved its vision and mission. When the Home Depot board had identified Blake as the new CEO, they stated that the firm's objectives were to improve its strategy and tie CEO pay more closely to firm performance.

In setting Blake's pay, three of the key considerations are: (1) Blake's prior compensation as an executive vice president of the company, (2) Nardelli's compensation as the former CEO, and (3) the compensation of the CEO of Home Depot's chief rival, Lowe's. These data are provided in Exhibit 13.10.

With Home Depot's objectives in mind, the board initially offered Mr. Blake a contract that included a mixture of incentives, including bonus payments, restricted stock, and stock

options. Surprisingly, Mr. Blake rejected the pay package because it was *too* generous and because he was opposed to restricted stock grants. His argument was that restricted stock didn't offer enough incentive because if the stock price declined he would still have some value in the shares make money. He ended up settling on the following package:[48]

Annual salary: $975,000

Annual bonus: A target 100 percent of salary, with the possibility of double salary if performance is high enough

Long-term bonus: A target of $2,500,000, contingent on performance over the next 3 years

Restricted stock awards: None

Stock options: A present value of $2,500,000, but contingent on increasing stock price

Exhibit 13.10 Pay Comparison Between CEOs at Home Depot and Lowe's

	Salary	Bonus	Restricted Stock	Stock Options
Blake's Pay as EVP	$685,000	$825,000	$2,900,000	$0
Nardelli's Pay as former CEO	$2,200,000	$7,000,000	$14,000,000	$0
CEO Pay at Lowe's	$850,000	$2,600,000	$4,000,000	$0

Corporate control literally refers to who controls the corporation. Thus, corporate control is achieved by having sufficient power and votes to choose the CEO and members of the board of directors of a company and to control all major decisions made by a company.[42] One of the principle ways of gaining corporate control is through mergers and acquisitions. Corporate raiders, competitors, and leveraged-buyout firms are investors who buy underperforming firms, restructure them, and then sell them for a profit. Because misbehavior or underperformance may lead to shareholders replacing the board and the CEO or other firms or investors attempting to buy out a firm and replace its management, the market for corporate control helps to keep managers in line.

The Trend Toward Takeovers and Buyouts   In the United States, the market for corporate control was spurred by hostile takeover activity and leveraged buyouts in the 1980s. Corporate raiders such as T. Boone Pickens, Carl Icahn, Saul Steinberg, Ted Turner, and Michael Milliken discovered great financial opportunities in seizing control of someone else's business, often at bargain prices. With millions of dollars at stake, these raiders aroused massive public attention and, depending on one's point of view, were either the villains or the saviors of American business.[43] The hostile takeover threat is alive and well today. Beginning in 2003 and eventually culminating in a successful acquisition in 2005, Oracle engaged in an 18-month battle to gain control of PeopleSoft.

Overall, researchers have concluded that corporate takeovers generate positive gains, that the target firm's shareholders benefit, and that the bidding firm's shareholders do not lose out. However, the success of a hostile takeover depends on the takeover premium paid. This work ties in well with the notion of resources and competitive advantage because the market for corporate control can be viewed as an arena in which managerial teams compete for the rights to manage corporate resources.[44]

Although the market for corporate control may indeed be the last line in the sand, in terms of corporate governance, it should also be evident that it is one of the most costly and emotion-wrenched governance remedies beyond the replacement of the CEO by a firm's board. When a firm is the target of a raider or a fight for control of a board, it is a potential signal that the firm's board and its management has been ineffective or, at the very least, that the board and management see no way to combat the competition without merging with or being acquired by another entity. In Chapter 10 on mergers and acquisitions, you learned that many of the gains associated with acquisitions go to the seller, not the buyer. Therefore, although the market for corporate control may serve to discipline management, it is a very costly and time-consuming remedy to implement, and its benefits to the buyer will always be of concern. Moreover, as you will learn in the following section, the market for corporate control can only be an effective governance mechanism to the extent that the capital markets and governance mechanisms in place in a country allow hostile acquisitions to occur in the first place.

The Faces of Corporate Governance Around the World

Although conflicts between managers and owners occur around the globe, the specific nature of the problems and the norms for guarding against them vary markedly. Governance problems are not unique to the United States, even though they may seem most visible to you; for instance, the Netherlands' Ahold Group (grocery stores), Italy's Parmalat (dairy and food products), France's Vivendi (entertainment), and the French-Belgian firm Elf (petroleum) are all very recent examples of scandal-ridden non-U.S. multinationals.

Most of these firms' problems can be traced to faulty governance and, in the end, fraudulent accounting and executive excess much like that which eventually brought down Enron,

MCI, and Tyco. Some of these differences are illustrated by recent cross-national comparisons of corporate governance practices, which differ considerably around the globe. For instance, ownership is heavily dispersed in the United States but is much more concentrated in Canada, Germany, Japan, and China. In the last three countries, national and state governments also often own major stakes of public companies. In countries where ownership is highly concentrated, owners typically have a corresponding high level of influence over corporate affairs. Finally, board composition differs greatly from country to country: Owners and workers typically sit on the board in France, Germany, Japan, and China, whereas outsiders and managers occupy those seats in U.S., U.K., and Canadian companies.[45]

DIFFERING NATIONAL GOVERNANCE PRACTICES

As implied by these differences in governance practices across the globe, the effects of particular governance mechanisms are somewhat dependent on the national context in question. For instance, a recent comparison of the relationship between ownership structure and R&D investment revealed that in the United States, the owner-manager relationship tends to be more adversarial, whereas in Japan it is more cooperative. Managers and shareholders in Japan are often members of the same *keiretsu,* which is a set of companies with interlocking business relationships and shareholdings. This often creates ties between potential adversaries.

On the basis of these differences, ownership concentration in the United States serves as a control mechanism and affects how resources are allocated in the firm; in Japan, because the relationship is not adversarial and monitoring in nature, it does not tend to have an effect on investment behaviors.[46] This difference is dramatized by T. Boone Pickens' hostile-takeover attempt of Japanese firm Koito Manufacturing in 1989. At the time, Pickens' firm Mesa Petroleum owned a 20-percent stake in Koito, which in the United States would guarantee him a position on the board and a large say in corporate matters. In Japan, Pickens was snubbed by the Japanese directors because of his hostile approach. As a result, he was unable to negotiate a board seat, ultimately foiling his takeover attempt. Although it appears that the governance environment is changing in Japan, as evidenced by the more recent successful hostile takeover of Yushiro Chemicals by American-led Steel Partners in 2004, these changes are taking effect very slowly.[47]

French and German firms have different types of owners than those found in the United States and the United Kingdom. In France, nonfinancial corporations and state governments are the largest shareholders, particularly with regard to some of the country's largest employers. The same holds true for Germany, but banks are also major owners there. It is not unusual for German banks to own both debt and equity in the same corporation. In addition to the direct voting power that banks have due to their ownership position, banks also control a significant number of proxy voting positions from depositors who use the bank as a trustee for ownership purposes.

THE CASE OF GERMANY

Boards of directors are structured very differently across countries. For instance, Germany has a two-board system (sometimes called a *two-tiered board*): the management board and the supervisory board. The management board is responsible for managing the enterprise. Its members are jointly accountable for the firm's management. The chair of the management board coordinates its work. The supervisory board appoints, supervises, and advises the members of the management board and is directly involved in decisions of fundamental importance to the enterprise. The chair of the supervisory board coordinates its work. The supervisory board is similar to the board of directors of U.S. firms, with two major exceptions. First, one-half of the board's seats are allocated to representatives of shareholders and one-half to representatives of labor. To break potential tie votes, the board chair (who is always a representative of owners) is given two votes. Second, executives are not permitted to serve on the supervisory board.

Contrast the situation in Germany with U.S. firms, where about 75 percent of the board's seats are occupied by outsiders and 25 percent by insiders. Much more often than not, the chair of the board in a U.S. firm is also the CEO of the firm. Also note that members of the board in U.S. firms are elected by shareholders; no seats are allocated to any other stakeholder by right. That would seem to give shareholders considerable power. However, potential board members nominated by people other than the current board are rarely elected to the board in the United States. Consequently, CEOs have considerable power over the board in many U.S. companies. Conversely, in France and Germany it is relatively easy for owners to nominate and elect members of the board. The board-election processes in Canada and the United Kingdom resemble those in the United States more so than in the continental European countries.

THE CASE OF CHINA

China is perhaps the newest market to face corporate governance issues. With its flagship stock exchanges set up in Shanghai and Shenzhen, the China securities market started in 1990. At that time, only 10 companies were listed on the stock exchanges. After 17 years of exponential growth, the Chinese securities market has reached a considerable size, and Chinese as well as non-Chinese individuals and firms are allowed to own stock. At the end of 2005, well over 1,000 firms were listed on Chinese exchanges, with shares owned by Chinese citizens (these types of shares being referred to as A-class shares). The number of companies listed in the local market with shares owned by foreign investors (B-class shares) was 108; among them, 26 companies issued B shares only, while the rest issued both A and B shares. Forty-six companies have overseas listings (H-class shares).[49]

Given China's history of operating as a closed economy, it is probably not surprising that the majority of companies listed on the Chinese exchanges started off as state-owned enterprises. This heritage is also evident in the ownership structure of public firms, where the percentage of state ownership remains relatively high across all industries. As a result, in virtually all cases, Chinese public firms are controlled by state-owned or state-controlled shareholders. The remaining trading shares are typically owned by a combination of individual and institutional investors.[50] Such government control of public corporations is most often seen in countries where, historically, the government owned the largest companies and gradually privatized them. In Brazil, for instance, the government still has veto power over the operations of Embraer and Petrobras, two of the world's largest airplane and oil companies, respectively. French and Russian residual ownership of many large organizations reflects this heritage, as well.

Summary of Challenges

1. *Describe what* corporate governance *means.* Corporate governance is the means and mechanisms used to ensure that managers act in accordance with investors' best interests. It encompasses the system by which organizations are directed and controlled by their owners. Corporate governance is related to strategy formulation and implementation in several ways. Corporate governance ensures that the firm's vision and mission are reflected in its strategy and the way that strategy is executed. Governance mechanisms include monitoring and incentive devices, such as pay and promotion, that can bring managements' actions in line with shareholders' interests.

2. *Explain how corporate governance relates to competitive advantage.* Evidence suggests that shareholders favor good governance and that it can help firms outperform those with poor governance characteristics. To the extent that governance helps firms maximize returns and minimize agency problems, firms with good governance may have a competitive advantage over those lacking appropriate oversight and incentives. Young firms with good governance outperform their counterparts with loose oversight and poor incentives. Corporate scandals, such as those at Enron, Tyco, and WorldCom, are more likely to affect firms with inappropriate incentives and lax boards.

3. *Identify the roles of owners and different types of ownership profiles in corporate governance.* A public firm is one that has sold shares to the general investing public. How those publicly traded shares are dispersed and traded in the stock market varies significantly. Some firms have a few select owners who control significant stakes in the firm. Consequently, these parties have so much voting power that they can have significant influence and control over the firm's strategy and governance. Generally, the presence of strong owners minimizes agency problems. However, the presence of a powerful owner does not remove all agency problems. One specific type of problem arises when a single powerful owner uses that power to extract private benefits from the company at the expense of other, less powerful owners.

4. *Show how boards of directors are structured and explain the roles they play in corporate governance.* One of the chief monitoring devices available to shareholders is the board of directors. The general responsibility of the board of directors is to ensure that executives act in shareholders' best interests. All publicly held companies are required to have a board of directors. The legal roles of the board include hiring and firing top executives, monitoring management, ensuring that shareholders' interests are pro-tected, establishing executive compensation, and reviewing and approving the firm's strategy. There is the presumption that independent outsiders make for a more vigilant board; however, insiders on the board can improve governance when the firm operates in highly technical areas and technical expertise is needed on the board to help board members better understand the firms' environment and internal resources. The three key roles played by boards include (1) monitoring the activities of senior executives, thereby protecting shareholders' interests; (2) providing advice to managers; and (3) using their power, influence, and networks in the business community and political circles to aid the company.

5. *Analyze and design executive incentives as a corporate governance device.* Incentives can be used to lessen potential conflicts of interests between executives and shareholders. Compensation can be structured so that managers are rewarded for doing what is in shareholders' best interests. Stock ownership is the strongest way to link shareholders' and executives' incentives. Bonus pay is a subjective incentive that can link pay to performance. Its potential drawbacks are short-term bias and that it provides executives with incentives to manipulate earnings. Stock options have been the most heavily used incentive. Although they provide upside financial benefits, such as stock ownership, they do not convey a downside financial risk beyond opportunity cost. Recently, restricted stock grants and long-term incentive plans have become popular because they seem to overcome the limitations of bonuses and options.

6. *Illustrate how the market for corporate control is related to corporate governance.* The threat that a firm may become the target of a battle for corporate control and takeover is an external governance mechanism that helps to limit the consequences of bad management. When management performs poorly, the firm may become the target of a hostile takeover, either by disgruntled investors who want to replace the management and the board or by opportunistic investors looking to buy a company on the cheap and reap profits through dramatic restructuring. In either case, the existing management team will typically be terminated. Thus, this mechanism is a draconian backstop to the other internal mechanisms.

7. *Compare and contrast corporate governance practices around the world.* Governance practices differ around the globe in accordance with local laws and societal norms. Governance in the United States and the United Kingdom is shareholder-centric; in other countries, other stakeholders have much greater formal standing. For instance, in Germany labor has the right to appoint one-half of the board members. Ownership structure in Europe and Asia differs dramatically from the ownership of U.S. companies, and these differences have profound consequences for strategy formulation and implementation. Large corporate and government ownership blocks are common in Europe and Asia, whereas in the United States the majority of stock ownership is through pension plans and mutual funds. These funds tend to own relatively small percentages of any given company.

Review Questions

1. Explain what is meant by corporate governance.

2. Who are the principals and agents in the modern corporation? How do their interests differ?

3. How does governance affect firm performance and competitive advantage?

4. How can large, powerful owners reduce the agency problem? How can they exacerbate the problem?

5. When are inside directors beneficial to the functioning of the board of directors?

6. What are the three primary roles played by boards? How do boards carry out these roles?

7. What is the difference between stock options and restricted stock? What are the advantages and disadvantages of each?

8. What is the market for corporate control? What role does it play in solving or exacerbating the agency problem?

9. What are some primary differences and similarities in governance practices between the United States and other countries?

Experiential Activities

Group Exercises

1. Prior to class, visit the Web site www.theyrule.net. This site provides a convenient way to map out the interlocking boards of directors of U.S. firms. Develop or pick from the various interlock arrangements, print out your example, and bring it to class for discussion. What are the implications of the interlocks you identified for strategy formulation and implementation? What is provocative about your network structure? How might it affect the formulation and implementation of strategy?

2. Identify a company that is currently subject to an attempted hostile takeover (the *Wall Street Journal* or various online sources can help you do this quickly). What are the dynamics that are involved in this potential takeover? Who are the key stakeholders in this battle? Who do you see benefiting and losing if this takeover is successful? Does it appear that this hostile takeover would create value?

Ethical Debates

1. In a business dinner at which a few board members and top executives are attending, you overhear directors mentioning that the CEO's office has been bugged because they think he is negotiating behind their backs for a sale of the company. What do you do with this information?

2. You work in the HR department of a large international high-tech company. During the annual process of preparing for the closing of year-end books, your manager comes to you and tells you to pull out the documents for executive stock option grants and change the grant date from April 1st to July 13th. Why would he do this? What should be done?

How Would YOU DO THAT?

1. Refer back to the box entitled Exhibit 13.6 which discussed the establishment of executive stock ownership requirements at Dendrite International. Many business press outlets, such as *Business Week* and *Fortune,* publish articles that are critical of the corporate governance practices, particularly executive compensation, of one firm or another. Using these outlets, identify a recent example of a company that has been criticized for its governance practices and determine whether executive or director stock ownership was a factor in this criticism. What action plan for remedying this situation would you propose?

2. Identify a firm that is looking for a new CEO (or pick one whose CEO you think should be replaced!). Using the box entitled "How Would *You* Do That? 13.1" as a model, imagine that a firm is turning toward a compensation model that requires the CEO to own stock. What, specifically, do you think the compensation package should look like? How different will your company be from the competition in terms of the compensation package offered to the new CEO? (Hint: Pull up competitors' 10-K statements on the Internet.) What are the implications of these differences?

Go on to see How Would You Do That at www.prenhall.com/ carpenter&sanders

Endnotes

1. A. Shleifer and R. W. Vishny, "A Survey of Corporate Governance," *The Journal of Finance* 52:2 (1997), 737–783.

2. E. F. Fama and M. C. Jensen, "Separation of Ownership and Control," *Journal of Law and Economics* 26 (1983), 301–325; A. Shleifer and R. W. Vishny, "A Survey of Corporate Governance," *The Journal of Finance* 52:2 (1997), 737–783.

3. A. Tuschke and W. G. Sanders, "Antecedents and Consequences of Corporate Governance Reform: The Case of Germany," *Strategic Management Journal* 24 (2003), 631–649.

4. Exchange News: Statements from Angelo Tantazzi, Chairman of Borsa Italiana and Massimo Capuano, CEO of Borsa Italiana, www.exchange-handbook.co.uk/news_story.cfm?id=50739 (accessed November 29, 2005); T. C. Hoschka, "A Market for the Well Governed," *The McKinsey Quarterly* 3 (2002), 26–27.

5. W. G. Sanders and S. Boivie, "Sorting Things Out: Valuation of New Firms in Uncertain Markets," *Strategic Management Journal* 25 (2004), 167–186.

6. This exhibit summarizes a press release from Governance Metrics International (GMI), a New York City organization that provides governance ratings on public companies around the world. Source: M. Maremont and R. Brooks, "Fresh Woes Batter Krispy Kreme; Doughnut Firm to Restate Results, Delay SEC Filing; Shares Take a 15% Tumble," *Wall Street Journal* (Eastern edition), January 5, 2005, A3.

7. For more information, see www.gmiratings.com and www.morningstar.com (accessed July 15, 2005).

8. E. F. Fama and M. C. Jensen, "Separation of Ownership and Control," *Journal of Law and Economics* 26 (1983), 301–325; M. C. Jensen and W. H. Meckling, "Theory of the Firm: Managerial Behavior, Agency Costs and Ownership Structure," *Journal of Financial Economics* 3 (1976), 305–360; Shleifer and Vishny, "A Survey of Corporate Governance"; J. P. Walsh and J. K. Seward, "On the Efficiency of Internal and External Corporate Control Mechanisms," *Academy of Management Review* 15 (1990), 421–458.

9. A. A. Berle, Jr. and G. C. Means, *The Modern Corporation and Private Property* (New York: McMillan, 1932).

10. E. Ofek and D. Yermack, "Taking Stock: Equity-Based Compensation and the Evolution of Managerial Ownership," *Journal of Finance* 55:3 (2000), 1367–1384.

11. P. Milgrom and J. Roberts, *Economics, Organization, and Management* (Upper Saddle River, NJ: Prentice Hall, 1992).

12. www.sec.gov (accessed July 15, 2005).

13. "Prosecutors Say Rigases Owe $2.5 Billion," *New York Times*, December 15, 2004, C2. Jack Hitt, "American Kabuki: The Ritual of Scandal." *New York Times*, July 18, 2004, 1.

14. www.calpers.org and www.swib.state.wi.us (accessed July 15, 2005).

15. R. E. Hoskisson, M. A. Hitt, R. A. Johnson, and W. Grossman, "Conflicting Voices: The Effects of Institutional Ownership Heterogeneity and Internal Governance on Corporate Strategies," *Academy of Management Journal* 45 (2002), 697–716.

16. M. Peers, J. Carreyrou, and B. Orwall, "Vivendi CEO Loses Key Board Support, Endangering His Job," *Wall Street Journal,* (2002) July 1: A1; L. Panetta, "It's Not Just What You Do, It's the Way You Do It," *Directors & Boards* 27 (2003), 17–21.

17. www.aicpa.org/info/sarbanes_oxley_summary.htm (accessed November 29, 2005).

18. B. Baysinger and R. E. Hoskisson, "The Composition of Boards of Directors and Strategic Control: Effects on Corporate Strategy," *Academy of Management Review* 15 (1990), 72–87.

19. Baysinger and Hoskisson, "The Composition of Boards of Directors and Strategic Control."

20. J. Dahya, A. Lonie, D. Power, "The Case for Separating the Roles of Chairman and CEO: An Analysis of Stock Market and Accounting Data," *Corporate Governance* 4 (1996), 71, 76. This study examined the impact of separating or combining the roles of CEO and chair in the United Kingdom. The authors found that a "significant positive market reaction…followed the separation of the responsibilities of chairman and CEO." Also, companies that announced a separation subsequently performed better than their counterparts based on several accounting measures. Conversely, companies that announced combination of the positions resulted in "the largest negative market response the day after the announcement."

21. "The function of the chairman is to run board meetings and oversee the process of hiring, firing, evaluating, and compensating the CEO … Without the direction of an independent leader, it is much more difficult for the board to perform its critical function," M. C. Jensen, "Presidential Address: The Modern Revolution, Exit and the Failure of Internal Control Systems," *Journal of Finance* 48 (1993), 831, 866; "Wearing both hats is like grading your own paper," A. Hansen, deputy director of the Council of Institutional Investors, as quoted in "A Walk on the Corporate Side," *Trustee* 49:10 (1996), 9, 10. See also, C. E. Bagley and Richard H. Koppes, "Leader of the Pack: A Proposal for Disclosure of Board Leadership Structure," *San Diego Law Review* 34:1 (1997), 149, 157–158.

22. Adapted from M. Wiersema, "Holes at the Top: Why CEO Firings Backfire," *Harvard Business Review* 80:12 (2002), 70–77.

23. C. Lucier, R. Schuyt, and J. Handa, "The Perils of Good Governance," *Strategy+Business* 35 (2004), 1–17.

24. J. D. Westphal, "Collaboration in the Boardroom: Behavioral and Performance Consequences of CEO–Board Social Ties," *Academy of Management Journal* 42 (1999), 7–24.

25. M. A. Carpenter and J. D. Westphal, "The Strategic Context of External Network Ties: Examining the Impact of Director Appointments on Board Involvement in Strategic Decision Making," *Academy of Management Journal* 44 (2001), 639–651.

26. G. Strauss, "Board Pay Gets Fatter as Job Gets Hairier," *USA TODAY*, March 7, 2005, B1; T. Johnson-Elie, "Boards Slowly Opening up to Women, Minorities—Time Is Right, Seasoned Executive Jackson Says," *Milwaukee Journal Sentinel*, June 1, 2005, 1.

27. B. Lechem, *Chairman of the Board* (London: Wiley, 2002).

28. www.thecorporatelibrary.com and www.issproxy.com (accessed July 15, 2005).

29. M. A. Carpenter and J. D. Westphal, "The Strategic Context of External Network Ties."

30. M. McDonald and J. D. Westphal, "Getting by with the Advice of Their Friends: CEOs' Advice Networks and Firms' Strategic Responses to Poor Performance," *Administrative Science Quarterly* 48 (2003), 1–32; J. D. Westphal and J. W. Fredrickson, "Who Directs Strategic Change? Director Experience, the Selection of New CEOs, and Change in Corporate Strategy," *Strategic Management Journal* 22 (2001), 1113–1138; J. D. Westphal, M. D. Seidel, and K. S. Stewart, "Second-Order Imitation: Uncovering Latent Effects of Board Network Ties," *Administrative Science Quarterly* 46 (2001), 717–747.

31. "Dendrite International Board Mandates New Executive Share Ownership Policy; Program Reflects Positive Expectations," *BusinessWire*, February 8, 2000; Standard and Poor's Quantitative Stock Report; DRTE (Dendrite International), December 17, 2005.

32. E. White, "Call It Sarbanes-Oxley Burnout: Finance-Chief Turnover Is Rising," *Wall Street Journal*, April 5, 2005, A1.

33. Adapted from Fredrick W. Cook & Co., Inc., "Stock Ownership Policies: Prevalence and Design of Executive and Director Ownership Policies Among the Top 250 Companies," www.fwcook.com/surveys.html (accessed November 29, 2005), September 2004.

34. P. M. Healy and J. M. Wahlen, "A Review of the Earnings Management Literature and Its Implications for Standard Setting," *Accounting Horizons* 13 (1999), 365–383.

35. R. E. Hoskisson, M. A. Hitt, and C. W. L. Hill, "Managerial Incentives and Investment in R&D in Large Multiproduct Firms," *Organization Science* 4 (1993), 325–341.

36. W. G. Sanders, "Behavioral Responses of CEOs to Stock Ownership and Stock Option Pay," *Academy of Management Journal* 44 (2001), 477–492; W. G. Sanders, "Incentive Alignment, CEO Pay Level, and Firm Performance: A Case of 'Heads I Win, Tails You Lose'?" *Human Resource Management* 40 (2001), 159–170.

37. W. G. Sanders, "Behavioral Responses of CEOs to Stock Ownership and Stock Option Pay," *Academy of Management Journal* 44 (2001), 477–492.

38. D. F. Larcker, "The Association Between Performance Plan Adoption and Corporate Capital Investment," *Journal of Accounting and Economics* 5 (1983), 3–30.

39. J. Dial and K. J. Murphy, "Incentives, Downsizing, and Value Creation at General Dynamics," *Journal of Financial Economics* 37 (1995), 261–314.

40. M. A. Carpenter and W. G. Sanders, "Top Management Team Compensation: The Missing Link Between CEO Pay and Firm Performance," *Strategic Management Journal* 23 (2002), 367–374.

41. M. Bloom and J. G. Michel, "The Relationships Among Organizational Context, Pay Dispersion, and Managerial Turnover," *Academy of Management Journal* 45 (2002), 33–42.

42. Berle and Means, *The Modern Corporation and Private Property*.

43. R. Slater, *The Titans of Takeover* (New York: Beard Books, 1999).

44. M. C. Jensen and R. S. Ruback, "The Market for Corporate Control: The Scientific Evidence," *Journal of Financial Economics* 11 (1983), 5–50.

45. E. R. Gedajlovic and D. M. Shapiro, "Management and Ownership Effects: Evidence from Five Countries," *Strategic Management Journal* 19 (1998), 533–553; R. Tricker, *Pocket Director* (London: The Economist Books, 1999).

46. P. M. Lee and H. M. O'Neill, "Ownership Structures and R&D Investments of U.S. and Japanese Firms: Agency and Stewardship Perspectives," *Academy of Management Journal* 46 (2003), 212–225.

47. B. Bremner and M. der Hovanesian, "So 'Takeover' Does Translate: Foreigners Are After Japanese Companies—With Better Governance as One Result," *BusinessWeek*, February 9, 2004, 51.

48. *Home Depot proxy statement filing (form DEF 14A), April 20, 2007.*

49. www.oecd.org (accessed July 15, 2005).

50. www.oecd.org (accessed July 15, 2005).

Glossary

acquisition Strategy by which one firm acquires another through stock purchase or exchange.

acquisition premium Difference between current market value of a target firm and purchase price paid to induce its shareholders to turn its control over to new owners.

agency problem Separation of its ownership from managerial control of a firm.

agent Party, such as a manager, who acts on behalf of another party.

ambidextrous structure Organizational structure for dynamic contexts in which project teams are organized as structurally independent units and encouraged to develop their own structures, systems, and processes.

arena Area (product, service, distribution channels, geographic markets, technology, etc.) in which a firm participates.

balanced scorecard Strategic management support system for measuring vision and strategy against business- and operating-unit-level performance.

barrier to entry Condition under which it is more difficult to join or compete in an industry.

behavioral controls Practice of tying rewards to criteria other than simply financial performance, such as those broadly identified in the balanced scorecard.

board of directors Group of individuals that formally represents the firm's shareholders and oversees the work of top executives.

bootstrapping Process of finding creative ways to support a startup business financially until it turns profitable.

business strategy Strategy for competing against rivals within a particular industry or industry segment.

buyer power Degree to which firms in the buying industry are able to dictate terms on purchase agreements that extract some of the profit that would otherwise go to competitors in the focal industry.

CAGE framework Tool that considers the dimensions of culture, administration, geography, and economics to assess the distance created by global expansion.

capabilities A firm's skill at using its resources to create goods and services; combination of procedures and expertise on which a firm relies to produce goods and services.

causal ambiguity Condition whereby the difficulty of identifying or understanding a resource or capability makes it valuable, rare, and inimitable.

codes of governance Ideal governance standards formulated by regulatory, market, and government institutions.

coevolution Process by which diversification causes two or more interdependent businesses to adapt not only to their environment, but to each other.

commoditization Process during industry evolution by which sales eventually come to depend less on unique product features and more on price.

competitive advantage A firm's ability to create value in a way that its rivals cannot

complementor Firm in one industry that provides products or services which tend to increase sales in another industry.

conglomerate Corporation consisting of many companies in different businesses or industries.

consortia Association of several companies and/or governments for some definite strategic purpose.

contractual agreements An exchange of promises or agreement between parties that is often enforceable by the law.

co-opetition Situation in which firms are simultaneously competitors in one market and collaborators in another.

core competence Capability which is central to a firm's main business operations and which allow it to generate new products and services.

corporate governance The system by which owners of firms direct and control the affairs of the firm.

corporate new-venturing New-venture creation by established firms.

corporate renewal Outcome of successful strategic change in the context of an established business.

corporate strategy Strategy for guiding a firm's entry and exit from different businesses, for determining how a parent company adds value to and manages its portfolio of businesses, and for creating value through diversification.

cross-subsidizing Practice by which a firm uses profits from one aspect of a product, service, or region to support other aspects of competitive activity.

culture Core organizational values widely held and shared by an organization's members.

differentiation Strategic position based on products or offers services with quality, reliability, or prestige that is discernibly higher than that of competitors and for which customers are willing to pay.

differentiator Feature or attribute of a company's product or service (e.g., image, customization, technical superiority, price, quality, and reliability) that helps it beat its competitors in the marketplace.

diseconomies of scope Condition under which the joint output of two or more products within a single firm results in increased average costs.

diseconomy of scale Condition under which average total costs per unit of production increases at higher levels of input.

disruptive technology Breakthrough product- or process-related technology that destroys the competencies of incumbent firms in an industry.

distinctive competence   Capability that sets a firm apart from other firms; something that a firm can do which competitors cannot.

diversification   Degree to which a firm conducts business in more than one arena.

divestiture   Strategy whereby a company sells off a business or division.

due diligence   Initial pre-closing screening, analysis, and negotiations for an acquisition.

dynamic capabilities   A firm's ability to modify, reconfigure, and upgrade resources and capabilities in order to strategically respond to or generate environmental changes.

economic logic   Means by which a firm will earn a profit by implementing a strategy.

economy of scale   Condition under which average total cost for a unit of production is lower at higher levels of output.

economy of scope   Condition under which lower total average costs result from sharing resources to produce more than one product or service.

entrepreneurial process   Integration of opportunity recognition, key resources and capabilities, and an entrepreneur and entrepreneurial team to create a new venture.

entrepreneurship   Recognition of opportunities and the use of resources and capabilities to implement innovative ideas for new ventures.

equity alliance   Alliance in which one or more partners assumes a greater ownership interest in either the alliance or another partner.

escalation of commitment   Decision-making bias under which people are willing to commit additional resources to a failing course of action.

ethnocentrism   Belief in the superiority of one's own ethnic group or, more broadly, the conviction that one's own national, group, or cultural characteristics are "normal."

exit barriers   Barriers that impose a high cost on the abandonment of a market or product.

exporting   Foreign-country entry vehicle in which a firm uses an intermediary to perform most foreign marketing functions.

first mover   The firm that is first to offer a new product or service a market.

five-forces model   Framework for evaluating industry structure according to the effects of rivalry, threat of entry, supplier power, buyer power, and the threat of substitutes.

focused cost leadership   Strategic position based on being a low-cost leader in a narrow market segment.

focused differentiation   Strategic position based on targeting products to relatively small segments.

foreign direct investment (FDI)   Foreign-country entry vehicle by which a firm commits to the direct ownership of a foreign subsidiary or division.

functional structure   Form of organization revolving around specific value-chain functions.

general resources   Resource that can be exploited across a wide range of activities.

generic strategies   Strategic position designed to reduce the effects of rivalry, including *low-cost, differentiation, focused cost leadership, focused differentiation, and integrated positions.*

geographic roll-up   Strategy whereby a firm acquires many other firms in the same industry segment by in different geographic arenas in an attempt to create significant scale and scope advantages.

geographic scope   Breadth and diversity of geographic arenas in which a firm operates.

globalization   Evolution of distinct geographic product markets into a state of globally interdependent product markets.

goals and objectives   Combination of a broad indication of organizational intentions (goals) and specific, measurable steps (objectives) for reaching them.

greenfield investment   Form of FDI in which a firm starts a new foreign business from the ground up.

high-end disruption   Strategy that may result in huge new markets in which new players redefine industry rules to unseat the largest incumbents.

horizontal alliance   Alliance involving a focal firm and another firm in the same industry.

horizontal scope   Extent to which firm participates in related market segments or industries outside its existing value-chain activities.

hubris   Exaggerated self-confidence that can result in managers' overestimating the value of a potential acquisition, having unrealistic assumptions about the ability to create synergies, and a willingness to pay too much for a transaction.

implementation levers   Mechanisms used by strategic leaders to help execute a firm's strategy.

importing   Internationalization strategy by which a firm brings a good, service, or capital into the home country from abroad.

incentive alignment   Use of incentives to align managerial self-interest with shareholders'.

industry life cycle   Pattern of evolution followed by an industry inception to current and future states.

initial public offering (IPO)   First sale of a company's stock to the public market.

innovator's dilemma   When incumbents avoid investing in innovative and disruptive technologies because those innovations do not satisfy the needs of their mainstream and most profitable clients.

institutional investors   Pension or mutual fund that manages large sums of money for third-party investors.

integrated position   Strategic position in which elements of one position support strong standing in another.

international strategy   Process by which a firm approaches its cross-border activities and those of competitors and plans to approach them in the future.

intrinsic value Present value of a company's future cash flows from existing assets and businesses.

joint venture Alliance in which two firms make equity investments in a third legal entity.

key success factor (KSF) Key asset or requisite skill that all firms in an industry must possess in order to be a viable competitor.

knowing-doing gap Phenomenon whereby firms tend to be better at generating new knowledge than at creating new products based on that knowledge.

learning curve Incremental production costs decline at a constant rate as production experience is gained; the steeper the learning curve, the more rapidly costs decline.

Level 5 Hierarchy Model of leadership skills calling for a wide range of abilities, some of which are hierarchical in natures.

long-tail When the selling of individual products that each have low sales volume add up to huge revenues.

low-cost leadership Strategic position based on producing a good or offering a service while maintaining total costs that are lower than what it takes competitors to offer the same product or service.

low-end disruption Strategy that appears at the low end of industry offerings, targeting the lest desirable of incumbents' customers.

managerialism Tendency of managers to make decisions based on personal self-interest rather than the best interests of shareholders.

market for corporate control Control over public corporations is traded, and this theoretically puts some pressure on managers to perform, otherwise their corporation can be taken over.

market value Current market capitalization of a firm.

matrix structure Form of organization in which specialists from functional departments are assigned to work for one or more product or geographic units.

merger Consolidation or combination of two or more firms.

minimum efficient scale (MES) The output level that delivers the lowest total average cost.

mission Declaration of what a firm is and what it stands for—its fundamental values and purpose.

monitoring Functioning of the board in exercising its legal and fiduciary responsibility to oversee executives' behavior and performance and to take action when it's necessary to replace management.

multidivisional structure Form of organization in which divisions are organized around product or geographic markets and are often self-sufficient in terms of functional expertise.

multipoint competition When a firm competes against another firm in multiple product markets or multiple geographic markets (or both).

network structure Form of organization in which small, semiautonomous, and potentially temporary groups are brought together for specific purposes.

new-venture creation Entrepreneurship and the creation of a new business from scratch.

nonequity alliance Alliance that involves neither the assumption of equity interest nor the creation of separate organizations.

offshoring Moving a value chain activity or set of activities to another country, typically where key costs are lower.

organizational structure Relatively stable arrangement of responsibilities, tasks, and people within an organization.

outcome controls Practice of tying rewards to narrowly defined financial criteria.

outsourcing Activity performed for a company by people other than its full-time employees.

patching Process of remapping businesses in accordance with changing market conditions and restitches them into new internal business structures.

peer-to-peer Where individual network members can engage in exchange with any other member of the network.

PESTEL analysis Tool for assessing the political, economic, sociocultural, technological, environmental, and legal contexts in which a firm operates.

portfolio planning Practice of mapping diversified businesses or products based on their relative strengths and market attractiveness.

principal Party, such as a shareholder, who hires an agent to act on his or her behalf.

profit pool Analytical tool that enables managers to calculate profits at various points along an industry value chain.

purchase price Final price actually paid to the target firm's shareholders of an acquired company.

real-options Process of maximizing the upside or limiting the downside of an investment opportunity by uncovering and quantifying the options and discussion points embedded within it.

related diversification Form of diversification in which the business units operated by a firm are highly related.

relational quality Principle identifying four key elements (initial conditions, negotiation process, reciprocal experiences, outside behavior) in establishing and maintaining interorganizational trust.

required performance improvements The increases in combined cash flow of the acquiror and target that are necessary to justify the acquisition premium.

resources Inputs used by firms to create products and services.

return on invested capital (ROIC) How effectively a company uses the money (borrowed or owned) invested in its operations.

revenue-enhancement synergy When total sales are greater if two products are sold and distributed within one company than when they are owned by separate companies.

reward system Bases on which employees are compensated and promoted.

rivalry Intensity of competition within an industry.

road show Series of presentations in which top management promotes an IPO to interested investors and analysts.

S-1 statement Legal document outlining a firm's financial position in preparation for an initial public stock offering.

second mover (often fast follower) Second significant company to move into a market, quickly following the first mover.

serial acquirers Company that engages in frequent acquisitions.

social capital The advantage created through the characteristics of a person's network

social network The collection of ties between people and the strength of those ties.

specialized resources Resource with a narrow range of applicability.

staging Timing and pace of strategic moves.

stakeholder Individual or group with an interest in an organization's ability to deliver intended results and maintain the viability of its products and services.

stereotyping Relying on a conventional or formulaic conception of another group based on some common characteristic.

stock options Incentive device giving an employee the right to buy a share of company stock at a later date for a predetermined price.

straddling Unsuccessful attempt to integrate both low-cost and differentiation positions.

strategic alliance Relationship in which two or more firms combine resources and capabilities in order to enhance the competitive advantage of all parties.

strategic change Significant changes in resource allocation choices, in the business and implementation activities that align the firm's strategy with its vision, or in its vision.

strategic coherence Symmetric coalignment of the five elements of the firm's strategy, the congruence of functional-area policies with these elements, and the overarching fit of various businesses under the corporate umbrella.

strategic group Subset of firms which, because of similar strategies, resources, and capabilities, compete against each other more intensely than with other firms in an industry.

strategic leadership Task of managing an overall enterprise and influencing key organizational outcomes.

strategic management Process by which a firm manages the formulation and implementation of a strategy.

strategic positioning Means by which managers situate a firm relative to its rivals.

strategic purpose Simplified, widely shared mental model of the organization and its future, including anticipated changes in its environment.

strategy The coordinated means by which an organization pursues its goals and objectives.

strategy formulation Process of developing a strategy.

strategy implementation Process of executing a strategy.

succession planning Process of managing a well-planned and well-executed transition from one CEO to the next with positive outcomes for all key stakeholders.

superordinate goal Overarching reference point for a host of hierarchical subgoals.

supplier power Degree to which firms in the supply industry are able to dictate terms to contracts and thereby extract some of the profit that would otherwise by available to competitors in the focal industry.

synergy Condition under which the combined benefits of activities in two or more arenas are greater than the simple sum of those benefits.

takeoff period Period during which a new product generates rapid growth and huge sales increases.

threat of new entry Degree to which new competitors can enter an industry and intensify rivalry.

threat of substitutes Degree to which products of one industry can satisfy the same demand as those of another.

unrelated diversification Form of diversification in which the business units that a firm operates are highly dissimilar.

value chain Total of primary and support value-adding activities by which a firm produces, distributes, and markets a product.

value curve A graphical depiction of how a firm and major groups of its competitors are competing across its industry's factors of completion.

value net model Map of a firm's existing and potential exchange relationships.

vertical alliance Alliance involving a focal firm and a supplier or customer.

vertical integration Diversification into upstream and/or downstream industries.

vertical scope The extent to which a firm is vertically integrated.

vision Simple statement or understanding of what the firm will be in the future.

VRINE model Analytical framework suggesting that a firm with resources and capabilities which are valuable, rare, inimitable, nonsubstitutable, and exploitable will gain a competitive advantage.

willingness to pay Principle of differentiation strategy by which customers are willing to pay more for certain product features.

winner's curse Situation in which a winning M&A bidder must live with the consequences of paying too much for the target.

Index

Photo Credits